I0884698

Errata

Figure 1 on page 351 should read: "Fig. 282 - Le Massif calcaire vers 250: nombre de pièces des villages étudiés." (From Georges Tate, *Les Campagnes de la Syrie du Nord du IIe au VIIe siècle* [Paris, 1992], I, 279. Published with permission, Librairie Orientaliste Paul Geuthner, Paris).

Figure 2 on page 355 should read: "Fig. 243. - Perspective d'ensemble des bâtiments 101 à 108 (J.-L. Biscop)." (From Jean-Pierre Sodini et al., *Déhès (Syrie du Nord): Campagnes I-III (1976-1978): Recherches sur l'habitat rural* [Paris, 1980], p. 181. Published with permission, Librairie Orientaliste Paul Geuthner, Paris).

Figure 3 on page 363 should read: The church at Gubelle (From E. Baccache and G. Tchalenko, *Eglises de village de la Syrie du Nord. Planches* [Paris, 1979], p. 107. Published with permission. Librairie Orientaliste Paul Geuthner, Paris).

Urban Centers and Rural Contexts in Late Antiquity

Urban Centers and Rural Contexts in Late Antiquity

EDITED BY
THOMAS S. BURNS
AND
JOHN W. EADIE

Michigan State University Press
East Lansing

♾ The paper used in this publication meets the minimum requirements of ANSI/NISO Z39.48–1992 (R 1997) (Permanence of Paper).

Michigan State University Press
East Lansing, Michigan 48823-5202

Printed and bound in the United States of America.

07 06 05 04 03 02 01 1 2 3, 4 5 6 7 8 9 10

LIBRARY OF CONGRESS CATALOGING-IN-PUBLICATION DATA
Urban centers and rural contexts in late antiquity /
edited by Thomas S. Burns and John W. Eadie.
p. cm.
Contributions to the Third Biennial Conference on Shifting Frontiers in Late Antiquity, Emory University, March 1999.
Includes bibliographical references.
ISBN 0-87013-585-6
1. Cities and towns—Rome—Congresses. I. Burns, Thomas S. II. Eadie, John William. III. Biennial Conference on Shifting Frontiers in Late Antiquity (3rd : 1999 : Emory University)
HT114 .U725 2001
307.76'0937—dc21
00-013228

Book and cover design by Sharp Des!gns, Lansing, MI

Visit Michigan State University Press on the World Wide Web at:
www.msu.edu/unit/msupress

Contents

TOWN AND COUNTRY

CHRISTIANIZATION

Editors

Thomas S. Burns, *Department of History, Emory University*
John W. Eadie, *Department of History, Michigan State University*

Contributors

Géza Alföldy, *Seminar für Alte Geschichte der Universität Heidelberg*
Helmut Bender, *Archäologie der Römischen Provinzen, Universität Passau*
Kim Bowes, *Department of Art and Archaeology, Princeton University*
E. G. Clark, *Depatment of Classics and Ancient History, University of Bristol*
Florin Curta, *Department of History, University of Florida*
J. F. Drinkwater, *Department of Classics, University of Nottingham*
Zbigniew T. Fiema, *Institutum Classicum, University of Helsinki*
David Graf, *Department of History, University of Miami*
Christopher Haas, *Department of History, Villanova University*
Linda Jones Hall, *Department of History, St. Mary's College of Maryland*
Kenneth Harl, *Department of History, Tulane University*
Frank L. Kidner, *Department of History, San Francisco State University*
Michael Kulikowski, *Department of History, Smith College*
Joseph Patrich, *Department of Archaeology, University of Haifa*
Marcus Rautman, *Department of Art and Archaeology, University of Missouri, Columbia*
David Riggs, *Christ Church, Oxford*
Zsolt Visy, *Department of Archaeology, Janus Pannonius University, Pecs*
Bailey Young, *Department of History, Eastern Illinois University*

Preface

TOM BURNS & JOHN EADIE

THIS VOLUME BEGAN AS THE TWO EDITORS SAT OVER COFFEE TOWARD THE END OF the Second Biennial Conference on Shifting Frontiers in Late Antiquity meeting at the University of South Carolina in March 1997. Like the previous conference of the Society for Late Antiquity, the Second was well attended and offered many opportunities for convivial association and intense scholarly discussion among specialists from around the world. By the last day of the conference, both of us had come away with the keen appreciation that many of the issues being raised, particularly outside the formal presentations, related to the shifting interface between late ancient towns and the countrysides around them. Two things were especially clear to us. First, we saw that to address one side of the urban-rural equation without approaching the other would neither yield answers to the questions that historians and archaeologists alike were beginning to ask about the changing nature of urban-rural interactions in the Roman Empire, nor would it permit one to take account of the burgeoning archaeological data on which revisionist interpretations had been predicated. Second, we realized that we needed to provide a forum for as much interdisciplinary discussion as possible. After refills of coffee, we decided to volunteer to host the Third Biennial

Conference on Shifting Frontiers in Late Antiquity, to meet at Emory University in Atlanta during March 1999.

Although there have been a number of recent publications on urbanism in Late Antiquity and several important scholarly investigations of changes in the rural environment, most of these studies explore a single region, a narrow chronological niche, or are predominantly either textual or archaeological. None has attempted the more ambitious task of bringing together diverse archaeological and textual studies within a multi-regional perspective and around common themes. *Urban Centers and Rural Contexts* seeks to redress this omission through the contributions of some of the historians and archaeologists who attended the conference at Emory.

Each author has been able to take advantage of the insights of colleagues who participated in the symposia and to explore, in somewhat greater detail than was possible in the presentations, some of the central themes of this volume. Every contribution is a fresh treatment of these themes based on hitherto unpublished or rarely adduced data and is informed by inquiries outside the author's primary field of specialization.

This volume could not have been produced without the generous support of Emory and Michigan State universities or the patience and good-humored efficiency of Shawn Myrda. We hope that everyone associated with this volume, and especially all the participants who made the three days of "shifting frontiers" in Atlanta so stimulating and memorable, will share the editors' pleasure in making the fresh insights contained in these papers accessible to a wider public.

Introduction

AT THE DAWN OF THE GREEK POLIS, THE POET ALCAEUS REMINDED HIS AUDIENCE that cities were "neither made of carefully hewn wood nor of finely dressed stone walls" but of men living inside them free to explore their horizons and defend their values. In late antiquity despite many changes in their physical appearance the heart of every city remained those men and women who lived there. Throughout antiquity especially creative individuals congregated in urban centers, while ordinary people too sought to better their lives in towns. The amenities of the great cities, particularly Rome and other very large urban centers such as Alexandria and Antioch, set the standards for all others. Throughout the first two centuries after Augustus people in the provinces followed his lead and transformed their cities from brick to marble. These new but classical Roman towns reflected society's concern for order through carefully designed urban space. Streets crossed at right angles and linked the populace to those amenities without which a Roman would have felt like a "barbarian": public latrines, bountiful supplies of fresh water, and well-maintained public buildings and temples. The key to finding your way around the classical city was to understand the layout of public space. Public buildings were sited with reference to water supplies, sewers, and major road access, and linked together by a grid-plan of streets. The work of city building was essentially over by the reign of Septimus Severus, but maintenance was an endless task.

The general features of urban life were ubiquitous, but, particularly in late antiquity, only the few truly great cities were so large as to distort the space around them for hundreds of miles, similar in that regard to today's megacities with their populations of many millions. But every regional urban center influenced the countryside around it. People needed food and work, and more people meant that supplies had to come from greater distances and that jobs became more diversified. In the case of major imperial centers supplies had to be shipped from all over their part of the Empire, and their populations mirrored those diverse locales. If it were possible to rewrite our lexicons, perhaps "city" could be reserved for a few major imperial centers: Rome, Carthage, and Trier in the West; Constantinople, Alexandria, and Antioch in the East; Serdica and Thessalonica in the Balkan Penisula, each a truly major city even by modern standards. All others, smaller but with public amenitites and classical design should then be called more appropriately "towns." But, unfortunately, authors of historical narratives gave up on such precision long ago. At the other end of the spectrum were agrarian communities: villas, villages, and hamlets. The villa transplanted Mediterranean urbanity to the countryside, whereas rural settlements remained essentially pre-Roman with a single, often winding path lined with houses made of wood and clay, gardens, and shelters for livestock. Cities had long given men and women much greater opportunity for personal development, but was this still true at the end of the fourth century or had tolerance for individual variation and enthusiasm for town life waned? Did progressive autocracy or Christianization reverse these traditional factors of urban vitality? Did a new ethos supplant the classical as urban space was reused for late antique purposes? Was the relative unity of the design of urban space, long fixed by the placement and maintenance requirements of public building, fractured in late antiquity? If so, then were there still commonalities in the urban experience shared across the Empire?

Whereas Roman literature and the physical remains of ancient cities reveal the power that urban values held over the lives of their inhabitants, the rural areas surrounding the towns are not so well served by the historical record. Only recently have archaeology and remote surveying techniques significantly enhanced our knowledge of the rural contexts in late antiquity, but even without this new data, much of it introduced for the first time in this volume, it would be clear that rural communities supported the urban elites, fed their populations, consumed their wares, and were home to the overwhelming majority of the Empire's residents. During the Principate, when townsmen were actively building their architectural infrastructure, rural values were secondary to urban successes. Rural contexts emerge from the shadows only rarely and then in unrealistic literary comparisons or as in dreams of a "simpler time." The reality, however, was that during the Principate town and country operated as a unit, within which the town was conceptually the dominant partner. Their symbiosis meant that neither the ancient city nor the countryside would survive unchanged if the other met with catastrophe, and starting in the third century crises were not hard to find. Traditionally scholars have singled out invasion and governmental crisis and restructuring as being primarily responsible for the reorientation of civilization away from the classical cities. This thesis had reached iconic stature by the 1960s.

More recently scholarship has again focused attention on the role that Christianity, with its new priorities in building and organization, played in a progressive transformation of urban space in late antiquity. Both traditionalists and revisionists have tended to concentrate on changes in the physical layout of urban space. Debate rages as to how to evaluate the general demographics of the era. Did all cities—great and small—decline in population or in density of settlement? Were local declines offset by increases elsewhere as people sought out greater safety and prosperity?

To a considerable degree the discussion of urban centers still follows postulates set forth at the end of the eighteenth century in Edward Gibbon's monumental *Decline and Fall of the Roman Empire.* Gibbon based his theories almost exclusively upon the extant literary materials, although inspired oddly enough by the ruins of Rome itself. Like Gibbon, many today still seek a single cause for a singularly defined result, in this case the collapse of the ancient city and its replacement by Byzantine or western medieval centers that were topographically, economically, and conceptually quite different from those that had dominated the ancient Mediterranean. This obsession with primary cause has also focused attention upon specific and datable crises, especially those of the third, fifth, and seventh centuries. The governmental crises of these centuries are traditionally assumed to be connected to, if not to have caused, a progressive decline in ancient urbanism, but is that correspondence real or imagined and to what degree are urban chronologies linked to governmental success or failure?

The essays in this volume deploy a wide assortment of new data, most of it unavailable just a decade ago, in order to reveal different alternatives within the theme of urban transformation: Alexandria [Haas], Beirut [Hall], Caesarea [Patrich], and Petra [Fiema] in the East; Trier [Bender], Pécs [Visy], Autun [Young], Tarraco, Emerita, Valentia, and Cordoba [Kulikowski] in the West; Rome stands astride geographic boundaries, as always it floats upon the earth. For these ancient cities no one model is sufficient, but there are certain factors that stand out as generally evocative of new branches being grafted upon old roots. In every case, the nonliterary data suggest that the grand crises of the late Empire were far more ephemeral than contemporary literature would have us believe. Everywhere the city remained at the conceptual core of Roman society until quite late. In absolute chronology, the sixth century was still dominated in those areas analyzed here by values rooted in the urban experience, but by then the physical landscape had changed considerably. Towns witnessed a gradual redirection of urban resources away from classical public spaces to more personal Christian construction, but they remained towns nonetheless. A clear demonstration of the hold classical urbanism had was the continuance of the traditional titles associated with civic government as sources of honor. At the royal level, the Visigothic king Leovigild (569-86) still thought it necessary to proclaim the founding of complete and classical Roman towns to validate his dynasty [Kulikowski].

Rome is perhaps the most unusual case addressed in these essays. For its political elite the hinterland seemed, on the one hand, to have remained as it had always been, irrelevant. On the other, the rural context of the Urbs Romana was conceived as being the entire Empire. By late antiquity in Rome, as elsewhere, the traditional elites were being challenged by ecclesiastical authorities, but for the Roman aristocracy this was not a religious competition but rather a political one. Rome's secular leaders thought of themselves as the living embodiment of the past, but others saw them and their culture as irrelevant [Alföldy]. The Roman aristocracy continued to ignore the fact that Rome, once Constantine left for the east in 312, had become a backwater. The papacy alone succeeded in disputing that relegation. Elsewhere we can recapture the attitudes of the citizenry more indirectly from the extant records of their daily lives. Out of this emerges a sense that in most places urbanity remained a core value. In towns such as Alexandria and Beirut, many people still went out into the countryside to work and returned to their urban homes at the end of the day. Saint Augustine was hardly alone when he posited as the fundamental dichotomy of his age the relationship of the *City* of Man to the *City* of God. Even in the West town councils existed long after their duties were of little consequence. In the cities under discussion, other than Rome, the leading elements of the community were demonstrably concerned with the rural areas, even though it is equally clear that they regarded their town as the hub of the region in whatever contemporary context we have evidence to explore.

Although the urban and rural elements composed a single community, there is no single relationship that linked them together. The records now becoming available suggest that, in most cases, the aristocracies had multiple sources of income, sometimes weighted toward rural landowning, sometimes not. Although the urban and rural elements were linked, change in one did not have a consistent impact upon the other, at least not a one-to-one correspondence. Their lives were too deeply intertwined for such a simple cause and effect relationship. The ancients themselves knew this. At Alexandria, there is clear evidence that all levels of government understood that the integrity of the Mareotis region was essential for the prosperity of its parts and that this prosperity was not based upon a single exchange [Haas]. Central to their thinking was the welfare of the entire community regardless of its political or architectural features. The newly published Petra papyri provide striking testimony to the survival of a classical urban spirit much later than previously thought and this occurred despite the departure to other locations of both civil and ecclesiastical government [Fiema].

Merely to survive was never sufficient for the wealthy. As individuals in succeeding generations evaluated their career options anew, they decided which path might lead them to the greatest prominence in their community. Some stayed in the occupations of their fathers; others did not. Regardless of their choice, the community remained central. In Petra, ultimately left out of all governmental, ecclesiastical, and economic networks, elites took up residence on their rural estates. Far into the Byzantine and Moslem eras, wealth in Beirut did not depend upon rural prosperity but rather upon industry, including that associated with higher education. Although fewer acres were cultivated or were used for less intensive agriculture and grazing, Beirut did not decline noticeably. Towns like Autun retained their prominence by gradually shifting from administrative and intellectual centers to focal points for religious observance. In Spain, towns remained primary conceptual images even in the most remote areas, and in successful towns new religious elites vied for power with their rural counterparts. The urban praetors in Rome went on extolling their accomplishments as if they alone mattered. In the cities explored in this volume, the ancient concepts of community proved to be truly eternal, surviving long after changed circumstances seemed to call for their abandonment.

Although based upon very tangible records—inscriptions, papyri, ceramics, coins—each case study in this volume also tries to delve into the conceptual world of the city's leading elements, explore ways in which the elites manifested their special relationship to those within and beyond their city, and assess changes that took place locally over the centuries comprising late antiquity. Natural disasters took a toll, and the public response too often seems inadequate. Perhaps more to the point, natural calamities offered opportunities to rebuild or build anew. From the fourth century onward, there seems to have been competing visions of what to do when events required new construction. Apparently gone were the days when a Trajan would rebuild Antioch, reproducing exactly its original plan, after it had been destroyed by earthquake. In late antiquity the repair of public works often took decades and in some cases was either not even contemplated or was done in such a poor manner as to be ineffective [Alföldy]. This lackadaisical attitude does not seem to have been a matter of technical or even financial capacity, but something else: perhaps new or conflicting ideas about community priorities, perhaps competing directions among community leadership. That there were competing ideas, however, may be evidence of urban vitality rather than stagnation.

The role of the imperial government seems remarkably slight in most of the cases under discussion, but there are exceptions. Wherever the emperor and his highest level staffs gathered the hand of the government was decisive in establishing priorities, including for example such cities as Serdica, Antioch, Alexandria, Trier, Milan, and Ravenna in addition to the imperial capitals. Elsewhere, towns functioned differentially because of decisions made by the imperial government. There seems to have been a curious relationship between community change and the government in that the more integrated the town had been in the imperial regime, the more new opportunities opened up as the governmental institutions themselves changed. In the case of Rome, the fourth-century departure of the emperor and his court for Milan, Trier, and ultimately Ravenna, left a vacuum of leadership in the ancient capital that the traditional aristocracy, historically identified with the welfare of the city, moved to fill as did the bishop of Rome. Whether an individual was pagan or Christian mattered little among the traditional elite. The validation of traditional leadership rested upon the secular elite's ability to convince the population that doing the time-honored things—holding office and maintaining the centuries-old public buildings—mattered as much or more to life in the metropolis than the comparable but purely Christian achievements of the bishops.

The essays exploring the rural experience remind us that, although it is commonplace today to say that Roman society was predominantly rural, there was a great variety of rural settings and experiences across the Empire. Even in the best of times natural disasters such as drought were frequent and immediate. Rather than being totally dependent upon urban markets, rural societies in the areas examined here were set in a web of local, subregional, and regional trade. Cyprus reveals the many levels of interaction in which rural producers had a stake, most of them far beyond their control: the demands of the great cities, the towns on the island, those who shared the valley, one's fellow villagers, and the isolated farms in the hills. In the

German provinces on the Rhine and uppermost Danube, rural life during the third century exhibited extraordinary prosperity and ended in fragmentation in the early fifth century. Over these centuries villa estates gradually but totally disappeared in some areas, were transformed into proto-medieval villages in others, or survived nestled near fortifications in still others. Regardless of the scenario, almost everywhere small groups sought to sustain agriculture from safe-havens. Concern for personal safety was paramount. Trier and Constantinople were imperial creations of a much larger size than anything around them, and both drew upon resources from throughout the Empire. Essentially civilian, each of these capitals nonetheless was protected by a special system of defense that significantly transformed rural society wherever troops were stationed.

In the Pannonian provinces (after ca. 400 renamed Illyrian), particularly Valeria, the fourth century witnessed a complex rural transformation [Visy]. Pécs (Sopianae), the capital of Valeria, acted as a diminutive Trier or Constantinople, supporting villa agriculture longest and concentrating wealth and monuments for its display. In this regard Pécs is a fine example of how an urban center of relatively modest size influenced its environs. In Pécs a few great landowners, probably associated with the late imperial bureaucracy, experienced a period of prosperity as judged from the remains of their estates, burials, and the few surviving inscriptions, but the poor rural inhabitants seem not to have fared so well. Into this social mix an increasing number of former barbarians were settled in the agricultural interior of the province as a result of the successful recruitment efforts of the Roman army, itself transformed during the last decades of the fourth century.

Ethnicity seems to have mattered less and less as it became progressively impossible to differentiate people by their cultural attributes. Settlement of barbarians inside the Empire had been going on for a very long time, but new circumstances may have accelerated the process during the latter half of the fourth century. More traditional Roman materials disappeared, replaced by new styles in ceramics, burials, and even certain strains of wheat brought from beyond the Danube and grown on the soils around their new homes. In many areas barbarians gradually took on the technology necessary to operate completely within the Roman provincial economy as they had earlier done along the frontiers. Essential mining activity continued at least into the fifth century in the Balkan provinces, where it was apparently still under traditional imperial supervision according to the *Notitia Dignitatum*. At some point, often but not always in the fifth century, the peripheral provinces ceased to have tangible significance to their local populations, which had shifted to barbarian markets and sources of protection, or had clustered around remaining Roman garrisons and fortified centers, or had departed the province altogether. This is especially true for the provinces along the Rhine and upper and middle Danube. For those in the Mediterranean provinces security was not such a concern, but nonetheless rural inhabitants there also responded to changes in their region. Like their peers in the frontier provinces, the rural populations of the interior provinces acted on a purely local level and without having any influence upon the overall factors changing their lives.

The role, or lack thereof, of the imperial government in rural life is an important factor in every case, and it varied according to time and place, but nowhere is its importance so clear as in the fifth- and sixth-century Balkans. Here villas and villages began to disappear in earnest around the middle of the fifth century, and by the reign of Justinian (527-65) the only supporter of organized towns was the central government, and the only town life was that of the camps. Villas remained in the neighborhood of Constantinople alone [Curta]. On the other hand, rural Cyprus, far from external disturbances until the Arab raids of the 640s, profited from the comings and goings of all types of merchant ships laden with goods for Constantinople or manufactured products coming in the reverse direction. Just as the Balkans was entering a death-spiral of both urban and rural life, Cyprus experienced two centuries of prosperity. In the West, there was little active intervention or stimulation by the imperial authorities, except for the area surrounding Trier. At Trier as at Constantinople, the presence of the imperial court, the attending governmental systems, and special defense forces assured the perpetuation of urban markets, good transportation, and a concentration of resources. Here in the fifth century, as around Constantinople in the sixth century, villa estates continued to prosper in their protected environment. These factors had a profound impact upon the immediately surrounding area. Much beyond Trier, however, rural society lost any single focus. The detailed work being conducted in the frontier provinces along the Rhine and upper Danube has revealed patterns of organization and behavior that were previously obscured. Although no one pattern dominates, a structure of principles for assessing causation and duration is beginning to take shape [Bender]. The great river frontiers of the German provinces went from being an interconnected and largely self-supportive regional system to a fractured series of valleys and strong-points where agriculturists eked out an existence virtually within sight of the walls.

Neither Petra nor Bostra, the provincial capital, dominated the landscape of Arabia; it remained a land of villages. The available evidence, especially from a few intensive surveys and excavations, is beginning to reveal many of the tensions that existed in the Arabian countryside [Graf]. There are hints of a late Roman development of a true landed elite and the presence of a variety of markets, similar in that regard to what is coming to light on Cyprus [Rautman]. Arabia and neighboring provinces also demonstrate the continued interaction of the rural elements of society and the imperial bureaucracy, particularly tax assessors and surveyors, who may have taken advantage of the survival of carefully established and durable field patterns in their assessments. In this regard, Egypt presents comparable material. The imprint of the central authority was also visible in the carefully prescribed districts around the urban centers, dividing up the area into effective townships. In those communities with populations large enough to be called towns, architecture, particularly of Christian churches, continued to be inspired by models in the great cities of the Empire, the capitals and major governmental and population centers such as Antioch, Alexandria, Milan, and Serdica. Other than these conceptual intrusions, the imperial centers mattered only indirectly as unseen agents rarely influencing local market conditions.

In these essays the authors use all varieties of available evidence, but archaeological material is preeminent. Literary sources very rarely mention even the most important rural areas and then usually only to denigrate the lifestyles of those living there. The attitude of the elite may not have been entirely genuine, however, as is carefully developed in one essay with a literary orientation. Many of our most valued authors in late antiquity in fact did know at first hand what rural life was all about. Their sporting activities took them there, and their livelihood depended to some degree upon the agricultural strength of their holdings and their own ability to manage it. Perhaps their intimacy explains why they could at once embrace its glories while mocking its allure. Gallic aristocrats lived in a world in which they had to know many of those features of life in the countryside that modern man has been able to put aside. The joys of the hunt were tempered by the fear of injury. Villagers were daily companions serving as aides, and they received a share of the meat—a tangible act of patronage. Horsemanship then was as important as driving an automobile today. A real master practiced in the fields and forests. Such intimacy with rural concerns, even if primarily inspired by elitist motives, suggests that the "frontier" between the world of the aristocrat and the tiller of the soil was paper thin, a matter of chosen illusion [Drinkwater].

There is nothing, however, illusory in the evidentiary base of these essays. Literary references, numismatics, ceramics, aerial surveys, field surveys, published and unpublished excavations, and chemical analysis, are all pressed to help unveil details of the rural environment. Collectively they allow us to grasp many of the factors influencing rural success or failure, considerations that aid our understanding throughout the Empire. They provide contexts for urban developments until quite recently unknowable.

It was in the urban centers that the "mission to the gentiles," the foundation of Christian universalism, first achieved some measure of public acceptance. Only in these population centers were resident communities of Jews available to translate the message, wealthy patrons able to provide the subventions required to sustain the agents of proselytism, and sufficient numbers of the political elite willing to offer some cover for activities routinely considered illegal and on examination possibly treasonous. Attempts to measure the growth of Christianity over time can be set aside: we do not possess reliable data on which to build a demographic profile of Christianity in the first century, when its separation from Judaism had not been completed, or in the fourth, when imperial favor, previously denied, transformed 'conversion' into a safe and politically advantageous option. What we can say is that when Constantine began to publicize his own preference, Christian communities were well-established in the population centers, had attracted converts from all social strata, and could rely on prominent, and often powerful, representatives to protect their corporate and individual interests before local and imperial administrators.

With the "conversion" of the political class, a gradual process in which 'mixed marriages' undoubtedly played a distinctive role, patronage no longer was expressed exclusively in games, the construction of public buildings and amenities, and conspicuous celebrations of pagan festivals. By the fourth century, and increasingly thereafter, many of the prominent residents of major urban centers preferred to allocate their resources for the endowment of churches and martyria and the promotion of elaborate observances of Christian holy days. How many patrons of paganism apostatized it is impossible to say, but the number was significant enough to transform the urban landscape by the beginning of the fifth century. Inspired by imperial legislation against pagan associations and practices, local patrons eagerly demonstrated their devotion by sponsoring urban renewal projects that not only asserted the Christian claim to public space but also threatened the survival of the artifacts of the pagan past. Only in Rome were pagan monuments in the urban core considered sacrosanct; until the fifth century most emperors, perhaps to preserve the historic buildings and certainly to placate the important pagan political class, were prepared to follow the example of Constantine, who had constructed the Lateran basilica outside the ancient pomoerium. Pagan architecture, of course, did not disappear from the urban landscape. One has only to inspect the topography of the "new Rome," the new model Christian city of Constantinople, to recognize that the traditional forms—basilica, hippodrome, baths, columns, bas-reliefs—remained the lexicon of architectural imagination in the new Christian Empire.

The pace and extent of Christianization are attested in Alexandria, where core and chora were linked by an extensive network of churches, martyria, and monasteries between the Mediterranean littoral and the southern shore of Lake Mareotis [Haas]. This prosperous Lake district had long supplied Alexandria with freshwater fish and agricultural products and in late antiquity supported a diverse population of merchants, landowners, farmers, pilgrims, miracle-workers, and monks. Reflecting the elevated status awarded the metropolitan bishops by the Council of Nicaea (325 C.E.), the authority of the Patriarch of Alexandria reached across the Lake to encompass the shrines, monasteries, and pilgrim routes on the western and southern shores. That he enjoyed higher status and greater authority is clear, but in origin and function the Patriarch was simply a superior representative of the episcopal infrastructure that Constantine had promoted and successive councils confirmed. Members of the urban political class, empowered by imperial decrees, and effectively autonomous within their sees (subject only to the judicial review of councils), bishops in late antiquity presided over basilican churches in the urban centers where the faithful were expected to gather for regular services and celebrations of major holy days in the Christian calendar. With friends in high places and with access to accumulated property and burgeoning revenues, the bishops not surprisingly became powerful civic personalities, to whom the entire Christian community, urban and rural, could turn for spiritual guidance and material support in times of trouble.

Bishops were clearly the principal agents of evangelization in the suburban districts and more distant towns and estates, the hinterland in which the majority of the late Roman population resided. It was in these rural areas—in the secondary towns and villages, the owner-occupied farms, the estates leased by urban magnates or managed on their behalf by vilici—that the urban representatives of Christianity, secular and ecclesiastical, competed with the pagan gods and their persistent devotees for the hearts and minds of the rustici. Some may have shared the traditional aristocratic disdain of country folk, but the more astute among them must have recognized that the Christianization of the urban centers would not be complete until the inhabitants of the countryside had abandoned the ancient gods. Some evidence that bishops appreciated the importance of the rustici is provided by Augustine, who took care to acknowledge the presence of country folk in his sermons and to craft a language that would render the message intelligible and attractive [Clark]. Alliance with Christian landowners in the countryside who had both the social position and the wealth required to underwrite the costs of church construction in the towns and on their rural estates was clearly an essential prerequisite in their efforts to complete the mission to the gentiles. Such alliances, however, were not without risk. Though the clergy attached to villa-churches would necessarily play an important role in the evangelization of the countryside, they derived their support from the local aristocracy and could conduct regular services and provide for the spiritual well-being of their parishioners without the direct supervision of bishops in the urban centers. It is unlikely that Hydatius of Merida and Ithacius of Ossonoba, who denounced the villa-churches as agents of the Priscillian heresy, were the only bishops of the fourth and fifth centuries to consider their independence as a threat to episcopal authority [Bowes]. Similarly, holy men may well have been a source of spiritual inspiration for the rustici, enhancing the popularity of Christianity through miracles and impressive displays of personal asceticism, but from the bishop's perspective they could be dangerous mavericks whose beliefs and practices were widely thought to have been sanctioned through direct communication with Higher Authority.

Whether imperial attempts to eradicate paganism through legislation, evolving from preferential treatment of Christian clergy and places of worship under Constantine to outright prohibition of pagan practices under Theodosius I and his successors, accelerated the conversion of the countryside is uncertain. Such legislation may well have been enforced in the urban centers, where the bishops could provide the necessary oversight and muscle, but it is unlikely to have persuaded individual pagans in the towns and rural estates to renounce practices of a lifetime or to reject the tangible support provided by pagan patrons. The countryside was much more complex than the urban accounts suggest, with conditions from region to region so remarkably different that it would be more accurate to speak of countrysides in late antiquity. In some, the bishops and their minions may have enjoyed considerable success; in others, notably in Africa and Anatolia, the indifference, if not outright resistance, of the pagani to the Christian message assured the survival of polytheistic alternatives into the fifth and sixth centuries [Harl, Riggs]. That Christianity, unlike most religions of the Roman Empire, could transcend local associations with particular towns or regions was a great advantage, but there is no reason to believe that the pagani would have considered a universal deity more attractive than their local gods. Had these gods not provided for their families and their community—assuring adequate rainfall for their crops, promoting health through sacred springs and miraculous cures, offering consolation in the cycle of birth and death? [Riggs]. Could the god of the Christians offer more? In the competition among religious patrons, the god or gods who promised the most compelling beneficia would be favored to win the allegiance of the countryside.

In modern assessments of the contribution of Constantine, his personal endorsement of Christianity and his patronage of clergy and individual bishops have figured prominently, but a case can be made that his promotion of a canonical ecclesiastical hierarchy at Nicaea and adoption of the basilica form for Christian churches provided even more enduring support for efforts to strengthen the appeal of Christianity beyond the urban centers. At Nicaea, Constantine declared the bishops stewards of imperial beneficia in the urban centers, resources that would make the bishop the patron *non pareil* and equip the Christian church with an infrastructure superior to anything pagans in the courtryside could marshal, as Julian clearly recognized. In borrowing the basilica from the pagan past he provided a model of religious architecture that could be reproduced, in grand or modest versions, in towns and villages throughout the Empire. Neither was sufficient to assure the success of evangelism, but coupled with a strategy to reduce the intellectual distance between town and countryside urban evangelists and local clergy alike were in a stronger position to compete with recalcitrant pagans and their patrons. That Christians recognized the need for a pragmatic approach can be seen in their willingness to shape the message and liturgy to accommodate local interests and expectations. A striking example of such accommodation has been detected in farming villages of the Belus Massif, 35 km east of Antioch. Here the basilica form that Constantine had employed in the construction of magnificent churches in Jerusalem and Constantinople was systematically modified to resemble the dominant architectural style of the region, the farmhouse complex [Kidner]. Modifications on this scale would not require unacceptable changes in church liturgy, but they may well have made unfamiliar beliefs and practices seem less threatening and more palatable to the inhabitants of the Belus Massif. The Christianization of the countryside had not been completed by the sixth century, and as the papers in this volume attest, the pace and character of the process was determined more by local conditions, in both the eastern and western halves of the Empire, than by imperial or ecclesiastical aspirations. We know something of the missionaries and their rate of success or failure in particular regions. What we should like to know is whether these representatives, in their zeal to banish the pagan gods, had created a hybrid Christianity for the countryside that differed fundamentally from that practiced in the basilicae of the urban centers.

Christianity altered the urban landscape in the Mareotis region of Alexandria as it did in Rome, Autun, Petra, Tarraco, and most other towns, but the question remains whether substantive change in the urban ethos underlay the physical changes attested archaeologically. When seeking the demise of the ancient city, we seem to have rushed to accept its collapse prematurely and simplistically. We need to recall Alcaeus reminding the Greeks that the people living in cities mattered more than their monuments. Those living in the cities of late antiquity were still exploring, but were their horizons as broad as those of their forefathers? How and why would they defend their individuality and that of their towns? In what ways were their fates and their values still linked to those beyond their town walls? These essays provide new insights and force us to abandon any single explanation or model of urban and rural change and to reevaluate cities as centers of habitation rather than as architectural museums. By using all the available evidence, material as well as literary, our authors provide access not only into the world of the elites, but also to the scarcely known lives of those without a voice in the surviving literature of the period, those men and women who worked in the shops, labored in the fields, and humbled themselves before their gods. To them the officeholders of Rome addressed inscriptions proclaiming their merits in hope that somebody would read them and agree. The poor were responsible for the middens of pottery, for the glass perfumeries, for grinding spices, for pressing tens of thousands of liters of olive oil. Their feet trampled the grapes, wore down the pilgrim's paths to holy shrines, and ultimately their houses buried the grid-patterns of the ancient streets over which their ancestors had walked from time out of mind. These essays bring us closer to the complexity of life in late ancient communities than the earlier simplifications and in that regard closer to the real citizens.

Urban Centers and Rural Contexts in Late Antiquity

EDITED BY

THOMAS S. BURNS

AND

JOHN W. EADIE

Michigan State University Press

East Lansing

Difficillima Tempora: Urban Life, Inscriptions, and Mentality in Late Antique Rome

GÉZA ALFÖLDY

IN HIS FAMOUS DESCRIPTIONS OF ROME WRITTEN IN THE LATE FOURTH CENTURY, the historian Ammianus Marcellinus presented a highly negative picture of the City in his age. He pointed out the decadence of both the senatorial aristocracy and the common people and closed by stating that due to immoral conduct nothing either memorable or serious came to pass at Rome.[1] Some decades later, Salvianus of Massilia could only bear witness to the tragical indifference of the Roman society in face of the danger of a total collapse: "Even in fear of captivity, we play games; frightened of death, we laugh. One might think that the whole Roman people has glutted Sardonian grass: it dies and laughs."[2]

As recent research has emphasized, it would be a mistake to consider the history of the Later Roman Empire only as a "decline" ending with the "fall" of its western part. In this way it was seen, under the influence of ancient authors like Ammianus or Salvianus, by almost all historians since Edward Gibbon. Scholars of the last generation have argued convincingly that the history of Rome during the fourth and even in the fifth century by no means only showed events and processes that could be interpreted as symptoms of a general decay, or at least as signs of a general transformation; on the contrary, the Later Roman Empire offers quite a lot of evidence for the continuity of the traditional order and for the willingness as well as for the ability of the Roman society to maintain this order even under the pressure of the Barbarians.[3] The imperial power, the administration of the state and of the numerous urban communities, several basic patterns of the social system, the Roman economy, the traditional way of urban life, and much of the Roman culture still existed and functioned in this time. Although they had to be reorganized after the so-called "crisis of the third century" and were confronted with growing difficulties during late antiquity, there was no fundamental change concerning all the basic structures—and they continued to exist not only up to the collapse of the Western Empire, but, even after the extinction of the imperial power in the West, lived on until the sixth century. The two most important processes of transformation during this time, the victory of Christianity and the growing success of barbarian invasions after the defeat of the Roman army at Hadrianopolis, did not change the fundaments of the traditional order with one stroke. It is, of course, true that there were great differences between various regions of the Empire as, e.g., between the northern frontier areas—which by no means had been removed from any form of Roman influence, but from the political dominance of Rome—and Italy, which remained under the rule of the emperors until 476 A.D. In the central areas of the Imperium Romanum, i.e., in the Mediterranean regions, the bonds of continuity and resistance against "decline and fall" were clearly present, including the conviction of large groups of the society that the Roman order was established to all eternity. If it was threatened, it had to be defended. "The Roman order is in collapse, but our neck does not bow down,"[4] wrote Saint Jerome. His pagan contemporaries like Symmachus or the author of the Historia Augusta thought the same.[5]

Within this setting, the urban life in the City of Rome and the mentality of its citizens in Late Antiquity offer a very interesting panorama. The City of the fourth and fifth centuries was not what she had been during the long period before, from Augustus to the late third century. From Diocletian and Constantine onward, the emperors had definitely removed their residence to other places. In consequence, Rome lost its role as the center of the political life of the Empire. But at the same time the Senate and also the senatorial aristocracy, which now ruled the City without standing in the permanent shadow of the Emperor, greatly improved their influence.[6] The administrative system established by Diocletian and Constantine, the social order with its fundamental dichotomy of the senatorial aristocracy and the *plebs*, now without an intermediary equestrian order, the system of food provisions for the metropolis with its enormous number of inhabitants, and the role of the *Urbs* as the most important cultural center of the Roman world—all this was distinguished by an astonishing continuity during the whole period of Late Antiquity. It did not break down even in the fifth and early sixth centuries; neither in consequence of the raids of the Goths in 410 or of the Vandals in 455, nor through the collapse of the Western Empire in 476 nor through the establishment of the kingdom of Theoderich in succession of Odoacer, killed in 493. The system of the senatorial government of the City also resisted internal conflicts, like the repeated hunger-revolts and other social upheavals, which resulted from the clash between pagans and Christians and from the fight for the leading role in the City between senatorial magistrates on the one side and the bishop of Rome on the other side.

Given this situation, it is highly interesting to learn how the inhabitants of Rome themselves considered the state and the development of their *Urbs* in this period. This article, therefore, poses the following questions: How did the ruling class of Rome in Late Antiquity present itself to the public, and what did it, to judge from the public media, think about its own situation and problems? In dealing with this topic, particular attention will be paid to the inscriptions of the *Urbs* that belong to the Late Empire; i.e. first of all to the epigraphic documents of the emperors, and even more to those of the magistrates of the City. It must be realized that in the Roman world inscriptions had a very important function as a medium of communication; in a certain sense, they were a substitute for the press, radio and television of our days.[7] They must always be compared, of course, with the testimonia given by other sources, like the contemporary literature, juridical texts, coins, architecture, sculpture etc.[8]

During the last years the inscriptions of emperors and senators from Rome, the *Tituli imperatorum domusque eorum* and the *Tituli magistratuum populi Romani*, have been systematically revised for some new fascicles of the *Corpus Inscriptionum Latinarum*, prepared by a group of scholars at Heidelberg in collaboration with Professor Silvio Panciera and his team at Rome. A volume dedicated to the inscriptions of monuments erected by the emperors or in their honor appeared in 1996, with a complete edition of some 600 new documents and *Addenda et corrigenda* to 800 inscriptions already published in the old volumes of the *CIL*. The next volume, which includes more than 600 new epigraphic documents concerning Roman magistrates and *Addenda et corrigenda* to almost another 1,000 texts of this kind, is forthcoming. A considerable part of these sources belong to the Late Empire.[9] Both the new documents and the inscriptions, which, already known, have undergone revision, improve our knowledge of urban life at Rome during the last centuries of Antiquity. In particular, they make us familiar with the situation of Rome the governing class intended to convey to both the visitors and the lower strata of the population of the City itself by means of monuments. The statues together with their inscriptions, supposed to serve this purpose, were erected on the public places of Rome—first of all the *forum Romanum* and the *forum Traiani*, but also other *fora*—as well as in the palaces of the aristocrats.

This picture did, of course, not necessarily correspond to the truth. In fact, it differed from it in several points. Nevertheless, the image of urban life expressed through the inscribed monuments may be very interesting in a double sense. Whenever we can assume a correspondence between historical reality and auto-representation, it is instructive to see in which fields people did not hesitate to confess the existence of real problems, also of rather grave ones, and which measures were publicly proposed for their solution. At the same time, whenever there was an evident gap between the official version of the situation of Rome and reality, it is very interesting to learn which problems were underestimated or consciously concealed behind the façade of an intact world.

It is certainly not true that official documents in any case have to be considered untruthful, i.e. that they always tell us the contrary of what was going on. In Roman literature it was indeed common to complain of the decadence of one's time in comparison with the noble past; in that manner Ammianus Marcellinus, in giving a negative description of Roman society at his time, clung to the old "biological" theory of decadence, which said that Rome, having grown up from childhood to youth and manhood, necessarily had to decline in its old age.[10] Inscriptions were, however, like public architecture, sculpture, reliefs, painting, and also coins, traditionally a medium of self-representation intending to glorify individuals or groups, i.e. to emphasize peoples' merits and achievements. They were not used to lament the bad times, in this point differing from what Roman historians so often did. In epigraphic documents it was common to mention difficulties only if one could praise the successful solution of these problems. This was a main subject of official inscriptions, for example, under Augustus, in an age in which the basis of the epigraphic culture in the Roman Empire was established: The Augustan epigraphy suggested that Augustus had created a new Golden Age after a long period of civil wars and external defeats.[11] The self-representation of his successors followed the same lines. In these circumstances it is interesting to notice that during Late Antiquity the tone of the inscriptions of Rome was by no means as optimistic as it had been during the first centuries of the Empire.

Like the coins with their catchwords, such as *fel(icium) temp(orum) reparatio, felicitas perpetua* or *beatitudo publica*,[12] the inscriptions of Rome, which glorified late Roman emperors were in fact intended to convey the impression that everything was in a good state thanks to the virtues and deeds of the rulers.[13] Diocletianus and Maximianus seem to be praised by an inscription of Rome even as the creators of the best of all ages.[14] Whenever inscriptions of this kind indicated problems of the public order at all, the texts pretended that they had been caused by "tyrants," i.e. by rivals of the present ruler who were, however, always defeated by the Emperor, with the consequence that public security, justice, peace, and prosperity were restored.[15] In the inscriptions of the late Roman aristocracy, however, there is no sign of a conviction that the age in which their heroes lived would have been generally regarded as a "good time," as it had been pretended not only in the imperial, but also in the senatorial inscriptions of the Early Empire. The senatorial epigraphy of the Late Empire pointed, sometimes very clearly, rather to the contrary, even if problems normally appeared in the usual manner, that is as already resolved. Memmius

Vitrasius Orfitus, prefect of the City for a second time from 357 to 359, at the end of his prefecture was honored with at least four statues set up in his house by different corporations. In fact, one of the texts written on the bases of these monuments tells us that the prefect had renewed the *status optimus* of the City. But all these inscriptions emphasize with the same wording, doubtlessly in correspondence to a formula established according to the wishes of the prefect himself, that the times in which the senator resolved a part of his former duties were *difficillima tempora*.[16] This terminology does not only refer to the revolt of Magnentius against Constantius II, but also to the situation after the defeat of the usurpator, which was characterized by the difficult position of the Senate in confrontation with the two rivals.[17] And more or less in the same manner as imperial constitutions that are preserved in our juridical sources, the inscriptions of late Roman magistrates noted the existence of some structural problems and difficulties which emerged again and again. I would like to concentrate myself on three of these topics: on the usurpation of privileges by unauthorized groups of the population and similar *fraudes*, on the food shortages, and on the dilapidation of public buildings. All these problems were, of course, by no means new ones. In the inscriptions of Roman magistrates of earlier periods, however, they never appeared so often and were certainly not described as drastically as in the epigraphic documents of the Later Empire.

I would like to start with the usurpation of privileges and the neglect of duties by individuals and groups. In the imperial constitutions of the Later Empire laws aiming at people who abused privileges or did not fulfill their obligatory tasks were a very common feature. Of course, we also know some epigraphic documents from earlier centuries, which referred to problems of this kind, e.g. the rescript of Septimius Severus and Caracalla concerning the *centonarii* of Solva in Noricum. According to this document, the emperors ordered that rich men who had abused the *vacatio munerum* of the *collegia* should be compelled to carry out their duties; at the same time, however, the emperors confirmed the *privilegia* of the *collegia*, which an over-zealous governor of the province had tried to abolish.[18]

From Rome we know some edicts of fourth-century urban prefects that deal with similar problems. One of the most interesting documents of this kind is the much discussed edict of Tarracius Bassus, published in 375 or 376 in several copies at different places of the *Urbs*. Numerous fragments of these inscriptions have been preserved; by studying them it has been possible not only to reconstruct the full text of the edict, but also to calculate the number of people concerned by the orders of the prefect.[19] The *tabernarii*, shop possessors, disregarding the edicts of former urban prefects and revolting against Roman discipline, misused money destined for public targets; they occupied seats in the theater, the amphitheater and the circus that did not correspond to their social status; and they laid claim to free bread, which was intended only for poor people: *qui sibi pecun[iam publicam, locum indebitum in] spectaculis, et panem populi contra disciplinam Romanam derel[ictis edictis praeff. urbi] vindicare consueverant.* The edict made public the names of all *tabernarii* who were to be punished. From the preserved fragments we can conclude that the list contained more than one hundred names, quite a high number, grouped into twelve columns. Those *tabernarii* came from all the regions of the City; among them we recognize representatives of different branches of trade, pagans as well as Christians and Jews. Even if the edict aimed at stopping all forms of abuse, the document made clear to everybody that there were large groups within the urban population that had to be forced by law to maintain the *disciplina Romana*.

We also know some edicts through which urban prefects of the fourth century attempted to stop illegal activities in the context of the food supply of the City, especially concerning meat and bread. In the same manner as imperial constitutions, these edicts describe the *fraudes*, i. e. the dishonest practices, and they lay down punishments for these abuses. But whereas imperial constitutions, e.g. with regard to the *suarii*, the swine collectors, nevertheless emphasize the general usefulness of these men who "display extremely vigilant exertions for the advantages of Roman people" and note "the special grant of imperial favour" given to them,[20] the edicts of the urban prefects restrict themselves to the description of privileges, duties, abuses and punishments.[21] They speak of the wide-spread abuses, e.g. of the *consueta fraudibus licentia* of the *molendinarii*, of the millers who worked in the mills constructed on the *Gianicolo;* but it is quite astonishing to see that the prefect, while announcing severe punishments, at the same time appealed to his *humanitas*.[22] This clear case of self-glorification makes it all too evident that not only the inscriptions set up in honor of the magistrates, but also those documents which presented their edicts and other official activities to the public, were a medium of the self-representation of Roman aristocrats. In their edicts, the magistrates appear as gentlemen confronted with a mass of defrauders and criminals who in some cases had to be threatened with capital punishment.[23] This was no longer the magnificent harmony of Roman society that the epigraphic culture of the Early Empire had intended to convey.

Another central problem of urban life in Rome during the Later Empire mentioned in the inscriptions of magistrates was the repeated food shortages.[24] Again, this phenomenon was not a new one, but in the inscriptions of earlier centuries it was considerably played down. Magistrates or private benefactors who, in the case of shortages, managed to reestablish the food situation of the towns of the Empire, were glorified as noble donators or good managers, but normally without giving a dramatic description of the situation that had caused their efforts.[25] In Rome, where, during the first centuries A.D., food supply was the concern of the emperor, food shortage was hardly a problem introduced into public documents. The *Res Gestae Divi Augusti,* where Augustus praised the role in the *curatio annonae,* which he, having disdained dictatorship, had taken upon himself *in summa frumenti penuria,* are an exception to the rule.[26] In the inscriptions of the magistrates of late Rome, however, their merits in this regard were emphasized in a specific manner. The best example is an inscription that can be read on the base of a statue erected in honor of Attius Insteius Tertullus, *praefectus urbi* in 307-8, a text we can now restore in a more complete form than before. We learn that the prefect helped the people of Rome through his energetic measures during an *inopia in[gens]* in the context of a general *miseria,* caused by an *incomparabili[s caritas]* of bread, which led to an *apertum periculum;* he also liberated those people who worked as bakers at this time from *gravis metus et discrimen,* from great fear and danger.[27] Another inscription seems to hint at an unrest in Rome in a similar situation, and the praise of the successful magistrate was of course increased by the description of the turbulence he had mastered in gloomy terms.[28] The general picture of urban life presented in these inscriptions to the public was, however, not quite a favorable one.

A third problem of urban life in Rome during the Later Empire, which ought to be mentioned here, was the dilapidation of public buildings, attested by a long series of inscriptions that refer to the renovation of *opera publica*. At this point, it is worthwhile noting that from Diocletian and Constantine onward and excluding ecclesiastical inscriptions, we know but very few epigraphic documents that mention the construction of *new* public buildings. They were, at least formally, initiated by the emperors or by the Senate. The last inscriptions of this category refer to the construction of an arch near the *pons Aelius* between 379 and 383, by order of Gratianus, Valentinianus II and Theodosius I,[29] and to the establishment of another arch in honor of Arcadius, Honorius, and Theodosius II ordered by the Senate on the occasion of Stilicho's victory over Radagaisus in 406.[30] The great majority of building inscriptions in late Rome, however, attests the renovation of older constructions.

During the fourth and at the beginning of the fifth century, some epigraphic documents mention the emperors as initiators of restorations in buildings like the baths of Agrippa and of Caracalla, the *thermae* of the late Severan palace of the Sessorianum or those of Diocletian, the theater of Pompeius, the embankments and the bridges of the Tiberis.[31] In one of his urban inscriptions, Constantius II was even praised as *restitutor urbis*.[32] According to the inscriptions above different gates of the City dedicated in 401 or 402, it had been the Senate who, taking up a *suggestio* made by Stilicho, had ordered the renovation of the Aurelian Wall together with the gates and towers.[33] However, by far the most building inscriptions of late Rome, and after the rule of Honorius all documents of this kind, refer to magistrates, usually to the urban prefects, who were responsible and took the initiative for the restoration of damaged or destroyed buildings until the reign of the Gothic kings,[34] and who were followed after the collapse of the Gothic rule in Italy by Byzantine magistrates.[35]

The language of these inscriptions is highly instructive; among the causes for the ruin of public buildings they not only mention their high age[36] or natural disasters like earthquake or fire,[37] but, in correspondence to a well-known topic that certainly had a realistic background, also human carelessness, *longa incuria* or *dissimulatio longa*.[38] In some cases, they hint at barbarian raids or other wars. The *fatalis ignis* which destroyed the *curia*, the Senate house, or the *fatalis casus* of a building in the southern *campus Martius* have certainly to be connected with the destruction of public buildings by the Goths under Alaric in 410;[39] the same seems to be true for the *civilis vel potius feralis clades*, by which the *thermae Constantinianae* were almost annihilated.[40] The *tumultus civilis* by which a statue set up on the *forum Romanum* was seriously damaged was the civil war between Ricimer and the emperor Anthemius in 472.[41] As to the wars before the collapse of the Western Empire, only the invasion of the Vandals in Rome in 455 were, without any euphemism, defined as an *hostilis impetus*;[42] and it was not before the *reconquista* of Justinian that an enemy of Rome who had been responsible for the destruction of a public building, the bridge of the via Salaria over the Tiberis, in 547, the *nefandissimus Totila tyrannus*, was mentioned by name.[43] All these epigraphic documents, including a long series of inscriptions with a similar wording, repeatedly containing the phrases *lapsus, ruina, squalor*,[44] did not present a very optimistic picture of the state of urban architecture, even if they emphasized the efforts of brave magistrates to restore public monuments "for the happiness of the age," *pro beatitudine temporum*, as we read in one document of that kind.[45]

The inscriptions sometimes also explicitly point at the long delay before a destroyed building was finally restored. It may be symptomatic that the restoration of the *curia*, which had been destroyed by Alaric's Goth in 410—and whose restoration was obviously considered a prime target after this catastrophe—was undertaken by at least four or five or possibly six urban prefects during the next decade.[46] Moreover, it seems to have taken more than thirty years to restore the baths of Constantine.[47] As exemplified by the restoration document of these baths, the inscriptions also speak of the *extremus occasus*, the total collapse, of public buildings, and of the *desperatio reparationis*, the hopelessness of their renewal, which underlines the merits of the renovator even more.[48] In inscriptions of Rome from the first centuries of the Empire, a formulation of this kind was absolutely unimaginable.

The individual achievements reported by the inscriptions may be different; their message is, however, always the same, as far as we can deduce it from the uniformity of their formulars and their wording. These epigraphic documents did not only intend to glorify individual senators and their families; by their stereotypical language and by the reference to the recurring qualities of their heroes, they wanted to convince everybody that the survival of Rome was guaranteed thanks to the virtues of its aristocracy. The inscriptions intended to create an image of Rome that did not correspond to that given by the contemporary juridical sources. In the latter it was normally the Emperor who offered a solution to the most urgent problems. This corresponds to the picture of the City presented by the epigraphic sources during the first three centuries of the Empire, in a period in which, from the middle of the rule of Augustus onward, the establishment or the restoration of public buildings had been a privilege of the emperor. In contrast to all that the inscriptions from the Later Empire emphasized the decisive role of the senatorial aristocracy in the government of the *Urbs*, its importance as a governing class that, in the opinion of its members, had always been able to cope with the affairs of the City. The main person whose achievements were praised was, it is true, the *praefectus urbi*, who substituted for the emperor; he was, however, at the same time the first man of the senatorial order.

The inscriptions reveal the idea mentioned before in a very clear manner. Everything done by senatorial magistrates executing their tasks did seem to be well done. Reading their inscriptions, the people should be convinced that these men would resolve all problems and difficulties of urban life; that they would always be able to defend and to renew the traditional order of Rome; that their activities would convert everything, to use the language of the epigraphic documents, *in pristinam faciem splendoremque.*[49] The inscriptions intended to give the impression that the efforts of the senators would always guarantee that the institutions of Rome, *recreatae atque confotae, redditis pristinis viribus, convalescerent et aeternum robur acciperent,*[50] that Rome, renewed and full of vitality, regaining its old vigor, would be sound and would have strength forever. "Forever," indeed. Not only did the emperors praise themselves in inscriptions, on coins or in constitutions collected in the juridical sources as *aeterni principes, perennes Augusti* or *perpetui Augusti.*[51] The same ideology is also present in the senatorial inscriptions of the Later Empire, as they mention that the monuments of the office-holders were set up *ad memoriam sempiternam, ad memoriam perpetui nominis,* as a *perenne monumentum,*[52] because senatorial magistrates themselves used to be a *testimonium sempiternum* of magnificent virtues.[53] In the epigraphic culture of the late Roman senatorial aristocracy, Rome was an *aeterna urbs*[54] first of all thanks to the eternity of its aristocracy, according to the well-known words of Symmachus the *pars melior generis humani.*[55]

This picture presented by the epigraphic sources was, of course, very one-sided. Individual weaknesses or even mistakes were not reported in the inscriptions. The difference between the idealized world of senatorial self-representation and reality may be exemplified by the contrast of the character-sketches of the famous Sex. Claudius Petronius Probus, consul in 371. Our main sources are his honorary inscriptions on the one hand and a well-known passage of Ammianus Marcellinus on the other hand. In his most important inscription found in Rome, Probus is praised as *nobilitatis culmen, litterarum et eloquentiae lumen, auctoritatis exemplum, provisionum et dispositionum magister, humanitatis auctor, moderationis patronus, devotionis antistes;* an inscription from Verona adds that he was *totius admirationis vir, civis eximiae bonitatis, disertissimus atque omnibus rebus eruditissimus*—in every respect a superman.[56] But what do we learn from Ammianus? Probus seemed "to be now generous and ready to advance his friends, but sometimes a cruel schemer, working harm by his deadly jealousies. And although he had great power so long as he lived, . . . he was sometimes timid when boldly confronted, though arrogant against those who feared him; so that in his moments of confidence he seemed to thunder from tragic buskin, and when he was afraid, to be more humble than any wearer of the slipper. . . . Yet he was suspicious, and fortified by his own character; he could smile rather bitterly and sometimes resorted to flattery in order to work harm. He had, moreover, what is a conspicuous evil in such characters, especially when one thinks to be able to conceal it, in that he was so merciless and unbending, that if he had made up his mind to injure anyone, he could not be made to relent nor induced to pardon errors. . . . At the very height of riches and honors he was worried and anxious, and hence always troubled with slight illnesses."[57]

The inscriptions also conceal basic problems and contradictions of the spiritual, social, and political life. In their world, the senatorial order, apart from some characteristics of the German army commanders of senatorial rank, always appears as a homogeneous class constituted of members with the same values, forms of behavior, and virtues. They seemed to hold the same high moral and intellectual qualities from their infancy onward, no matter whether they were pagans or Christians;[58] they appeared equally as men of the same high culture and as the heirs of the most important traditions of Rome. As my pupil Heike Niquet pointed out in her Ph.D. thesis on the monuments of late Roman senators in Rome, the most important virtue of late Roman aristocrats, of pagans as well as Christians, was, according to the inscriptions, their education in the spirit of classical Roman culture.[59]

Outside the funerary setting, the religious confession of the aristocracy was only indicated by mentioning the priesthoods of pagan senators (the last document of this kind set up in public was a monument for the Elder Symmachus, erected in 377, as it seems, on the *forum Traiani*),[60] or by reference to the construction of ecclesiastic buildings.[61] In all other cases the stereotype language of the honorific inscriptions makes it impossible to decide whether the senator in question was a partisan of the old or of the new religion.[62] The notion of *religio,* emphasized in some senatorial inscriptions as a virtue, could cover pagan religiosity as well as Christian belief.[63] Confessional antagonism does not appear in the epigraphic documentation of the aristocracy at all. If a spiritual behavior with an emotional background was praised in the inscriptions of Roman nobles, it was usually not religion, but rather patriotism, once more a virtue common to pagan senators and their Christian fellows, as we learn also by the literary works of pagan and Christian intellectual élites.[64] It is highly impressive that prefects of Rome in their edicts still expressed their *amor patriae* even under the rule the Gothic kings.[65]

Political or social conflicts were mentioned in the inscriptions only when they already seemed to be settled to everyone's satisfaction, like the problems of urban life mentioned above. Accordingly, we learn from an inscription of Virius Nicomachus Flavianus, an ardent pagan who had been a partisan of the usurpator Eugenius and had committed suicide in 394, that his sad destiny was due to the *casus condicionis humanae,* with the consequence that he had lost the reputation gained by his virtues. But this inscription, dedicated to the memory of Flavianus, was set up in 431, at the moment when the senator, thirty-seven years after his death, was publicly rehabilitated by the emperors.[66] Even less important conflicts were mentioned in the inscriptions only if they had already been completely resolved, like a dispute between the *mensores Portuenses* and the *caudicarii* (who were responsible for delivering the grain to Rome) in 389, which was settled by the *praefectus annonae* Ragonius Vincentius Celsus.[67]

Late Roman aristocrats lived in a real world, and they realized the problems existing around them, being aware of the fact that, according to the maxim of Symmachus, all orders of life could be shaken by vicissitudes of time and by changes of the political situation.[68] In their inscriptions, however, they created an ideal world for themselves and for the society of their City—as did Symmachus as well as other authors of his class up to a certain degree also in their literary works, in which important contemporary themes are omitted.[69] The crucial message of the epigraphic culture of the late Roman aristocracy, which does not differ substantially from that of their literary products, can be formulated as follows: Rome will survive forever, because it is governed by an aristocracy that represents the eternal virtues. That is to say, the main message of the public documents of Rome during the Later Empire finally appears to have been a fiction.

Fiction, it is true, can be an important spiritual force, if it is accepted by everyone. The history of Rome knew several fictions of a *longue durée,* which contributed, through their influence on morale and mentality, to the continuity of the social and political order of the Romans, as did, for instance, the fiction that the Roman gentleman was a *bonus agricola.*[70] Despite some contemporary criticism of Roman hypocrisy, there is hardly any doubt that during the Later Empire not only the aristocracy of Rome, but also large groups of the population of the *Urbs* were pleased with the ideal world of the inscriptions, which offered not only temporary solutions to some repeated difficulties like the food supply realized by aristocratic magistrates of the same profile, but could also nourish the hope that this would always be the same. There was no place, however, for a vision of structural reforms of the social and political system. Rome in Late Antiquity was certainly a vivid town with real problems and conflicts, but the monuments and their inscriptions, which expressed the values of the senatorial aristocracy, were more suitable for a museum than for the scenes of real life.

Iamne constat, fortunam nobilitatis consentire temporibus?, asked Symmachus:[71] "Is it not a fact that the fate of the aristocracy corresponds to the character of the times in which it lives?" The time we have dealt with in this contribution was characterized by the contradictions between continuity and change of the Roman order; and the mentality of the late Roman aristocracy was dominated by the contradiction between the dream that good old Rome would survive, and the dramatic experience that Rome was no longer what it had been before. In such a situation, a museum, which presents valuable and nice old things, not only with the message that they will have their value forever, but also with the pretension that they were more important than everything else, does not seem the ideal source of strength to cope with the problems of the future. It may rather serve as a refuge. Let us hope, at the threshold of a new millenium, that the cultivation of our own cultural heritage, including classical tradition, will not have its place only in such a museum.

NOTES

1. Amm. Marc. 14,6,2 ff. and 28,4,6 ff. Cf. W. Hartke, *Römische Kinderkaiser* (Berlin, 1051), 62 ff.; R. Pach, *TAPhA* 84, 1953, 181 ff.; J. Matthews, *The Roman Empire of Ammianus* (London, 1980), 414 ff. I am very indebted to Thomas S. Burns and John W. Eadie because of the kind invitation to the Conference "Urban and Rural in Late Antiquity" as well as to Heike Niquet and Christian Witschel for their help in preparing this contribution, which, in the actual form, intentionally preserves some elements of the original style of a lecture.
2. Salv., De gub. Dei 7,6.
3. The picture of the Late Roman Empire given in my book *The Social History of Rome* (rev. ed., London 1988; American ed., Baltimore, 1988), 186 ff. is, following the earlier *communis opinio,* certainly too negative (see also the original German version in: *Römische*

Sozialgeschichte [Wiesbaden, 1975], 165 ff. and in the third German edition [Stuttgart, 1984], 154 ff.). For the necessity of the revision of this picture cf. the *Remarques complémentaires* in the French edition of the mentioned book: *Histoire sociale de Rome,* (Paris, 1991), 199 f. In short terms, I share the opinion of Av. Cameron, who characterized the history of the fourth century a.d. in the following way: "During that period we can see both the resilience of the Roman imperial system and the inertia of pre-modern society" (*The Later Roman Empire AD 284–430* [Cambridge, Mass., 1993], 193). Cf. ead., *The Mediterranean World in Late Antiquity AD 395–600* (London-New York, 1993), especially 81 ff.

4. Hier., Ep. 60,16.
5. On "historical self-evidence" in the Late Roman Empire, cf., in particular, F. Vittinghoff, *Zum geschichtlichen Selbstverständnis der Spätantike.* Historische Zeitschrift 198, 1964, 529 ff. = id., *Civitas Romana. Stadt und politisch-soziale Integration im Imperium Romanum der Kaiserzeit* (Stuttgart, 1994), 435 ff.
6. On the senatorial aristocracy of the Late Empire, cf. especially A. Chastagnol, *La préfecture urbaine à Rome sous le Bas-Empire* (Paris, 1960); id., *Le sénat romain sous le règne d'Odoacre. Recherches sur l'Épigraphie du Colisée an Ve siècle* (Bonn, 1966); J. Matthews, *Western Aristocracies and Imperial Court a.d. 364–425* (Oxford, 1975; Reprint, 1990 with Addenda); A. Demandt, *Die Spätantike. Römische Geschichte von Diocletian bis Justinian 284–565 n. Chr.* (München, 1989), 276 ff.; A. Chastagnol, *Le sénat romain à l'époque impériale. Recherches sur la composition de l'Assemblé et le statut de ses membres* (Paris, 1992), 233 ff.; id., *Aspects de l'antiquité tardive* (Roma, 1994); D. Schlinkert, *Ordo senatorius und nobilitas. Die Konstitution des Senatsadels in der Spätantike* (Stuttgart, 1996).
7. Inscriptions as a medium of communication and self-representation: see, in particular, G. Alföldy, *Die Rolle des Einzelnen in der Gesellschaft des Römischen Kaiserreiches. Erwartungen und Wertmaßstäbe* (Heidelberg, 1980) = id., *Die römische Gesellschaft. Ausgewählte Beiträge* (Stuttgart, 1986), 334 ff.; id., *Individualität und Kollektivnorm in der Epigraphik des römischen Senatorenstandes,* Tituli 4 (1982): 37 ff. = id., *Die römische Gesellschaft,* 378 ff.; W. Eck, "Senatorial Self-Representation: Developments in the Augustan Period," in *Caesar Augustus. Seven Aspects,* edited by F. Millar and E. Segal (Oxford, 1984), 129 ff. (in Italian: id., *Tra epigrafia, prosopografia e archeologia. Scritti scelti, rielaborati ed aggiornati* [Roma, 1996], 271 ff.). G. Alföldy, *Augustus und die Inschriften: Tradition und Innovation. Die Geburt der imperialen Epigraphik,* Gymnasium 98, 1991, 289 ff. (in Italian: *Scienze dell'Antichità. Storia, Archeologia, Antropologia.* Dipartimento di Scienze Storiche, Archeologiche, Antropologiche dell'Antichità. Università degli di Studi di Roma "La Sapienza" 5 1991 [1994], 573 ff.); id., *Studi sull'epigrafia augustea e tiberiana di Roma* (Roma, 1992); id., "La cultura epigráfica de la Hispania romana: inscripciones, auto-representación y orden social," in *Hispania. El legado de Roma,* edited by M. Almagro-Gorbea and J. M. Alvarez Martínez et al. (Zaragoza, 1998), 289 ff. (also in: eid., *Hispania. El legado de Roma* [Zaragoza, 1999], 324 ff). Cf. also O. Salomies, *Observations on the Development of the Style of Latin Honorific Inscriptions during the Empire. Arctos* 28, 1994, 63 ff. On senatorial inscriptions of Rome in Late Antiquity under this aspect see now H. Niquet, *Monumenta virtutum titulique. Denkmäler, ihre Inschriften und senatorische Selbstdarstellung im spätantiken Rom* (Stuttgart, 2000); cf., moreover, V. Neri, *L'elogio della cultura e l'elogio delle virtù politiche*

nell'epigrafia latina del IV secolo d. C. Epigraphica 43 (1981): 175 ff.; M. Horster, Ehrungen spätantiker Statthalter. *AnTard* 6 (1998): 37 ff.

8. Self-representation of senators in late Roman literature: see, in particular, B. Näf, *Senatorisches Standesbewußtsein in spätrömischer Zeit* (Freiburg/Schweiz, 1995); by means of coins: A. Alföldi, *Die Kontorniaten. Ein verkanntes Propagandamittel der stadtrömischen heidnischen Aristokratie in ihrem Kampfe gegen das christliche Kaisertum* (Leipzig, 1943) (rev. catalogue: A. Alföldi and E. Alföldi, *Die Kontorniat-Medaillons*, Teil 1: Katalog, [Berlin 1976]). Monuments: P. Zanker, *Augustus und die Macht der Bilder* (München, 1987) (English version: *The Power of Images in the Age of Augustus* [Ann Arbor, 1988]); for Late Rome cf. F. A. Bauer, *Stadt, Platz und Denkmal in der Spätantike. Untersuchungen zur Ausstattung des öffentlichen Raumes in den spätantiken Städten Rom, Konstantinopel und Ephesos* (Mainz, 1996), 1 ff.
9. On the actual situation and on the perspectives of the CIL see G. Alföldy, *Epigraphica* 57 (1995 [1996]): 292 ff. = in *XI Congresso Internazionale di Epigrafia Greca e Latina*, Roma, 18–24 settembre 1997, Preatti, Roma 1997, 89 ff. The fascicle which contains the urban inscriptions of the rulers is CIL VI 8, 2, the other one is CIL VI 8, 3.
10. Amm. Marc. 14,6,3 ff. It is true, however, that for Ammianus the "old age" of the Roman state, despite the "decadence" of the *Urbs* itself (cf. above with note 1), by no means corresponded to "senility," cf. Matthews, *The Roman Empire of Ammianus* (see note 1) 250, 279; bibliography on this theory ibid. 553n. 40; cf. also G. Alföldy, *Die Krise des Römischen Reiches. Geschichte, Geschichtsschreibung und Geschichtsbetrachtung.* Ausgewählte Beiträge (Stuttgart, 1989), 107n. 66. On the whole, however, the picture of contemporary Rome given by Ammianus in the quoted passage is a pessimistic one, see now T. D. Barnes, *Ammianus Marcellinus and the Representation of Historical Reality* (Ithaca–London, 1998), 174 f. with further bibliography.
11. See my contributions on *Augustus und die Inschriften* and *Studi sull'epigrafia augustea e tiberiana di Roma*, quoted in note 7, and also G. Alföldy, *Der Obelisk auf dem Petersplatz in Rom. Ein historisches Monument der Antike* (Heidelberg, 1990), particularly 68 ff.
12. Cf. e. g. RIC VIII 557. 563 f. 566 ff.
13. For the "happiness of times" cf. e. g. CIL VI 1130 = 31242 (cf. p. 4326 f.) = ILS 646, the dedication of the *thermae felices Diocletianae* by the rulers of the second tetrarchy; CIL VI 36954 (cf. p. 4355) = ILS 726, where Constans is praised as *felicitatem publicam clementia et virtute cumulans;* CIL VI 1175 (cf. p. 4332) = ILS 771 on the construction of the *pons felicis nominis Gratiani* by Valentinian I, Valens and Gratianus; CIL VI 1196 (cf. p. 4334 f.) = ILS 798, where Arcadius, Honorius and Theodosius are praised as *imperatores felicissimi.* On this topic, cf. O. Salomies, *Arctos* 28 (1994): 87 f. with note 82.
14. CIL VI 40716 (= 31382), with the proposed restoration of the wording *felicissimum omni[um saeculorum]*.
15. Restoration of liberty or public order after the victory on internal enemies: CIL VI 1139 (cf. p. 4328) = ILS 694; CIL VI 1158 (cf. p. 4330) = ILS 731; CIL VI 3791 *a-b* = 31413–31414 (cf. p. 4338) = ILS 789 (CIL VI 3791 *a*); CIL VI 40768; cf. CIL VI 1145 (cf. p. 4329). 1146 (cf. *ibid.*). 1163 (cf. p. 4331). 1187 = 31256 (cf. p. 4333 f.) = ILS 794 and 8951; CIL VI 40768a.
16. CIL VI 1739–1742 = ILS 1243 (CIL VI 1741). On Memmius Vitrasius Orfitus, see A. Chastagnol,

Les fastes de la préfecture de Rome au Bas-Empire (Paris, 1962), 139 ff. no. 59; PLRE I Orfitus 3 (bibliography in CIL VI p. 4330 s. and in CIL VI 8, 3, *Add. et Corr.* to CIL VI 1739).

17. Cf. P. Heather, in *The Cambridge Ancient History*[2] *XIII. The Late Empire 337–425* (Cambridge, 1998), 200.
18. See G. Alföldy, *Historia* 15 (1966): 433 ff. and id., *Noricum* (London–Boston, 1974), 269, in each case with bibliography.
19. See, first of all, CIL VI 41328–41330 with a new restoration and with bibliography (before, these inscriptions were edited as CIL VI 1766 = 31894. 31893. 10099 = 31899, cf. ILS 6072; concerning earlier tentative reconstructions cf. N. Purcell, in *The Transformations of Urbs Roma in Late Antiquity* [Portsmouth, 1999], 144); to copies of this edict seem also to belong the fragments CIL VI 9103 = 31895 and 31900, probably also the fragments CIL VI 31896–98. 31901. 37111 (cf. on all these texts CIL VI 8, 3, *Add. et Corr.*).
20. CTh 14,4,6.
21. See, in particular, CIL VI 1771 (cf. CIL VI 8, 3, *Add. et Corr.* with bibliography), edict of Turcius Apronianus, praefectus urbi 362–364; on this senator Chastagnol, *Fastes* (note 16) 156 ff. no. 65; PLRE I Apronianus 10. See also CIL VI 41327 = C. Ricci, in S. Panciera, ed., *Iscrizioni greche e latine del Foro Romano e del Palatino. Inventario generale, inediti, revisioni* (Roma, 1996), 218 ff. no. 68, an edict probably of Vettius Agorius Praetextatus, *praefectus urbi* 367–368; on him Chastagnol, Fastes 171 ff. no. 69; PLRE I Praetextatus 1; recently Niquet, *Monumenta virtutum titulique* (note 7), under press, and CIL VI 8, 3, *Add. et Corr.* to CIL VI 1779 = ILS 1259, with bibliography. Perhaps to the same edict belong the fragments CIL VI 1784 *a-b* (cf. CIL VI 8, 3, *Add. et Corr.* with a hypothetical reconstruction of the document).
22. CIL VI 1711 (cf. CIL VI 8, 3, *Add. et Corr.* with bibliography).
23. CIL VI 1770 (cf. CIL VI 8, 3, *Add. et Corr.* with bibliography).
24. On the problems of food supply in late Rome, see especially H. P. Kohns, *Versorgungskrisen und Hungerrevolten im spätantiken Rom* (Bonn, 1961); E. Tengström, *Bread for the People. Studies of the Corn-Supply of Rome during the Late Empire* (Stockholm, 1974); P. Herz, *Studien zur römischen Wirtschaftsgesetzgebung. Die Lebensmittelversorgung* (Stuttgart, 1988); B. Sirks, *Food for Rome. The Legal Structure of the Transportation and Processing of Supplies for the Imperial Distributions in Rome and Constantinople* (Amsterdam, 1991).
25. Cf. e. g. the relevant inscriptions from Italian and African towns: St. Mrozek, in "Le ravitaillement en blé de Rome et des centres urbains des débuts de la République jusqu'au Haut Empire," *Actes du colloque international, Naples, 14–16 Février 1991* (Naples–Rome, 1994), 97 f.; G. Wesch-Klein, *Liberalitas in rem publicam. Private Aufwendungen zugunsten von Gemeinden im römischen Afrika bis 284 n. Chr.* (Bonn, 1990), 32 f.
26. RGDA 5. On the reforms of the *frumentatio* under Augustus cf. D. Van Berchem, *Les distributions de blé et d'argent à la plèbe romaine sous l'Empire* (Genève, 1939), 27 ff. etc.; G. Rickman, *The Corn Supply of Ancient Rome* (Oxford, 1980), 61 ff.; C. Virlouvet, in *Nourrir la plèbe. Actes du Colloque tenue a Genève les 28 et 29. IX. 1989 en hommage à Denis Van Berchem* (Basel–Kassel, 1991), 43 ff.; ead., *Tessera frumentaria. Les procédures de la distribution du blé public à Rome* (Paris–Roma, 1995), 186 ff.
27. CIL VI 1696 (cf. CIL VI 8, 3, *Add. et Corr.*). On Tertullus, see Chastagnol, *Fastes* (note 16) 48 ff. no. 17; PLRE I Tertullus 6. Augustus had already spoken of the liberation of the people from

metus and *peric(u)lum* in the similar situation of 22 a.d., see note 26.

28. CIL VI 1784 *a-b* (cf. CIL VI 8, 3, *Add. et Corr.*).
29. CIL VI 1184 (cf. p. 4333) = ILS 781. One of the earlier inscriptions of this kind commemorates the inauguration of the *thermae* of Diocletian by the rulers of the second tetrarchy: CIL VI 1130 = 31242 (cf. p. 4326 f.) = ILS 646. Other documents of the same type belong to the reign of Valentinian I: The inscription CIL VI 3866 = 31963 (cf. CIL VI 8, 3, *Add. et Corr.),* where has to be restored *iussu [mode]rationis Augustae* (see Chastagnol, Fastes [note 15] 168), testifies the establishment of a new *castellum aquae* for the Claudian aquaeduct in the first *regio* of the City in 365, ordered by the emperors Valentinianus I and Valens, executed by the *praefectus urbi* and the *curator aquarum;* CIL VI 1175 = ILS 771 and CIL VI 1176 = ILS 772 (on both inscriptions cf. p. 4332) mention the construction of the *pons Gratiani.* The inscription CIL VI 1177 (cf. p. 4332) = ILS 776 which refers to a *forum* (so-called "forum Palatinum") built by Valentinian I and his colleagues, seems to attest a restoration of this public place and not a new construction, see R. L. Bauer, in R. L. Colella et al., ed., *Pratum Romanum. Richard Krautheimer zum 100. Geburtstag* (Wiesbaden, 1997), 45 f.; recently Niquet, *Monumenta virtutum titulique* (note 7), 204, with bibliography.
30. CIL VI 1196 (cf. p. 4334 f.) = ILS 798. An earlier case of this kind was the dedication of the arch of Constantine I by the Senate: CIL VI 1139 (cf. p. 4328) = ILS 694.
31. *Thermae* of Caracalla, restored by Constantine I and his sons: CIL VI 40772; those of the Sessorianum, restored by Helena: CIL VI 1136 (cf. p. 4327); those of Agrippa, restored by Constantius II and Constans: CIL VI 1165 (cf. p. 4331); *[al]bei Tiberis ripae et pontes tredecim,* restored by Valentinianus I and Valens: CIL VI 40793; *theatrum Pompei,* restored by Arcadius and Honorius: CIL VI 1191 (cf. p. 4334) = ILS 793; *thermae* of Diocletian, restored probably by an emperor: CIL VI 1131 (cf. p. 4327).
32. CIL VI 1158 (cf. p. 4330) = ILS 731.
33. CIL VI 1188–1190 (cf. p. 4334)= ILS 797 (CIL VI 1189).
34. On the responsibility for the *opera publica* in late Rome see Chastagnol, *La préfecture urbaine* (note 6) 43 ff.; on the supreme role of the *praefectus urbi* in this field of the urban administration, institutionalized by Constantine I in 332/333, see ibid. 52 f.; concerning the date see the commentary on CIL VI 1651 (CIL VI 8, 3, *Add. et Corr.*) and on 41320 (= 32016 = 37116).
35. The latest inscription of Rome that refers to the renovation of a public construction is that of the bridge of the via Salaria, restored in 565 by Narses (PLRE III Narses 1) *ex praeposito sacri palatii, ex cons(ule) atque patricius:* CIL VI 1199 (cf. p. 4335) = ILS 832. The last example of public dedications in ancient Rome, the column of Phocas with the statue of this emperor, was erected on the forum Romanum in 608 by Smaragdus (PLRE III B 7) *ex praepos(ito) sacri palatii ac patricius et exarchus Italiae:* CIL VI 1200 (cf. p. 4335) = ILS 837.
36. Renovation of the columns of the *atrium libertatis* (i. e. the *curia*), which had been *vetus[tate ac temporis] carie [f]ere con[fectae]:* CIL VI 40807 (= 1794) = ILS 825; restoration of a *colymbum nemus vetustate lapsum:* CIL VI 1179 (cf. p. 4333) = ILS 5732; cf. also the restoration of the *thermae* of Agrippa, which had been *vetustate labefactae,* by an urban prefect on the order of the emperors: CIL VI 1165 (cf. p. 4331). The formula *vetustate conlapsum* and similar formulae can, in an euphemistic manner, also refer to negligence or to historical events

which one did not want to mention, cf. E. Thomas - Ch. Witschel, "Constructing Reconstruction: Claim and Reality of Roman Rebuilding Inscriptions from the Latin West," *PBSR* 60 (1992): 135 ff., also with several testimonia for the epigraphic formulae from different parts of Roman West treated in this paper.

37. Renovation of the Colosseum after a *terrae motus:* CIL VI 1716 *a-c* = 32094 *a-c* (cf. CIL VI 8, 3, *Add. et Corr.*) = ILS 5365 (CIL VI 1716 *b* = 32094 *b*). On other renovations of this building in the fifth century (cf. especially CIL VI 1763 = 32089 = ILS 5633), see now S. Orlandi, in *Transformations of the Urbs Roma* (note 19), 249 ff. The inscription CIL VI 41397 (= 31993) probably refers to arches restored after an earthquake. On restored buildings which had been destroyed by fire (including arson by foreign invaders), see CIL VI 1136 (cf. p. 4327); CIL VI 526 = 1664 (cf. CIL VI 8, 3, *Add. et Corr.)* = ILS 3132; CIL VI 1718 (cf. CIL VI 8, 3, *Add. et Corr.)* = ILS 5522.
38. CIL VI 1750 (cf. CIL VI 8, 3, *Add. et Corr.*) = ILS 5703; CIL VI 40793.
39. CIL VI 1718 (cf. CIL VI 8, 3, *Add. et Corr.*) = ILS 5522; CIL VI 1676 (cf. CIL VI 8, 3, *Add. et Corr.*).
40. CIL VI 1750 (cf. CIL VI 8, 3, *Add. et Corr.*) = ILS 5703. Cf. also CIL VI 3864 *a* = 31883 and 3864 *b* = 31884 (cf. CIL VI 8, 3, *Add. et Corr.*) on the restoration of statues on the forum Romanum which had been destroyed by a *fatalis necessitas;* Gabinius Vettius Probianus, who was responsible for the renovation of these statues, seems to have been urban prefect in 377 (cf. Chastagnol, Fastes [note 15] 201 f. no. 80; PLRE I Probianus 4), but it cannot be excluded that he is Probianus, *praefectus urbi* in 416 (contra: Chastagnol, Fastes 275 f. no. 124; cf. PLRE II Probianus 1), in which case *fatalis necessitas* refers to the Gothic invasion of the City in 410.
41. CIL VI 526 = 1664 (cf. CIL VI 8, 3, *Add. et Corr.)* = ILS 3132.
42. CIL VI 41403 (= 31890 = 37106) and 41404 (= 1788 = 31891).
43. CIL VI 1199 (cf. p. 4335) = ILS 832.
44. CIL VI 1703 = ILS 5715; CIL VI 1716 *a-c* = 32094 *a-c* = ILS 5365 (CIL VI 1716 *b* = 32094 *b*). 1728 *a*. 1728 *b*. 1790. 3865 = 31945. 31912 = ILS 5733; CIL VI 37134 (on all these documents cf. CIL VI 8, 3, *Add. et Corr.*); CIL VI 40805. 41388. 41416. 41423.
45. CIL VI 526 = 1664 (cf. CIL VI 8, 3, *Add. et Corr.)* = ILS 3132.
46. See CIL VI 41378 (between 410 and 420); CIL VI 41386–41387 (between 410 and 420); CIL VI 37128 (cf. CIL VI 8, 3, *Add. et Corr.*, probably in 412); CIL VI 1718 (cf. CIL VI 8, 3, *Add. et Corr.*) = ILS 5522 (between 412 and 414); CIL VI 41376 (= 39182 + 32061 = 37117, between 418 and 420); cf. also the inscriptions mentioned in note 39, which are perhaps from the year 416.
47. CIL VI 1750 (cf. CIL VI 8, 3, *Add. et Corr.*) = ILS 5703.
48. See ibid.
49. See once more again CIL VI 1750 (cf. CIL VI 8, 3, *Add. et Corr.*) = ILS 5703.
50. CIL VI 1696 (cf. CIL VI 8, 3, *Add. et Corr.*).
51. Cf. e. g. CIL VI 1749 (cf. CIL VI 8, 3, *Add. et Corr.*) = ILS 809 on *aeterni principes;* CIL VI 31987 (cf. CIL VI 8, 3. *Add. et Corr.*) = ILS 799 on *perennes Augusti*, CIL VI 41389 on *perpetui Augusti*, CIL VI 1184 (cf. CIL VI 8, 3, *Add. et Corr.*) = ILS 781 on the *aeternum nomen* of the emperors.
52. Formulae of this kind: CIL VI 1706. 1710 = ILS 2949; CIL VI 1735. 1749 = ILS 809; CIL VI 1768 = ILS 1229; CIL VI 1772 = ILS 1230; CIL VI 32051 = ILS 1237 (on all these inscriptions cf. CIL VI 8, 3, *Add. et Corr.*); CIL VI 41336.

53. CIL VI 1769 (cf. CIL VI 8, 3, *Add. et Corr.*): on L. Turcius Apronianus (PLRE I Apronianus 10): *constantiae abstinentiae exemplum sempiternum.* It is interesting to learn that, at the same time, the punishments aristocratic magistrates ordered for criminals were considered as a *perpetuum periculum* for this people: CIL VI 1770 (cf. CIL VI 8, 3, *Add. et Corr.* with bibliography).
54. See, e. g., CIL VI 1793. 32083 (on both inscriptions cf. CIL VI 8, 3, *Add. et Corr.*); CIL VI 41344a (= 36968).
55. Symm., Ep. 1,52. Cf. Näf, *Senatorisches Standesbewußtsein* (note 8) 63 f.; on Symmachus' views concerning the senatorial aristocracy see ibid. 60 ff.
56. CIL VI 1751 (cf. CIL VI 8, 3, *Add. et Corr.*) = ILS 1265; CIL V 3344 = ILS 1266. On Probus cf. PLRE I Probus 5; see now M. G. Schmidt, *Hermes* 127 (1999): 99 ff. (on the unfavorable judgement of Ammianus Marcellinus ibid. 100 f. and note 5 with bibliography; see also Barnes, Ammianus [note 10] 117 ff.). On senatorial virtues in the inscriptions of Rome in Late Antiquity see Niquet, *Monumenta virtutum titulique* (note 7), under press.
57. Amm. Marc. 27,11,2 ff., in the translation of J. C. Rolfe (*Ammianus Marcellinus III* [Cambridge, Mass.–London, 1958]).
58. Virtues and merits from infancy onward: CIL VI 1679 = ILS 1262; CIL VI 1724 = ILS 2950; CIL VI 1727 = ILS 1275; CIL VI 1730 = ILS 1277; CIL VI 1735. 1742. 1759 = ILS 1272; CIL VI 1760. 1761 = ILS 1285 (on all these inscriptions cf. CIL VI 8, 3, *Add. et Corr.*).
59. Niquet, *Monumenta virtutum titulique* (note 7), 167 ff. Cf. what Av. Cameron recently said on "the relation of Christian and pagan literature" in Late Antiquity: "Appropriation and assimilation provide better tools of analysis" than "conflict," see in *The Cambridge Ancient History*[2] *XIII* (note 17), 705. Cf. now also Al. Cameron, in *Transformations of Urbs Roma* (note 19), 109 ff.
60. CIL VI 1698 (cf. CIL VI 8, 3, *Add. et Corr.*) = ILS 1257, cf. Niquet, *Monumenta virtutum titulique* (note 7), under press; on the Elder Symmachus see Chastagnol, *Fastes* (note 16), 159 ff. no. 66; PLRE I Symmachus 1.
61. See e. g. the inscriptions that refer to *praefecti urbi,* who were responsible for constructions of the basilicae of St. Peter and St. Paul, and of other members of the senatorial order who contributed to these constructions: CIL VI 41331a = ICVR, N. S. II 4097; CIL VI 41336a = ICVR, N. S. II 4122; CIL VI 41400 = ICVR, N. S. II 4125; respectively CIL VI 1666 = ICVR, N. S. II 4793; CIL VI 1668 = ICVR , N. S. II 4781 (on both inscriptions cf. CIL VI 8, 3, *Add. et Corr.*); CIL VI 41399 (= 1762) = ICVR, N. S. II 4782; ICVR, N. S. II 4778.
62. Niquet, *Monumenta virtutum titulique* (note 7), 134 ff., 151 ff., 175 ff.
63. Cf. CIL VI 1678 = ILS 1281; CIL VI 1783 = ILS 2948; CIL VI 37112 (= 1723 + 1757) = ILS 1225 + 1232 cum add. (on all these inscriptions cf. CIL VI 8, 3, *Add. et Corr.*).
64. See F. Paschoud, *Roma aeterna. Études sur le patriotisme romain dans l'Occident latin à l'époque des grandes invasions* (Rome, 1967), esp. 323 ff. This patriotism was focused, of course, on the City of Rome with its tradition, cf. A. Alföldi, *A Conflict of Ideas in the Later Roman Empire. The Clash between the Senate and Valentinian I* (Oxford, 1952), 52, on Symmachus.
65. CIL VI 1711 (cf. CIL VI 8, 3, *Add. et Corr.*).
66. CIL VI 1783 (cf. CIL VI 8, 3, *Add. et Corr.*) = ILS 2948; cf., more recently, Th. Grünewald,

Historia 41 (1992): 462 ff.

67. CIL VI 1759 (cf. CIL VI 8, 3, *Add. et Corr.*, with bibliography) = ILS 1272. On Celsus cf. PLRE I Celsus 9.
68. Symm., Or. 1,6.
69. Cf. Paschoud, *Roma aeterna* (note 64), 105 ff., on Symmachus.
70. On this topic recently H. Niquet, "Virum bonum laudabant bonum agricolam bonumque colonum (Cato agr. praef. 2): The Ideal of the Senatorial Agriculturist and Reality during Roman Republic and Empire," in *The Acts of the International Symposium "Doppelmoral in Antike und Mittelalter" / "Double Standards in the Ancient and Mediaeval World,"* St. Andrews, 12.-16. 8. 1998 (forthcoming).
71. Symm., Or. 4,9.

Autun and the Civitas Aeduorum: Maintaining and Transforming a Regional Identity in Late Antiquity

BAILEY K. YOUNG

ONE DAY IN A.D. 312, PERHAPS 31 MARCH, A PROFESSIONAL ORATOR SPEAKING before the Imperial court in Trier, evoked the glorious past and difficult present of his home town, Augustodunum.[1] "Is there anywhere in the whole universe a people more strongly attached to the name of Rome than the Aeduens?" he asks, reminding the Emperor Constantine how in the days of Cicero the Aeduans had been called brothers of the Roman people, how Julius Caesar had first marched into Gaul at their appeal. In the more recent, past the town had paid a bitter price for supporting the legitimate Roman Emperor Claudius Gothicus against the Gallic usurper Tetricus: in 270, after a 7-month siege, the city had been taken and sacked by rebel troops. The orator himself, then a small child, had survived these terrible events, whose ravages, forty years later, still offended the eye. Had not the Emperor himself wept—during his visit the previous year—to see the fields abandoned and given over to weeds, the ruined vineyards, the gaping breaches in the town walls, the roads in such poor repair that even half-empty wagons could barely get by? Despite the citizens' brave display of welcome in his honor, the Emperor had understood their underlying need and would surely respond by remission of taxes, that fourth-century analogue for Federal

Disaster Aid.

This speech throws precious light on one of the largest and most prestigious of the 100-odd Gallic *civitates* at a crucial moment of transition.[2] It also confronts us with the thorny problem of interrelating written and archaeological sources, a problem well illustrated by the complex story of the Aeduan civitas. The catastrophic view of the "fall of the Roman empire" has, of course, been associated with the fifth-century invasions that led to the end of the Western Empire and the establishment of barbarian polities by Goths, Vandals, Burgundians, Franks, and so forth. But the impression of catastrophic rupture in third century Gaul, in a context of power struggles and invasions, growing fiscal pressures, manpower shortages, and social revolts has been receiving growing support among scholars.[3] Paul-Albert Février, however, reviewing the evidence ca. 1980 in *Histoire de la France urbaine* puts the emphasis on the revival (*Renovatio*) of Gallo-Roman cities in the early fourth century and of their subsequent transformation as they adopted a new religious identity (*Christiana tempora*). Between the third and the sixth centuries, Février argues, these towns mixed tradition with innovation (*vetera et nova*) to re-invent themselves as Christian capitals, thus providing the urban core from which the medieval town would later grow.[4] The excavations, which Christian Sapin and I began in 1976, in the hamlet of Saint-Pierre l'Estrier on the outskirts of Autun, of vestiges of a medieval church surviving as a nineteenth-century barn have developed into a multidisciplinary, multi-site investigation of the interplay of *vetera* with *nova* in the Aeduan territory.[5] It will be useful to look first at the *vetera* side.

When Caesar marched north into Gaul in 58 B.C. the Aeduans controlled an immense tribal territory between the Saone River valley to the east and the Loire to the west, stretching to the plains of the Auxerrois in the north and to the hills and forests of the Beaujolais/Lyonnais mountains to the south. Stressing their hegemony over such neighboring peoples as the Aulerques, the Mandubiens, the Segusiaves, and the Ambarres, and their traditional rivalry with the Arvernes for leadership among the Gauls, Camille Jullian spoke of this ascendency as an Aeduan Empire. At the center stood the ancient Morvan massif, with their capitol, the *oppidum* of Bibracte, towering over the landscape from the peak of Mont Beuvray. Its important role during the Gallic Wars (indeed they were in great part written there) has long made this a familiar name to historians. Thanks to the pioneering excavations of J. B. Bulliot and his son-in-law Joseph Déchelette between 1867 and 1895, and to the international and multi-disciplinary research program underway since 1984, Bibracte is now one of the best-known archaeological sites in the Celto-Roman west.[6] It was impressive in its dimensions: Bulliot/Déchelette gave it some 5 km of ramparts, enclosing 135 ha (by comparison, Greek Marseille at that time was under 50 ha), and recent topographical survey would extend that to more like 200 ha. The contemporary excavations both confirm the reliability of much of the early work and furnish new evidence, such as aristocratic residences in the Italian manner (*domus*) and a monumental stone basin, in form an elegant oval (10.48 × 3.65 m) that seems to derive from Pythagorean geometry, to suggest that the hilltop *oppidum* was being impressively transformed into an urban center in the generation or so after the Gallic Wars. Abruptly, this stopped. The monumental fountain was abandoned, its excavators think, by the beginning of the Christian era, around the time of the last transformation of the *domus* at the Parc aux Chevaux. The Aeduen elite, attuned to broad historical changes, was about to shift its focus, and not for the last time.

The shift was to a new site, 26 km to the east, on a slope rising from the Arroux river to the mountain to the south. Today the magnificent Romanesque cathedral dedicated to Saint Lazarus dominates the view of Autun, but the visitor is soon struck by the prominence of Roman vestiges.[7] There is a stone temple with a square Celtic plan ("temple of Janus"), a handsome and sober monumental gateway marking the northern entry to the city (Porte de l'Arroux), an *intra-muros* theater, originally excavated in the 1870s and recently restored, that was among the largest in the Roman world (diameter 148 m). Nearby there once existed a large amphitheater as well (154 × 130 m), but of this no trace survives. The Musée Rolin displays imposing vestiges of the monumental ornament that adorned public buildings during the *Pax Romana*, and hints of the luxurious domestic life of the elite also abound, such as splendid polychrome floor mosaics recovered from urban residences. Most impressive of all, the ramparts (over 2 km survive of the original 6-km circuit, incorporating 53 or 54 towers), which date to the days of Augustus (tradition here confirmed by recent controlled excavation). Like the very name chosen for the brand-new *civitas* capital, *Augustodunum*, they were a strong symbol of the privileged ties between the Aeduan aristocracy and the new Imperial government in Rome.

And yet, despite such hints and such splendors, it is striking how little we know about the Aeduans, their capital and their extensive territory during that Imperial heyday. Monumental inscriptions are few. Literary evidence throws light mostly on episodes of trouble: a revolt in Tiberius's day with an Aeduan ringleader; another brief episode in A.D. 70, connected with the Imperial crisis following Nero's death; repercussions that can be inferred in the aftermath of Septimius Severus's victory over Clodius Albinus in 197. Although Tacitus refers off-handedly to the presence of students in connection with such events, it is only chance that has preserved a panegyric pronounced in 298 by a native rhetor named Eumenes, who is donating his salary to aid the restoration of the town's famed schools, that allows us to see Augustodunum as a kind of Ivy League equivalent for well-born boys from all over Gaul. This text, like that of the anonymous rhetor in Trier examined earlier, invites us to return to the question of Late Antiquity.

Augustodunum's other surviving monumental gateway, known as the Porte de Saint-Andoche, seems to have been restored under Constantine, a sign of the Emperor's favorable response to the rhetor's appeal. From it wound the eastern highway, leading toward the Saone Valley where the port town of Chalon had already developed such commercial and military importance that it would soon be classed by Ammianus Marcellinus among the principal towns of the First Lyonnaise Province. Whether this vitality—which would make Chalon a capital of the Burgundian kingdom in the sixth century and a bustling medieval town later—had already led to its detachment from the Aeduan *civitas* is not known. Saint-Pierre 1'Estrier is located at the top of a rise, about 3 km from the Saint-Andoche gateway, just north of this road. By antiquarian tradition it was included within a vast eastern necropolis on either side of this highway, the pendant of another off the Lyon road south of town, whose toponym, *le champ des urnes*, betrays its origin. But was Saint-Pierre indeed the site of an *early Roman* cremation

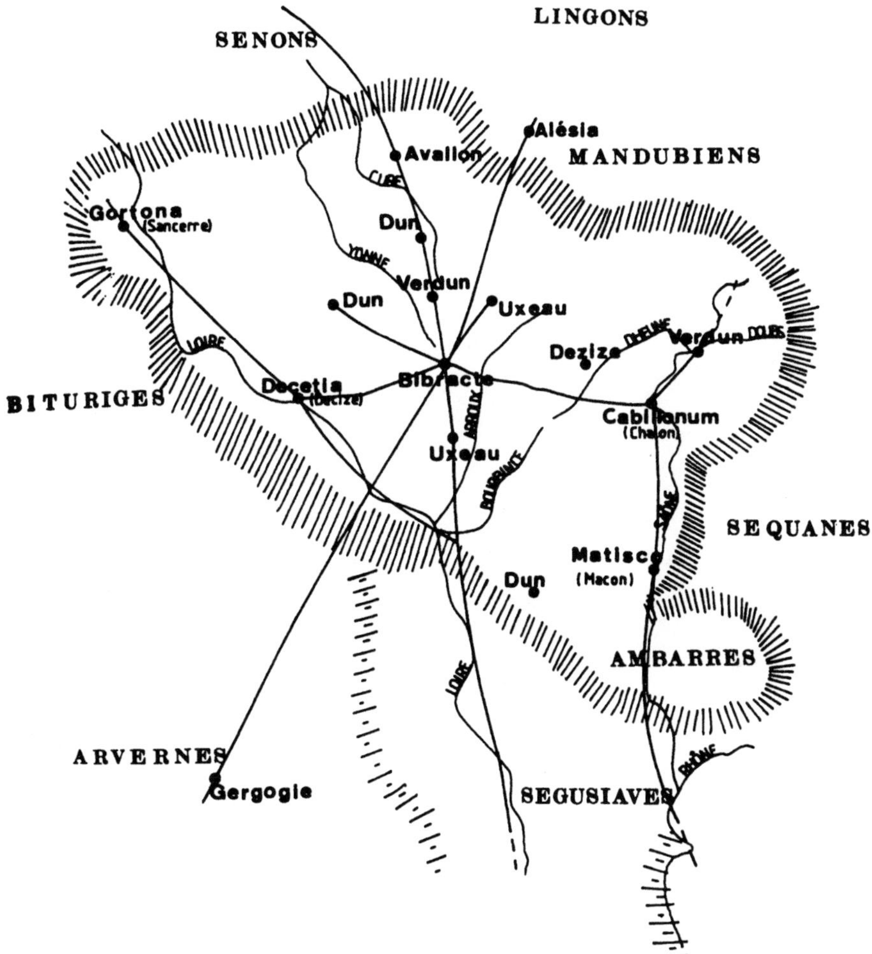

Map of the Aeduan *civitas* at the time of Julius Caesar's residence at Bibracte. *Augustodumum* will be built along the Arroux River, 26 km to the east. Courtesy of the BURGONDIE Research Group, Centre d'études médiévales, Auxerre.

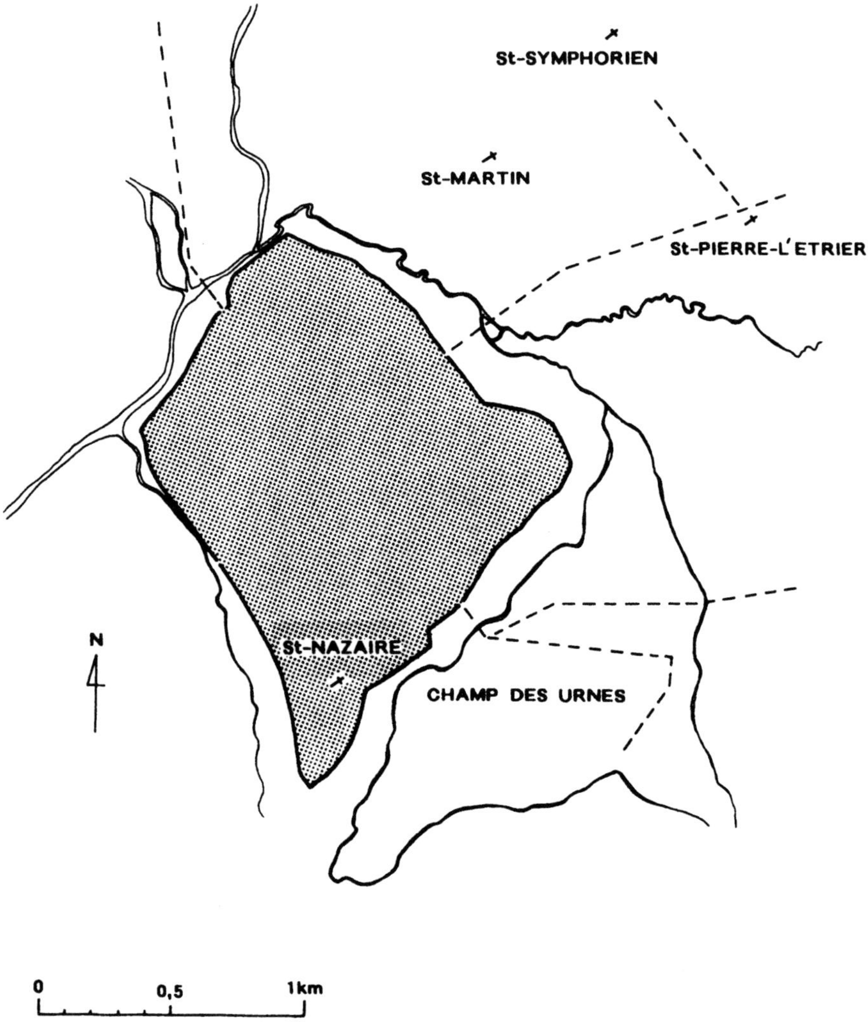

Map of *Augustodunum* in Late Antiquity. The cathedral of St. Nazaire was located *intra muros*; Saint-Pierre l'Estrier was off the highway to the northeast, in the same general area as the later monastary of Saint-Martin, and the church honoring the local martyr Saint-Symphorien. The *Champ des Urnes*, off the Lyon highway to the south, was the major early Roman necropolis. Courtesy of the BURGONDIE Research Group, Centre d'études médiévales, Auxerre.

cemetery, as had always been assumed, and as was certainly the case for the southern cemetery? There was no clear archaeological evidence that it was—none of the funerary urns or the carved grave stele so well represented in the collections of the Musée Rolin, for example, can be shown to have been found in the vicinity of Saint-Pierre. There is, however, strong evidence that Saint-Pierre was an important burial place in Late Antiquity. In 1839, the versified funerary inscription of Pectorios was found in a farmyard just east of the surviving building. Its allusive literary style, in Greek, has led some scholars to date it as pre-Constantinian, while others would place it as late as the fourth century. In any case, its presence corroborates the testimony of Gregory of Tours, who tells us that in his day (ca. 571-593) this area was so renowned as a Christian burial site that pilgrims came from afar—as he did himself—to venerate the sepultures of the early bishops.[8] This evidence raised two questions in our minds. Could the medieval church, whose vestiges survive at Saint-Pierre today, derive from a Late Antique funerary basilica associated with these venerated burials? And, if so, had the site of Saint-Pierre been selected because it had always been a necropolis? Was this choice thus an expression of essential continuity of urban life from the founding of Augustodunum through Late Antiquity? Or, on the contrary, did this choice mark a departure, of a deliberate restructuring of the urban landscape in keeping with the new times, *christiana tempora?*

To the first question we may respond positively. Although the site was badly disturbed and we were able to investigate only a limited sector, we argue that the medieval church on the site developed from a Late Antique vaulted mausoleum (4 × 8 m), probably built in the early fourth century.[9] This was soon linked by a new wall to an older building with a square plan just west of it. Two graves dug on the north side of the new wall—one a child in a lead coffin with an X scratched into the cover over the head; the other a man associated with a coin—suggest a funerary basilica linked with a monumental tomb was in place by the latter fourth century. There is good evidence of intensive burial activity around the building; the grave of a young woman with a glass vial by her head fits into this chronological horizon. Although the evidence is fragmentary, we believe that it supports the conclusion that the basilica was expanded early in the Merovingian period,

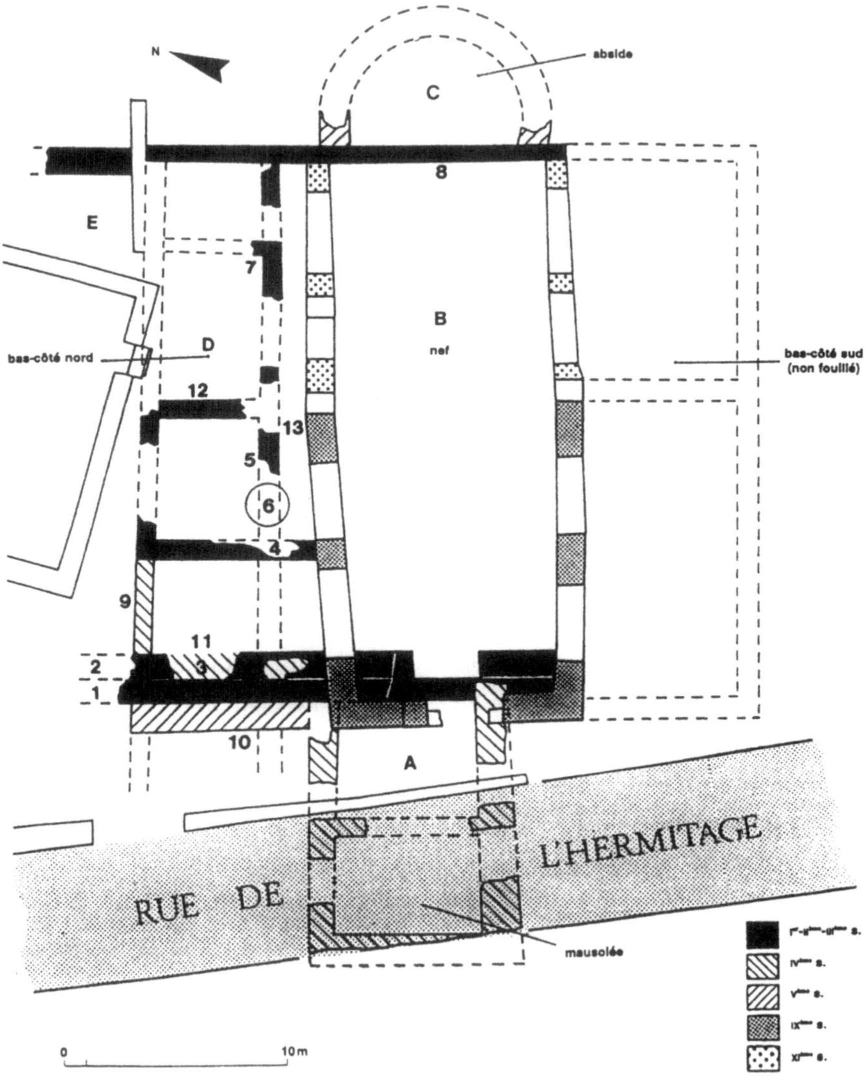

Plan of Saint-Pierre l'Estrier. The early Roman structures are dark black; the *memoria* was built to the west of them, and then incorporated into a funerary basilica (diagonal hatching). Courtesy of the BURGONDIE Research Group, Centre d'études médiévales, Auxerre.

with the western facade extended some 8 m, incorporating the mausoleum into a funerary annex filled with expensive, high-status stone sarcophagi. The enlarged basilica would have been composed of a central nave and two side aisles; with an apse to the east. There is also some evidence for a monumental sepulchre in arcosolium against one wall, a type of arrangement that would be consistent with later traditions that the tombs of the first bishops of Autun were preserved in Saint-Pierre. The excavation of a Merovingian funerary basilica at Saint-Julien-en-Genevois offers a parallel for arrangements of this sort.[10] Thus, although Gregory of Tours does not expressly mention the presence of a funerary basilica on the site of Saint-Pierre when he came to venerate the tombs there in the late sixth century, we can now be quite confident that there was one.

In response to the second question, the evidence points more to rupture than to continuity. We found no signs of incineration burials typical of the early empire. While it could be argued none could have survived in the limited and much-disturbed zones that were excavated, the analysis of the residual Roman pottery shows that most of this is late antique, and what is earlier is domestic rather than funerary in type. We did discover, east of the church structure, a horizon of inhumation burials. None included grave-goods, but a series of later third or fourth century bronze coins found in this horizon help date it, though they do not prove, in my view, a pagan burial environment. We did find a large funerary stele of a pagan sort, depicting a standing figure holding a cup, but it had been placed face down in the doorway of a medieval structure—no doubt a piece of *spolia* carted in to serve as a threshold lintel. We did find evidence of two pre-Christian structures. One was a building with a square plan (11 m on a side) and the other a well-founded double wall (55 and 90 cm thick) running north/south immediately under the facade of our proposed fourth-century basilica. Both structures seem to date to the third century, and could have been part of a suburban villa. There is also some very limited evidence, in one area sampled in 1985, that suggests first-century agricultural activity on the site. Our conclusions must be very tentative, but they do point to a radical change of function at Saint-Pierre in the later third and early fourth century. What had until then been a domestic or agricultural site took on a funerary function. The

Pectorios inscription, the glass vial, the lead coffin, the stone sarcophagi, and the mausoleum all point to elite usage. To correlate these changes with the mid-third century devastation and the renewal attested by the rhetors' speeches a generation later does not appear far-fetched.

Recent research has drawn attention to the impact of funerary monuments on restructuring the urban environment in many Gallic cities.[11] A particularly famous example concerns Saint Martin of Tours. Sulpicius Severus describes the triumphant funeral cortege accompanying his body back to Tours, in 397, but the tomb itself was a fairly modest affair in a small structure, *modicum sacellum,* no doubt when compared to the style of aristocratic burial characteristic of Sulpicius's circle. It was only under Bishop Perpetuus (461-490) that this was replaced by a splendid funerary basilica (53 × 20 m) with its 120 columns, 52 windows and 8 doors.[12] Henri Galinié's recent and ongoing archaeological studies in Tours show that the burial site was in an abandoned zone of the original Roman town, far (2 km) from the tiny (9 ha) Late Antique urban area now surrounded by walls.[13] By the time of Gregory's episcopate, a century later, it had given birth to what was in effect a thriving new settlement, which Gregory called the *vicus Christianorum,* or *Martinopolis.* Merovingian Paris, Patrick Périn has shown, was ringed with sanctuaries associated with tombs. Marcellus, the first reliably attested Bishop, was no doubt honored by a basilica in a necropolis located a good distance from town, off the southern highway; unfortunately the data from nineteenth-century observations are too vague to let us guess when it was built. But we do know that when St. Géneviève died about 502 her sepulcre, atop the hill that still bears her name, soon attracted the Frankish king Clovis to build a private royal funerary church there. This example, Périn argues, inspired such subsequent builders as his grandson Childebert, who graced his burial basilica (today St. Germain des Pres) with relics he obtained in his wars in Spain.[14]

In Geneva, Charles Bonnet has provided us with a particularly well-documented example of the genesis and growth of a suburban funerary basilica.[15] Here the port of the Roman town was destroyed during the third-century invasions, and the ruins became the site of inhumation burials in wooden coffins. One of them was set off by the fifth century by a small con-

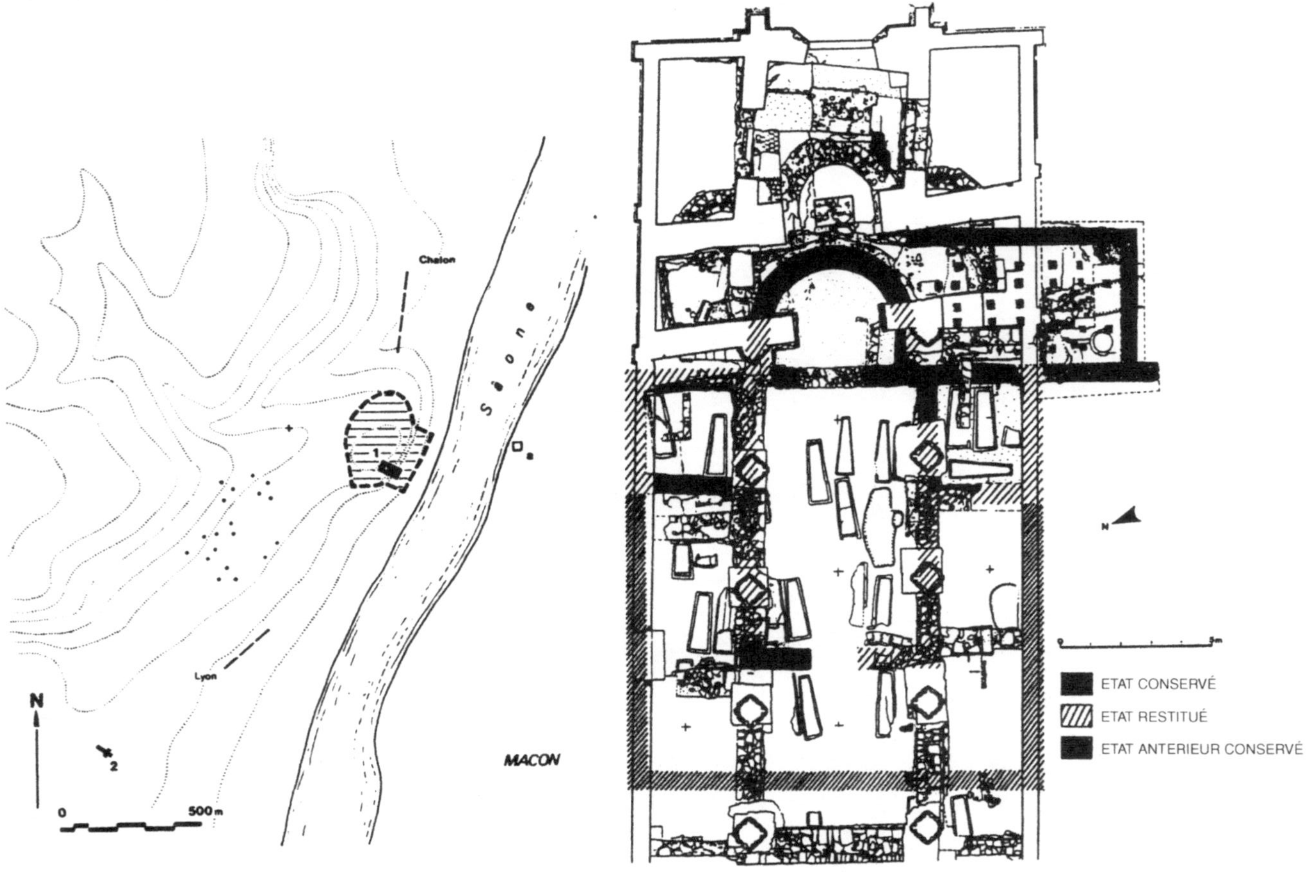

État de l'église au VIe siècle ; première église (Dessin : G. Fèvre/O. Juffard).

Map showing the location of Saint-Clément in Macon with the plan of the sixth-century funerary church. Courtesy of the BURGONDIE Research Group, Centre d'études médiévales, Auxerre.

struction, half-sunken in the ground, built of woodwork and river-stone. This *memoria* was to be preserved as an annex beside the apse of a single-nave funerary church in use by the sixth century, and enlarged around 600 with a lateral portico to meet the heightened demand for *ad sanctos* burial space. The identity of the personage so honored is unknown, as was the very existence of Late Antique structures under the medieval Madeleine church until Bonnet's excavations—and this despite excavation done in the 1920s. But the impressive three-aisled structure, with a semi-circular apse and an underground gallery under its western façade, excavated in the 1970s in Lyon by Jean-Francois Reynaud can be identified with a funerary basilica celebrated by Sidonius Apollinarius, who attended a ceremony there in 469.[16] It housed the tomb of Iustus, a local Bishop attested in 381, whose body was brought back to be honored after he died in Egypt. Here, too, the site chosen was in a ruined quarter of the earlier Roman city.

About 50 km north of Lyon, up the Saone River, Macon, known as *Matisco,* guarded the entrance into Aeduan territory in the days of Caesar and Constantine.[17] During Late Antiquity it was known as a *castrum,* implying it was fortified, like the other Aeduan port town of Chalon to the north. From historical sources we know that, by the mid–sixth century, Macon had become the center of an independent Bishopric, as indeed had Chalon, which may have been administratively separated from Aeduan territory even earlier. Very little was known archaeologically of the Roman and Late Antique town, however, when in 1985 we were asked to evaluate the archaeological interest of Saint-Clement, a disaffected church slated for demolition to make way for a traffic roundabout. The standing church had been extensively remodeled in the nineteenth century, although the western bell tower dates back to the late gothic period, and the church had always been assumed to have been a medieval creation. Archival research revealed, however, a late Carolingian reference to a *parrochia sancti Clemantis,* and mention was made to two Late Antique saints from Lyon (one of them our friend Justus) venerated there, as well as a certain Eusebius, who could have been a Bishop of that name attested in 583. Considering the location of the site beside the road to Lyon, just about 2 km south of the late antique castrum, we wondered if this was not another case where a late antique funerary church came to fix a durable pole of urban Christian identity. Excavations between 1985 and 1992 proved that this was so. A funerary basilica, decorated with gold-backed mosaics, was built during the sixth century on a suburban site with no previous funerary vocation; it is not unreasonable to conjecture that the decorated sarcophagus in the central axis was intended for a noted local figure, such as Bishop Eusebius or his predecessor Placidius, active from 538 to 552, perhaps the very first bishop.[18] Why this new construction, at this time?

The reason lies in the intersection of a new political landscape with new cultural patterns. Until the 530s, the Aeduan territories had been part of the Burgundian kingdom, which itself had essentially prolonged the Late Roman administrative structures. The Frankish conquest was followed by new political and territorial divisions: King Theodobert took Autun and Chalon, while King Childebert took Macon as well as Lyon, just to the south. Lyon was a very important Christian center, its Bishop was Metropolitan of the Province that included most of Burgundy and was indeed the Primate, or honorary senior Bishop of all Gaul. Childebert might have chosen to merge the modest *castrum* of *Matisco* into this established bishopric, but he did not; instead he chose to give the former chunk of Aeduan territory its own identity, creating a brand-new bishopric. Is it unreasonable to suppose that the Frankish ruler was thus acceding to the wishes and conciliating the loyalties of the local elite? By the mid–sixth century, the distinctive signs of *christiana tempora* marked the urban landscapes of Gaul: just outside the walls of the fortified center, where the living bishop presided over the liturgies in his cathedral, the glorified local heroes, those inventors of local Christianity (their relics often re-enforced by those of martyrs from the Universal Church), continued to guard and guide the community from their venerated tombs. By the mid–sixth century this pattern had been established, but when had its basic elements begun to coalesce?

The process can be studied with some precision in the case of Auxerre, thanks to a happy conjunction of written sources, monumental remains, and an interdisciplinary team of historians and archaeologists who have been studying them. A site dominating the Yonne River, *Autessioduro* belonged to the *civitas* of the Senones, the immediate northern neighbors of the Aeduans, and some scholars argue that its region may have been subject to their influence at their height of power. Very little is known of the agglomeration in the days of the Pax Romana, not even its necropolis, but Auxerre emerged as an important place in Late Antiquity.[19] During the fourth century, it was raised to the rank of city and its topography utterly transformed by the construction of a 6-ha hilltop fortification—a site apparently previously unoccupied. The Christian origins are shadowy—in 346, a Bishop is attested by his signature on a document, but that is all we know for certain of him. Of Bishop Amator, who was active around 400, little was remembered by the later sixth century except the location of his tomb; but as this was to be included in a new liturgical circuit, a hagiographic account of his life was composed from standardized stories (*topoi*) plundered from older saints' lives and relocated to Auxerre. As Jean-Charles Picard, that keen scholar of Late Antiquity so tragically taken from us in 1992, remarks aptly, the first really well-attested historical figure was Bishop Germanus (418-448).[20] Germanus was a local aristocrat and a major player on the stage of fifth century Gaul: his travels to the Imperial court in Italy to defend Gallic interests, or to beleaguered Britannia where he helped repel a barbarian attack with a Hallelujah chorus are well known from his biography by Constantius of Lyon, written in the 470s, within a generation of the saint's death. Today, as throughout the Middle Ages, his influence on his hometown is preserved and symbolized by the mighty abbey church erected over his tomb. But, as Picard tells it, this funerary sanctification was an ex-post facto affair with enormous import for the topographic re-invention of Auxerre as a Christian city. Germanus had chosen to be buried in a private mausoleum, erected atop a hill on his own lands, just north of the *castrum*—all this quite in keeping with aristocratic traditions. For these traditions, burial was essentially a private, family affair, but, like other contemporary Christian aristocrats, Germanus added a new touch by including holy relics. After his death the domain would become the property of the Church, with the mausoleum-cum-relics transformed into an oratory where a new cult in honor of this local saint could develop. But this did not happen overnight, Picard cautions. After all, the first saint's life was written not in Auxerre but in distant Lyon, and this makes no reference to an active funerary cult in its time (ca. 480). When was the modest oratory replaced by a splendid funerary basilica? Perhaps the claim of a Carolingian writer that Queen Clotilde herself (493-545) was the grand patroness of this transformation can be trusted, Picard says, but we are certain of its existence only during the reign of Bishop Aunarius (561-605). Aunarius emerges as the great impressario of Christian Auxerre; it was he who hired an African writer named Stephanus to compose a life of Germanus's predecessor, Amator, even as he was building a funerary basilica over the latter's long-neglected sepulcher in the Late Roman necropolis at Montarte, south of town. Aunarius also instituted regular Rogation processions to link these extra-mural memorials to the local Christian founding Bishops Germanus and Amator (audaciously compared by Stephanus to the universal saints Peter and Paul buried around Rome) with the ongoing liturgies of the Christian town.

Aunarius was a contemporary of Gregory of Tours, to whose testimony that the sepulchers of the founding bishops of Autun at Saint-Pierre l'Estrier attracted pilgrims from near and far.[21] Was the capital of the Aeduans, so badly shaken by the third-century troubles, then succored, in the days of Constantine by Imperial and private benefaction, among the first in Gaul to reinvent itself as a Christian capital? This is not an implausible suggestion.

Augustodunum was one of only sixteen Gallic cities with a solid-enough Christian organization to be represented at the first general council of Arles in 314. Furthermore its bishop, Rheticus, was one of only three Gallic bishops summoned by the Emperor to a council in Rome, where his role was prominent enough to draw comment from St. Augustine. Rheticus also wrote a treatise on the Song of Songs that interested St. Jerome. Did this Christian intellectual statesman—who was to be buried at Saint Pierre l'Estrier—regularly cross paths with Aeduan notables still as firmly committed to old-fashioned pagan traditions as were such great Senatorial families of that day as the Symmachi in Rome? Neither written nor archaeological sources provide much in the way of reliable clues to pagan resistance and Christian advance in Autun. Gregory of Tours does recount an episode when a shadowy bishop Simplicius (whose life is variously ascribed to about 346 and about 418) encounters a procession of *rustici* taking the statue of the fertility goddess Berecynthe through field and vineyard, but there is no violent confrontation.[22] Sulpicius Severus depicts Saint Martin (d. 397) destroying a pagan temple site in a rural area of the *civitas aeduorum;* I have elsewhere criticized Bulliot's and Emile Mâle's attempt to fix this event at Bibracte.[23] The tradition that Martin started a monastery in Autun itself on the site of an abandoned temple is rejected by Picard as an unreliable medieval legend, seeking to attach this latterly famous abbey, located in the northwest *suburbium* and much endowed, if not actually founded by the disreputable Merovingian queen Brunehaut (d. 612) to the saint himself.[24] But, though St. Martin's Abbey may not go back to the saint's personal initiative, by the seventh century it was famed for its wealth and learning, not only within the region but also nationally, as though continuing in this Christian form the town's venerable reputation as a center of learning and culture. The abbey church, where Brunehaut's sepulcher was preserved as late as the fifteenth century in a special chapel extending beyond the apse, was richly decorated with re-used marble columns and an apse mosaic.[25]

Brunehaut's patronage undoubtedly cast shade on the neighboring monastery of Saint Symphorien, whose Abbot, Germanus, became one of the leading figures of the sixth-century Frankish church when he was made Bishop of Paris in 555.[26] This foundation is particularly important for the story of Christian origins in Autun, as it commemorates a local martyr. There is also a hagiographical narrative; the *Passion of Saint Symphorien* tells the story of a boy from the Aeduan nobility who became a Christian in the days of persecution (under Aurelian?) and was beheaded. Although the precise chronology and some details of this account are suspect, it does appear to commemorate a local martyr, for the *Passio* was composed about 450 for bishop Euphronius. Euphronius also erected a basilica over the tomb, making it the earliest Autunois church whose construction is attested in literary sources.[27] Two archaeological vestiges point to the Late Antique splendor of this foundation: a white marble plaque decorated with a fine engraving of a lamb, which probably decorated the altar around A.D. 500, and a decorated white marble sarcophagus dated to the sixth century, which in the Middle Ages housed saintly relics.[28] Taken together, texts and material remains suggest that within a generation or so of its erection as a funerary basilica Saint-Symphorien had become the center of a thriving monastic community. Thus it would seem that by 500, and perhaps considerably earlier, a Christian funerary landscape was in place outside the walls of Autun.

I wish I could complete the picture by describing the intra-muros transformations. What we now know can be quickly said.[29] The highest part of the Roman town was made defensible by linking the west and east ramparts of the old wall with a new southern stretch closing off the hilltop. A cathedral was built within these walls. We cannot precisely date its origins, although we do know that at some time it acquired relics of the Milanese Saint Nazarus (these relics were found ca. 397 by Saint Ambrose). This early cathedral was not located on the same site as the current one, the famous Romanesque church dedicated to St. Lazarus, but quite nearby, just to the east. Our group was able to excavate a courtyard, where we found vestiges of Saint Nazaire's Carolingian cloister, as well some earlier burials and underlying Roman levels. The site of the cathedral basilica itself, and of the adjacent baptistry attested in literary sources, lies farther south.[30]

At the time Gregory of Tours came to visit, bishop Syagrius of Autun was one of the leading churchmen of the day.[31] He was a trusted counselor of the Burgundian King Guntram, who resided normally in the formerly Aeduan town of Chalon; and later of Queen Brunehaut, with whom he built the richly decorated monastery dedicated to Saint Martin near that older foundation to the local martyr Symphorian, which it soon eclipsed. Syagrius redecorated his cathedral of Saint Nazarus with mosaics so splendid that they became famous throughout Gaul, and were later imitated elsewhere. He built a hospice by one of the gateways to the lower city, which became the medieval church of Saint Andoche. When Pope Gregory the Great sent Augustine and his monks to convert the English he sent them via Autun, and, more remarkably, he sent to Syagrius the pallium, an honor usually reserved for archbishops. The famous poet Venantius Fortunatus, himself by this time Bishop of Poitiers, composed a complex figurative acrostic poem (it had 30 verses of 33 letters each, numbers symbolic of the life of Christ) to thank him for an act of generosity. This was displayed as a painted mural on the wall of the vestibule in the episcopal palace.[32] Although the seventh century was to prove more troublesome, Autun continued to play a major role in regional and national politics. In 663, Queen Batilde put an end to a presumably local quarrel over the vacant bishopric by imposing an outsider, Leudgar (Léger), a Frankish aristocrat from a Rhineland family, who restored the walls of the *castrum* and the cathedral as well.[33] He also played a leading role in rallying the Burgundian nobles against the Neustrian Mayor of the Palace, Ebroïn. After complicated intrigues, Autun was besieged (in 673); the bishop surrendered to spare the town a sack (though not, it seems, a pillage) and was later blinded and martyred.[34]

Perhaps future research will allow us to further refine and develop this picture of Autun's Late Antique urban splendors, and also take us out into the countryside, still so little studied.[35] Nevertheless, the Aeduan story, from the days of Caesar and Diviaticus at Bibracte to those of Syagrius and Brunehaut constructing the Abbey of Saint Martin, suggests a remarkable continuity in the ability of the local elite to maintain the prestige of the *civitas* within Gaul as a whole. In taking leave of the Aeduans, let us return once again to that text, the *Passio* of St. Symphorian, which reflects a particularly threatening moment about midway through the span of time covered in this study. As the boy was led out to execution, his noble mother called to him from the ramparts: "Have no fear! Life does not end. It is transformed!" Such a statement, attributed to the grim days after the mid–third century sack, seems to prophesy the Christian reinvention of the community, which was about to begin.

BIBLIOGRAPHY

Autun/Augustodunum. Capitale des Eduens. 1985. Catalogue of the exhibition held at the Musée Rolin, 16 March–27 October 1985. Ville d'Autun/Musée Rolin.

Berry, Walter E. 1987. "Southern Burgundy in Late Antiquity and the Middle Ages." In *Regional Dynamics. Burgundian Landscapes in Historical Perspective,* edited by Carole L. Crumley and William H. Marquardt. Academic Press, 447–607.

Boëll, Charles. 1949. "Les origines de l'église d'Autun." *Mémoires de la Société éduenne* 49:213–26.

Bonnet, Charles. 1977. *Les premiers édifices chrétiens de la Madeleine à Genève.* Geneva.

Buckley, Bridget. 1981. "The Aeduan Area in the Third Century." In *The Roman West in the Third Century,* edited by A. King and M. Henig, BAR Int'nl Ser 109(i), 287–315.

Colardelle, Michel. 1983. *Sépultures et traditions funéraires du Ve au XIIIe siècle ap. J.-C.*

dans les Alpes Françaises du Nord, 57–87, esp fig. 28. Grenoble.

Crumley, Carole L. 1987. "Celtic Settlement before the Conquest: The Dialectics of Landscape and Power." In *Regional Dynamics,* 403–29.

Duval, Noël. 1991. "*L'ecclesia,* espace de la communauté chrétienne dans la cité," In *Naissance des Arts Chrétiens. Atlas des Monuments paléochrétiens de la France,* 50–69. Paris: Ministère de la Culture.

Fontenay, Harold de. 1889. *Autun et ses monuments,* avec un précis historique par A. de Charmasse. Autun.

Février, Paul-Albert. 1981. "*Vetera et nova:* le poids du passé, les germes de l'avenir, IIIe-VIe siècle." In *Histoire de la France urbaine. Tome I: La ville antique des origines qu IXe siècle,* 399–493. Paris.

Février et Patrick Périn. 1991. "*Basiliques et oratories suburbaines, le culte autour de la ville.*" In *Naissance des Arts Chrétiens. Atlas des Monuments paléochrétiens de la France,* 88–93. Paris: Ministère de la Culture.

Galinié Henri. 1997. "Tours de Grégoire, Tours des archives du sol." In *Grégoire de Tours et l'espace gaulois. Actes du Congrès International Tours, 3–5 novembre 1994,* edited by Nancy Gauthier and Henri Galinié, 13e Supplément à la *Revue archéologique de l'Est,* 65–80. Tour.

Gauthier, Nancy, and Picard, Jean-Charles, eds. 1986. *Topographie Chrétienne des Cités de la Gaule IV: Province ecclesiastique de Lyon (Lugdunensis Prima).* Paris.

Goudineau, Christian, and Christian Peyre. 1993. *Bibracte et les Eduens.* Centre archéologique européen du Mont-Beuvray, Ed. Errance.

Griffe E. 1964–1966. *La Gaule chrétienne à 1 époque romaine.* 3 Vols. Rev. Ed. Paris.

Grivot, Denis. 1967. *Autun,* Lyon.

Hatt, Jean-Jacques. 1970 *Histoire de la Gaule romaine.* 3rd Edition. Paris.

Périn Patrick. 1985. "Paris, capitale mérovingienne." In *Collections mérovingiennes du Musée Carnavalet.* Paris: Imprimerie municipale.

Picard, Jean-Charles. 1976. "Espace urbaine et sépultures épiscopales à Auxerre." In *Evêques, saints et cités en Italie et en Gaule. Etudes d'archéologie et d'histoire,* Collection de l'Ecole Francaise de Rome 242 (1998): 275–92. First published in *Revue historique de l'Eglise de France* 62 (1976): 205–22.

———. 1989. "Les premiers sanctuaires chrétiens des cités de Bourgogne." In J.-Ch. Picard, *Evêques, saints et cités en Italie et en Gaule. Etudes d'archéologie et d'histoire,* Collection de l'Ecole Francaise de Rome 242 (1998): 293–309. First published in *Revista di storia et letteratura religiosa* 25 (1989): 3–19.

Sapin, Christian. 1982. "L'ancienne église de Saint Pierre-l'Estrier à Autun: premier bilan d'une étude archéologique en cours." *Archéologie médiévale* 12:51–105.

———. 1985. "Les tombeaux des premiers évêques et l'occupation du cimtière d'Autun: archéologie du site." *Actes du 109e Congrès national des sociétés savantes, Dijon, 1984: Section archéologie* 1:113–29.

———. 1986. *La Bourgogne préromane.* Paris.

Sapin, Ch., and W. Berry. 1984. "Un sarcophage de plomb découvert sur le site de Saint-Pierre l'Estrier à Autun." *Mém. De la soc. éduenne* 54:285–89.

Sapin, Christian, and Bailey K. Young. 1986. "Saint-Pierre l'Estrier (Autun, France)." *Gesta* 25 (1): 39–46.

Young, Bailey K. 1997. "Que restait-il de l'ancien paysage religieux à l'époque de Grégoire de Tours?" In *Grégoire de Tours et l'espace gaulois. Actes du Congrès International Tours, 3–5 novembre 1994,* edited by Nancy Gauthier and Henri Galinié, 13e Supplément à la *Revue archéologique de l'Est,* 241–50. Tours.

NOTES

1. E. Galletier, *Panégyriques latins* (Paris: Les Belles Lettres, T. I , 1949). I have drawn upon Grivot's translation of the fifth panegyric: D. Grivot, *Autun* (Lyon, 1967), 33-35.
2. Buckley Bridget, "The Aeduan Area in the Third Century," in *The Roman West in the Third Century,* ed. A. King and M. Henig, BAR Int'nl Ser 109(i) (Oxford, 1981), 287-315.
3. A. King and M. Henig, eds., *The Roman West in the Third Century,* BAR Int'nl Ser 109(i, ii) (Oxford, 1981).
4. Paul-Albert Février, "*Vetera et nova*: le poids du passé, les germes de l'avenir, IIIe-VIe siècle" in *Histoire de la France urbaine. Tome I: La ville antique des origines qu IXe siècle* (Paris, 1981), 399-493.
5. Christian Sapin, "L'ancienne église de Saint Pierre-l'Estrier à Autun: premier bilan d'une étude archéologique en cours," *Archéologie médiévale* 12 (1982): 51-105; Christian Sapin and Bailey K. Young, with the participation of Walter Berry, "Saint-Pierre l'Estrier (Autun, France)," *Gesta* 25, no. 1 (1986): 39-46.
6. For a recent introduction to the history of research on Mont Beuvray, see Christian Goudineau and Christian Peyre, *Bibracte et les Eduens.* Centre archéologique européen du Mont-Beuvray, ed. Errance (1993).
7. For a well-illustrated historical introduction see Denis Grivot, *Autun* (Lyon,1967). There is much of interest also in *Autun/Augustodunum. Capitale des Eduens.* Catalogue of the exhibition held at the Musée Rolin, 16 March–27 October 1985. Ville d'Autun/Musée Rolin (1985). Older but still essential studies are Harold de Fontenay, *Autun et ses monuments,* avec un précis historique par A. de Charmasse (Autun, 1889).
8. C. Sapin "Les tombeaux des premiers évêques et l'occupation du cimtière d'Autun: archéologie du site," *Actes du 109e Congrès national des sociétés savantes, Dijon, 1984: Section archéologie,* vol. 1 (1985), 113-29. For an analysis of the evidence concerning the ancient and late antique topography of Autun, see the notice "Autun" by Ch Pietri and J.-Ch. Picard in *Topographie Chrétienne des Cités de la Gaule IV: Province ecclesiastique de Lyon,* ed. Nancy Gauthier and Jean-Charles Picard *(Lugdunensis Prima)* (Paris, 1986), 37-45. For the *Pectorios* inscription, see H. Leclercq., "*Pectorios,*" *DACL* 13, no. 2 (1938): col. 2884-98; and, most recently, N. Gauthier, "Autun et les débuts du christianisme" in *Sept siècles de civilisation gallo-romaine vus d'Autun,* Société éduenne des lettres, sciences et arts (Autun, 1985), 101-9.
9. The full publication of these excavations is being prepared. Besides the preliminary

studies cited in note 5 *supra*, Saint-Pierre is treated in the 1985 catalogue (note 7, *supra*, pp. 364-75) and in *Atlas des monuments paléochrétiens de la France*. For the lead sarcophagus, see, Ch. Sapin and W. Berry, "Un sarcophage de plomb découvert sur le site de Saint-Pierre l'Estrier à Autun," in *Mém. De la soc. éduenne* 54 (1984): 285-89.

10. M. Colardelle, *Sépultures et traditions funéraires du Ve au XIIIe siècle ap. J.-C. dans les Alpes Françaises du Nord* (Grenoble, 1983), 57-87, esp. fig. 28.
11. For an introduction to the question, see Paul-Albert Février et Patrick Périn, "*Basiliques et oratories suburbaines, le culte autour de la ville*", in *Naissance des Arts Chrétiens. Atlas des Monuments paléochrétiens de la France* (Paris: Ministère de la Culture, 1991), 88-93.
12. Ibid., 90.
13. Henri Galinié, "Tours de Grégoire, Tours des archives du sol," in *Grégoire de Tours et l'espace gaulois. Actes du Congrès International Tours, 3-5 novembre 1994*, ed. Nancy Gauthier and Henri Galinié, 13e Supplément à la *Revue archéologique de l'Est* (Tours, 1997), 65-80.
14. Patrick Périn, "Paris, capitale mérovingienne" in *Collections mérovingiennes du Musée Carnavalet* (Paris: Imprimerie municipale, 1985).
15. Charles Bonnet, *Les premiers édifices chrétiens de la Madeleine à Genève* (Geneva, 1977).
16. See the notice "Lyon" by P.-A Février, Ch Pietri , J.-Ch. Picard and J-F Reynaud, in *Topographie Chrétienne des Cités de la Gaule IV: Province ecclesiastique de Lyon (Lugdunensis Prima)*, ed. Nancy Gauthier and Jean-Charles Picard (Paris, 1986), 27-28. For a fuller treatment, Jean-François Reynaud, *Lugdunum christianum. Lyon du Ive au VIIIe siècle: topographie, nécropoles et édifices religieux* (Paris, 1989).
17. See the notice "Macon" by J.-Ch. Picard in *Topographie Chrétienne des Cités de la Gaule IV: Province ecclesiastique de Lyon (Lugdunensis Prima)* (Paris, 1986), 75-80.
18. Publication of these excavations is being prepared by Christian Sapin, Alain Guerreau, and Bailey K. Young.
19. See the notice "Auxerre," by J.-Ch Picard, in *Topographie Chrétienne des Cités de la Gaule VIII: Province ecclesiastique de Sens*, ed. Nancy Gauthier, and Jean-Charles Picard (Paris, 1992), 47-65.
20. Jean-Charles Picard, "Espace urbaine et sépultures épiscopales à Auxerre," in *Evêques, saints et cités en Italie et en Gaule. Etudes d'archéologie et d'histoire*, Collection de l'Ecole Francaise de Rome 242 (1998), 275-92. First published in *Revue historique de l'Eglise de France* 62 (1976): 205-22.
21. Jean-Charles Picard, "Les premiers sanctuaires chrétiens des cités de Bourgogne", in J.-Ch. Picard, *Evêques, saints et cités en Italie et en Gaule. Etudes d'archéologie et d'histoire*, Collection de l'Ecole Francaise de Rome 242 (1998), 293-309. First published in *Revista di storia et letteratura religiosa* 25 (1989): 3-19.
22. Gregory of Tours, *Glory of the Confessors*, 76 trans. R. Van Dam (Liverpool: Translated Texts for Historians, Latin Series IV), 80.
23. Emile Mâle, *La fin du paganisme en Gaule* (Paris, 1950; Reprint, 1962), chap. 2. For my

critique: Bailey K. Young "Que restait-il de l'ancien paysage religieux à l'époque de Grégoire de Tours?", in *Grégoire de Tours et l'espace gaulois*, ed. N. Gauthier and H. Galinié, 241–50.

24. J.-Ch. Picard, notice on "Autun et Saint Martin" in *Autun/Augustodunum. Capitale des Eduens.* (1985) Catalogue of the exhibition held at the Musée Rolin, 16 March-27 October 1985. Ville d'Autun/Musée Rolin, 380.
25. Ch. Sapin, "Abbaye de Saint-Martin," ibid., 379.
26. Grivot, *op. cit.*, 46–47.
27. The *Passio*, which is published in the *Acta Sanctorum* t. XXXVIII (22 August): 496–97, is considered by Charles Boell "Les origines de l'église d'Autun," *Mémoires de la Société éduenne* 49, pp. 215–17, to have been redacted by the middle of the fifth century, to incorporate verbatim parts of the judicial interrogatory, and to have been widely copied. Grivot, *op. cit.*, note 1, 26, is more skeptical about the historical value of this source. See also E. Griffe, *La Gaule chrétienne à l époque romaine*, vol. I (Paris, 1964), 152–53, 160.
28. *Autun/Augustodunum. Capitale des Eduens* (1985). Catalogue of the exhibition held at the Musée Rolin, 16 March–27 October 1985. Ville d'Autun/Musée Rolin., nos. 743 and 744, pp. 377–78.
29. See Christian Sapin, "Le *Castrum* ou enceinte réduite d'Autun" and "Le groupe episcopale" in *Autun/Augustodunum. Capitale des Eduens* (1985). Catalogue of the exhibition held at the Musée Rolin, 16 March–27 October 1985. Ville d'Autun/Musée Rolin., 351–53.
30. Ibid. For Saint-Nazaire and the episcopal group, also see notice "Autun" by Ch Pietri and J.-Ch. Picard in *Topographie Chrétienne des Cités de la Gaule IV: Province ecclesiastique de Lyon (Lugdunensis Prima)*, ed. Nancy Gauthier and Jean-Charles Picard (Paris, 1986), 41–42; and Christian Sapin, *La Bourgogne préromane* (Paris, 1986), 29–31.
31. For Syagrius, see Grivot, *op. Cit.*, 49–50.
32. This poem was reconstituted for the 1985 exhibition and is displayed in the catalogue (no. 716, p. 357).
33. A square tower in the ramparts, at a point where they join the episcopal residence, is called by tradition "*la tour de Saint Léger*" and it is considered not implausible that it incorporates masonry from this phase of reconstruction; most of the wall towers are round.
34. Grivot, *op. cit.*, 51–54.
35. Walter Berry's thesis at the University of Missouri studies the Arroux Valley upriver from Autun, and offers a model for the Late Antique and early medieval parish development in that area; see his chapter, "Southern Burgundy in Late Antiquity and the Middle Ages," in *Regional Dynamics. Burgundian Landscapes in Historical Perspective*, ed. Carole L. Crumley and William H. Marquardt (Academic Press, 1987), 447–607.

Alexandria and the Mareotis Region

CHRISTOPHER HAAS

ON THE 13TH OF JULY, 494, TWO WEALTHY ALEXANDRIANS PAID OFF PART OF A DEBT they owed to a certain Flavius Maximus, *scholasticus* and advocate in the court of *praefectus Augustalis*. The two debtors were themselves wealthy and powerful men in the city. Flavius Olympiodorus was, like Maximus, an advocate and *scholasticus*. The other debtor, Flavius Julianus, was a *notarius sacri palatii* and held the rank of *clarissimus*. The two men lived in different parts of the city: Olympiodorus dwelt near the Great Tetrapylon in the city center, while Julianus's home was near the former Serapeum. Their debt amounted to more than mere pocket-change: 1,455 *nomismata*, that is, more than 20 Roman pounds of gold. In order to pay off 675 *nomismata* of the debt, Julianus surrendered to Maximus "two orchards and their appurtenances, situated in the Strip (or *Taenia*) of Taphosiris . . . near Lake Marea."[1]

In this recently edited papyrus, we witness one aspect of the multifaceted relationship that grew between the city of Alexandria and its immediate hinterland surrounding Lake Mareotis. Our understanding of this city/hinterland system is still in its early stages, due in large part to scholarly preoccupation with the regions up the Nile. However, archaeological field surveys and more focused excavation over the past two decades in

Mareotis have provided tantalizing pieces of information that allow for a preliminary reconstruction of this system.[2]

Far and away, the overwhelming volume of agricultural goods shipped to Alexandria came from middle and upper Egypt, facilitated by the inexpensive and efficient transport provided by the Nile. However, most of these goods (principally wheat and barley) were trans-shipped in Alexandria, and sent in vast quantities to Rome, Constantinople, and the imperial armies. The main supplier of agricultural produce to Alexandria itself was its immediate hinterland within a radius of some 30 to 40 miles.[3] This hinterland may be divided, for the sake of convenience, into two distinct geographic areas: Mareotis, comprising the lands to the south and west of the lake, and the so-called "territory (*chôra*/*regio*) of the Alexandrians," which extended from the lake's eastern shore as far as the Nile. This latter district became a separate nome sometime in the early Roman period with its metropolis at Hermopolis Parva. Throughout antiquity, the region contained extensive landholdings of Alexandrians, and helped to furnish the city's needs in meats and vegetables.[4]

Yet, of the two hinterland regions subordinate to Alexandria, Mareotis was clearly the more important, not only because of its abundant output of agricultural goods, but also owing to its closer political and economic ties to the city. Mareotis itself was made up of two zones, which need to be distinguished very carefully when the term is encountered in the ancient sources.[5] The first of these refers to the main eastern body of the lake itself, which covered approximately three times its current area during antiquity.[6] A good measure of its size can be found in Palladius, the mid–fifth century hagiographer, who informs us that it took him a full day and a half to cross from Alexandria to the monastic settlement of Nitria at the lake's southernmost shore.[7] During the late Roman period, its waters teemed with fish and waterfowl, and it was noted for its many papyrus marshes.[8] The inhabitants of Lake Mareotis carried on an existence not too much different from that of today's lake dwellers: living in reed huts either along the shoreline or on islands, and maneuvering among the maze of reeds in shallow-draft boats.[9] The lake was fed by canals, which linked up with the Canopic branch of the Nile at Schedia and Charaeu. As a consequence, Lake Mareotis delimited the southern boundaries of Alexandria. With the Mediterranean and the lake on

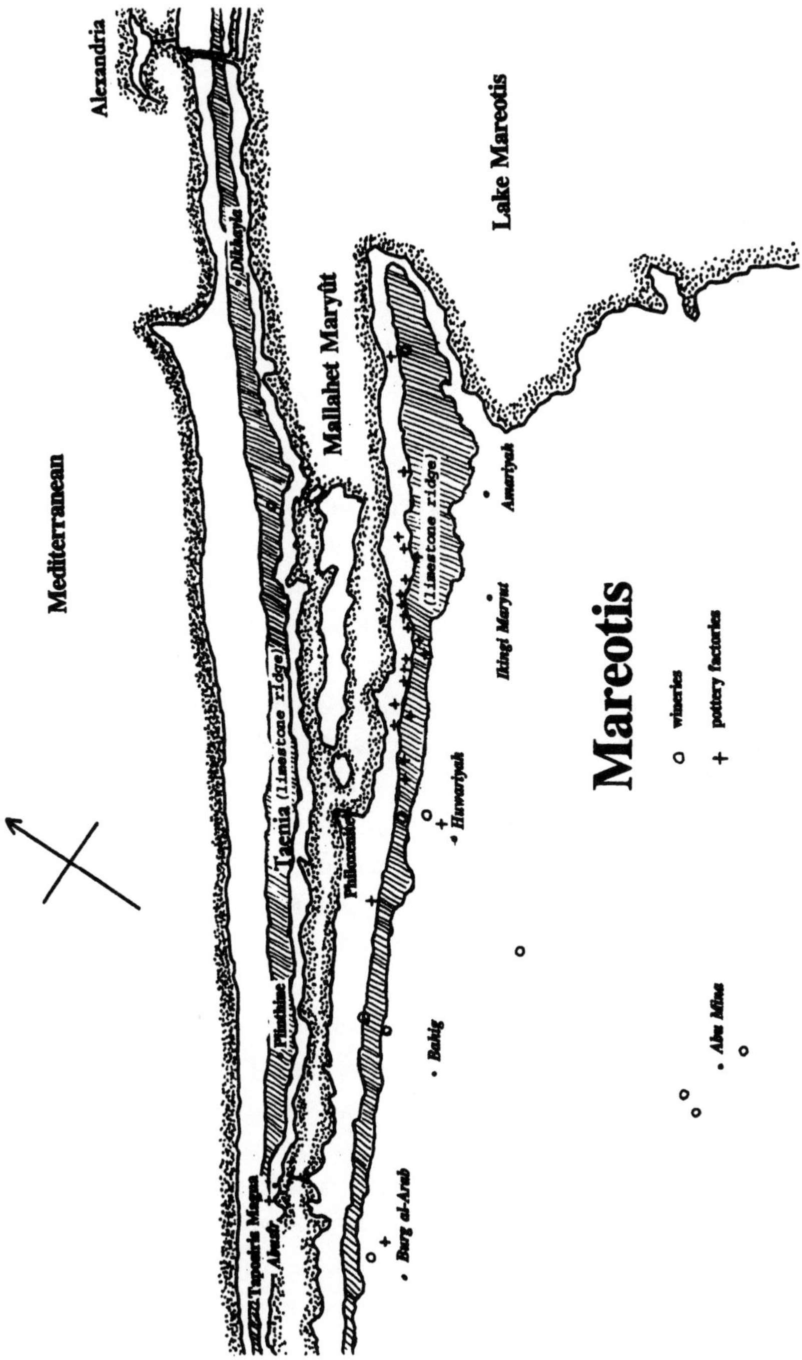
Alexandria
Lake Mareotis
Mallahet Maryût
Mediterranean
Taenia (limestone ridge)
(limestone ridge)
Amariyah
Ikingi Maryut
Hawariyah
Bahig
Burg al-Arab
Abu Mina
Mareotis
wineries
pottery factories

either side, the city's unique location led the anonymous fourth-century author of the *Expositio totius mundi* to marvel that Alexandria' s inhabitants could partake of "something no other province has: river fish, lake fish, and salt-water fish."[10]

The fifth-century historian, Socrates, tells us that the name Mareotis also referred to "a district of Alexandria, in which are contained very many villages, and an abundant population."[11] This semi-rural region south and west of the lake possessed ten or more villages and a larger urban center named Marea, dating back to Pharonic times, around which there was a countryside dotted with prosperous villas. Until Justinian detached Mareotis from Aegyptus Prima, and transferred it to the jurisdiction of the Libyan diocese in 538, the region was clearly subordinate to Alexandrian authorities.[12] During the fourth century, it had a separate tax assessor sent out by the prefect in Alexandria. Though the district could boast numerous churches, the fifteen priests and fifteen deacons of Mareotis remained under the direct control of the Alexandrian patriarch. The region was never served by its own bishop or even by a *chôrepiscopos* sent out from Alexandria; the patriarch himself inspected these churches. This tight control enhanced the severity of the charges leveled at Athanasius at the Council of Tyre in 335, that he had ordered the altar of a dissenting priest overthrown and had approved the breaking of a holy chalice at a church in Mareotis.[13]

The main geographical feature that endows this region with its distinct character is the long westward arm of Lake Mareotis, known today as the Mallahet Maryût, which extends some 60 km west from the main basin. The lake is separated from the Mediterranean by a narrow limestone ridge, between 10 and 30 m in height which begins near Canopus and runs along the coastline through Alexandria and well past the end of the lake. The presence of the ridge led Alexander to situate his city on this first solid ground west of the marshy Delta. This narrow strip, or *taenia*, of land was famed in antiquity for its papyrus and for a flavorful wine much praised by the ancients. Athenaeus tells us, "The wines there are somewhat pale, disclosing an oily quality in them which is dissolved by the gradual mixture of water, like the honey of Attica when water is added. This Taeniotic wine, beside being pleasant, has also an aromatic quality, and is mildly astringent."[14] South of the lake, the ground gradually rises by some 200 m to the top of yet another ridge, parallel to the first, which is situated approximately 2 km south of the lake.

Although this entire district was well off the main corridor of goods and services moving between Alexandria and the rest of Egypt, archaeological remains testify to the agricultural wealth of Mareotis. Well-appointed villas and country houses have been excavated at Huwarriyah, Burg al-Arab, and Taposiris Magna.[15] The prosperity of the region was based largely on viticulture, as evidenced by more than two dozen wineries that have been surveyed recently—four alone in the vicinity of Huwarriyah.[16] Mareotic wine, though not on a par with that of Taenia, was one of the Mediterranean' s most sought after varieties. Strabo, Virgil, and Horace all sing the praises of Mareotic wine, though the seventh-century patriarch, John the Almsgiver, claimed that "its taste is nothing to boast of and its price is low"—doubtless because of its local production.[17] Our late second-century connoisseur, Athenaeus, comments: "The vine is abundant in this region, and its grapes are very good to eat. The wine made from them is excellent; it is white and pleasant, fragrant, easily assimilated, thin, and does not go to the head."[18]

Wine production was supplemented by grains and olive oil, attested by several mills and presses. Faunal remains at Philoxenite indicate that pigs were common, and to a lesser degree, sheep and goats. Skeletal remains of duck and gazelle suggest that hunting supplemented the local diet. Fish, however, are by far the most abundant in the archaeological record, reminding us of the lake's important role as a source of food, as well as of fresh water and transport.[19]

One of the most remarkable aspects of recent archaeological work around the Mallahet Maryût is the presence of numerous pottery factories. Rubbish dumps of ill-formed or broken amphoras, as well as several actual kilns, bring the current total of these pottery workshops to near thirty, many of which are arranged in a chain along the southern shore of the lake.[20] The easternmost of these kilns, located near Amriyah, is a medium sized, double-chambered pit kiln which could fire nearly one hundred pots at a time.[21] In 1982-83, just north of Burg el-Arab, archaeologists uncovered a huge pit kiln from the early Roman period. This kiln has a diameter of 12 m and is 2 m deep with large access vents for depositing fuel. Holes in the floor of the kiln, arranged in the form of 5 concentric circles, could accommodate well over one hundred amphoras, making the kiln the largest in Egypt and one of the largest in the Mediterranean.[22]

Even more striking are the mounds of pottery sherds along the lake's southern shore. One the largest, near Amriyah, is nearly 30 × 50 m, and rises to a height of 20 m. Thousands of broken pots alternate in layers with ashes from a nearby kiln. A similar tale could be told of refuse mounds on the lakeward slope near Huwarriyah and Bahig. Most of these pottery mounds date back as early the late Ptolemaic period. Late antique amphoras seem to predominate, and the sequence generally ends in the seventh century. Thus far, there is no evidence of Coptic glazed pottery of the eighth to tenth centuries in the lakeside mounds associated with the pottery workshops. The close connection between these pottery workshops and viticulture in the Mareotic economy may be observed at several sites, notably at Burg el-Arab, where a large winery built of carefully dressed limestone and dated to the fourth/fifth centuries was discovered only 150 m to the west of the enormous pit kiln described above.[23] The contents of the amphoras produced in these workshops were clearly for export since Mareotic pottery has been found in abundance in Roman shipwrecks in the western Mediterranean and at sites well up the Rhone valley.[24]

The prosperity generated by this far-flung trade in wine is manifested by the close proximity of wineries to spacious villas throughout the region. At Abu Mina, a two-storied sixth-century villa was connected by a courtyard to a winery that is nearly as large as the villa itself. Even more sumptuous is the villa/winery complex at Huwarriyah. Sometime in the early fifth century, a large double-peristyle villa was constructed atop the limestone ridge south of the lake. Not more than 200 m to the northeast, an extensive winery of the same date has been excavated. The arrangement and relationship of the vats, as well as the four coats of red plaster that protected the precious fluid they contained, are common to wine factories in the region. In the large upper basin the grapes were initially crushed, and the sloping floor directed the juice toward a marble lion's head spout. The smaller upper basin containing the press probably was used to extract the last bits of juice from the previously crushed grapes. The juice then flowed into the large basin, after it had been strained through a cloth suspended beneath the spouts. The main collection basin, nearly 2.5 m deep, is one of the biggest in the eastern Mediterranean. After some initial fermentation, the wine was then poured into amphoras produced in one of the nearby workshops.[25] It was taken down to the lake and loaded at one of the many ancient jetties, which can still be seen along the western coasts.[26]

From the scale of the villas and country houses in the region, it appears that the economy of Mareotis was in the hands of landowners of good-sized farms and vineyards. As we have seen, some of these landowners, like Flavius Julianus, were Alexandrians. To protect this wealthy district, Alexandria's rulers, from the Ptolemies down to Byzantine emperors, developed the important garrison town of Taposiris Magna. Ptolemy II constructed a large temple to Osiris here, and the remains of this precinct are some of the most impressive north of Gizah. Visitors to the site are also drawn by the 19 m-high copy of the Alexandrian Pharos, which functioned here, not as a beacon to sailors, but as a magnificent funerary monument. The tower stands atop a typical late Ptolemaic chamber tomb and is in the midst of Taposiris Magna's necropolis. Of greater importance for the entire region were the defensive works that guarded the only landward approach to Alexandria from the west. More than a century ago, Mahmoud el-Falaki traced the course of a wall which cuts across the entire Taenia ridge, from the Mediterranean to the lake. Dubbed the "barbarian's wall," it makes use of an adjacent wadi running down to the lake to create a formidable combined barrier of ditch and wall. It has one gate, which guards the ancient road from Alexandria to Cyrenaica, and can only be approached by entering a narrow lane formed by parallel walls on either side of the road.[27]

Defensive works on the lake are no less impressive. A dike of stone quarried from the Taenia ridge extends across the lake from the south until, just off shore, it meets a perpendicular harbor mole, thereby creating a long narrow channel. The harbor mole is joined to the shore by a bridge, under which all lake traffic would have to pass. Between these installations on both land and water, the Ptolemies and their successors could effectively regulate all movement on the routes west of Alexandria.

The Romans recognized the defensive capabilities of this strategic site. Its value continued throughout the late antique period, as evidenced by a Roman camp, which was built inside the walls of the temple precinct. This conversion to a military camp occurred sometime in the late fourth or early fifth century, after the cessation of pagan cult. Well-ordered barracks were built along three sides the precinct, newly-installed flights of stairs led to the top of the walls, and a single-apsidal church was built to serve the needs of the soldiers and surrounding population.

Obviously, if the main function of Taposiris Magna was to protect Alexandria from the west, there were even better sites closer to the city where defensive works could have been built. Its establishment here filled the additional role of guarding the most intensely cultivated and inhabited regions along the Mallahet Maryût. Nearly all of the excavated villas, wineries, and pottery workshops are situated between Taposiris Magna and the main basin of the lake.

It comes as no surprise that Alexandria's Mareotic hinterland was drawn into contests for the military control of the city. Some of the bitterest fighting that took place late in 609, during the rebellion of Heraclius against Phocas, occurred in the Mareotic regions near Alexandria. Once Heraclius' lieutenant, Nicetas, overwhelmed the defenses of Mareotis and gained access to the canal system just west of Alexandria, it was just a matter of time until Phocas' appointed prefect was defeated and his impaled head was displayed over Alexandria's Gate of the Moon. The capture of Alexandria was a major stepping stone in Heraclius's eventual victory over Phocas.[28]

The rise of Christianity influenced the relationship between Alexandria and the Mareotis region in several different ways, and, in part, created a strong counter-current of goods and people travelling from Alexandria to the hinterland. During the late fourth century, the shrine of St. Menas, a Tetrarchic military martyr, grew enormously in popularity due to his reputation as a miracle-worker. The shrine was situated in a desert region, even in antiquity, and was 17 km from Lake Mareotis. Despite the distance, a veritable city—called by contemporaries, Martyroupolis—sprang up in the desert during the fifth and sixth centuries. Successive Alexandrian patriarchs endowed the shrine with a lavish basilica, a renovated martyr-crypt and martyr church, a baptistery, markets, hostels and baths for pilgrims; and barracks for a protecting garrison. The crowds who flocked here took home with them flasks of holy water, which depicted the saint between two camels. The wide distribution of these flasks around the Mediterranean testifies to St. Menas's high regard during the early Byzantine period.[29]

The Coptic *Encomium of Apa Mena* relates that the emperor Anastasius's praetorian prefect:

> saw the hardships suffered by the many multitudes coming to the shrine. For when they left the lake and entered upon the desert there, they found no place of lodgement or water till they reached the holy shrine. And the prefect built hospices by the lake and rest-houses for the multitudes to stay at. And he had the market-place established there in order that the multitudes might find and buy all their needs. He had spacious depositories constructed where the multitudes could leave their clothes and baggage and everything which they brought to the shrine. When he had completed everything he called it Philoxenite after himself. He also set up porticoes at different places where the people might rest. And he established watering places along the roads, leaving at them waterjars, from the hospices as far as the church. . . . And this continued till the time of Heraclius when the Saracens took the land.[30]

The port facility built for this pilgrim traffic remains today as one of the most impressive archaeological sites in the entire Mareotis region. Though it has sometimes been identified as the Pharonic administrative center of Marea, its architectural remains cannot be dated before the fifth century A.D., and it lacks any *terra sigillata* pottery, common at Egyptian sites prior to the late fourth century. It is built almost entirely of limestone quarried from the Taenia ridge just across the lake. Philoxenite's main purpose was neither defense nor trade, since it lacks any fortifications or warehouses. Its three well-preserved quays vary in length from 64 to 146 m in length. This variation would enable the port to be used regardless of the seasonal level of the lake's water. Over the past two decades, archaeologists have uncovered a double-bath complex, a slipway that served as a dry-dock, and a row of five shops that fronted on a covered portico. On the eastern promontory forming the harbor area, there is a public latrine, an oil press, and a large three-aisle transept basilica, of which only one apse has been fully excavated. A causeway over 0.5 km in length connects the mainland with a small island, which probably functioned as a fort and also as a lighthouse or customs post. The port lacks a substantial residential section, and the nearby encroaching necropolis suggests that the local population was rather small, only enough to serve the needs of pilgrim traffic.[31]

The hagiographic sources connected with the cult of St. Menas vividly depict life in this bustling transit port for pilgrims. One tale speaks of a slave boy miraculously saved from drowning who searches for his master among the many ships ranged along the docks of Philoxenite. Frequently, the miracles of St. Menas concern his heavenly protection of naive pilgrims from the unscrupulous and predatory inhabitants of Philoxenite. In one typical story, a rich pilgrim is murdered and dismembered by a dockside storekeeper, only to be restored to life again by the saint. In another, an Alexandrian woman is delivered from the lecherous designs of a innkeeper by the miraculous appearance of the mounted military saint. In the full regalia of a *spatharius*, St. Menas breaks down the doors of the hostelry and afflicts the wicked innkeeper with a paralysis that can only be cured by oil from the saint's shrine.[32]

The effect this flow of fervent pilgrims had on the Mareotic countryside can be seen just over 2 km south of the lake, at the villa near Huwarriyah. This double-peristyle villa was the luxurious country residence associated with the elaborate winery discussed above. It is one of the very few peristyle villas known from Egypt and it covered an area of more than 1,500 m^2. Sometime in the mid-to-late sixth century, the villa received an extensive renovation. Additional latrines were installed—far more than would be needed in a typical villa. More telling is the renovation of the northern peristyle in which a church was built, incorporating two rooms from the eastern wing of the building. To the north of the church, a baptistery was added, in form quite similar to the sixth-century baptistery at Abu Mina. Since this villa was located on a direct line between Philoxenite and Abu Mina, and stood just at the crest of the limestone ridge that sloped up from the lake, it is very likely that the Huwarriyah villa was transformed, in its last phase, into a pilgrim *xenodochion* or *hospitium*.[33]

Christianity also influenced the landscape in Mareotis, once the monastic ideal caught the imaginations of town dwellers. By the fifth century, Alexandria was ringed by notable monastic communities, among them Metanoia at Canopus and Nitria south of the lake, so that Palladius could speak of "the monasteries in the neighborhood of Alexandria with their some two thousand most noble and zealous inhabitants."[34] Likewise, to the west of Alexandria, along the narrow limestone ridge separating the Mediterranean from Lake Mareotis, a number of monasteries sprang up in the late fourth and early fifth centuries. These monasteries, which flourished just prior to the Sassanian and Arab conquests, took their names from the nearest milestone marking the distance from the city—thus, Pempton (5th), Enaton (9th), and Oktokaidekaton (18th).[35] In addition, the sources speak of a monastery within the settlement at Taposiris Magna.[36] While this intermural monastery has not yet been found, some 100 m west of Taposiris Magna a large church complex was discovered. It included a spacious basilica church with an attached chapel. Broad courts on either side of the churches open onto rows of rooms. The precise function of the complex has not been determined, but it may have been one of the Taenia monasteries.[37]

Among the monasteries ranged along the Taenia ridge, undoubtedly the most important was Enaton, which was the home of several famous abbots and miracle-workers during late antiquity.[38] The spiritual writer, John Climacus, collected much of the material for his *Ladder of Divine Ascent* during a lengthy sojourn at Enaton.[39] The monastery became large enough that it eventually comprised a handful of churches and monastic sub-communities all under the hegemony of the larger community. It became a center of Monophysite opposition to Chalcedonian authority within Alexandria, and, for a time, was the seat of the Coptic patriarchate.[40] Nearly a century ago, the remains of a small monastic settlement at Dikayla were identified as Enaton, however it seems to be both too small and too close to Alexandria to merit this identification. It is more likely to be Pempton, that is, if it is even one of monasteries known to us from the sources.[41]

Given this picture of late antique prosperity, with wine, oil, grain, and other produce being shipped to Alexandria, and with pilgrims, ascetics, and officials traveling to the Mareotis—why did this region decline so rapidly at the end of Antiquity? The pottery record at Philoxenite shows various North African and Cypriot wares, along with local pottery, but the sequence abruptly ceases in the seventh century. The Huwarriyah villa likewise seems to have been abandoned in the seventh century. It is only in scattered settlements south of the villa that we find Coptic glazed pottery of the eighth to tenth centuries. A similar tale could be told of sites from Taposiris Magna to Amriyah: steep decline in habitation during the seventh century, and more gradual abandonment until the end of the tenth century. Thus far, there has been no Mamluk pottery of the eleventh century found at any of these sites.[42]

The reasons for this decline go far beyond simply pointing a finger at 'Amr ibn al-'As and his Arab army. Just as the Syrian cities of the limestone massif east of Antioch and the agricultural towns of Egypt's Fayyûm experienced decline largely due to ecological factors, so too the prosperity of the Mareotis region began to deteriorate when its delicate environmental structure was disrupted.[43] The Arab conquest is just one piece of a much larger puzzle.

The stability of this city/hinterland system was predicated upon the water-borne transport afforded by Lake Mareotis and the Mallahet Maryût. This "dendritic" system (in the parlance of regional systems analysis) grew out of a two-way flow of goods, services, taxes, and people between Alexandria and its principal hinterland of Mareotis.[44] Fed by canals from the Canopic branch of the Nile, Lake Mareotis was the lifeblood of the entire region. These canals suffered from the neglect of Byzantine authorities and from deliberate military violence during Heraclius' war against Phocas, during the devastating Sassanian invasion of 619, and also at the time of Alexandria's capture by 'Amr ibn al-'As. The lake was dealt a final death blow in the ninth and tenth centuries when the Canopic branch of Nile dried up. It is no wonder that Alexandria's new city walls, built by Ibn Tulun in the ninth century, were far removed from the former shores of Lake Mareotis. Habitation continued on the highlands south of the lake, but was dependent upon wells and cisterns. By that time, both ends of this great city/hinterland system had turned away from the other and had learned to rely instead on their own resources. Flavius Julianus, the elite Alexandrian owner of the Mareotic orchards, was fortunate to have paid off his debt when he did.

NOTES

1. *P.Oxy.* 63.4394, ed. J. R. Rea.
2. A foundational discussion of the region's archaeology is M. Rodziewicz, "Alexandria and the District of Mareotis," *Graeco-Arabica* 2 (1983): 199–216. A wide range of specialized studies resulting from recent surveys may be found in J.-Y. Empereur, ed., *Commerce et Artisanat dans 1'Alexandrie Hellénistique et Romaine: Actes du Colloque d'Athènes, 12–12 decembre 1988 BCH* Supplément 33 (Athens, 1998); summarized, in part, in J.-Y. Empereur, *Alexandrie redécouverte* (Paris, 1998); Engl. ed., *Alexandria Rediscovered,* trans., M. Maehler (New York, 1998), 213–39.
3. The abundance of this district was such that many Egyptians from upriver sought sustenance here during a particularly severe famine in the mid–seventh century; *History of the Patriarchs* 1. 14 (ed., Evetts), p. 501, <237>.
4. *P.Oxy.* 7.1045, 10.1274, 12.1462; John of Nikiu *Chron.* (ed., R. H. Charles), 94. 18. See also A. Calderini, *Dizionario dei nomi geografici e topografici dell'Egitto greco-romano* (Milan, 1935), 1:208–9.
5. For surveys of the ancient literature, see Kees, *RE,* Bd. 14. 2, s.v. "Marea" cols. 1676–1678; A. de Cosson, *Mareotis* (London, 1935); and Calderini, *Dizionario,* 3:233–34.
6. Strabo 17. 1. 14; also de Cosson, pp. 70–82.
7. *Hist. Laus.* 7. 1.
8. *Expositio totius mundi et gentium* (ed., J. Rougé) 35. 3–5, 36. 1–7; *P.Tebt.* 3.867 (3rd century b.c.); Pliny *HN* 13. 76; Sophron. H. *v. Jo. Eleem.* 8; *Hist. Monach.* 27. 10.
9. Strabo tells us that the lake "contains eight islands, and all the shores around it are well inhabited," 17. 1. 14.
10. *Expositio* 36. 9–15, 35. 3–5. M. Rodziewicz, *Les Habitations Romaines Tardives d' Alexandrie à la lumière des fouilles polonaises à Kôm el-Dikka, Alexandrie* III (Warsaw, 1984), 219, describes graffiti of lake- and sea-going craft as the most numerous of all the genre scenes found at the late antique site of Kôm el-Dikka, in the center of Alexandria.
11. Soc. *HE* 1. 27 cols. 153c-156a. Athanasius refers to it as the chôra of Alexandria, (*Apol. contra Ar.* 85 col. 400b-c).
12. During the period just prior to the Arab conquest, Mareotis was counted as a Byzantine province, (John of Nikiu 107. 4, 12; Justinian *Edict* 13. 1, 9, 17–22).
13. Athan. *Apol. c. Ar.* 17, 46, 63–4, 74, 85; Epiph. *Haer.* 68. 7. 5-8. 5.
14. *Deipnosophistae* 1. 33.
15. F. el-Fakharani, "Recent Excavations at Marea in Egypt," in *Das römisch-byzantinische*

Ägypten: Akten des internationalen Symposions 26.-30. September 1978 in Trier, Aegyptiaca Treverensia: Trierer Studien zum Griechisch-Römischen Ägypten, Band 2, edited by G. Grimm, H. Heinen, and E. Winter (Mainz, 1983), 175–86, at 184–86; M. Rodziewicz, "Remarks on the Peristyle House in Alexandria and Mareotis," *Papers of the Twelfth International Congress for Classical Archaeology in Athens* (Athens, 1983); idem, "Remarks on the Domestic and Monastic Architecture in Alexandria and Surroundings," *Archaeology of the Nile Delta* (Amsterdam, 1988), 267–77; idem, "Taenia and Mareotis: Archaeological Research West of Alexandria," *Annual of the Egyptian Society of Greek and Roman Studies* 1 (1990): 62–78.

16. M. Rodziewicz, "Classification of Wineries from Mareotis," *in Commerce et Artisanat dans l'Alexandrie,* edited by J.-Y. Empereur, 27–36.
17. Strabo 17. 1. 15; Virgil *Georg.* 2. 91; Horace *Odes* 1. 37; Jo. Moschus *Prat. Spir.* 162; Severus ibn al-Muqaffa' *History of the Patriarchs* (ed. and trans. B. Evetts), 4 <pp. 56–57>; Sophr. H. *v. Jo. Eleem.* 10.
18. *Deipnosophistae* 1. 33.
19. K. Petruso and C. Gabel, "Marea: A Byzantine Port on Egypt' s Northwestern Frontier," *Archaeology* 36, no. 5 (1983): 62–63, 76–77 (at p. 77).
20. The pottery workshops are catalogued in J.-Y. Empereur and M. Picon, "Les ateliers d' amphores du Lac Mariout," in *Commerce et Artisanat dans 1' Alexandrie,* ed. J.-Y. Empereur, 75–91.
21. A. Abd el-Fattah, "Recent Discoveries in Alexandria and the Chora," in *Commerce et Artisanat dans 1' Alexandrie,* ed. J.-Y. Empereur, 43–45. Catalogue of pottery workshops, number 1, in Empereur/Picon, "Les ateliers d' amphores du Lac Mariout," 85.
22. F. el-Ashhawi, "Pottery Kiln and Wine Factory at Burg el-Arab," in *Commerce et Artisanat dans 1' Alexandrie,* ed. J.-Y. Empereur, 55–64; Rodziewicz, "Taenia and Mareotis," 62–78; J.-Y. Empereur, "La production viticole dans 1' Égypte ptolémaïque et romaine," in *La production du vin et de 1' huile en Méditerranée, Bulletin de Correspondance Hellenique: Supplement XXVI,* edited by M.-C. Amouretti and J.-P. Brun (Paris, 1993), 39–47; idem, *Alexandria Rediscovered,* 217–18. Burg el-Arab pottery workshop: Catalogue of pottery workshops, number 27, in Empereur/Picon, "Les ateliers d' amphores du Lac Mariout," 88.
23. F. el-Ashhawi, "Pottery Kiln and Wine Factory at Burg el-Arab"; M. Rodziewicz, "Classification of Wineries from Mareotis," 27–36.
24. Empereur, *Alexandria Rediscovered,* 218–19; Petruso and Gabel, "Marea: A Byzantine Port," 62–63, 76–77.
25. El-Fakharani, "Recent Excavations at Marea," 183–84; M. Rodziewicz, "Classification of Wineries from Mareotis," 35–36.
26. M. Rodziewicz, "From Alexandria to the West by Land and by Waterways," in *Commerce et Artisanat dans 1' Alexandrie,* ed. J.-Y. Empereur, 93–103.
27. For Taposiris Magna, its tower, and its defensive structures, see de Cosson, *Mareotis,* 109–15; idem, "Note on the Taenia Ridge" *Bulletin de la Société Archéologique d' Alexandrie* 32 (1938): 162–75; J. Drescher, "Topographical notes for Alexandria and District" *BSAA* 38 (1949): 15–16; A. Adriani, "Travaux des fouilles et de restaurations

dans la région d' Abousir (Maréotis)" *Annales du Musée Gréco-Romain* 3 (1940–50): 129–39; Rodziewicz, "Taenia and Mareotis," 72–74; idem, "From Alexandria to the West by Land and by Waterways," 102–3; Empereur, *Alexandria Rediscovered,* 222–25.

28. John of Nikiu *Chron.*, 103–9. See also Z. Borkowski, *Inscriptions des Factions à Alexandrie, Alexandrie* II, Centre d' Archéologie Méditerranéenne de 1' Académie Polonaise des Sciences (Warsaw, 1981), and the review of same by R. Bagnall and Alan Cameron, *BASP* 20 (1983): 75–84. For a readable reconstruction of these events, see A. J. Butler, *The Arab Conquest of Egypt and the Last Thirty Years of the Roman Dominion,* 2nd ed. by P. M. Fraser (Oxford, 1978), 1–41.
29. P. Grossmann, *Abu Mina: A Guide to the Ancient Pilgrimage Center* (Cairo, 1986); idem, "Abû Mînâ," in *CoptEncy* 1:24–29; Z. Kiss, *Les Ampoules de Saint Ménas découvertes à Kôm el-Dikka (1961–1981), Alexandrie* V (Warsaw, 1989); idem, "Ampulla," in *CoptEncy* 1:116–18.
30. *Encom. Apa Mena* in *Apa Mena: A Selection of Coptic Texts Relating to St. Menas,* edited and translated by J. Drescher (Cairo, 1946), 147–48.
31. El-Fakharani, "Recent Excavations at Marea," 178–82; M. Sadek, "The Ancient Port of Marea," *Cahiers des Études Anciennes* (Quebec) 8 (1978): 67–77; idem, "The Baths at the Ancient Harbour of Marea," *Sesto Congresso internazionale di Egittologia,* vol. 1 (Turin, 1992), 549–53; Rodziewicz, "Taenia and Mareotis," 73–74; idem, "Alexandria and the District of Mareotis," 202–4; idem, "From Alexandria to the West by Land and by Waterways," 95–97, 101–2; K. Petruso and C. Gabel, "Marea: A Byzantine Port."
32. *The Miracles of Apa Mena* 2, 3, 16 (in J. Drescher, *Apa Mena*), 111–12, 114–16, 119–20.
33. M. Rodziewicz, "Remarks on the Domestic and Monastic Architecture in Alexandria and Surroundings," *Archaeology of the Nile Delta* (Amsterdam, 1988), 267–77; idem, "Remarks on the Peristyle House in Alexandria and Mareotis," *Papers of the Twelfth International Congress for Classical Archaeology in Athens* (Athens, 1983); idem, "Opus sectile mosaics from Alexandria and Mareotis," in *Tesserae: Festscrift für J. Engemann, JAC* Ergänzungsband 18 (1991): 204–14; el-Fakharani, "Recent Excavations at Marea," 184–86.
34. *Hist. Laus.* 7. 1.
35. The most thorough examination of these monasteries during the period of their greatest influence remains P. van Cauwenberg, *Études sur les moines d' Égypte depuis le Councile de Chalcédoine jusqu' à 1' invasion arabe* (Louvain, 1914), 63–81. Valuable recent assessments may be found in J. Gascou, "Oktokaidekaton," in *CoptEncy* 6:1826–27; idem, "Pempton," in *CoptEncy* 6:1931.
36. Severus ibn al-Muqaffa' Hist. Patr. in PO vol. 5, p. 26 <280>. J. B. Ward-Perkins identified the Roman garrison structures within the enclosure walls as the monastery at Taposiris Magna, "The Monastery of Taposiris Magna," *BSAA* 36 (1945): 48–53. More recently, M. Rodziewicz has shown that this identification is mistaken, by comparing the purported monastery's architecture with excavations of similar structures in both Alexandria and in the Mareotis region—structures which are undoubtedly domestic in nature: "Taenia and Mareotis," 62–63; idem, "Remarks on the Domestic and Monastic Architecture."

37. P. Grossmann, "Die Kirche extra muros von Taposiris Magna," *Mitteilungen des Deutschen Archäologischen Instituts Kairo* 38 (1982): 152–54.
38. Zachariah Scholasticus *v. Sev.*, ed. M.-A. Kugener, *Patrologia Orientalis* 2:14–35; John Moschus, *Prat. Spir.* 145, 146, 171, 178.
39. *Scala Paradisi* 4. 20–39.
40. Zach. Mityl. *HE* 3. 2, 6. 1–2; Arabic-Jacobite *Synaxarium* 'Amshîr 2 (ed. and trans., R. Basset, Patrologia Orientalis 11 <732> p. 766; Severus ibn al-Muqaffa' *History of the Patriarchs* (ed. and trans. B. Evetts), p. 447 <183>. See also, C. Haas, *Alexandria in Late Antiquity* (Baltimore, 1997), 324–30.
41. For a thorough discussion, see J. Gascou, "Enaton," in *CoptEncy* 3:954–58.
42. Rodziewicz, "Alexandria and Mareotis," 201–5; idem, "Taenia and Mareotis," 69–70. See also C. Décobert and M. Martin, "La Maréotique médiévale, notes d' histoire religieuse," in C. Décobert and J.-Y. Empereur, eds., *Études alexandrines 4*, Supplement to *BIFAO* (forthcoming).
43. G. Tate, *Les campagnes de la Syrie du nord* (Paris, 1992); C. Foss, "The Near Eastern countryside in late antiquity: a review article," *The Roman and Byzantine Near East, Journal of Roman Archaeology* Suppl. 14 (1995): 213–34; P. van Minnen, "Deserted Villages: Two Late Antique Town Sites in Egypt," *BSAP* 32 (1995): 41–56.
44. C. A. Smith, ed., *Regional Analysis* (New York, 1976); N. Oppenheim, *Applied Models in Urban and Regional Analysis* (Englewood Cliffs, N.J., 1980).

The Case of Late Antique Berytus: Urban Wealth and Rural Sustenance— A Different Economic Dynamic

LINDA JONES HALL

THE TRADITIONAL VIEW OF THE LATE ROMAN ECONOMY HAS BEEN THAT WEALTH and prestige in Late Antique cities accrued primarily to "leading citizens" who drew on income from agriculture.[1] Jones, Finley, and their successors such as Hopkins and Garnsey,[2] have asserted that social prestige in the cities was linked to wealth based on the productivity of the land. However, Pleket, in a series of articles, has suggested, ever more strongly, that in certain coastal cities, such as Tyre and Berytus, merchants and artisans dealing in luxury textiles and dyes rose to prominence in the conduct of affairs in their *civitates*.[3]

The archeological evidence, both agricultural survey and urban excavation in this area of Phoenicia, appears to support Pleket's theory. The relatively smaller size of the farms in the hilly terrain around Berytus, when coupled with the evidence for great urban wealth from trade, calls for a re-evaluation of the relationship of agriculture and artisan production as sources of social status and wealth in the cities of Berytus and Tyre.

First let us turn to an examination of the potential for wealth from agriculture in the area surrounding Berytus. The original farms were small allotments assigned to the soldier-settlers (about 10-20 *jugera*)[4] at the time the *colonia Romana* was established in the reign of Augustus. The chronological sequence of inscriptions and land development suggests a gradual expansion of terracing the uplands and draining the lowlands; that is, the inscriptions show progressive settlement toward the hills. Archeological survey indicates that the villagers of the highlands near Berytus developed terraced farming for the production of a well-known Syrian wine.[5] The western part of the Biqa'a Valley, with drier and gentler slopes, was cultivated for olive and fig production.[6] Leon Marfoe has suggested that the farmers practiced intercropping with cereals in the olive orchards and produced a fine Levantine wheat, which was more expensive than Egyptian wheat, but was of a superior quality.[7]

In the Late Antique period, although there was a pattern of some settlement abandonment, the overall density of settlement remained higher than in any other period except the Roman. However, there seems to have been a shift from the cultivation of crops on the valley sides to goat pastoralism on the slopes.[8] Marfoe has found evidence that the slopes were now dominated by a degraded maquis which would have provided an ideal pasture for both cattle and caprines. Such a change to animal husbandry may have been prompted by a desire to evade taxes on richer agricultural lands and by the realization that fewer laborers were required for the tending of animals than for the maintenance of terraces, vineyards, and olive orchards. Such a transition might have begun with "mixed farming," that is, sheep pastoralism combined with olive culture.[9] To Marfoe, it seems evident that settlements in the valleys also converted to animal husbandry and relied on transhumance between the valley bottom and the now sparsely settled slopes. In summary, Marfoe found a decline in the settled area of the Biqa'a Valley from 280 ha in the Roman period to 240 hectares in the Byzantine period, a drop of 14 percent.[10]

On the other hand, the literary record supports the theory of a wealthy, influential class of merchants and artisans in Tyre and Berytus. Libanius (*Oratio* 62.21) suggested that students from the artisan classes even attended the law schools of Berytus.

> But indeed, on the one hand, formerly one could see the youths from the workshops [artisans] who are concerned about a barely sufficient livelihood, going to Phoenicia to study the laws. On the other hand, those young men of the wealthy houses who have distinguished lineage, wealth, and fathers who have carried out their curial duties remained among us.[11]

Although it was Libanius' intention to praise his students from the curial classes who pursued the traditional curriculum of rhetorical training in Antioch[12] by contrasting them with the "working class" students who studied law in Berytus, logic would suggest that the families of the latter students had "surplus income" in order to provide such an education for their sons. Procopius characterized the city's traders and craftsmen who were involved in the production and distribution of luxury textiles as well-to-do:

> Garments made of silk had been produced from ancient times in the cities of Beirut and Tyre in Phoenicia. And the merchants and craftsmen and artisans of these stuffs had lived there from ancient times, and this merchandise was carried from there to the whole world.[13]

Procopius says explicitly that the economy of Berytus and Tyre had been dependent upon the silk-weaving industry and that all classes of artisans and traders in silk and purple had been quite prosperous before the move to Constantinople, in the reign of Justinian while Theodora was alive (giving thus an end date of 548 A.D.).

There is further evidence for the level of wealth that could be gained from the production and sale of silk garments. The silk merchants (*metaxarii*) of Justinian's time were classed with the *argentarii* (silversmiths and bankers) and were among those forbidden to buy "court sinecures" for themselves and their sons.[14] Such a ruling indicates both the means and ambition for advancement through wealth by these merchants and their heirs.

In addition, both Tyre and Berytus produced and sold linen, as reported by the writer of the *Expositio totius mundi et gentium*. "The following [cities] are in the trade [or production] of linen cloth: Scythopolis, Laodiceia [*ad mare*], Byblos, Tyrus, and Berytus. These [cities] export linen cloth to all the world and are outstanding in every kind of wealth. . . ."[15] The possibility of great profit such merchandise might provide has been demonstrated by Christopher Haas in his study of the income for both the weavers and the traders in the finished cloth in Late Antique Alexandria.[16]

Further confirmation for both diversity of textiles and high levels of income from a range of merchandise can be gleaned from Jerome's description of Tyre, which can be applied to Berytus as well. Jerome noted that the merchants of Tyre were able to accrue riches even in unstable times through their business acumen and the quality of their merchandise.

> Even today, however, there remains in the Syrians an inborn zeal for transacting business; they go about the whole world with a desire for money, and they have such a frenzy for trading, that even now when the Roman world has been beset upon, they seek riches in the midst of swords and the slaughter of unfortunate ones, and they flee poverty by means of dangers. Men of this kind are the business people of Tyre; who trade damask, purple, and checked garments; linen also, and silk and cotton they place in their trade.[17]

Jerome's testimony confirms the types of textiles and adds the details of special weaving techniques used to produce "damask" and "checked" fabrics.[18] The variety of goods described seems to suggest reliable and varied sources of the traded textiles; the merchants appear to have had secure contacts for obtaining goods to sell and the necessary capital for transport. Inscriptions from other parts of the Mediterranean reflect the widespread trade in silk.[19] A "Syrian" *holosericoprata* (silk merchant) is known from a sixth-century papyrus.[20] The testimony of Western writers such as Salvian, Jerome, and Gregory of Tours suggests that Syrian merchants in Italy sold luxury garments that well may have been woven in Berytus and Tyre.[21]

Direct evidence for active maritime trade between Beirut and faraway ports, such as Brundisium, is supplied from the *Digest* by the description of legal arrangements made to secure a cargo.

> Callimachus received a bottomry loan from Stichus, slave of Seius, in the province of Syria, city of Beirut, destination Brundisi; sum in credit: two hundred

> sesterces for each day of the voyage: pledged as security: the goods bought at Beirut for carriage to Brundisi and any goods to be bought at Brundisi for return carriage to Beirut. And it was agreed between them that on arrival at Brundisi Callimachus should before 13 September following buy other goods, load them, and sail back to Syria, or that if by due date he had not bought other goods and left that city he should repay the whole sum as if the voyage were now terminated, and provide all necessary expenses for those persons carrying the money to enable them to take it to Rome. Promise for proper performance of all these things was called for by Stichus, slave of L. Titus, duly given by Callimachus.[22]

The use of Berytus as an example in this case of maritime law by Scaevola, the teacher of Paulus, who was one of the Severan jurists, suggests that ships with rich cargoes routinely made the trans-Mediterranean sailing.[23]

Archeological excavations in Beirut have revealed a comfortable and successful artisan quarter in Late Antique Berytus, which had beautiful houses and well-appointed shops.[24] Large finds of Late Antique coinage support the conjecture of prosperity[25] based on trade, particularly with Constantinople. Kevin Butcher, writing in a recent publication about these finds, notes:

> Most of the coins which have been found belong to the period A.D. 498-518, during the reign of Anastasius I. Coins of Anastasius' successors Justin and Justinian have been found, but not in any significant numbers. The prevalence of the coins of Anastasius is interesting, especially as most of them come from Constantinople.[26]

Late Antique descriptions of the damage from the earthquake of 551 emphasize the beauty of the city's buildings and the wealth of its inhabitants. Agathias described sixth-century Berytus as a city graced by elegant, undoubtedly expensive buildings, which were famed throughout the world.[27]

> In summer time, roughly during the same period, there was a violent earthquake in Constantinople and in many parts of the Empire, with the result that several cities both on the islands and the mainland were razed to the ground and their inhabitants wiped out. The lovely city of Berytus, the jewel of Phoenicia, was completely ruined and its world-famous architectural treasures were reduced to a heap of rubble, practically nothing but the bare pavements of the buildings being left. Many of the local inhabitants were crushed to death under the weight of the wreckage, as were many cultivated young men of distinguished parentage who had come to study the Law. There was, in fact, a long tradition of legal studies in the city, and the law schools conferred an aura of peculiar privilege and distinction on the place. At this point, then, the professors of law moved to the neighboring city of Sidon and the schools were transferred there, until Berytus was rebuilt. The restored city was very different from what it had been in the past, though it was not changed beyond recognition, since it still preserved a few traces of its former self. But this rebuilding of the city and the subsequent return of the schools was not to take place for some time yet.[28]

Agathias who was about twenty years old at the time of the earthquake seems to have had first-hand information about the city's appearance and status, both before and after the disaster. Subsequent chroniclers emphasize not only the damage done to the buildings but also the loss of great ships in the harbor. The impression of great wealth, based on trade, is confirmed by the description of the inhabitants' behavior during the tidal wave, which accompanied the earthquake. Malalas preserves this scene of the efforts to salvage the cargoes from ships sinking in the harbor:

> The sea also along the whole Phoenician coast retreated and went back nearly two miles . . . we have decided to report for posterity a terrible disaster and a great and remarkable portent which happened in the city of Beirut in Phoenicia during the earthquake which destroyed the cities. For in the terrible confusion, when the sea at God's will had retreated and withdrawn from Beirut and the other coastal cities of Phoenicia for a distance of nearly two miles, the dreadful depths of the sea became visible. Suddenly, wonderful,

> varied and amazing sights could be seen—sunken ships full of different cargoes, and other things too when the waters had retreated from the land. Some ships which were moored in the harbors settled on the sea-bottom since at God's command they had been left high and dry as the water flowed away. . . . For the inhabitants of the cities and towns on the coast immediately rushed into the sea on a bold and determined impulse, to steal with wicked avarice the huge overturned treasures which were at the bottom of the sea—an impulse which cost them their lives.
>
> Therefore when many thousands of people, rushing into the depths of the sea on a deadly impulse, had begun to take treasures and remove them quickly and others, seeing them laden with deadly wealth, had rushed up with great enthusiasm so as not to be deprived of the hidden treasures which had suddenly been revealed by the earthquake, when some of them had rushed down to the bottom others were hastening above, others were trying their utmost in the middle, and all were rushing around in confusion, then a tremendous surge of the sea, rushing up unobserved to return to its original depth, overwhelmed and consumed in the depths of its eddying waters all those wretched people who had rushed to find wealth from the bottom of the sea. . . .[29]

The moralizing tone of the chronographer cannot conceal that for many of the inhabitants of Berytus, the rich cargoes of varied merchandise were worth great risks of all sorts.

A reference in John Chrysostom to the occupation of weaver (*gynaeciarius*) suggests not only that men were engaged in this craft but that the economic rewards were so great that a prejudice against the work was frequently overlooked.

> For (God) neither entrusted everything to the husband, nor all to the wife; but also dividing these things to each: on the one hand entrusting to her the house, on the other hand entrusting to him the market; and to him the task of support, for he tills the ground; and to her that of clothing, for loom and distaff are the wife's, for He Himself gave to the woman skill in woven work. But beware the covetousness, which does not remit this apparent difference!

> For the foolishness of the many has introduced our men to the looms, and put shuttles in their hands, and the woof, and threads.30

Another measure of increased wealth is the ability to pay taxes in gold. During the reign of Anastasius (late fifth to early sixth century), artisans were required to pay the *chrysargyon*, which amounted to 140 pounds of gold every four years for the artisans of Edessa. When this tax was abolished in 498, the residents of the entire city celebrated by a procession to the church of St. Sergius and St. Simeon. "They then reentered the city, and kept a glad and merry festival during the whole week, and enacted that they should celebrate this festival every year. All the artisans were reclining and enjoying themselves, bathing and feasting in the court of the [great] Church and in all the porticoes of the city."[31] Clearly, the artisans had attained wealth to be able to pay such a tax, but more importantly, they had acquired a substantial level of status to be honored by a public festival that involved every aspect of urban life.

Just how much wealth could be realized from the trade and production of textiles is suggested by Suetonius' description of the sources of income for Q. Remmius Palaemon from Vicetia (a freed slave in the reign of Tiberius and Claudius) who

> took in 400,000 sesterces a year from his school and not much less from his private assets; these he oversaw very conscientiously, for he ran workshops that produced garments to be sold on the open market, and he was so keen on agriculture—that as a matter of established fact—a vine set in place by his own hand produced grapes for 365 days every year. (*de. Gramm, 23*)[32]

Interestingly, this well-to-do grammarian supplemented his income both through artisan and agricultural investments. Such a diversification of money-making strategies may well have been possible in Late Antique Berytus as well.

Thus, wealth from trade in textiles and dyes is clearly documented for the people of Berytus and Tyre in all our sources. However, social status could be acquired in Berytus by another route. Libanius complained bitterly about the status that could be gained by persons who mastered Latin and legal studies.

> Moreover, as regards my studies [in Greek and rhetoric], they had now lost ground to Latin even more than before, so that I am afraid that they may, through the agency of law, become completely superseded. Yet it is not law or edicts that have brought this about, but the honour and power reserved for those acquainted with Latin.[33]

In another passage, Libanius, as a "hostile witness," offers more testimony concerning the rewards awaiting those students who acquired mastery of Latin to enhance their entree and promotion through the imperial bureaucracy.[34]

> And, moreover, you are open to reproof on the following grounds. Every spring you see the sons of present, or past, members of the council sailing off to Berytus or to Rome, and you are not angry or annoyed, nor do you seek audience with the governors and complain as you should. But who is so dull-witted, such a fool or a simpleton as to be incapable of understanding what their trip implies for them? It is out of no concern for justice or to avoid any inadvertent breach of the laws that they set sail for Phoenicia, nor do they sail to the other place so as to assist the council by their proficiency in both languages; their concern is to have their legal or linguistic qualifications as a means of getting out of membership of council. Nor have they been deceived in their ambition.[35]

Real wealth from textile trade and production may have preceded or paid for success-oriented education which may then have led to even more influence by "upward mobility" in the imperial service. Ramsay MacMullen and others have noted that the legislation in the Theodosian Code, designed to control social fluidity, in fact attests to the very possibility of advancement, particularly through the avenue of bureaucratic promotion.[36]

John Chrysostom pinpointed quite crisply the political and social advancement that would come to young men who gained competence in

Latin and the law. Although the highly educated bishop may have been referring to the training available in Antioch or Constantinople rather than in Berytus, clearly such benefits would have enticed ambitious young men to consider obtaining legal training. Chrysostom described the advice a father might give his son on how to get ahead in the Later Roman Empire:

> . . . but one may hear some fathers speaking to their sons to encourage them to the study of rhetoric and they would use such words. . . . Again, another person says such and such a one having learnt Latin [the language of the Romans] has a brilliant position in the imperial service and administers all internal matters.[37]

In conclusion, the evidence suggests the following socioeconomic dynamic at work in the city of Berytus:

Agriculture in the Biqa' did not produce either the same volume of produce or income that accrued to the landowning, curial classes in other cities. However, wealth and material success did enrich the merchants[38] and artisans who were associated with the production of luxury textiles and dyes. Even greater economic status and social prominence could be gained by those young men who were willing to study Latin and law in the schools of Berytus. Such a course of legal study and social advancement appears to have been open to even the young men from the workshops of Berytus, as well as to the sons of the curial classes from throughout the empire. Thus artisan wealth could pave the way for the acquisition of not only material goods but for an improved social standing in a society which increasingly measured success by movement through the imperial strata of Late Antique bureaucracy and by propinquity to the emperors.[39] It, therefore, appears that the landowning *curiales* did not enjoy a level of wealth in Berytus that marked them out for leadership in other cities. Instead, it appears that wealthy artisans and merchants dominated the economic life of the city, and that there was a close relationship between the teachers and practitioners of the law and the members of these economically successful families.

NOTES

See Linda Jones Hall, "Berytus, 'Mother of Laws': Studies in the Social History of Beirut from the Third to Sixth Centuries A.D." (Ph.D. diss., Ohio State University, 1996) for fuller presentation of the evidence for this essay. Grateful acknowledgment is made to Professors Timothy E. Gregory and J. H. W(olf) G. Liebeschuetz who have made many useful comments on this essay.

1. See Peter Garnsey and Richard Saller, *The Roman Empire: Economy, Society, and Culture* (Berkeley and Los Angeles, 1987), 46–51, for an excellent survey of the ideas of Jones and his successors.
2. A substantial summary is offered by Keith Hopkins in the Introduction to Peter Garnsey, Keith Hopkins, and C. R. Whittaker, *Trade in the Ancient Economy* (Berkeley, 1983), i–xxv. C R. Whittaker, "Late Roman Trade and Traders," 163–80 in the same volume, specifically addresses the question of trade in the Late Antique period.
3. H. W. Pleket, "Urban Elites and Business in the Greek Part of the Roman Empire," in *Trade*, ed. Garnsey, Sailor, and Whittaker, 131–44. See also H. W. Pleket, "Urban Elites and the Economy in the Greek cities of the Roman Empire," *Münstersche Beiträge zur antiken Handelsgeschichte* 3 (1984): 3–26. H. W. Pleket, "The Roman State and the Economy: The Case of Ephesus," in *Économie antique, Les échanges dans l'Antiquité: le rôle de l'État*, Entretiens d'Archéologie et d'Histoire (1994), 115–26 at 120, referring to his earlier study of Tyre and Beirut: H. W. Pleket, "Greek Epigraphy and Comparative Ancient History: Two Case Studies," *Epigraphica Anatolica* 12 (1988): 25–38.
4. See Henry Innes MacAdam, "Some Aspects of Land Tenure and Social Development in the Roman Near East," in *Land Tenure and Social Transformation in the Middle East*, edited by T. Khalidi (Syracuse, N.Y., 1984), 45–62. See also Leon Marfoe, "Empire and Ethnicity in Syrian Society: 'From Archeology to Historical Sociology Revisited' Revisited," in *Archéologie au Levant. Recueil a la memoire de Roger Saidah: Coll. de la Maison de l'Orient mediterr.*, XII Ser. archeol. IX (Lyon, 1983), 463–79 at 470.
5. See Pliny *NH* XIV, 74 and XV, 74 for reference to Syrian wine which was exported as far as India.
6. Marfoe (1983), 471. For full treatment of the results of archaeological survey in the region, see Leon Marfoe, "Between Qadesh and Kumidi: A History of Frontier Settlement and Land Use in the Biqa'" (Ph.D. diss., University of Chicago, 1978). *IGLS* VI 2945–6 has relevant inscriptions from the Biqa'a.
7. Marfoe (1978), 683–84.
8. Ibid., 681.
9. Ibid., 682–83.
10. Ibid., 685.
11. Libanius, *Oratio* 62.21, Foerster ed., 4:356. Discussion and French translation in Paul Collinet, *Histoire de L'École de Droit de Beyrouth* (Paris, 1925), 37–38.

12. See P. Petit, *Libanius et la vie municipale à Antioche au IVe siècle après J.-C.* (Paris, 1955) and P. Petit, *Les Étudiants de Libanius* (Paris, 1957), for detailed study of Libanius' students and the intellectual life of Antioch. J. H. W. G. Liebeschuetz, *Antioch: City and Imperial Administration in the Later Roman Empire* (Oxford, 1972), provides additional citations and discussion of these topics.
13. Procopius, *Anecdota or Secret History* 25.13. Translation based on Dewing, 6:297–98.
14. *Cod. Just.* 8.13.27. Jones assumes that this ruling applied to the merchants of Constantinople after the transfer of the monopoly to the capital. See A.H.M. Jones, "The Cloth Industry under the Roman Empire," *Economic History Review* 13 (1960): 183–92, reprinted as XVIII in A.H.M. Jones, *The Roman Economy: Studies in Ancient Economic and Administrative History*, edited by P.A. Brunt (Oxford, 1974).
15. In linteamina sunt hae: Scythopolis, Laodicia, Byblus, Tyrus, Berytus quae linteamen omni orbi terrarum emittunt, et sunt eminentes in omni abundantia. Latin text from Rouge, ed., *Expositio totius mundi et gentium* (XXXI E), pp. 163–64. My translation.
16. Christopher Haas, *Alexandria in Late Antiquity: Topography and Social Conflict* (Baltimore and London, 1997), 33–35, discusses the wealth realized from the trade in and production of linen woven goods.
17. Jerome, *In Ezech.* 27.15–16. *PL* 25.267C (see also *Corpus Christianorum Series Latina*, vol. 75). Latin text and English translation given in M. Jamesetta Kelly, *Life and Times as Revealed in the Writings of Jerome Exclusive of his Letters* (Ph.D. diss., The Catholic University of America, 1944), 32. Since it has been demonstrated by David S. Wiesen, *St. Jerome as a Satirist: A Study in Christian Latin Thought and Letters* (Ithaca, 1964) and J. N. D. Kelly, *Jerome: His Life, Writings, and Controversies* (London, 1975) that Jerome was heavily influenced by Juvenal in his acerbic manner of writing attacks of various kinds, we should note the animosity against the Tyrians. However, his account of their items of trade seems correct and expands our knowledge of the textiles that were traded. Jerome described the citizens of Tyre as Syrians; this may be a Western construction of identity rather than the view of the citizens of Tyre themselves.
18. H. Granger-Taylor, "Two Silk Textiles from Rome and Some Thoughts on the silk-weaving industry," *Bulletin du Centre International d'Études des Textiles Anciens* 65 (1987): 13–31, provides a detailed analysis of the sophisticated designs, dyes, and workmanship by a study of Late Antique silk fragments, found in a tomb at Rome and now kept in the Vatican museum. The range of colors and motifs is impressive in fabrics used for clothing and ecclesiastical purposes.
19. Inscriptions referring to silk workers include *CIL* VI.9678. *CIL* XIV.2793 = *ILS* 5449 and *CIL* XIV.2812 = *ILS* 7681.
20. Latin papyrus referring to George of Antioch, a silk merchant, who was in business at Ravenna in the sixth century a.d. See J. O. Tjäder, *Die nichtliterarischen lateinischen Papyri Italiens*, no. 4–5, B.V.13, VI. 14.
21. See Theodor Mommsen, *The Provinces of the Roman Empire from Caesar to Diocletian* (London, 1909; Reprint, Chicago, 1974), 2:139–40 for discussion of Salvian *De gub. Dei* 4.14 for multitude of Syrian merchants in Gaul; Gregory of Tours 8.1 and 10.26; Jerome *in Ezech.* 27; and inscriptions from Treves. The diffusion of "Syrian" silk merchants

may be suggested by C. P. Jones, "A Syrian in Lyons," *AJP* 99 (1978): 336–53 and by the evidence collected in A.H.M. Jones, "The Cloth Industry under the Roman Empire," *Economic History Review* 13 (1960); reprinted in A.H.M. Jones, *The Roman Economy: Studies in Ancient Economic and Administrative History* (Oxford, 1974).

22. *Digest* 45.1.122. Quoted and discussed in J. A. Crook, *Law and Life of Rome, 90 B.C–a.d. 212* (Ithaca, 1967), 224 and 326. Crook thinks that the case is imaginary because the slave's owner is listed with two different names, but he suggests that the contract follows the usual format.
23. See L. J. Hall, "*Latinitas* in the Late Antique Greek East: Cultural Assimilation and Ethnic Distinctions," in *Veritatis Amicitiaeque Causa: Essays in Honor of Anna Lydia Motto and John R. Clark*, edited by S. Byrne and E. Cueva (Chicago, 1999), for full documentation of Berytus' reinvented Phoenician identity, from the time of Septimius Severus onward. See also Cod. Theod. 13.9.1 (Pharr translation, p. 399) for a law which was given and posted at Berytus in 372 a.d. concerning the possibility of imperial compensation for loss due to shipwreck. This law clearly indicates that the potential for both gain and loss for shipping from the port of Berytus was substantial.
24. K. Butcher and R. Thorpe, "A Note on Excavations in Central Beirut 1994–96," *JRA* 10 (1997): 291–306. Dominic Perring, Helga Seeden, Peter Sheehan and Tim Williams, "Archeological Excavations in the Souks Area of Downtown Beirut; Interim Report of the UAB Project BEY 006, 1994–1995," *BAAL (Bulletin d'Archeologie et d'Architecture Libanaise)* 1 (1996): 1–13, at 7–9. The mosaics from fourteen artisan shops and an extensive domus dated to the "Byzantine" period are to be conserved in an archeological park to be constructed in Beirut, according to Helga Seeden, public lecture and private discussion, New York City, May 1996.
25. Compare with the richer record for Alexandria, as demonstrated by Haas (1997). See also the studies of Antioch, as well documented by Liebeschuetz, *Antioch*, and by Glanville Downey, *A History of Antioch in Syria* (Princeton, 1961). See also T. Williams et al., "Archaeological Excavations in the Souks Area of Downtown Beirut 1994–1995. Interim Report," (1996) World Wide Web Internet publication: *http://www.aub.ac.lb/aub-online/faculties/ arts_and_sciences/ archaeology/ index.html.* See now Dominic Perring, "Excavations in the Souks of Beirut," *Berytus* 43 (1997–98): 9–34. The entire issue should be consulted for recent fuller publication of the finds of pottery, glass, and mosaics from Roman and Late Roman Berytus.
26. See Kevin E. T. Butcher, "The Coins from BEY 006; Preliminary Report," *BAAL (Bulletin d'Archeologie et d'Architecture Libanaise)* 1 (1996): 14–16. This pattern of coin finds correlates well with evidence collected in the chapters on imperial support for the church in Berytus and the monastic movement outside the city, as discussed in Hall, *Berytus*, 145–243, and for imperial support for rebuilding the city after the earthquake in 551 a.d., Hall, *Berytus*, 131–44. See now Kevin Butcher, "Coinage in Sixth Century Beirut: Preliminary Observations," *Berytus* 43 (1997–98): 173–80, for fuller presentation of the coin finds.
27. See K. W. Russell, "The Earthquake Chronology of Palestine and Northwest Arabia from the 2nd through the Mid-8th Century a.d.," *Bulletin of the American Schools of*

Oriental Research in Jerusalem and Baghdad 260 (1985): 37–58, for a recent study of earthquake chronologies in the region.

28. Agathias 2.15.1–4. *Agathias: The Histories*, translated by D. Frendo (Berlin and New York, 1975), 47–48.
29. See John Malalas, *The Chronicle*, translated by E. Jeffreys, M. Jeffreys, and R. Scott, (Melbourne, 1986), 291–92.
30. John Chrysostom, translated and discussed in Douglas A. O'Roark, "Urban Family Structure in Late Antiquity as Evidenced by John Chrysostom" (Ph.D. diss., The Ohio State University, Columbus, 1994), 90–91, translating *In epistulam I ad Corinthos argumentum et homilia 34* (*PG* 61.291).
31. W. Wright, *The Chronicle of Joshua the Stylite* (Cambridge, 1882), 22.
32. Robert A. Kaster, *C. Suetonius Tranquillus, De Grammaticis et Rhetoribus* (Oxford, 1995), 26–27.
33. Libanius, *Autobiography* 234, in Libanius, *Autobiography and Selected Letters*, translated by A. F. Norman, 2 vols. (London and Cambridge, Mass., 1992), 1:291.
34. Note the careers of these lawyers who studied or taught in Berytus: from *PLRE I*, Apringius, Anatolius 3, Celsinus 3, Fl. Domitius Leontius 20, Lupercus 1, Scylacius 2, Severinus 1, and Theodorus 11; from *PLRE II*, Zacharias 4, Severus 12, Patricius 10, Leontius 20, and Leontius 23; from *PLRE III*, Anatolius.
35. Libanius *Opera* (Foerster, ed.), 3:438–39, *Oratio* 48.22, *Libanii oratio ad Senatum Antiochen*. Also in Libanius' *Selected Works*, trans. A. F. Norman (London and Cambridge, Mass., 1969–77), 2:438–41.
36. Ramsay MacMullen, "Social Mobility and the Theodosian Code," *JRS* 54 (1964): 49–53.
37. John Chrysostom, *Adversus oppugn. vitae monasticae* III.5, in *PG* 47.357. See Carl R. Trahman, "The Latin Language and Literature in the Greek World" (Ph.D. diss., University of Cincinnati, 1942), 70.
38. Revelation 18:11–13 implies that the wealth of merchants was proverbial in the Roman Empire. Their cargoes included not only "fine linen, purple, silk, and scarlet cloth" but also "gold, silver, precious stones and pearls . . . every sort of citron wood, and articles of every kind, made of ivory, costly wood, bronze, iron, and marble; . . . cinnamon and spice . . . incense, myrrh and frankincense, of wine and olive oil, of fine flour and wheat, cattle and sheep, horses and carriages and bodies and souls of men [slaves?]." New International Version translation. A Late Antique patristic commentary on this passage might well reveal the perceived status and wealth of merchants in the Late Roman period.
39. See Ammianus Marcellinus, Procopius, and John Lydus for the evidence, discussed in Hall, *Berytus*, 244–61.

Urban Space in Caesarea Maritima, Israel

JOSEPH PATRICH

CAESAREA MARITIMA WAS FOUNDED BY HEROD, KING OF JUDAEA, IN 22-10/9 B.C.E. on the site of a deserted Hellenistic coastal town called Straton's Tower. According to Josephus (*War* 1.408-15; *Antiquities* 15.331-41), Herod founded there an elaborate harbor called Sebastos, and a city with streets laid in a grid pattern. The city, like the harbor, was named after emperor Caesar Augustus, Herod's patron in Rome. In the city Herod erected a temple, which he dedicated to Rome and Augustus, a theater and an amphitheater, a royal palace, market places, dwellings, and an underground sewer system.

Caesarea served as the main harbor and capital city of Herod's kingdom, and of the later Roman province of *Judaea/Syria Palaestina*, the seat of the Roman governors and of the financial procurators of the province. Vespasian made Caesarea a Roman colony, and Alexander Severus raised it to the rank of metropolis. In the Byzantine period[1] it was the capital of *Palaestina Prima*, and a Metropolitan See. During this period urban space expanded about three times relative to the Herodian period, reflecting a large increase in population. It was a prosperous maritime city, of a heterogeneous ethnicity and a cosmopolitan flavor, as is reflected by the archaeological record: the city coins, statuary, and inscriptions, attesting to its pantheon, and the imported ware and numismatic finds, attesting to its international commerce. During the third and fourth centuries it was the seat of a Jewish academy, led by Rabbi Oshayah and Rabbi Abbahu, and of a Christian academy, founded by Origen. The Christian community suffered martyrdom in the persecutions under Decius, Valerian, and Diocletian. The Samaritans were another vital component in the Caesarean society, representing the lucrative peasantry of the fertile agricultural hinterland of the city—the Sharon plain and the hilly country of Samaria.

The division of the province of *Syria Palaestina* into smaller provinces during the fourth or early fifth centuries (*T.A.Q.* 409 C.E.), and the emergence of Scythopolis as a capital of Palaestina Secunda, resulted in a decrease in the administrative status of the city within the Empire, and in the economic prosperity associated with it. Similarly, in the mid-fifth century the ecclesiastical status of the city decreased, when the Metropolitan of Caesarea became subordinate to the Patriarch of Jerusalem. The demise of the harbor, and three Samaritan revolts in the years 484, 529-30, and 555, were other causes of gradual deterioration, yet it was a thriving city throughout late antiquity.

The Arab conquest in 640 or 641 brought a sharp decline of urban life, a process that had already begun following the Persian conquest of 614. Islamic and Crusader Qaisariye was a small town of marginal importance, located around its decaying harbor.[2]

LATE ANTIQUE/BYZANTINE CAESAREA[3]

The excavations, since the 1950s to the present, have shed light mainly on the Harbor, the Temple Platform, and SW Zone. But good information, though segmented, has accumulated in other sectors as well. In most of the excavated areas the Late Antique/Byzantine stratum was exposed in its entirety. Our information on this period in the history of the city is, therefore, far better than for any of the earlier periods.

The local *kurkar* stone continued to be the major building material, although public *kurkar* structures of the Herodian age were gradually replaced in the Roman period by marble structures. This is evident in the *skenefrons* of the theater, as well as in the main temple. Marble was applied for column shafts, capitals and bases, entablature, statuary, pavement and wall revetment. Isotope analysis of Corinthian marble capitals has indicated that major locations of marble import were Proconnesos and Afyon/Aphrodisias.[4] Marble, reused as well as imported, continued to be applied in Late Antiquity, as is evident in the octagonal church, but in some cases marble floor-plates were replaced by mosaic floors, and in some rare cases marble columns were whitewashed. The intensive burning under the Islamic regime of marble architectural members in lime kilns in order to produce slake lime, encountered in Caesarea as in so many ancient Roman cities, has masked the extent to which the Roman and Late Antique city was clad in marble. *Opus sectile* floors of a rich pallet of colorful stones and of intricate patterns—mostly geometric and floral, but depicting dolphins and crosses as well—became popular in the sixth century, but mosaic floors were prevalent in the private as well as in the public domain.[5] Frescoes depicting Christian saints and crosses were applied even in structures of mundane function.[6]

The Herodian, orthogonal city-plan was maintained throughout antiquity with only minor modifications, expressed in narrowing the Roman streets, elevating the street level in accordance with the raised sills of the adjoining buildings, and replacing thick lime-stone pavers by thinner pavers of the local *kurkar*. The latest re-pavement of *cardo* W1 took place in the mid–sixth century, and on the same occasion a comprehensive renovation of the sewer system and a replacement of lead water pipes by terracotta pipes were carried out.[7] Roman trabeated colonnades gave way to arcades supported by square pilasters.

The Late Antique/Byzantine city extended beyond the Herodian wall, reflecting a great increase of population, but it seems that the settlement of this zone had started already in the second and third centuries, following the construction of the eastern hippodrome and the amphitheater. But since no excavations were carried out in this zone, other than those of the hippodrome, we have no information about the exact process of habitation of this zone during the second to the fourth century. However, the addition of the lower level aqueduct in ca. 385 C.E. may indicate that a significant increase of population was reached already before the end of the fourth century, and it seems that the settlement of this zone was dense enough by the time the wall was erected in the fifth century to dictate its line. This wall suffered during the three Samaritan revolts mentioned above and the Arab siege that lasted seven years (633/34-640/41 C.E.). In the latter, some of the urban statuary was piled up in the southern city gate to block it against the penetration of the Arab troops.[8] And indeed, monumental Roman statuary was reused in the urban sphere of the Byzantine city to decorate its streets, plazas, and nymphaea.[9]

The estimated population at its apogee, when it occupied an area of ca. 111.5 ha, varies between ca. 35,000 and 100,000.[10] As for ethnicity, as everywhere throughout the east after the crisis of the third century and the reforms of Diocletian and Constantine, the Latinate element in the provincial and municipal administration gave way to Greek speaking *officiales*. The Late Antique inscriptions are all in Greek or in the local Semitic scripts and languages (Aramaic, Hebrew and Samaritan[11]). The Greek that returned as the language of administration in the entire east was spoken by all three religious groups: Christians, Jews, and Samaritans.

The Jewish quarter is considered to be in the northern part of the city, at the site of ancient Straton Tower, around the third-century synagogue. The synagogue, which yielded Jewish inscriptions in Hebrew and Greek, and Corinthian capitals with the *menorah* symbol, was destroyed by fire in the mid–fourth century and rebuilt in the mid–fifth. After the death of R. Abbahu, the head of the local Jewish academy, in 309, there was no Jewish leader of his magnitude. Beryllos, archisynagogue and *phrontistes* (treasurer or administrator), who made a mosaic floor from his own funds, is mentioned in a Greek inscription from the synagogue.[12] The predominance of Greek inscriptions, as well as references in the Rabbinic sources, attest to the high degree of Hellenization and acculturation of the local community, as in other urban Jewish congregations in Palestine and in the Jewish diaspora.[13] Despite the fact that in the literary sources there is almost no reference to the Jews of Caesarea in the Byzantine period, the Jewish community continued to form a significant component of the local population, though its status declined relative to that of the third and early fourth century.[14] The general Jewish revolt against Gallus in 351-52 might have been a decisive factor in this decline. The Jews of Caesarea joined ranks with the Samaritans in the revolt of 555, burning Christian churches and slaughtering the provincial governor in his *praetorium;* one of them assisted the Arab troops in sneaking into the besieged city through a secret water tunnel in 640/41.[15]

As for the Samaritans, a large quantity of "Samaritan" oil lamps retrieved from the excavated area in the SW zone provide evidence of their presence and activity in this part of the city. According to a Rabbinic source, the staff (*taxis*) of the Byzantine governor of the province in the city (as opposed to that of the *dux*) was composed mainly of Samaritans. There were also separate Samaritan troops in the Roman army.[16] Their involvement in the provincial administration might be alluded to by two Greek mosaic inscriptions found in Area NN in the SW zone. One, of the fifth century, reads: "May the one and only God (*heis theos monos*), help Eusebius the accountant (*noumerarios*)." On the one hand, there is no cross at the beginning of the inscription, as was common in Christian epigraphy, and on the other hand, the opening formula was very common among the Samaritans.[17] The second inscription, of the sixth century, reads: "May the peace of the Christians persist,"[18] a declaration that suggests that its author was a non-Christian, perhaps a Samaritan, or a nominal Christian.[19] In this case the inscription may be conceived as a declaration of loyalty related perhaps to one of the Samaritan revolts of the sixth century. A notable Samaritan of Palestine who accepted nominal Christianity was Faustinus, of an old Samaritan family. Under Justinian he assumed the senatorial rank of *clarissimus* and became governor (*consularis*) of his province. Later, he became *epitropos* of the imperial domains in Palestine and Phoenicia.[20] Inscriptions from Scythopolis and literary sources provide some interesting details about another prominent Samaritan family of that city. Silvanus and his brother Sallustius, both lawyers (*scholastici*), acted as patrons of the city and obtained grants from emperor Anastasius for the erection of public buildings in Scythopolis (year 515/16). Silvanus had a consular rank and maintained close connections with the emperor. His son, Arsenius, accepted the Christian faith, and had a successful career at the imperial court of Justinian and Theodora, yet he maintained close relations with his family in Scythopolis. He had procured an imperial donation for rebuilding the walls of Scythopolis.[21] Similar Samaritan families, involved in municipal and provincial affairs, might have existed also in Caesarea. The basilical structure to the south of the deserted Herodian hippodrome might have been a Samaritan synagogue, rather than a Christian church.

The Christians constituted the majority of the population. Their major church in the sixth century was the octagonal church on the site of the former Roman temple—the most prominent position in Caesarea landscape, overlooking the entire city and the harbor. The bishop, assisted by the clergy, was most influential in municipal affairs, second only to the governor. Being renowned since the days of Origen in the third century and Eusebius in the fourth as a center of learning and Christian theology, Caesarea preserved its prestige down to the sixth century as a school of theology, rhetoric, and law.[22] Procopius of Caesarea, the famous historian at the courts of Belisarius and Justinian, was its most renowned author (although his writing was done remote from his city of origin). Another prominent author was John the Grammarian, an important Neochalcedonian theologian in the late fifth and early sixth century, against whom the Monophysite leader Severus of Antioch composed in 520 a polemical treatise.[23] An echo of the Christological controversy of the sixth century can be heard in a Greek mosaic inscription found at the site of the inner harbor (Area I1), reading: "May the Lord sustain the Orthodoxy forever."[24]

THE ARCHAEOLOGICAL RESEARCH[25]

Archaeological excavations started in the early 1950s, and included many expeditions, both Israeli and foreign, working in many locations: Yeivin, Avi Yonah and Negev,[26] and the Italian Mission headed by Frova excavated there during the 1950s and early 1960s.[27] The Joint Expedition to Caesarea Maritima (JECM)—a consortium of American colleges and universities, headed by Bull,[28] that worked at the site in the 1970s and early 1980s—has been followed since the late 1980s to the present by the Combined Caesarea

Excavations (CCE) headed by Holum, in cooperation with Raban from the University of Haifa.[29] The Hebrew University excavations in the 1970s, headed by Netzer and Levine,[30] were followed by the University of Pennsylvania excavations, led by Borrell and Gleason.[31] The large scale excavations in the SW zone of the city during the last seven years (1992-98), undertaken within the framework of the Caesarea Tourist Development Project—the Israel Antiquities Authority (IAA), directed by Porath, and the University of Haifa, directed by Raban and myself—have augmented tremendously the previous archaeological record.[32] This SW zone, ca. 80 m wide and 800 m long, extending along the sea from the Harbor and the Temple Platform in the North to the Roman theater in the South (inclusively), is today almost entirely exposed to its Byzantine and Roman layers. Our information about the northern and eastern sectors of the city is segmented and fragmentary, yet informative and significant.

Underwater work, started in 1960 under Link,[33] was followed in the 1980s by the Caesarea Ancient Harbors Excavation Project (CAHEP),[34] moderated by Raban of the Center for Maritime Studies of the University of Haifa, and since the late 1980s by the underwater team of the CCE.[35] This research supplied a wealth of information on the construction of the harbor, its later history and its gradual demise.

The *Harbor* was a huge enterprise, compared by Josephus (*War* 1.410; *Antiquities* 15.332) to Piraeus, with many quays, landing places, and secondary anchorages. It was constructed of huge stones, including *pozzolana*—volcanic ashes imported from Italy, used by Romans for making hydraulic cement applied in harbor architecture, and other advanced Roman harbor technology.[36] The outer mole and breakwater, on the S and W, penetrated ca. 400 m into the sea, enclosing the outer and intermediate basins; the inner basin was rock cut in land incorporating the closed harbor (*limen kleistos*) of the Hellenistic Straton's Tower. Work of recent years indicated that the inner harbor extended over a much vaster area than previously assumed. Its E pier extended to the S beyond the Crusaders' wall, and it encompassed an area 250 m long (NS) by 150 m broad (EW). The entrance to the outer harbor, flanked by three colossal statues on either side, was from N, at the W end of the N mole. Several inscribed lead ingots found in 1993 over the NW end of the mole[37] suggest that this section of the pier was submerged already at the end of the first century C.E. due to tectonic slumping, causing a rapid silting of parts of the inner harbor, which became a lagoon.[38] The intermediate and outer harbors underwent a large-scale reconstruction by Anastasius in the late fifth–early sixth century.[39] By that time the inner harbor was already silted, giving new ground for the construction of new buildings, and later, under Arab dominion, of a new neighborhood of dwellings.

Although no lighthouse is mentioned in Josephus' narrative, we may assume its existence. However, its exact location is a matter of dispute.[40]

Walls and Gates: Two semi-circular city walls are still recognizable in aerial photographs, beyond the rectilinear shorter line of the Arab-Crusader wall. The inner line is Herodian and the outer Byzantine. The Herodian wall had an N gate flanked by two circular towers. A third, rectilinear tower was exposed nearby.[41] At the S part of the Herodian city wall, to the S of the Roman Theater, another circular tower was exposed in the recent years' excavations, attached to the external face of the wall. Later during the Roman period the round tower was encompassed in a rectilinear encasement. The fortification line was abandoned in mid–fourth century.

Like other Roman cities, such as Jerusalem, Gerasa, Scythopolis, and Neapolis, the Roman and Early Byzantine city that extended beyond the Herodian wall had no outer wall for more than three centuries. These extramural quarters comprised also an amphitheater and a hippodrome. So far there are not enough data to reconstruct in detail the history of this extramural settlement. It is also not clear to what extent the Herodian wall retained its defensive features during this period. But while Roman Jerusalem and Gerasa were encircled by walls in ca. 300 C.E., Caesarea got its wall more than a century later, only in the fifth century. The southern quarter of Jerusalem likewise got a wall under Eudocia in the first half of the fifth century. The date of construction of the wall of Scythopolis is as yet unknown; what is known is that it was renovated in the first quarter of the sixth century.[42]

Segments of the Byzantine wall of Caesarea, in the N, E, and S, have been exposed and explored by four different expeditions.[43] It encompassed an area of 111.5 ha (1500 × 830 m maximal dimensions), two to three times larger than before. The road system emerging from the city[44] suggests the

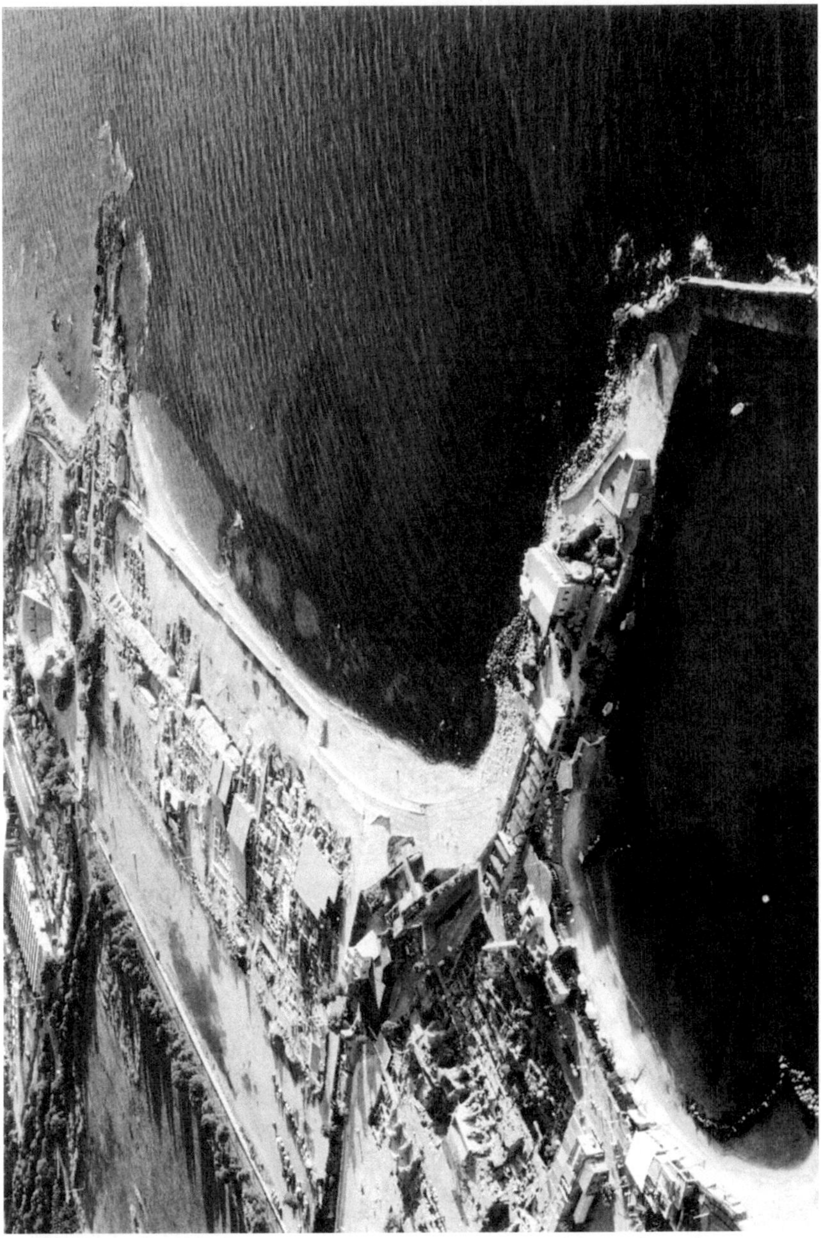

Two semi-circular city walls are still recognizable in aerial photographs, beyond the rectilinear shorter line of the Arab-Crusader wall. The inner line is Herodian and the outer Byzantine.

existence of four gates. The north Byzantine gate was eroded by the sea, the southern was a triple entrance monumental gate.[45] A Greek inscription mentioning a *bourgos* was uncovered near the conjectural location of the E gate.[46] A Roman monumental arch with a Greek inscription referring to the city as metropolis, a rank granted to the city by Alexander Severus, was located nearby;[47] as in the case of Gerasa, Jerusalem, Scythopolis, and Gadara (and Athens), the outskirts of the city were indicated by a monumental arch long before a city wall was actually constructed.

In the sixth century an inner fortress or citadel (*kastron*) with semicircular towers was constructed around the theater that went out of use during the fourth century.[48] Byzantine cities from the sixth century onward were usually equipped with citadels. Zenobia with its *Praetorium*, on the Euphrates, fortified by Justinian, is a nice example.[49]

The Street System and Urban Plan: Archaeology has confirmed Josephus' account (*Antiquities* 15.340; *War* 1.408, 413) that Herod laid a magnificent city plan, with equal distance between its streets, and a sophisticated sewage system underneath. The JECM as well as the recent excavations in the SW zone uncovered at least three successive street levels, adhering to the same urban plan.[50] In this regard Caesarea is the exception in the cities built by Herod. Jerusalem and Samaria followed an entirely different city plan, with a main thoroughfare leading from the city gate to the main temple. So far there are not enough data to indicate whether the extra-mural quarters, developed in the Roman and Byzantine periods beyond the Herodian city wall, followed throughout the same grid pattern recognized within the inner perimeter wall.[51]

Cardo W1, exposed in the SW zone for a length of ca. 400 m, was not a colonnaded street. Its width–ca. 5 m, was slightly reduced during the centuries of its existence due to retaining the walls of the buildings along its course. The line of the *cardo maximus* is marked by the line of the eastern crusader wall. Several columns are still preserved on the inside of the northern section of this wall, suggesting that it was a colonnaded street. As for the *decumanus maximus,* its western end was exposed in the recent excavations by the IAA team at the north-eastern corner of the Temple Platform, its line being parallel to *decumani* S2 and S3 (see map). Its course eastward is suggested by the remains of a *tetrapylon* in the eastern gate of the Crusader

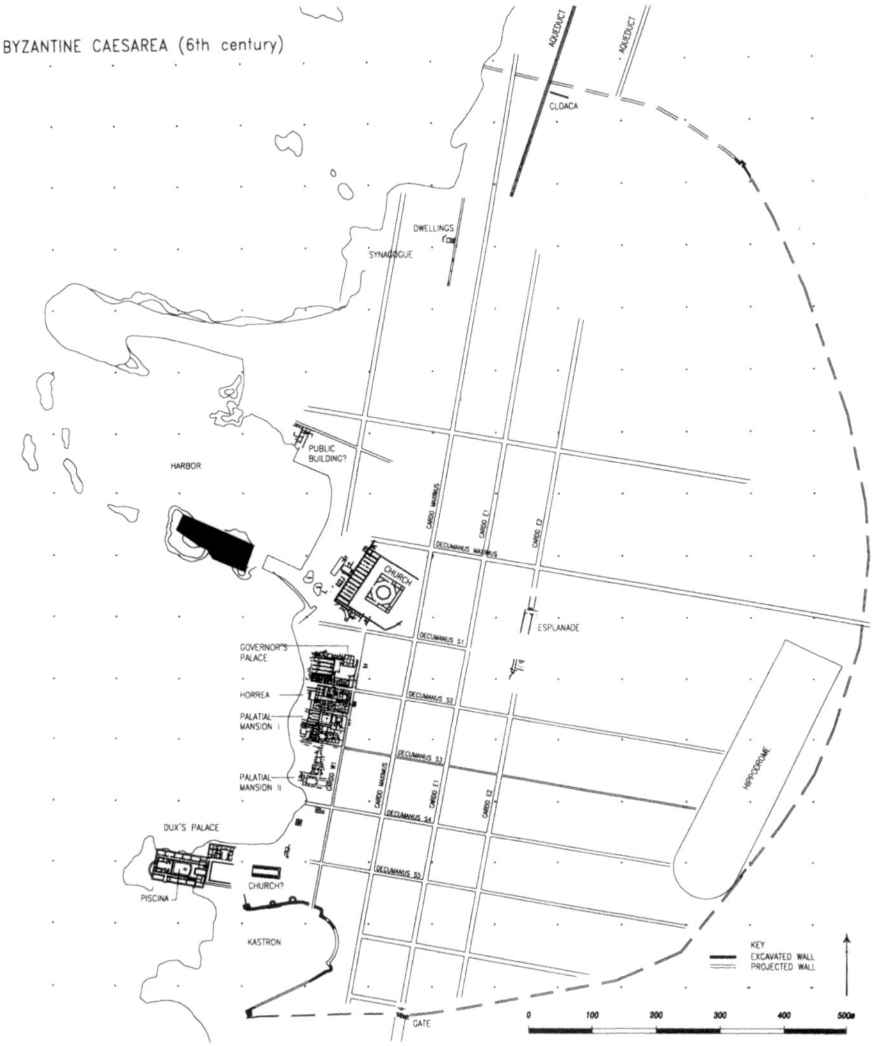

Byzantine Caesarea (sixth century). Drawn by Anna Iamim, based on the Caesarea Graphics Archive.

wall. So far, no remains indicate that it was a colonnaded street. But colonnaded streets (*platea* and *stoa*) in Caesarea are mentioned in Rabbinic and Christian sources (*Jerusalem Talmud, Nazir* VII, 1, 56a; *Tosefta Oholot* XVIII, 13; Eusebius, *Mart. Pal.* 9.12).

The N-S street exposed by the JECM in the NW zone of the city indicates that the size of the urban *insulae* in this zone, a neighborhood of dwellings (see plan), was different in size than in the SW zone. In Gerasa as well, the dimensions of the residential *insulae* in the eastern part of the city were different from those of the *insulae* in the western part of the city, comprising mainly public structures.

RELIGIOUS BUILDINGS

Temples: Of the many temples suggested by the deities depicted on the city coins (Tyche, Isis, Sertapis, Demeter, Apollo),[52] and inscriptions (Jupiter Dolichenus),[53] only three temples are attested by architectural remains. As for the evidence of the statuary of deities (Tyche, Isis and Serapis, Apollo, Aphrodite, Athena, Asklepius and Hygieia, the Ephesian Artemis, Cybele or Nemesis, and the Dioscuri),[54] one should not interpret each statue as an indication of the existence of a temple for that particular deity. Statues were commonly used for decoration alone, though expressing religious piety.

On top of the temple platform, dominating both city and harbor, the foundations and scattered architectural members of Herod's temple to Roma and Augustus (*War* 1.415; *Antiquities* 15.339) were found.[55] The podium, 28.6 × 46.4 m in dimensions, was constructed on top of a U-shaped elevated platform, leaving an open esplanade below, to the W, in a lower terrace along the E mole of the inner harbor.[56] In ca. 300, twelve vaults were erected on the esplanade, between the arms of the elevated platform, whose roof established an additional square in front of the Roman temple. Certain modifications in the façade of the temple might have occurred on this occasion.

The Imperial cult is also attested by two inscriptions, one in Latin, mentioning a *Tiberieum*,[57] and the second in Greek, a *Hadrianeion*. The porphyry statue of Hadrian, found reused, decorating a Byzantine esplanade, originated perhaps from his temple.[58] A marble head of Hadrian, of almost life size, was found during the recent excavations in a late seventh-century layer of debris. Its original location is unknown.

In the SW zone a Mithraeum was installed in the second or third century in one of the vaults underneath the audience hall of the *praetorium* of the Roman financial procurator.[59] A *naos* (presumably of this *praetorium*) is mentioned in a Greek papyrus from Egypt.[60] The shrine (*sacellum*) of the western hippodrome (Herod's *amphitheatron*) was, seemingly, dedicated to Kore, since a dedicatory inscription to her on a marble foot—one of seven—was found therein. Snakes—a common attribute of Isis—entwining four of the ex-voto feet suggest an assimilation between Kore and Isis. Kore was the principal deity of the adjacent city of Samaria in Roman times. A Greek inscription found in the stadium there reads: "One god, the ruler of all, great Kore, the invincible." In Samaria Kore was also assimilated with Isis.[61]

Of the various *synagogues* that existed in Caesarea, only one has been exposed in the N part of the city,[62] the site of Straton's tower. Another Jewish synagogue was converted by Vespasian into an odeum (Malalas, *Chronographia*, X, 338, ed. Niebuhr, Bonn 1831, p. 261). A Jewish house of learning (*bêt midrasâ*) open to the agora of Caesarea is mentioned in the Babylonian Talmud, *Hulin* 86d.

Several *Christian Buildings* associated with New Testament events and with the persecutions of martyrs are mentioned in the Byzantine *itineraria:* the houses of Philip (*Acts* 8:40; 21:8) and of Cornelius (*Acts* 10:1-48), the chamber of the four virgin prophetesses (Philip's daughters), the burial place of Pamphilius and Procopius, and the latter's chapel.[63] More chapels and churches are known from literary sources. In the Acts and Miracles of Saint Anastasius (Martyred 627 C.E.) are mentioned the following churches: St. Euphemia, St. Mary the Younger (perhaps not distinct from the unspecified St. Mary), a chapel of Saint Anastasius the Persian, the "most holy church of Christ," and a building associated with the martyr Cornelius.[64] The church of St. Procopius was set on fire in the Samaritan revolt of year 484.

Of these only two churches (one being dubious) have so far been exposed. In ca. 525-50 C.E., an octagonal church, decorated and revetted in marble, replaced Herod's temple to Rome and Augustus. Access from the W was by means of a monumental staircase raised over a broad arch.[65] The W end of this staircase was founded on a platform of huge stones laid inside the partially silted inner harbor, adjoining the edge of the Herodian mole.[66] The E end of the staircase was leaning against the vaults. A second, simple staircase gave access from the south.[67]

The process of Christianization of urban space at Caesarea was slower than has been assumed.[68] The temple, although ruinous, was replaced by a Christian monument many decades after such a process occurred in Jerusalem (under Constantine) or in Gaza (under Theodosius I and Eudoxia).[69]

A second structure identified as a church was exposed during the recent excavation to the south of the deserted Herodian hippodrome, overlying the NE part of the Roman *praetorium*. It is a basilica, 32 × 17.5 m in dimensions, with a 16 m long atrium to its west and a small cistern in its center.[70] It seems that the *sacellum* of the western hippodrome (Herod's *amphitheatron*) was converted in the fourth century to a martyrs chapel.

Palaces and Praetoria: Herod's palace, constructed on a promontory to the south of the harbor, was enlarged and elaborated, becoming the *praetorium* of the Roman governors.[71] Late in the first century, a second *praetorium* was constructed in the first urban insula to the south of the harbor, for the use of the financial procurators of the province. This palace became later the residence and *officium* of the Byzantine governor.[72] Both *praetoria* had vast courtyards, gardens, and elaborate bathhouses. Two other palatial mansions were constructed in Late Antiquity in the SW zone, between the two *praetoria* mentioned above. The northern one, exposed in its entirety, has an elaborate bathhouse in a good state of preservation.[73] It was constructed in the fourth century over a first-century Roman "villa" that extended over a vaster area. The second, constructed in the sixth century, had a two-story peristyle courtyard with a tri-conch triclinium. In a lower terrace, on the west, a garden and a fountain were installed, leading to a private beach.[74] A unique *opus sectile* workshop with magnificent designs was uncovered in one of the side rooms of this Byzantine palace. Urban dwelling quarters of palatial mansions are known in many Late Antique cities—Apamea in Syria, Ephesus and Aphrodisias in Asia Minor, Paphos in Cyprus, Volubilis in Morocco and elsewhere.[75]

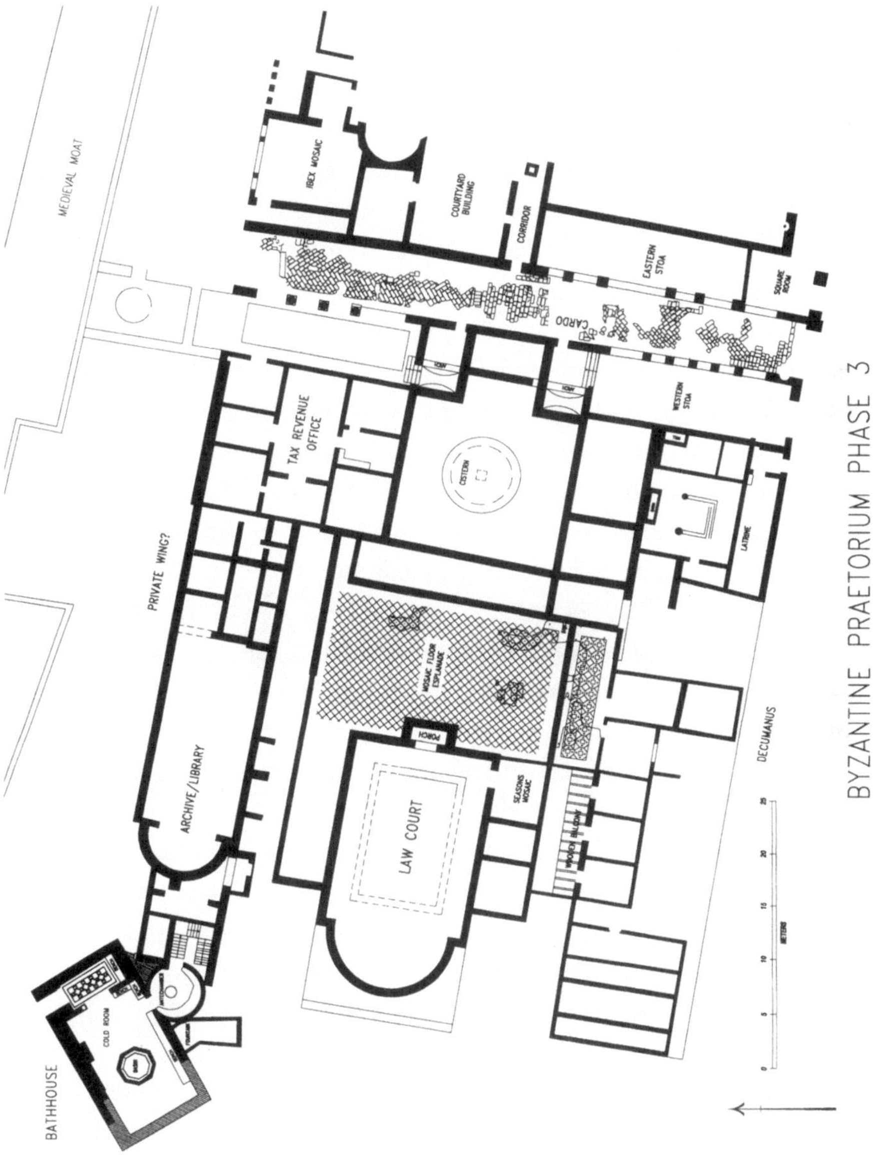
BYZANTINE PRAETORIUM PHASE 3
MEDIEVAL MOAT
IBEX MOSAIC
COURTYARD BUILDING
CORRIDOR
EASTERN STOA
SQUARE ROOM
CARDO
WESTERN STOA
TAX REVENUE OFFICE
CISTERN
LATRINE
PRIVATE WING?
MOSAIC FLOOR ESPLANADE
PORCH
ARCHIVE/LIBRARY
LAW COURT
SEASONS MOSAIC
DECUMANUS
COLD ROOM
BATHHOUSE
METERS

Dwellings of a more regular type, yet quite spacious, were uncovered in several locations in Caesarea, mainly in the NW zone.[76]

Sports Arenas: Herod's theater is located at the southern end of the city. Comprising two blocks of seats, it accommodated ca. 4,000 spectators.[77] Herod's *amphitheatron* (*Antiquities* 15.341; *War* 1.415),[78] uncovered in the recent excavation along the sea between the palace and the harbor, turned out to be a hippodrome.[79] The estimated number of spectators is 13,000. The arrangement of the starting gates, five on either side of a central wide gate, and their layout parallel to each other rather than radial indicate that the races established by Herod followed the Olympian tradition of chariot racing, rather than that of the Roman circus, with its four factions. Later transformations in the arrangement of the starting gates with a radial layout, and the introduction of a *spina,* reflect a process of Romanization.[80] Chronologically, this architectural and cultural transformation is contemporary with the re-foundation of Caesarea as a Roman colony by Vespasian. The Latin factor associated with the Roman army and administration became dominant from that time until the Diocletianic reforms in the late third and early fourth century, as is reflected by the language of the local inscriptions.[81] At the final phase of the hippodrome, perhaps in the early- or mid-third century, the arena was truncated and the hippodrome was converted to an amphitheater; it was deserted later in that century due to erosion by the sea waves. Similar conversion of a hippodrome to an oval amphitheater was encountered in Gerasa, Neapolis, and Scythopolis. But while the converted amphitheaters at Scythopolis and Neapolis were monumental in their truncated end, that at Gerasa has a thin wall; at Caesarea there are four distinct lines of thin walls, just one stone thick, suggesting a casual or temporary construction, perhaps on occasion of special events.[82]

A "canonical," oval, Roman amphitheater (recognized only by aerial photographs),[83] and a second hippodrome were installed in the NE and SE zones respectively, presumably in the early second century. The eastern hippodrome, with obelisques and *metae* decorating its *spina,* continued to function during the Byzantine period until it went out of use and was systematically demolished well before the end of that era, perhaps early in the sixth century.[84]

According to Malalas (*Chronographia*, X, 338, ed. Niebuhr, Bonn 1831, p. 261), Vespasian converted a Jewish synagogue into an *odeum*. Its location is so far unknown.

Other monuments and buildings are mentioned in the literary sources, both Greco-Roman and Rabbinic,[85] and in the inscriptions: a *tetrapylon*,[86] remains of which are still recognized inside the East Gate of the Crusaders wall, porticos (one of which, *the portico of Iunia Ba( )ae*, was used for displaying petitions and statutes concerning the Roman soldiers serving in the province),[87] stoas and colonnaded streets (*platea*), a dome-like structure overlaying a public thoroughfare, and market places.[88] A sigma-shaped market building of Roman and Byzantine date was exposed in recent excavations on the S side of the temple platform.[89]

Warehouses and Horrea: As a maritime city and provincial capital, the city was provided with plenty of warehouses and *horrea* for both import-export trade, and for stocking foodstuffs in adequate quantities to prevent inflation of prices. Warehouses of several types were uncovered in the SW zone and around the harbor, mostly dated to the late Roman and early Byzantine periods: long vaulted *horrea* and warehouses of the "courtyard" and "corridor" types.[90] Particular features of these warehouses are vast halls with crude mosaic floors that held large *dolia* for the storage of oil (*dolium olearium*), and under ground granaries with thick walls revetted by well-drafted blocks imbedded in a thick layer of oily lime mortar. Granaries of similar structure were found in Shuni—a site of an Askelapeion and water celebration near Caesarea—and in Apollonia, the adjacent city to Caesarea on the south. Warehouses with *dolia* were uncovered in Iamnia, another maritime city of *Palaestina*, and in Sepphoris.

THE WATER SUPPLY SYSTEM[91]

The Roman city got its water supply from the north by means of two aqueducts. The high level aqueduct reached the city as a double arcade supporting two channels. The western, later one is dated by inscriptions to the reign of Hadrian. The earlier channel is attributed, alternatively, to Herod, the

Roman procurators, or Vespasian. The lower level aqueduct is a masonry tunnel, ca. 1.20 m wide and 2.00 m high, that got its water from an artificial lake constructed in the late fourth century (ca. 385 C.E.).[92] A Byzantine terra cotta pipeline reached the city from the north.[93] A network of lead and terra cotta pipes running under the paved streets led the water to various public amenities: fountains, *nymphaea*, bathhouses, latrines, and gardens. The palaces and rich mansions benefited from this net of pipes, enjoying a private water supply. In the late Byzantine period the water system deteriorated, and wells replaced the pipelines in some parts of the city. Stephanus, the governor of *Palaestina Prima* in the early 630s is praised in his encomium, written by Choricius of Gaza in 534/36, for improving the water supply system of Caesarea by maintenance work, clearing the high-level aqueduct's channels of obstructions. [94]

Bathhouses, Nymphaea and Latrines: All the bathhouses uncovered so far in Caesarea are associated with the palaces and villas mentioned above. A possible exception is a small bathhouse, in an impressive state of preservation, exposed in the recent excavations (1997-98) below the temple platform, to the east. This one might have been an urban *balaneum*, unless it formed a part of another palace, perhaps that of the metropolites, that might have existed adjacent to the octagonal church. But until the excavated area has been extended, this suggestion is a mere speculation. None of the Caesarean bathhouses uncovered so far was a huge *therma* of the Roman imperial type, like those known at Scythopolis, Eleutheropolis, Gerasa, Gadara, or Bostra.[95] Yet, according to Malalas (*Chronographia*, XI, 367, ed. Niebuhr, Bonn 1831, p. 281), Antoninus Pius erected a public bath at Caesarea. The 'baths of Cornelius' are mentioned in the fourth century *Itinerarium Burdigalense* (CCSL 175, p. 13).

Nymphaea, fountains[96] and latrines,[97] both public and private, were abundant throughout the city. A network of lead and terra-cotta pipes conducted water to street and private fountains and to the latrines. An elaborate *nymphaeum*, with three niches holding statues, adorned the NW projections of the temple platform;[98] yet, it is not as elaborate as the *nymphaea* of Philadelphia, Gerasa, or Bostra.[99] Smaller fountains were located at street corners and in the private domain fountains and reflecting pools that were incorporated in the gardens and courtyards. Being located on the seashore, Caesarea also enjoyed the pleasant and refreshing panorama of the sea.

The *necropolis* extended on all three sides around the city wall, but mainly to the east, as is attested by burial caves, burial inscriptions and sarcophagi.[100] A first/second-century Roman cemetery with cremation burials was uncovered in the recent IAA excavations to the south of the theater, adjacent to the Herodian city wall, on the outside. This alien burial practice should be attributed to the Latinate element in the population, associated with the governor's *praetorium*, located nearby.

The *extra-mural* territory was densely settled and cultivated. Dwellings and Suburban Villas with mosaic floors were encountered in several locations,[101] and Roman and Byzantine farmsteads have been found farther away in the agricultural countryside.[102]

The southern part of the SW zone was occupied in the sixth century by the citadel (*kastron*) erected around the theater; it was a military zone. [103] The adjacent, former *Praetorium* of the Roman governor on the site of Herod's Palace was partially dismantled during the construction of the *kastron.* In its reduced size it might have served the *Dux* while in the city. In the northern part of this zone extended the *praetorium* of the Byzantine governor, the public part of which comprised a revenue office flanked by waiting rooms with benches, an audience hall that served as a law court, offices for the clerks, and an archive or library. [104] The *officiales* mentioned in the inscriptions from the *praetorium* of Caesarea included *ypoboethoi, chartularioi, noumerarioi,* a *magister* or *magistrianos,* and various staff of the law court. [105] Another Late Antique *praetorium* with a law court was found in Gortyn (Crete), the capital of Roman province of Crete and Cyrene. Inscriptions of the fourth and fifth century specify that they originally stood beside, or before, the doors of Justice. [106]

The rest of the SW zone was occupied by two or three palatial mansions of the local landowners (*ktetores*), each having its own complex of warehouses. In Late Antique Apamea, we encounter along its *cardo maximus* the same phenomenon of a neighborhood of palatial mansions, one of which—the house called "*au triclinos*"—is supposed to be the palace of the governor of Syria II.[107] Neither in Apamea, nor in Caesarea, was the governor's palace the most elaborate residence. The provincial governors who resided in the *praetorium* were replaced quite frequently, after a relatively short period of office, while the other mansions served as the permanent residences of the aristocracy of the city. The more simple dwellings, in the NW zone, were quite spacious as well, reflecting the wealth of the population. In one of them, comprising a peristyle courtyard, and three shops in the street front, an under-floor hoard of ninety-nine gold coins, dated to the second half of the fourth century, was found.[108]

The wealth of the city and its functions as a commercial center are also reflected in its warehouses. The imported ware, both amphorae and tableware, reflect commercial contacts with large parts of the Mediterranean basin: North Africa, Egypt, Cyprus, Asia Minor and the Aegean.[109] The harbor, undergoing a gradual demise, was renovated by emperor Anastasius, but its inner basin was already silted by sand, and it never re-assumed the grandeur of the Herodian and early imperial times.[110]

The eastern hippodrome was the sole sports arena that survived into Late Antiquity. Chariot races and circus factions were popular in Caesarea, as they were in other cities of the eastern Mediterranean.[111] The "*hyppotrophoi* inscription" found not far from the eastern hippodrome, specifies sums of money expended from various municipal taxes and levies to pay for the maintenance of the stables and the races.[112] In the Samaritan revolt of 484, Justasas, their leader, presided over victory celebration games in this circus.[113] As in many cities of the East, other spectacles lost their popularity.[114] The theater went out of use by the fourth century, and in the sixth century its site was surrounded by a *kastron*. The amphitheater, not yet excavated, might have gone out of use much earlier. The hippodrome went out of use and was systematically demolished in the first half of the sixth century. So far no public *thermae* have been uncovered, but bathing in the private sphere, in the palatial mansions mentioned above, was a popular entertainment among the local elite.

CONCLUSION

It seems that the city reached its apogee at the end of the fourth century, after serving for more than four centuries as the capital of a large province. As was mentioned above, the division of the Roman province of *Judaea Palaestina* into two, and later three smaller provinces in the mid–fourth to early fifth centuries, decreased its administrative and ecclesiastical status. A further decrease in the ecclesiastical status was caused by the proclamation of Jerusalem as the fifth Patriarchate of the Christian world, recognizing the superiority of its *episcopos* over the *metropolites* of Caesarea. The anti-Jewish and anti-Samaritan imperial legislation affected the security and prosperity of these important ethnic groups in the local society. All parties suffered due to the Samaritan revolts. Especially severe were the damages and casualties caused in the 529/30 revolt that inflicted a severe blow on the Samaritan peasantry and on the agricultural estates. All these were causes of a gradual process of decline in urban life and economy. [115] Some improvement was realized by the partial restoration of the harbor by emperor Anastasius, and the erection of the octagonal church, perhaps under this emperor as well.

The demise of Caesarea following its capture by the Muslim troops, after a prolonged siege, was quite abrupt. Deserted by its elite during the siege, it underwent a rapid transformation, although there is no evidence for a large-scale hostile destruction. The Islamic town occupied only a small area, centered in the immediate vicinity of the harbor, reflecting a severe decrease of population. The buildings of the Roman and Byzantine city were stripped of their masonry, marble elements were burned for lime. The SW zone, the administrative and aristocratic center, underwent a process of ruralization by being converted, already in the second half of the seventh century, to terraced gardens fed by wells. [116] The fate of Caesarea, the capital of *Palaestina Prima,* located on the sea shore in an easy reach for the Byzantine fleet, was different from that of Scythopolis, the provincial capital of *Palaestina Secunda,* and of Jerusalem, the religious capital of *Palaestina,* both located inland. All of them survived, though more humbly, under the new regime.

NOTES

This article was written while I was on Sabbatical at the University of Miami, Coral Gables, Florida. I am grateful for the facilities and services offered me there.

1. The term *Byzantine* denotes here the period from Constantine's conquest of the East in 324, to the Arab conquest of Palestine in ca. 640 as is common in Israeli archaeology. For the rationale behind this terminology pertaining to the Holy Land see, for example, Tsafrir and Foerster, *Dumbarton Oaks Papers* [henceforth *DOP*] 50, p. 85n. 1. However, being aware that the period from Diocletian to the mid-sixth, or early seventh century is considered by many historians as *Late Antiquity*, the terms *Byzantine period* or *Late Antiquity* will be used here indifferently.
2. For historical studies see: F. M. Abel, *Histoire de la Palestine depuis la conquête d'Alexandre jusqu' à 1'invasion arabe* (Paris, 1952), 1: 369–70, 470, 478; 2: 182–84, 250–53, 404–5; J. Ringel, *Césarée de Palestine: Étude Historique et Archéologique* (Paris, 1975); I. L. Levine, *Caesarea Under Roman Rule* (Leiden, 1975); Ch. T. Fritch, *Studies in the History of Caesarea Maritima* [*Bulletin of the American Schools of Oriental Research* (henceforth *BASOR), Supplement Studies* 19], Misssoula, Mont. 1975; B. J. Lifshitz, "Césarée de Palestine, son histoire et ses institutions," in *Aufstieg und Niedergang des Römischen Welt,* vol. II, ed. H. I. Temporini (Berlin 1977), 490–518; E. Schürer, *The History of the Jewish People in the Age of Jesus Christ,* ed. G. Vermes, F. Millar, and M. Black (Edinburgh, 1979), 2:34–35, 115–18; K. G. Holum et al., *King Herod's Dream* (New York and London, 1988). For comprehensive references to the literary sources and scholarly studies see: Y. Tsafrir, Leah Di Segni and Judith Green, *Tabula Imperii Romanii. Iudaea/Palaestina* (Jerusalem, 1994), 94–96.
3. Since so far only preliminary reports on the large-scale 1992–98 excavations have appeared, and the huge amount of new data is still being processed, this synthesis should be considered as preliminary.
4. M. L. Fisher, M. Magaritz, and Z. Pearl, "Decoration and Marble Sources of Sarcophagi from Caesarea: a casestudy," *Caesarea Papers. Straton's Tower, Herod's Harbor, and Roman and Byzantine Caesarea, Journal of Roman Archaeology* Supplementary Series 5 (Ann Arbor, Mich., 1992), 214–21. [Henceforth *Caesarea Papers* I.]
5. M. Spiro, "Some Byzantine mosaics from Caesarea," *Caesarea Papers* I, 244–60.
6. T. Avner, "Early Byzantine Wall Paintings from Caesarea," *Caesarea Papers* II, *Journal of Roman Archaeology,* Supplement Series 35 (Ann Arbor, Mich., 1999), 109–28; J. Patrich, "Warehouses and Granaries in Caesarea Maritima," *Caesrea Retrospective,* 169–71, figs. 22–24; Fred L. Horton, "A Sixth-Century Bath in Caesarea's Suburbs and the Transformation of Bathing Culture in Late Antiquity," *Caesarea Retrospective,* 180, fig. 2.
7. J. Patrich et al., "The warehouse complex and governor's palace (areas KK, CC, and NN, May 1993-December 1995), in *Caesarea Papers* II, 75.

8. M. Peleg and R. Reich, "Excavation of a Segment of the Byzantine City Wall of Caesarea," *Atiqot* 21 (1992): 137–70.
9. S. Yevin, "Excavations at Caesarea Maritima," *Archaeology* 8 (1955):122–29; idem, "Césarée, Chronique archéologique," *Révue Biblique* 64 (1957): 259–60. M. Avi Yonah, *Israel Exploration Journal* [henceforth *IEJ*] 6 (1956): 260–61; Y. Porath, *ESI* 17 (1998): 47, fig. 11; R. Gersht, "Roman Statuary used in Byzantine Caesarea," *Caesarea Papers* II, 389–98. The view that ancient temple statuary have artistic value, deprived of their previous pagan connotation, was expressed by the early fifth-century Christian poet Prudentius (*Contra Symmachum*, 1.499–505). On this, and in general on Late Antique legislative attitudes toward urban buildings of the past, see J. Alchermes, "*Spolia* in Roman Cities of the Late Empire: Legislative Rationales and Architectural Reuse," *DOP* 48 (1994): 167–78; Helen Saradi-Mendelovici, "Christian Attitude toward Pagan Monuments in Late Antiquity and Their Legacy in Later Byzantine Centuries," *DOP* 44 (1990): 47–61.
10. The lower figure can be gleaned from M. Broshi, "The Population of Western Palestine in the Roman-Byzantine Period," *BASOR* 236 (1980): 5, if we correct the figure of the city area to 124.5 hectars instead of 95 hectars given by Broshi. A population of 100,000 is given by M. Avi Yonah, "Survey of Population Density, and Settlements Quantity in Ancient Eretz Israel," *Essays and Studies in the Lore of the Holy Land* (Tel Aviv, 1964), 121 (Hebrew) and Levine, *Caesarea Under Roman Rule*, 9 and n. 37, who refers to even higher, purely speculative estimates of 200,000 inhabitants. Holum et al., *King Herod's Dream*, 174, adhere also to the 100,000 figure, but more recently ("Identity and the Late Antique City: The Case of Caesarea," in *Religious and Ethnic Communities in Later Roman Palestine*, edited by H. Lapin [Bethesda, 1998], 163–64 and n. 20), he speaks of a population of only 25,000 people within the Byzantine fortification wall. Broshi discusses various methods for calculating population density and size. According to al-Baladhuri (*Futuh al-buldan* 141–42), in his account of the Arab conquest of the city, the entire number of soldiers was 700,000 [*sic*!, clearly a mistake], the Jews numbered 20,000, the Samaritans 30,000, and the city was guarded every night by 100,000 men stationed on its wall. See Ph. Kh. Hitti, ed. and trans., *The Origins of the Islamic State* (New York, 1916), 217–18.
11. A. Hamburger, "A Greco-Samaritan Amulet from Caesarea," *Israel Exploration Journal* 9 (1959): 43–45 and pl. 4 A, B). I. Ben Zvi, "A Lamp with a Samaritan Inscription," *IEJ* 11 (1961): 139–42. On the use of the old Hebrew script by the Samaritans see Babylonian Talmud, *Sanhedrin* 21b; Jerome, *Comm. In Ezech.* 3.9.4., CCSL 75, 106. According to A. D. Crown, "The Byzantine and Moslem Period," in *The Samaritans*, ed. A. D. Crown (Tubingen, 1989), 59, the Samaritans at Caesarea comprised about one third of the population.
12. Roth-Gerson, *The Greek Inscriptions from the Synagogues in Eretz-Israel* (Jerusalem, 1987), 115, inscr. 27. Capitals and architectural fragments with Jewish symbols are presented there (pp. 122–24). A marble column with the Hebrew inscription "shalom" (peace) was found by Netzer and Levine in their principal area of excavation, to the NW of the inner harbor (*Excavations at Caesarea Maritima 1975, 1976, 1979—Final*

Report, Qedem, Monographs of the Institute of Archaeology, Hebrew University 21 [Jerusalem, 1986], 45, ill. 64). A fragment of a stone slab decorated with a *menorah* was found to the S of the temple platform (Area Z). See A. Raban, "Caesarea Maritima—Land and Sea Excavations," CMS News, University of Haifa, Report No. 24–25 (1998): 32, fig. 4.

13. I. L. Levine, "Synagogue Officials: The Evidence from Caesarea and Its Implications for Palestine and the Diaspora," *Caesarea Maritima. A Retrospective after Two Millennia.* (Leiden - New York – Köln, 1996), 392–400 [henceforth *Caesarea Retrospective*].
14. For their number in the local population at the end of the period, see above, note 10.
15. John Malalas, *Chronographia,* XV, ed. Dindorf (Bonn, 1831), 487–88; Theophanes, *Chronographia,* A. M. 6048, ed. De Boor (Leipzig, 1883), 1:230; al-Baladhuri, above, note 10.
16. *Jerusalem Talmud, Avodah Zarah* 1.2 - 39c; S. Lieberman, "The Martyrs of Caesarea," *Annuaire de l'Institute de Philologie et d'Hisoire Orientales et Slaves* 7 (1939–44): 405–6. The period alluded to in this text is the time of the Diocletianic persecutions. Samaritan troops suppressed the uprising of the Monophysite monks against Juvenal in the wake of the Council of Chalcedon (Ps. Zacharias Rhetor, *Historia Ecclesiastica,* 3.5, trans. Brooks, CSCO, ser. 3, vol. 5, 109). According to Malalas (note 113, below), following the Samaritan revolt of 484, Zeno issued an edict that no Samaritans be admitted into the army. But the exclusion of the Samaritans from the army (and the civil services), was first issued by Honorius in 404 (*Cod. Theod.* 16.8.12) and repeated by Theodosius II in his *Novella* 3 of 438 or 439. A re-enactment by Zeno is not mentioned either in *Cod. Just.* 1.5.18, issued between 527 and 531, where Justinian repeated it, or in his *Novellae.* See Di Segni, "The Samaritans in Roman-Byzantine Palestine: Some Misapprehensions," in *Religious and Ethnic Communities in Later Roman Palestine,* ed. H. Lapin (Bethesda, 1998), 65.
17. Three *heis theos* inscriptions were found at Caesarea (C. Lehmann and K. G. Holum, *The Greek and Latin Inscriptions of Caesarea Maritima* [forthcoming], inscriptions 138–40), suggesting the existence of Samaritan synagogues in the city. As was noted by Leah Di Segni, "The Church of Mary Theotokos on Mount Gerizim: the Inscriptions," in *Christian Archaeology in the Holy Land. New Discoveries,* ed. G. C. Bottini, L. Di Segni, and E. Alliata (Jerusalem, 1990), 346; *eadem.*, "E((((((in Palestinian inscriptions," *Scripta Classica Israelica* 13 (1994): 94–115, although this formula is known in Jewish and Christian circles, in Palestine most inscriptions of this kind come from a Samaritan milieu.
18. For a drawing and a photo of the inscriptions, see J. Patrich *et. al. Caesarea Papers* II, 96–97, figs. 31, 32.
19. As a result of the anti-Samaritan legislation many of them assumed nominal Christianity. See Procopius, *Anecdota* XI, 15. 24–30.
20. Procopius, *Anecdota* XXVII. 8–10.
21. Y. Tsafrir and G. Foerster, "Urbanism at Scythopolis-BetShean in the Fourth to Seventh Centuries," *DOP* 51 (1997): 65–146, 124–26. For the Samaritans at Caesarea,

see K. G. Holum, "Caesarea and the Samaritans," in *City, Town, and Countryside in the Early Byzantine Era* [East European Monographs, 120, Byzantine Series, 1], ed. R. L. Hohlfelder (Boulder, 1983), 65–73.

22. F. Schemmel, "Die Schule von Caesarea in Palastina," *Philologische Wochenschrift* 45 (1925): 1277–80; G. Downey, "The Christians Schools of Palestine," *Harvard Library Bulletin* 12 (1958): 301f.
23. John of Caesarea, *Opera quae supersunt,* (ed. M. Richard, *appendicem suppeditante* M. Aubineau), Corpus *Christianorum. Series Graeca* I, Turnhout 1977; idem, *Capitula XVII contra Monophysita,* ibid., 59–66. Severus of Antioch, *Liber contra impium grammaticum* (ed. J. Lebon), *Corpus Scriptorum Christianorum Orientalium, Scriptores Syri IV, 4, 5, 6,* Paris-Louvain 1928, 1929, 1933.
24. A. Raban, *ESI* 17: 63–64, fig. 35.
25. For the history of research, and summary of archaeological finds, excluding the 1992–98 large-scale excavations, see I. L. Levine, *Roman Caesarea: An Archaeological-Topographical Study.* [Qedem, Monographs of the Institute of Archaeology, Hebrew University, 2]. (Jerusalem 1975); K. G. Holum et al., "Caesarea," in *New Encyclopaedia of Archaeological Excavations in the Holy Land,* ed. E. Stern (Jerusalem, 1993), 1:270–91; K. G. Holum, "Caesarea," in *The Oxford Encyclopedia of Archaeology in the Near East,* ed. E. Meyers (New York and Oxford, 1997), 1:399–404; J. Patrich, "Caesarea Maritima, Israel," in *Ciutats antigues de la Mediterrània,* ed. M. Mayers and I. Rodà (Barcelona, 1997), 302–5; K. G. Holum and A. Raban, "Introduction: Caesarea and Recent Scholarship," in *Caesarea Retrospective,* ed. A. Raban and K. G. Holum.
26. S. Yevin, "Excavations at Caesarea Maritima," *Archaeology* 8 (1955): 122–29; idem, "Césarée, Chronique archéologique," *Révue Biblique* 64 (1957): 259–60. M. Avi Yonah, *Israel Exploration Journal* [henceforth *IEJ*] 6 (1956): 260–61; idem and A. Negev, *IEJ* 13 (1963): 146–48. A. Negev, "Where Vespasian Was Proclaimed Emperor, Caesarea Maritima on the Coast of Israel," *Illustrated London News* 6482 (1963): 684–86, idem "The *Palimpsest of Caesarea Maritima,*" ibid., 6483 (1963): 728–31; idem, *Caesarea* (Tel-Aviv, 1967); idem, "Caesarea," in *Encyclopedia of Archaeological Excavations in the Holy Land,* ed. M. Avi-Yonah (Jerusalem, 1975), 270–85.
27. A. Frova et al., *Scavi di Caesarea Maritima* (Rome, 1966), and see also note 43 below.
28. R. Bull et al., *The Joint Expedition to Caesarea Maritima: Preliminary Reports.* Madison (1985), Drew University Institute for Archaeological Research (microfiche), with reference to earlier reports.
29. K. G. Holum et al., "Roman and Byzantine Caesarea," in *Caesarea Papers* I, ed. Vann, 79–193; A. Raban, K. G. Holum, and J. A. Blakely, *The Combined Caesarea Expeditions Field Report of the 1992 Season* (Haifa, 1993) [henceforth–*1992 Field Report*]; and see also Raban's contributions in notes 32 and 35 below, and the field reports in K. G. Holum, A. Raban, and J. Patrich, eds., *Caesarea Papers* II.
30. L. I. Levine and E. Netzer, *Excavations at Caesarea Maritima 1975, 1976, 1979—Final Report, Qedem, Monographs of the Institute of Archaeology,* Hebrew University 21 (Jerusalem, 1986).
31. B. Burrell, K. Gleason, and E. Netzer, "Uncovering Herod's Seaside Palace," *Biblical*

Archaeology Review 19 (1993): 50–57, 76; B. Burrell and K. L. Gleason, *American Journal of Archaeology* 99 (1995): 306–7; E. Netzer, "The Promontory Palace," in *Caesarea Retrospective,* (above, note 13), 193–207; Kathryn L. Gleason, "Ruler and Spectacle: The Promontory Palace," ibid., 208–28; Barbara Burrell, "Palace to Praetorium: The Romanization of Caesarea," ibid. 228–47; K. L. Gleason et al., "The Promontory Palace at Caesarea Maritima: Preliminary Evidence for Herod's *Praetorium,*" *Journal of Roman Archaeology* 11 (1998): 23–52.

32. Y. Porath, J. Patrich and A. Raban, "The Caesarea Excavation Project–March 1992–June 1994," *Excavations and Surveys in Israel* [henceforth *ESI*] 17 (1998): 39–77; Y. Porath, "The Evolution of the Urban Plan of Caesarea's Southwest Zone: New Evidence from the Current Excavations," in *Caesarea Retrospective,* 105–20; J. Patrich, "Warehouses and Granaries in Caesarea Maritima," ibid., 146–76. See also Patrich's et al. and Raban's et al. contribution to *Caesarea Papers* II; and notes 72, 79, and 80 below.
33. Ch. T. Fritsch, and I. Ben-Dor, "'The Link Expedition to Israel," *Biblical Archaeologist* 24 (1961): 50–56. See also R. Hohlfelder in A. Raban et al., *The Harbours of Caesarea Maritima,* 1: *The Site and the Excavations: Results of the Caesarea Ancient Harbour Excavation Project 1980–1985* (BAR S 491, Oxford, 1989), 65–71; idem, "The first three decades of marine explorations," *Caesarea Papers* I, 291–94.
34. Raban et al., *The Harbours of Caesarea Maritima,* 1; J. P. Oleson et al., *The Harbours of Caesarea Maritima,* 2: *The Finds and the Ship* (BAR S594, Oxford).
35. A. Raban, "The Inner Harbor Basin of Caesarea: Archaeological Evidence for its Gradual Demise," *Caesarea Retrospective,* 628–66; and see also Raban's et al., contributions in *Caesarea Papers* I and II, in *1992 Field Report,* and his periodical reports in the *University of Haifa Center for Maritime Studies News Reports.*
36. A. Raban, "Sebastos, the Herodian Harbor of Caesarea: How It Was Built and Operated," *University of Haifa Center for Maritime Studies News, Report no. 19* (1992); J. P. Oleson and G. Branton, "The Technology of King Herod's Harbour," *Caesarea Papers* I, 49–67; Ch. Brandon, "Cements, Concrete, and Settling Barges at Sebastos: Comparisons with Other Roman Harbor Examples and the Descriptions of Vitruvius," *Caesarea Retrospective,* 25–40; R. L. Vann, "Herod's Harbor Construction Recovered Underwater," *Biblical Archaeology Review* 9, no. 3 (May/June 1983): 10–14.
37. A. Raban, "The Lead Ingots from the Wreck Site (Area K8)," in *Caesarea Papers* II, 179–88.
38. A. Raban, above, note 35; B. Yule et al., "Evaluation of the Inner Harbour;" in *Caesarea Papers* II, 261–357; R. Tweig, "History of the Inner Harbor in Caesarea," *University of Haifa Center for Maritime Studies News,* Report no. 24–25, December 1998, pp. 16–18.
39. Procopius of Gaza, *Panagyr. Anast.* 19, *Patrologia Graeca* 87: 2817.
40. R. L. Vann, "The Drusion: a candidate for Herod's lighthouse at Caesarea Maritima," *International Journal of Nautical Archaeology* 20 (1991): 123–39; R. Hohlfelder, "Caesarea's Master Harbor Builders: Lessons Learned, Lessons Applied?," *Caesarea Retrospective,* p. 85; G. Alföldy, "Pontius Pilatus und das Tiberieum von Caesarea Maritima," *Scripta Classica Israelica* 18 (1999): 85–108.
41. Finocchi, in Frova (above, note 27), 247–92; A construction date within the first cen-

tury b.c. was concluded by J. Blakely, "A Stratigraphically Determined Date for the Inner Fortification Wall of Caesarea Maritima," in *The Answers Lie Below: Essays in Honor of Laurence Edmund Toombs*, ed. H. O. Thompson (Lanham, 1984), 3–38, who excavated near its NE tower. See also idem, "Stratigraphy and the North Fortification wall of Herod's Caesarea," *Caesarea Papers* I, 26–41. The Herodian date suggested by the Italians was questioned by Levine (above note 25), 10–12, Negev, and disputed by Raban, "The City Walls of Straton's Tower: Some New Archaeological Data," *BASOR* 268 (1987): 71–88. Excavating in the northernmost vault of the Temple Platform, and noticing that the stones of its lower courses have similar margin drafts, Raban claimed that the remains of the towers and wall in the north belong to the Hellenistic town of Straton's Tower. See also A. Raban, "In Search of Straton's Tower," *Caesarea Papers* I, 7–22. T. W. Hillard, "A Mid-st c. b.c. Date for the Walls of Straton's Tower?," ibid., 42–48 favors a Gabinian date. The more recent excavations in the vaults of the Temple Platform have called into question Raban's claim. The present prevalent opinion is that the fortification remains at the north are Herodian. On the abandonment of this fortification line, see Blakely, *op. cit.* The city gates are mentioned in the early fourth century by Eusebius, *Mart. Pal.* 9–12.

42. Y. Tsafrir and G. Foerster, "Urbanism at Scythopolis-BetShean in the Fourth to Seventh Centuries," *DOP* 51 (1997): 65–146, at 102.
43. A. Frova, *Caesarea Maritima (Israele): Rapporto preliminare della prima campano della Missione Archeologica Italiana*, Milan 1959; idem, Gli Scavi della Missione Archeologica Italiana a Cesarea (Israele). *Annuario della Scuala Archeologica di Atene* 39–40, n. s. 23–24 (1961–62): 649–57; J. Humphrey, "A Summary of the 1974 Excavations in the Caesarea Hippodrome," *BASOR* 218 (1975): 1–24; M. Peleg and R. Reich, "Excavation of a Segment of the Byzantine City Wall of Caesarea," *Atiqot* 21 (1992): 137–70; C. M. Lehmann, "The Combined Caesarea Expeditions: The Excavation of Caesarea's Byzantine City Wall, 1989," *Annual of the American Schools of Oriental Research* 52 (1994): 121–31.
44. I. Roll, "Roman Roads to Caesarea Maritima," in *Caesarea Retrospective*, 549–58.
45. Peleg and Reich (note 43 above).
46. M. Schwabe, "The Bourgos Inscription from Caesarea Palaestina," *Tarbiz* 20 (1950): 273–83 (Hebrew); B. Lifshitz, "Inscriptions grecques de Césarée en Palestine." *Révue Biblique* 68 (1961): 115–26, inscr. no. 16.
47. F. M. Abel and A. Barrois, "Fragment de Césarée la metropole," *Révue Biblique* 40 (1931): 294–95.
48. A. Frova (note 27 above), 57–159, 165–86.
49. C. Foss and D. Winfield, *Byzantine Fortifications - An Introduction* (Pretoria, 1986), 7–14.
50. R. L. Vann, "Byzantine Street Construction at Caesarea Maritima," in *City, Town, and Countryside in the Early Byzantine Era* [East European Monographs, 120, Byzantine Series, 1], edited by R. L. Hohlfelder (Boulder, 1983), 161–74; J. Patrich et al., "The warehouse complex and governor's palace (areas KK, CC, and NN, May 1993-December 1995)," in *Caesarea Papers* II, 74–75; Y. Porath, "The Evolution of the Urban

Plan of Caesarea's Southwest Zone: New Evidence from the Current Excavations," *Caesarea Retrospective*, 105–120; idem, *ESI* 17 (1998): 41–42.

51. Therefore Holum was right in refraining from depicting the grid beyond the Herodian wall in the city plan of year 500 c.e. See *Caesarea Retrospective*, map 3 (The Byzantine/Late Antique Period).
52. L. Kadman, *The Coins of Caesarea Maritima* [*Corpus Nummorum Palaestinensium* 2] (Tel Aviv–Jerusalem, 1957); J. Ringel (above note 2), 151–62.
53. B. Lifshitz, "Le culte de Jupiter Dolichenus à Césarée. Notes d'épigraphie palestinienne." *Révue Biblique* 73 (1966): 255–56.
54. R. Gerst, "The Sculpture of Caesarea Maritima" (Ph.D diss., Tel Aviv University, 1987) [Hebrew]; idem, "The Tyche of Caesarea Maritima," *Palestine Exploration Quarterly* 116 (1984): 110–14; idem, "Seven New Sculptural Pieces from Caesarea," in *The Roman and Byzantine Near East* [*Journal of Roman Archaeology* Suppl. Series 14], ed. J. Humphrey (Ann Arbor, 1995), 108–20; idem, "Representation of Deities and the Cults of Caesarea," in *Caesarea Retrospective*, 305–24; idem, "Roman Statuary used in Byzantine Caesarea," *Caesarea Papers* II, 389–98; A. Frova, "La statua di Artemide Efesia a 'Caesarea Maritima'" *Bollettino d'Arte* 4 (1962): 305–13; R. Wenning, "Die Stadtgöttin von Caesarea Maritima," *Boreas* 9 (1986): 113–29.
55. K. G. Holum et al., *Caesarea Papers* I, 100–9; Raban and Holum in *1992 Field Report*, 53–60; A. Raban, *ESI* 17 (1998): 68–69; For a summary of recent excavations see K. G. Holum, "The Temple Platform Excavation: A Progress Report," *Caesarea Papers* II, 13–34. For the reconstruction of the temple on the evidence of scattered architectural fragments see L. Kahn, "King Herod's Temple of Roma and Augustus at Caesarea Maritima," *Caesarea Retrospective*, 130–45.
56. See drawing in Y. Porath, *ESI* 17 (1998): 46, fig. 10. The dimensions of the podium are given in p. 21 in Holum's recent report (previous note).
57. The common opinion is that despite Tiberius' refrain from encouraging his veneration as a god, the inscription attests to this cult. Recently G. Alföldy has suggested that the reference is to a light tower, a twin of the "Druseion" tower mentioned by Josephus (*War* 1.413; *Antiquities* 15.336), called after Drusus—Tiberius' brother. See note 40 above.
58. The *Hadrianeion* is mentioned in a sixth-century Greek inscription at the site: W. Moulton, "Gleaning in Archaeology and Epigraphy: A Caesarean Inscription," *Annual of the American Schools of Oriental Research* 1 (1919–20): 86–90; M. Avi Yonah, "The Caesarea Porphyry Statue." *Israel Exploration Journal* 20 (1970): 203–8; On the presumed visit of Hadrian to Caesarea, and his endowments to the city, see K. G. Holum, "Hadrian and Caesarea: An Episode in the Romanization of Palestine," *Ancient World* 23 (1992): 51–61.
59. R. Bull, "Mithraic Medallion from Caesarea," *Israel Exploration Journal* 22 (1972): 187–90; "The Mithraeum at Caesarea Maritima." *Études Mithraiques, textes et memoires* 4 (1978): 75–89. (At the time when these articles by Bull were published the relation of this sanctuary to the *praetorium* of the Roman procurator was not perceived yet).

60. J. Rea, "Two Legates and a Procurator of Syria Palaestina, *ZPE* 26 (1977): 217–22; W. Eck, "Ein Prokuratorenpaar von Syria Palaestina in P. Berol. 21652," *ZPE* 123 (1998): 249–55.
61. D. Fluser, "The Great Goddess of Samaria," *Israel Exploration Journal* 25 (1975): 13–20. For the ex-voto feet and the dedicatory inscription for Kore, see R. Gersht *Caesarea Retrospective* (above note 54), 310–11; Y. Porath, "Herod's 'amphitheatre' at Caesarea: a multipurpose entertainment building," in *The Roman and Byzantine Near East* [*Journal of Roman Archaeology* Suppl. Series 14], ed. J. Humphrey (Ann Arbor, 1995), 23, fig. 10; a photograph of the *Sacellum* is given there on p. 21, fig. 9a, and p. 272, color fig. 9. For a picture of the feet see also idem, *ESI* 17 (1998): 41, fig. 3.
62. M. Avi Yonah, (note 26 above); idem, "The Synagogue at Caesarea," *Louis M. Rabinowitz Fund for the Exploration of Ancient Synagogues, Bulletin* 3 (1960): 44–48. For the Synagogue inscriptions see: M. Schwabe, "The Synagogue of Caesarea and its Inscriptions." in *Alexander Marx Jubille Volume*, ed. S. Lieberman (New York, 1950), 433–50, pls. 1–4 [Hebrew]; B. Lifshitz, "Donateurs et fondateurs dans les synagogues juives." *Cahiers de la Révue Biblique* 7 (1967): 50–54, nos. 64–68; L. Roth-Gerson, *The Greek Inscriptions from the Synagogues in Eretz-Israel* (Jerusalem, 1987), nos. 25–29 [Hebrew]. See also Levine (above note 25), 40–45.
63. G. Downey, "Caesarea and the Christian Church," in *Studies in the History of Caesarea Maritima* [*BASOR Supplement Studies* 19], ed. Ch. T. Fritch (Misssoula, Mont., 1975), 23–42; E. Krenz, "Caesarea and Early Christianity," *Caesarea Papers* I, 261–67; Levine (above note 25), 45–46. *Acts* 21:13; Jerome, *Epistulae* 108.8; *PPTS* VI, p. 32 (a thirteenth-century anonymous travelogue; reference to the chamber of the four virgin prophetesses). Antoninus of Placentia, *Itinerarium* 45 [*CCSL* 175, p. 174] (reference to the burial place of Pamphilius and Procopius). Malalas, *Chronographia*, XIV, ed. Dindorf (Bonn, 1831), 93–94; *Chronicon Paschale*, 327, PG 92, 840–41 (reference to the chapel of Procopius).
64. W. E. Kaegi Jr., "Some Seventh-Century Sources on Caesarea," *IEJ* 28 (1978): 177–81; B. Flusin, *Saint Anastase le Perse* (Paris, 1992), 231–43.
65. K. G. Holum et al., *Caesarea Papers* I, 100–7; Raban et al., *1992 Field Report*, 37–42, 50–51, 53–55. For the date of construction of the octagonal church see most recently: K. G. Holum (above note 55), p. 26.
66. Raban, *Caesarea Retrospective*, 657–58, and fig. 23, refers to this platform as a "reflecting pool." In my opinion this is an erroneous interpretation. The massive platform was needed to retain the staircase and to provide reasonable open space to its front. A later looting of some of the *kurkar* blocks of this platform gave the wrong impression that the extant remains are those of a basin.
67. F. H. Stanley, Jr., "The South Flank of the Temple Platform," *Caesarea Papers* II, 35–40.
68. For the intentional preservation of pagan or Jewish precincts as void spaces in Christian town-planning see A. J. Wharton, *Refiguring the Post-Classical City: Dura Europos, Jerash, Jerusalem and Ravenna* (Cambridge, 1995).
69. See Eusebius, *Life of Constantine* III. cc. xxvi-xl on the erection of the church of the holy sepulcher in Jerusalem, at the order of Constantine, on the site of the temple of

Aphrodite; Marc le Diacre, *Vita Porphyrii*, ed. H. Gregoire and M. A. Kugener (Paris, 1930), concerning the erection of Eudoxia church at Gaza on the site of the local temple of Marnas. On the conversion of temples to churches and the christianization of the urban space in Palestine, see K. G. Holum, "In the Blinking of an Eye: The Christianizing of Classical Cities in the Levant," in *Religion and Politics in the Ancient Near East*, ed. A. Berlin (Bethesda, Md., 1996), 131–50; Y. Tsafrir, "The Fate of Pagan Cult-Places in Palestine: The Archaeological Evidence with Emphasis on Bet Shean," in *Religious and Ethnic Communities in Later Roman Palestine*, ed. H. Lapin (Bethesda, Md., 1998), 197–218.

70. However, since the Greek inscriptions of this basilical building, with its apse oriented east, do not commence with a cross, as is common with Christian inscriptions, this interpretation of the architectural remains (Porath, *ESI* 17 [1998]: 44, fig. 8) is dubious. The eastern orientation of the apse can befit also a Samaritan synagogue, since Mt. Garizim, to which Samaritan synagogues were oriented, is located to the east of Caesarea.

71. See note 31 above, and E. Netzer and R. Bar Nathan, "The Promontory Palace," in *Excavations at Caesarea Maritima 1975, 1976, 1979*, ed. Levine and Netzer (note 30 above), 149–77.

72. J. Patrich, "A Government Compound in Roman-Byzantine Caesarea," *Acts of The Twelfth World Congress of Jewish Studies, Jerusalem, July 29th-August 5th, 1997* (Jerusalem, 1999); idem et al., "The warehouse complex and governor's palace (areas KK, CC and NN, May 1993-December 1995)," *Caesarea Papers* II, 70–108.

73. Y. Porath, *ESI* 17 (1998): 42–43, fig. 4. During the IAA excavations this complex was identified as a bathhouse. However, now, after being entirely exposed, it is clear that the bathhouse, being the first part to be exposed, formed just a wing of this palatial mansion.

74. See plan in Y. Porath, *ESI* 17 (1998): 43–44, fig. 6; and garden reconstruction in: *Caesarea Retrospective*, 118–19, figs. 2, 3.

75. For bibliographical references see J. P. Sodini, "Habitat de l'antiquité tardive" 1 & 2, *Topoi* 5 (1995): 151–218; 7 (1997): 435–577.

76. See, for example, R. J. Bull and O. Storvick, "The Gold Coin Hoard at Caesarea," *Biblical Archaerologist* 56 (1993): 116–20.

77. A. Albricci, in Frova (note 27 above), 93–120; Levine (note 25 above), 23–26. The diameter of the theater was 90 m, and that of the orchestra 30 m. It is not clear how A. Segal, *The Theatres in Roman Palestine and Provincia Arabia* (Leiden, 1995), 99, derived his dimensions of 62 m and 16 m respectively. Just a glance at the plans reproduced as figs. 70 and 71 in that book indicate that these dimensions are wrong.

78. On the ambiguity in applying technical terms to spectacle structures that existed in the Late Hellenistic/Late Republican and Early Imperial periods, see J. Humphrey, "'Amphitheatrical' Hippo-Stadia," in *Caesarea Retrospective*, 121–29, and Y. Porath, "Herod's 'Amphitheatre' at Caesarea: A Multipurpose Entertainment Building," in *The Roman and Byzantine Near East* [*Journal of Roman Archaeology* Suppl. Series 14], ed. J. Humphrey (Ann Arbor, 1995), 23–27.

79. Y. Porath, (note 78 above), 15–27, 269–72 (color pls.); idem, "Herod's Amphitheatre at Caesarea, Preliminary Notice," *Atiqot* 25 (1994): 11–19 [Hebrew]; idem, *ESI* 17 (1998): 40–41; idem, "Herod's "Ampitheatre" at Caesarea," *Qadmoniot* 29, no. 112 (1996): 93–99 [Hebrew].
80. J. Patrich, "The Starting Gates of the Herod's Hippodrome at Caesarea," *JRA* (forthcoming). For a thorough survey of Roman circuses and the two major styles of chariot races, see J. Humphrey, *Roman Circuses: Arenas for Chariot Racing* (London, 1986), 1–24.
81. B. J. Lifshitz, "Inscriptions grecques de Césarée en Palestine," *Révue Biblique* 68 (1961): 115–26, pls. I.a-d, II.a.c; 70 (1963): 256; 72 (1965): 98–107, pl. VII, a-c; 73 (1966): 248–57, pl. XI. a-d.; 74 (1967): 50–59, pl. IV, a-g; idem, "Inscriptions latines de Césarée en Palestine." *Latomus* 21 (1962): 149–50, pls. IV.1–2, V.3–6; 22 (1963): 783–84, pls. LXIII-LXIV.1–3; A. Negev, "Inscription hébraïques, grecques et latines de Césarée Maritime." *Révue Biblique* 78 (1971): 247–63, pl. I-IX; W. Eck, "Zu Lateinischen Inschriften aus Caesarea in Iudaea / Palaestina," *ZPE* 113 (1996): 129–43; C. Lehmann and K. G. Holum, *The Greek and Latin Inscriptions of Caesarea Maritima* (forthcoming).
82. E. B. Müller, "The Hippodrome," in *Gerasa–City of the Decapolis,* ed. C. H. Kraeling (New Haven, 1938), 85–100; A. Ostrasz, "The Hippodrome of Gerasa: A Report on Excavation and Research, 1982–1987," *Syria* 66 (1989): 51–77; Y. Magen, *New Encyclopaedia of Archaeological Excavations in the Holy Land,* vol. 4 (Jerusalem, 1993), 1357–58; Y. Tsafrir and G. Foerster (note 42 above), 99 and fig. E on p. 91.
83. A. Reifenberg, "Archaeological Discoveries by Air Photographs in Israel." *Archaeology* 3 (1950): 40–46; idem, "Caesarea: A Study in the Decline of a Town," *Israel Exploration Journal* 1 (1951): 20–32.
84. J. Humphrey, "A Summary of the 1974 Excavations in the Caesarea Hippodrome." *BASOR* 218 (1975): 6; L. E. Toombs, "The Stratigraphy of Caesarea Maritima," in *Archaeology in the Levant: Essays for Kathleen Kenhon,* ed. R.P.S. Moorey and P. J. Parr (Warminster, 1978), 229; On this hippodrome of Caesarea in the wider context of Eastern hippodromes, see also J. Humphrey, "Prolegomena to the Study of the Hippodrome at Caesarea Maritima," *Bulletin of the American Schools of Oriental Research* 213 (1974): 2–45; idem (note 80 above), 438–540 (*Caesarea,* 477–91). See also J. Jeremias, "Der Taraxippos im Hippodrom von Caesarea Palaestinae," *Zeitschrift des Deutschen Palästina-Vereins* 54 (1931): 279–89, pls. XII–XIII.
85. E. Habas, "The Halachic Status of Caesarea as Reflected in the Talmudic Literature," in *Caesarea Retrospective,* 454–68; Z. Weiss, "The Jews and the Games in Roman Caesarea," ibid., 443–53; Levine (note 25 above), throughout.
86. K. G. Holum, "Hadrian and Caesarea: An Episode in the Romanization of Caesarea," *Ancient World* 23 (1992): 51–61.
87. This portico is mentioned in a Greek papyrus from Egypt, *Papiri Greci e Latini–Publicazioni della Sicieta Italiana,* IX, 36f, no. 1026. See also A. Degrassi, "Il papiro 1026 della Società italiana e I diplomi militari romani," *Aegyptus* 10 (1926): 242–54.

88. Levine (note 25 above), 38–40.
89. A. Raban and R. Stieglitz, "Caesarea, Ancient Harbor, 1987," *IEJ* 38 (1988): 276–78. A much larger *sigma* complex, dated to early sixth century was exposed in Beth Shean. See R. Bar Nathan and G. Mazor, "City Center (South) and Tel Iztaba Area; Excavations of the Antiquities Authority Expedition," *ESI* 11 (1992): 43–44; 17 (1998): 15; Tsafrir and Foerster (note 42 above), 120–21.
90. J. Patrich, "Warehouses and Granaries in Caesarea Maritima," *Caesrea Retrospective*, 146–76. For a comprehensive survey, see G. Rickman, *Roman Granaries and Store Buildings* (Cambridge, 1971), 148–55.
91. A. Negev, "The High Level Aqueduct at Caesarea," *Israel Exploration Journal* 14 (1964): 237–49, pl. 17C; Olami and Ringel *IEJ* 25 (1975): 148–50; Y. Peleg, "The Water Supply system of Caesarea," *Mitteilungen des Leichtweiss-Institut für Wasserbau der Technischen Universität Braunschweig* 89 (1986): 1–15; D. Everman, "Survey of the Coastal Area of Caesarea and of the Aqueducts: Preliminary Report," *Caesarea Papers* I, 184–93; Y. Porath, "The Aqueducts of Caesarea," in *Ancient Aqueducts in Judaea / Palaestina* [*Journal of Roman Archaeology, Supplement Series*], ed. D. Amit, J. Patrich, and Y. Hirschfeld (forthcoming).
92. A. Negev, "A New Inscription from the High Level Aqueduct at Caesarea." *Israel Exploration Journal* 22 (1972): 52–53; L. Di Segni, "Epigraphical and Literary Sources on Aqueducts," in *Ancient Aqueducts in Judaea / Palaestina*, ed. D. Amit et al.; D. Barag., "An Inscription from the High Aquaduct at Caesarea–Reconsidered," *Israel Exploration Journal* 14 (1964): 250–52, pl. 45.a-d.
93. Y. Porath, "Pipelines of the Caesarea Water Supply System," *Atiqot* 10 (1990): 100–10 [Hebrew; English Summary].
94. Ph. Mayerson, "Choricius of Gaza on the Watersupply System of Caesarea," *Israel Exploration Journal* 36 (1986): 269–72.
95. Yegul, *Bath and Bathing in Classical Antiquity*, New York 1992; I. Nielsen, *Thermae et Balnea: The Architectural and Cultural History of Roman Public Baths* (Aarhus, 1990). See also A. Berger, *Das Bad in der byzantinischen Zeit* [*Miscellanea Byzantina Monacensia* 27] (Munich, 1982), 90–93. The bathhouse below the temple platform, occupied in this period by the octagonal church, can be compared with the Baths of Bishop Placcus at Gerasa, erected in 454/55, and renovated in 584. The baths are located to the north of St. Theodore Church, in the ecclesiastical complex that comprised also of the "Cathedral" and the clergy house. See Kraeling, note 82 above, 265–81, pls. XLIV-XLV, LIII-LVI.
96. The following is a list of nymphaea and fountains found so far in the city: two small niche fountains on E facade of the "western stoa," Area KK; a fountain to the W of vault 4 in Area CV; the central, garden fountain in the *praetorium* of the financial procurator, phases 1 and 2, and a second, "mundane" fountain in CC 59; a niche fountain in the "library" of that *praetorium*, phases 1 and 2; two fountains and an octagonal basin in the bathhouse of that *praetorium;* an elaborate latrine fountain in IAA "bathhouse" (*ESI* 17:43, fig. 5), and several "basin fountains" in the "palaestra" and "frigidarium" of that "bathhouse"; a central, portico fountain in the upper terrace

of the IAA "Byzantine palace," and a second, garden fountain, in its lower terrace (*ESI* 17:43, fig. 6); an apse fountain in the triclinium of Herod's lower palace, and a courtyard fountain in the N wing of the upper palace; a nymphaeum in the facade of the NW projection of the Temple Platform (*ESI* 17:47, fig. 11).

97. The following is a list of latrines—Public: at the cardo-decumanus junction in Area CC; in the N passage to the Hippodrome; Private: adjacent to the "Ibex Mosaics" hall in Area NN; in vault 54 of area CC; in IAA "bathhouse"; in CCE Area I, over the Herodian mole (Byzantine in date; first exposed by Negev).
98. Levine (note 25 above), pl. 3:2; Y. Porath, *ESI* 17 (1998): 47, fig. 11.
99. See A. Segal, *From Function to Monumentality: Urban Landscapes of Roman Palestine, Syria and Provincia Arabia* (Oxford, 1997), 161–80.
100. Mishnah, *Oholoth* 17:49; B. Lifshitz, "La necropole juive de Cesaree," *Revue Biblique* 71 (1964): 384–87. It seems that the Tell Mevorakh (3 km distant from the city) sarcophagi were found in the confines of a private estate; they should not be conceived as an indicator for the continuous extension of the urban necropolis of Caesarea. See E. Stern, *Excavations at Tel Mevorakh (1973–1976). Part. 1: From the Iron Age to the Roman Period,* [Qedem, Monographs of the Institute of Archaeology, Hebrew University, 9] (Jerusalem, 1978); R. Gersht, "Imported Marble Sarcophagi from Caesarea," *Assaph, Studies in Art History* 2 (1996): 13–26.
101. G. Struffolino, in *Scavi di Caesarea Maritima,* ed. Frova, 294–304; R. Reich, "On Some Byzantine Remains," *Atiqot* (Eng. Ser.) 17 (1985): 206–13; F. L. Horton, "A Sixth-Century Bath in Caesarea's Suburbs and the Transformation of Bathing Culture in Late Antiquity," *Caesarea Retrospective,* 177–89.
102. Y. Hirschfeld and R. Birger-Calderon, "Early Roman and Byzantine Estate near Caesarea," *Israel Exploration Journal* 41 (1991): 81–111; Y. Hirschfeld, "The Early Roman Bath and Fortress at Ramat Hanadiv near Caesarea," in *The Roman and Byzantine Near East* [*Journal of Roman Archaeology* Suppl. Series 14], ed. J. Humphrey (Ann Arbor, 1995), 28–55.
103. A police chief or sheriff (*lestodioktes*) and a garrison of Arcadiani is mentioned in Caesarea in conjunction with the suppression of Samaritan revolt of 484 (Ps. Zacharias Rhetor, note 16 above; Jo. Malalas, *Chron.* XV.8, ed. L. Dindorf (Bonn, 1831), 382–83.
104. J. Patrich, note 72 above; K. G. Holum, "Inscriptions from the imperial revenue office of Byzantine Caesarea Palaestinae," in *The Roman and Byzantine Near East,* ed. Humphrey, 333–45.
105. The final epigraphical report on the new inscriptions from the Byzantine *praetorium* is being prepared for publication by Leah Di Segni. For previous publications of some of them see Patrich et al. in *Caesarea Papers* II, and Holum et al., above note 25.
106. See B. Burrell, above, note 13 (*Caesarea Retrospective*), where she discusses also the Roman palace of the *Dux Ripae* at Dura Europos, the *praetorium* at Cologne, and the governor's palace at Aquincum.
107. J. C. Balty, "L'edifice dit 'au triclinos,'" *Apamee de Syrie* (Miscellanea fasc. 6) (Bruxelles, 1969), 105–16. For the other mansions in that quarter of Apamea see J. Balty, ed.,

Apamee de Syrie [Bilan des recherches archeologiques 1973–1979, aspects de l'architecture domestique d'apamee], (Bruxelles, 1984). For other palatial mansions that belong to this group see S. Ellis, "The 'Palace of the Dux' at Apollonia, and Related Houses," in *Cyrenaica in Antiquity* [BAR International Series 236], ed. G. Barker et al. (1985): 15–25; K. Erim, "The Ninth Campaign of Excavations at Aphrodisias in Caria," *Turk Arkeoloji Dergisi* 18, no. 2 (1969): 87–110, the so-called "Governor's Palace" with a private bath suite. Another quarter of wealthy mansions in a late antique city is the NE quadrant in Ptolemais (Cyrene). See J. Little, "Urban Change at Ptolemais," in *Cyrenaica in Antiquity*, ed. Barker et al., 43–47.

108. P. Lampinen, "The Gold Hoard of 4th C. Solidi Found in 1993," *Caesarea Papers* II, 368–88; Bull and Storvick, "The Gold Coin Hoard at Caesarea," *Biblical Archaerologist* 56 (1993): 116–20.
109. The final reports on the imported amphorae and the table ware from Areas KK, CC and NN are in the final stages of preparation by two of our staff members: Michal Oren-Pascal and Orit Tzuf.
110. A. Raban, note 35, above.
111. J. Humphrey, above, note 85, "Prolegomena . . ."; A. Cameron, *Circus Factions. Blues and Greens at Rome and Byzantium* (Oxford, 1976); W. Liebeschuetz, "The Circus Factions," *Saggi di Storia Antica* 13 [Convegno per Santo Mazzarino, Roma 9–11 maggio 1991], (Bretschneider, 1991), 163–85; Y. Dan, "Circus Factions (Blues and the Greens) in Byzantine Palestine," in *The Jerusalem Cathedra: Studies in the History, Archaeology, Geography and Ethnography of the Land of Israel*, vol. 1, ed. I. L. Levine (Jerusalem and Toronto, 1981), 105–19.
112. B. Lifshitz, "Césarée de Palestine, son histoire et ses institutions," in *Aufstieg und Niedergang des Römischen Welt*, ed. H. I. Temporini (Berlin, 1977), 2:510–12; Lehmann and Holum, above, note 81, inscr. 110.
113. Jo. Malalas, *Chron.* XV.8, ed. L. Dindorf (Bonn, 1831), 382–83; A. D. Crown, "The Byzantine and Moslem Period," in *The Samaritans*, ed. A. D. Crown (Tubingen, 1989), 72. According to Leah Di Segni, "The Samaritans in Roman-Byzantine Palestine: Some Misapprehensions," in *Religious and Ethnic Communities*, ed. Lapin, 60, Justasas just attended the chariot races, and did not preside over them.
114. H. Kennedy, "From *Polis* to *Medina:* Urban Change in Late Antique and Early Islamic Syria," *Past and Present* 106 (1985): 3–27; W. Liebeschuetz, "The End of the Ancient City," in *The City in Late Antiquity*, ed. J. Rich (London and New York, 1992), 1–49.
115. In this I share the opinion expressed by Levine (*Caesarea Under Roman Rule*, 135–39), about Byzantine Caesarea.
116. J. Patrich, "Urban Ruralization in Provincia Palaestina: The Demise of the Byzantine *Praetorium* at Caesarea," *Twenty-Fourth Annual Byzantine Studies Conference Abstracts*, 5–8 November 1998, University of Kentucky, p. 41; K. G. Holum, "Caesarea Palaestinae: The Byzantine-Islamic Transition," ibid., 42–43.

Byzantine Petra—A Reassessment

ZBIGNIEW T. FIEMA

INTRODUCTION

The ancient city of Petra in southern Jordan is associated with the Nabataean Arab population that built and inhabited the city. The importance of the city between the second century B.C. and the third century A.D. is attributed to the economics of long distance trade in spices and aromatics between the East and the West, in which the Nabataeans achieved a manifest success. The economic growth in the area and a need for trade-related infrastructure and protection triggered the rise of the Nabataean Kingdom in the first century B.C., with the attendant political and administrative centralization, as well as the urbanization of the area, the intensive agricultural production, and the diversity of material culture as exemplified in the capital city of Petra.[1]

Following the annexation of the Nabataean Kingdom by Rome in A.D. 106, Petra continued to be the most prominent political, economic, and cultural center of Roman Arabia, if not its de facto "capital." The impressive honorific titles of Petra—Augustocolonia, Antoniana, Metrocolonia, Hadriana, Petra Metropolis—still in use in the sixth century,[2] well reflect the process of the Romanization of the city in terms of the administrative and status-related advancement. A substantial urban development had already occurred during the Nabataean period. However, recent excavations in the city center (infra) revealed that some major improvements and additions to the city plan also took place in the Roman period. This effectively undermines a lately expressed opinion that Petra in the Roman period was ". . . a smallish provincial town . . . with little development."[3]

Furthermore, there is no reason to assume that the significance of Petra in relation to the international trade had been diminished with the annexation of the Nabataean Kingdom, or by the rise of Palmyra. On the contrary, the unguent/perfume container (unguentarium) manufacturing and processing industries at Petra undoubtedly continued between the first and the third centuries A.D.,[4] which confirms the continuity of the Petra's involvement in trade. However, during the later third century—a period of economic crisis and sociopolitical transformation—the importance of the city, as related to the long-distance caravan trade, may have dwindled. The diminished demand for Oriental goods in the Roman empire would have been related to the unstable political conditions, continuous wars, impoverishment of towns and regions, and the concomitant change in pattern of main trade routes. The latter shifted farther north (Persian Gulf–Mesopotamia–Armenia–North Syria) and south (South Arabia–Ethiopia– Red Sea) of the Petra area. Although some Oriental goods might still have been transported overland and through Petra, no large-scale traffic appear to have occurred there during the Byzantine period.

DATA

The historical information concerning Petra in the Byzantine period is limited.[5] Following the extensive and poorly known rearrangements of the provincial administration and boundaries in the fourth century,[6] Petra emerged as the capital of Palaestina Salutaris (Notitia Dignitatum, Or. II 9, 14, 16, 17), later known as Tertia (Cod. Theod. VII.4.30, 1905: 322; A.D. 409). This status was apparently retained at least until the end of the sixth century, as implied in the handbooks of Hierocles and Georgius Cyprius, dated to about A.D. 535 and the last quarter of the sixth century respectively (Synekdèmos 1939; 721.2, p. 43; line 1044, p. 68). The city remained the bastion of paganism and idolatry, even in the later fourth and the early fifth centuries (Sozomen, HE VII.15,11, 1960: 321; Epiphanius, Panarion haer. II.51.22.11, 1980: 286-87).[7] In A.D. 363, Petra was considerably damaged by an earthquake.[8] No bishops of Petra attended major Church Councils in the fifth and sixth century. The only known exception is Bishop Theodoros, who attended the anti-Monophysite Synod in Jerusalem in A.D. 536.[9] At the turn of the fifth century, Petra became a place of exile for ecclesiastics and common criminals (John Malalas XVI.5, 1986: 222; John of Nikiu LXXXIX.69-70, 1916: 129-30; John of Ephesus XIII, 1923: 188; Zacharias of Mitylene VIII.5, 1899: 208-9).

Scarce historical information and the depressing appearance of the city following the 363 earthquake prompted an opinion that the city experienced a serious political and economic decline, caused by the loss of revenues from the participation in the Oriental trade, and by the earthquakes that shattered local infrastructure. It was suggested that by the mid–sixth century the city was reduced to rubble and even abandoned.[10] However, the archaeological and historical information now available allows for more substantive statements concerning the late periods at Petra.

In particular, the Petra Church Project excavations by the American Center of Oriental Research (ACOR) uncovered a magnificently decorated church complex constructed in the later fifth century. Following a fire at the end of the sixth century, the church was ecclesiastically abandoned, yet the space and the buildings were occupied well into the seventh century.[11] The recent ACOR excavations of several shops along the main, colonnaded street of Petra attested the continuity of their utilization, even following the 363 earthquake. However, later gradual abandonment of the shops was finally completed by the mid–seventh century.[12] The Swiss ez Zantur excavations documented that the domestic structures there were largely abandoned after the 363 earthquake, while the final stage of occupation in that area of the city ends in the early fifth century.[13] The same disaster destroyed the nearby Great Temple, excavated by Brown University. The following occupation of the lower temenos—lime burning and dumping of debris—

continued in the fifth/sixth century.[14] The Swiss explorations in the Siq of Petra—a natural canyon and a major approach road to the city—revealed that the 363 disaster destroyed some vital dams, which protected the Petra valley against the torrential floods. The following repair of the dams was neither sufficient nor durable. The road itself appears to have been no longer in use by the mid–seventh century.[15] Petra's hinterland during the sixth/seventh century, recently investigated by surveys,[16] is marked by a notable reduction in the number of sites, comparing with the Nabataean-Roman periods. Significant information comes from the recent Finnish excavations at the mountain of Aaron, located ca. 5 km SW of Petra. That mountain was already in the Byzantine times associated with the place of death of Moses's brother (Eusebius, Onom. 176.7-8); the tradition continued in the Islamic period.[17] The excavations there detected the presence of a large church, probably of the fifth-century date, and presumably associated with the monastic presence and a pilgrimage center. The occupation there may have continued, with probable gaps, until the twelfth century.[18]

The historical research on the sixth-century Petra has been particularly enhanced by the discovery of the Petra Papyri—the largest corpus of written sources ever found in Jordan. This archive of carbonized Greek documents was found in the Petra church complex.[19] The documents belong to an extended family, and concern the possession, disposition and acquisition of real estate, including contracts, loans, settlements of disputes, receipts of taxes, divisions, inheritance and registrations of properties, mortgage, and marriage contracts. The dated documents cover the time-span from A.D. 528 (or earlier, most probably 513) to A.D. 592.

ANALYSIS

The most important conclusion derived from the recent archaeological work and the Petra texts is that the city continued its existence beyond the sixth century. The administration, including tax-collecting, remained active throughout the sixth century, although probably as a transformed organization, elsewhere defined as a "post-curial government," dominated by the local clergy and landowners.[20] The Petra papyri never mention a boule of Petra or its bouleutai.[21] The politeuomenoi occur in the texts, often assisting in the registration of landed property, but it is uncertain whether these are the members of the curial order, or the actual magistrates of a still existent boule.[22] The tax collectors and officials (Êpodektai) in the land-tax office in Petra, judging from their Flavius designation, belong to the upper-class possessores, which may indicate the shift of fiscal and legal responsibilities from the imperial administration to local wealthy landowners.[23] The increased importance of the Church in non-ecclesiastical affairs is reflected by the common occurrence of the church officials, such as bishops, archdeacons, and presbyters in the Petra texts. The settlements out of court, which appear to be common in Petra, are usually cemented by taking sacred oaths in the church.

It is also apparent that Petra remained under the control of the central government, as exemplified by the military presence in the Petra area during the sixth century. The tax-system in the Petra texts included annona militaris exemplified by special taxes (roga)[24] for the army provision. The presence of regular army personnel, limitanei rather than foederati, is attested in Kastron Zadacathon near Petra. This effectively questions previous suggestions that by the sixth century most of the military garrisons along the so-called "Limes Arabicus" had been abandoned,[25] and the administrative-military control over southern Jordan had been relinquished to the Arab phylarchs who commanded forces of foederati, such as the Ghassanids.[26] However, the Ghassanids are also present in the Petra text, through the appearance of Abu Karib ibn Jabala, the phylarch of Palaestina Tertia and a leader of foederati.

The Petra texts present a prosperous, although highly selective, image of the economic standing of some of Petra's citizens, since they are all wealthy landowners. Churches and charitable institutions are mentioned in Petra, but not public institutions. A pious donation to a religious institution is expressed in the will of one individual, thus confirming the suspected pattern of private generosity, but no indication of private filotimia for civic purpose is preserved. An example of this new attitude would be the monumental Petra church, which stands out among impoverished buildings in post-363 Petra, most probably financed through private donations administered by ecclesiastic authority. The general lack of enthusiasm for financing civic maintenance works or embellishment by the higher classes of Petra was probably similar to the situation in other cities.[27] This does not necessarily imply a communal poverty, but rather a selective financial commitment and an attitude toward civic duties much changed from the Roman period. Wherever activities are more ostentatious, they are redirected toward goals more transcendental and considered more worthy, as exemplified by the church construction.

The most tangible indication of the urban transformation of Petra from the flourishing international metropolis into a stagnant provincial town is the appearance of the city center in the sixth century A.D. While the authors of the Petra Papyri conducted successful business, the center of Petra hardly resembled the orderliness and aesthetics of the Nabataean-Roman metropolis. Undoubtedly, when the Petra church was built, remodeled and frequented, some major architectural landmarks of Petra (Temple of the Winged Lions, the Qasr el-Bint Temple, the Great Southern Temple, the Colonnaded Street, and the theater), either lay in ruins, following the A.D. 363 disaster, or were only hastily or partially restored. Admittedly, some of these structures were pagan temples, thus of interest to the Christian Petraeans, yet, in some cases, no attempt was even made to clear the ruins.[28] Sixth-century Petra was a fortified settlement—a typical feature for Late Antique cities—with walls made of reused material, but still enclosing a considerable space.[29] Within this enclosure, large parts of the city were already abandoned, especially the central-south area. The Colonnaded Street might have already lost a part of its portico, and some shops were already abandoned. Simple structures built upon the sidewalk and encroaching even on the street itself—an ancestor of a Middle Eastern suq—had been constructed in the fifth or sixth century.[30] The inadequate restoration of the anti–flash flood installations, following their damage in 363, caused the growing deposition of alluvial material in the city center.[31] However, in the northern part of Petra, between the church with the mosaic floors and the Ridge Church, also recently excavated,[32] the occupation continued and new structures were built, often of reused material.

The emergent image of Late Antique Petra is similar to many late Byzantine cities in the Middle East. Although it should not convey an instantaneous thought of the city's total decline, it implies an increased material deterioration, and signals profound changes in the nature of urban life, which would have continued into the Early Islamic period. This pattern of urbanism, defined elsewhere as a transformation from "polis to madina," had been underway well before the conquests of the seventh century.[33] Late Antique urban landscape displays substantial differences compared with its Classical predecessor. Churches are often surrounded by ruins and rubble. Secondary walls and shops often encroach upon public spaces.[34] Buildings and spaces are abandoned or remodeled to serve commercial or industrial utilitarian purposes. The symmetry and the grid-plan of city centers are often retained, but the expanding suburbs represent much more spontaneous development into networks of small and irregular streets. In short, a practical approach to urban existence and extreme pragmatism in solving problems of urban expansion and functioning take over from the classical aesthetics and orderliness. In this respect, Late Antique Petra is no different than late sixth-century Scythopolis or Gerasa.[35]

Little is known about the economic conditions of Petra in the Byzantine period, but these would certainly have been less favorable than in the times when Petra was a major trading emporium. The fourth-century Expositio Totius Mundi, while presenting the economic wealth of Syro-Palestinian cities derived from trade and industry, does not mention Petra at all. Suggestions that the international long-distance trade in spices and aromatics continued overland from South Arabia to Palestine and Syria are anachronistic for the Byzantine period.[36] There is no indication that Petra benefited from the Red Sea–maritime trade.[37] The city is never mentioned in accounts related to interregional trade, including the Meccan network and its reflection in pre- and early-Islamic tradition. The Petra Papyri do not refer to any form of commerce, local or international. Fortunately, the symbiotic relationship between Petra and its rural hinterland is better known through the Petra texts. The hinterland features villages, gardens, vineyards, seed land, and agricultural installations. The source of landowners' income included the land produce (wine, grain, fruit), the lease of landed property, and the rental of housing. Some families possessed substantial land holdings. Compulsory farming is also, as in Egypt, attested in the texts. The Church appears as landowner, leasing out its land through permanent leases. Unfortunately, the hierarchy and structure of landownership is unknown, and the information on taxes paid by landlords is fragmentary. With the exception of an abandoned village near Petra, the overall picture conveys the relative prosperity of the agrarian economy in the area. Yet, the economic standing of some of the Petra's citizens should not be equated with the general state of the economic affairs of Petra as an urban center.

Although Christian pilgrimages to the Mountain of Aaron are not recorded, the recent excavations there would support such a proposition. The pilgrim traffic would generate donations to ecclesiastical foundations, and produce additional income for Petra, by supporting local market economy and services. The continuing of market-oriented economy should be partially reflected in coin distribution. Indicative of the situation is the chronological pattern of coins recovered from the Petra church area. Out of 239 identifiable coins, the fourth century is represented by 92 coins (38%), the later fourth/fifth century by 38 coins (16%), the fifth century by 9 (4%), and the sixth by 58 (24%) with only one (0.4%) coin dated to the post–sixth century period. Out of 190 identifiable coins found by the Roman Street in Petra Project, 52 (= 27%) are definitely post-363.[38] This should imply that the commercial activities in the street area had, at least partially, recovered from 363 disaster. However, only two coins from there can be dated to the sixth century.

DISCUSSION

Although the currently available archaeological evidence extends the continuity of settled life in Petra well into the seventh century, the latest historical information concerns Athenogenes, the Bishop of Petra at the turn of the sixth century (John Moschus CXXVII, 1865: 2987-88; CXXVIII, 1865: 2991-92). This disappearance of Petra from the records has generally discouraged the scholars from speculation on the later periods there. Thus, Petra is omitted from the scholarly debate concerning the differential survival of cities at the twilight of Antiquity, characterized by chaotic socioeconomic conditions, further affected by invasions, natural disasters, collapse of political entities, and appearance of new states between the fifth and eighth century.[39] The centrality of city as the physical entity and socioeconomic institution, its survival, and its role in the departing world of Antiquity and the emerging complexity of early Middle Ages is hardly accidental. The fabric of Classical Antiquity was an urban structure, with the city being the primary unit that determined and encompassed the sociopolitical and economic relationships.[40] Hence, the fate of cities in the Late Antiquity transition is of capital importance in understanding the process of change from the agglomeration of poleis of the Roman empire to the administratively centralized network of village economies of the Byzantine state.[41]

The "urban catastrophe" of the seventh century, associated with Persian, Arab, Avar, and Slav invasions in the Byzantine East and the Balkans respectively, has been long postulated. That was preceded by the gradual sociopolitical decline and economic stagnation of cities in the fifth-sixth centuries, and followed by a virtual "Dark Age" of the eighth century. While accepting the general ramification, opinion is divided with regard to the degree and nature of the survival of urbanism.[42] Some scholars point to the disappearance of the polis during the fifth-seventh centuries, indicated by the loss of fiscal and economic autonomy of the cities in favor of imperial administration, and resulting in physical deterioration of the cities and their general impoverishment.[43] This, on occasions, could have led either to an abandonment of the city and the ruralization of the region, or to the transformation from a classical polis into a totally new form, deprived of classical landmarks and institutions, be it a Greek kastron, or Islamic madina.[44] The invasions and disasters were the final blows to ancient polis, which already had lost its vitality and ability to recover or rebuild its infrastructure.[45] This approach emphasizes the dominance of Christian ideology and new elites, and their impact on attendant municipal institutions, economy, and perception of life, all distant from their Classical predecessor.[46] An alternative view emphasizes the linkages of Byzantine society with its classical predecessors and the continuity of antique culture in its new, Christian attire. The polis did not survive intact through the violence of Late Antiquity, but no sudden disruption of urban life is proposed; rather, a relatively late change.[47] Phenomena considered otherwise as negative, such as the decline of urban magistracies or confiscation of civic lands, are understood here as necessary institutional and economic rearrangements, which, in fact, revitalized the cities affected by the real crisis of the third and fourth centuries.[48]

The inevitable gap between these approaches is closed by the concept of transformation or urban change, which emphasizes neither discontinuity nor continuity. The overall fate of the cities was the result of gradually changed patterns of political, social and economic relationships—a process that had already begun in the third or fourth century and concluded in the seventh.[49] The appearance, function, and attendant relationships of post-classical cities considerably differed from their predecessors; the original polis had indeed disappeared, but the continuity of the settlement and tradition remained throughout the fifth to eighth centuries. This view is reinforced by the new archaeological data from the Middle East, which support the survival of the urbanism during the "Dark Age," although in a clearly altered pattern.[50]

For example, the previously postulated total decline and frequent abandonment of cities, as associated with the Persian invasions and the Islamic conquest in the Near East, cannot stand closer scrutiny.[51] Yet, while some cities survived the political upheaval of the seventh century and continued in a more or less changed political-economic form, other old urban centers rapidly declined and even disappeared during that century or later.[52] For example, the administrative changes initiated by the Umayyad rulers in the Middle East must have had a deep impact on the fate of cities. The Byzantine administrative districts were soon reduced by almost two-thirds.[53] This centralization and limitation of the focal points of local power would have favored the position of some cities versus the others. From the economic standpoint, the Islamic conquest would have temporarily disrupted patterns of commerce, which linked the inland cities with the Mediterranean littoral and beyond, but that factor would have primarily affected the coastal cities. On the other hand, an increased interregional commerce between inland cities and rural or nomadic populations of Arabia is noticeable already in the later sixth century (vide Meccan trade).[54] The cities of northern and central Jordan, (Pella, Madaba, or Umm ar Rasas) which benefited from that trade, continued in prosperity during the seventh century and later. Since the rural countryside fared well under the Umayyads, the state of market-oriented economy would have become a major factor determining the survival of an urban center. As a gateway of exchange with the countryside and other regions, the city would have attracted goods, industrial and artistic production, and provided sufficient luxuries for the élites to entice them to remain urban.[55]

What was the position of Petra in the new political and economic reality is virtually unknown. Since the city was never mentioned in the texts, it was obviously of no political importance to the Umayyads. The administrative capital of the district of al-Shara in Southern Jordan had been established at nearby Adhruh (Udhruh).[56] Petra's status in the ecclesiastical hierarchy had been substantially diminished after the metropolitan see was transferred to al-Rabba, shortly after the conquest.[57] But it remains inexplicable why Petra would not continue as an important interregional market, despite its rich countryside. Notable is the survival of the major settlements in the Petra area—Udhruh and Humeima—which although smaller than Petra, certainly thrived under the Umayyads, both in political and economic capacity.[58]

In this context, the review of archaeologically discerned settlement hierarchy in the Petra area is instructive.[59] During the Nabataean-Roman period, the hierarchy was well-developed: from the major urban center (Petra), through smaller towns and villages, down to numerous hamlets and farms. This pattern appears radically changed during the Early Islamic period. What survived were smaller towns such as Udhruh, Humeima, Kastron Zadacathon, and large "concentrated" villages such as Wadi Musa, Dhaha, Basta, or Jabal al-Tahuna,[60] all surrounded by large agricultural fields. Characteristically, the highest level (Petra) and lowest level settlements (hamlets, farmsteads) either declined or disappeared. The smaller average size and less accentuated hierarchy among outlying settlements would imply only a minimal development of the administrative and economic structures that are concomitants of centralized control. Undoubtedly, changes in settlement patterns reflect changes in subsistence strategies, from international commercial activities supported by a well-developed agricultural base and an extensive trade-related infrastructure, into lower level economics of increasingly regionalized and fairly isolated large farming communities based upon agriculture and local exchange.

Despite the recent expansion of data on the Byzantine Petra, the problem of the city's decline and disappearance is not easily solved. The emergent image of the sixth century Petra is precisely that of a typical provincial urban center. However, the pre–sixth-century information on the Early Byzantine transformation is critically missing, and the post–sixth century continues to be shrouded in uncertainty. Our strongest data then reflect the point in Petra's history in which the transformation is in full progress, and not when and why it began or how it ended.[61]

Undoubtedly, Petra had fallen victim to various trends, patterns, and changes that affected the Middle East in the Roman-Byzantine periods. The loss of the privileged status in the international trade would have had an impact by the end of the third century A.D. The postulated "urban change" in the Byzantine period, while more or less typical elsewhere, is more dramatic in Petra because of the already existent economic stagnation of the city, although not necessarily of its inhabitants. At the turn of the sixth century, Petra lived in a sort of provincial "splendid isolation," neither representing a real decline, nor showing signs of economic vitality. The Petra Papyri display an almost sentimental attachment to the past, through the repetition in purely local documents of impressive honorifics, which, by that time, did not mean much, yet promoted the continuity of the polis status.[62] But only ca. forty years afterwards, the city did not warrant a mention in the Muslim conquest account; certainly not an oversight. Jerusalem, Gaza, Elusa, Aila, Scythopolis, Gerasa, Pella, and Philadelphia have all been mentioned either in the conquest narratives or in the later records. The "Dark Age" of the Persian occupation of the Near East in the decades directly prior to the Muslim conquest may be relevant here. Perhaps, from the political standpoint, the Umayyads preferred less Romanized towns such as Udhruh or Humeima. At any rate, if a "decline"—rapid descent toward greater insignificance in sociopolitical and economic affairs—is a preferred term, it must have characterized the situation of Petra in the Early Islamic period.

This rapid decline is particularly dramatic when compared against the relative prosperity and economic stability not only of Palestine during the Umayyad period,[63] but also of Petra's own countryside, exemplified by the continuity at Udhruh or Humeima. While other towns readjusted to the new political situation, and economically gained from new trading patterns, Petra must have reached a stage of political-economic stagnation in which the disappearance of its urban status became inevitable. Already in the sixth century, the attention of the wealthy class seems to have been directed toward their extensive land holdings, rural residences, and farmhouses. Country life became more comfortable and secure, as the city could hardly provide incentives for staying on, such as market and business opportunities, or political promotion. With the reduced status in the ecclesiastical hierarchy, and the lost political status, the city had little to offer to justify the preservation of its urban status and appearance. As the new excavations extend occupation in the Petra Valley into the seventh century, and possibly beyond, no dramatic abandonment of the settlement should be envisaged. However, Petra as a polis and an urban center probably disappeared sometime in the later seventh century.

ABBREVIATIONS

ACO	Acta Conciliorum Oecumenicorum
ACOR News	American Center of Oriental Research Newsletter.
ADAJ	Annual of the Department of Antiquities of Jordan
BASOR	Bulletin of the American Schools of Oriental Research
BF	Byzantinische Forschungen
BSOAS	Bulletin of the School of Oriental and African Studies
BZ	Byzantinische Zeitschrift
DOP	Dumbarton Oaks Papers
IEJ	Israel Exploration Journal
JJP	The Journal of Juristic Papyrology
JRA	Journal of Roman Archaeology
JRS	Journal of Roman Studies
ODB	The Oxford Dictionary of Byzantium
PG	Patrologia Graeca
PO	Patrologia Orientalis

SHAJ	Studies in the History and Archaeology of Jordan
ZPE	Zeitschrift für Papyrologie und Epigraphik

BIBLIOGRAPHICAL LISTINGS

Abrahamse, D. Z. 1967. "Hagiographic Sources for Byzantine Cities, 500–900 a.d." Ph.D. Dissertation, University of Michigan. Ann Arbor.

'Amr, Kh., A. al-Momani, S. Farajat, and H. Falahat. 1998. "Archaeological Survey of the Wadi Musa Water Supply and Wastewater Project Area." *ADAJ* XLII.

Barnish, S. J. B. 1989. "The Transformation of Classical Cities and the Pirenne Debate." *JRA* 2:385–401.

Ball, W., J. Bowsher, I. Kehrberg, A. Walmsley, and P. Watson. 1986. "The North Decumanus and North Tetrapylon at Jerash." In *Jerash Archaeological Project 1981–1983*, edited by I. Fawzi Zayadine, 351–411. Amman: Department of Antiquities.

Bikai, Patricia M. 1996. "The Ridge Church at Petra." *ADAJ* 40:481–86.

Bikai, Pierre M. 1995. "Update on the Scrolls." *ACOR Newsletter* 7(2):11.

———. 1996. "Petra Church Project, Petra Papyri." *ADAJ* 40:487–89.

Bouras, Ch. 1981. "City and Village: Urban Design and Architecture." *Jahrbuch der Österreichischen Byzantinistik*, 611–53.

Bowersock, G. W. 1982. Review of "A. Spijkerman, *The Coins of the Decapolis and the Provincia Arabia*." *JRS* 72:197–98.

———. 1983. *Roman Arabia*. Cambridge, Mass.

Brandes, W. 1988. "Die byzantinische Stadt Kleinasiens im 7. und 8. Jahrhundert - ein Forschungsbericht." *Klio* 70:176–208.

Brock, S. 1977. "A Letter Attributed to Cyril of Jerusalem on the Rebuilding of the Temple." *BSOAS* 40 (2):267–86.

Brünnow R., and Domaszewski, A. von. 1909. *Die Provincia Arabia III*. Strassburg.

Cameron, Averil. 1993. *The Mediterranean World in Late Antiquity, AD 395–600*. London.

———. 1997 "Hellenism and the Emergence of Islam." DIALOGOS. *Hellenic Studies Review* 4:4–18.

Cappel, A.J. 1991. Roga. In *ODB*, p. 1801.

Claude, D. 1969. D*ie byzantinische Stadt im 6. Jahrhundert*. München.

Codex Theodosianus. 1905. *Theodosiani Libri XVI cum Constitutionibus Sirmondianis. Vol I Pars Posterior*. Edited by Th. Mommsen and P. Krueger. Berlin.

Dagron, G. 1977. Le Christianisme dans la ville byzantine. *DOP* 31:3–25.

Daniel, R. 1996. "The Petra Papyri in Historical Perspective: The Dating Formulas." *ACOR Newsletter* 8(2):1–3.

———. 1998. "Toponomastic Mal in P. Nessana 22 and P. Petra Inv. 10 (Papyrus Petra Khaled & Suha Shoman)." *ZPE* 122:195–96.

Daniel, R., and T. Gagos. 1996. "Update on the Petra Papyri." *ACOR Newsletter* 8(1):11.

Di Segni, L. 1995. "The Involvement of Local, Municipal and Provincial Authorities in

Urban Building in Late Antique Palestine and Arabia." In *The Roman and Byzantine Near East: Some Recent Archaeological Research*, edited by J. Humphrey, 312–32. *JRA* Supplementary Series 14.

Epiphanius. 1980. Panarion haer. 34–64. K. Holl and J. Dummer. Berlin.

Expositio Totius Mundi et Gentium. 1966. Expositio Totius Mundi et Gentium, edited and trans. by J. Rougé. Sources Chrétiennes, No. 124. Série Annexe de Textes non Chrétiens. Paris: Editions du Cerf.

Fiema, Z. T. 1991. "Economics, Administration and Demography of Late Roman and Byzantine Southern Transjordan." Ph.D. Dissertation, University of Utah. Salt Lake City.

———. 1994. "Jordanie: une eglise byzantin a Petra." *Archaeologia* 302:26–35.

———. 1998. "The 1997 Roman Street in Petra Project—A Preliminary Report." *ADAJ* XLII.

———. forth.a. "Conclusions. To appear in the Petra Church Project."

———. forth.b "Reconstructing the Culture History of the Petra Church—The Data and Phasing." To appear in the Petra Church Project.

Fiema, Z.T., L. Koenen, and F. Zayadine. 1997. "Petra Romana, Byzantina et Islamica." Pp. 145–160 in Petra. *Antike Felsstadt zwischen Arabischer Tradition und Griechischer Norm*, edited by T. Weber and R. Wenning. Mainz.

Fiema, Z.T., R. Schick, and Kh. 'Amr. 1995. "The Petra Church Project 1992–1994." In *The Roman and Byzantine Near East: Some Recent Archaeological Research*, edited by J. Humphrey, 289–303. *JRA* Supplementary Series, 14.

Frösén, Jaakko, and Zbigniew T. Fiema. 1994. "The Petra Papyri." *ACOR Newsletter* 6(2):1–3.

Frösén, J., Z. T. Fiema, H. Haggrén, K. Koistinen, M. Lavento, and G. L. Peterman. 1998. "The Finnish Jabal Haroun Project—A Preliminary Report on the 1997 Season." *ADAJ* XLII.

Frösén, Jaakko, Z. T. Fiema, M. Lavento, and K. Koistinen. Forth. "The 1998 Finnish Jabal Haroun Project—A Preliminary Report." To appear in *ADAJ*.

Frances, E. 1966. "La ville byzantine et la monnaie aux VIIe-VIIIe siècles." *ByzantinoBulgarica* 2:3–14.

Gagos, T. 1997. "Update of the Scrolls." *ACOR Newsletter* 9(1):11–12.

Gascou, J. 1985. "Les grandes domains, la cité et l'état en Égypte byzantine." *Travaux et Mémoires* 9:1–90.

Gawlikowski, M. 1997. "The Oriental City and the Advent of Islam." In *Die Orientalische Stadt: Kontinuität, Wandel, Bruch*, edited by G. Wilhelm, 339–50. Saarbrücken.

Geremek, H. 1981. "Les politeuomenoi égyptiens sont-ils identique aux bouleutai?" *Anagennesis* 1(2):231–47.

———. 1990. "Sur la question des boulai dans les villes égyptiennes aux Ve-VIIe siècles." *JJP* 20: 47–54.

Graf, D. F. 1995a. "The Via Nova Traiana in Arabia Petraea." In *The Roman and Byzantine Near East: Some Recent Archaeological Research*, edited by J. Humphrey, 241–65. JRA Supplementary Series 14.

———. 1995b. "The Via Militaris and the Limes Arabicus." In *Roman Frontier Studies 1995. Proceedings of the XVIth International Congress of Roman Frontier Studies*, edited by

W. Groenman-van Waateringe, B. L. van Beek, W. J. H. Willems, and S. L. Wynia. Oxford.

Haldon, J. F. 1985. "Some Considerations on Byzantine Society and Economy in the Seventh Century." *BF* 10:75–112.

———. 1990. *Byzantium in the Seventh Century. The Transformation of a Culture.* Cambridge.

Hierocles. 1939. *Le Synekdemos d'Hierokles et l'Opuscule geographique de Georges de Chypre,* edited by E. Honigmann. Corpus Bruxellense Historiae Byzantinae. Forma Imperii Byzantini—Fasciculus I. Bruxelles.

John of Ephesus. 1923. *Lives of the Eastern Saints.* Syriac text edited and translated by E.W. Books. PO, vol. 17. Paris.

John Malalas. 1986. *The Chronicle of John Malalas,* trans. by E. Jeffreys, M. Jeffreys and R. Scott. Melbourne: Australian Association for Byzantine Studies.

John Moschus. 1865. Pratum Spirituale. PG LXXXVII/3, edited by J.-P. Migne. Paris.

John, Bishop of Nikiu. 1916. *The Chronicle of John, Bishop of Nikiu,* translated from Zotenberg's Ethiopic Text by R.H. Charles. London: Williams and Northgate.

Johnson, D. J. 1987. "Nabataean Trade: Intensification and Culture Change." Ph.D. Diss., University of Utah, Salt Lake City.

Jones, A. H. M. 1964. *The Later Roman Empire, 284–602. A Social, Economic and Administrative Survey.* Norman.

Joukowsky, Martha Sharp. 1998. "Brown University 1997 Excavations at the Petra Great Temple." *ADAJ* 42.

Kaegi, W. E. 1985. "The Annona Militaris in the Early Seventh Century." *Byzantina* 13(1):591–96.

Kaimio, M. 1996. "Update on the Scrolls." *ACOR Newsletter* 8(2):4.

Kazhdan, A., and Cutler, A. 1982. "Continuity and Discontinuity in Byzantine History." *Byzantion* 52:429–70.

Kennedy, H. 1985a. "From Polis to Medina: Urban Change in Late Antique and Early Medieval Syria." *Past and Present* 106:3–27.

———. 1985b. "The Last Century of Byzantine Syria: A Reinterpretation." *BF* 10:141–85.

———. 1986. "The Towns of Bilad al-Sham and the Arab Conquest." In *Proceedings of the Symposium on Bilad al-Sham during the Byzantine Period 2,* edited by M.A. Bakhit and M. Asfour. Amman.

———. 1989. "Change and Continuity in Syria and Palestine at the Time of the Moslem Conquest." *Aram* 1(2):258–67.

———. 1992. "Antioch: From Byzantium to Islam and Back Again. In *The City in Late Antiquity,* edited by John Rich. London & New York: Routledge.

Kirsten, E. 1958. *Die byzantinische Stadt. Berichte zum XI Internationalen Byzantinisten-Kongress.* München.

Kirkbride, D. 1960. "A Short Account of the Excavations at Petra in 1955–56." *ADAJ* 4-5:117–22.

Koenen, L. 1995. "Phoenix from the Ashes: Update on the Petra Papyri." *ACOR Newsletter* 7(1):9–10.

———.1996a. "The Phoenix from the Ashes: The Burnt Archive from Petra." *Michigan*

Quarterly Review 35:513–31.

———. 1996b. "The Carbonized Archive from Petra." *JRA* 9:177–88.

Kolb, B. 1996. "Die Spätrömische Bauten." In *Petra. Ez Zantur I. Ergebnisse des Schweizerisch-Liechtensteinischen Ausgrabungen 1988–1992*, ed. A. Bignasca, N. Desse-Berset, R. Fellmann Brogli, R. Glutz, S. Karg, D. Keller, B. Kolb, Ch. Kramar, M. Peter, S.G. Schmid, Ch. Schneider, R. A. Stucky, J. Studer, I. Zanoni. Terra Archaeologica II. Mainz.

Kraeling, Carl H. 1938. *Gerasa. City of the Decapolis*. New Haven: American Schools of Oriental Research

Laniado, A. 1997. "Bouleutai et politeuomenoi." *Chronique d'Egypte* 72 (fasc 143): pp. 130–44.

Liebeschuetz, W. 1992. "The End of the Ancient City." In *The City in Late Antiquity*, edited by John Rich, 1–9. London and New York.

———. 1996. "Civic Finance in the Byzantine Period: The Laws and Egypt." *BZ* 89(2):389–408.

Mansi, J. D. 1762. *Sacrorum Conciliorum Nova et Amplissima Collectio. Vol VIII*, 492–536. Florence.

Mayerson, Ph. 1984. "'Palaestina' vs. 'Arabia' in the Byzantine Sources." *ZPE* 56:223–30.

———. 1987. "Libanius and the Administration of Palestine." *ZPE* 69:251–60.

———. 1994. "Rouzikon and Rogë in the Post-Conquest Papyri." *ZPE* 100:126–28.

Millar, F. 1993. *The Roman Near East, 31 b.c.-a.d.337*. London and Cambridge, Mass.

Nau, F. 1927. "Deux épisodes de l'histoire juive sous Théodose II (423 et 438) d'après la vie de Barsauma le Syrien." *Revue des Etudes Juives* 83:184–206.

Notitia Dignitatum. 1876. *Notitia Dignitatum*, ed. O. Seeck. Berlin.

Oleson, J. P., Kh. 'Amr, R. M. Foote, and R. Schick. 1995. "Preliminary Report of the Humayma Excavation Project, 1993." *ADAJ* 39:317–54.

Ostrogorsky, G. 1959. "Byzantine Cities in the Early Middle Ages." *DOP* 13:45–66.

Ovadiah, Asher. 1993. "Early Churches." In *The New Encyclopedia of Archaeological Excavations in the Holy Land*, edited by E. Stern, A. Lewinson-Gilboa, J. Aviram, 305–9. Jerusalem: The Israel Exploration Society, Carta.

Parker, S. Thomas. 1986. *Romans and Saracens: A History of the Arabian Frontier*. Philadelphia.

Parr, P. 1986. "The Last Days of Petra." In *Proceedings of the Symposium on Bilad al-Sham during the Byzantine Period 2*, edited by M.A. Bakhit and M. Asfour, 182–205. Amman.

Peterman, G. O., and R. Schick. 1996. "The Monastery of Saint Aaron." *ADAJ* 40:473–80.

Petit, P. 1955. *Libanius et la vie municipale à Antioche au IVe siècle après J.-C.* Paris.

Russell, J. 1986. "Transformations in Early Byzantine Urban Life: The Contribution and Limitations of Archaeological Evidence." In *The 17th International Byzantine Congress, Washington, D.C. Major Papers*, 137–54. New York.

Russell, K. W. 1980. "The Earthquake of May 19, a.d. 363." *BASOR* 238:47–64.

———. 1985. "The Earthquake Chronology of Palestine and Northwest Arabia from the 2nd through the Mid-8th Century A.D." *BASOR* 260:37–59.

Saradi-Mendelovici, H. 1988. "The Demise of the Ancient City and the Emergence of the

Medieval City in the Eastern Roman Empire." *Echos du Monde Classique/Classical Views* XXXII, n.s. 7; pp. 365–401.

———. 1994. "The Dissolution of the Urban Space in the Early Byzantine Centuries: The Evidence of the Imperial Legislation." In Summeikta. Tomos Enatos, 295–308. MNMH D. ZAKUYHNOU.

Schick, Robert. 1994. "The Settlement Pattern of Southern Jordan: The Nature of the Evidence." In *The Byzantine and Early Islamic Near East II*, edited by G.R.D. King and Averil Cameron, 133–54. Princeton: The Darwin Press.

———. 1998. "Palestine in the Early Islamic Period: Luxuriant Legacy." *Near Eastern Archaeology* 61(2):74–108.

Schick, R., Z.T. Fiema, and Kh. 'Amr. 1993. "The Petra Church Project, 1992–93." *ADAJ* 37:55–66.

Schieffer, R. 1982. "Index Generalis Tomorum I-IIII." Pars Secunda. *Index Prosopographicus.* [ACO., Tomus IV, Volumen III, edited by E. Schwartz and J. Straub]. Berlin.

Schwartz, E. 1940. *Collectio Sabbaitica. ACO., Tomus III.* Berlin.

Shahid, I. 1995. *Byzantium and the Arabs in the Sixth Century 1.1 and 2.* Washington, D.C.

Sozomenus. 1960. *Kirchengeschichte*, edited by J. Bidez and G. Ch. Hansen. Berlin.

Spieser, J.-M. 1989. "L'évolution de la ville byzantine de ;'époque paléochrétienne à l'iconoclasme." In *Hommes et richesses dans l'Empire byzantin. Tome I. IVe-VIIe siècle*, 97–106. Paris.

Spijkerman, A. 1978. *The Coins of the Decapolis and Provincia Arabia.* Jerusalem.

Tholbecq, L. In Press. "The Hinterland of Petra from the Edomite to the Islamic Periods: The Jabal Shara Survey (1996–1997)." To appear in the *Proceedings of the xx Conference on the History and Archaeology of Jordan.*

Tsafrir, Y. 1986. "The Transfer of the Negev, Sinai and Southern Transjordan from Arabia to Palaestina." *IEJ* 36(1–2):77–86.

Tsafrir Y., and G. Foerster. 1994. "From Scythopolis to Baysan—Changing Concepts of Urbanism." In *The Byzantine and Early Islamic Near East 2*, edited by G.R.D. King and Averil Cameron, 95–116. Princeton.

Vavrínek, V. 1985. "The Eastern Roman Empire or Early Byzantium? A Society in Transition." In *From Late Antiquity to Early Byzantium. Proceedings of the Byzantinological Symposium in the 16th International Eirene Conference*, edited by V. Vavrínek, 9–20. Praha.

Walmsley, A. 1992a. "Fihl (Pella) and the Cities of North Jordan during the Umayyad and Abbasid Periods." In *SHAJ* 4:377–84. Amman.

———. 1992b. "Vestiges of the Decapolis in North Jordan during the Late Antique and Early Islamic Periods." *Aram* 4(1 & 2):343–55.

———. 1996. "Byzantine Palestine and Arabia: Urban Properity in Late Antiquity." In *Towns in Transition*, edited by N. Christie and S. T. Loseby, 126–58. Aldershot.

Weber, T., and R. Wenning, eds. 1997. *Petra. Antike Felsstadt zwischen Arabischer Tradition und Griechischer Norm.* Mainz

Whittow, M. 1990. "Ruling the Late Roman and Byzantine City: A Continuous History." *Past and Present* 129:3–29.

Zacharias of Mitylene. 1899. *The Syriac Chronicle Known as that of Zacharias of Mitylene*, trans. F. J. Hamilton and E. W. Brooks. London.

Zayadine, Fawzi. 1971. "Deux Inscriptions Grecques de Rabbat Moab (Areopolis)." *ADAJ* 16:71–76.

NOTES

1. For the recent treatment of Petra and the Nabataeans, see Weber and Wenning 1997.
2. As in the Petra Papyri (see note 20 below). Some honorifics are evidenced by the city coins (Spijkerman 1978: 218, 220–21, 236–37), and a monumental inscription of a.d.114 (Bowersock 1982: 198; 1983: 84–85n. 28).
3. Millar 1993: 421.
4. Johnson 1987: 64, 66.
5. For full presentation, see Fiema 1991, and Fiema, Koenen and Zayadine 1997.
6. For these see Brünnow and Domaszewski 1909: 273–80; Mayerson 1984, 1987; Tsafrir 1986; and Fiema 1991: 128–33.
7. See also the story of the Monk Bar Sauma at Petra (Nau 1927: 186–87).
8. As reported in Harvard Syriac 99 (Brock 1977); see also Russell 1980.
9. Mansi 1762: 1173; Schwartz 1940: 188; Schieffer 1982: 462n. 49.
10. Russell 1985: 45; Fiema 1991: 214–17.
11. See, Schick, Fiema, and 'Amr 1993; Fiema 1994; and Fiema, Schick, and 'Amr 1995. These early reports attributed the end of the church's occupation to the earthquake of a.d. 551. For the most recent view and discussion, see Fiema, forth b. The impact of the 551 earthquake on Petra, as implied in previous publications, is now seriously contested (Fiema, forth a).
12. Fiema 1998.
13. Kolb 1996: 51, 89.
14. Joukowsky 1998, Phases V and VI.
15. I am thankful to Daniel Keller, University of Basel, for this still unpublished information.
16. 'Amr et al. 1998; and Tholbecq, forth. I am thankful to both authors who have recently surveyed in the Petra area, for their comments and preliminary reports.
17. See Peterman and Schick 1996, for references and pre-excavation description.
18. Frösén, Fiema et al. 1998, and forth.
19. All information here which concerns the Petra Papyri derives from the published material. To date, the more extensive reports on the Petra Papyri include Koenen 1996a and 1996b, Bikai (Pierre) 1996, Fiema, Koenen and Zayadine 1997, and Daniel 1998. *ACOR Newsletter* features short articles by Frösén and Fiema 1994, Koenen 1995, Bikai 1995, Daniel and Gagos 1996, Daniel 1996, Kaimio 1996, and Gagos 1997. Short notes appeared in *AJA* 99, 1995 (by J. Frösén and Z.T. Fiema); 100, 1996 (by P. M. Bikai); 101/3, 1997 (by M. Kaimio and R. Daniel), and 102/3, 1998 (by T. Gagos). I am indebted

in my analysis to R. Daniel, J. Frösén, T. Gagos, L. Koenen, and M. Lehtinen for their comments and advices.

20. Liebeschuetz 1996: 390.
21. The presence of bouleutai may indicate the existence of city councils in Egypt, even in the sixth century (Geremek 1990: 53–54). Specific references to curiae in the East could have become increasingly rare in the sixth century as a consequence of decuriones not considering it worthwhile to mention their curial membership (Liebeschuetz 1992: 26–27).
22. Whether politeuomenoi are synonymous with bouleutai is debatable. For discussion, see Geremek 1981, Petit 1955: 30, and Laniado 1997: 141–42.
23. Perhaps similarly to Egypt, the local fiscal administration was increasingly assumed by oikoi—the great "houses" of local potentates? For that, see Gascou 1985 and Liebeschuetz 1996.
24. From rogai—the "issues" of footstuff for the soldiers (Jones 1964: 674). For roga as a cash payment, even in the early seventh century, see Cappel 1991: 1801, while the non-military context for roga is treated by Mayerson 1994: 128. For the survival of annona militaris, in the early seventh century, see Kaegi 1985.
25. Parker 1986: 149, 152–53, 158.
26. For the Ghassanid phylarchates, see Shahid 1995.
27. For specific comments, see Di Segni 1995; esp. 312, 329–32.
28. Ovadiah (1993: 308) assumes that it was not customary in Palestine to convert pagan temples into churches, but he mentions Christian tradition ruling that a ruined temple should be rebuilt as a church.
29. Parr 1986: 200, for details.
30. At any rate, presumably after the 363 earthquake (Parr 1986: 195–96; Kirkbride 1960: 119; Fiema 1998).
31. As evidenced in some shops along the Colonnaded Street (Fiema, 1998).
32. Bikai (Patricia) 1996.
33. For discussion, see Kennedy 1985a, 1989.
34. Gawlikowski (1997: 350) suggests that the actual trespassing of buildings into public space did not occur before the second half of the seventh century. At least in Petra, this process must have occurred earlier than that.
35. Tsafrir and Foerster 1994: 109–15, for Late Byzantine–Early Islamic Scythopolis; Kraeling 1938: 67–69, and Ball et al. 1986: 393 for the contemporary Jerash. General remarks are offered by Jones 1964: 736–37, and Cameron 1993: 159–162.
36. Kennedy 1989: 266–67.
37. See, Fiema 1991, chapter VIII.
38. The coins from both projects were read by J. Betlyon and H. Sokolov. The calculations were made by the author.
39. For discussion, see Barnish 1989; Brandes 1988; Claude 1969; Kazhdan and Cutler 1982, Kirsten 1958: 1–19; Liebeschuetz 1992; Saradi-Mendelovici 1988; Whittow 1990; all with extensive bibliographies
40. Kazhdan and Cutler 1982: 434–35.

41. Haldon 1985: 77.
42. See Vavrinek 1985 and Russell 1986: 137n. 3 for summaries of views.
43. E.g., Saradi-Mendelovici 1988; 1994: 300–7.
44. See Kirsten 1958: 19–34, for kastron, and Kennedy 1985a, for madina.
45. Kennedy 1985b: 181.
46. E.g., Saradi-Mendelovici 1988: 367–93; Dagron 1977; Frances 1966: 6, 9–10; Bouras 1981: 615–16, 638–40; Russell 1986: 138, 144.
47. E.g., Abrahamse 1967: 94, 331, 334; Cameron 1997; Ostrogorsky 1959.
48. Whittow 1990: 3, 8–9.
49. See, Haldon 1985: 85–92, Spieser 1989: 105–6, for further evaluation.
50. Walmsley 1996; Whittow 1990: 13–14, 21–29.
51. Walmsley 1992a; esp. 377–378; see also Haldon 1990: 93–93, for overview of opposing opinions.
52. Kennedy 1986; 1992: 196–97, and Haldon 1990: 102–14, for historical survey, and differential survival.
53. Walmsley 1992b: 345.
54. Kennedy 1989: 267.
55. Barnish 1989: 394.
56. Most convincingly identified with the town of Augustopolis in the Petra Papyri. Al-Ya'qubi mentions Adhruh as the capital of al-Shara region (Schick 1994: 144).
57. Zayadine 1971: 75–76.
58. For the summary of written sources concerning these towns in the Early Islamic period, see Schick 1994. For archaeological exploration at Humeima, see Oleson et al. (1995).
59. For presentation and a preliminary assessment, see Fiema 1992, although propositions concerning the Byzantine-Early Islamic periods need to be assessed in light of the most recent archaeological evidence.
60. See Graf 1995a and 1995b, for surveys in the Petra area.
61. For the ramifications of such situation see Kazhdan and Cutler 1992: 435–36.
62. In the hagiographic texts of the sixth to ninth centuries, polis is never confused with terms which mean a village, fortress or a camp (Abrahamse 1962: 346).
63. See Schick 1998, for discussion and extensive bibliography.

Town and Country

Women and Horses and Power and War

J. F. DRINKWATER

INTRODUCTION

This article was inspired by Hagith Sivan's evocative reconstruction of the warm relationship between Ausonius and his pupil, Paulinus of Nola, in those convivial days before the latter devoted himself to Christian asceticism. She pictures them both, resident in their country villas, reveling in their mutual correspondence:

> One can nearly visualize these two men lounging in their beautiful gardens on a pleasant evening, eating delicacies, drinking Bordeaux wine and reading aloud poetry.[1]

I have to admit that I found this image at first appealing, but then appalling, as it struck me what an extraordinarily precious pair these two must have been—hardly the sort to go drinking with after a hard day's work. I then fell to wondering what "ordinary people" (or rather, given the nature of our sources, "ordinary male landowners") talked about. My first working-title was, therefore, "Soccer, cricket, cars or women?" When something more sonorous and less politically incorrect was required, I borrowed a line from Rudyard Kipling's dramatic poem describing a meeting on India's North-West Frontier between an English intelligence officer, investigating possible Russian winter troop-movements into Afghanistan, and a native trader, at the height of the British Raj:

> We cleansed our beards of mutton-grease,
> We lay on the mats and were filled with peace,
> And the talk slid north and the talk slid south,
> With the sliding puffs of the hookah-mouth.
> Four things greater than all things are,
> Women and Horses and Power and War.
> We spake of them all, but the last the most,
> For I sought a word of a Russian post,
> Of a shifting promise, an unsheathed sword,
> And a grey-coat guard on the Helmund ford.[2]

In what follows, therefore, in pursuing thoughts of "women and horses and power and war" in the minds of the well-to-do, I hope to raise a range of questions about the nature of the "frontier" between "urban" and "rural" in Gaul in late antiquity. In particular, by emphasizing the presence and significance of non-intellectual, non-urban experiences and skills, I wish to demonstrate the need to treat the countryside on its own terms. For it appears to me that modern historians and archaeologists, taking their tone from the literary sources, still too frequently prioritize the city over the land, treating the latter as an adjunct to the former instead of a powerful socio-economic entity in its own right.

AUSONIUS AND THEON

In a letter written to Theon, a Gallic landowner of the Médoc, Ausonius gently mocks his rural lifestyle and draws attention to its dangers:

> Or with thy brother amid impenetrable thickets dost thou surround the wandering harts with mesh and feathers in a wide circle? Or dost thou urge on with shouts the foaming boar's career and lay wait for the monster? Yet I warn thee ever to avoid wielding thy spear at close quarters with a bolt-like foe. Take warning from thy brother, who pulls back his clothes displaying ugly scars near his privy parts, and bares his breech to show how awkwardly t'was pierced. Then to display his wounds he flits away to be admired by Gedippa and his friend Ursinus. . . .[3]

It is all too easy to miss the full force of this passage. Green, for example, comments on manuscript tradition and style, and offers help on a few words and allusions, but no more.[4] All the modern reader is likely to register is the closing burlesque of a rude rustic's baring his bottom in mixed company. The gravity of Ausonius' warning can be appreciated only after explanation of the risks of ancient boar-hunting. This is provided by Anderson, drawing on Xenophon's *Cynegeticus*.[5] Basically, the European wild boar is a very dangerous animal to dispatch armed only with a short hunting-spear. A major danger is the losing—through dropping, excessive penetration, or snapping—of this weapon, leaving the huntsman defenseless in the presence of a wound-maddened animal. If this occurs he should protect the soft parts of his belly and groin by falling on his face and laying a tight hold on any available ground vegetation to prevent the boar from turning him. However, he will then still probably have his back and sides gored by the animal's tusks, and his buttocks and possibly his anus and crotch torn by its sharp and powerful front trotters. This will be an agonizing and terrifying experience. (In terms of noise alone, for example, one can imagine the grunting and squealing of the boar, the huntsman's screams of pain and cries for help, and the encouraging shouts of his fellows and the yelping of their dogs as they crash through the undergrowth to his rescue.) However, the survivor of such an ordeal would be entitled to boast about it to his friends and, especially, his women friends: in a tough and violent world, still perilously close to nature, he will have proved his virility, and his justification (if still able) to breed.

This brings me to my first main point. Nowadays, no one takes exception to the characterization of the Roman world as predominantly rural.[6]

However, as in the case of Theon's brother and his boar, modern historians of that world still need to deploy an immense amount of historical imagination in order to appreciate precisely what the phrase signifies. We require this alien world to be explained to us. Ausonius did not: his references to it are humorous, but not ignorant. Though, as townsman, university professor, poet, courtier and magistrate of the Empire, one of the most sophisticated products of Greco-Roman civilization, he was still very close to the soil. He had no choice; the wealth and skills that maintained civilized city-life were all essentially rural. So, like the younger Pliny in Italy before him and Sidonius Apollinaris and his circle in Gaul a century or so later, Ausonius had to spend long periods of time in the country supervising the estates that fed his table and filled his purse.[7] As a result, for all his cultural sophistication and pretensions he knew, because he had to know, a great deal about rural activities. Most famously, of course, in his *De Herediolio* but also in his letter about his problems with his steward, Philo, he reveals himself knowledgeable about the theory and practice of estate-management;[8] and in both his private and public capacities, he shows himself very concerned about the state of the annual harvest.[9] Perhaps more illuminating, however, because closer to our own experience, we find him remarkably familiar with various types and qualities of horseflesh and wheeled conveyances.[10] Taken completely for granted, this is the ancient equivalent of the modern obsession with the motorcar, but centered firmly on the products and technology of the countryside, not the factory. The same close familiarity with the horse is found in Sidonius Apollinaris, together with a more surprising reminder of the place of rural skills in late antique society.[11] Success at the imperial court could sometimes turn on spontaneous composition of a polished phrase or verse.[12] However, in a completely different sort of contest Sidonius' friend, Consentius, must have drawn on all his considerable practical knowledge of horses and driving when, as a junior palatine official under the emperor Valentinian III, he had to compete in a dangerous chariot race.[13] Animal power and violence intruded into palace life.

In this respect it is significant that Ausonius' grumbles about town-life are essentially rural. His general complaints about the town's crowds, noise and narrow streets sound modern, but his specific examples—the fleeing pig, the mad dog, and the straining oxen—remind us how much the sights, sounds and smells of the countryside must equally have been part of the ancient city.[14] Settlements were small; through their gates or over their walls the country was always visible. My second proposition is, therefore, that in absolute terms the "frontier" between town and country was more mental than actual, and that Ausonius played up the difference because of his acute awareness of the proximity and power of the countryside. The land was essential and could be celebrated as fecund and even attractive; but it was also perilous and potentially brutalizing.[15] We return to Ausonius' complex, allusive, and elusive correspondence with Theon. It is clear that, despite Ausonius' jests, Theon cannot have been a real country bumpkin. Rather, what worries Ausonius is the lesson of Circe's pigs: the potential reversion of the educated man to country ways if he is exposed to these for too long. Indeed, he gives a specific example: if, presumably like other rural gentry, Theon chooses to deal with robbers in his neighborhood, he will become a robber himself by association.[16] In similar vein, Ausonius fretted in case Paulinus of Nola went native among the rude peasantry of Spain.[17]

There was, therefore, in Ausonius an acute awareness of a boundary between town and country. He knew and loved the land, but he could see its dangers both real and cultural. However, we also have to take into account the existence of Theon's brother and those local squires who felt no compunction in consorting with bandits, and to ask whether all the Gallic well-to-do were as sensitive as Ausonius to the urban/rural divide, and as positive as him as to merits of town- over country-living.

THE NON-INTELLECTUALS

There has been a tendency to see all Gallic landowners as men of letters.[18] However, it is unlikely that such as Ausonius and Paulinus of Nola were entirely typical of their class. In historiographical terms they are best categorized as early members of Wood's "single social group," comprising highly educated, intellectual, ambitious, secular, and (later) ecclesiastical dignitaries, whose culture and careers depended on town-life and whose writings dominate the source-tradition, but the generalizability of whose views should not be accepted without question.[19] Common sense should tell us that, with nature constantly mixing the gene-pool, even in the wealthiest and most educated families not everyone would be willing or able to interest themselves in learned activities and imperial careers and so be acutely aware of town/country differences. Again given the nature of the sources, I expected alternative interests to be difficult to identify, but this was not the case. The best evidence comes from Ausonius' grandson, Paulinus of Pella.[20] McLynn must be right in arguing that Paulinus was not so "artless" as he presents himself in his *Eucharisticos* when, toward the end of his life, he returned to the literary activity that he had left in his youth.[21] However, it is also undeniable that the young Paulinus had abandoned high culture. Having been an (apparently unwilling) youthful "swot," he suffered some sort of breakdown and was then allowed and even encouraged by his parents to give up his studies.[22] Subsequently, he filled his time with hunting, sexual activity (with slave-girls), and, after marriage, farming.[23] Discussion of Paulinus' adult career could be taken a number of ways. For example, it is interesting to note that although his father, Thalassius, Ausonius' son-in-law, had a distinguished imperial career, Paulinus himself did not, until the awkward episode of his service under the usurper Attalus.[24] In his adolescence, therefore, it appears, he was not pushed or promoted by his family. One is bound to wonder whether he owed the lack of pressure to a reaction on the part of his father: was the latter advanced to high office by Ausonius when he would have preferred a quiet life? Likewise, one could perhaps make more of Paulinus' enthusiasm for the life of the improving farmer, not only in his youth but also, as McLynn has again pointed out, possibly in later life.[25] As I have proposed elsewhere, such activity may have been more common in later Roman Gaul than is usually allowed, as a necessary means of increasing wealth.[26] It is, therefore, possible that Ausonius' Theon and some of Sidonius Apollinaris' "delinquents"—those who "hid" themselves in the countryside and refused to take up their responsibilities in the cities—were similar improvers:[27] like Paulinus, simply intent on increasing their agricultural incomes and (a nice indication that not all Gallic landowners were the same) actually proud of paying their tax on time![28] Here, however, I wish to develop the reference to hunting. Paulinus of Pella's father was apparently very much taken by his son's abandonment of education. He had been a keen hunter, but had given up the sport so as not to disrupt his son's studies. When Paulinus was prescribed hunting to regain his health his father joined him.[29] Heredity may have played an important part here. According to Ausonius, his father-in-law spent all his life "in hunting and husbandry and all the pleasures of a refined life, despising public affairs."[30]

HUNTING

Led to the hunt by Paulinus of Pella, I was surprised both by the richness of the seam in the sources, and by how little the topic is listed in indices of modern works on the late Roman west.

Hunting was clearly an enormous field of activity throughout the Roman period.[31] It was economically significant: the countryside was an important reservoir of food. Moreover, when it involved the larger mammals it was also a high-status activity, recorded on inscriptions, reliefs, and mosaics throughout the Empire. In the so-called *Testamentum Galli Lingonis* an early Gallo-Roman aristocrat made elaborate provision for his funeral, including the instruction that all his hunting gear be burned with his body.[32] The later grave-monuments of the Gallic commercial class reveal that as they grew richer they aped the lifestyle of their betters, including hunting on horseback.[33] In a martial society hunting, with its undeniable discomforts and dangers, was legitimately seen as an important preparation for office, especially imperial office.[34] It was therefore one of the pursuits of emperors. In this respect, of course, the name of Hadrian springs first to mind, but it should not be forgotten that the later western ruler, Constans, was also a notorious devotee.[35] Hunting also permitted aristocratic generosity. Gifts of produce and the exchange of seasonal delicacies and dainties among aristocratic households were clearly very welcome in a taste-starved society.[36] As a "polite attention" their arrival was probably as much appreciated as that of a letter or a poem.[37] Here, once more, it is possible for discussion to go a number of ways. For all its popularity there was, for example, a dark side to hunting: it could be taken too far. Hadrian went beyond respectable convention in commemorating his hunting activities;[38] and Constans' obsession with the chase, we are told, was a major factor in his overthrow by Magnentius.[39] Possibly Gallus' boorishness was ascribed the same cause.[40] We seem again to be in the presence of urban fear of the brutalizing effect of rural life. Hunting could be both the mark of the gentleman and of the semi-savage.[41] The huntsman wanders far from the town; he is physically removed from the urban life; and to hunt successfully he has to know and care for his prey, almost to become one of them. Furthermore, in the period of the Christian Empire, with the city now virtually colonized by the Church with its great buildings and annual festivals, the huntsman may have incurred suspicion because of his twofold "pagan" activities: literally, because of his country-rambling, and spiritually, because in the rural solitudes he may stumble into the presence of non–Christian religious powers: hunting was always closely related to sacrifice and dedication to the Olympian gods.[42] However, having earlier touched upon "Women and Horses," I would end by taking a brief look at the relationship between hunting and "Power and War."

There can be no doubt that Caesar's Gauls were great warriors. After the Conquest, the Gallic aristocratic military tradition was not suppressed, but was diverted into service in the Roman army. This continued into the first century A.D., but then died out and was never re-established.[43] As a result, we are accustomed to the Gauls of the later Empire, like Ausonius and Sidonius, as teachers, rhetoricians, courtiers, and clergy, but not as generals.[44] As long as the imperial structure was maintained, and military responsibilities could be taken up by "outsiders," Roman or German, this hardly mattered. Civil office, centered on the great metropolis of the Empire, was as distinguished as, and probably more profitable than, military office. As a result, urban activities and urban skills continued to flourish and be prized. Against such a background, it has to be said, we are probably not surprised by the fact that during the fifth century Gaul fell to a relatively small number of Germanic invaders. In other words, we accept that without imperial support the Roman west could not defend itself; that the urban skills of its local leaders were out of date; indeed, that it had become "soft." Yet a moment's reflection should suggest that, given the likely popularity and demands of hunting, as argued above, weakness of physique or character on the part of the ruling class and its servants cannot be adduced to explain the collapse of the west. Aristocratic hunting demanded the possession of considerable personal courage and experience and expertise in the handling of weapons and mounts. It also demanded access to significant numbers of people to act as bearers, beaters, sutlers etc.

These helpers would have to be recruited and organized; and would be expected to have their own courage and specialist knowledge. Significant numbers of leading Gauls would, therefore, have been in a position to rely on themselves and on their dependants; and, as imperial power shrank in extent and potency, these rural skills would have had the chance to come into their own. In terms of the relative positions of town and country, the latter could now advance its "frontier." Most famous is Ecdidius, Sidonius' brother-in-law. In his youth he had amused himself with "ball and dice-box, hawk and hound, horse and bow"; as an adult he organized a spirited defense of Clermont against the Goths, at one point raising a private army.[45] However, as the Goths began to take over the land, other Gauls served them as senior officers: we know of Arborius, Vincentius, Victorius, Calminius, and Namatius.[46] It should be noted that Sidonius refers to the last of these, who became one of Euric's admirals, specifically as a farmer and hunter.[47] However, in respect of Gallo-German cooperation hunting must have had a more direct role. The Germans were also great hunters. We are told, for example, that hunting played a large part in the life of the Gothic king Theoderic II (453-466), who was particularly proud of his bowmanship.[48] Hunting would therefore, I propose, have created another link, in addition to the literary and religious, between Gallic and German leaders: most liked hunting, and at the end of the day, casting aside their many differences, most would have been able to use the language of hunting to mix, socialize, and drift into "men's talk"—of "Women and Horses and Power and War."

By way of a coda, I would add that acceptance of hunting as a means of maintaining the Gallic warrior tradition points up even more an oddity which I have drawn attention to in earlier publications: the peculiar rarity and lateness of the late antique Gallic warlord.[49]

REFERENCES

Anderson, J. K. 1985. *Hunting in the Ancient World.* Berkeley, Los Angeles, London.

Dill, S. [1898]. 1905 *Roman Society in the Last Century of the Western Empire.* Oxford.

Drinkwater, J. F. 1983. *Roman Gaul: the Three Provinces 58 B.C.- A.D. 260.* London and New York.

———.1989. "Gallic Attitudes to the Roman Empire in the Fourth Century a.d.: Continuity or Change?" In *Labor Omnibus Unus* (Historia Einzelschriften 6), edited by H. Herzig and R. Frei-Stolba, 136–53. Stuttgart.

———. 1992. "The Bacaudae of Fifth-Century Gaul." In *Fifth-Century Gaul: a Crisis of Identity?,* edited by J. Drinkwater and H. Elton, 208–17. Cambridge.

———.1998. "The Usurpers Constantine III (407–411) and Jovinus (411–413)." *Britannia* 29, 269–97.

Green, R. P. H. 1991. *The Works of Ausonius.* Oxford.

Harries, J. 1994. *Sidonius Apollinaris and the Fall of Rome.* Oxford.

Hatt, J.-J. [1951]. 1986. *La tombe gallo-romaine.* Paris.

Heather, P. 1992. "The Emergence of the Visigothic Kingdom." In *Fifth-Century Gaul: a Crisis of Identity?,* edited by J. Drinkwater and H. Elton, 84–94. Cambridge.

Heinen, H. 1985. *Trier und das Trevererland in römischer Zeit.* Trier.

Jones, A. H. M. 1964. *The Later Roman Empire, 284–602.* Oxford.

Jullian, C. 1926. *Histoire de la Gaule.* Vol. 8. Paris.

Kipling, R. 1940. "The Ballad of the King's Jest." In *The Definitive Edition of Kipling's Verse,* 247–50. London.

Lane-Fox, R. 1996. "Ancient Hunting: From Homer to Polybius." In *Human Landscape in Classical Antiquity* (Leicester-Nottingham Studies in Ancient Society 6), edited by G. Shipley and J. B. Salmon, 119–53. London.

Matthews, J. F. 1974. "The Letters of Symmachus." In *Latin Literature of the Fourth Century,* edited by J. W. Binns, 58–99. London.

———. 1975. *Western Aristocracies and Imperial Court a.d. 364–425.* Oxford.

Mause, M. 1994. *Die Darstellung des Kaisers in der lateinischen Panegyrik* (Palingenesia Bd. 50). Stuttgart.

McLynn, N. 1995. "Paulinus the Impenitent: A Study of the *Eucharisticos.*" *Journal of Early Christian Studies* 3, no. 4: 461–86.

Numrich, B. 1997. *Die Architektur der römischen Grabdenkmäler aus Neumagen* (Trierer Zeitschrift Beiheft 22). Trier.

Parlasca, K. 1998. "Hasenjagd bei den Treveren und anderswo." *Trierer Zeitschrift* 61: 129–36.

Sivan, H. 1989. "Not a *civis?* A note on Ausonius' *Parentalia* 8 (Schenkl 10.6)." *Latomus* 48: 879–80.

———. 1993. *Ausonius of Bordeaux. Genesis of a Gallic Aristocracy.* London.

Wood, I. 1992. "Continuity or Calamity: The Constraints of the Literary Models." In *Fifth-*

Century Gaul: a Crisis of Identity?, edited by J. Drinkwater and H. Elton, 9–18. Cambridge.

NOTES

1. Sivan, *Ausonius of Bordeaux. Genesis of a Gallic Aristocracy* (London, 1993), 72.
2. R. Kipling, "The Ballad of the King's Jest," in *The Definitive Edition of Kipling's Verse* (London, 1940), 248.
3. *Ep.* 14 Peiper [=13 Green], trans. White.
4. Green 1991, 629.
5. Anderson 1985, 148 with 52–3; *Cynegeticus* 10.10–14.
6. See for example, amongst many, Jones 1964, 1041: "The Roman empire was a country of peasants. . . ."
7. Ausonius: *Ep.* 4[2].1–3; 11[11].11–12; 16[15].5–6; 27[23].91–6. Sidonius: *Ep.* 2.2; 2.9.
8. *Carm.* 3.1[6]; *Epp.* 26[28].
9. Private: *Ep.* 26 [20a, 9–10]. Public: *Carm.* 3.5[20.2].; cf. Sidonius Apollinaris, *Ep.* 3.6.3.
10. E.g. Ausonius, *Ep.* 4[2].5–8; 10[8].13–16; 25b[21b].33–6.
11. Sidonius, *Ep.* 2.9.2, 7; 3.12.2; 4.18.1.
12. E.g. Sidonius Apollinaris, *Ep.* 1.96; 1.11.14–15; 9.13.4–5.
13. Consentius: *PLRE* 2, 308–9. The contest: Sidonius Apollinaris, *Carm.* 23.307–427; Consentius' horsemanship in later life: ibid. 23.12. Matthews 1975, 340, has Consentius being "represented" by a team in the race, but this is inconsistent with Sidonius Apollinaris' long and detailed account of the event and with the impression of Consentius' colorful and daring character that emerges from the poem as a whole. Harries (1994, 130) refers to him briefly, but I am sure correctly, as a "charioteer."
14. *Ep.* 6[4].19–28. Green 1991, 611 identifies Ausonius' reworking of Horace (*Ep.* 2.2.74–5) here. If the Italian countryside could so intrude into the high imperial capital, the Gallic must have had an even stronger presence in late-antique Bordeaux.
15. On the beauty of the countryside see Ausonius, *Mosella* (*Carm.* 10[16]).150–68, 189–99, etc.
16. *Ep.* 14[13].23–7.
17. *Ep.* 31[-].208–10 [Paulinus to Ausonius].
18. Cf. Jullian 1926, 139.
19. Wood 1992, 11.
20. Paulinus of Pella: *PLRE* 1, 677–78.
21. McLynn 1995, 462–63.
22. Paulinus of Pella, *Euch.* 72–84; 113–40.
23. Ibid., 127–34, 141–45; 154–68; 188–97.
24. Thalassius: *PLRE* 1, 887–88.
25. McLynn 1995, 477–78.

26. Drinkwater 1992, 212.
27. Sidonius Apollinaris *Ep.* 1.6.3–4 (Eutropius), 2.14 (Maurusius), 8.8 (Syagrius).
28. Paulinus of Pella, *Euch.* 198–200.
29. Ibid., 127–33.
30. *Parent.* (*Carm.* 4[10])8.7–8 (cf. Sivan 1989).
31. See Anderson 1985; and, for a recent brief, but very stimulating, survey of the Greek background see Lane-Fox 1996.
32. *CIL* 13.5708 = *ILS* 8379. Hatt 1986, 68–9: "I also wish all my hunting- and fowling-equipment to be burned with me, with my spears, swords, knives, nets, traps, snares, arrows (or rods?), tents and scares . . ."
33. Heinen 1985, 168 (Abb. 59); Numrich 1997, 114–17; Parlasca 1998.
34. Ausonius, *Epig.* 27[2], 30[6] [Gratian]; Sidonius Apollinaris, *Carm.* 7.187–206 [Avitus], *Carm.*5.153–54 Majorian, *Carm.* 2.144–48 [Anthemius]. In general, see Mause 1994, 81.
35. *Epitome* 41.22.
36. E.g., two examples from many: Ausonius, *Ep.* 15[14] (again, Theon); Sidonius Apollinaris, *Carm.* 21.
37. Dill 1905, 153: a letter from Symmachus as a "visiting card," "polite attention." Cf. Matthews 1974, 62.
38. *Historia Augusta* "Life of Hadrian," 20.12.
39. Zosimus 2.42.2.
40. Julian, *Ep. ad Ath.* 271D.
41. Sidonius Apollinaris, *Carm.* 2.42–3.
42. For the importance of aristocratic presence in the city to attend the Christian festivals see Ausonius, *Ep.* 4[2].9, 6[4].17–18; and Sidonius Apollinaris. *Ep.* 4.18.1. On the pagan gods and hunting, see Anderson 1985, 101, 144 (the Piazza Armerina mosaic). Though Sidonius hunted in his youth (*Ep.* 4.4.1) and continued to fish (*Ep.* 2.12.1, *Carm.* 21), there is no mention of hunting in his detailed descriptions of the villa parties of his adult years (*Ep.* 2.2, 2.9).
43. Drinkwater 1983, 194–95.
44. Cf. Drinkwater 1989, 143–46, 151–52.
45. Sidonius, *Ep.* 3.3.4,7.
46. Heather 1992, 91–92.
47. Sidonius, *Ep.* 8.6.10–13.
48. Ibid., 1.2.5.
49. E.g., Drinkwater 1998, 296.

The Interdependence of Town and Country in Late Antique Spain

MICHAEL KULIKOWSKI

IN SPEAKING ABOUT TOWN AND COUNTRY IN ROMAN SPAIN, THE TEMPTATION TO descend into polemic is built right into the framework of discussion. The assumption that town and country are perfect opposites is commonplace and instantly polarizes the discourse. Another assumption—that growth in the country of necessity implies decline in the town—has shaped our entire understanding of late Roman Spain. It is nearly impossible to find a study of Spain in late antiquity that is not couched in terms of *ruralización*, a word that in itself embodies a whole set of assumptions about social decay from a high imperial, urbanized norm.[1]

This article will try to resist the siren call of this polarized debate. Instead, it will start with the proposition that any discussion of town and country in Roman Spain ought to include a dialogue between archaeology and history, in which archaeologists and historians actually listen to one another. Precisely this sort of dialogue has become much easier in the past decade or so, for a variety of reasons. The most important of these is the brave new world into which Spanish archaeology has only recently entered. In the past two decades, Spanish archaeology has undergone a methodological revolution, the results of which are just now beginning to be published in useable quantity. Rather than attempting to link all their findings to such tiny scraps of literary evidence as we happen to possess, Spanish archaeologists have become willing to describe the material evidence they uncover on its own terms, and according to its own internal chronology. That is to say, the archaeological record is finally being published as an autonomous source of evidence, independent of known or hypothetical narratives. The new breed of site report is thus quite often a conscious repudiation of its ancestors; it embraces technical specificity and shuns generalizing extrapolation from local findings.[2]

As such, the results can be bewildering for the historian who blunders into this specialist world. Nevertheless, the only way we can make any progress in our understanding of late Roman and post-Roman Spain is if archaeologists and historians begin a dialogue in which the autonomy of the two disciplines is recognized on both sides. Historians must realize that archaeology cannot answer the sort of questions historians like to ask—questions about political history and the precise course of events. At the same time, historians must also try to incorporate the sort of answers archaeology does provide into our understanding of the past. For the historian weaned on the written word, doing this is not always easy, since we instinctively privilege our written sources and let them dictate the framework into which we fit our material evidence. However, for the Spain of Late Antiquity, the growing body of archaeological evidence is very much fuller than is our sparse literary record. If for no other reason than its bulk, this evidence demands the historian's attention. But it demands to be heard on its own terms, if we are to discover what implications it might have for our literary sources.

What follows is my own unscientific attempt at listening to the material evidence. It may be no more than a historian's misplaced enthusiasm. But I think the material evidence provides the essential background against which we must place our scattered written sources, and the new archaeology allows us to do so in a way that was simply not possible even ten years ago. The great achievement of the new archaeology has been its systematic dissociation of change in the material record from the well-known crises and transitions of political history. The years 260 and 409, in each of which barbarian groups crossed the Pyrenees into Spain, have lost their totemic significance thanks to the new archaeology.[3] Indeed, the third-century crisis and the early fifth-century crisis have no archaeological existence. This is tremendously important, and quite humbling for the historian hoping to eke out a mention in Jerome or Hydatius with material evidence of barbarian rapacity. Change in the material record is gradual change. More importantly, the gradual changes we can observe take place in ways and at times which simply cannot be hitched to our political narrative.[4] This means that a large number of sacred topoi in our modern reconstructions no longer explain, or can be explained by, the material record. If the Spanish city declines from a high imperial apex and power gravitates to the countryside in a process of ruralization, archaeology no longer allows us to blame this on a Moorish invasion under Marcus, or the civil wars of Severus and Albinus, or even the Frankish invasion of the year 260. The interpretative suture of third-century crisis and third-century ruralization has been ripped.

Whether there was a decline in the monumentality of the urban environment is open to question, though it does seem certain that urban élites had ceased to patronize large-scale building projects by the beginning of the third century. However, a falling-off of urban euergetism tells us nothing about change in urban population or urban economic vitality. Fashion and taste are not solely economic phenomena, and even some second-tier cities like Gerunda and Valentia had larger populations in the late than in the early empire.[5] Similarly, the sumptuous villa culture of the fourth century is not a phoenix rising out of late third-century ashes; fourth-century villas rest on late second- and early third-century foundations. As a superb spatial analysis of ancient land use in Extremadura has shown, the founding of these villas represents not ruralization in some pejorative sense, but rather the systematic extension of economic life across all the readily exploitable land, and in many places quite far into marginal areas.[6]

What all this means is that material change in both town and country, having been detached from its causal connection to a mid–third-century crisis, has now been spread across an intrinsically more plausible chronology of a century and a half. Something similar has happened at the other end of our period as well. It has become increasingly difficult to maintain that the year 409 represents any significant turning point in either town or country. In that year, in the midst of a Roman civil war, a group of Vandals, Alans, and Sueves crossed the Pyrenees into Spain. Historians, for the most part, remain willing to accept this event as the moment at which Roman Spain came to an end.[7] The new archaeology is showing that this is simply not so. The fifth-century scene has been less well-served than the third by spatial analyses, since such studies have to rely upon an older breed of site report that takes 409 as its a priori *terminus ante quem*. More recent excavations are challenging the old models at every juncture. The case is clearest in the countryside. Rural digs, at both deluxe and much humbler sites, are beginning to show a generalized continuity of fourth-century amenities until late in the fifth century. At many low status sites, village cemeteries stay in use alongside the cottages whose owners are buried in them.[8] More spectacularly, at villa sites everywhere the constant urge to trump one's ancestors and make the family pile bigger and better keeps going in those very years in which our literary sources paint a picture of smoking Spanish ruins. At many sites, this pattern starts to trail off by the 460s or the 470s, in some places it starts a bit earlier. Nowhere, significantly, is there evidence of sudden change.[9]

If the chronology of rural sites is in nearly every case to be dissociated from the narrative record of fifth-century history, the case of the towns is considerably more ambiguous. Part of the problem lies with the nature of urban archaeology. It is not easy to dig systematically in towns that remain heavily occupied in the present day, as most of the late Roman towns of Spain are. Too much important data has to be gathered piecemeal, while the foundations of the new supermarket are dug simultaneously, and it is hard to speculate meaningfully about urban change when it is unclear what precisely is changing. As matters stand, there are relatively few Spanish cities where the high imperial town plan is well enough known to make speculation about late antique changes meaningful. There are exceptions, primarily Tarraco and Emerita, but also smaller sites like Gerunda, Barcino, and Ilerda, or Valentia and Carthago Nova.[10] All of these sites, and others where less extensive work has as of yet been done, have benefitted both from painstaking archaeological research and unprecedentedly scrupulous and efficient publication. What their findings actually tell us is rather more difficult to say. At Emerita alone is there evidence of the sort of material change that can be linked to historically attested events: the coetaneous razing of much inframural housing, the ruin of the patron saint's shrine, and a spoliage-filled repair of the city's walls can be associated more or less plausibly with a Suevic visit in 429.[11] Elsewhere, changing uses of public space are well-documented, but show no signs of correlating with the historical record.

By the late fifth century, the townscape of most Spanish cities was profoundly different from what it had been in the third or early fourth centuries. Instead of an urban space organized around public buildings, there was an urban public space organized around holy places. None of the cities from which we have meaningful late antique data are recognizable as models of the high imperial Roman city. At only one or two did the fora remain living public spaces into the sixth century, though even that fact is significant. At Tarraco, a provincial capital and a city that no one has ever suggested suffered during the fifth-century instability, the old municipal forum had probably been destroyed toward the end of the fourth century. On the other hand, the provincial forum in the upper town remained intact and in use till around 440, when the uprooting of its paving stones, and the digging of a large rubbish dump in one corner, testify to the new residential uses to which the forum was being put.[12] At a comparable site like Corduba, however, the vast official complex of Cercadilla shows signs of active use into the middle of the fifth century.[13] Elsewhere, changes in the townscape seem to have come gradually, and on the whole not till late in the fifth century. They consist, in the main, of churches built where once there had been older types of public building. Valentia offers a good example of this, and there as elsewhere, the ecclesiastical structures most readily identifiable date from the sixth not the fifth century.[14] But there as elsewhere sixth-century churches rest on fifth-century foundations and it is significant that at Emerita, where we have ample signs of fifth-century destruction, the damage was done to a townscape that had already experienced the reorientation toward a Christian use of public space.

The foregoing has been a rough and ready sketch, as it could hardly fail to be in the present context. A more detailed sketch would be fenced with caveats and also take note of all the many exceptions to the trends mooted here. Nevertheless—and still speaking generally—all of the new archaeology seems to suggest that the cities of Spain underwent a series of *gradual* material changes in the course of their late antique history, and that these changes obeyed a rhythm that is neither susceptible of simple explanation nor easily tied to our written record. The townscape of the fifth and later centuries is clearly no longer the townscape of the first or the second century. But the evidence for urban vitality, as opposed to monumentality, is much stronger than we could have realized ten years ago. Tarraco's provincial forum may have lost its paving stones in the 440s, but the town's inhabitants enjoyed the produce of the whole Mediterranean world for many decades thereafter.[15] There is an important corollary to this new evidence of urban vitality—if towns and town life neither contracted nor decayed in quite so simple a fashion as we have long believed, then it is no longer possible to treat late antique Spain as culturally rural, and explain political events by appeal to that ruralization. We cannot, that is, take as the premise of our social history a social structure in which real power is located outside the towns, in the hands of rural *possessores* or *latifundisti* or whatever we want to call them. Instead, we need to go back to our written sources with an awareness of the complexity of the material record, and an awareness of the fact that town and country are not polar opposites which can only flourish at one another's expense.

When we do this, what we find is the continued dominance of the town in both the actual power nexus of late antique Spain and in the expectations and imaginations of late antique Spaniards. This is perhaps not the place to delve too deeply into the evidence of church councils, well-sifted as they have been in various contexts. The canons of Elvira are well-known, largely for their constructions of Christian sexuality, but it is worth noticing how many *flamines, sacerdotes,* and duumvirs turn up as well.[16] The vitality of such quintessentially urban municipal and cultic offices so early in the fourth century is perhaps not very surprising, but it is important nevertheless. It tells us that a fundamentally urban expression of status like the flaminate was still worth having in precisely those years when the rural villa culture of the Spanish provinces was at its height. The evidence of other church councils is equally suggestive. In both the late and the post-Roman councils there is a constant sense that the town is superior to the country, that the locus of power both is and ought to be the town, and that it is the job of an urban elite—in this case a clerical elite—to control the life of the country. The peculiarly Spanish strain of ascetic heresy that we loosely, though not always accurately, describe as Priscillianism, probably began as an urban, high status heresy. On the other hand, much of what made it so abhorrent to its detractors was its advocacy of retreat to the countryside.[17] The search for the wilderness is, to be sure, common to early Christian ascetic movements in general, whether they were endorsed as orthodox or proscribed as heretical. The rejection of the world that asceticism demanded was enacted as a flight from the city. What we should realize, however, is that for this strategy of spiritual fulfillment to work, there had to be an urban world from which to flee, and indeed an ideologically dominant urban world to which ascetic retreat could provide a spiritual alternative. That Priscillianism and its analogues persisted in Spain for decades must be explained, at least in part, by the vitality of urban culture. The Priscillianist ascetic alternative presupposes an urban world to rebel against, and the lack of analogous movements in fifth-century Gaul may point up an important contrast between Gaul and Spain in this period. As we shall see shortly, our evidence for orthodox asceticism points to similar conclusions, but let us first turn to our more traditional narrative sources.

The chronicle of Hydatius is well-known, and much has been done in recent years to explicate its author's techniques. Richard Burgess has demonstrated the chronicler's apocalyptic preoccupations, while Javier Arce has illuminated several important instances in which the Hydatian narrative systematically misleads those who would take it literally.[18] Hydatius is emerging as a far more tendentious writer than we once thought, and the unrelievedly bleak picture he draws is in many places a demonstrable overstatement. On the other hand, Hydatius remains by far the fullest source we possess for Spanish affairs at any time during the Roman period. The chronicle is rich enough in incident that the present article might easily have become "town and country in the work of Hydatius." Rather than let this happen, we might point out one or two key parts of the Hydatian evidence before moving on to other sources. Though we find at least one rural potentate in the chronicle, the vast majority of it is taken up with the people and affairs of cities.[19] Bishops and local notables dominate the pages of the work, and it is in the cities that these men are usually to be found. In the earlier part of the chronicle, the importance of the city is displayed mainly by the efforts various people make to take or retake different peninsular sites. The narrative climax comes when the emperor Avitus' Gothic allies sack Bracara in 456.[20] Later, after the emperor Majorian leaves Tarraconensis and the last imperial officials depart from Spain, the prominence of cities in the chronicle actually increases. It is now, in the 460s, that we learn of the urban notable Lusidius who betrays Olisippo, and of the *familiam nobilem Cantabri* of Conimbriga, despoiled and kidnapped by the Sueves.[21] In Hydatius, regardless of political vicissitudes or barbarian anarchy, the Hispano-Roman city remains the core of political life.

The Hydatian evidence is paralleled quite closely, though with considerably less incidental detail, in the chronicle of John of Biclar, written more than a hundred years later.[22] Some time after 590, John set out to add yet another link to a long chain of continuations to the chronicle of Eusebius-Jerome. A Catholic of Gothic parentage, John's chronicle is in essence the story of the conversion of the Visigoths from heresy to orthodoxy. But John is far from being a crude Catholic apologist, and his portrayal of the Arian king Leovigild is far from condemnatory.[23] The chronicle narrates Leovigild's creation of a genuine Visigothic kingdom in Spain, but like Hydatius, John is a valuable witness to the relationship of town and country. John shows us that despite the passage of a hundred years since the last imperial administrators were active in the peninsula, Spain remained a world of towns. Leovigild's reign, as John describes it, is a series of conquests, the process by which he imposes the rule of a Gothic monarch on a whole series of independent polities, Hispano-Roman, Gothic and Byzantine. That conquest, however, is almost entirely a conquest of towns—John assumes that the taking of a town means *ipso facto* the taking of a region.[24] He thus implies that Spanish towns in the post-Roman period retained the same sort of importance they had

had in the Roman period, that is to say, they remained administrative and governmental centers, the control of which brought with it control of their dependent territories.

Another episode in Leovigild's career is still more important. The king's reliance on consciously imperial symbolism is well known, and he was wont to celebrate his triumphs in the most truly imperial fashion available to him—by the foundation of a town. In and of itself the foundation of a town implies nothing more than ostentation. What is revelatory is the way Leovigild conceived of at least one of his new towns. Of Victoriacum, planted in Vasconia after a victory over some Basques, we know nothing at all. More considered, or so it seems, was Reccopolis, named after his younger son Reccared. Reccopolis was founded ex nihilo with all the *privilegia* of a new town, with walls and with suburbs, that is to say with the suburbium that was the integral concomitant of a Roman city.[25] This suggests that for Leovigild, the town retained the same ideological predominance it had possessed for his imperial Roman predecessors. We do not know how successfully Leovigild realized his project, but one point is clear. It is impossible to reconcile Leovigild's conception of what made a town a town with any image of citizen squatters huddled around a church, the sole living site amidst despoiled ruins. If the real focus of life, the real power in this world, lay out on the estates of the *possessores* neither Leovigild nor his historian John show any signs of having realized it.

Indeed, what is so striking about the Spanish literary sources from the fourth through the sixth centuries is how hard it is to actually find the *possessores* and *latifundisti* of whom we hear so much in our modern narratives. Didymus and Verinianus, the Theodosian cousins of Honorius who waged war against the usurper Constantine III in 408 or 409, can be cited as prime specimens of this rural *dirigent* class, and they very well may have been.[26] We should realize, however, that we encounter them in circumstances that cannot prove the case one way or another. It is true that the brothers raise an army off their estates to fight the forces of Constantine III, but they do not necessarily do so from choice. The bureaucracy of the Spanish provinces, based in the towns and with its hands on the machinery of government, had already declared for the usurper.[27] Didymus and

Verinianus were constrained by force of circumstance to turn to the resources of their estates—that they did so is not in itself evidence that they were primarily rural latifundists or would not normally have resided in one of the towns, which were still flourishing as the archaeological evidence now shows us. Even the evidence of the Theodosian cousins is not at all clear cut, which should only serve to highlight how very little evidence for a dominant rural milieu there really is.

All the evidence so far cited for the city as the enduring focus of public life in the peninsula has been confined to the greatest of the peninsula's towns, precisely where we would expect to find it. We have not yet seen anything comparable from Spain's lesser cities, places like Termes, where heroic archaeological efforts have uncovered a shifting late antique townscape of staggering complexity.[28] It may therefore be useful to close with an example drawn from a somewhat less predictable context. The life of the sixth-century saint Aemilian was lived within the narrow confines of the Sierra de Cantabria and the Sierra de la Demanda, though his fame spread much further than that. Braulio, Bishop of Zaragoza composed his life of Aemelian some time early in the seventh century, and it provides precious insight into the life of northern Iberia before the conversion of the Visigothic kingdom to orthodoxy in 589.[29] The whole of Aemilian's long career was played out far from the great urban centers of late Roman Spain, in a region traditionally regarded as the least urbanized in all of Roman Iberia. Yet even here, the lives of the local populace were centered on towns. Their social interactions and their power relationships had their gravitational center not in the countryside, as we might expect, but rather in the public world of the town.

Braulio's *vita* abounds in familiar topoi, both literary and historical, but it distinguishes carefully between three existential spaces—the town, the country, and the wilderness. Aemelian spends his early life trying to flee the countryside for the wilderness.[30] He does so because the townspeople keep trying to find him and have him exercise his sanctity in the place where the lives of the worldly take place, that is to say in the towns.[31] Aemilian dwells forty years in the wilderness, but however far he flees the fame of his sanctity pursues him. Finally, Didimus of Tirasona, the bishop within whose diocese Aemelian's wilderness retreat lay, felt compelled to pursue the saint, drag him from his solitude, and have him ordained a priest in his own village of Vergegium,[32] in what was the familiar early Christian means of dealing with an unauthorized holy man. But all did not work out as Didimus hoped. Aemelian began to systematically alienate the property of the church at Vergegium, which, fortuitously or not, caused Didimus to dismiss him from his post. For the rest of his life, Aemelian was permitted to dwell at his oratory near Vergegium and enjoy the contemplative life for which he had so long striven.[33]

As is so often the case with saints' lives, it is hard to localize the various miracle stories that accompany Aemelian's long life. It is more or less impossible to place Aemelian's various miraculous achievements during his forty years as a hermit, his short period as a priest, or his retirement at his oratory at Vergegium. It is clear, however, that Aemelian's retreats existed between two urban poles, one at Tirasona, where Didimus was bishop, and the other at Amaia in Cantabria. Aemelian may have dwelt in the wilderness, but it was in the towns that his fame spread. It was from the towns that people sought his aid, and equally from the towns that the secular clergy attempted to impose their control on the saint. The conflict between the active and contemplative life dramatized in Braulio's *vita* is also a conflict between town and country. Here, as with the Prisicillianists of an earlier era, the ascetic retreat from the world is enacted as an escape from the city. What is so striking is that even in the wilds of sixth-century Cantabria, this retreat had meaningful content.

In Aemilian's Cantabria, it is in the towns that the normal world of social relations takes place. Aemilian exists outside this world, and the people who seek him are city folk who return to their urban milieu upon being cured. Braulio's *vita* records a steady stream of visitors. Some come from named villages, which we can no longer locate, but others come from the town of Amaia. A recent English translation makes Amaia a village, but the Latin implies difference in kind from the actual little villages it records.[34] Sick and diseased people are brought from Amaia to Aemelian—no small distance, one might add—and then return to town. That we have to do with a real town is made clear by the titles certain men bear. We may leave aside the various senators, and the mysterious *senatus Cantabriae* that appears several times before meeting its doom in the shape of Leovigild.[35] The nature of this senate has never been adequately explained and the existence of the senatorial title need not imply a thriving town life. The case of the *curialis* Maximus, whose daughter Columba Aemilian exorcises, is more significant. The curial office is necessarily urban and we cannot dismiss it as mere elegant variation on Braulio's part, for he is scrupulous in his nomenclature. Admittedly, alongside the curial Maximus, we meet the *senator* Honorius whose haunted *domus* almost certainly lies on a rural estate.[36] Nevertheless, we need to give due weight to the remarkable fact that even in the mountain fastnesses of post-Roman Cantabria men still took up seats on town councils, with all that this implies for the vitality of the town, and of the idea of the town, in late antique Spain.

As has been said already, the foregoing is at best a rough and ready sketch. There is massive work to be done, and to do it will require a very thorough interaction with not just the written but also the archaeological evidence. I will not be at all surprised if the argument of the present paper proves somewhat overstated—its insistence on a more than token continuity of Spanish town life is in large part a reaction to the demonstrably overstated arguments for ruralization. Further understanding can only come if historians listen sensitively to archaeologists and handle their own evidence accordingly. The present work is one small attempt at doing just that.

NOTES

1. One thinks of each and every book on Roman Spain in the numerous multi-volume *Historias de España* although few specialist studies are immune, even the otherwise sensibly revisionist F. J. García de Castro, "La trayectoria histórica de Hispania romana durante el siglo IV d.c.," *Hispania Antiqua* 19 (1995): 327–61.
2. Particularly the work of the Taller Escola d'Arqueologia, e.g. X. Dupré i Reventós, *El circ Romà de Tarragona I: les voltes de Sant Ermenegild* (Barcelona, 1988); TED'A, *Un abocador del segle V d.c. en el fòrum provincial de Tarraco* (Tarragona, 1989); TED'A, *L'amfiteatre romà de Tarragona, la basílica visigòtica i l'església romànica* (Tarragona, 1990).
3. The traditional catastrophic approach, which still reigns in some circles, is best exemplified by M. Tarradell, "Sobre las invasiones germánicas del siglo III d.J.C. en la penín-

sula ibérica," *Estudios Clásicos* 3 (1955): 95–110. The literary evidence for the 260 invasion is Aurelius Victor 33.3, Eutropius 8.8.2, and Jerome, s.a. 2280, all derived from the *Kaisergeschichte*. For 409: Orosius, *Adv. paganos* 7.41.2 and Hydatius 34 (the latter must now be cited from the edition of R. W. Burgess, *The Chronicle of Hydatius and the Consularia Constantinopolitana* [Oxford, 1993] which supersedes all previous editions and solves the notoriously difficult Hydatian system of chronological reckoning).

4. A salutary example is the villa of Vilauba in the modern province of Girona. The site report of A. Roure i Bonaventura et al., *La vil.la romana de Vilauba (Camós)* (Girona, 1988) is a model of its kind, and reports its evidence with the transparency a reader needs to check the excavators' conclusions. At Vilauba, a massive destruction layer has been stratigraphically dated to c. 325, a period for which our historical record is entirely silent.
5. J. M. Nolla, "Gerunda: dels orígens a la fi del món antic," *Fonaments* 7 (1988): 69–108; J. Blasco, et al., "Estat actual de la investigació arqueològica de l'antiguitat tardana a la ciutat de València," in *III Reunió d'arqueologia cristiana hispànica* (Barcelona, 1994), 185–99.
6. J. M. Fernández Corrales, *El asentamiento romano en Extremadura y su analisis espacial* (Cáceres, 1988); similar conclusions are reached by J. Gomez Santa Cruz, "Aproximación al poblamiento rural hispano-romano en la provincia de Soria," in *Actas del segundo symposium de arqueología soriana* (Soria, 1989), 937–56.
7. Thus even J. Arce, whose work has consistently challenged received opinion, uses 409 as the terminal date for *El último siglo de la España romana, 284–409* (Madrid, 1982).
8. E.g., A. Fuentes Domínguez, "Necropolis tardorromanas en Soria," in *Actas del segundo symposium de arqueología soriana* (Soria, 1989), 991–1006; id., *La necropolis tardorromana de Albalate de las Nogueras (Cuenca) y el problema de las denominadas "necropolis del Duero"* (Cuenca, 1989); D. Pradales Ciprés and L. Sagredo San Eustoquio, "Un asentamiento romano en la provincia de Palencia: La Sotilla (Lantadilla)," in *Actas del segundo congreso de historia de Palencia* (Palencia, 1990), 1:405–16.
9. There is an enormous quantity of research on villa sites throughout Spain and the standard catalogue of J.-G. Gorges, *Les villas hispano-romaines: inventaires et problématique archéologiques* (Paris, 1979) is now badly out of date. Perhaps the best place to look for recent work on Hispano-Roman villas is the fine new journal *Extremadura Arqueológica*, volumes 2 (1991) and 5 (1995) of which are particularly useful for up-to-date research on the villas around Emerita. There is no space to list the growing number of carefully published villas around Spain, but the many Iberian regional journals nowadays repay the effort it takes to keep track of them.
10. Gerunda: J. M. Nolla, *Girona romana* (Girona, 1987) and id., above note 5; Barcino: J.O. Granados, "La transformación de la colonia Barcino," in *Actas del II congreso de la arqueología medieval española* (Madrid, 1987), 2:353–61; Ilerda: A. Pérez Almoguera, "La ciutat d'Ilerda de la conquesta romana al Baix Imperi (s. II a.C.-V. d.C.)," *Fonaments* 9 (1996): 145–201; Valentia: R. Soriano Sánchez, *La arqueología cristiana en la ciudad de Valencia: de la leyenda a la realidad* (València, 1990) and Blasco et al., note 5 above; Carthago Nova: S. F. Ramallo Asensio, *La ciudad de Carthago Nova: la*

documentación arqueológica (Murcia, 1989).

11. See P. Mateos Cruz, "El culto a santa Eulalia y su influencia en el urbanismo emeritense (siglos IV-VI)," *Extremadura Arqueológica* 3 (1992): 57–79; id., "Proyecto de arqueología urbana en Mérida: desarollo y primeros resultados," *Extremadura Arqueológica* 4 (1995): 191–215; L. Caballero Zoreda and P. Mateos Cruz, "Excavaciones arqueológicas en la basílica de Santa Eulalia de Merida," in *IV Reunió de arqueologia cristiana hispànica* (Barcelona, 1995), 297–307.
12. See TED'A, *Un abocador del segle V d.c.* (above note 2).
13. See R. Hidalgo, *Espacio público y espacio privado en el conjunto palatina de Cercadilla (Córdoba): el aula central y las Termas* (Seville, 1996), with J. Arce, "Emperadores, palacios y *villae* (a propósito de la villa romana de Cercadilla, Córdoba)," *AnTard* 5 (1997): 293–302.
14. Soriano Sánchez and Blasco et al., note 10 above.
15. As is revealed by the various TED'A publications, and also by J.-M. Carreté, S. J. Keay and M. Millett, *A Roman Provincial Capital and Its Hinterland: The Survey of the Territory of Tarragona, Spain, 1985–1990.* Journal of Roman Archaeology Supplementary Series 15 (Ann Arbor, Mich., 1995) which is to be consulted in preference to several summaries published by Keay in various conference proceedings and journal articles.
16. Most easily accessible in J. Vives, *Concilios visigóticos e hispano-romanos* (Barcelona-Madrid, 1963), 1–15, though the canons of individual councils are edited critically in the ongoing edition of G. Martínez Díez, *La colleción canónica Hispana* (Madrid, 1965ff.).
17. The literature on Priscillianism grows constantly, though H. Chadwick, *Priscilian of Avila* (Oxford, 1976) remains fundamental on matters of doctrine and practice. V. Burrus, *The Making of a Heretic* (Berkeley and Los Angeles, 1996), though it glosses over every textual and chronological difficulty in the Priscillianist dossier, is nevertheless very successful in problematizing the whole question. She argues that the word 'Priscillianist' loses its connection to the beliefs and person of the actual Priscillian very quickly and becomes instead a generic term of abuse. We therefore can never tell whether those stigmatized as Priscillianists in our literary sources professed beliefs in common to those of Priscillian and his companions, or for that matter whether so-called Priscillianists were unorthodox at all. This means that we are not justified in accepting fifth-century allegations of Priscillianism as evidence of its actual existence. The point is well taken, but not entirely germane. The objective content of the beliefs of those whom our fifth-century sources call Priscillianists is not what matters. What matters is the fear engendered by the beliefs which these orthodox sources call Priscillianist, or attribute to those whom they call Priscillianist. As Kim Bowes demonstrates in the present volume, whether we can objectively identify a particular group of people as Priscillianist is irrelevant. At different times in different parts of Spain, bishops living in cities reacted violently against groups of people whom they associated with a rural retreat, whom they categorized as unorthodox, and whom they labelled Priscillianists.

18. See R.W. Burgess, "Hydatius: A late Roman chronicler in post-Roman Spain" (D.Phil. Oxon., 1989) and J. Arce, "El catastrofismo de Hydacio y los camellos de la Gallaecia," in *Los últimos Romanos en Lusitania*, Cuadernos Emeritenses, ed. A. Velázquez, E. Cerillo, and P. Mateos. 10 (Mérida, 1995), 219–29.
19. This is Andevotus (Hyd. 106).
20. Hyd. 167.
21. Lusidius: Hyd. 240; Cantaber: Hyd. 225.
22. Edited by Mommsen in *Chronica Minora* 2 (Monumenta Germaniae Historica, Auctores Antiquissimi 11): 207–220.
23. All studies of Leovigild's reign have to base themselves on John: K.F. Stroheker, "Leowigild," in *Germanentum und Spätantike* (Zurich, 1965), 134–91; J.N. Hillgarth, "Coins and Chronicles: propaganda in sixth-century Spain and the Byzantine background," *Historia* 15 (1966): 483–508; L.A. García Moreno, *Historia de España Visigoda* (Madrid, 1989): 113–31.
24. E.g., Malaca: John, s.a. 570; Asidonia: s.a. 571; Corduba: s.a. 572.
25. Victoriacum: John, s.a. 581; Reccopolis: John, s.a. 578.
26. The evidence is Sozomen, *Historia ecclesiastica* 9.11.4; 9.12.1; Orosius 7.40.5–6.
27. As is shown by Oros. 7.40.5: [*Constantinus*] *misit in Hispanias iudices: quos cum provinciae obedienter accepissent, duo fratres* . . . etc.
28. J. L. Argente Oliver, et al., *Tiermes II (Campañas de 1979 y 1980)* (Madrid, 1984) and id., et al., *Tiermes III (Campañas de 1981–1984)* (Madrid, 1994), which actually describes the findings through 1986.
29. The only reliable edition is L. Vazquéz de Parga, ed., *Sancti Braulionis Caesaraugustani Episcopi Vita S. Emiliani* (Madrid, 1943).
30. *VSE* 9.
31. *VSE* 10.
32. *VSE* 12.
33. *VSE* 13.
34. A. T. Fear, *Lives of the Visigothic Fathers*. Translated Texts for Historians (Liverpool, 1997), 28.
35. *VSE* 26.
36. Maximus and Columba: *VSE* 16; Honorius: *VSE* 17.

Towns, Vici and Villae: Late Roman Military Society on the Frontiers of the Province Valeria

ZS. VISY

DIOCLETIAN REORGANIZED THE PROVINCES OF THE ENTIRE ROMAN EMPIRE AND their administration: their number increased to almost one hundred and their governmental structure was divided into military and civilian spheres. Out of the two Pannoniae he created four provinces, and his colleague Galerius named the northeastern one after his wife, the daughter of Diocletian, Valeria. The province of Valeria corresponded to what is now the eastern half of the Hungarian territory west of the Danube, its eastern boundary, but its exact western boundary with the province Pannonia Prima is still a matter of discussion. To its the south lay the province Pannonia secunda. The two provinces were generally separated by the river Drava, but a short sector north of the Drava fell within Pannonia Secunda (Ad Militare [Batina, Kisköszeg] in Valeria: Not. Dign. Occ. XXXIII 45 - Ad Novas [Zmaje-vac, Vörösmart] in Pannonia Secunda: Not Dign. Occ. XXXII 40). The capital of the new province, Valeria, remained Aquincum (Budapest-Óbuda), but only for the military government under the *dux provinciae*. The head of the civil government was the *praeses provinciae*, who first had his seat in Aquincum (Alföldi 1942, 699; Mócsy 1974, 273), but after Constantine was in Sopianae (Pécs) (Amm. Marc. XXVIII 1,5). Instead of Sopianae, Fitz proposed

Herculia (Fitz 1984, 279- and Fitz 1993-95, 1181), but this hypothesis remains unproven and has not been widely accepted (Tóth 1982, 55f.). Since a *praeses provinciae* for Valeria is not mentioned in the *Notitia Dignitatum*, Mócsy (1962, 611) and Várady (1969, 38) suggested that the governor of this province was a *dux et praeses*. Fitz rejects this theory (Fitz 1993-95, 1187-).

The military situation in Valeria was complex, particularly because of the invasions and disruptions caused by various Germanic groups. From the north came the *Quadi*, from the east the *Vandali*, but foremost were the desperate *Sarmati*, who wanted to escape conflict with their Germanic foes by admission into the Empire and the security of its provinces. The division of Pannonia inferior took place in 296, the year of the victory over the Carpi by Galerius, who settled them in Valeria (Aur. Victor Caes. 39, 43, cf. Eutrop. VIII 25, 2) in the region around Sopianae (Amm. Marc. XXVIII 1,5). After the Sarmatian wars at the end of the third and at the beginning of the fourth century, an extensive system of walls was erected in the Hungarian plain from the Danube bend to the Iron gate, which continued in existence up to the death of Valens at Adrianople in 378. After the major losses of the third and first half of the fourth centuries the frontier system was again reorganized. There was still another major phase of building and remodeling fortifications under Valentinian (364-75), but after 378 this activity all but ceased. It seems that the last turrets were erected in a corner of some former fortresses during the final years of the fourth or at the beginning of the fifth century. It is obvious from their scale that only a few soldiers could serve in these turrets, and according to scholarly opinion the soldiers served not for money but for land. The main question is, who were these soldiers? Were they provincials or newcomers? Although the details and exact dates cannot be ascertained, it is clear that the province Valeria was ceded to the Huns as *foederati*. Although the surrender was made in 433, the Huns may have acquired Valeria as early as 425, as a reward for helping Aetius in the civil war (Bóna 1993, 46).

Since there were a great many military centers in the interior of the province as well as along the Danube—primarily the troops of the army of the *comitatenses* in Valeria—the army determined the structure of the society. One can imagine that an exception could have existed in the towns, but

legionary fortress
auxiliary fortress
colonia or municipium
other locality
road
bridge
summit
above 300 meter
above 500 meter
NORICVM
PANNONIA
PRIMA
SAVIA
DALMATIA
PANNONIA
SECVNDA
100 km

there were very few civil centers and towns without military elements. A similar non-military evolution could have theoretically taken place in the small villages and on the villas, but in reality a significant portion of the rural proprietors were veterans or other military people. According to the archaeological evidence, the demographics of the rural communities was somewhat changed in the fourth century by the increasing number of newly admitted barbarians of various origins. This gradual change in the population accelerated during the last decades of the fourth and the first decades of the fifth century, particularly in the frontier zone, in the *vici* of the fortresses and in the fortresses themselves.

A mobile field army was organized in Illyricum in the last years of Constantius II's reign, while he was concluding his campaign against the Sarmatians (A. Demandt, RE Suppl. XII 1970, 553-). He placed it under the command of a *magister militum*. In 396, as the empire was divided, Arcadius received two Illyrian *dioeceses*, Dacia and Macedonia, and 26 corps of the mobile army of the former Illyrian *dioeceses* were stationed in them, while there remained 22 with a strength of about 15,000 men in the Pannonian *dioeceses* administered by Honorius (Várady 1961, 49; Demandt 1970, 622) under the command of the *comes Illyrici* (*Not.Dign. Occ.* VII 40). The location of the fortresses of the mobile army are quite unknown, but there are some suggestions for probable or possible bases for this army Valeria: Környe, Herculia, Ságvár, and Alsóheténypuszta in Valeria; Fenekpuszta in Valeria; and Ludbreg in Savia. The various theories concerning the purposes of these forts have been generated primarily to account for the fact that within their huge perimeter walls, with thicknesses of 2.3-2.6 m, no barracks or similar structures for the soldiers have been found. Each fortress contains a huge magazin, a headquarters-type building with bath, and some small buildings. So much military building precludes a purely economic function, but their purpose could be—as several scholars have recently pointed out—of a military character. Fitz sees them as the military bases of the 15,000 man-strong mobile army of western Illyricum (Fitz 1993-95, 1191-). Lacking any signs of barrack-buildings, however, this remains only a hypothesis, albeit a credible one. He dates their first phase to the era of Constantine, which would correlate with the Illyrian stay of the army of Constantine at the time of his joint rule with Licinius, and the second phase to the time of Constantius II. This dating seems to be too early. In the second phase the U-shaped turrets were changed to round ones. Since no round turrets have been found in fortresses in the frontier zone, and since the building of their U-shaped turrets can be dated to the time of Constantius II (Lőrincz and Visy 1980, 697-), it must be assumed that the second period of the inner fortresses, during which their U-shaped turrets were modified, was later, in the 370s (Tóth 1987-88, 30-) or even later still (Barkóczi 1994, 91-).

The mobile army, *comitatensis*, was altered after 395, but not withdrawn or dispersed. The *Notitia Dignitatum* mentions three units, which were organized or reorganized after 395 A.D.: *Honoriani victores, Mauri Honoriani seniores,* and *Mattiari Honoriani Gallicani,* all under the leadership of the *comes Illyrici* (*Not. Dign. Occ.* VII 48-52). In 406-7 the Illyrian army received the *legiones pseudocomitatenses* organized from other units of the frontier troops (Hoffmann 1969-70, 408n. 479). This augmentation might have been connected to the appointment of Alaric as *magister militum* for western Illyricum by Honorius in 406 (he had held this same rank for Eastern Illyricum since 395 (Fitz 1993-95, 1318). Since Generidus received the military post for Raetia, Noricum and Pannonia Prima, and later for Dalmatia in 408, it can be suggested that he was also the commander—as a kind of *comes Illyrici* (Hoffmann 1969-70, 213)—of Savia and Valeria simultaneously. According to Fitz, the mobile army was withdrawn from Valeria to Dalmatia at this time (Fitz 1980, 58; Fitz 1993-95, 1319).

The *limitanei* were reduced at the beginning of the fifth century. Some units became part of the *legiones pseudocomitatenses;* others, like the *Taurunenses* (*Not. Dign. occ.* V 262) and the *Antianenses* (*Not. Dign. occ.* V 262), left their post on the frontier (Hoffmann 1969-70, 73). The *Acincenses* (*Not. Dign. occ.* VII 101), the *Cornacenses* (*Not. Dign. occ.* 102), and perhaps the *Martenses* (*Not. Dign. occ.* VII 91) left Illyricum under Valentinian (Hoffmann 1969-70, 224-) or between 395-98 (Alföldi 1924-26, II 77). It seems that after 395 the best units were removed and only the weaker troops were left as kind of a peasant-militia organization (Fitz 1993-95, 1321). The overwhelming majority of those soldiers who remained were barbarian *foederati* (Soproni 1978, 202-; Fitz 1993-95, 1321).

The weakened frontier no longer played an important role in the province of Valeria, and it may be supposed that it was at this time that small towers were built instead of fortresses or that turrets were erected in a corner of some of the earlier fortifications while the remainder of the fort was allowed to crumble or was used as a quarry (Visy 1988b). There is a hint of this final realignment of manpower in the *Notitia Dignitatum*, according to which some troops were routinely being transferred from their former posts to new duty stations from the time of Constantine to about 425-30 (Várady 1969, 262; Soproni 1978, 161-; Fitz 1993-95, 1322-), but surely those duty stations indicated by the word *nunc* in the *Notitia Dignitatum* were the units' most recent postings. These assignments took place according to Soproni in 378-80, according to Várady in 409 (Várady 1961, 83), and according to Fitz at the time of the last notices in the *Notitia Dignitatum*, that is at the end of the 420s. Fitz's arguments regarding the Roman reoccupation of Pannonia Secunda and possibly Valeria from the Huns in 427 after fifty years of Hunnic occupation (*Pannoniae, quae per quinquaginta annos ab Hunnis retinebanur, a Romanis receptae sunt.* – Marcellinus, Chron. Min. II 76) are insufficient. So I am led back to the beginning of the fifth century, when most other changes demonstrably took place in this area, as being the most likely date for these events, ca. 407-9 as suggested by Várady.

Four units were transferred at this time from one place to another within Valeria. The reassignments are worthy of discussion. Two of them were taken from frontier fortresses on one side of the Danube and relocated to the other side: the *cuneus equitum stablesianorum* from Ripa Alta (Tolna) to Conradcuha (but for Conradcuha as *contra* see Soproni 1978, 162) and the *equites sagittarii* from Altinum (Kölked) to contra Florentiam (Dunafalva). This relocation must have been made at a time when the contra-fortresses were still in use. On the basis of stamped tiles their first period of occupation should be dated to the late Constantinian era, and the second to the reign of Valentinian. There are no hints of any later garrisonings except in the *Notitia Dignitatum*—that is, if the contra-fortresses listed there include some of these—but any such identification must remain tentative. The archaeological finds of those opposite Valeria do not support their military use later than the fourth century. If the *Notitia Dignitatum* mentions not these, but some others as yet unidentified fortresses on the left side of the Danube, we certainly cannot reckon a strong Roman frontier defense controlling *Barbaricum* as well after the end of the century despite the *Notitia.* Since it can at best be argued that these fortifications were probably manned up to the eve of the battle at Hadrianople in 378, and perhaps were still garrisoned under Theodosius (that is until 395) or even up to the last known reorganization of the frontier of Valeria in 407-8, any hypothesis that seeks to describe the left-bank fortresses as viable Roman military posts in the late 420s has no solid basis. Therefore, it seems that the last redistribution of units on the frontier of Valeria took place earlier, at the latest in about 407-8.

The *equites sagittarii* of Altinum lay according to the *Notitia Dignitatum occ.* (XXXIII 44) *nunc in burgo contra Florentiam.* The *equites sagittarii* was in theory a 500-800 man strong unit (Várady 1961), but this is only its earlier paper-strength; nothing proves that it maintained this size at the end of the fourth or at the beginning of the fifth century. One should assume, on the contrary, that the decreasing significance of the *limitanei,* the increasing number of *foederati* deployed in the frontier zone, and the decline in the fiscal means at the empire's disposal, did not allow it to sustain the former troop strengths of these units.

A further point in this discussion is that the *Notitia Dignitatum* uses the word *burgo* for the fortress of the *equites sagittarii* in contra Florentiam. If this reference is to the fortlet known on the left bank of the Danube opposite the fortress Florentia (Lugio) in Dunaszekcs, it could not possibly have housed a mounted unit of 500-800 men, for it was only about 30 × 60 m in size. These dimensions are approximately the same for all the other known contra-fortlets. Taking into account the excavated fortlets in Nógrádverce (Paulovics 1934, 210; Visy 1988a, 74), there was only one larger building in this territory and it was most probably used as a storehouse rather than as a barrack (Nagy 1998, 37). A few years ago what appears to be traces of a small fortress were noted near the contra-fortlet of Dunafalva, but this unverified structure would also have been too small to have held a mounted unit of 500-800 men, since it measures but ca. 60 × 100 m. The known or proposed forts on the left side of the Danube at Florentia (Lugio) were only large enough then for a small unit. These archaeologically attested or supposed defenses were contemporary to the last transfer of units attested in the *Notitia* and could not have involved a high number of soldiers. Also the word *burgus* is significant. It had the meaning of a small fortlet, mostly in the form of a turret. Such turrets are known from Valeria and represent the last building activity on the *limes* there. Since they date to the last years of the 4th century at the earliest (Visy 1988b; Soproni dates them earlier, just right after 378; Soproni 1978, 204; Soproni 1985, 95-), we must assume that the *burgus* of the *Notitia Dignitatum* was such a fortlet.

TOWNS

The towns in Valeria consisted of the former *coloniae* Aquincum and Brigetio, and some other settlements such as Floriana (Csákvár), Herculia (Tác) and Sopianae (Pécs), which played the role of territorial centers without a formal Roman municipal organization. Two more urban centers should be mentioned: the settlements at Tricciana (Ságvár) and Felsleperd. The latter lies north of Dombóvár, but except for surface observations nothing is known about it. Perhaps its role was taken over by the fortified settlement of Iovia nearby at Alsóheténypuszta. All these towns had defensive walls built in the third century. Near the *coloniae* of Aquincum and Brigetio, at a distance of 2-2.5 km, lay the legionary camps. Three other centers, Környe, Tricciana, and Iovia belonged to the chain of the late Roman fortified settlements of Valeria, but it is possible that Herculia, which has a same fortification system as the others, should be included in this system (Toth 1987-88, 32). Nothing is known in this respect about Floriana, where only the mere existence of the town wall has been detected.

VICI

The *vici* of the *castella* on the frontier comprised the second major group of settlements. They differ in shape and extent, but some may have been regional centers such as Solva (Esztergom), Constantia (Szentendre),

Intercisa (Dunaújváros), Lussonium (Dunakömld), and Lugio (Dunaszekcs). An interesting development can be detected in the late Roman fortress of Lussonium, which will serve us here as a good case study of this type. In the northwest corner of the fortress, in the front corridor of the main house that had a canal heating system, two large pits with plastered walls have been unearthed. Both storage pits can be generally dated to the end of the reign of Valentinian or soon thereafter. Their exact date cannot be assigned, but the latest coins found in them were those of Valens (364-65). Their beehive shape and plastered walls make it clear that they were used as granaries, but at the moment of their abandonment some precious things were hidden in them: lamps, spindle weights, a bronze scale, knives, an arrow head, a shieldboss, iron helmets, stamped tiles and various other items (Visy 1991, 263-; Kiss 1993a, 89-). The shieldboss with its conical form was not a Roman artifact but a barbarian one. According to stylistic parallels it is a Germanic type. Similar bosses were found in graves on the Hungarian plain: in Csongrád (in Berzsenyi street), in Tiszavalk and in Újhartyán (Lengvári 1992-95, 26). Lengvári notes that the helmets are typical late Roman forms—*typus Intercisa*—and it is clear they were used by both Romans and barbarians (Germans), who were in all probability barbarian *foederati.* Although no grain was found in the pits, enough burned wheat could be gathered in the surrounding area for analysis. The analysis of the material revealed that both *triticum aestivum* and *triticum sp.* were used here, but *triticum dicoccum Schrank* was also available in significant quantities. The last type was also used in the *Barbaricum,* and its presence in Roman territory suggests once again that at this time the inhabitants of the fort of Lussonium were not only indigenous Romans but included (German) *foederati* as well (Lengvári 1992-95, 27; Lengvári 1995, 113-).

VILLAE

During late Roman times the number of the large estates in Pannonia increased. The political and the economic crisis of the empire brought on a collapse of rural society, and only the bigger and richer owners could survive. The concentration of the landownership helped the emperor, on the one hand, and the richer owners on the other, to obtain large estates. Mócsy suggested that the fluctuating political situation toward the end of the third century and especially under the tetrarchy led to confiscations that accelerated this tendency (Mócsy 1974, 299f.). Though his general observation may be correct, one point in his argumentation needs modification. In his opinion the inland fortifications were fortified settlements, centers of imperial estates. The strongest support for his argument was the existence at each of these sites of a large granary *(horreum)*. These sites, however, could have been the fortifications of the mobile army, as discussed above, and there is no reason to believe that they were at the same time centers of large estates. The *horreum* and the main building could easily have served military purposes. The main building, often in the form of a peristyle villa, may have been the house of the commanding officer, and the granary may have held the wheat gathered for the army. If so, it means that the army bought the grain or obtained it in other ways—a great amount of it—to preserve the harvest and guarantee food first of all for the soldiers. From the measurements of such a granary we can determine the extent of the territory from which the grain was gathered, but this does not correspond to the area of a single, large estate.

Some years ago I tried to determine the extent of the lands associated with late Roman fortified settlements. From the capacity of the *horreum* in Fenékpuszta—4,500 m²—I deduced a harvest from about 5,000 ha of land. Through several calculations I got a harvested area of 10 × 10 km in extent (Visy 1994, 430). This calculation may be further elucidated. The granaries were to hold the harvest of the territory around the fortified settlement according to the needs anticipated for the army, but their existence and the related finds do not point to only one imperial estate, but several estates. It is quite certain that the grain was partly brought from some imperial estates as well as from some other large estates, which in extraordinary situations might have been confiscated. There is another possibility. In time of war the owners could transport their harvest into these granaries to keep it safe from the enemy.

Based on the analysis of villas and especially of small villages, it may be observed that the houses and their inhabitants preserved their culture and traditions during the fourth century, including the little clay cottages, partly cut into the earth. These rural dwellings too were still used in the late Roman times (Visy 1994, 425). Generally, the number of the villas increased and the quality of their buildings became higher. In the vicinity of Sopianae, surveys have shown that more villas were built. This could have been a consequence of the increasing significance of the town itself (Visy 1994, 428). Excavations of one such villa have now made substantial progress.

A Roman villa was found near Babarc, and Emory University, the Universität Passau, and the University of Pécs have been working in the recent years to understand its function and development. Investigations were carried out at first only on the surface with various kinds of the geophysical and remote sensing methods (Bender, Burns, and Visy 1992, 89-152). Excavation began in 1996 and continued in 1998. The SW corner of the villa and another building were partially uncovered, revealing the stone wall of the courtyard and a kiln. The Babarc villa had several occupation phases. The first can be dated to the second/third century, the second one to the fourth, and another very probably to the beginning of the fifth century. The evaluation of the rich archaeological material is underway, but already the analysis of the numismatic finds supports the suggested chronology of occupation. The latest coins are those of Valentinian and Valens, but it is certain that life went on after their rule.

The region of Lake Balaton was still preferred in the fourth century. The biggest and richest *villae* were built here. Mócsy supposed a concentration of the imperial domains in this region on the basis of the name of the village of Caesariana, not far from Veszprém. For many years excavation has proceeded at a *villa* north of the Balaton at Nemesvámos-Baláca. It is one of the greatest and richest villas known in Pannonia. Its first period belonged to the second century, but it was also in use in the fourth century. Not far from here excavations are on-going at another richly appointed villa at Szabadbattyán. The archaeological evidence gained up to now suggests that it might have been the center of a large (imperial?) domain. It should be mentioned that a richly decorated silver *tripus* was found not far from here in Polgárdi at the opening of the twentieth century, and that the Hungarian scholars remain convinced that the extremely rich SEVSO-treasure came to light in the same area (Mango 1990, 70f; Nagy and Tóth, 1990, 5f.; Mango and Bennett 1994). The fourteen plates, jugs, and other precious items of the SEVSO hoard were found in a large bronze kettle. Inscribed on the richest of its decorated silver plates was PELSO, that is, Lake Balaton. This treasure and the rich villas demonstrate that prior to ca. 380 Valeria ranked among the rich provinces of the empire, and that there was no sign of concern for an imminent collapse.

Some years ago I tabulated the number of *vici* and *villae* in Pannonia inferior/Valeria. The result was a total of 251 findspots. Many villas could be identified in the region of Aquincum, and smaller groups were concentrated around Sopianae and in the Kapos valley. Their density partly reflects the intensity of local archaeological activity, but the great number of the villas at Sopianae might also be a consequence of the growing importance of the town in the fourth century. As in most cases, we have only scarce finds gathered from the surface, and their exact identification and date cannot be known. It is important, nonetheless, that 106 out of the 251 were definitely active sites in the fourth century, and 9 of them also in the fifth. This number may be increased further because of the excavations made in the villas or in the *vici* such as in Szakály and Rétiföldek, where the excavations of D. Gabler have proven that they were also used in the fifth century (Gabler and Ottományi 1990, 161f.). This observation demonstrates, once again, that the fourth century was not a period of decline but was a flourishing time in Valeria. Developments in the villages and in the *villae* parallel that of the towns. An increasing number of the new inhabitants—*foederati* or those of a similar status—used the old settlements and the old buildings, but we cannot attribute the building activity to them, except the little domiciles with wooden posts, clay, plaster, and reused Roman building material.

THE ECONOMY

In late Roman times, especially under the Constantinian dynasty, the economy of the province expanded. This last economic flourish is attested in building activity in the towns, in the fortresses, and in their civil settlements, but primarily by the testimony of the cemeteries. It is a pity that the practice of setting up inscriptions was reduced to a minimum.

There are some clues for determining the industrial organization of Illyricum. We know of imperial workshops for cotton in Sirmium and in Bassiana (in Pannonia Secunda) under *procuratores gynaecii.* Imperial workshops for weaponry were organized in Sirmium, Carnuntum, and also in Valeria at Aquincum (*Not. Dign. Occ.* IX 18-20). They were under the administrative direction of the *praefectus praetorio,* and after 390 that of the *magister officiorum.* Although the precise location of the workshop in Aquincum is unknown, it can be assumed that the *fabrica* of the legionary fortress and later the *scutaria,* which took its origin from the *fabrica,* of the late Roman fortress were the most important centers of this activity. The *scutaria* was situated between the legionary fortress and the Danube. The richly decorated bronze plates of the wooden caskets from Valeria and from Illyricum (Gáspár 1971; Gáspár 1986) reveal the existence of a very high level of skilled craftsmenship. Such quality was most likely achieved in imperial workshops (Mócsy 1962, 766). Archaeological materials indicate that there was a similar workshop in Brigetio, although it is not mentioned in the *Notitia Dignitatum* (Láng 1938, 175; L. Nagy 1942, 614f.).

The economic activity declined at the beginning of the fifth century. Two textile workshops were transferred from Savia (Bassiana and Iovia) to Dalmatia. As Fitz pointed out, this could have been connected with the withdrawal of the mobile army from Pannonia into Dalmatia (Fitz 1993-95, 1320). The continuance of the *Acincensis scutaria* at this time is highly likely, since it belonged—along with the assumed Brigetio workshop—to the frontier army, which clearly existed into the first decades of the fifth century.

CEMETERIES

The larger the settlement, the more cemeteries there were, and in them some graves demonstrate that a rich upper class had separated itself from the other strata of the local society. One can also adduce religious differences.

Some finds and some grave forms also show new, partly barbarian elements. Society became poorer after the battle of Hadrianople, and adopted more barbarian characteristics, at least in part because many people fled to safer provinces and more barbarian groups settled in Valeria. The newcomers settled partly in the frontier zone and partly in the interior of the province. From the fifth century it becomes very difficult to distinguish between Roman and barbarian finds and groups in Pannonia.

From the analysis of the grave goods in the cemetery at Csákvár (Floriana), Barkóczi and Salamon observed that there were some significant differences among the graves. These fell into two groups: one belonging to the provincial Roman population of the fourth century and a second belonging to a new mixed group. In the first group most graves were built from tiles with a main W-E orientation, and their content was only or mostly made up of items with Roman characteristics. The other group had simpler graves with a primary orientation of S-N. Here were discovered finds such as earrings with polygonal knobs, double combs made of bone, brooches with bent feet, and a great variety of beads. Many of these finds have parallels in the late Sarmatian cemetery of Tápé and Malajdok or in the cemeteries of the Cernjahov and Marosszentanna Culture of Gothic origin. The glass conical beakers, sometimes decorated with blue dots, may have originated in the area of the Black Sea (Barkóczi and Salamon 1970, 56-; Barkóczi and Salamon 1978-79, 76). Barkóczi and Salamon proposed that the new specimens be connected with the *foederati* people arriving in 379-80 or at the end of the century. Their presence can be traced until about 427, when the Huns took over the governance of Valeria.

The analysis of the Szabadbattyán cemetery revealed that Roman craft traditions still existed under and beyond Attila's rule, as indicated by brooches without onion shapes and by bracelets with animal heads or made of bone. New artifact types make their appearance; for example, mirrors typical of the steppe nomads and the polygonal earrings with round stems. To this archaeological horizon also belong the iron buckles and the iron brooches with bent feet (Barkóczi and Salamon 1974-75, 104-; Barkóczi and Salamon 1978-79, 76-). Other examples of nomadic mirrors were unearthed from tile graves in Szekszárd-Palánk (Mészáros, Rég. Füz. 1, 1960, 70),

Kővágószölös (Burger, 1985-86), and from a stone grave at Környe (unpubl.). Various examples of cicada brooches are also associated with this horizon (Untersiebenbrunn, Intercisa, Aquincum - Nagy T., BpR 13, 1943, 383, fig. 28., Gorsium (Bánki, AR 15, 1976, plate I/6) as are certain plate brooches (Szekszárd and Palánk, Intercisa).

The three brick graves in Babarc belong to the late Roman era, possibly to the fifth century (Gy. Török, Majorossy Imre Múzeum Ért. 1941, 3-). In the grave of a child here was found a jug of the Muzsla type. Not far from these graves lies the remains of the Roman villa discussed above. Three brick-graves were excavated within the area of the villa and just outside of it. The graves contained no archaeological material, but it is clear from the location that they represent the latest phase of the villa. Some parts of the villa lay in ruins with only some poorly made huts standing there. These huts were similar to the small dwellings found in Lussonium and elsewhere, but before this undiscovered in Babarc. In many other places, and when the analyses are complete probably also at Babarc, the stratgraphy and ceramic finds make it clear that the provincial way of life went on for decades after the last coins were struck.

ROMAN PROVINCIALS AND FOEDERATI

The new materials coming to light in the cemeteries of the old Roman towns and villages have such strong relationships with the archaeological material of the Carpathian basin and occasionally with the Pontic region that a continuous connection must have existed from at least 380 between two sides of the frontiers. These interconnections led to an ethnographically diverse population. The newcomers were of different ethnic origins—some Sarmatian, some Gothic, others possibly Vandalic or Hunnic—but regardless of their ethnicity their material culture had many similar or even identical features with Roman provincial types. It is evident that barbarian culture had acquired many Roman skills and techniques, but simultaneously their various cultures, art, workmanship, and customs had mixed with each other. The striking fact is that the differences on both sides of the frontiers became less, little by little achieving a great many similar characteristics (Ottományi 1991; Barkóczi and Salamon passim).

After the battle of Hadrianople, a Gothic-Alanic-Hunnic group arrived in Valeria with Alatheus and Saphrac in 379. Before they got a territory of their own, they raided towns like Mursa and devastated many settlements. The only written source for them is the epitaph of Amantinus, bishop of Iovia (CIL V 1623 = Dobó 602), who is also mentioned as their bishop. It is not known whether this reference to an Iovia is identical with the town at Alsóheténypuszta or at Ludbreg, and so scholarly opinion is divided as to their precise settlement area.

Some new ceramic forms and techniques are of importance for the fourth century, and especially for its later decades. The intensive distribution of glazed ceramics began after ca. 380, and this type was also produced in the fifth century. Smooth ceramics also began to appear widely after ca. 380, and are associated with the *foederati*. Although this type of decoration was used throughout Roman times, its late Roman form had certain peculiar features—parallel vertical and horizontal lines as well as wave and X-decorations on the surface of the vessels. The form and decorative technique of the late Roman items are quite similar to or identical with contemporary examples found on the Hungarian Plain, but it must be emphasized that their technique of manufacture is Roman. Their occurrence in the frontier zone has become a kind of detector of *foederati* of some Sarmatian or Germanic (Vandalic perhaps) extraction. In Pilismarót a pottery kiln used to make this material was unearthed along with other finds. Soproni assumed that the inhabitants of this small fortlet, occupied during the first decades of the fifth century as well a bit earlier, were Germanic *foederati*. He believed that the ceramics that came to light together here along with pieces of handmade pottery indicated their presence, but Ottományi pointed out that this hypothesis cannot be proven. Because the context and the locations of their discovery in the frontier zone of Valeria varies considerably, we cannot use this ceramic type to determine the location of settlements of the new *foederati* within the province (Ottományi 1991, 51).

This same kind of pottery and related finds, such as certain types of brooches, knives and other utensils, as well as some weapons, have come to light at other places. In Lussonium we found a great number of examples of smoothed pottery, and M. Kiss has demonstrated that they were used at the end of the fourth and at the beginning of the fifth century (Kiss 1993a, 89-; Kiss 1993b, 185-; Kiss 1994, 249-). At Lussonium the location of parallel rows of postholes reveal that the site was still in use after the collapse of the Valentinianic building in the corner of the fortress. The pottery could have been made and used by the inhabitants, living not as soldiers within a camp but as *foederati coloni* in its ruins. A huge tower was discovered in the south corner of the fortress. This tower could also have been built and used in the fifth century, as is suggested by the dating of the finds associated with it. Although it is not easy to detect such buildings because of the thin and fragile layers in which they lie, often just above the last main phase of building, similar ones have been found in other fortresses on the Danubian frontier where sufficiently careful excavations have been made—e.g. Kiss has assembled a list of these and their publication (for a comprehensive list see Kiss 1995, 411f.), in Carnuntum, Odiavum (Vékony 1985, 86f.), and in Campona (Fülep 1968, 357f.)—and we know also of similar structures at Gorsium and from the military fortress of Intercisa.

The years after the death of Theodosius brought sorrow to Valeria. Stilicho permitted some barbarian groups from the Hungarian Plain to settle in the province, and traces have been identified by Barkóczi and Salamon in the cemeteries of Sárvár (Floriana) (Barkóczi and Salamon 1970, 35-), Brigetio (Barkóczi and Salamon 1978-79, 76-), Castra ad Herculem (Pilismarót) (Barkóczi 1960, 111-) and Intercisa (Barkóczi and Salamon 1973, 73-). They suggest that some items (brooches, combs, amulets, spinningwurls) found mixed with the Roman material were artifacts of the newcomers. The materials have analogies in the Tisza region (Bóna 1971, 223-) but assigning them to any specific ethnic group remains hazardous (perhaps Alans or Vandals). A similar cemetery has recently been excavated in Visegrád and Lepence. The chronology of these cemeteries lies between the end of the fourth century and the thirties of the fifth, around the time when Valeria fell into the hands of the Huns. In the extensive cemetery in Csákvár (Floriana), *solidi* of Honorius and Johannes together with some mintings of Theodosius II struck from 430 came to light in a grave. All these coins might have had as their origin the recompense for the Hunnic aid given to Aetieus in 425. Deformed skulls and horse skeletons were found in the latest graves, indicating that the inhumation traditionally practiced by the Roman population had come to an end here by this time (Bóna 1993, 46). New cemeteries were opened, sometimes within the old towns and amidst the houses (Bánki 1975, 303; Fitz 1993-95, 1328), making it is clear that these buildings were not still in use. The graves reveal some Roman characteristics as well; for example, they are made from bricks. Nomadic mirrors, earrings with polygonal knobs, and brooches in the form of a cicada, are the finds with the most important identifying characteristics: eg. at Intercisa (Visy 1981, 211-) and at Szabadbattyán (Barkóczi and Salamon 1974-75, 89-). In Sopianae the *cella trichora* and the grave chapels were used as houses by the old and new inhabitants (Fülep 1973, 323).

After Hunnic rule collapsed various Germanic peoples arrived in Valeria. East Goths settled south of Lake Balaton, and Suevi to the north of it (Bóna 1971, 227-). While this immigration was taking place, there was an emigration of the Roman population to Dalmatia and Italy, leaving only the southwestern part of Pannonia as Roman territory. Towns in this area, like Poetovio or Emona, have preserved their Roman names whereas elsewhere the placenames were lost to the languages of the new populations. To replace Valeria a new province, Valeria Media, was created in about 433 in the southwestern corner of Savia (Tóth 1989, 222-). Here the Roman population could preserve its culture; the Germans—Goths in the fifth and the Langobards in the sixth century—could not settle south of the line Savaria–Keszthely–Sopianae (Bóna 1971, 296). The territory of the new province remained a Roman enclave, and its freedom continued into the early Avar era (Keszthely culture—Alföldi 1924-26, II 55-; Kiss 1967, 51-).

SUMMARY

Ethnic relations were profoundly changed in late Roman times in Valeria, and these changes accelerated with time. Under the Tetrarchy the Carpi were settled in Valeria, and there is a *communis opinio* that the location of this resettlement was the territory south of Lake Balaton and in the Mecsek region. Some handmade pottery found in the neighborhood of Ságvár can be ascribed to them (Visy 1994, 430). Between 322 and 334 there were more admissions: Sarmatians and Vandalic groups arrived, but the first Sarmatians to arrive were assigned to other provinces. A. Mócsy and M. Nagy proposed that the group admitted in 322 could have been partly Vandalian from the fact that their king's name, Rausimodus, was Germanic (Nagy 1993). According to Jordanes the Hasdingian Vandals were allowed to settle in Valeria after they had been defeated by the Goths. Nagy tried to locate them within the province. He believed that the W-E orientation of the graves with weaponry (spearheads, lanceshafts, shieldbosses, knives), spoons, and wooden buckets might be an indicator of their Vandalian ethnicity, because these features and finds began to be present in the cemeteries from the second third of the fourth century and correspond chronologically to the reference in Jordanes. Strikingly enough, these were found in the same general area in southern Valeria where earlier barbarian materials have come to light. The German character of these burials was pointed out previously by other scholars; for example, Dombay associated this horizon with the West Germans. L. Barkóczi has recently dealt with some of the special finds from this horizon, such as engraved belt decorations in propeller form and other items with peculiar characteristics. He associates these with a Germanic military group, specifically with the commanders of the mobile field army of Constantius II transferred to Valeria from Gaul (Barkóczi 1994).

Regarding the mobile army it can be shown that toward the end of the fourth century new Moorish and Gallic units arrived in Pannonia, and according to our archaeological and literary sources more "foreign" troops may have been stationed in the Danube region at this time. Unquestionably the Gallic–Hunnic–Alanian group brought the greatest changes to the ethnic composition of Valeria. Unlike other new arrivals who were provincials, old neighbors, or people allied to Rome, these new settlers had not enough time and involvement with Romans to be accustomed to Roman culture. Although they took over the defense of the frontier as *foederati,* their activity was directed toward creating their own rule, not furthering that of the Roman Empire. One can assume that the little fortlets on the frontier, in the form of towers like those in Pilismarót, Azaum, Cirpi, Lussonium and other sites along the Danube, were manned by this type of the *limitanei.* They took over the surrounding territory step by step and used it as their own.

The towns and the larger settlements preserved their Roman heritage in Valeria the longest. Although at the end of the fourth and at the beginning of the fifth century many provincials fled to Dalmatia and Italy, many other people did not flee but remained in their settlements and tried to live their own lives. Their cemeteries were in use until at least the thirties of the fifth century, and the newcomers opened cemeteries in separate places near the towns and vici. Some of the Roman population was able to go to the newly organized province ofValeria Media in the Save region, while other elements of the remaining population merged within a few generations with the newer peoples ofValeria.

BIBLIOGRAPHY

Alföldi A. 1924–1926. *Der Untergang der Römerherrschaft in Pannonien* I-II. Berlin.

———. 1942. *Budapest az ókorban.* In *Budapest története* I-II. Budapest.

Bánki, Zs. 1975. "Forschungen in Gorsium im Jahre 1973." *Alba Regia* 14:329–33.

Barkóczi, L. 1960. "Ein spätrömisches Gräberfeld in Pilismarót." *Folia Arch.* 12:111–32.

———. 1994. "Beiträge zur Geschichte der Provinz Valeria im IV-VI. Jh." *Specimina. nova* [1995] 10:57–135.

Barkóczi, L., and Á. Salamon. 1970. "Bestattungen von Csákvár aus dem Ende des 4. und dem Anfang des 5. Jahrhunderts." *Alba Regia* 11:35–80.

———. 1973. "Archäologische Angaben zur spätrömischen Geschichte des pannoniaschen Limes-Gräberfeld von Intercisa, I." *Mitt. Arch. Inst.* 4:73–95.

———. 1974–75. "Das Gräberfeld von Szabadbattyán," *Mitt. Arch. Inst.* 5:89–111.

———. 1978–79. "Archäologische Angaben zur spätrömischen Periodisation Pannoniens (378–476)," *Mitt. Arch. Inst.* 8–9:76–78.

Bender, H., T. Burns, and Zs. Visy. 1992. "Die Römische Ansiedlung bei Babarc, Komit Baranya, Ungarn. Die Prospektionsarbeiten in den Jahren 1989, 91," *Specimina nova* [1994] 7:89–152.

Bóna, I. 1993. *A hunok és nagykirályaik.* Budapest (Also in English).

———. 1994. *Roman Frontier Studies 1989.* (Rec.). *Acta Arch. Hung.* 46:450–53.

Burger, A. 1985–86. "Die spätrömische Villa in Kővágószöllös." *Janus Pannonius Múzeum Évkönye* 30–31:65f.

Dobó, Á. 1975. *Inscriptiones extra fines Pannoniae Daciaeque repertae ad res earundem provinciarum pertinentes*. Budapest.

Fitz, J. 1980. "Die Innenbefestigungen der Provinz Valeria." *Alba Regia* 18:53–60.

———. 1984. "Gorsium und Herculia." *Alba Regia* 20:273–74.

———. 1993–95. *Die Verwaltung Pannoniens in der Römerzeit* I-IV. Budapest.

Fülep, F. 1968. "Campona," *RE* Suppl. 11:357–68.

———. 1973. "Beiträge zur frühmittelalterlichen Geschichte von Pécs (Sopianae - Quinque Basilicae - Fünfkirchen)," *Acta Arch. Hung.* 25:307–26.

———. 1984. *Sopianae. The history of Pécs during the Roman era, and the problem of the continuity of the late Roman population*. Budapest.

Gabler, D., and K. Ottományi. 1990. "Késo római házak Szakályban." *Archaeologiai Értesitö* 117: 161–88.

Gáspár, D. 1971. *Die spätrömischen Kästchenbeschläge in Pannonien*, Acta Ant. et Arch. Szeged, 15.

———.1986. *Römishe Kästchen in Pannonien*. Antaeus.

Hoffmann, D. 1969–70. *Das spätrömische Bewegungsheer und die Notitia Dignitatum* I-II. Bonn.

Jones, A. H. M. 1964. *The later Roman Empire 284 - 602*. I-III. Oxford.

Kiss, A. 1967. "Die Stellung der Keszthely-Kultur in der Frage der römischen Kontinuität Pannoniens." *Janus Pannonius Múzeum Évkönye* 12:49–59.

Kiss, M. 1993a. "Lussonium erödje a 4. század végén - 5. század elején." *A Herman Ottó Múzeum Évkönye (Miskolc)* 30–31:89–106.

———. 1993b. "Zum Problem der barbarischen Ansiedlungen in Pannonien." *Spec. nova* [1994] 9:185–220.

———. 1994. "Adatok a Murga-típusú korsók kérdéséhez (Daten zur Frage der Krüge vom Murga-Typus)." In *A kökortól a középkorig*, 249–57. Szeged.

———. 1995. "Bauspuren mit Pfostenkonstruktion vom Ende des 4. Anfang des 5. Jh. in der Festung Lussonium." In *Roman Frontier Studies*, 411–15.

Láng, N. 1938. "Das Dolichenum von Brigetio." In *Dissertationes Pannonicae ex intstituto numismatico et archaeologico universitatis P. Pázmány nominatae Budapestiensis*, ser. 2, 11: 165–81.

Lengvári, I. 1995. "Grain Storage Pits from *Lussonium* Roman Fort," *Spec. nova* 11: 113–25.

———. 1992–95. "A wallersteini modell és a késö 'barbár' - római kapcsolatok." *Savaria* 22–23: 26ff.

Lörincz, B., and Zs. Visy. 1980. "Die Baugeschichte des Auxiliarkastells von Intercisa," *BAR* Int. Ser. 71, 681–701.

Mango, M. 1990. "Der Sevso Schatzfund: eine Ensemble westlichen und ostlichen Kunstschaffen," *Antike Welt* 21:70–88.

Mango, M., and A. Bennett. 1994. *The Sevso Treasure : art historical description and inscriptions*. JRA Suppl. Ser., Supp. 12. Ann Arbor.

Mócsy, A. 1962. "Pannonia." *RE* Suppl. 9:515–776.

———. 1974. *Pannonia and Upper Moesia. A History of the Middle Danube Provinces of the Roman Empire*. London-Boston.

Mócsy, A., and J. Fitz, eds. 1990. *Pannonia régészeti kézikönyve*. Budapest.

Nagy, L. 1942. "Fémmüvesség." In *Budepest az ókorban* 1–2 (Budapest in Antiquity). Budapest története I, edited by A. Alföldi, L. Nagy, and Gy. László. Budapest.

Nagy, M. 1993 "The Hasdingian Vandals in the Carpathian Basin (a Preliminary Report)." *Spec.nova* [1994] 9:157–84.

———. 1998. "Nagy Lajor, a Dunakanyar késö romai védrendszerének kutatoja." *Budapest Régiségei* 32: 35–43.

Nagy, M., and E. Tóth. 1990. "The Seuso Treasure. The Pannonian Connection?" *Minerva* 1.7:4–11.

Ottományi, K. 1991. "Késö római kerámia a leányfalui örtoronyból." *Studia Comitatensia* 22:51ff.

———. 1996. "Ein Töpferwerkstatt der spätrömischen Keramik mit Glättverzierung in Pilismarót-Malompatak." *Acta Arch. Hung.* 48:71ff.

Paulovics, I. 1934. "Freilegung einer Römerfestung in Nógrádveröce." *Arch. Ért.* 81:158–63, 210.

Soproni, S. 1978. *Der spätrömische Limes zwischen Esztergom und Szentendre. Das Verteidigungs-system der Provinz Valeria im 4. Jahrhundert.* Budapest.

———. 1985. *Die letzten Jahrzehnte des pannonischen Limes.* Münchner Beiträge zur Vor- und Frühgeschichte 38. München.

Tóth, E. 1982. "Tetrarchiezeitliche Namensgebung von Iovia-Herculia in Pannonien?" *Arch. Ért.* 109:55–72.

———. 1987–88. "Az alsóhetényi 4. századi eröd és temetö kutatása, 1981–1986. Eredmények és vitás kérdések." *Arch Ért.* 114:22–61.

———. 1989. "Provincia Valeria Media." *Acta Arch. Hung.* 41:197–226.

Vaday, A. 1994. "Late Sarmatian Graves and Their Connections within the Great Hungarian Plain." *Slov. Arch.* 42:105–24.

Várady, L. 1961. *Késörómai hadügyek és társadalmi alapjaik.* Budapest.

———. 1969. *Das letzte Jahrhundert Pannoniens 376 - 476.* Budapest 1969.

Vékony, G. 1985. "Koranépvándorláskori telepnyomok Pilismaróton. Frühvölkerwanderungszeitliche Siedlungsspuren in Pilismarót." *Communicationes Archaeologicae Hungariae.* 85–96.

Visy, Zs. 1981. "V. századi sír Intercisában (A grave in Intercisa from the 5th century)." *Arch. Ért.* 108:211–17.

———. 1988a. *Der pannonische Limes in Ungarn.* Budapest.

———. 1988b. Rec.: S. Soproni: *Die letzten Jahrzehnte des pannonischen Limes.* München 1984. - *Századok* 122:697–99.

———. 1991. "Lussonium: archaeological excavations 1988–1989." In *RFS* 1989, 263–67.

———. 1994. "Die ländliche Besiedlung und Landwirtschaft in Niederpannonien." In *Die ländliche Besiedlung und Landwirtschaft in den Rhein- und Donauprovinzen,* edited by H. Bender - H. Wolff, 421–50. Passau.

Archaeological Perspectives on Rural Settlement in Late Antiquity in the Rhine and Danube Area

HELMUT BENDER

THE REGIONS I WANT TO DEAL WITH LIE ALONG THE RHINE-DANUBE LINE AND include the Roman provinces of Germania Inferior and Superior, eastern Belgica, Raetia, and Noricum and the late Roman provinces of Germania Prima and Secunda, Belgica Prima, Maxima Sequanorum, Raetia Prima and Secunda, Noricum Ripense and Mediterraneum respectively.

Whereas the borders of these provinces were without natural barriers to the west and south-west in the direction of inner Gaul and eastward toward Pannonia, the central and eastern Alps made up a natural border toward south and south-east. The geographic conditions are extraordinarily different in climate, in soil conditions and in hydrology. Regions with dense populations, even in late antiquity, lay beside ones with sparse or no population at all (for example, in the high Alps); a significant portion of the area under consideration is comprised of low mountain ranges, which were almost unpopulated in Roman times up to a height of 1.506 m/5,000 ft.

A well-planned road system existed from the first century A.D., running east and west as well as toward the south to southern Gaul, Italy and the Balkans. Two large river systems, the Rhine and Danube, completed in an ideal manner the transportation network.

The distribution of large civil settlements, villages, forts, and farms varied greatly, and this had, in part, historical reasons. In the west and southwest, more or less along the Rhine, there was a close and productive network. Germania Inferior, Germania Superior, and Belgica with justification may be called economically strong. The foothills of the Alps across to Noricum, that is the regions along the upper and middle Danube, were sparsely settled. The south of Noricum, later Roman Noricum Mediterraneum, was full of towns and was highly developed economically. From the end of the first century A.D., the military was the dominant influence along the Rhine and the Danube. Both rivers were connected by a *limes* built over many decades and extending more than 500 km/300 miles through modern Germany. Together with the rivers, this Upper German-Raetian *limes* made up a long border with so-called Barbaricum or Germania, which exerted a not insignificant influence on the history of the provinces.

After the collapse of the Upper German-Raetian limes (about 270 A.D.) it took until the times of Diocletian before conditions had consolidated along the Rhine and Danube. By about 300 A.D. the so-called Danube–Iller– Rhine–*limes* was established, with the latest construction activities so far discovered dating from the reign of Valentinian I. The defensive line essentially ran along these rivers in late antiquity, and only the short piece from Lake Constance to Kempten crossed overland.

The number of troops stationed in the Rhine Danube provinces—consisting of legions, auxiliary troops, and numeri—can only be estimated. It might have amounted to 90,000 men at the end of the second century A.D. These men, their relatives, townspeople, tradesmen and manual workers all had to be supplied with basic food—cereals, meat, vegetables, and salads. Their needs for wine and oil also had to be met. Except for those items provided by import, which was very easy to accomplish because of the river system, everything was produced on the spot or in the surrounding areas. Establishing an agrarian structure in these regions was possible, in fact essential, because the stationing of the army here was an absolute necessity for the Romans. This will be illustrated later when we examine the hinterland of Regensburg. I estimate the total number of rural sites as having been at a minimum of 10,000 and a maximum of 15,000. This working hypothesis

The Passau Region. Published with permission R. Brulet, Louvain–La Neuve.

is extrapolated from the total number of securely identified sites that existed in Roman Germany at the end of the second century A.D., of which there are at least 5,000. It is very difficult to determine to what degree indigenous settlements, scarcely apparent in the archaeological record, truly existed, because of the fact that their buildings, which were mostly wooden or half-timbered, can only rarely be evaluated today. Contrary to the popular and pessimistic opinion of the Roman agrarian structure in the northwestern provinces up to era of the Severan emperors, my study of Germany's agrarian history paints a picture that is essentially positive with effective market structures, surplus production, settlements of manual workers, secure supplies of food and finished products, regularly met needs for imported goods—especially wine and oil—security on land and water, and finally, good and dependable transportation.[1] The troops and towns along the Rhine and Danube, the classical centers of consumption, never revolted because of food shortage or famine, for surely our sources would have recorded that.

Archaeobotanic[2] and archaeozoologic[3] studies of specimens from towns, forts, and estates done in the last three decades reveal a very sophisticated agriculture. Close to the larger settlements there were special plantations for perishable food that needed to be sold quickly. There were many types of special development and organization. To give but one example, specially constructed grain ships transported cereals planted in the southern part of Germania Inferior on good soil downstream to the delta of the Rhine.[4] Therefore, we can better understand how quite large estates were built in the best producing areas, such as the villa of Voerendaal with its gigantic *horreum*, where it was calculated that 235,000 kg of cereals could be stored. Here the area of the farmyard is 3.5 ha/8.6 acres, the whole estate about 250 ha/620 acres. I think it is about time that the discussion of economic structures, which remains at present very theoretical, is reoriented to take account of these new discoveries.

The well-balanced system of relationships between towns, military camps, and the countryside that developed up to the middle of the third century A.D. collapsed in late antiquity. It began to falter because of external threats and internal conflicts during the third century A.D. It would be

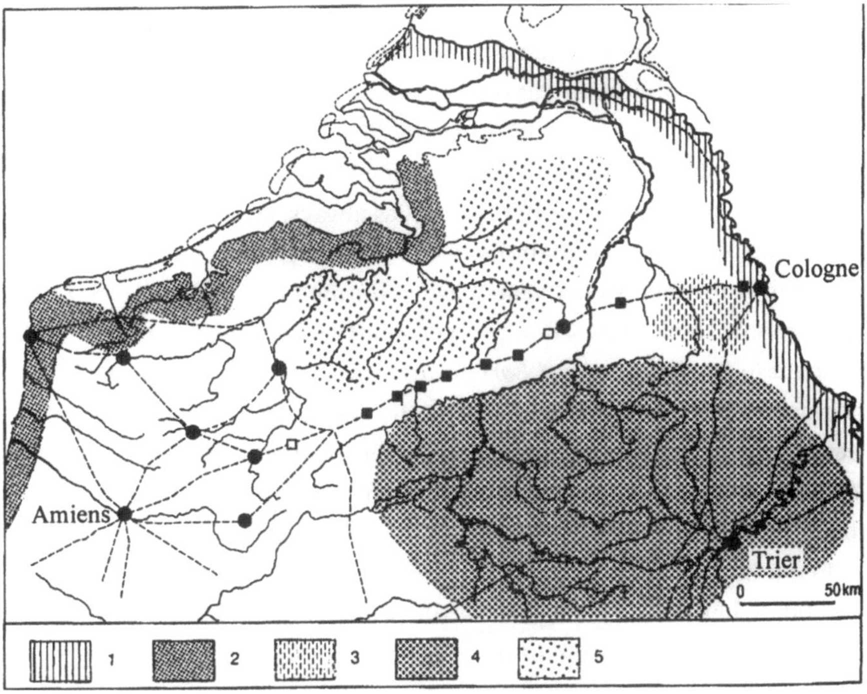

Germania Prima and Belgica Prima in Late Antiquity. 1. Limes, 2. Litus Saxonicum, 3. Area of fortified rural settlements, 4. Area of highground settlement—hilltop fortifications, 5. Toxandria. Published with permission R. Brulet, Louvain–La Neuve.

wrong, however, to describe these changes as decline, culmination, or radical change. After 300 A.D. people confronted new internal and external conditions and learned to react to developments in a flexible way. A new arrangement arose with very diverse local and regional structures that enabled the transition to the Middle Ages. With regard to the epoch after approximately the beginning of the fifth century A.D., it would be wrong again to speak of an abrupt break or radical change.

Before exploring some case studies of various regions, I would like to conclude my introductory remarks with reference to the region of Passau.[5] In Passau, ancient Batavis and Boiotro, communities lying across the river Inn from each other, or one might say, at the furthest tip of Raetia Secunda or in the most western part of Noricum Ripense respectively, there were regular troops stationed around 460. According to the *vita Severini* of Eugippius, the soldiers in Passau sent out a patrol in order to escort the expected arrival of pay to the fort safely.[6] The inhabitants are depicted as working in the fields from a secure, fortified place. The Roman way of life continued just as in many other regions, as always, even in the fifth century A.D. Archaeological examinations in the forts of Batavis and Boiotro conducted over the last twenty years have confirmed this image drawn from a hagiographic source. E. A.Thompson devoted a whole chapter specifically to Noricum in his *Romans and Barbarians* (1982), and now he would have to include the results of archaeology. By the way, in this chapter Thompson describes very nicely how public and military order have dissolved around Favianis in Noricum, where traditional borders have ceased to have any function at all.

Just a bit upstream of Passau is Künzing/Quintanis lying in the fertile Gäuboden, beyond which lay the territory of Gibuld, ruler of the Alemanni. Today we know his people quite well because of recent examinations of their burials.[7] The border—for the lack of better term—of the cultural and economic exchange that Eugippius mentions quite often, runs inside the former Roman province. At the time of Severinus when one passed upstream from Quintanis one moved from an area essentially Roman and to one Barbarian in nature; or expressed chronologically, from that which had characterized late antiquity to one that has more in common with the middle ages, but here they existed side by side.

The recent publication of regional and supra-regional collections of archaeological materials allows us to analyze rural settlement in late antiquity much more precisely. P. vanOssel[8] has critically analyzed the whole north-east of Gaul; K. H. Lenz[9] has examined the Aldenhovenes Platte in the Jülichen Börde; H. Bernhard[10] the area around Speyer and the Rhine-Palatinate respectively and high-ground settlements in the hinterland. There are three works on settlement archaeology having to do primarily with eastern Raetia from Regensburg to Passau: (Th. Fischer,[11] M. Struck, and G. Moosbauer[12]). Northwestern Switzerland, that is the area of Maxima Sequanorum from Basileia, Vindonissa to the border of Raetia Prima, was examined by M. Martin[13] and K. Roth-Rubi.[14] Finally, the valley of the Alpine Rhineland south of Lake Constance can be readily surveyed because of two works (B. Overbeck,[15] and G. Schneider-Schnekenburger[16]). Unfortunately, there is no such published examination for Noricum, but some yet to be published excavations offer valuable information.[17]

Settlement in the later Roman provinces—those along the Rhine and Danube—can be generalized as fitting into four basic patterns:

- A relocation of settlement, often corresponding to an overall reduction of the populated area[18] (For example, Kempten; Arlon).
- A concentration of settlement, again a reduction of total area[19] (For example, Tongern).
- A retreat behind the walls of forts as we see in the hinterland of Regensburg and in Noricum.
- High-ground fortifications or settlement[20] (For example, in the south of Belgica Prima, in Raetia Secunda, or in the Palatinate).

Although, as stated above, until the middle of the third century A.D., 80-90 percent of the population lived in the open countryside, outside of towns, villages and forts, this situation must have been largely overturned afterwards, at least in the areas along Rhine and Danube. There, instead of open agriculture, we find fields, pastures, and forests being cultivated from secure places. This process started at the beginning of the fourth century A.D. and had developed so far that, for example, the countrysides near towns from Regensburg downstream to Künzing[21] were no longer settled in the second half of the fourth century A.D. Archaeological finds leave no doubt as to this conclusion. South of Passau across the river Inn and into Noricum villas or rural estates continued to exist far from the forts even into late fourth and beginning of the fifth century A.D. The situation in the heart of Raetia Secunda was completely different than either of the two above.

Here there was a large number of rural settlements, which fall into two types: (1) the high-ground settlements and (2) a new type of nucleated settlement. Examples of the latter type have been found in several areas far removed from each other as well as in Raetia Secunda. These are nucleated settlements, with or without palisades, and are both reminiscent of pre-Roman agriculture and the post-Roman village. In Raetia Secunda these nucleated settlements are concentrated in Munich's gravel plain near the Augsburg-Salzburg road.[22] The high-ground settlements lie about 10 km to the south and west of the road. Some of the nucleated settlements were given up after the invasions of the Juthungi of 357 A.D., according to recent studies of their burial grounds, but a lesser number continued in operation until the early fifth century. Nucleated settlements such as Weßling,[23] 25 km west of Munich, were fortified with palisades, but they are really small villages and do not have anything in common with the classical *villa rustica*.

A very instructive cartographic summary was published by R. Brulet for Germania Prima and Belgica Prima.[24] Brulet proposes five areas, of these three stand out most clearly: first, the zone of the *limes* on the Rhine; second, the area of fortified rural settlements to the west and southwest of Cologne in flat or hilly country; and third, the area of the highground settlements to the south, across the Mosel from Trier and far into Gaul. Although called "defense sectors" by Brulet, these zones also contained distinctive settlement patterns: (1) the area near the hilltop fortifications, where agricultural tools have often been found and from which the surrounding fields in the valley were cultivated; (2) the area where massive, trench-provided towers served as refuges or structures for storing cereals;[25] and (3) the *limes* area where few rural settlements continued beyond the middle of the fourth century.

I will now take an instructive example from the Palatinate, basing my conclusions upon the work of H. Bernhard.[26] Here on a central axial estate that was in operation from the times from Augustus to the middle of the third century A.D. on the best wine-growing terrain available, the fourth-century owner could afford to build an annex to the villa. Concurrently in the first half of the fourth century a high-ground fortification 3.5 km away was constructed. Finally only half a kilometer from the site of the villa, still then a going concern, a "castle," that is to say a *burgus*, a heavily fortified installation of 54 × 35 m internal dimension, was erected in the second half of the fourth century. This castle is situated in the heart of today's village and carried the settlement over into the early Middle Ages.

On the territory of the former colony of Augusta Raurica in northwestern Switzerland, were originally about 280 estates, of these 32 estates held on until 364 A.D.[27] At the beginning of the fifth century A.D. a minimum of 16 survived. When plotted on a map, a pattern seems evident. As late as 364, settlement was distributed fairly evenly on the best soils, but by the early fifth century, those few that survived were to be found only in the proximity of the fortified centers in the north that still offered protection.

So far I have avoided discussing Trier, the imperial and episcopal residence.[28] This omission was intentional. Trier fascinates the archaeologist because of the richness of its finds. Its written records can blind the historian and the archaeologist alike, but because of its richness Trier and its outskirts are not good examples with which to illustrate rural settlement in late antiquity. The hinterland must have been organized in late antiquity in an abnormal way because of the presence of the imperial court, officials, and soldiers with orders to protect it. There were several magnificent villas in the suburbs where emperors are noted as having drawn up documents.[29] Other peculiarities included the extension of viticulture, magnificent buildings in the town, no visible reduction of settlement into a small nucleus as in other cities in the area. Just outside town in the so-called "district of the long walls" lay an imperial domain with the magnificently equipped villa of Welschbillig.[30]

We should not allow this picture of Trier as an enclave of the classical Roman city to distort our analysis of its countryside. The areas beyond the immediate vicinity of Trier,[31] including the district of the long walls, witnessed substantial changes in the rural landscape, such as the building of high-ground settlements and the transformation of Roman villas. The physical fabric of villa life in some cases changed markedly as kilns for drying grain and ovens for metal processing were set up in the midst of main buildings. It seems that only small parts of vast residential areas were still used for habitation, the remainder having often been converted to handicrafts such as at Newel.

The typical Roman *villa rustica*, an isolated estate upon its own land, had no future. It had been a pattern imported from the Mediterranean area and had fulfilled for a few centuries those tasks for which it had evolved in the lands to the south, that is a system of agriculture that produced surpluses for large-scale centralized markets. The well-appointed residential buildings disappeared, the separation of living and working quarters in the manner of special buildings was discarded. In its place housing that combined stables and a residential quarter, which had been common in pre-Roman times, made a comeback. As vanOssel put it so nicely when describing pre-Roman housing—everything was under one roof.[32]

In conclusion, if we survey the development of rural settlement in the later Roman provinces on Rhine and Danube, we must bear in mind one essential fact. There were no general tendencies valid overall; no single pattern of development; no supra-regional causation. What had for a few centuries seemed uniform, at least from our distant vantage point, dissolved according to intrinsic factors of natural and human geography. Each area demands exact analysis, for only then can we approach an understanding of its unique characteristics. The only evidence we possess is archaeological.

ABBREVIATIONS

Bender, "Agrargeschichte Kaiserzeit" = H.Bender, "Agrargeschichte Deutschlands in der römischen Kaiserzeit innerhalb der Grenzen des Imperium Romanum," in J.Lüning, A.Jockenhövel, et al. (eds.), *Deutsche Agrargeschichte. Vor- und Frühgeschichte*, Stuttgart, 1997, 263–374.

Bender - Wolff, *Ländliche Besiedlung* = H.Bender and H.Wolff, eds., *Ländliche Besiedlung und Landwirtschaft in den Rhein-Donau-Provinzen des Römischen Reiches.* (Passauer Universitätsschr. z. Arch. 2), Espelkamp, 1994.

Fischer, *Umland* = Th.Fischer, *Das Umland des römischen Regensburg* (Münchner Beitr. Vor- u. Frühgesch. 42), Munich, 1990.

Moosbauer, *Östliches Raetien* = G.Moosbauer, *Die ländliche Besiedlung im östlichen Raetien während der römischen Kaiserzeit* (Passauer Universitätsschr. z. Arch. 4), Espelkamp, 1997.

NOTES

1. Bender, "Agrargeschichte Kaiserzeit," 349–52, see also the realistic appraisal by A. Kreuz in *Ber. Komm. Archäolog. Landesforsch. Hessen* 3 (1994/95): 78–83.

2. Bender, "Agrargeschichte Kaiserzeit," 304–9; H.-P Stika, *Römerzeitliche Pflanzenreste aus Baden-Württemberg*, Materialh. Archäologie Baden-Württemberg, 36 (Stuttgart, 1996); Kreuz (as in note 1 above); L. I. Kooistra, *Borderland Farming. Possibilities and Limitations of Farming in the Roman Period and Early Middle Ages between the Rhine and Meuse* (Amersfoort, 1996); *Ber. Bayer. Bodendenkmalpflege* 24/25 (1983/84): 76–166.
3. J. Peters, *Römische Tierhaltung und Tierzucht. Eine Synthese aus archäozoologischer Untersuchung und schriftlich-bildlicher Überlieferung*, Passauer Universitätsschr. z. Archäologie5, (Rahden, 1998). On a chicken farm that included a specialized facility for preparing roast rooster in Annecy (Boutae/France), see C. Olive and S. Deschler-Erb, *Arch. Schweiz* 22 (1999): 35–36. Likewise their revelation that a farm near Neftenbach advertised its speciality, red deer, on its trademark.
4. The ship found at Woerden (Netherlands) had a carrying capacity of 60 tons. On the special cereals that could have been harvested only on the weedless chalk soils found in southern Germania Inferior, see J. K. Haaleboos et al., *Jahrb. RGZM* 43 (1996): 475–509; on the ship, R. Bockius, ibid., 511–30.
5. On the role of Passau in this era, see E. Boshof et al., eds., *Geschichte der Stadt Passau* (1999), "Spätantike," 51–60; with a discussion of the basic problems and the extent to which archaeological materials can be used in conjunction with the reports contained in hagiographic sources, namely the *vita S. Severini* by Eugippius, On the archaeological material see Moosbauer, *Östliches Raetien* 199–200; Fischer, *Umland*, 116–20.
6. H.-J. Kellner, *Veröff. Tiroler Landesmus.* 78, 1998, 89–114, esp. 94–95, 98, the last pay for the soldiers in Batavis.
7. H. Geisler, *Das frühbairische Gräberfeld Straubing-Bajuwarenstraße*, Internationale Archäologie 30, (Rahden, 1998); M. Martin, "Historische Schlagzeilen, archäologische Trümmer," in *Die Alamannen* (Stuttgart, 1997), 163–70, ed. the Archäolog. Landesmuseum Baden-Württemberg; R.Koch, "S-förmige Schlußhaken für Halsketten aus dem 4. und 5. Jahrh.n.Chr.," in *Beitr. Arch. Mittelfranken* 4, Büchenbach (1998): 211–20; on both the ethnographic problems relating to the establishment of the Bavarians and the ethnogenesis of the Alamanns and Franks see the catalogues of the extensive exhibitions entitled "Die Alamannen" [above] and "Die Franken," A. Wieczorek - P. Périn et al., eds., *Die Franken - Wegbereiter Europas*, 2d ed. (Mainz, 1996).
8. P. VanOssel, *Etablissements ruraux de l'Antiquité tardive dans le nord de la Gaule.* 51e suppl. *Gallia* (Paris, 1992).
9. K.H.Lenz, *Siedlungen der römischen Kaiserzeit auf der Aldenhovenes Platte (Jülichen Börde)*, Rhein. Ausgr. 45 (Bonn, 1999).
10. H. Bernhard, *Mitt. Hist. Ver. Pfalz* 73 (1976): 37–165; and by the same author, *Saalbg.-Jahrb.* 37 (1981): 23–85; and in *Arch. Korrbl.* 12 (1982): 217–30; and in *Mitt. Hist. Ver. Pfalz* 95 (1997): 7–106, esp. 61–67.
11. Fischer, *Umland*, 116–18 (Auswertung); on the interior of the province see M.Struck, *Römische Grabfunde und Siedlungen im Isartal bei Ergolding, Landkreis Landshut.* Materialh. Bayer. Vorgesch., A71 (Kallmünz, 1996).
12. Moosbauer, *Östliches Raetien*, 195–203.

13. M. Martin, "Die spätrömisch-frühmittelalterliche Besiedlung am Hochrhein und im schweizerischen Jura und Mittelland," in *Von der Spätantike zum frühen Mittelalter.* (Vortr. u. Forsch. 25), ed. J. Werner and E. Ewig (Sigmaringen, 1979), 411–46; also M. Martin, *Das spätrömisch-frühmittelalterliche Gräberfeld von Kaiseraugst, Kt. Aargau.* Basler Beitr. Ur- u. Frühgesch., 5A (Derendingen, 1991); U.Giesler, "Völker am Hochrhein," in *Die Alamannen* (as in note 7), 209–18.
14. K. Roth-Rubi, in Bender and Wolff, *Ländliche Besiedlung,* 314; for a useful overview see A. Furger, C. Jaggi et al., *Die Schweiz zwischen Antike und Mittelalter. Archäologie und Geschichte des 4. bis 9.Jahrhunderts* (Zürich, 1996).
15. B.Overbeck, *Das Alpenrheintal in römischer Zeit auf Grund der archäologischen Zeugnisse.* Pt.1. Topographie, Fundvorlage und historische Auswertung, Münchner Beitr. Vor- u. Frühgesch. 20 (Munich, 1982), 197–228; and Pt.2. Die Fundmünzen, Münchner Beitr. Vor- u. Frühgesch., 21 (Munich, 1973), esp. charts 7–10.
16. G. Schneider-Schnekenburger, *Churrätien im Frühmittelalter auf Grund der archäologischen Funde.* Münchner Beitr. Vor- u. Frühgesch. 26, (Munich, 1980); the inventories in both Overbeck (note 15) and Schneider-Schnekenburger may be supplemented by the new data coming out in the *Jahrb. SGUF.*
17. Research on rural settlement during late antiquity in this province has only commenced in the last few years. Excavation of a villa in Schönering near Wilhering a.d. Donau (Oberösterreich) has been carried out by Chr. Schwanzar (Materials from the fourth and fifth centuries, unpublished.) and at Antiesenhofen near Schärdinga.Inn by J.Offenberger (Building from the fourth century); for now see K. Genser, in Bender - Wolff, *Ländliche Besiedlung,* 331–76.
18. On Kempten (Bayern) see G. Weber, "Das spätrömische Cambodunum," in *Geschichte der Stadt Kempten,* ed. V.Dotterweich et al.(Kempten, 1989), 56–62; on Arlon (Belgium) see A. Wankenne, *La Belgique à l'époque Romaine; Sites urbains, villageois, religieux et militaires.* Centre Nat. Rech. Arch. en Belgique. Ser. C, 3 (Brussels, 1972), 163–85, plan4.
19. On Tongern (Belgium) see Wankenne (note 18), 75–98, plan 3.
20. For the northwestern part of this region see VanOssel (note 8), 111–20; and also in this work the analysis of the settlement pattern, 85–100; as well as R. Brulet, *La Gaule septentrionale au Bas-Empire. Occupation du sol et défense du territoire dans l'arrière-pays du Limes aux IVe et Ve siècles,* Trierer Zeitschr., Beih. 11 (Trier, 1990). For the area to the southeast see S. Ciglenecki, *Höhenbefestigungen aus der Zeit vom 3. bis 6. Jh. im Ostalpenraum.* Slovenska Akademija Znanesti in Umetnosti, Dela 31, Institut za Arheologijo 15 (Ljubljana, 1987); and C. Bridger and K.-J. Gilles, eds., *Spätrömische Befestigungsanlagen in den Rhein- und Donauprovinzen.* BAR Internat. Ser. 704 (Oxford 1998).
21. On the areas surrounding Regensburg and Straubing, see note 11 (Fischer, *Umland*) and note 12.
22. Fundamental still E.Keller, *Die spätrömischen Grabfunde in Südbayern,* Münchner Beitr. z. Vor- u. Frühgesch. 14 (Munich, 1971), 145–55; and Keller et al., "Die urnenfelderzeitliche Siedlung und das spätrömische Kalkbrennerviertel in Unterhaching,

Lkr. München," *Ber. Bayer. Bodendenkmalpfl.* 36/37 (1995/96): 124–68, esp. 157–58; M. Pietsch, *Das Archäolog. Jahr in Bayern* 1997, 121–24; W. Czysz, "Das Umland von Augsburg in der römischen Kaiserzeit," in *Vor- und Frühgeschichte, Archäologie einer Landschaft. Der Landkreis Augsburg,* ed. W. Pötzl and O. Schneider (Augsburg, 1996), 254–66; on the Christianization of the rural areas in Raetia Secunda, see H. Bender, "Die Christianisierung von Flachlandraetien nach den archäologischen Zeugnissen bis zur Mitte des 5.Jahrhunderts," in *Das Christentum im bairischen Raum. Von den Anfängen bis ins 11.Jahrhundert,* Passauer Hist. Forsch. 8, ed. E. Boshof and H. Wolff (Cologne, Weimar, Vienna, 1994), 63–77; in this same volume, see also the report on the organization of the church in Raetia and Noricum (H. Wolff, 1–27); and on the archaeology from the era of S. Severinus in Künzing and Passau (Th. Fischer, 93–127), on the Christianization of Noricum Ripense (Hj. Ubl, 129–51), on Mautern (M. Pollak, 153–69) and on Enns-Lorch, St. Laurentius (Chr. Schwanzar, 171–91). On Noricum Ripense, see also M. S. Handke, *A Social and Economic History of Noricum Ripense in the Fifth Century* (1987).

23. H. Bender (forthcoming), *Die römische Siedlung von Weßling-Frauenwiese. Untersuchungen zum ländlichen Siedlungswesen in der Spätantike.* (Habil. Schr. Universität Passau, 1988), to appear in Passauer Universitätsschr. z. Archäologie; On the settlement of Münchner Schotterebene, see Keller (note 22, Unterhaching), 157–58.
24. R. Brulet, "Das spätrömische Verteidigungssystem zwischen Mosel und Nordseeküste," in *Die römische Reichsgrenze von der Mosel bis zur Nordseeküste,* ed. T. Bechert and W. J. H. Willems (Stuttgart, 1995), 103–19 with illus. 101; see also n. 20 (Brulet); for an outstanding regional analysis see, W. J. H. Willems, *Romans and Batavians, a Regional Study in the Dutch Eastern River Area,* Pt.1 Report. ROB 31 (1981): 7–217; Pt. 2, 34 (1984): 39–331, esp. 272–301 (Late Antiquity and Early Middle Ages).
25. In general, VanOssel (see note 8), 156–59.
26. See note 10; and H. Bernhard, "Bad Dürkheim/Ungstein," in *Die Römer in Rheinland-Pfalz,* ed. H. Cüppers (Stuttgart, 1990), 317–20; for northernmost Rheinhessen (the area surrounding Mainz), see H.Ament and J.Oldenstein, *Ber. RGK* 62 (1981): 261–316.
27. See note 13 (Martin); also by him, "Die Zeit um 400n.Chr.," in *Ur- und frühgeschichtliche Archäologie der Schweiz. Die römische Epoche,* ed. W. Drack (Basel, 1975), 171–84 with illus.2; and W. Drack and R. Fellmann, *Die Römer in der Schweiz* (Stuttgart and Jona, 1988), 276–315, esp. illus. 279.
28. H. Cüppers, ed., *Trier, Kaiserresidenz und Bischofssitz. Die Stadt in spätantiker und frühchristlicher Zeit* (Mainz, 1984); and also his contribution in *Die Römer in Rheinland-Pfalz* (Stuttgart, 1990), 577–648.
29. Pfalzel, Konz, in *Die Römer in Rheinland Pfalz,* 649–53 and 425–26 respectively; and in *Trier, Kaiserresidenz und Bischofssitz,* 319–22 and 310–18 respectively.
30. Ibid., *Trier, Kaiserresidenz und Bischofssitz,* 286–91 and *Römer in Rheinland-Pfalz,* 665–67 respectively.
31. Assembled by VanOssel (note 8), 236–79, esp. Newel in the Langmauer area, 259–64;

also the chart in *Trier, Kaiserresidenz und Bischofssitz,* 323, noting the locations of the late ancient fortifications running along the Mosel to its mouth on the Rhine. These had the purpose of local defense.

32. H. Bender, *Bonner Jahrb.* 196 (1996): 859–61 (review of VanOssel); the shift from a Roman domestic mentalité of separation to that of combining functions (that is, the change to the single farm dwelling for both humans and animals, the *Wohnstallhaus*).

Peasants as "Makeshift Soldiers for the Occasion": Sixth-Century Settlement Patterns in the Balkans

FLORIN CURTA

THE STUDY OF LATE ANTIQUE CITIES IN THE BALKANS TYPICALLY IS FOCUSED either on textual evidence of public institutional change or on the archaeology of early Christian monuments. The crucial issue of how the urban life ended in the Balkans has often been approached from a rather narrow perspective, in an attempt to link archaeologically observable phenomena with historical narratives, with particular barbarian raids or earthquakes. Historians and archaeologists alike have examined the sixth-century Balkans for evidence confirming or contradicting Procopius' description of Justinian's building program (*Buildings* IV). Beyond individual cities and forts, however, little attention has been paid to settlement patterns at a micro- and macro-regional level. Settlement pattern analysis is, nevertheless, the strategic point for interpreting the archaeological evidence as reflecting institutions of social interaction and control.[1]

In this article, I intend to examine the archaeological evidence of settlement patterns in the sixth-century Balkans, both at the intrasite and the macro-regional levels. I will argue that, despite some variation, a pattern of change is easily recognizable. In most cases, ancient cities contracted and regrouped around a defensible acropolis, usually dominated by the church.

The process of disintegration of the urban nucleus into small settlement areas was accompanied by the subdivision into smaller rooms of formerly finer buildings, by the re-use of various architectural elements, and by the construction of new buildings with mud and brick walls. Large *civitates* were replaced by comparatively smaller forts and the urban population of the Balkans concentrated primarily in coastal cities, such as Thessalonica, Mesembria, Salona, and Constantinople.[2] Since no evidence exists of contemporary rural settlements, I will attempt to answer the key question of how the remaining population in urban centers and forts was supplied with food. In doing so, I will propose a model of distribution based on *annona*. I will argue that the implementation of Justinian's building program in the mid–sixth century proved to be an unbearable burden for the provincial administration. Disruption of distribution networks may explain the eventual collapse of the defense system, the final withdrawal of Roman troops from the Balkans, and the abandonment of both urban centers and forts.

In the late 500s, according to Theophylact Simocatta, there were thirty towns in Dacia and Moesia with a cluster of cities between Novae and Iatrus. He called them πόλεις.[3] At Novae, the excavations conducted since 1960 by a joint Bulgarian-Polish team showed that in its last phase of existence, tentatively dated to the fifth or sixth centuries, the fourth-century building with peristyled courtyard located in the northwest corner of the city was subdivided into smaller rooms by walls of stone bonded with clay, while its northern portico was blocked. Between 470 and 480, Novae was ruled by Theodoric the Great and it may be during this period that the episcopal basilica was built on top of the city's abandoned bath. Around 500 the first intramural burials appeared near the episcopal basilica, probably of some wealthy sponsors.[4]

A similar picture emerges from the Bulgarian excavations at Pernik, near Sofia. Within the area enclosed by walls, archaeologists found houses built in stone, mortar, and adobe, some provided with brick ovens. The settlement had two basilicas, one of which was destroyed during the second half of the sixth century.[5]

The most important city in the region, however, was Justiniana Prima, built shortly before 535. When describing the city in his *Buildings*, Procopius speaks of administrative buildings, but mentions no civic administration, and no structures of that sort have been found. Excavations at Caričin Grad revealed that at first the acropolis was occupied by a large episcopal church with a baptistery and a residential area to the north, which was interpreted as episcopal residence. The rampart itself was built only later, during the second half of Justinian's reign, together with the upper city bath, a two-aisled basilica, and a cistern. The main purpose of this building phase seems to have been to include as many churches and public buildings as possible within the city's walls. Soon, however, many such buildings were abandoned and an encroachment phase seems to have taken place. This last building phase, dated after ca. 565 until about 615, is characterized by houses with walls built in stone bonded with clay.[6]

At Stobi, in Macedonia, large palatial residences with elaborate courtyards decorated fountains, floors with pavements of mosaic, and walls covered with frescoes were still in use in the early 500s. At that time, however, the theater was only a quarry for building material. Small houses with walls of stone and clay were built in its ruins. After the early sixth-century earthquake, the episcopal church was modified to accommodate galleries built above the aisles and an enormous terrace was built along the south side between the church and the baptistery. The lower walls of the church were covered with marble revetment, with molded and brightly colored stucco above and fresco along the upper parts. The narthex and the south aisle were repaved with fine mosaics. The care and expense needed to restore the episcopal basilica so lavishly are in sharp contrast to the refurbishment of other buildings in the city. By 500, a *villa urbana* built in the early fourth century and known as the House of the Fuller (the name is derived from the quantity of murex-shells found to the north of the apsidal hall), was divided by rough walls of brick bonded with clay into a storehouse and a workshop. Both produced a considerable quantity of spindle-whorls and loom weights.[7]

At Corinth, any use of the forum as a public square or for private housing ceased by 500. By the mid–sixth century, burial activity was well established in this area, with tombs in the ruins of the fourth-century shops and baths to the rear of the South Stoa. Whether or not these burials were intramural, remains an object of dispute, for it is not yet clear what exactly constituted the city of Corinth during the 500s. The corridors along the east and northern sides of the peristyled courtyard known as the Peribolos of Apollon were transformed in the early 500s into small rooms. A house was built with re-used material in the northern half of the Great Bath on the Lechaion Road. Shortly after the mid-sixth century, a group of houses emerged in the ruins of the H. Leonidas basilica at Lechaion. All had water wells or cisterns and small, inner courtyards. Baking ovens, querns and *dolia* bespeak the agricultural character of this small settlement.[8]

A different picture results from the examination of Thessalonica. We know from Procopius' *Secret History* that both the grandfather and the father of Belisarius' wife, Antonina, demonstrated their skills as charioteers in Thessalonica. This suggests that the city's hippodrome was still in operation during the early sixth century. Archbishop John, the author of the first book of the *Miracles of St. Demetrius,* mentions both the city's stadium and the theater. During the plague shortly preceding the siege of 586 by Avars and Slavs, the sick who had taken refuge in the church of St. Demetrius were making their way every morning to the baths. Unlike all other Balkan cities, in Thessalonica the agora retained its commercial significance, as suggested by the association of the Megalophoros' western side with the copper trade from Late Antiquity through the present day. The *Miracles of St. Demetrius* show that, on at least two occasions, the Slavs launched attacks against the city while its citizens were busy harvesting their crops on their estates and small holdings outside the city walls. But at the same time, Thessalonica relied heavily on its rations of public grain (*annona*), as evidenced by the eighth homily of Book I. Preventing corn supplies from reaching the city must have been one of the main reasons behind the attempt of the Slavs, sometime during the first decade of Heraclius' reign, to block the port with their fleet of canoes and to attack Thessalonica by sea. This further suggests that a crucial element in the city's survival was its role as a harbor open to outside shipping. As long as Egypt was under Byzantine control, Thessalonica continued to receive regular supplies of corn to supplement the foods its population cultivated locally. With the Persian conquest of Egypt in 619, the Empire's main source of grain was lost, and the city could no longer expect shipments of public corn. Thessalonica was thus forced to depend on the products of its own hinterland and on those brought from the neighboring regions. During the siege of 677, citizens of Thessalonica relied on supplies of corn from the Slavic settlements in Thessaly. [9]

The process of encroachment and change of use indicates an urban change, which cannot be attributed to particular local causes such as plague or invasion, but must have been connected to economic and administrative factors, above all to a new relation between urban centers and central administration. It is important to note, for example, that cities in the interior of the Balkans lack the signs of long-distance trade so evident in those of the Black Sea coast or in Greece. Phocaean Red Slip wares (also known as Late Roman C), produced in western Asia Minor, began to appear in significant quantities on the Black Sea coast after 470 and remained relatively frequent until about 580. They are also abundant at Argos during the first half of the sixth century. By 600, they were still in use on the site of Diocletian's palace in Split. By contrast, sites in the interior produced only small quantities. At Sadovec, in western Bulgaria, Phocaean Red Slip wares are completely absent. All sites in the interior, however, produced large quantities of amphora shards, an indication that the relative absence of Phocaean Red Slip Ware is not an accident. This picture is confirmed by finds of lead seals (fig. 1). Among eight-two sixth- to seventh-century specimens known from the northern Balkans, forty-six have only the name of the owner, without office or title. They were most likely commercial seals. The largest number was found at Constanţa (Tomis). The westernmost specimen found is that from Călăraşi, on the left bank of the Danube. No seals were found in the interior of the Balkans, an indication that commodities traded by seal owners did not reach that region. The commercial network revealed by lead seal finds included only a small area easily accessible by sea. Disruption of commercial links between coastal trade centers and settlements in the interior illustrates the degree of autonomy of the northern Balkan cities, which Procopius listed by regions, rather than by provinces.[10]

That this phenomenon was also associated with significant social changes is shown by the quality of buildings now erected within the urban area. The inhabitants of early Byzantine cities displayed their wealth and

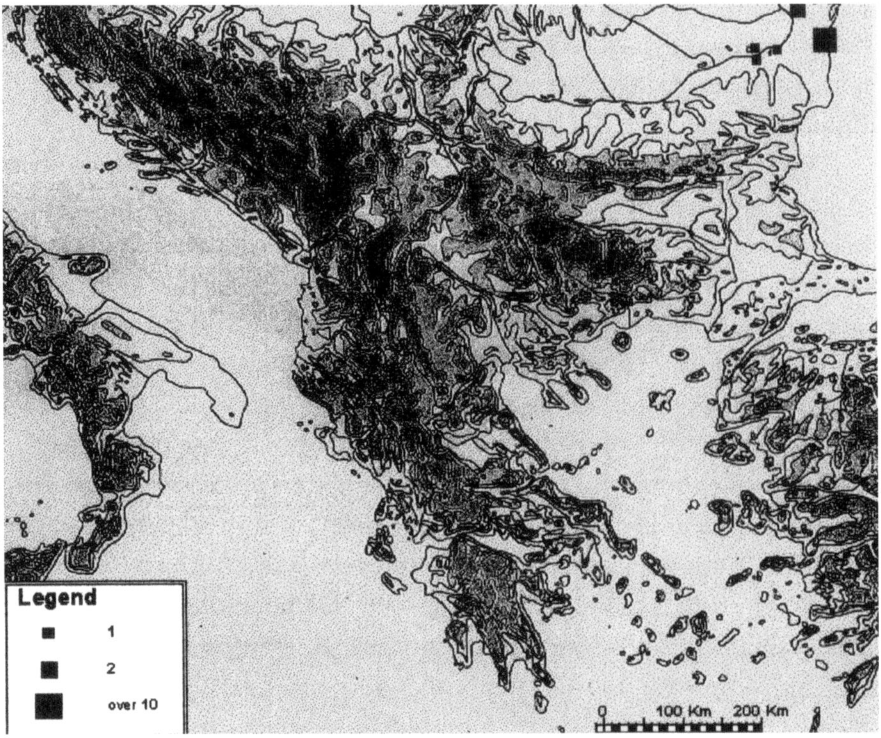

Figure 1. Distribution of sixth- and seventh-century commercial seals in the Balkans.

status by building churches and paying for their lavish decoration with mosaic floors. No evidence exists for any other public buildings erected at that time. Caričin Grad was dominated by the acropolis on which the episcopal church was located. Newly built churches often obstructed or even obliterated the old street grid. In some cases, such as Histria, archaeological excavations revealed the existence of houses with peristyled courtyards and apsed *triclinia.* These were probably residences of the rich, but any attempts to identify their inhabitants with the new urban elite (e.g., bishops) should be treated with extreme caution. In any case, these buildings are in sharp contrast with houses built in stone bonded with clay, which represent the last building phase in the urban landscape. Since these houses encroached into earlier *villae urbanae,* they might indicate that the place of the rich was taken by the less well off. It has been suggested, therefore, that the last decades of the Balkan cities witnessed a rise in the number of poorer citizens. Querns, spindle whorls, baking ovens, and smithies indicate a process of ruralization, which may have started before, but was encouraged by the Slavic invasions. The existing archaeological evidence, however, suggests a much more complex picture. First, there is no evidence to support the idea that these houses were a hasty, if provisory, solution to the problem of countless refugees from the countryside, now savagely raided by the Slavs. Second, the artifacts associated with this building phase suggest a military occupation, which is otherwise comparable to that of contemporary forts.[11]

This trend seems to have coincided with and been related to one of the most curious phenomena of the sixth-century Balkan provinces: the absence of rural settlements. To be sure, archaeologists have identified significant numbers of *villae rusticae* and rural settlements dated to the first four centuries A.D. After the middle of the fifth century, however, medium-sized estates seem to have completely disappeared. By 450, the last *villae rusticae,* which have survived until then in the sheltered areas of Dalmatia and northeast Bosnia, were completely abandoned.[12]

The evidence for peasant settlements is also scarce. According to Procopius, Justinian "made the defenses so continuous in the estates, that each farm either had been converted into a stronghold or lies adjacent to one which is fortified." He even cites an example of a village entirely transformed into a stronghold, due to Justinian's munificence. But he also describes how, at Thermopylae, local peasants "suddenly changed their mode of life, and becoming makeshift soldiers for the occasion," kept guard on the defenses at Thermopylae. Procopius suggests that agricultural occupations were now abandoned, albeit only temporarily, until Emperor Justinian replaced the inexperienced garrison with regular troops. His evidence is further corroborated by other sources. According to Agathias, when Zabergan's Cutrigurs invaded the Balkans in 558, they quickly reached Thrace, after crossing many *deserted* villages in Moesia and Scythia Minor. The only evidence for the survival of a significant peasant population comes from the hinterland of Constantinople. Theophylact Simocatta mentions a χωρίον at about 15 miles distance from Heraclea (Perinthus), which had a large population and supplied the imperial armies with food. Elsewhere the existence of open settlements with exclusively agricultural functions remains doubtful. It is true that the early Byzantine archaeology in the Balkans focused mainly on urban centers. Much has been done in recent decades, however, for the study of the countryside during the Early and Late Roman period. The evidence for rural settlements after ca. 500 is remarkably scanty: a single-roomed house at Kurt Baiâr in Scythia Minor and the remains of two others at Novgrad, not far from the ancient site at Iatrus, in Moesia. There is nothing comparable to the village at Qasrin, in the Golan highlands, nothing similar to the two-storied peasant houses found in the hinterland of the city of Kyaneai, in Lycia.[13]

The rarity of rural settlements may be explained in reference to contemporary legislation. In 505, Emperor Anastasius was compelled to acknowledge the impossibility of collecting the *annona* in Thrace and to introduce the *coemptio.* Thirty years later, Justinian issued novel 32, which attempted to stop an ever-accelerating decline of peasantry in Haemimons and Moesia inferior. Because of high-interest loan rates, peasants forfeited their lands. Some fled and others died of starvation, the general situation being described as worse than after a barbarian invasion. Ten years later, the emperor introduced the *epibole* to the fiscal law, in order to cope with the demographic instability of the countryside upsetting the process of tax collection. Every farmer was now burdened with liability for taxes from the abandoned land of his next-door neighbor. Justinian's successor, Justin II, twice granted tax exemptions for peasants in Moesia and Scythia minor. In both cases, at stake were food supplies for troops stationed in these two provinces.[14]

During the sixth century, the Balkans witnessed a serious contraction, but the complex readjustments taking place almost everywhere did not involve rural sites. The urban life in the Balkans was not based on a thriving rural economy. The rarity of rural settlements may explain the rarity of monasteries. Literary sources indirectly suggest the existence of monastic life in the Balkans. During Justinian's reign, the "Scythian monks" were zealous supporters of a formula attempting to reconcile adherents of the Council of Chalcedon with the Monophysites. A few decades later, at the time of Tiberius and Maurice, John Moschus wrote about hermitages around Thessalonica in his biographies of abbot Palladius and David the Ascetic. However, there is no mention of large cenobitic communities beyond the walls of Constantinople. The archaeological evidence for sixth-century monasteries in the Balkans is also meager: a small *coenobium* on the island of Majsan, near Korčula; a monastic complex at Isperihovo, near Plovdiv, in Thrace; and a complex of buildings interpreted as a laura at Slava Rusă, in Scythia Minor.[15]

With this rarity of monasteries and rural settlements, the problem of urban change in the Balkans can be rephrased in new terms. The only other settlement category that was omnipresent in the Balkans was that of forts. Archaeological surveys show that the majority were small, often no larger than 0.5 hectare. They could not have been manned by more than three to four hundred soldiers. It has been argued that, in order to defend his walls and forts in the Balkans, Justinian depended either on local farmers, serving in rural militias (i.e., *ad-hoc* troops that were not part of the *limitanei*) or on local landowners and their *bucellarii.* To be sure, there is no evidence in the sixth century for either local landowners employing private armies or *limitanei.* As for rural militias, both the absence of rural settlements and the great number of forts, especially in the northern Balkans, make this interpretation very problematic, notwithstanding Procopius' description of the pre-Justinianic defense of Thermopylae. It would not have made much sense for the state to undertake such expensive building projects, only to leave defense of these fortifications in the hands of local farmers. Procopius clearly indicates that at Thermopylae, Emperor Justinian replaced bands of peasants with a garrison of two thousand. Whether or not the troops that manned the forts remained there for a longer term cannot be decided on the basis of the archaeological evidence alone. There is some indication, however, that, in some cases, fort garrisons were permanent. According to the author of a sixth-century military treatise entitled *De re strategica,* "the men in the garrison [of forts] should not have their wives and children with them." However, "if a fort is extremely strong, so that there is no danger of its being besieged, and we can keep it provisioned without any problems," soldiers may have their families reside with them. The general picture obtained from the archaeological evidence is also one of permanent garrisons, at least in those forts that produced evidence of houses, amenities, and churches.[16]

An important problem raised by the evidence of sixth-century forts and urban centers, which so far no archaeologist has approached in a systematic way, is that of how cities and forts were supplied with ammunition, weapons, and, more important, food. The *Miracles of St. Demetrius* suggest that a large city, such as Thessalonica, relied heavily on supplies of public corn, but it is dangerous to extrapolate this evidence to other Balkan cases. The explanation may lie at a more structural level, in the military and building programs implemented in the Balkans, especially under Emperor Justinian.

Justinian's defense system was completed shortly before 554, when Procopius ended book IV of his *Buildings*. In contrast to other regions, where Justinian's program simply consisted of restoring older constructions, the building activity in the northern Balkans seems to have been taken more seriously. Local quarries, such as those of oölithic limestone in the Svishtov-Ruse area, which supplied all sites in the Iantra Valley, provided most of the building materials for the forts. Who took the responsibility for all these forts? Even if local aristocrats and their personal armies would have taken the provincial defense into their own hands, it remains unclear how forts were supplied with ammunition, weapons, and food. Themistius indicates that, in the late fourth century, the army's supply system largely depended upon the central government and the imperial administration. There is some indication that the system was still in use during the sixth century.[17]

Ever since A. H. M. Jones interpreted the *quaestura exercitus* as an administrative reform designed to ensure a continuous food supply for troops stationed on the Thracian border, scholars have insisted that the attributions of the *quaestor* were primarily financial. He was directly responsible for the *annona* of the army in Moesia Secunda and Scythia Minor. In addition, lead seals found in the region point to communication of some regularity between the two Balkan provinces included in the *quaestura exercitus* and the central government. Thirteen imperial seals, nine of which belong to Justinian, demonstrate that officials in Scythia Minor frequently received letters and written orders from the emperor.[18]

The archaeological evidence points to a similar conclusion. Egyptian papyri show that the daily food ration for a soldier consisted of three pounds of bread, two pounds of meat, two *sextarii* of wine and ⅛ *sextarii* of olive oil. At least three elements of this ratio were commodities usually transported in amphorae. These vessels come in two basic categories: squat and elongated. The most common squat amphora is Late Roman 2. Produced in the Aegean, LR 2 was used for transporting either wine (as indicated by grape seeds found in some cargo amphorae on the Yassi Ada shipwreck) or olive oil. They were common on sixth-century sites in Greece, such as Argos, as well as in forts on the Danube frontier and in the central Balkan region. Elongated amphorae known as Late Roman 1 were also a familiar presence. Produced in the region of Antioch, in Cyprus, as well as in Rhodes, they were used for transporting wine, oil, or grain. These were the most common amphorae at Argos, in Constantinople, and on many military sites in the Balkans. A second variant of the elongated type is known under the rather improper name of *spatheion*. *Spatheia* were most probably produced in the east Mediterranean area and may have been used for carrying olive oil, though other commodities, such as *garum* or honey, should not be excluded. Such amphorae were relatively rare at Argos and in Constantinople. The Yassi Ada shipwreck produced only two specimens, but they were very common in the northern Balkans, and the only type of early Byzantine amphorae found on hilltop sites in Bosnia, Dalmatia, and Slovenia.[19]

By contrast, there is comparatively little evidence of amphorae produced in Palestine (Late Roman 4, 5, and 6), which frequently appear in the western Mediterranean area and in Gaul, where they certainly transported wine. Only a few fragments were found in Constantinople and on the Black Sea coast. Relatively large quantities come from Argos and from some other coastal sites in Greece, where LR 1 and LR 2 do not occur too frequently. It is important to note that the distribution of LR 4, 5, and 6 overlaps that of Phocaean Red Slip ware, but sharply contrasts with that of LR 1, LR 2 and *spatheion*-type amphorae (figs. 2 and 3). Catherine Abadie-Reynal first attempted to explain this difference in distribution patterns by pointing to different distribution networks. She argued that Palestinian amphorae, in

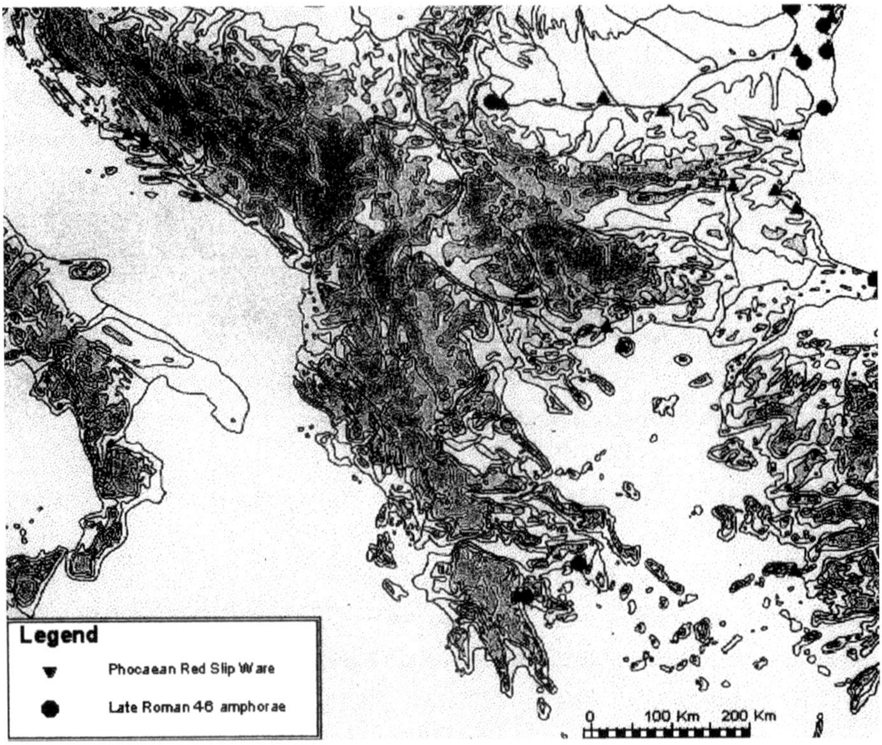

Figure 2. Distribution of Phocaean Red Slip wares (triangle) and Late Roman 4, 5, and 6 amphorae (circle) in the Balkans.

particular the so-called "Gaza amphora" (LR 4), seem to indicate "free-market commerce," for they crossed the Mediterranean and reached Gaul in significant quantities. Their relatively lower frequency in the Aegean area and total absence in the Balkans (except a few trade centers on the coast) suggest that the Balkans were an area of state-run distribution. The frequency curves for LR 1, LR 2, and *spatheion*-type amphorae seem, therefore, to support the hypothesis of *annona*-type distributions to the army. This is also suggested by the constant association of these amphorae with military sites, as well as by their relatively homogeneous typology.[20]

That the sixth-century *limes* still relied heavily on central distribution of grain also results from legislative measures taken by emperors from Anastasius to Justin II. All attempted to provide a solution to the remediless

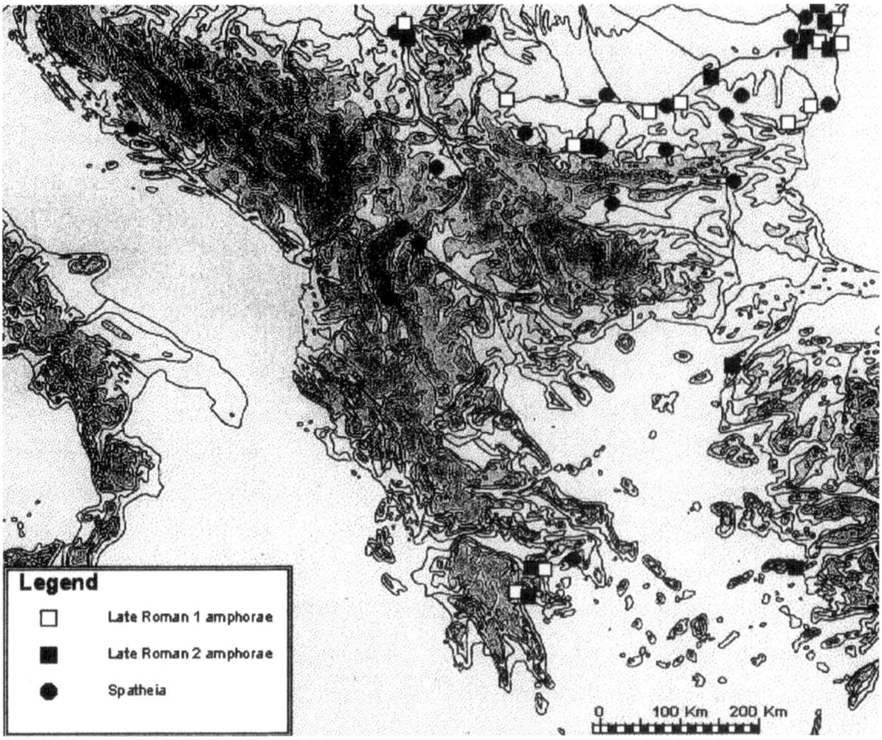

Figure 3. Distribution of Late Roman 1 (square), Late Roman 2 (full square), and spatheion-type (circle) amphorae in the Balkans.

problem of making a much impoverished and depopulated region of the empire capable of producing enough food for the troops coming to its defense. Approaches to this problem ranged from compulsory collection of the *annona* to tax exemptions, but in all cases at stake were food supplies for troops stationed in Thrace or Moesia Inferior. Some scholars have rightly assumed that the creation of the *quaestura exercitus* in 536 was in fact a solution to the problem of helping Scythia Minor and Moesia Inferior feed their troops with supplies from the rich overseas provinces.[21] That none of these measures proved to be successful is indirectly shown by the late sixth- or early seventh-century treatise known as the *Strategikon*. Its author, an experienced military officer, recommends that when campaigning north of the Danube, in Sclavene territory, Roman troops do not destroy provisions found in the surrounding countryside, but ship them on pack animals and boats "to our own country." The evidence of the *Strategikon* is archaeologically confirmed by changing consumption patterns. In addition to shipments of *annona*, the soldiers of the fort at Iatrus relied heavily on hunting for meat procurement. Garden cultivation of millet and legumes is documented at Iatrus and Nicopolis, and suggests that the *annona* was not sufficient for the subsistence of the frontier troops. On the other hand, that Roman soldiers may have relied on food captured from the enemy is a good indication of the ongoing crisis.[22]

A project of gigantic proportions and overall excellent execution, Justinian's system failed to provide the expected solutions because its maintenance would have required efforts far beyond the potential of the Roman state, particularly of the Balkan provinces. After Justinian's death, if not earlier, the emperor's building program, whose implementation coincides with the last phase of a sharp decline of the rural population in the Balkans, proved to be an unbearable burden for the provincial administration. When the central distribution of *annona* completely ceased, maintaining the troops on the frontier became impossible. During Maurice's reign, the Roman army on the Danube *limes* twice mutinied, and the second rebellion brought about the emperor's rapid fall. In both cases, at stake were the deterioration of the living standards and the social status of the field army as a consequence of Maurice's intended reforms.

The *communis opinio* is that as soon as Phocas' rebellion broke out, the *limes* crumbled and the Slavic tide invaded the Balkans. In fact, Phocas' purge of the army did not prevent it from returning to the Danube front after overthrowing Maurice, in order to continue operations against the Avars and the Slavs. Emperor Heraclius eventually moved troops to the Persian front, in 620. The general withdrawal of troops from the Balkan front and the definite cessation of grain supplies from Egypt, now occupied by the Persians, cannot be a mere coincidence. The effects the fall of Egypt had on corn supplies for Thessalonica are well, if indirectly, documented by the *Miracles of St. Demetrius*. The Muslim conquest of Syria and the subsequent developments prevented the return of troops to Thrace. They would be relocated in western Anatolia, while Thrace remained without any Byzantine troops until 690, when Justinian II created the Thracian theme. By that time, however, Justinian I's system of defense was already history.[23]

NOTES

1. Bruce G. Trigger, "Settlement Patterns in Archaeology," in *Introductory Readings in Archaeology*, ed. B. M. Fagan (Boston, 1970), 237–62.
2. Ivan Mikulčić, "Spätantike Fortifikationen in der SR Makedonien," *Corso di cultura sull'arte ravennate e bizantina* 33 (1986): 269. See also Archibald Dunn, "The Transition from *Polis* to *Kastron* in the Balkans (III-VII cc.): General and Regional Perspectives," *Byzantine and Modern Greek Studies* 18 (1994): 72–73.
3. Peter Schreiner, "Städte und Wegenetz in Mösien, Dakien und Thrakien nach dem Zeugnis des Theophylaktos Simokates," *Österreichische Akademie der Wissenschaften. Schriften der Balkankommission. Antiqu. Abt.* 16 (1985): 62–64. To Procopius, both Novae and Iatrus were mere φρούρια (*Buildings* IV 11.20 and 7.6). For Iatrus as πόλις, see Theophylact Simocatta VII 2.16 and VII 13.9.
4. Ludwika Press and Tadeusz Sarnowski, "Novae. Römisches Legionslager und frühbyzantinische Stadt an der unteren Donau," *Antike Welt* 21, no. 4 (1990): 242–43. See also Stefan Parnicki-Pudelko, "The Early Christian Episcopal Basilica in Novae," *Archaeologia Polona* 21–22 (1983): 242 and 268–69.
5. Veneciia Liubenova, "Selishteto ot rimskata i rannovizantiiskata epokha," in *Pernik I. Poselishten zhivot na khălma Krakra ot V khil. pr.n.e. do VI v. na n.e.*, ed. Teofil Ivanov (Sofia, 1981), 107–203, esp. 112 and 195.
6. Procopius, *Buildings* IV 1. See also Noel Duval and Vladislav Popović, "Urbanisme et topographie chrétienne dans les provinces septentrionales de l'Illyricum," in *Actes du X-e Congrès international d'archéologie chrétienne, Thessalonique, 28 septembre-4 octobre 1980*, vol. 1 (Thessaloniki/Vatican City, 1984), 549; Bernard Bavant, "La ville dans le nord de l'Illyricum (Pannonie, Mésie I, Dacie et Dardanie)," in *Villes et peuplement dans l'Illyricum protobyzantin. Actes du colloque organisé par l'Ecole française de Rome (Rome, 12–14 mai 1982)* (Rome, 1984), 273 and 282–85. For houses built in the stone-cum-clay technique, see Dorde Mano-Zisi, "Iskopavanja na Caričinomu Gradu 1955 i 1956 godine," *Starinar* 7–8 (1958): 312–13.
7. Ivan Mikulčić, "Über die Größe der spätantiker Städte in Makedonien," *Živa Antika* 24 (1974): 200; Ivan Mikulčić, "Der Untergang der Paläste im spätantiken Stobi, Nordmakedonien," in *Palast und Hütte. Beiträge zum Bauen und Wohnen im Altertum von Archäologen, Vor- und Frühgeschichtlern*, edited by Dietrich Papenfuss and Volker Michael Strocka (Mainz, 1982), 536–37; James R. Wiseman, "The City in Macedonia Secunda," in *Villes et peuplement*, 310; Kara Hattersley-Smith, "Byzantine Public Architecture, Between the Fourth and Early Seventh Centuries a.d., with Special Reference to the Towns of Macedonia," Ph.D. diss. (University of Oxford, 1988), 107–9.

8. Eric A. Ivison, "Burial and urbanism at Late Antique and Early Byzantine Corinth (c. a.d. 400–700)," in *Towns in Transition. Urban Evolution in Late Antiquity and the Early Middle Ages*, ed. N. Christie and S. T. Loseby (Hants, 1996), 104 and 112; Hattersley-Smith, "Byzantine Public Architecture," 403; Jane C. Biers, *The Great Bath on the Lechaion Road* (Princeton, 1985), 12; Jean-Pierre Sodini, "L'habitat urbain en Grèce à la veille des invasions," in *Villes et peuplement*, 372.
9. Procopius, *Secret History* I 11; *Miracles of St. Demetrius* I 1.24, 3.39, 13.127, and 14.132; II 1.180, 2.199, and 4.254. For the early Byzantine *annona* and Thessalonica, see Jean Durliat, *De la ville antique à la ville byzantine. Le problème des subsistances* (Rome, 1990), 389–99.
10. For Phocaean Red Slip wares, see A. Minchev, "The late Roman fine ware import to the western Black Sea coast," in *Ancient Bulgaria. Papers presented to the International Symposium on the Ancient History and Archaeology of Bulgaria, University of Nottingham, 1981*, ed. A. G. Poulter (Nottingham, 1983), 197; Michael Mackensen, "Mediterrane Sigillata, Lampen und Amphoren," in *Invillino-Ibligo in Friaul I. Die römische Siedlung und das spätantik-frumittelalterliche Castrum*, ed. Volker Bierbrauer (Munich, 1987), 235; Ivančica Dvoržak-Schrunk, "Dioklecijanova palača od 4. do 7. stoljeća u svjetlu keramičkih nalaza," *Vjesnik Arheoloskog Muzeja u Zagrebu* 22 (1989): 94; Catherine Abadie-Reynal, "Céramique et commerce dans le bassin égéen du IV-e au VII-e siècle," in *Hommes et richesses dans l'Empire byzantin*, vol. 1, ed. Gilbert Dagron (Paris, 1989), 155; Michael Mackensen, "Amphoren und Spatheia von Golemannovo Kale," in *Die spätantiken Befestigungen von Sadovec (Bulgarien). Ergebnisse der deutsch-bulgarisch-österreichischen Ausgrabungen 1934–1937*, ed. Syna Uenze (Munich, 1992), 235. For seal finds in Constanţa, see Ioan Barnea, "Sigilii bizantine din colecţia MIRSR," *Studii şi cercetări de numismatică* 8 (1984): 95–104. For specimens from Călăraşi, see Ioan Barnea, "Noi sigilii bizantine la Dunărea de Jos," *Studii şi cercetări de istorie veche* 17, no. 2 (1966): 277–97. For a detailed discussion and a complete catalogue of finds, see Florin Curta, "Making an Early Medieval *Ethnie*: The Case of the Early Slavs (Sixth to Seventh Century a.d.)," Ph.D. diss. (Western Michigan University, 1998), 322 and 837–41.
11. Mark Whittow, "Ruling the Late Roman and Early Byzantine City: A Continuous History," *Past & Present* 129 (1990): 18. For the episcopal church at Caričin Grad, see Noel Duval, "L'architecture réligieuse de Tsaritchin Grad dans le cadre de l'Illyricum oriental au VI-e siècle," in *Villes et peuplement*, 407–14. For newly built churches obstructing the old street grid, see Elena Kessiakova, "Une nouvelle basilique à Philippopolis," in *Actes du XI-e Congrès international d'archéologie chrétienne. Lyon, Vienne, Grenoble, Genève et Aoste (21–28 septembre 1986)*, vol. 3 (Rome, 1989), 2539–59. For "aristocratic houses" at Histria, see Emil Condurachi, "Quelques maisons byzantines des villes pontiques," in *Studies in Memory of David Talbot Rice*, ed. G. Robertson and G. Henderson (Edinburgh, 1975), 174–79. For Slavic invasions, refugees and poorer houses, see Alexandru Barnea et al., *Tropaeum Traiani I. Cetatea*, vol. 1 (Bucharest, 1979), 101.
12. Joachim Henning, *Südosteuropa zwischen Antike und Mittelalter. Archäologische*

Beiträge zur Landwirtschaft des I. Jahrtausends u.Z. (Berlin, 1987), 22–35 and figs. 7–11; Andrew Poulter, "The Use and Abuse of Urbanism in the Danubian Provinces during the Later Roman Empire," in *The City in Late Antiquity*, ed. John Rich (New York, 1992), 122.

13. Procopius, *Buildings* IV 1, 2, and 10; Agathias V 11; Theophylact Simocatta VI 1.4. For sixth-century rural settlements, see A. Opaiţ and T. Bănică, "Das ländliche Territorium der Stadt Ibida (2.-7. Jh.) und einige Betrachtungen zum Leben auf dem Land an der unteren Donau," in *Die Schwarzmeerküste in der Spätantike und im frühen Mittelalter*, ed. R. Pillinger, A. Pülz, and H. Vetters (Vienna, 1992), 105–6; Stefan Stefanov, "Novgrad. Starinni selishta," *Izvestiia na Arkheologicheskiia Institut* 34 (1974): 291–92. For contemporary rural settlements in the East, see Jean-Pierre Sodini, "La contribution de l'archéologie à la connaissance du monde byzantin (IV-e-VIIe siècles)," *Dumbarton Oaks Papers* 47 (1993): 152 (with bibliography).
14. *Codex Iustinianus* 10.27.2; *Novellae* 32, 128, 148, and 162. See also Michel Kaplan, *Les hommes et la terre à Byzance du VI-e au XI-e siècle. Propriété et exploitation du sol* (Paris, 1992), 378 and 382.
15. For the "Scythian monks," see Jacques Zeiller, *Les origines chrétiennes dans les provinces danubiennes de l'Empire romain* (Paris, 1918), 383–84. For hermitages around Thessalonica, see the *Life of St. David of Thessalonica*, edited by Valentin Rose (Berlin, 1887), 15–16. For the archaeological evidence for monasteries, see Cvito Fisković, "Ranosrednjovjekovne ruševine na Majsanu," *Starohrvatska prosvjeta* 11 (1981): 137–62; Khristo Dzhambov, "Rannokhristiianska cărkva pri s. Isperikhovo, Peshterska okoliia," *Godishnik na Narodniia Arkheologicheski Muzei Plovdiv* 2 (1956): 175–92; Andrei Opaiţ, Cristian Opaiţ, and Teodor Bănică, "Der frühchristliche Komplex von Slava Rusă," in *Die Schwarzmeerküste in der Spätantike*, 113–22.
16. *De re strategica* 9, edited by George Dennis (Washington, 1985), 27. For small-size forts in Bulgaria, see Dimităr Ovcharov, *Vizantiiski i bălgarski kreposti V-X vek* (Sofia, 1982), 22. For the relation between the size of the fort and that of its garrison, see Nick P. Kardulias, "Anthropology and population estimates for the Byzantine fortress at Isthmia," in *The Corinthia in the Roman Period Including the Papers Given at a Symposium Held at the Ohio State University on 7–9 March, 1991*, ed. Timothy E. Gregory (Ann Arbor, 1993), 139–48. For Justinian's forts, rural militias and *bucellarii*, see Frank E. Wozniak, "The Justinianic Fortification of Interior Illyricum," in *City, Town, and Countryside in the Early Byzantine Era*, ed. R. L. Hohlfelder (New York, 1982), 204; John Rosser, "The Role of the Great Isthmus Corridor in the Slavonic Invasions of Greece," *Byzantinische Forschungen* 9 (1983): 253.
17. Themistius, *Or.* 10.136, tr. by Peter Heather and John Matthews (Liverpool, 1991), 44. See also Velizar Velkov, "Der Donaulimes in Bulgarien und das Vordringen der Slawen," in *Die Völker Südosteuropas im 6. bis 8. Jahrhundert*, edited by Bernhard Hänsel (Berlin, 1987), 147. A system of central distribution for the army was already in place under the early Empire. See C. R. Whittaker, *Frontiers of the Roman Empire. A Social and Economic Study* (Baltimore/London, 1994), 103 and 105. For the date of Book IV of Procopius' *Buildings*, see Geoffrey Greatrex, "The Dates of Procopius' Works,"

Byzantine and Modern Greek Studies 18 (1994): 113.

18. For imperial seals, see Barnea, "Sigilii bizantine," 95; S. Schultz, "Streufunde aus Isaccea (Noviodunum)," *Pontica* 11 (1978): 100; Vasile Culică, "Plumburi comerciale din cetatea romano-bizantină de la Izvoarele (Dobrogea)," *Pontica* 8 (1975): 246; Ioan Barnea, "Plombs byzantins dans la collection Michel C. Soutzou," *Revue des études sud-est-européennes* 7, no. 1 (1969): 29–30; Vasilka Gerasimova-Tomova, "Bleiplomben aus Durostorum," in *Die Schwarzmeerküste in der Spätantike*, 70.The sigillographic evidence from the Balkans includes an abundance of official seals: prefects, eparchs, consuls, *chartularii, magistri,* and *a secretis*. They must have belonged to the local administration. Three seals belong to *stratelates*, one of whom may have been the last king of the Gepids, Cunimund. For the attributions of the *quaestor exercitus*, see A. H. M. Jones, *The Later Roman Empire, 284–602: A Social, Economic, and Administrative Survey* (Oxford, 1964), 280; Sergei Torbatov, "Quaestura exercitus: Moesia Secunda and Scythia under Justinian," *Archaeologia Bulgarica* 1, no. 3 (1997): 78 and 80.
19. For daily food rations and amphorae, see Burkhard Böttger, "Zur Lebensmittelversorgungen des niedermösischen Kastells Iatrus (4.-6. Jh.)," in *Akten des 14. Internationalen Limeskongresses 1986 in Carnuntum*, edited by H. Vetters and M. Kandler (Vienna, 1990), 926. For Late Roman 2 amphorae, see Wolfgang Hautumm, *Studien zu Amphoren der spätrömischen und frühbyzantinischen Zeit* (Fulda, 1981), 48; Catherine Abadie-Reynal, "Les amphores protobyzantines d'Argos (IVe-VIe siècles)," in *Recherches sur la céramique byzantine*, ed. V. Déroche and J.-M. Spieser (Athens/Paris, 1989), 53; Georgi Kuzmanov, "Ceramica del primo periodo bizantino a Ratiaria," *Ratiariensia* 3–4 (1987): 115; Marko Popović, "Svetinja, novi podaci o ranovizantijskom Viminacijumu," *Starinar* 38 (1987): 13. For Late Roman 1 amphorae, see Mackensen, "Amphoren und Spatheia," 252; J. W. Hayes, *Excavations at Saraçhane in Istanbul*, vol. 2 (Princeton, 1992), 64. For *spatheia*, see Mackensen, "Mediterrane Sigillata," 258; Timotej Knific, "Vranje near Sevnica: a Late Roman settlement in the light of certain pottery finds," *Arheološki Vestnik* 45 (1994): 220. For amphorae found on the Yassi Ada shipwreck, see F. H. Van Doorninck, "The Cargo Amphoras on the 7th Century Yassi Ada and 11th century Serçe Liman Shipwrecks: Two Examples of a Reuse of Byzantine Amphoras as Transport Jars," in *Recherches sur la céramique byzantine*, 247–52.
20. Abadie-Reynal, "Céramique et commerce," 159. For Palestinian amphorae in Gaul, see Michel Bonifay and Dominique Piéri, "Amphores du Ve au VIIe s. à Marseille: nouvelles données sur la typologie et le contenu," *Journal of Roman Archaeology* 8 (1995): 97. The cargo on the Yassı Ada shipwreck has been associated with food supplies for the army, perhaps in connection with the *quaestura exercitus*. It is possible that the ship sunk off the south-west coast of Turkey shortly after 625 transported *annona* distributions to the Byzantine army in the East. See Peter G. van Alfen, "New Light on the 7th-c. Yassı Ada Shipwreck: Capacities and Standard Sizes of LRA1 Amphoras," *Journal of Roman Archaeology* 9 (1996): 213.
21. Velizar Velkov, "Les campagnes et la population rurale en Thrace au IVe-VIe siècles," *Byzantinobulgarica* 1 (1962): 58–59.

22. *Strategikon* XI 4.8. For changing consumption patterns, see L. Bartosiewicz and A. M. Choyke, "Animal Remains from the 1970–1972 Excavations of Iatrus (Krivina), Bulgaria," *Acta Archaeologica Academiae Scientiarum Hungaricae* 43 (1991): 191; Eva Hajnalová, "Archäobotanische Funde aus Krivina," in *Iatrus-Krivina. Spätantike Befestigung und frühmittelalterliche Siedlung an der unteren Donau*, vol. 2 (Berlin, 1982), 232; Andrew Poulter, *Nicopolis ad Istrum: A Roman, Late Roman, and Early Byzantine City* (London, 1995), 42–46.
23. For a.d. 602 as the end of the Danube *limes*, see Robert Roesler, "Über den Zeitpunkt der slavischen Ansiedlung an der unteren Donau," *Sitzungsberichte der kaiserlichen Akademie der Wissenschaften. Philosophisch-historische Klasse* 73 (1873): 77–126. For Phocas' troops returning to the Danube frontier, see David Michael Olster, *The Politics of Usurpation in the Seventh Century: Rhetoric and Revolution in Byzantium* (Amsterdam, 1993), 69. For the Thracian theme, see R.-J. Lilie, "'Thrakien' und 'Thrakesion.' Zur byzantinischen Provinzorganisation am Ende des 7. Jahrhunderts," *Jahrbuch der österreichischen Byzantinistik* 26 (1977): 7–47.

Town and Countryside in Roman Arabia during Late Antiquity

DAVID F. GRAF

AS ELSEWHERE IN THE ROMAN WORLD, THE COUNTRYSIDE OF ARABIA HAS BEEN neglected by archaeological enterprises until recently.[1] The former fascination here as elsewhere was with excavations of urban complexes such as the Decapolis cities in the north—Jerash (Gerasa), Philadelphia (Amman), Pella, Umm Qeis (Gadara)—and Petra, Udhruh, Humayma, and 'Aqaba (Aila) in the south. Civic architecture, temples, churches, and forts have been the priority, despite the fact that Arabia was for all essential purposes a world of villages. This urban myopia has been particularly unfortunate for studies of late antiquity, where it is generally believed there was urban decline and a greater presence of élites in the countryside, marked by extravagant villa estates and elaborate mausoleums, particularly in the fourth century and afterwards. This phenomenon is not uniform across the Mediterranean world and regional differences should be anticipated.[2] But for the East, in Syria at least, the countryside is marked by prospering rural villages and the concentration of a dense population.[3] As for Arabia, there has been a proliferation of surveys on the Transjordan plateau in the past quarter century which have marshaled important data for the state of the region during late antiquity. Their results provide a comparative basis for earlier explorations, but still remain in a quantitative state that begs for some qualitative analysis.

The advances in our archaeological knowledge of Byzantine Arabia have come in dramatic spurts. The first stage is marked by Brünnow and Domaszewski's exploration of Transjordan in the 1890s, followed shortly after by the Princeton Expedition (1904-9) and Alois Musil's efforts (1908-15). After WWI, and a short hiatus, there was another spurt, represented by the pioneering surveys of Transjordan by N. Glueck, A. Alt, and Sir Aurel Stein in the 1930s. After WWII, there was and even lengthier hiatus, but in the last third of the twentieth century, there has been a virtual explosion of projects in every region of the country. These extensive surveys have embraced the whole Transjordan plateau and desert steppe. The results have been used as a demographic index for the rise and fall of the population in various periods. Attempts to summarize this material for the Byzantine Era (fourth-seventh centuries) have already been provided by Michele Piccirillo in 1985, S. T. Parker in 1992, and Henry MacAdam and Robert Schick in 1994.[4] Unfortunately, the first study is now seriously outdated and the others appeared on the cusp of the publication of some of the important survey results. A fresh summary of the results is therefore needed and may serve as a beginning point for an analysis of the Arabian towns and countryside in late antiquity.

S. Mittmann's exploration of the area between the Yarmouk and Zarqa rivers in the 1960s marked the revival of these large-scale regional surveys. More than 364 sites were recorded in this sector of northern Transjordan, 170 of which showed traces of the Roman period and an impressive 240 of the Byzantine era.[5] In the Amman region, the Madaba Plains project between 1968-76 conducted a 10 km radius survey around Hesban.[6] Some 148 sites were recorded, of which 57 had Early Roman pottery (38%) and 45 others Late Roman (30%), whereas Byzantine increased to 126 sites (85%). Further south the "Central Moab survey," directed by J. Maxwell Miller between 1978 and 1982, recorded 443 sites on the Kerak plateau between the Wadi Mujib and Wadi al-Hasa.[7] Nabataean sites were predominant (65%), only 115 were Late Roman (26%) and 107 Early Byzantine (24%), but there was a slight rise of 132 sites that were designated as Late Byzantine (30%) and another 75

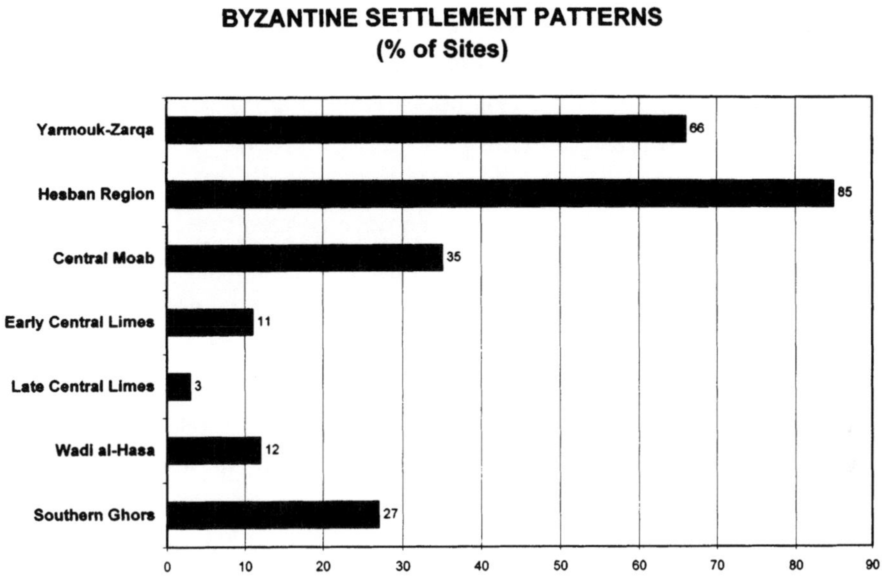
BYZANTINE SETTLEMENT PATTERNS
(% of Sites)
Yarmouk-Zarqa
66
Hesban Region
85
Central Moab
35
Early Central Limes
11
Late Central Limes
3
Wadi al-Hasa
12
Southern Ghors
27
0
10
20
30
40
50
60
70
80
90

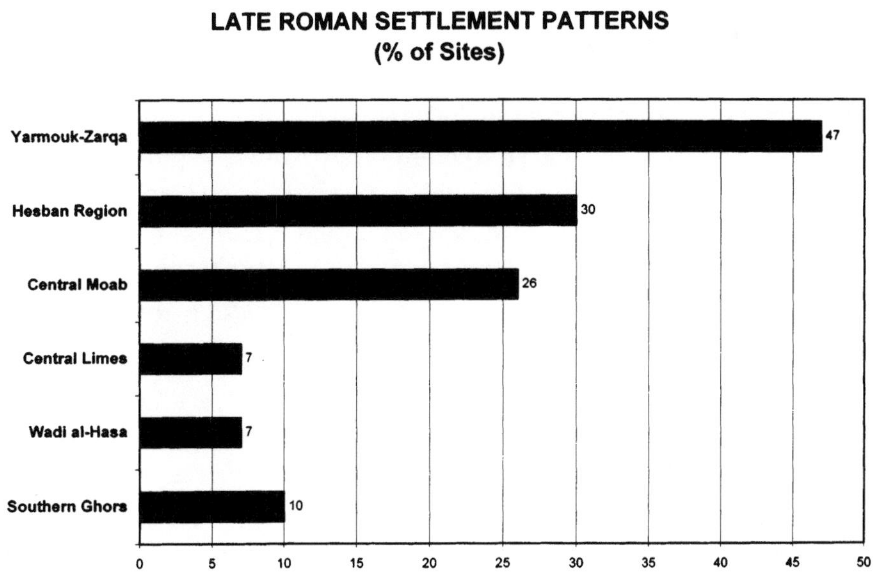
LATE ROMAN SETTLEMENT PATTERNS
(% of Sites)
Yarmouk-Zarqa
47
Hesban Region
30
Central Moab
26
Central Limes
7
Wadi al-Hasa
7
Southern Ghors
10
0
5
10
15
20
25
30
35
40
45
50

sites labeled merely "Byzantine" (17%). In contrast, the *Limes Arabicus* survey, directed by S. Thomas Parker between 1980 and 1987 in the territory just east of Miller's survey, showed a decrease in Byzantine occupation.[8] Of the 557 sites recorded, 334 (60%) yielded Nabataean and Early Roman pottery, but Late Roman was found on only 38 sites (7%), Early Byzantine on a mere 59 sites (11%), and only a meager 18 had Late Byzantine sherds (3% of the total). Most of the late Byzantine sites were concentrated in the western zone adjacent to Miller's survey. Although an additional 100 sites (18%) were designated as merely Byzantine, the decline in the Byzantine era is still dramatic.

Farther south in Transjordan, the Wadi al-Hasa survey, directed by Burton MacDonald between 1979 and 1982, recorded 1,074 sites between the Wadi al-Hasa and Tafila.[9] Of these, 195 (18%) had Nabataean and early Roman sherds, but Late Roman sites diminished to 71 sites (7%), with only another 25 yielding pottery of "Late Roman-Byzantine" date and a mere 125 (12% of total) designated purely "Byzantine," and most of these were concentrated west of the *Via Nova Traiana* and in small clusters to the east of this main artery. In 1985-86, MacDonald directed another important project between the Southern Ghors at the northern edge of the Lisan peninsula in the northeastern Arabah.[10] Some 240 sites were recorded, of which only 24 (10%) had Roman pottery and 64 Byzantine (27%). This marked increase in the number of Byzantine sites includes some of major importance, such as the Wadi Faynan which has yielded important evidence from the fifth and sixth centuries from ancient Phaeno, a Byzantine penal colony, and the extensive Byzantine cemetery discovered at Ghor Safi.[11] For the area further south, surveys have been less extensive and coordinated, but the impression is that the southern plateau and Hismâ desert also had a healthy proportion of Roman and Byzantine sites.

In sum, the results of these surveys have revealed a disparate settlement pattern for late antiquity. Between the Yarmuk river and Wadi al-Hasa, Roman and particularly Byzantine sites dominate. However, east of central Moab and south of the Wadi al-Hasa, the slight increase of Early Byzantine sites (fourth and fifth centuries) is followed by a dramatic decline in the Late Byzantine period (sixth and seventh centuries). Nevertheless, it must be emphasized that these results are subject to various interpretations and are inconclusive by nature. The tabulation of sites includes everything from sherd scatters to villages, and rarely define the size of the majority of the sites. Did larger sites merely replace scattered smaller sites? Declines in the number of sites may only represent a shift of the population to another region. Moreover, and more serious, the ceramic typology utilized by most of the surveys is derived primarily from excavations at Hesban near Amman in the 1970s and leaves in abeyance consideration of regional pottery. This perhaps accounts for the majority of the sherds collected in the surveys being unidentified and the fact that subsequent excavations have frequently produced results entirely different than the surface pottery collected.[12] Furthermore, David Kennedy's study of aerial photography is exposing many sites missed in the surveys.[13] Obviously, more *intensive* surveys with selected *sondages* and excavations in villages and the countryside would be of immense help in forming a more definitive picture of demographic trends, the organization of territory, land use, and surplus production from natural resources. In the present state of affairs, the results reflecting rises and declines of Byzantine occupation can only be regarded as impressionistic. Far more unsettling are certain features missing from the Arabian landscape that are typical of Roman provincial life elsewhere. Three particular features may be singled out: the evidence for land-divisions, large rural estates or villas, and rural markets.

TERRITORIAL DIVISIONS

Investigation of the Roman road system in the region has helped to expose the fundamental provincial and territorial divisions of the region. Geographically they are represented by the great drainage systems of the Wadi Mujib and Wadi al-Hasa, which cut across the landscape in an east-west direction, dividing the country into three separate spheres: the urban north, the fertile plains of Moab dominated by villages, and the more desolate southern regions. After the annexation of the province in 106, the *Via Nova Traiana* was constructed between 111 and 114, connecting the Arabian capital at Bostra in the Haurân to Aila on the Gulf of -Aqaba, *a finibus Syriae usque ad mare rubrum*, some 430 km in length. This central transportation spine cut directly across the major dividing wadi systems, helping to unite the new province. More than 200 milestone inscriptions from Trajan to Julian document the itinerary and path of this route.

These milestones also are indicators of the territorial divisions that dominate the landscape. Initially, it is clear, Petra served as the *caput viae* for the whole route of the major Trajanic road. However, in 181 under Commodus, at least as far as the XLVIII Roman mile south of Bostra, the Arabian capital replaced Petra as the *caput viae*.[14] Afterwards, city territories begin to mark the distances on the milestones along the *Via Nova Traiana*, just as they had elsewhere in the province. For example, Jacque Seigne's recent discoveries of milestones and other inscriptions help clarify the territorial limits between the two major Decapolis cities of Gerasa (Jerash) and Philadelphia.[15] To the west, milestones on the Roman road to Pella in the Jordan Valley indicate Jerash's territory extended as far as the XII mile.[16] The boundaries of other Decapolis cities remain unknown, but the pattern of this civic triad indicates what may have existed elsewhere.[17] The same pattern seems clear from the milestones along the *Via Nova Traiana* between Amman (Philadelphia) and Petra farther south. South of Madaba, the milestones reflect distances from this town until the descent into the Wadi Mujib.[18] On the southern banks of the great divide of the Mujib, the milestones are marked with distances to Rabba and to the south as far as al-Mote near the Wadi al-Hasa, the other great dividing line of Transjordan, with milestones also marked from Rabba, dated like that marking its northern limit to the reign of Pertinax in 193 A.D.[19]

At this point such civic markers virtually disappear, but there are indications the system continued. At 52 km and 90 km north of Petra along the *Via Nova Traiana*, two fragmentary boundary markers are found, but the names of the respective villages are either missing or illegible.[20] The location of one is just south of the Wadi al-Hasa, and the other near Shobak. The Peutinger Table indicates that the village of Thornia (Thawana) and Negla (Nejl) were the major road stations in the region, and either could be the unidentified villages mentioned on the milestones. Of course, this region is dominated by Petra, the former capital of the Nabataean kingdom, and it may be one of the intended villages. Further south, none of the milestones divulge city territories, but it is likely that Petra dominated the plateau up to escarpment above the Hisma desert.[21] For the last segment of this major route, Humayma (ancient Hawara/Auara) and 'Aqaba (Aila) are the best candidates for the civic territories demarcating the region. In essence, from north to south, cities seem to command the landscape of Roman Transjordan. What the relationship of the urban centers was to their rural regions is difficult to determine without documentation, but the tendency has been to emphasize the extension of the urban aristocratic elite into the countryside, elite who expanded their wealth by extracting rents and surpluses from the rural hinterland.[22] Whatever the case, the fate of the official Roman road system during late antiquity is more obscure.

It has been suggested that the Roman road system fell into disuse in the East during late antiquity, centuries before the Islamic conquests. The reason proposed for this development is the replacement of wheeled vehicles by camels for transporting goods throughout the Near East.[23] Diocletian's Edict of Maximum Prices in 301 supposedly marks the transition by placing the charges of transporting by ox cart at a rate 20 percent more than by camel load. Thereafter, at different times and in different places, presumably the traditional paved roads soon fell into disrepair. Dated epigraphic milestones end throughout the Levant in the fourth century, with the reigns of Constantine in Syria, Julian in Arabia, and Arcadius in Palestine. Imperial rescripts in the *Theodosian Code* do speak of difficulties in maintaining the road system and the "immense ruin of the highways" at the time (*CT* 15.3.4), but this popular hypothesis is belied by various kinds of documentary and archaeological evidence. During the fourth century, Eusebius and the *Itinerarium Egeriae* use the milestones to locate holy places in Palestine, showing that official roads are still in use. The responsibility for the repair of roads in the fifth century was even enlarged to include all citizens, without "distinction of any honors, persons or privileges" (Valentinian, *Nov.* 10.3), including the formerly excluded members of the imperial household, dignitaries, and the clergy. The *Justinianic Code* also preserves rescripts for maintaining the *cursus publicus* into the early fifth century (XII.51.1-23). During the reign of Justinian, Procopius records that roads were constructed for wagons in Europe, North Africa, Asia Minor, and Syria, where some of the physical evidence still survives.[24] In Egypt, Greek and Coptic papyri indicate donkeys and ox-carts were still being used in the seventh centuty.[25] Ottoman sources also indicate wheeled vehicles were still used for transporting goods in Eastern Turkey and Syria in the seventeenth century.[26] In essence, vehicular traffic and the road system appears to have continued unabated into the Islamic period throughout the Near East.

Internal divisions within the rural landscape need also to be addressed. Property divisions of the farmlands in the hinterland are virtually unknown in the region, but there are other kinds of evidence for field patterns. During the early Roman era, the system of land-division known as "centuriation" was strongly linked to the foundation of veteran colonies and the allocation of land to the new settlers. Aerial photographs have revealed such arrangements throughout the Roman empire.[27] In the Levantine Near East, such field divisions have appeared in Lebanon, Syria, and Palestine.[28] For the province of Arabia, the only such grid patterns detected are in the Syrian Hauran. At the capital of Bostra, where the legionary camp of the *III Cyrenaica* was located, regular land divisions have been observed in the western and southwestern suburbs of the city, and nearby at Salkhad and Imtan.[29] Elsewhere in the province, any traces of regular field divisions are minimal, appearing only at Umm al-Quttayn in northern Jordan and El-Tilah about 25 km south of the Dead Sea on the eastern side of the Wadi Araba.[30] The latter consists of a regular pattern of square terraced walls adjacent to a small fort (40 × 40 m), reservoir, and aqueduct system that appear to date to the Late Roman and Byzantine periods.[31] The site can be identified with *Toloha*, where the *Ala Constantiana* was stationed (*Notitia Dignitatum*, Or. XXXIV.34). But the irregularity of the plot sizes and shapes in Arabia suggests that not all the plots were necessarily assigned to military veterans. In Roman Syria, some of the regular field divisions appear to be the product of fiscal policy related to rural development.[32] In Tunisia, such grid patterns are associated with city lands, private and imperial estates, and even lands assigned for settlements of tribesmen.[33] The same may be the case in Arabia.

The most striking case of defining territory by imperial authorities is that of the Tetrarchic land surveyors, who left evidence of their work scattered across the Near East, including Commagene in eastern Turkey, the vicinity of Aleppo and the Orontes Valley in Syria, the Golan Heights and Huleh Valley in Galilee, and Egypt.[34] This evidence consists of boundary inscriptions clearly connected with the Tetrarchic tax-reform of 297. Traces of the land demarcating activity of the Tetrarchic *censitores* occur also in the southern Hauran (Batanaea and Auranitis) of Syria, but not anywhere within the borders of the province of Arabia.[35] Since the enterprise appears to have comprised the entire Roman Near East, this seems curious. In fact, the same *censitor,* Aelius Statutus, was active in Damascus, Gaulanitis, and the Huleh Valley, and another *censitor,* Julius Septimius Sabinus was active in Syria and the Arsinoite nome in Heptanomia in Egypt, where the process continued until at least 309.[36] But neither of the two cadasters known from northern Jordan appear to reflect the activity of the Tertrachic *censitores.* These boundary markers merely define the boundaries of private property and imperial estates.[37] This lacuna in Arabia for the Tetrarchic land surveyors would seem to be purely accidental, and likely eliminated by some future epigraphic discovery.

VILLAS

Large estates are a typical feature of the Roman and Byzantine landscape in the western provinces and Greece.[38] Thousands have been excavated in Britain, Belgium, Gaul, Spain, the Upper Danube and Rhineland, as well as Italy. In contrast, villas appear to be strikingly rare in the Near East.[39] Part of the reason for their seeming absence is the tyranny of an overly-precise definition that emphasized only the luxury and leisure aspects of the Italian rural complexes, neglecting their productivity (*fructuaria*). Emphasis on the sterility of the *villae* in the Latin literary tradition also contributed to the perception that villas were "a little island of urban uselessness marooned in the real countryside."[40] The reality is that production of a surplus and exploitation of the countryside was just as much a part of their essential function as the elements of privacy. Of course, the large villa estates with their luxurious baths, porticoes, and mosaics that were common in the West are unlikely to be found in the East. In fact, there is a wide variety of types even in the West, reflecting regional diversity and the tastes of the indigenous local elite society.[41] It is now recognized that a provincial villa was not a "slavish reproduction of the Italian one," but one exhibiting its own unique properties.[42] Those in the East took on a different form than elsewhere, where there was already a long tradition of the Oriental *paradeisos*, with its productive gardens and water resources.

In the Levant, many of the villas are linked to nucleated villages and cities, intermingled among the farmsteads in the nearby surrounding suburbs. They are also typically associated with garden estates and plantations for supplying food for the owner's household. Libanius indicates that the wealthy citizens of Antioch escaped in the summer to their villas in the suburb of Daphne (*Ep.* 419), where senators and emperors also erected villas. Such villas near Antioch had been excavated before 1980 as well as others in the environs of Beirut and Baalbek in Lebanon, and Ascalon, Beth-Shean, and Emmaus in Palestine.[43] But the list from Palestine has been significantly expanded since 1980, with Byzantine *villa rusticae* now known throughout Palestine, especially along the coastal plain northeast of Caesarea, and from Hebron to the northern Negev.[44] A number date to the early Roman era (first century B.C.–first century A.D.), including even the possibility that the settlement at Qumran was originally a *villa rustica* before its possible conversion to an Essene center.[45] These large complexes occupy several hundred square yards, including adjacent industrial areas, with sometimes a fortified tower connected to the residential quarter. The estates appear to be the product of wealthy and powerful magnates, and involved a significant work-force.

The recent surveys in Jordan have revealed the intensity of rural settlements, but few villas have been identified. Villeneuve has drawn attention to several *villae rusticae* in the environs of Bostra.[46] There are also a number of large farm houses with towers in the area near Suweida in the Hauran, similar to those in Palestine. Other rural estates might be expected in the vicinity of the Transjordanian urban centers, at Jerash, Amman, Madaba, and Petra, such as the badly destroyed large Byzantine villa complex Pam Watson discovered about 2 km north of Pella overlooking the hot springs at

Wadi al-Hammeh. It appears to be connected to the adjacent bath house structures, and produced abundant late sixth and early seventh century pottery.[47] The identification and excavation of such sites elsewhere in Jordan should be a desideratum for the future. The focus should be the field systems rather than just the palatial elements. Such rural complexes have been observed elsewhere. In Egypt, papyri suggest one of the most noticeable demographic changes in late antiquity is the increased number of large land-owners of "great domains" in the third to the sixth centuries and a decline in village organization.[48] During this period, the tendency was for a permanent agricultural work-force living on subsistence wages on larger estates operated by the so-called magnates of these "great domains."[49]

Although such "great domains" are almost unknown in the Levant, the recent discovery in 1993 of more than 150 scrolls of carbonized papyri in a sixth century Byzantine church at Petra illustrates the phenomenon may exist also in Arabia.[50] As Petra was the former capital of the Nabataean kingdom, the tendency had been to search for the socioeconomic decline of the city after its annexation in 106. Earthquakes in 363 or 561 were thought to have brought the once proud capital to an end. But the papyri demonstrate the city was flourishing across the sixth century as the center of *Palaestina Tertia.* Most of the scrolls are economic documents ranging in date from 528 across the sixth century until 583 or later. They record the property and possessions in the agricultural hinterland owned by prominent families at Petra that extend from 10 to 30 km from the city. Listed are the names of nearby towns, villages, and farmlands in the region such as Augustopolis (Udru), Ammatha (Al-ammam) and Kastron Zadakathon (Sadaqa). Mention is also made of what may be regarded as an urban villa in Petra and a rustic villa in the village Serila. In both cases the Greek term used is *aulê*, originally "courtyard" but in later Greek by extension "farmhouse," "villa," and the text fortunately preserves the Arabic equivalent *dâra* transcribed in Greek letters. The archive is dominated by the Christian clergy as frequent references to monks, priests, deacons, archdeacons, and bishops indicate. With the sixth century Nessana papyri found in the Negev a half century ago, these documents provide insights into the rural landscape of Third Palestine that help illuminate the archaeological record. Elsewhere in Arabia, similar tendencies may be reflected in the disappearance of the traditional village institutions and the prominence of the clergy in public building in late antiquity.[51] This investment in the countryside should also be reflected in villas.

RURAL MARKETS

Urban and rural markets and periodic and annual commercial fairs are a well documented phenomenon across the empire.[52] It has been observed that "of all aspects of Roman commerce there is none so neglected as the arrangements for markets within a short radius."[53] The recent discovery of the *macellum* at Gerasa, known previously only from dedicatory inscriptions of the Hadrianic era, provides now an excellent example of an urban market in Arabia.[54] Rural markets, organized around central towns and their satellite villages, and usually located on or near important junctions of local roads, are also well known. According to Libanius (*Or.* 11.230), in the vicinity of Antioch, large and well populated villages (*kômai*), exchanged with one another their goods and crafts through festivals (*panêgyreis*), having "'little need of the city' (*mikra tês poleôs chrêizousai*), because of their exchange among themselves." This depiction of economic self-sufficiency in rural villages may seem to be merely a *topos* for the "glorification of the country life," but Brent Shaw has demonstrated that in Roman North Africa at least, the rural markets were strikingly not integrated into the urban market centers.[55] At such markets, farmers and pastoralists could exchange common goods, and village craftsmen sell their wares. Most villagers would have their common needs satisfied in this fashion, especially those who lived some distance from major urban markets.[56] These locals could purchase here the necessary clothing, pottery, metal or wood implements, salt, and other items to satisfy their basic needs, and perhaps even a few luxuries like gold and silver jewelry. Slaves, land, and animals also could be sold in such locations. Estate owners often provided the location for the event, clearing a space on their property for such exchanges. Any doubts about the realistic nature of this picture are dispelled by the mounting evidence for the monetarization of the rural economy and the stratification of peasant society.[57]

Nor should the volume of peasant demand be underestimated, since they represented more than 80 percent of the total population of the Roman empire.

Of course, the fairs (*panygereis* or *nundinae*) were of greater magnitude, attended by both local population and foreigners. These periodic events attracted itinerant merchants, peddlers, and caravans from afar who traveled from fair to fair. Many of these merchants received a tax or customs exemption from the emperor, since their large-scale trade involved expensive items. In the fourth century, Ammianus mentions the annual fair at the town of Batne, just east of the Euphrates from Zeugma, where crowds gathered to purchase wares from India and Persia (14.3.3). Shortly after, another Syrian describes the festival at Immae near Antioch, where merchants from afar gathered and attracted a crowd "beyond number" (Theodoretus, *Hist rel.* 7 = PG 82.1365). Such large gatherings of locals and foreigners could arouse the suspicions of the authorities, especially in the frontier provinces, where security could be threatened. Consequently, legal permission was required before holding such affairs, and supervision and monitoring must have been demanded during the events. Since long-distance trade was conducted mainly by ship, many of the fairs were located in port cities along the Mediterranean coast from Gaza to Tyre, but others were inland. For example, a famous fair was located at Botnah (Beth Ilanim), near Hebron in Palestine. Herod is known to have enclosed the location with a massive wall, and after its destruction in the Bar Kokhba revolt, it was rebuilt by Hadrian and Constantine later added to it a church. Numismatic evidence from the site indicates that it flourished throughout the Roman and Byzantine periods, with its inter-regional nature reflected by coins from Egypt, Syria, Asia Minor, Greece, Italy, Spain, and Gaul.[58]

The location of such open-air fairs and markets may be difficult to determine in the absence of any literary material such as the Rabbincal sources that attest to Botnah, but, as Ramsay MacMullen has suggested, the archaeologist "might find at a cross-roads an area littered with coins, pottery, and other small objects attesting to the presence of crowds of people."[59] Perhaps more specific is Shaw's suggestion that rural markets should be sought along regularly used routes connecting disparate zones, such as the frontiers zones, rather than villages or small towns. The preference is for a neutral ground for rural periodic markets, a place juxtaposed between adjacent populations in a kind of "no man's land."[60] It is also evident that such affairs were of pre-Roman vintage. In fact, our first literary reference to the Nabataeans refers precisely to their participation in just such a regional fair in Arabia during the early Hellenistic period (Diodorus Siculus 19.95). This is a reminder that rural markets are of pre-Roman vintage and of eastern vintage. Both the Latin term *mercatus* and *macellum* are of Semitic derivation, suggesting that the phenomenon was imported to the West from the East.[61] *Ex Oriente Lux* should not be forgotten.

This world of small markets and exchange is predicated on a world of diversity and complexity that includes merchants and artisans, not just farmers and pastoralists. The tendency to bifurcate the ancient population into a small urban elite and an overwhelming majority of peasants has obscured this variety of lifestyles in the countryside. Recent emphasis has been placed on the self-sufficiency of ancient towns and villages in regard to their common needs, which were supplied by local craftsmen.[62] Their workshops should be sought in villages interspersed among agricultural contexts, not just the cities. Even the small villages in Egypt had seven to twelve tradesmen and a small town like Korykos in Rough Cilicia in Asia Minor had over 100 different tradesmen. When compared to only 80 trades and occupations at Pompeii and slightly over 200 from Rome, the differences and distinctions between urban and rural begin to diminish somewhat.[63] Epigraphic evidence from Syria has already signalled what can be expected from villages elsewhere in the Near East, but a systematic study of artisans and tradesmen in Arabia is still needed.[64] This variegated population of craftsmen and merchants may constitute only a minority of the village population who were predominantly agriculturists, but it is an important minority who should not be neglected.

The fate of this prospering countryside in late antiquity has been regarded as one of decline, the result of military withdrawal and plague, with the final blow delivered by the Islamic conquests. The literary and archaeological evidence has been marshaled to conclude that the forts along the Arabian frontier were abandoned by the early sixth century.[65] But this picture of the central sector of the Transjordan frontier is not matched by the evidence from either the northeastern sector (see below) nor that of Third Palestine (southern Jordan and the Negev of Palestine) in the sixth century. For the latter region, the Nessana papyri are particularly important, as they suggest the garrisons at Eboda (Avdat), Nessana, and Sobita in the Negev were installed first in the sixth century. Archaeological evidence also suggests that important road posts in the Negev at Mezad Thamar, Ein Boqeq, Upper Zohar, and Horvat Ma'agora existed in the sixth century and may have even been constructed at that time.[66] For the eastern sector of Third Palestine, the recently discovered Petra papyri in the sixth century also mention the military sites at Augustopolis (Udru), Ammatha, and Sadaqa in southern Transjordan. Before the seventh century, there is little evidence to suggest there was any large-scale systematic reduction of the provincial army in *Palaestina Tertia:* epigraphic texts even indicate military officers in the Negev as late as 613.[67] Islamic sources are silent about military troops at Udru or Aila at the time of the Muslim conquests, but these same sources fail to mention the important military road posts at Humayma, Sadaqa, and Petra. The evidence is far from conclusive on this point.

Between 542 and 749, a series of plagues also struck the Near East. The outbreak began under Justinian's reign, arising first in Egypt before spreading elsewhere in the Levant.[68] Afterwards, it appears to have erupted periodically in fifteen year intervals across the Mediterranean into at least the seventh century, with an impact even on Ireland and England.[69] The disease seemed to have traveled along the imperial routes and coastal areas, striking both Antioch and Constantinople, so the impact was considerable. The reverberations of the earlier Antonine plague have gained greater respect as a result of the analysis of census documents from Egypt.[70] It is even possible that both the Antonine plague and the Justinianic one appeared earlier in South Arabia prior to their impact on the Mediterranean world.[71] Its effect on the towns and countryside of Arabia is difficult to ascertain, but epigraphic testimony suggests the plague did have its effect on the region. Construction of civic buildings and churches reached a zenith in Palestine and Arabia in the reign of Justinian, yet only three churches and no civic buildings were constructed in the crucial decade of 540-550 when the plague struck. Afterwards, Jerash has only four dated inscriptions, while villages on the desert fringe some 25 km distant were still flourishing and erecting no less than eight post-Justinian churches.[72] Any effects of the Justinian plague on the countryside of Arabia have yet to be detected.

Even the impact of the Islamic conquests upon the prosperous Arabian countryside in late antiquity is under revision. The traditional view of the violent conquest of the towns and countryside of the Levant by the Muslims is now generally rejected. The theme is now diplomacy and survival of the Christian communities of Arabia and Palaestine.[73] The prosperity of the towns and villages in late antiquity is now considered to have continued into the Umayyad period and declined only late in the Abassid period at the end of the eighth century or early ninth.[74] This theme of survival is illustrated by three settlements on the desert fringe. The extensive thriving rural settlement at Umm al-Jimal, consisting of over a hundred houses and fifteen churches in northeast Jordan, located in the black basalt desert east of Mafraq, may have dwindled some after the Islamic conquest, but its complete collapse was not until it suffered a plague and earthquake in the mid–eighth century.[75] Just to the south, excavations at Khirbet es-Samra have recovered evidence of an enclave of Melkite Christians at a fort and settlement that was flourishing in the sixth century. More than eighty funerary stele inscribed in their peculiar script, once classed merely as Syro-Palestinian, testify not only to the effort of Chalcedonians to preserve their orthodoxy, but the fact that their community survived into the seventh and eighth centuries.[76] Finally, the rectangular fortified camp at Umm er-Rasas became the center of a small cluster of churches and village in late antiquity.[77] Eighth century mosaics of one of the churches positively identify the site as Kastron Mefaa, known from Eusebius' *Onomasticon* (128.21) and the *Notitia Dignitatum,* and depict a number of towns in Transjordan, Palestine, and Egypt. For Arabia, these include Kastron Mefaa itself, along with Amman, Madaba, Hesban, Ma'in, Rabba, Karak, Limbon, and Diblaton. The indications are that these towns survived into the early ninth century.[78] These impressions of survival seem to be the case across the whole Moabite plateau. Many of the Greek funerary inscriptions collected by R. Canova from twenty-nine villages in the Kerak region date across the fifth and sixth centuries, but even extend into the seventh century and beyond, with the latest dated to 736 and 785.[79] I hope that such fringe settlements and my discussion demonstrate that the Arabian towns and countryside are a topic worth pursuing further.

NOTES

1. See R. Hohlfelder, ed., *City, Town and Countryside in the Early Byzantine Era* (New York, 1982), and G. Barker and J. Lloyd, eds., *Roman Landscapes: Archaeological Survey in the Mediterranean Region* (London, 1991).
2. See S. Saïd, "Countryside," 398–99 and J. Percival, "Villas," 741–42, in *Late Antiquity: A Guide to the Postclassical World,* ed. G. Bowersock, P. Brown, and O. Grabar (Cambridge, 1999).
3. G. Tate, "The Syrian Countryside during the Roman Era," in *The Early Roman Empire in the East,* ed. S. E. Alcock (Oxford, 1997), 55–71.
4. M. Piccirillo, "Rural Settlements in Byzantine Jordan," *Studies in the History and Archaeology of Jordan* II, ed. A. Hadidi (Amman, 1985), 257–61; S. T. Parker, "The Limes and Settlement Patterns in Central Jordan in the Roman and Byzantine Periods," *Studies in the History and Archaeology of Jordan* IV (Amman, 1992), 321–25; H. I. MacAdam, "Settlements and Settlement Patterns in Northern and Central Transjordan, ca. 550-ca 750," 49–93, and R. Schick, "The Settlement Pattern of Southern Jordan: The Nature of the Evidence," in *The Byzantine and Early Islamic Near East* II: *Land Use and Settlement Patterns,* ed. G. R. D. King and A. Cameron (Princeton, 1994), 133–54.
5. S. Mittmann, *Beiträge zur Siedlungs- und Territorialgeschichte des nördlichen Ostjordanlandes* (Wiesbaden, 1970), 256–64.
6. R. D. Ibach, Jr., *Archaeological Survey of the Hesban Region: Catalogue of Sites and Characterizations of Periods: Hesban 5* (Berrien Springs, 1987), 174–83. The project has expanded the survey in the 1990s, but the results are not yet available.
7. J. Maxwell Miller, ed., *Archaeological Survey of the Kerak Plateau* (Atlanta, 1991).
8. F. L. Kouchy, "Survey of the Limes Zone," 41–106, and V. A. Clark "The Desert Survey," 107–64 in *The Roman Frontier in Jordan,* edited by S. T. Parker (Oxford, 1987).
9. B. MacDonald, *The Wadi el-Hasa Archaeological Survey 1979–1983, West Central Jordan* (Waterloo, Ontario, 1988), 190–249.
10. B. MacDonald, *The Southern Ghors and Northeast 'Arabah Archaeological Survey* (Sheffield, 1992), 89–97.
11. For the Wadi Faynan, see A. McQuitty et al. in *Levant* 30 (1998): 1–83, and for Ghor Safi, K. D. Politis, *American Journal of Archaeology* 103 (1999): 518–20.
12. For two recent examples, see E. B. Banning, "Highlands and Lowlands: Problems and Survey Frameworks for Rural Archaeology in the Near East," *Bulletin of the American*

Schools of Oriental Research 301 (1996): 25–45, and P. Bienkowski et al., "Soundings at Ash-Shorabat and Khirbet Dubab in the Wadi Hasa, Jordan: The Stratigraphy," *Levant* 29 (1997): 41–70.

13. D. Kennedy, "Aerial Archaeology in Jordan," *Levant* 30 (1998): 91–96.
14. T. Bauzou, "Le secteur nord de la via nova en Arabie de Bostra à Philadelphia," in *Fouilles de Khirbet es-Samra en Jordanie* I, ed. J.-B. Humbert and A. Desreumaux (Turnhout, 1998), 242.
15. A.-M. Rasson-Seigne and J. Seigne, "Notes préliminaires à l'étude de la voie romaine Gerasa/Philadelphia," *ADAJ* 39 (1995): 193–210, J. Seigne and S. Agusta-Boularot, "Milliaires anciens et nouveaux de Gerasa," *Mélanges de l'École Française de Rome antiquité* 110 (1998): 261–95, and J. Seigne, "Les limites orientale et méridionale du territoire de Gerasa," *Syria* 74 (1997): 121–38.
16. P. Thomsen, "Die römischen Meilensteine der Provinzen Syria, Arabia, und Palastina," *ZDPV* 40, nos. 221–22 (1917).
17. See now S. Mittmann, Römerstrassen in Nordwestjordanien und ihr Nachleben in der Kreuzfahrerzeit," *ZDPV* 115 (1999): 24–48.
18. Thomsen, *ZDPV* 40, nos. 116, 118–19, 125–26 (1917).
19. Thomsen, *ZDPV* 40, no. 185 (1917).
20. M. Sartre, *IGLS* 21/*IJ* 4, nos. 116 and 118 (1993).
21. For this region see my discussion of "The *Via Nova Traiana* in Arabia Petraea," in *The Roman and Byzantine Near East: Some Recent Archaeological Research*, JRA Supplementary Series, no. 14 (Ann Arbor, 1995), 241–67.
22. C. R. Whittaker, "Do Theories of the Ancient City Matter?," *Urban Society in Roman Italy*, edited by T. Cornell and K. Lomas (New York, 1995), 9–37, provides a recent critique of the various models for interpreting the role of cities.
23. Richard Bulliet, *The Camel and the Wheel* (Cambridge, 1975), 19–26; cf. W. H. McNeill, "The Eccentricity of Wheels, or Eurasian Transportation in Historical Perspective," *American Historical Review* 92 (1987): 1111–26.
24. See my discussion in "Camels, Roads and Wheels in Late Antiquity," *Donum Amicitiae*, ed. E. Dabrowa (Kraków: Jagiellonian University Press) = *Electrum* 1 (1997): 43–49, and more briefly in "Roads," in *Late Antiquity: A Guide to the Postclassical World*, ed. G. Bowersock, P. Brown, and O. Grabar (Cambridge, 1999), 671–73. For the archaeological evidence, see D. French, "A Road Problem: Roman or Byzantine?," *Istanbuler Mitteilungen* 43 (1993): 445–54.
25. R. S. Bagnall, "The Camel, the Wagon, and the Donkey in Later Roman Egypt, *Bulletin of the American Society of Papyrologists* 22 (1986): 1–6.
26. S. Faroqhi, "Camels, Wagons and the Ottoman State in the Sixteenth and Seventeenth Centuries," *International Journal of Middle East Studies* 14 (1982): 523–39.
27. For a general discussion, see J. Bradford, "Roman Centuriation: A Planned Landscape," in *Ancient Landscapes: Studies in Field Archaeology* (London, 1957), 145–216, and O. A. W. Dilke, *The Roman Land Surveyors: An Introduction to the Agrimensores* (Newton Abbot, 1971).
28. J. Sauvaget, "Le plan de Laodicea sur mer," *Bulletin d'Études Orientales* 4 (1934):

81–1113; W. J. Van Liere, "*Ager Centuriatus* of the Roman Colonia of Emesa (Homs)," *Annales Archéologiques Syriennes* 8–9 (1958–59): 55–58; L. Marfoe, *Between Qadesh and Kumidi: A History of Frontier Settlement and Land Use in the Biqa'* (Ph.D. diss., University of Chicago, 1978), and "Empire and Ethnicity in Syrian Society: 'From Archaeology to Historical Society' Revisited," in *Archéologie au Levant: Recueil à la mémoire de Roger Saidah* (Lyon, 1982), 470; M. Dodinet, J. Leblanc, J.-P. Vallat and F. Villeneuve, "Le paysage antique en Syrie: l'exemple de Damas," *Syria* 67 (1990): 339–55; cf. G. Tate, "A propos des cadastres romains du Nord de la Syrie," in *Structures rurales et sociétés antiques*, ed. P. N. Doakellis and L. G. Mendoni (Besançon, 1994), 443–51; and S. Applebaum, "The Roman Colony of Ptolemais-Akko," in *Greece and Rome in Eretz Israel*, ed. A. Kasher et al. (Jerusalem, 1990), 135–40.

29. M. Dodinet, J. Leblanc, and J.-P. Vallat, "Étude morphologique des paysages antiques de Syrie," in *Structures rurales et sociétés antiques*, ed. P. N. Doakellis and L. G. Mendoni (Besançon, 1994), 427–42, D. Kennedy, "Aerial Photography: Ancient Settlements in Syria," *Popular Archaeology* (September 1985): 42–44, and F. Villeneuve in *Hauran I*, ed. J.-M. Dentzer (Paris, 1985), 128 with pl. VIIb.
30. D. Kennedy, H. MacAdam, and D. Riley, "Preliminary Report on the Southern auran Survey, 1985," *ADAJ* 30 (1986): 151–53 with fig. 2, and H. MacAdam, *The Byzantine and Early Islamic Near East*, vol. II (1994), 61n. 68; D. Kennedy and D. Riley, *Rome's Desert Frontier from the Air* (Austin, 1990), 205–7.
31. For the pottery see Graf, *Wadi 'Arabah Survey* (Amman, 1980) and MacDonald, *The Southern Ghors and Northeast Arabah Archaeological Survey* (1992), 89 and 105.
32. G. Tate, "The Syrian Countryside during the Roman Era," in *The Early Roman Empire in the East*, ed. S. E. Alcock (Oxford, 1997), 60–62.
33. J. Bradford, *Ancient Landscapes: Studies in Field Archaeology* (London, 1957), 213–14.
34. See F. Millar, *The Roman Near East 31 BC-AD 337* (Cambridge, 1993), 535–44, for the details.
35. M. Sartre, "Nouvelles bornes cadastrales du Hauran sous la Tétrachie," *Ktema* 17 (1992): 111–31.
36. Millar, *Roman Near East*, 536 [Aelius Statutus]; A. H. M. Jones, J. Martindale and J. Norris, *The Prosopography of the Later Roman Empire*, vol. 1 (Cambridge, 1971), 794 [Iulius Septimius Sabinus 17].
37. E. Littmann, *Princeton Archaeological Expedition to Syria* IIIA (Leiden, 1907), no. 28 (Sama) and *SEG* 17 (1960), no. 760 (Jabin). Each text has the Greek equivalent (*engion tamiakon*) for the Roman Latin *ager fiscalis*, indicating imperial land.
38. J. Percival, *The Roman Villa: An Historical Introduction* (Berkeley, 1976) and B. Bergmann, "Visualizing Pliny's Villas," *JRA* 8 (1995): 406–20.
39. J. J. Rossiter, "Roman villas of the Greek east and the villa in Gregory of Nyssa *Ep.* 20," *Journal of Roman Archaeology* 2 (1989): 101–10, and H.-P. Kuhnen, *Palästina in griechisch-römischer Zeit* (Munich, 1990), 241.
40. N. Purcell, "The Roman *Villa* and the Landscape of Production," *Urban Society in Roman Italy*, edited by T. Cornell and K. Lomas (New York, 1995), 173, a remarkably perceptive essay.

41. See now J. T. Smith, *Roman Villas: A Study in Social Structure* (New York/London, 1998).
42. J. Percival, "The Villa in Italy and the Provinces," *The Roman World* II, edited by J. Wacher (London/New York, 1987), 542.
43. See Rossiter, *JRA* 2 (1989): 102n. 8, for a list.
44. Y. Hirschfeld, "Farms and Village in Byzantine Palestine," *Dumbarton Oaks Papers* 51 (1997): 44–59.
45. Y. Hirschfeld and R. Birger-Calderon, "Early Roman and Byzantine Estates near Caesarea," *Israel Exploration Journal* 41 (1991): 81–111; R. Donceel and P. Donceel-Voûte, "The Archaeology of Khirbet Qumran," *Methods of Investigation of the Dead Sea Scrolls and the Khirbet Qumran Site: Present Realities and Future Prospects*, ed. M. O. Wise et al. (New York, 1994), 26–27, and Y. Hirschfeld, "Early Roman Manor Houses in Judea and the Site of Khirbet Qumran," *Journal of Near Eastern Studies* 57 (1998): 161–89. But cf. J. Magness, "A Villa at Khirbet Qumran?," *Revue de Qumran* 16 (1994): 397–419.
46. Villeneuve in *Hauran I* (1985), 76 and 114.
47. P. Watson, "Pella Hinterland Survey 1994: Preliminary Report," *Levant* 8 (1996): 69–71.
48. R. S. Bagnall, *Egypt in Late Antiquity* (Princeton, 1993), 133–38 and 159–60.
49. J. Gascou, "Les grand domaines, le cité et l'état en Egypte byzantine (recherches d'histoire agraire, fiscale et administrative," *Travaux et Mémoires* 9 (1985): 1–90.
50. L. Koenen, "The Carbonized Archive from Petra," *Journal of Roman Archaeology* 9 (1996): 177–88. My appreciation to Ludwig Koenen and Bob Daniels for supplying information about the scrolls.
51. P.-L. Gatier, "Villages du Proche-Orient protobyzantin (4ème-7ème s.). Étude régionale," *The Byzantine and Early Islamic Near East* II, edited by G. King and A. Cameron (Princeton, 1994), 38–41, and L. Di Segni, "The Involvement of Local, Municipal and Provincial Authorities in Urban Building in Late Antique Palestine and Arabia," *The Roman and Byzantine Near East* (Ann Arbor, 1995), 312–32.
52. See J. M. Frayne, *Markets and Fairs in Roman Italy. Their Social and Economic Importance from the Second Century BC to the Third Century AD* (Oxford, 1993), L. De Ligt, *Fairs and Markets in the Roman Empire: Economic and Social Aspects of Periodic Trade in a Pre-Industrial Society* (Amsterdam, 1993), and D. Sperber, *The City in Roman Palestine* (Oxford, 1998), 9–47.
53. D. Peacock, *Pottery in the Roman World* (New York/London, 1982), 156.
54. A. Uscatescu and M. Martín-Bueno, "The *Macellum* of Gerasa (Jerash, Jordan): From a Market Place to an Industrial Area," *BASOR* 307 (1997): 67–88, and T. Marot, *Las monedas del Macellum de Gerasa ('aras, Jordania)* (Madrid, 1998).
55. B. Shaw, "Rural Markets in North Africa and the Political Economy of the Roman Empire," *Antiquités Africaines* 17 (1981): 67.
56. A. H. M. Jones, "The Economic Life of the Towns of the Roman Empire," *The Roman Economy* (Oxford, 1974), 38.
57. L. de Ligt, "Demand, Supply, Distribution: The Roman Peasantry between Town and Countryside: Rural Monetization and Peasant Demand," *MBAH* 9 (1990): 24–56, and

"The Roman Peasantry: Demand, Supply and Distribution between Town and Countryside. II: Supply, Distribution and a Comparative Perspective," *MBAH* 10 (1991): 33–77.

58. I Magen, "Mamre," *The New Encyclopedia of Archaeological Excavations in the Holy Land,* edited by E. Stern (Jerusalem, 1993), 3:939–42; cf. Z. Safrai, *The Economy of Roman Palestine* (New York/London, 1994): 254–56.
59. R. MacMullen, "Market-Days in the Roman Empire," *Phoenix* 24 (1970): 33; cf. K. W. Harl, "Coins in Taxes and Markets of the Roman World," *Ancient World* 27, no. 2 (1996): 197–204.
60. Shaw, *Antiquités africaines* 17 (1981): 40–41.
61. L. De Myer, "L'etymologie de *marcellum,* marché," *L'Antiquité Classique* 31 (1962): 148–52, and E. Gabba, "Mercati e fiere nell'Italia romana," *Studi Classici e Orientali* 24 (1975): 141–60 at 145.
62. A. H. M. Jones, "The Economic Life of the Towns of the Roman Empire," *The Roman Economy,* ed. P. A. Brunt (Oxford, 1974), 38.
63. K. Hopkins, "Economic Growth and Towns in Classical Antiquity," *Towns in Societies,* edited by P. Abrams and E. Wrigley (Cambridge, 1978), 71–72, who emphasizes that the distinction between village and town in antiquity is arbitrary.
64. See A. Bounni, "Métiers et fonctions à Palmyre," *Études et Travaux* 15 (Warsaw, 1988), 78–86, and G. Tate, "Les métiers dans les villages de la Syrie du Nord," *Ktèma* 16 (1991), 73–78. Such a study is still needed for Roman-Byzantine Arabia, but a beginning is made by L.-A. Hunt, "The Byzantine Mosaics of Jordan in Context: Remarks on Imagery, Donors, and Mosaicists," *Palestine Exploration Quarterly* 126 (1994): 106–26.
65. Parker, *SHAJ* 4 (1992): 324.
66. B. Isaac, "The Army in the Late Roman East: the Persian Wars and the Defense of the Byzantine Provinces," *The Byzantine and early Islamic Near East* III, ed. A. Cameron (Princeton, 1995), 125–51. For the argument that some of these forts are actually creations of the middle of the sixth century, see J. Magness, "Redating the forts at Ein Boqeq, Upper Zohar and other sites in SE Judaea, and the implications for the nature of the *Limes Palestinae,*" in *The Roman and Byzantine Near East,* vol. 2, ed. J. H. Humprey (Portsmouth, 1999), 189–206.
67. Issac, *The Byzantine and Early Islamic Near East* III (1995), 149.
68. L. I. Conrad, *The Plague in the Early Medieval Near East* (Ph.D. diss., Princeton University, 1981) summarized in "The Plague in Bil'd al-Sh'm in Pre-Islamic Times," *Proceedings of the Symposium on Bil'd al-Sh'm during the Byzantine Period* II, ed. M. Bakhit and M. Asfour (Amman, 1986), 142–63.
69. J. R. Madicott, "Plague in Seventh-Century England," *Past & Present* 156 (1997): 7–54.
70. R. S. Bagnall and B. W. Frier, *The Demography of Roman Egypt* (Cambridge, 1994), 173–78; a view shared recently by D. W. Rathbone, "Villages, Land and Population in Graeco-Roman Egypt," *Proceedings of the Cambridge Philological Society* 36 (1990): 114- 19, and R. P. Duncan-Jones, "The Impact of the Antonine Plague," *Journal of Roman Archaeology* 9 (1996): 108–36.
71. C. Robin, "Guerre et épidémie dans les royaumes d'Arabie du sud, d'après une inscrip-

tion datée (IIe siècle l'ère chrétienne)," *CRAI* (1992): 215–34.

72. L. Di Segni, "Epigraphic Documentation on Building in the Provinces of *Palaestina* and *Arabia,* 4th-7th c.," in *The Roman and Byzantine Near East,* vol. 2 (Portsmouth, 1999) 149–78, esp. 161–65.
73. See F. Donner, *The Early Islamic Conquests* (Princeton, 1981).
74. A. G. Walmsley, "Byzantine Palestine and Arabia: Urban Prosperity in Late Antiquity" in *Towns in Transition: Urban Evolution in Late Antiquity and the Early Middle Ages,* ed. N. Christie and S. Loseby (Aldershot, 1996), 126–58, and R. Schick, *The Christian Communities of Palestine from Byzantine to Islamic Rule: A Historical and Archaeological Study* (Princeton, 1995).
75. B. de Vries, *Umm el-Jimal: A Frontier Town and its Landscape in Northern Jordan,* vol. 1 (Portsmouth, 1998), 229–41. For the plague, see M. Dols, "Plague in Early Islamic History," *JAOS* 94 (1974): 371–83, and D. Turner, "The Politics of Despair: the Plague of 746–647 and Iconoclasm in the Byzantine Empire," *BSA* 85 (1990): 419–34.
76. A. Desreumaux, "Introduction: Histoire des documents araméens melkites: L'invention du christo-palestinien," in *Fouilles de Khirbet es-Samra en Jordanie* I (Turnhout, 1998), 1–17.
77. M. Piccirillo and E. Alliata, *Umm al-Rasas Mafa'ah I: Gli scavi del complesso di Santo Stefano* (Jerusalem, 1994).
78. For the dating of the mosaics to 718 and 756 see Schick, *Christian Communities of Palestine,* 472–76.
79. R. Canova, *Iscrizioni e Monumenti Protocristiani del Paese di Moab* (Rome, 1954).

Rural Society and Economy in Late Roman Cyprus

MARCUS RAUTMAN

THE COMPLEX AND VARIED INTERRELATIONS OF TOWN AND COUNTRY ASSUME AN additional dynamic among the islands of *mare nostrum*. Physical insularity presents any society with distinct challenges and advantages, which are conditioned by internal resources and locational proximities. Environmental factors, for example, acquire special importance within a confined space, and brief topographic spans can belie vast cultural differences. In the case of Cyprus, the third largest island of the Mediterranean, which lies less than 100 km from the Cilician and Syro-Palestinian coasts, the sea offers both barrier and bridge to contact with the mainland. Despite its geographical diversity, Cyprus today conveys an inescapable impression of an island nation, its modern landscape a historical palimpsest of external relations.[1]

Located astride traditional Levantine sea routes, Cyprus has always played a role in regional power structures. Early inhabitants recognized the island's land and mineral wealth, which drew the attention of Mycenaean and Phoenician settlers in the late Bronze Age. Ten or more independent polities emerged in the Iron Age, but by the mid first millennium B.C. these had come under outside domination, first by Assyria and then by Persia. Cyprus was annexed by the Ptolemies, who valued its rich timber and mineral resources as well as its strategic position for staging campaigns on Seleucid Syria. These virtues were recognized equally by Rome, which held the island from 58 B.C. until the Arab campaigns of the mid–seventh century C.E.[2]

This peripheral island province played a small and often overlooked part in the late empire.[3] Originally administered by a proconsul as a senatorial province, Cyprus was reassigned by Diocletian to a consular governor reporting to Antioch. The spread of Christianity among its cities brought autocephalous status to the island in 488, and in 536 Justinian reassigned Cyprus to the *quaestura exercitus*, reporting directly to Constantinople.[4] This slow climb from provincial backwater to strategic outpost has been written as a predominately urban tale.[5] Contemporary sources speak of a prosperous and productive land that supported such great cities as Paphos, Kourion, Amathus, and Salamis, while also contributing to the empire's needs for foods and minerals. The Peutinger Table identifies a dozen of these urban points along a circumferential highway, together with a road passing through the Mesaoria plain between the Troodos and Kyreneia mountain ranges (fig. 1). This basic network appears to have been a Roman initiative to link the island's preexisting cities, ports, and shrines, and to integrate the radially diverging settlement systems carried over from earlier times.[6]

In antiquity as today, the threshold between town and country in Cyprus could appear reinforced by the contrast between coast and hinterland. Written sources focus on the cities and largely neglect the inland chora. The apocryphal Acts of Barnabas, for example, describes the south coastal road to Kition as passing through a wasteland.[7] Historical chronicles and saints lives naturally focus on urban affairs and offer only indirect witness to the life of most of the island's residents.[8] Rural Cyprus was best known to Roman authors as a passive landscape regarded for its mineral resources and agricultural bounty. Strabo (*Geog.* 14.6.5) introduces the province as "not inferior in fertility to any of the islands, for it produces both good wine and good oil, and also enough grain for its own use," and goes on to mention the wealth of its copper and silver mines.[9] Ammianus Marcellinus (*Res Gestae* 14.8.14) tells us that Cyprus was so fertile and abounding in various products that it had all the resources needed to build and equip transport ships.[10] The

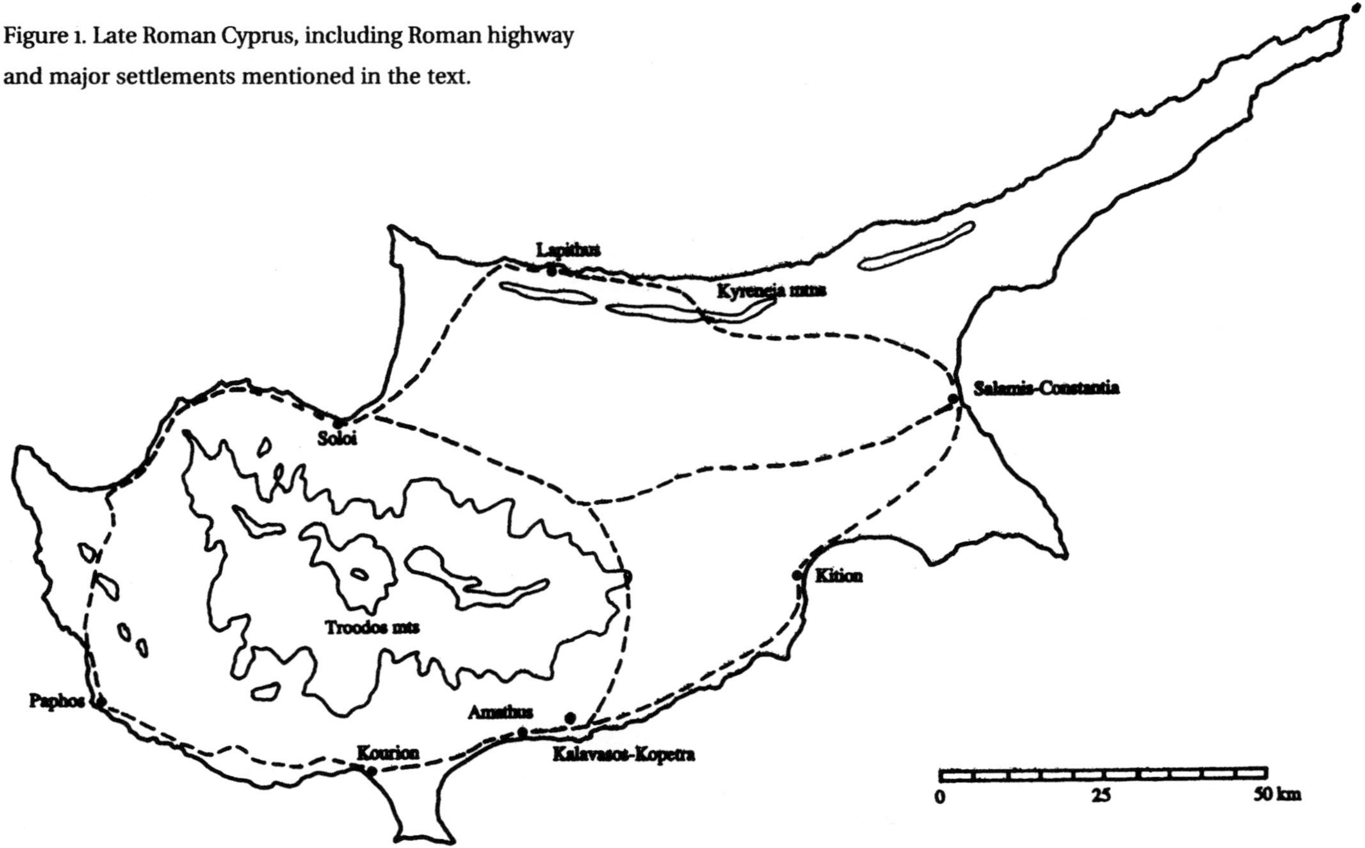

Figure 1. Late Roman Cyprus, including Roman highway and major settlements mentioned in the text.

Troodos and Kyreneia mountains were sufficiently wooded that timber was available in abundance for fuel, architecture, and ship building.[11] From the first century grain, wine, and oil were regarded as the island's most important products, which were distributed as far as Rome (Pliny, *Nat.Hist.* 18.12.67-68), and in later antiquity reached Constantinople.[12] Minor food stuffs included almonds, figs, and other fruits, while various Cypriot plants and minerals were credited with wholesome and medicinal properties.[13] As late as the sixth century, John Lydus (*de Mag.* 2.29) includes Cyprus among the most prosperous provinces of the late empire.[14]

Most of these commodities were both derived and processed in the countryside. Copper and silver were worked near mines in the Troodos, which also provided fuel for the environmentally messy task of smelting.[15] Remains of pressing equipment document the processing of grapes and olives at inland locales as well as near coastal cities.[16] Oil and wine were shipped in ceramic transport amphoras that were made at various rural and suburban kilns.[17] The most important ceramic products were the high-quality tablewares known as Cypriot Sigillata and Cypriot Red Slip, both of which apparently were made in western Cyprus.[18] Since fine ceramics usually were traded not by themselves but together with other products, their wide distribution can be understood as illustrating the paths of perishable commodities like grain, oil, and wine across the Mediterranean.[19] Other manufacturing on the island included the spinning and weaving of flax, the production of mattresses, and the dyeing of fabrics.[20]

The textual and material record provides a general framework for exploring the late antique Cypriot countryside. Despite recent interest in the field, the available evidence is still quite uneven and it is premature to sketch more than a general picture. Literary sources are primarily of early date and oblique relevance. Archaeology holds the promise of more immediate access to the chora, yet so far has directed little attention to this modest level of settled life.[21] Most rural exploration has been limited to salvage study of isolated churches and villas encountered in the course of modern construction. More coherent evidence for reconstructing the countryside comes from regionally based diachronic survey projects, which offer broad overviews of different parts of the island.[22]

Our earliest reliable information comes from extensive reconnaissance carried out in the 1950s by the Cyprus Survey Department, which observed that much of the long north coast had prospered under Roman rule. Settlement of the Cape Kormakiti region reached a high point in the Late Bronze Age and again in the sixth and seventh centuries, when a large number of farmsteads and *komai* dotted the coast and the Kyreneia foothills.[23] The city of Lapithus had formed the region's urban focus since the Iron Age. The remains of churches were noted at some of the larger settlement sites, but none of these possessed civic features that would raise them above the village level. Western Cyprus also flourished in Roman times, encouraged no doubt by the establishment of Paphos as provincial capital. The surrounding countryside was extensively occupied in the first century C.E. but apparently declined in the second-fourth centuries, before expanding again in the fifth-seventh centuries. Recent surveys have noted sub-regional variations in this pattern, with a gradual contraction beginning in the later sixth century across both the rugged Akamas Peninsula and the environs of Palaipaphos.[24] Farther east, the island's south shore and coastal plain between the Akrotiri peninsula and Cape Greco have been extensively explored. Particular attention has been paid to the suburban environs of Kourion, Amathus, and Larnaca, but also to the more remote Maroni and Vasilikos river valleys, where excavations provide a stratigraphic anchor for local surface finds. Much of this region seems to have languished in the third-fourth centuries but prospered again in later antiquity.[25]

The growth of rural settlement was accompanied by the construction of small churches, conspicuous monuments that record the spread of religion and culture into the countryside.[26] The usual building form was the three-aisle basilica with a single projecting apse opening onto the nave and a narthex to the west. While admitting considerable variation, the overall dimensions average 16-18 m long by 11-14 m wide, with an approximate area of 200-250 m^2. In most cases five paired columns or piers supported the nave arcades. Architectural sculpture included capitals, chancel screens, and tables, which were usually cut from local gypsum, locally known as *marmara,* but occasionally were made of imported marble. Floor mosaics and stucco plaster sometimes decorated the interiors. In most respects these modest buildings reflect at small scale the architecture of the coastal cities, and especially the great churches at Salamis-Constantia.[27] Similar liturgical arrangements are found here, including for example, secondary offering tables, lateral chapels, and funerary annexes. The widespread appearance of these churches in the fifth and sixth centuries reflects equally the spread of Christianity and the rising economic importance of the inland regions.

The available evidence suggests a generally consistent impression of rural Cyprus. Settlement expanded in late Hellenistic and early Roman times, saw a significant retreat between 100/150 and 350, but recovered during the fifth-seventh centuries. This sequence is apparent in the cities but appears quite clearly in the countryside.[28] The reasons for these alternating demographic trends during a period of prolonged political stability are not immediately clear. Environmental factors such as earthquakes and climatic fluctuation no doubt affected life on the island, in antiquity as today, but their impact would have been mitigated by Cyprus' provincial membership.[29] More likely the shifting fortunes of the Cypriot chora reflect wider economic and political conditions and the importance of those social networks to which the island belonged.[30] In late antiquity these included the shift of government to Constantinople and the rising importance of the eastern provinces, which benefited both coastal *poleis* and inland *komai.* The dispersion of settlement presumably reflects the presence of small villages, farmsteads, and seasonal camps. Increasing activity on previously neglected terrain implies a turn to more intensive land-use methods, with terraced cultivation extending onto marginal lands in the upper valleys.[31]

A more detailed view is possible by focusing on a single sub-regional landscape. The Vasilikos valley in south central Cyprus is one of several large catchment systems that originates in the eastern Troodos mountains.[32] For much of its length the Vasilikos river extends through a rugged valley used today for summer pasturage, with a few terraced orchards set among its maquis-covered slopes. Slag heaps at Spilious in the upper valley mark the copper mines that were worked in the Late Bronze Age, in late antiquity, and as recently as the 1970s. About 5 km from the shore, just below the present village of Kalavasos, the valley opens onto the south coastal plain, a gently sloping limestone shelf whose rich terra rossa soils are planted with cereals, pulses, olives, vines, and carobs—foundations of the local economy in recent times.[33] The river meets the sea at Vasiliko, a toponym that recalls the legendary landing near here of Helena Augusta on her return from the Holy Land.

The Vasilikos valley presents a cross-section of the island's geography and history. Continuing work by the Vasilikos Valley Project has been able to trace long-term settlement patterns and has noted cycles of growth during the Neolithic period (sixth millennium B.C.) and Late Bronze Age (mid–second millennium B.C.). Sparsely inhabited during the Iron Age, the valley experienced a Roman-era expansion that culminated in the sixth and early seventh centuries C.E. Over forty sites have been assigned to this period, including seasonal agricultural shelters, isolated oil and wine presses, and permanent villages (fig. 2).[34] Many of these are found across the coastal plain with ready access to their respective fields. By contrast, sites above modern Kalavasos looked toward terraced orchards and vineyards, and to the mines at Spilious.

Two sites stand out among the identified Roman settlements in the valley. One of these is at Sokopra, a flat plateau that lies along the lower river channel about 1 km from the coast. The other site is at Kopetra, a bluff ridge located about 3 km to the north. Both Sokopra and Kopetra were initially identified by a broad scatter of sherds and building debris. Closer study suggests that they were year-round settlements that apparently acted as central places within the local agricultural system, substantial *komai* that served as gathering points for local products as well as rural markets. Both sites preserve evidence of earlier Hellenistic or Roman activity, but achieved their greatest extent within the expanding economy of late antiquity. Yet despite these similarities, the two sites are very different. Sokopra grew up on the lower river near its agricultural base, a natural collection point for the plain close to the seaside anchorage at Zygi-Petrini. Kopetra, on the other hand, was built on a high ridge overlooking the river, a natural promontory within sight of both sea and upper valley. Its location capitalized on two local resources: the agricultural products of the adjacent plain and the nearby outcrops of good-quality gypsum, an easily worked building material that

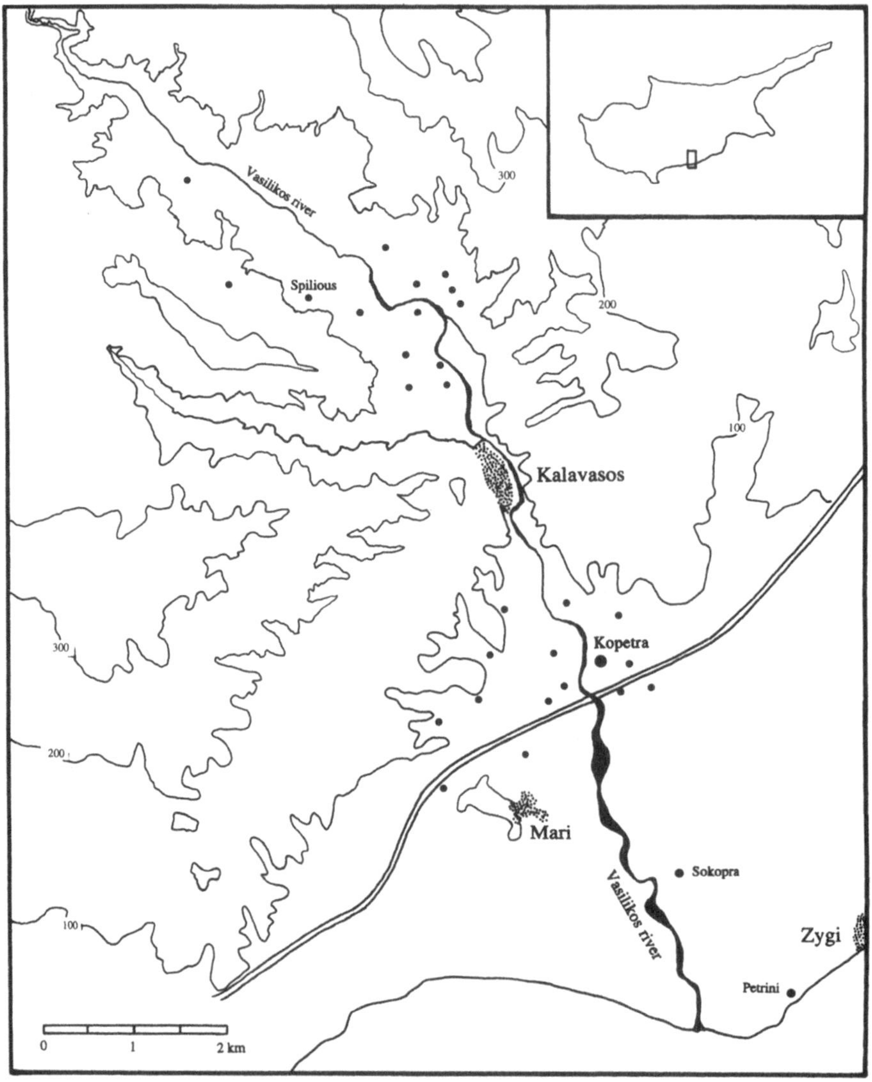

Figure 2. Vasilikos Valley, distribution of Late Roman sites.

may have been exported as well. Equally important, Kopetra lies about halfway between the coast and the copper mines at Spilious. Finally, the site lies near the presumed intersection of the valley's traditional north-south axis and the coastal highway between Amathus and Kition.[35] In truth, the choice was not an original one: dominant places of the Neolithic, Chalcolithic, and

Late Bronze Age periods are found close by.[36] In this light, the growth of both settlements seems a logical result of an agricultural and mining boom of the sixth century.

This background set the stage for the intensive survey and selective excavation of the settlement at Kopetra.[37] Today the site bears little resemblance to its anonymous Roman predecessor: the open, gently sloping terrain is mostly covered by wheat and barley fields, dotted with carob and olive, and punctuated by several small, rubble-covered mounds. Systematic recording of the surface pottery and building debris suggested that the unwalled settlement stretched some 200 m along the ridge and had an area of about 4 ha (fig. 3). Excavations carried out near the north and south peripheries of the inhabited site located two substantial basilicas, and a third church was discovered standing atop a low mound to the east. Two

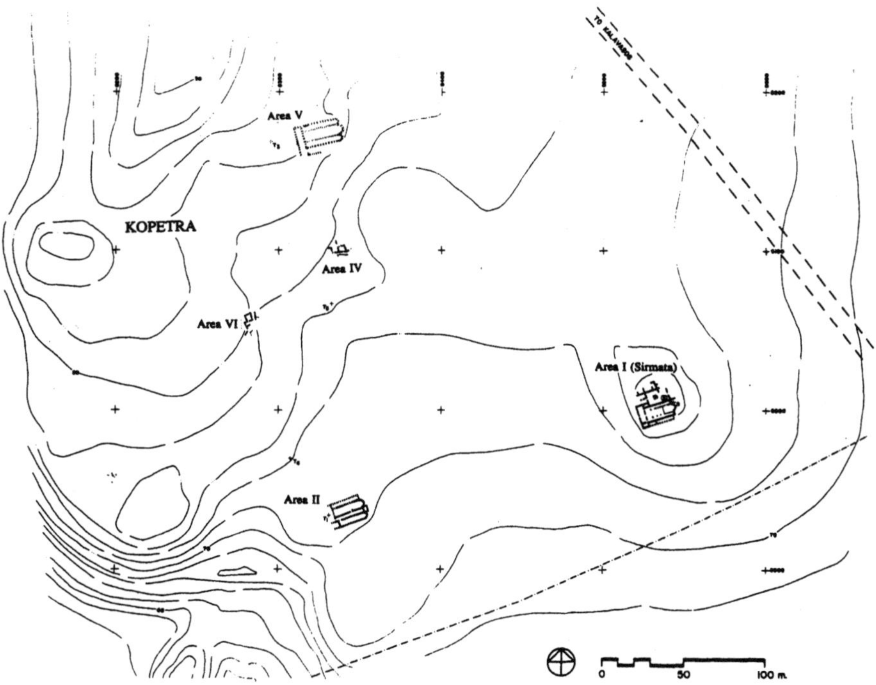

Figure 3. Kalavasos-Kopetra, site plan with excavated buildings.

residential quarters also were explored on the central ridge, and like the churches date to the sixth and early seventh centuries.

The most direct evidence for understanding the local economy comes from the site's central area. Copper slag found on the surface and in stratified contexts points to ongoing contact with the Spilious mines. Fragments of agricultural stone occasionally turn up in plowing and often are built into fieldwalls and terraces. Several large stone press-weights found along the settlement's perimeter indicates that olives and perhaps grapes were processed locally. One likely processing area (Area IV) includes two small domestic structures separated by a narrow alley. Irregularly shaped rooms were enclosed by walls of mortared gypsum and fieldstone and had *marmara* floors. The presence of a calcarenite crushing basin together with a large press-weight provides good evidence that olives were processed on at least a household scale. Multiple layers of controlled burning beneath one floor may reflect light industrial activity as well.

Limited excavation at a rocky escarpment about 60 m to the southwest (Area VI) revealed a different level of habitation. Five rooms were identified as belonging to a multi-level, terraced building with heavily mortared and plastered walls and gypsum floors. Two small trapezoidal rooms apparently opened to the south onto an open, unpaved court; both rooms were paved and had glazed windows and an upper story. A wide variety of pottery, glass, and metal artifacts was found on the floors. Two other rooms lie at a lower level and may belong to either the same complex or an adjacent structure. The irregular building plans are not clearly organized and belong to a rural vernacular known at rural sites throughout the Near East.[38]

Farming, agricultural processing, and perhaps metalworking formed the base of Kopetra's economy, whose scale can best be judged by the three identified churches. These tangible expressions of wealth donated to pious ends constitute the most conspicuous features of the site. All were carefully built of mortared fieldstone and gypsum, paved with *marmara*, and decorated with molded plaster, or *gypsiplasia*. All were timber-roofed basilicas with three aisles separated by cylindrical piers, a narthex, and one or more flanking spaces. Their peripheral locations near probable roadways to the village suggest that they were intended to serve as public landmarks as well as centers of spiritual life. Indeed, they were the most enduring structures on the ridge.

The north church (Area V) was the earliest and largest of the three churches with a reconstructed area of about 275 m^2. It was built around the middle of the sixth century with a triapsidal sanctuary that was decorated with an opus sectile floor and vault mosaics. The south church (Area II) was slightly later and smaller, with a total area of roughly 180 m^2. Floor mosaics were found in the side chapel and bema, together with the remains of an apse mosaic. The building was decorated with a complex set of plaster sculpture, which included architectural moldings, capitals, and such images as baskets, birds, a leaping quadruped, a small shrine, and a panel depicting the Theotokos and child. One of several marble tables bears the monogram of a possible patron, Menalaos. The east church complex (Area I, or Sirmata) was built around the turn of the century some 200 m to the east. This group comprised a small basilica, approximately 140 m^2 in area, with narthex, south lateral space, and an enclosed court to the north. The hall was paved with *marmara* and divided by two rows of cylindrical piers, including at the west end a pair of transverse cruciform piers that appear to be unique on the island. The sanctuary included a raised bema, an altar and secondary table, and in the apse a two-tier synthonon with a projecting axial seat. A small crypt with multiple burials lay below the narthex floor. The court contained a deep cistern and a large central foundation, together with bins or troughs for animals. Small rectangular rooms lay along the north side of the court, and similar spaces may have flanked the other sides. The peripheral location and organization of this ensemble suggest that it may have housed a small monastery during the early seventh century.

In sum, survey and excavation at Kopetra document a substantial village that drew on valley resources but looked to the cities for its public architecture. Earlier habitation was limited and the identified buildings date for the most part to the sixth century. The settlement was situated to benefit from farming, mining, and trade within the valley and lasted until the mid–seventh century, when it was extensively damaged and substantially abandoned. This abrupt demise appears most clearly at the east church complex, where the skeletal remains of two adults and four or more children were summarily dumped in the cistern. Despite the lack of specific textual evidence, this incident likely reflects the disruption caused by the Arab campaigns, including attacks on Cyprus in 649 and 650.[39] Apart from a small chapel raised amid the ruins of the south church (Area II), the village was not rebuilt and the ridge was permanently abandoned by the survivors, probably in favor of more transient lifeways in the upper valley.

The buildings give some idea of the physical organization and relative prosperity of this Cypriot village. The small objects help refine this picture by tracing the site's economic relations—that is, the paths of exchange that fueled its growth in the sixth century. Some of this material takes the form of tangible goods, such as marble vessels and furniture imported from the mainland. Survey and excavation coins offer further information. The few identifiable coins are half or full *folles* that were issued at Constantinople or Nicomedia under Heraclius or Constans II. The relative scarcity of coinage, and especially small currency, at the site implies that the local economy may have remained largely unmonetized.[40] Yet, by far the most important data for understanding the site's history and economy are the ceramics.

The fine pottery indicates that Kopetra's floruit was short-lived. Three major fine wares were used in the sixth and seventh centuries and were most abundant in the years around 600. About a third of all fine pottery came from north Africa and western Asia Minor, with Phocean Red Slip maintaining an important place in the local market. Their relatively high numbers here may reflect the lingering prestige of these imported wares or the mechanisms of their distribution. Commercial traffic between the east Mediterranean granaries, on the one hand, and Constantinople and the Balkans, on the other, would have offered a convenient return route for Phocean Red Slip and other low-volume, high-value products originating in the east Aegean.[41] One can imagine that the Phocean ware may have posed a viable alternative to Cypriot Red Slip at such seaside markets as Amathus and Zygi-Petrini, and from these reached minor places like Kopetra. As elsewhere in the east Mediterranean, the small but steady supply of African Red Slip probably reached Cyprus via Aegean middlemen.[42]

Amphoras offer further evidence for understanding Kopetra's commercial contacts. Despite recent interest in exploring the origin, contents, and distribution of Roman amphoras, Cyprus occupies an uncertain place in our understanding of Mediterranean trade. Most are LR1 type vessels, which were produced throughout Cyprus, Cilicia, and coastal north Syria in late antiquity. Compositional analysis suggests that many of these were made on Cyprus with 10-20 percent originating in the south central coastlands and lower Mesaoria plain.[43] Others, perhaps accounting for half of the total, came from the mainland. The predominance of LR1 amphoras suggests that the settlement's agricultural imports consisted primarily of oil and wine. Many of these vessels may have been recycled for storage or to carry local products away from the valley. These exports probably included oil, wine, and cereals, although in the latter case non-ceramic containers were more likely.[44] While the details of exchange remain uncertain, the village clearly attracted a range of commodities from beyond its immediate vicinity.

This impression of a primarily local market with important regional components is reinforced by the smaller numbers of other non-Cypriot amphoras found at the site. In descending order of frequency, these include vessels from Palestine (LR4, LR5/6), the Aegean (LR2, LR3), and Egypt (LR7). Most of these amphora types have been associated with the oil and wine trade, but individual examples may have been used for other products as well. In general, Kopetra seems to have shared closer economic ties with Cilicia and north Syria than with the coastlands to south and southeast. The scarcity of Aegean amphoras contrasts with the abundance of Phocean Red Slip, which apparently was the preferred cargo for ships returning along the grain route to Cyprus and Egypt.[45]

The market for cooking wares may have been more restricted, for most cooking pots are of standard, widely distributed Cypriot types.[46] There was also a distinctive series of handmade cooking vessels found in late habitation levels at the site. Compositional study shows that many of these pots were made locally, perhaps in small workshops at Kopetra itself. In other settings, the production of pottery at the household or neighborhood level often is seen to have been a way to manage agricultural risk from economic and environmental factors. In Cyprus, such circumstances surely would have encouraged the household production of pottery and other crafts as regional supply routes collapsed around the mid–seventh century, when in fact handmade pottery became more common elsewhere on the island.[47]

This picture of provincial exchange at the village level can be expanded by considering the roof tiles. Typically regarded as mundane building materials, roof tiles in fact constitute an important part of any ceramic environment. Three main systems were used here: an elongated Lakonian-style tile in a fine red fabric, a small Corinthian-style tile in a light yellow fabric, and a large Corinthian-style tile in a coarse dark fabric. Compositional analysis of representative tiles, other pottery wares, and surviving clay sources on the island suggests production areas for all three types. The Lakonian-style tiles are closely related to Cypriot Red Slip ware and probably were made in the same part of western Cyprus. The fabric of the small Corinthian-style roof tiles resembles Late Bronze Age pottery from the lower Mesoaria valley and likely originated in eastern Cyprus, perhaps near Salamis. The large Corinthian-style roof tiles, on the other hand, turn out to have been made in the valley of the same clay used for large storage pithoi.[48]

The significance of roof tiles becomes clear in the context of village exchange. The three tile systems were made at the same time and often appeared on the same buildings. In sheer bulk the red and yellow tiles formed a major part of local imports, far exceeding in weight all table and kitchen wares, and perhaps surpassed only by fully loaded LR1 amphoras. Most of these tiles entered the valley at the Zygi-Petrini anchorage, whence they were carried overland to sites like Sokopra and Kopetra. Secondary roads reached from the latter to scattered *komai* in the upper valley, the mines at Spilious, and into the Troodos foothills. Unsurprisingly, imported tiles are best represented at these two large settlements and their numbers dwindle farther north.

This varied evidence shows that Kopetra's interdependence with both higher and lesser order settlements is central to understanding this rural landscape. While only one of many villages in the hinterland of Amathus, Kopetra was a key component of the Vasilikos valley, where it functioned as a middle-tier collection point for local products and a redistribution center for larger markets. Advantageously sited near both coastal highway and valley road, halfway between mines and coast, Kopetra was a logical nexus for local exchange. Major products included copper and timber from the Troodos foothills; wheat, barley, olives, and grapes from the surrounding plain; and gypsum from nearby quarries. Many of these would have been shipped via Zygi-Petrini to other island ports in return for cash and commodities of corresponding value from the east Mediterranean and beyond. Despite the strong presence of imported goods, Cypriot products dominated the local market for pottery and foodstuffs, and monopolized the traffic in roof tiles. In this light Kopetra appears as a second-order central place within a dendritic, sub-regional hierarchy that clearly benefited from its location.[49] Its growth encouraged by a rising tide of regional prosperity, this small settlement faded as established exchange networks dissolved in the seventh century.

The inhabitants of late Roman Kopetra can at least be glimpsed within this social-economic framework. The topographic extent of settlement and the size of the three churches suggest that at its peak the village may have comprised several hundred people.[50] Most of these would have been tenant farmers or free *coloni* who primarily worked the surrounding fields, mines, and quarries. Individual families also cultivated household gardens on the nearby river plain while herding sheep and goats around the upper valley.[51] Increasingly vulnerable to climatic and market fluctuations, some of these families apparently turned to making pottery and other domestic crafts for the local market. Women and perhaps children likely played important roles in this small-scale industry, which was intended to meet household needs as well as sub-regional demand. Independent merchants may have participated in local trade, but Kopetra's greater prosperity also suggests the presence of a rural elite that may have controlled exchange and distribution.[52] Social stratification appears in the varying quality of local buildings; the abundance of imported comestibles, fine pottery, and glass; and especially the foundation of three substantial churches and their decoration by artisans called from the coastal cities. Visible from across the valley, the churches were essential landmarks of civic identity; as producers and consumers of wealth they also would have played an important economic role in village life. As in nearby Kalavasos in recent times, the resident priests and lesser clergy probably came under the jurisdiction of nearby Amathus and helped administer village affairs.[53]

It remains unclear to what extent the Vasilikos valley was representative of rural life elsewhere on Cyprus. The island varies a great deal from its coastal plains to inland valleys and wooded uplands, and yet a broad harmony runs through the available evidence from surveys and excavations. A general prosperity was fostered by early Roman policies that encouraged rural exploitation and urban growth. Thanks to its economic and political integration with the mainland, Cyprus shared in the regional slump of the second-fourth centuries but also revived after the founding of Constantinople. The island's location along the grain route from Egypt surely strengthened contacts with the capital, which were reinforced by the shift from Antioch to Constantinople of first ecclesiastical allegiance in the late fifth century and then political accountability in the early sixth century. The Persian invasion of Palestine, together with subsequent campaigns of reconquest, may even have briefly increased the island's strategic and commercial importance to the late empire in the early seventh century. This westward orientation was interrupted by the Arab victories of the 640s, which permanently altered centuries-old trading patterns and relegated the island to an uncertain frontier status.[54] As elsewhere across the Mediterranean, the Cypriot *chora* needs to be viewed as part of a continuous settlement system, a provincial landscape whose urban and rural features were inextricable from the web of empire.

NOTES

1. J. V. Thirgood, Cyprus. *A Chronicle of its Forests, Land, and People* (Vancouver, 1987); E. Malamut, *Les isles de l'empire byzantin, VIIIe-XIIe siècles* (Paris, 1988), 1:26; M. Patton, *Islands in Time. Island Sociogeography and Mediterranean Prehistory* (London, 1996), 1–34.
2. G. F. Hill, *A History of Cyprus*, I (Cambridge, 1940); R. S. Bagnall, *The Administration of the Ptolemaic Possessions Outside Egypt* (Leiden, 1976); A. T. Reyes, *Archaic Cyprus* (Oxford, 1994).
3. Cyprus is largely bypassed by such recent surveys as A. Cameron, *The Mediterranean World of Late Antiquity* (London, 1993); S. E. Alcock, ed., *The Early Roman Empire in the East* (Oxford, 1997); J. Haldon, *Byzantium in the Seventh Century. The Transformation of a Culture*, rev. ed. (Cambridge, 1997).

4. Hill, *History*, 226–83; 276–77 for the date of ecclesiastical independence; A.H.M. Jones, *The Later Roman Empire, 284–602* (Oxford, 1964), 482–83; E. Chrysos, "Cyprus in Early Byzantine Times," in *"The Sweet Land of Cyprus." Papers Given at the Twenty-fifth Jubilee Spring Symposium of Byzantine Studies*, ed. A. A. M. Bryer, G. S. Georghallides eds. (Nicosia, 1993), 3–14.
5. T. B. Mitford, "Roman Cyprus," *Aufstieg und Niedergang der römischen Welt* II, 7.2 (1980) ,1285–1384. E.g., J. Matthews, *The Roman Empire of Ammianus Marcellinus* (Baltimore, 1989), 388–403.
6. Mitford, "Roman Cyprus," 1332–37; T. Bekker-Nielsen, "Centres and Road Networks in Hellenistic Cyprus," in *Center and Periphery in the Hellenistic World*, ed. P. Bilde, T. Engberg-Pedersen, L. Hannestad, J. Zahle, K. Randsborg (Aarhus, 1994), 176–91 at 183–90.
7. "Acta Barnabae," ed. M. Bonnet, *Acta Apostolorum Apocrypha* II, 2 (rep. Hildesheim, 1959), 292–302; R. Janin, "Chypre," *Dictionnaire d'histoire et géographie ecclésiastiques* 12 (Paris, 1953): 791–820 at 792. The text presumably dates from the fifth or sixth century.
8. H. Delehaye, "Saints de Chypre," *Analecta Bollandiana* 26 (1907): 161–301; D. Krueger, *Symeon the Holy Fool* (Berkeley, 1996): 4–11.
9. *Geography of Strabo* VI, ed. H. L. Jones, rep. (Cambridge, 1960), 382–83.
10. *Ammianus Marcellinus* I, ed. J.C. Rolfe (Cambridge, 1963), 72–73.
11. *Geographi Graeci Minores* II, ed. C. Müller (Paris, 1861), 527–28, 63; Thirgood, *Cyprus*, 70–72.
12. Pliny, *Natural History* V, ed. H. Rackham (Reprint; Cambridge, 1961), 232–33; J.L. Teall, "The Grain Supply of the Byzantine Empire, 330–1025," *Dumbarton Oaks Papers* 13 (1959): 87–139; Ch. Bakirtzis, "The Role of Cyprus in the Grain Supply of Constantinople in the Early Christian period," in *Proceedings of the International Archaeological Conference "Cyprus and the Sea,"* ed. V. Karageorghis and D. Michaelides (Nicosia, 1995), 247–53.
13. D. Michaelides, "The Economy of Cyprus during the Hellenistic and Roman Periods," in *The Development of the Cypriot Economy from the Prehistoric Period to the Present Day*, edited by V. Karageorghis and D. Michaelides (Nicosia, 1996), 139–52 at 146–48.
14. A. C. Bandy, *Ioannes Lydus on Powers, or the Magistracies of the Roman State* (Philadelphia, 1983), 126–27.
15. For copper mining see L. M. Bear, *The Mineral Resources and Mining Industry of Cyprus* (Nicosia, 1963); Thirgood, *Cyprus*, 72; A. B. Knapp, *The Archaeology of Late Bronze Age Cypriot Society: The Study of Settlement, Survey and Landscape* (Glasgow, 1997), 43.
16. S. Hadjisavvas, *Olive Oil Processing in Cyprus from the Bronze Age to the Byzantine Period* (Nicosia, 1992), fig. 34.
17. See in general D. P. S. Peacock and D. F. Williams, *Amphorae and the Roman Economy* (London, 1986). Likely production regions on Cyprus include the environs of Paphos, Amathus, and Salamis-Constantia; see below note 43.
18. M. Rautman, "Neutron Activation Analysis of Cypriot and Related Ceramics at the

University of Missouri," in *Hellenistic and Roman Pottery in the Eastern Mediterranean. Advances in Scientific Studies*, ed. H. Meyza and J. Mlynarczyk (Warsaw, 1995), 331–49; B. Gomez, M. L. Rautman, H. Neff, M. D. Glascock, "Clays Used in the Manufacture of Cypriot Red Slip Pottery and Related Ceramics," *Report of the Department of Antiquities, Cyprus* (1996): 69–82.

19. R. Tomber, "Quantitative approaches to the Investigation of Long-Distance Trade," *Journal of Roman Archaeology* 6 (1993): 142–66; P. Reynolds, *Trade in the Western Mediterranean, a.d. 400–700: The Ceramic Evidence* (BAR S604, Oxford, 1995), 126–30.

20. A league of linen weavers (*linyphoi*) is attested at Salamis in the early second century (T.B. Mitford and I. Nicolaou, *Salamis* I. *Inscriptions from Salamis* [Nicosia, 1974], 28–29, no. 13; J. Pouilloux, P. Roesch, J. Marcillet-Jaubert, *Salamine de Chypre* XIII. *Testimonia Salaminia* 2 [Paris, 1987], 63–64, no. 143.). The production of varying grades of linen bedding is noted in the Price Edict of Diocletian at 28.47 (T. Frank, *An Economic Survey of Ancient Rome* V. *Rome and Italy of the Empire* [Baltimore, 1940], Appendix 404–5). Libanius in Epistula 1362 mentions dyeworks on the island in the fourth century (*Libanii Opera*, edited by R. Foerster XI [Stuttgart, 1922; Reprint, Hildesheim, 1963], 409). See also Jones, *The Later Roman Empire*, 849, 836.

21. A. Papageorghiou, "Cities and Countryside at the End of Antiquity and the Beginning of the Middle Ages in Cyprus," in *"The Sweet Land of Cyprus,"* ed. Bryer and Georghallides, 27–51. The textual sources are discussed by G. Dagron, "Entre village et cité: La bourgade rurale des IVe-VIIe siécles en Orient," *Koinonia* 3 (1979): 29–52; M. Kaplan, *Les hommes et la terre à Byzance du Vie au Xie siècle* (Paris, 1992). For the mainland see F. Villeneuve, "L'économie rurale et la vie des campagnes dans le Hauran antique (Ier siècle av. J.-C.-VIIe siècle ap. J.-C.)," in *Hauran* I. *Recherches archéologiques sur la Syrie du sud a l'époque hellénistique et romaine*, edited by J.-M. Dentzer (Paris, 1985), 63–136; C. Dauphin, "Les 'komai' de Palestine," *Proche Orient chrétien* 37 (1987): 251–67; Y. Hirschfeld, "Farms and Villages in Byzantine Palestine," *Dumbarton Oaks Papers* 51 (1997): 33–71. The potential contribution of archaeology is also limited by the island's thin stratigraphy and rapid pace of modern development; see Knapp, *Archaeology*, 36–37.

22. G. Barker and J. Lloyd, *Roman Landscapes. Archaeological Survey in the Mediterranean Region* (London, 1991); S. E. Alcock, *Graecia Capta. The Landscapes of Roman Greece* (Cambridge, 1993).

23. H. W. Catling, "An Early Byzantine Pottery Factory at Dhiorios in Cyprus," *Levant* 4 (1972): 1–82, at 5. The seventh-eighth century dates now can be revised to the sixth-seventh centuries; A. H. S. Megaw, "'Betwixt Greeks and Saracens,'" in *Acts of the International Archaeological Symposium "Cyprus between the Orient and the Occident,"* ed. V. Karageorghis (Nicosia, 1986), 505–19 at 505.

24. J. Lund, "Pottery of the Classical, Hellenistic and Roman Periods," in *The Land of the Paphian Aphrodite 2. The Canadian Palaipaphos Survey Project. Artifact and Ecofactual Studies*, ed. L.W. Sørensen and D. W. Rupp (SIMA CIV:2, Göteborg, 1993), 79–155; J. Fejfer, ed., *Ancient Akamas* I. *Settlement and Environment* (Aarhus, 1995); D. W. Rupp, "'Metro' Nea Paphos: Suburban Sprawl in Southwestern Cyprus in the

Hellenistic and Earlier Roman Periods," in *Urbanism in Antiquity from Mesopotamia to Crete,* ed. W. E. Aufrecht, N. A. Mirau, and S. W. Gauley (Sheffield, 1997), 236–62.

25. I. A. Todd, "Vasilikos Valley Project: Fourth Preliminary Report, 1979–1980," *Journal of Field Archaeology* 9 (1982): 35–77; S. W. Manning, D. L. Bolger, A. Swinton, and M.J. Ponting, "Maroni Valley Archaeological Survey Project: Preliminary Report on the 1992–1993 Seasons," *Report of the Department of Antiquities, Cyprus* (1994): 345–67. Cf. Lund, "Pottery," 141–42.
26. No rural church or chapel from this period survives intact. Certainly many buildings have been dismantled over the years while others have been reconstructed. Field survey alone rarely is able to identify and closely date such buildings without the aid of architectural sculpture. The handful of known, partially excavated examples thus constitutes a random sample of churches, frequently lacking a regional context, that only hints at the presence of larger villages in the landscape.
27. A. H. S. Megaw, "Byzantine Architecture and Decoration in Cyprus: Metropolitan or Provincial?" *Dumbarton Oaks Papers* 28 (1974): 57–88; A. Papageorghiou, "L'architecture paléochrétienne de Chypre," *Corsi di cultura sull'arte ravennate e bizantina* 32 (1985): 299–324; G. Roux, *Salamine de Chypre* XV. *La basilique de la Campanopetra* (Paris, 1998).
28. Comparison of this surface data nevertheless requires much caution regarding both the physical environments and collection methods employed, see Alcock, *Graecia Capta,* 49–53; Knapp, *Archaeology,* 11–13.
29. Chrysos, "Cyprus in Early Byzantine Times," 7–9. Cyprus experiences drought every three years and severe drought every ten years; Thirgood, *Cyprus,* 19–20, cf. 59.
30. P.-L. Gatier, "Villages du Proche-Orient protobyzantin (4ème-7èmes.). Étude regionale," in *The Byzantine and Early Islamic Near East* II. *Land Use and Settlement Patterns,* ed. G. R. D. King and A. Cameron (Princeton, 1989), 17–48; J. Durlait, "Les conditions du commerce au VI siècle," in *The Sixth Century. Production, Distribution, and Demand,* ed. R. Hodges and W. Bowden (Leiden, 1998), 89–117.
31. D. Christodoulou, *The Evolution of the Rural Land Use Pattern in Cyprus* (Cornwall, 1959); Thirgood, *Cyprus.*
32. B. Gomez, J. Hansen, and J. M. Wagstaff, "The Vasilikos Valley," in *Vasilikos Valley Project,* ed. I. A. Todd, 6: *Excavations at Kalavasos-Tenta* I (Göteborg, 1987), 3–10; M. Wagstaff, "The Tenta Catchment: Resource Exploitation in Neolithic Cyprus," in *Conceptual Issues in Environmental Archaeology,* edited by J. L. Bintliff, D. A. Davidson, and E.G. Grant (Edinburgh, 1988), 64–71
33. Christodoulou, *Evolution;* Thirgood, *Cyprus,* 60–61.
34. The distribution of sites in figure 2 is based on I. A. Todd, "Vasilikos Valley Project, 1977–1978: An Interim Report," *Report of the Department of Antiquities, Cyprus* (1979): 13–66 at 31–35; *idem,* "Vasilikos Valley Project: Fourth Preliminary Report," 64–66. These will be discussed by I. A. Todd, *Vasilikos Valley Project* 9. *The Field Survey of The Vasilikos Valley* (forthcoming). My thanks to Ian Todd for allowing me to study the pottery from the field survey.
35. The location is also near Mitford's conjectured intersection with a cross-insular road

from Tamassus; see Mitford, "Roman Cyprus," 1333, fig. 1.

36. For Neolithic Tenta, Chalcolithic Ayious, and Late Bronze Age Ayios Demetrios see I. A. Todd, "Excavations in the Vasilikos Valley," in *Archaeology in Cyprus, 1960–1985*, ed. V. Karageorghis (Nicosia, 1985), 81–91.
37. Major fieldwork was conducted in 1987–91. See most recently M. C. McClellan and M. L. Rautman, "The 1991–1993 Field Seasons at Kalavasos-Kopetra," *Report of the Department of Antiquities, Cyprus* (1994): 289–307. The final report is forthcoming.
38. Cf. the townhouses of Paphos, Kourion and Salamis-Constantia. For contemporary rural structures see Catling, "An Early Byzantine Pottery Factory," 6–9 (Dhiorios-Mersineri); Fejfer ed., *Ancient Akamas*, 78–86 (Ayios Kononas); and for comparison S. Sinos, "Types of Rural Dwellings in Cyprus," in *"Cyprus Between the Orient and the Occident,"* ed. Karageorghis, 520–33. For the mainland see Y. Hirschfeld, *The Palestinian Dwelling in the Roman-Byzantine Period* (Jerusalem, 1995); *idem*, "Farms and Villages."
39. Megaw, "'Betwixt Greeks and Saracens,'" 506–13; A. Cameron, "Cyprus at the Time of the Arab Conquests," *Epeteris tes Kypriake Etaireias Istorikon Spoudon* 1 (1992): 27–50 (Reprinted in A. Cameron, *Changing Cultures in Early Byzantium* [Aldershot, 1996]); L. Conrad, "The Conquest of Arwad: A Source-Critical Study in the Historiography of the Early Medieval Near East," in *The Byzantine and Early Islamic Near East* I. *Problems in the Literary Source Material*, ed. A. Cameron and L. I. Conrad (Princeton, 1989), 317–401, at 328–30.
40. P. Yannopoulos, "Chypre au milieu du VIIe siècle à lumière des sources numismatiques," *Epeteris tou Kentrou Epistimonikon Ereunon* 12 (1983): 69–77; M. Hendy, *Studies in the Byzantine Monetary Economy, c. 300–1450* (Cambridge, 1985), 640–45. Compare the paucity of coins reported above Palaepaphos (Sørensen and Rupp, eds., *The Land of the Paphian Aphrodite*) and on the Akamas peninsula (Fejfer, ed., *Ancient Akamas*).
41. J. W. Hayes, *Late Roman Pottery* (London, 1972), 368–69; Bakirtzis, "The Role of Cyprus in the Grain Supply of Constantinople," 247–53; F. Curta, "Peasants as 'Makeshift Soldiers for the Occasion:' Sixth-Century Settlement Patterns in the Balkans," this volume.
42. C. Abadie-Reynal, "Céramique et commerce dans le bassin égéen du IVe au VIIe siècle," in *Hommes et richesses dans l'empire byzantin* I. *IVe-VIIe siècle* (Paris, 1989), 143–59.
43. M. L. Rautman, H. Neff, B. Gomez, S. Vaughan, and M. D. Glascock, "Amphoras and Rooftiles from Late Roman Cyprus: A Compositional Study of Calcareous Ceramics from Kalavasos-Kopetra," *Journal of Roman Archaeology* 12 (1999): 377–91. At least one fabric originated in central Cyprus, with possible kiln sites noted at Amathus and Zygi-Petrini.
44. Peacock and Williams, *Amphorae and the Roman Economy*, 185–87. Processed copper ore similarly would have been transported in bags or baskets.
45. Peacock and Williams, *Amphorae and the Roman Economy*, 182–205; P. Ballet, "Relations céramiques entre l'Egypte et Chypre à l'époque gréco-romaine et byzan-

tine," in *Hellenistic and Roman Pottery*, ed. Meyza and Mlynarczyk, 11–25, at 16–19; P. Arthur and E. D. Oren, "The North Sinai Survey and the Evidence of Transport Amphorae for Roman and Byzantine Trading Patterns," *Journal of Roman Archaeology* 11 (1998): 193–212.

46. Catling, "An Early Byzantine Pottery Factory," 57–64; J.W. Hayes, "Problèmes de la céramique des VIIème-IXème siècles à Salamine et à Chypre," in *Salamine de Chypre. Histoire et archéologie* (Paris, 1980), 375–87; C. Williams, *Anemurium. The Roman and Early Byzantine Pottery* (Toronto, 1989), 68–70.
47. M. Rautman, "Handmade Pottery and Social Change: The View from Late Roman Cyprus," *Journal of Mediterranean Archaeology* 11 (1998): 81–104.
48. Rautman et al., "Amphoras and Rooftiles."
49. B. K. Roberts, *Landscapes of Settlement, Prehistory to the Present* (London, 1996), 15–37; cf. Rupp, "'Metro' Nea Paphos," 241–46 on the settlement hierarchy of western Cyprus in the Hellenistic and Early Roman periods.
50. Population estimates based on site area are notoriously hazardous but can suggest a likely upper range for local habitation. Modern village populations in the Near East vary between about 120 and 200 persons/ha, with greater densities noted at enclosed sites and in nucleated landscapes. The lack of a clear boundary at Kopetra together with the valley's relatively dispersed settlement pattern suggest a low density of perhaps 125–150 persons/ha., which would yield a maximum population range of 500–600. Cf. the urban approximations in J.C. Russell, "Late Antique and Medieval Populations," *Transactions of the American Philosophical Society* 48, no. 3 (1958): 77–83, 92–93; and representative cautions by F. A. Hassan, *Demographic Archaeology* (New York, 1991), 66–75; J. R. Zorn, "Estimating the Population Size of Ancient Settlements: Methods, Problems, Solutions, and a Case Study," *Bulletin of the American Schools of Oriental Research* 295 (1994): 31–48; Knapp, *Archaeology*, 37–38. The figure for Kopetra roughly coincides with the estimated capacity of the three churches (about 600), assuming one person per square meter of interior space.
51. P. Halstead, "Traditional and Ancient Rural Economy in Mediterranean Europe: Plus ça change?" *Journal of Hellenic Studies* 107 (1987): 77–87; Kaplan, *Les hommes et la terre;* P. Garnsey, "Prolegomenon to a Study of the Land in the Later Roman Empire," in *Cities, Peasants, and Food in Classical Antiquity* (Cambridge, 1998), 151–65. For Cyprus today see Christodoulou, *Evolution;* Thirgood, *Cyprus*, 60–61.
52. C. A. Smith, "Exchange Systems and the Spatial Distribution of Elites: The Organization of Stratification in Agrarian Societies," in *Regional Analysis* 2. *Social Systems*, edited by C. A. Smith (New York, 1976), 309–74; R. Hodges, *Primitive and Peasant Markets* (Oxford, 1988); P. van Dommelen, "Roman Peasants and Rural Organisation in Central Italy: An Archaeological Perspective," in *Theoretical Roman Archaeology: First Conference Proceedings*, ed. E. Scott (Avebury, 1993), 167–86.
53. Dagron, "Entre village et cité," 44–47; Gatier, "Villages du Proche-Orient protobyzantin," 42; Kaplan, *Les hommes et la terre*, 202–3, 230–31; Haldon, *Byzantium*, 132–41.
54. A.I. Dikigoropoulos, "The Political Status of Cyprus a.d. 648–965," *Report of the Department of Antiquities, Cyprus* (1940–48), 94–114; R. Browning, "Byzantium and

Islam in Cyprus in the Early Middle Ages," *Epeteris tou Kentrou Epistemonikon Ereunon* 9 (1977–79): 101–16; C. Kyrris, "Cyprus as a Trade Station Between East and West in the Middle Ages," *Epeteris tou Kentrou Epistemonikon Ereunon* 12 (1983): 1–3; Cameron, "Cyprus at the Time of the Arab Conquests," 27–50; Th. Papadopoulos, "Frontier Status and Frontier Processes in Cyprus," in *The Sweet Land of Cyprus*, ed. Bryer and Georghallides, 15–24.

Christianization

Pastoral Care: Town and Country in Late-Antique Preaching

E. G. CLARK

"LET IT BE SAID IN WHAT PLACES THESE PRECEPTS OF GODS WHO TEACH WERE habitually read out and often heard by the people who worship them, in the same way that we point to churches built for that purpose, wherever the Christian religion spreads."[1]

Augustine, arguing in *City of God* against the claim that the gods of Rome had especially blessed the city, pointed to the absence of moral instruction in traditional Roman religion. Mystery cults might teach initiates, but why make morality a mystery? Philosophers did their best, but are only human; and, he could have added, philosophy also was accessible only to the select few who could understand its debates and could afford the time.[2]

If it is true that Christians built churches wherever their religion spread, and that those churches offered religious instruction to anyone who cared to come, late antiquity saw a cultural revolution. Educated preachers now expounded texts and precepts to people who could not pay for education or had been thought unfit for education: manual workers, women, the urban poor, and the particular concern of this paper, the "rustics" who lived away from towns.

But is it true? The more strongly late antiquity has established itself as a field of study, the more its scholars have been wary of claims that Christianity transformed Roman culture and conduct. Instead, they have emphasized the continuity of Christian moral precepts, and of early Christian theology and exegesis, with the morality and philosophy and textual culture of the Greco-Roman world within which Christianity developed.[3] The brilliant preachers of the fourth and early fifth centuries—Basil, John Chrysostom, Ambrose, Augustine—were uncomfortably aware that they were products of the traditional Greco-Roman educational system. Did Christian preaching also perpetuate the social conventions of Greco-Roman rhetoric? If so, much of the population continued to be excluded. They were too far from the towns where preaching happened, or obviously too poor to be allowed into grand buildings. They were alienated by the carefully classical speech, based on texts four to eight hundred years old, which was the mark of the educated orator; they might not even understand the language, Greek or Latin, of the dominant urban culture. If late-antique preaching was a rhetorical performance, it was the educated elite talking to the social elite in the language of books. There was no expectation that it would discuss or affect what was actually happening. The poor were not having the Good News brought to them, and there was no late-antique cultural revolution.

Preaching has a special relevance to the relationship of town and country. If preaching is performance, it is an urban art, dependent on both highly trained speakers and sophisticated audiences who can pick up allusions, appreciate skill, affirm and be affirmed by the speaker. A person from the country—*rusticus* in Latin, *agroikos* in Greek—could not be expected to do this. The category "country person" implied more than a domicile and a way of living. Latin *rusticanus* seems to be simply descriptive, "of the country," but just as English "rustic" used to connote "slow" or "simple," Latin *rusticus* or *agrestis,* and Greek *agroikos,* also mean "unsophisticated," "untaught," "uncultured," "crude."[4] The opposite words are *urbanus* in Latin, *asteios* in Greek: a person from the town is urbane, sophisticated in understanding and repartee. Unless *rustici* came into town, they could not get practice in listening to speeches.[5] The duty to preach might take educated clergy out to the country, but that would not necessarily bridge the cultural gap. *Rustici* might not speak Greek or Latin at all, let alone well enough to appreciate a good speaker, and educated preachers might have very little idea how country people lived and what kind of instruction they needed.

To trace the spread of Christian churches in the country, and to reveal the diversity of "country" in late antiquity, regional case-studies are essential. Archaeologists interpret some non-urban areas as almost without human habitation, others as hinterland supplying towns and suburbs, others again as populated with rural villas and villages and hamlets, or provided with strong points and occasional markets that could function as centers when needed. They note the complexities of identifying buildings, or rooms in villas, as churches, and of deciding how much of the rural population these churches served.[6] This diversity and complexity is also apparent in texts.

Augustine, for instance, describes a "country heresy" (*haeresis rusticana*) which required people to marry but abstain from intercourse:

> There is a country heresy in our campus, that is the campus of Hippo, or rather there was: it gradually decreased until it survived only in one little villa, where there were indeed very few people, but they all belonged to it [. . .] They were called Abeloim, in the Punic declension of the word.[7]

Campus, like Greek *chôra*, is the surrounding territory or hinterland of a city, thought of in relation to the city. The "little *villa*" is an estate on which people live as a group. Both categories warn against any easy assumption that country people lived in rural isolation, scattered over large areas and inaccessible to preachers. People came, according to Augustine in a sermon, from farms (*fundi*) and from desert places: "they come suddenly from the bush [*silva*], from the desert, from steep and most remote mountains to church." He is evidently dramatizing the distance, but his point is that God's word has reached them and they are making the effort to come and hear preaching.[8] The "country heresy" shows a *villa* with a small population, but the biographer of the Roman aristocrat Melania said that her *villa*, near Augustine's birthplace Tagaste, was bigger than the town of which his friend Alypius was bishop and had two bishops of its own, one for Catholics and one for "heretics," presumably Donatists.[9]

The "country heresy" also raises the question of language. Its name had a Punic case-ending: could those who belonged to it understand Latin? Augustine's diocese certainly included Punic speakers, but we should not assume that someone leaving the city walls entered a different language environment, that outside Hippo people spoke Punic or outside Antioch people spoke Syriac.[10] Those whose home language was Punic or Syriac or Celtic might well have enough Latin or Greek to make themselves understood in the town, or when trading, or talking to travelers or officials, or else there would be someone who could interpret. Augustine tells the story of his bishop Valerius talking to a group of *rusticani*.[11] Some were Punic speakers, and at least one was monoglot Punic. But when the monoglot asked one who spoke both Punic and Latin for a translation of *salus*, Valerius was delighted to discover that the Punic for "salvation" was *tria*, "three" in Latin: Trinitarian doctrine was embedded in language. Augustine comments that "our *rustici*," asked what they are, reply in Punic *"chanani."* [12] They are, he says, obviously Canaanites, related to the Canaanite woman of the Gospels who said to Jesus that even the dogs eat the crumbs that fall from the master's table.

So the Punic-speaking *rustici* are included in the gospels, and the language barrier is permeable. Augustine was aware of language problems and made efforts to overcome them. He tried to find a Punic-speaking bishop for Fussala, a *castellum* forty (Roman) miles from Hippo which had been won back from the Donatists.[13] The strength of Donatism in rural areas was confirmed by his friend Alypius, who had it minuted, in the records of the Council of Carthage, that some of the bishops in the impressive Donatist list belonged to *villae* and *fundi*, not to *civitates*.[14] Augustine also declined to release one of his deacons to a fellow-bishop, arguing that the deacon was more urgently needed in Augustine's diocese for reasons of language. The text of the relevant sentence is in doubt, so it is not certain that the deacon spoke Punic: perhaps he spoke Greek, or simply had good Latin.[15] Augustine's concern for accessible teaching is not in doubt.

But how accessible was the teaching Augustine provided, and how closely was it related to the concerns of country people? Augustine himself preached in small towns, especially those on the route from Hippo to

Carthage. One of the sermons recently rediscovered by Francois Dolbeau was preached at Boseth, a small place in Numidia or Proconsularis not yet securely identified.[16] Pagans were allowed in, and Augustine was preaching to impress. He reached a favorite theme: we cannot see the soul, but we can see what it does. To illustrate its works, he contrasted town and country:

> What delights you in human affairs? Look around at the order of things, the beauty of cultivated fields with thickets cleared and grafted trees bearing fruit, and all we see and love in the fields; the order of the civic community with imposing buildings, variety of skills, abundance of languages, depth of memory, richness of eloquence.[17]

Civic order requires rhetorical skill, rural order requires productive cultivation. This is a stylized countryside, in which tilled fields, cleared thickets, and grafted trees exemplify human effort to produce food. But agriculture is not only stylized, it supplies favorite themes for allegory. When Augustine uses agricultural images, derived or developed from the text he is expounding, he interprets them as the cultivation of the soul to bear spiritual fruit. Adam was told "in the sweat of thy face shalt thou eat bread," but the labor of ground-clearing and plowing, pruning and irrigating, threshing grain and pressing olives, even trenching and manuring, is transformed into the struggle against sin. Dung in the wrong place, such as a heap of wheat-grains, is dirt, but in the right place it helps the wheat to grow; dung symbolizes sadness, but sadness rightly used promotes spiritual growth, just as dung applied to the roots of a barren fig-tree will help the tree bear fruit.[18] Augustine explicitly seeks a spiritual meaning:

> This psalm has the heading *To the end, for the oil-pressers, fifth of the sabbath, a psalm of Asaph.* [. . .] I'm going to talk about oil-pressers, but don't expect me to say anything about the vat and the beam and the baskets, because the psalm doesn't, and that is a further sign of a hidden meaning. For if the text of the psalm did say something like that, someone would be sure to think the press should be taken literally, and there's nothing further to be looked for there, no hidden meaning, nothing conveyed by a holy sign: the psalm is

> simply talking about oil-presses, he'd say, and you're telling me you suspect there's something else in it.[19]

Take "you who judge the earth" literally, he observed in another sermon, and you will think it is addressed to farmers.[20]

Rhetorical tradition, stylization, and allegory, all contribute to the widely held opinion that late-antique preaching had no social relevance. Preachers, it is argued, did not discuss the experience of their congregations even when they understood it: they used what they did know, namely theological debate and rhetorical commonplace. Consequently, sermons have little to tell present-day students of late antiquity. There is a forceful statement of this position in the pioneering (1964) survey by A. H. M. Jones, *The Later Roman Empire:*

> As I explored the ancient sources I regretfully came to the conclusion that a lifetime would not suffice to read them all; anyone who surveys only the relevant shelves of Migne's *Patrologiae* will understand. I soon decided to abandon theological treatises and commentaries on the Scriptures and secular *belles-lettres* (with obvious exceptions such as Ausonius and Claudian). There are a few grains of wheat in these, but the quantity of chaff (from my point of view) is overwhelming. [. . .] I next, after reading a fair sample, abandoned sermons, having discovered that most consisted of exegesis of the Scriptures or of vague and generalized moralisation.[21]

It is only to be expected that sermons would expound Scripture, but Jones's frustration is understandable. The *Patrologiae* collect an astonishing range of sermons from different times, countries, and contexts, yet they do not supply many "grains of wheat," that is items of historical or socio-historical interest, and Jones was probably right to say that most of these had already been collected by the great church historians of earlier centuries.

Since 1964, historians have become increasingly interested in what Jones counts as "chaff" and increasingly reluctant to separate the "grain" from its elegant protective sheath. They are concerned for texts, techniques of communication, and reception. But this interest in the uses of rhetoric has led to a stronger sense of Christian texts as rhetoric, perpetuating and exploiting the traditions of public speech. Ten years ago, Ramsay MacMullen argued in a classic article that the preacher's audience was nothing new in social terms: the elite were still talking mostly to the elite and failing to reach the poor, the uneducated, women and rustics.[22] This article makes use especially of John Chrysostom, all of whose sermons were preached in the great urban centers of Antioch and Constantinople. MacMullen comments that John's audiences "were remarkably patient of rhetoric pitched at a high level of stylistic and exegetical sophistication," and that John assumes they have had an expensive education. "Can this be confirmed? Certainly; for he may be heard to call his audience the rich, comparing them to the poor who are not before him."[23]

It is not so certain that John Chrysostom's homilies assume a high level of education. He earned the name of "golden mouth" by eloquence, but his style is lively and fluent rather than complex, and his exegesis adopts the manner of the patient teacher asking and answering the questions he thinks his students will have. His allusions to classical culture are brief and disparaging, designed to show the moral superiority of the Christian scriptures: Plato said that women should be held in common, and in the works of the great classical dramatists, a man marries his mother, then blinds himself, and a woman falls for her stepson.[24]

It is also not certain that Chrysostom's repeated denunciations of "you rich" imply an audience composed entirely, or mostly, of rich people. Like the Hebrew prophets, he addresses those whom he wishes to challenge, but we cannot assume that the audience addressed in the text (the "encoded" audience) is the audience actually present and listening. No doubt the congregations of Antioch and Constantinople included some very rich people, though we must allow for Chrysostom's taste for exaggeration: one memorable passage suggests that women who wear gold ornaments and twist gold in their hair will move on to gold-plating the hair itself, and their eyebrows and lashes.[25] But denunciation of the very rich would also appeal to the not so rich, and Chrysostom had a challenge for them too. His most constant concern was the failure of the rich to help the poor, and, as he often pointed out, anyone was rich in comparison with the desperate people who depended on charity. Beggars crowded at the exit from the church, and were disregarded as if they were a row of pillars; the poor were in the church, standing in rags at the altar beside the rich in their silk and gold.[26]

So one social group—the very rich—addressed in Chrysostom's sermons was not necessarily there, or at least did not necessarily form the majority of the congregation. MacMullen uses the reverse argument, suggesting that social groups not addressed, or rarely addressed, in the sermons were not usually there, or were in a small minority. This applies to poor people, slaves (except those in attendance on their rich owners), and country people. But the case of women, which MacMullen rightly sees as problematic, casts doubt on this argument.

John Chrysostom frequently refers to women, especially to their extravagant dress, their weakness, and their effect on the male. But it is rare to find women addressed directly—that is, collectively and in gendered language—in the sermons of John Chrysostom or of anyone else.[27] Does this mean that women were rarely present in church? Here, again, we need to distinguish the "encoded" audience, the audience addressed or targeted by the text, from the empirical audience that the preacher could never exactly predict.[28] On one occasion when Augustine commented on sex-ratios in his congregation, he implied that the absence of women was unusual. He was preaching a long sermon because, as he acknowledged in his closing remarks, he wanted to keep his congregation away from a pagan spectacle, and he was pleased to see that so many had come to church instead.

> As for the number of brothers, it's hard to imagine that any man would be carried away by that festival; as for the number of sisters, it distresses us, and this is a further reason for grief, that they did not run to the church: modesty, if not fear, should have called them away from being in public.[29]

(The festival honored "the blood of some woman": if it honored Cybele and the self-castrated Attis, though this is difficult to prove,[30] that might explain why the men stayed away.)

It would be very surprising if Christian women did not attend church, and there are reasons why they are not directly addressed. Congregations were a mixed, though usually segregated, public gathering. Decorum forbade a male preacher to speak to women directly and at length, or to focus attention on them. In another of the recently rediscovered sermons, Augustine encourages men who really want to undergo the new-style martyrdom of post-marital celibacy, but are held back by their parents and especially by their wives. Late in the sermon, he adds a brief "consolation to the weaker sex": there have been women martyrs too.[31] Did he think it very unlikely that women wanted marital celibacy, had he forgotten about women until then, or would it have been embarrassing for everyone if he had discussed women controlling their desires and resisting the blandishments of their husbands?

Comments addressed specifically to women are the more noticeable because Greek and Latin speakers (like English speakers until the late 1960s) took it for granted that the masculine includes the feminine. Audiences are addressed in the grammatical masculine, as *fratres, carissimi, agapêtoi,* with the one exception of abstract nouns used as a collective, for instance *caritas vestra* or *sanctitas vestra;* but it is also rare for men to be addressed as a group of males rather than as the standard variety of human being.[32] On the one occasion when Chrysostom explicitly says "listen, women; listen, men!" he is making a specific point about Christian teaching on adultery, which rejects the double standard permitted by Roman law.[33]

The case of women may shed light on the case of country people, who are also rarely addressed. It might, for instance, have been impolite or patronizing or simply irrelevant for an urban speaker to single out the country people in his congregation. The Christian message does not need to be prefaced with "listen, rustics; listen, townspeople!" The "vague and generalised moralisation" that frustrated A. H. M. Jones could be read as a wish to unite the congregation, to focus on shared moral concerns and a common effort to understand the Scriptures, not on distinctions of social status or of gender.

Preachers of course differed in their expectations. Augustine does not usually specify that there are farmers in his congregation, but he apparently takes it for granted that there will be some. Here he is deploying a favorite pun on *colere,* which means both "to offer cult" and "to cultivate," and wanting his congregation to contribute:

> What does a farmer (*agricola*) do? I'm asking you who are farmers, what does a farmer do? I think he farms the land (*agrum colit*).[34]

But John Chrysostom twice makes it clear that the presence of country people in his church deserves comment, and what he says is a striking example of rhetorical convention in preaching. One of these occasions can (unusually) be precisely dated and assigned to Antioch rather than Constantinople. Homily 19 of the series *On the Statues*, preached in 387, begins with a regret that John has missed several days of a martyr-festival, because he was ill. But, he says, this is the best day, because of the presence of our brothers.

> This is a people differing from us in language, but agreeing with us in faith; a people living in tranquillity, leading a temperate and austere life.[35]

These people have come in from the country and, presumably, speak Syriac. For the next two columns of the *Patrologia*, ten minutes' preaching time on the standard calculation, John describes the moral excellence of country life. It is free from city temptations: there are "no theatres of lawlessness, no horse-races, no prostituted women [. . .] among them are no women living in luxury, no decoration of clothes, no makeup and eyeliner: all such corruption of behaviour is exiled." The lifestyle of these farmers manifests their belief that worldly delights are hollow, and their Bible-based wisdom surpasses any pagan philosopher. They clear the earth of thorn-bushes and souls of the thorns of sin; one minute they are harnessing plow-oxen, the next they are up in the pulpit furrowing souls.

Possibly the Syriac speakers understood enough Greek to follow this, or helpful members of the congregation explained, but John's account of country life is obviously aimed at exhortation of his urban audience rather than praise of the visitors. After his ten minutes of preaching, he says an affectionate farewell to the visitors and returns to his previous topic (oaths) on which he preaches for at least another hour.[36] It is equally obvious that his description of country life is not derived from experience and intended as social history. There is a very close parallel in one of a series of baptismal catechizes, in which country visitors are welcomed and eulogized, then

John reverts to previous concerns.[37] Here, not only does the *agroikos* surpass pagan philosophers, but the idealized country life is equated with the angelic life of minimal food, absence of luxury, and concentration on hymns and prayers, exemplified by monastic communities.[38]

John Chrysostom uses an idealized account of rustics to rebuke the self-indulgence of his urban audience, just as he uses a negative account of females to rebuke explicitly the self-indulgence and lapse into effeminacy of a male audience, and implicitly the extravagance and provocation of a female audience. His account of the angelic country life and the deep spirituality of rustic ascetics is undercut by another sermon, preached (almost certainly) at Constantinople, in which he departs from his exegesis of the Acts of the Apostles and exhorts landowners to build churches on their villages and country estates (*kômai kai chôria*).[39] This time, the rustics do not provide for their own salvation by prayer and preaching. The landowner organizes clearance of the ground, but not clearance of the farmers' souls: "how can the farmer be a Christian when he sees you neglecting his salvation like that?" The owner should build a church and support its clergy. This will also contribute to the safety of the estate, because the priest will be respected, and churches are much better for farmers than baths and shops, which make them self-indulgent, or markets and fiestas, which make them over-excited.

This looks like a clear example of preaching that deploys rhetorical *topoi* and fails to engage with a new audience, with the result that it cannot provide present-day historians with useful information. Here, again, the comparison with women may be helpful. It has often been argued that we know nothing about women in the ancient world: all we have is texts and artifacts made by men and used for male purposes. Is this also true of rustics, who are described by urban authors and deployed to target urban audiences, whether to make the city people feel superior or to make them feel guilty? Women and rustics have much in common. They are objects of preaching not agents of preaching: women were explicitly forbidden to preach even if they had the skill,[40] *rustici* (except in John Chrysostom's fantasy) did not have the skill. But Christian preaching reworked the tradition it inherited, and consciously valorized what had once been despised or pitied in women and in rustics.

Christian transformation of gender-roles has been extensively studied. Virginity until death had been considered the ultimate tragedy for a woman, now it was the highest spiritual status: she was the bride of Christ not the bride of Hades. A half-starved female body, de-sexed and disfigured by fasting, could be presented as having a special beauty, a new female heroism. Similarly, a man was no longer dismissed as effeminate if he opted out of the competition for social and political status, refused to provide grandchildren for his parents and new citizens and surplus wealth for his city, and allowed or even encouraged his male physical strength to lapse into weakness. Instead, he was a spiritual athlete, a new model hero.[41] Professed celibacy had been an option only for a few male philosophers who had the education and the resources to sustain the simple life, but the churches offered institutional support for celibates, male or female.

Rustics had been despised for the ignorance that excluded them from so much of human culture, and even, perhaps, from the possibility of virtue. There was a tradition of uncorrupted rustic piety and morality, which goes back to Homer's pigman Eumaios (a kidnapped prince) in the *Odyssey*. But followers of Plato and Aristotle found it hard to see how an ignorant person could actually be good. Someone who has not been taught to assess reactions, to ascend by reason beyond immediate experience and reach some understanding of goodness, cannot act in accordance with goodness. The philosopher Porphyry, a third-century Platonist and author of the fullest account of non-Christian asceticism, is openly contemptuous of ordinary people, with their muddled ideas and their material values, who cannot make the intellectual effort to understand Plato.[42] But Christians proclaimed a gospel preached by Peter the fisherman and Paul the tentmaker, and could not despise *rustici* or artisans, *banausoi,* who worked with their hands.

Pagan philosophers, following Aristotle, argued that such people were inevitably narrow-minded, unable to think beyond their immediate needs. But when Basil saw that a group of *banausoi* had come to hear one of his sermons on the six days of creation, the *Hexaemeron,* his response was not to exclude them from teaching, but to shorten the sermon so that they should not lose too much of the working time which earned their daily bread.[43] Christian ascetics praised the discipline of routine physical work and exploited the paradox of the uneducated but spiritually aware peasant. Antony of Egypt could confute any philosopher, and Arsenius, former tutor to the future emperors Arcadius and Honorius, sought guidance from a peasant monk.

> "Abba Arsenius, how is it that you, with such a good Roman and Greek education, ask this *agroikos* about your thoughts?" He replied, "I have had a Latin and Greek education, but I have not yet learned the alphabet of this *agroikos*."[44]

The educated pagans become the *rustici*, untaught and inarticulate; this may well be the primary meaning of "pagan," someone who lives in a *pagus*. Even Porphyry, who lived for a time in Sicily, was labeled "Porphyrius Siculus," with the implication that he was an untaught Sicel not a cultivated Greek. Meanwhile, Christian rustics were offered institutional support in that they could join communities or live as solitaries, uttering brief and pungent sayings, which were reverently transmitted.

But the new valuation of rusticity, like that of gender roles, is still presented by male, urban, expert speakers. Even if Christian ascetic teaching undermined traditional male dominance by physical strength, political and economic influence, and education, male ascetics continued to dominate by words, either by preaching them or by withholding them from the eager disciple or the visiting grandee who begs "Father, speak a word to me."[45] Sermons were preached neither by women nor by rustics, and we have neither female-authored nor rustic-authored texts. Instead, we find "rusticity" deployed as a defensive tactic, or as mock-modesty, by educated speakers apologizing for their lack of style or of culture. The device works particularly well when the self-defined rustic is living a retired life in the country.

Zeno of Verona provides a fine example of rhetorical rusticity. Before he expounds Isaiah's image of the vineyard, which yielded only sour grapes, he apologizes to a congregation that knows more than he does about vine-cultivation: "most blessed farmers (*agricultores*), please forgive me, your *rusticus*, if my uselessness detracts from your expertise when I explain about the vineyard."[46] But Zeno the *rusticus* reestablishes himself by describing the cultivation of the vine in language that is far too elaborate for real *rustici.* Either he was not adapting to his audience, or the *agricultores* were estate owners.

When real *rustici* were present in church, how much of the preaching could they understand? Augustine gave advice on preaching to a deacon, working in Carthage, who was anxious not to alienate the people he prepared for baptism. The treatise has the title *On catechising the uninstructed, de catechizandis rudibus.* The "uninstructed" are *rudes* in the Christian sense: they are not people generally uneducated, but people uninstructed in the faith.[47] But, Augustine says, there are different kinds of *rudes,* and it is important to distinguish between the future reader of a text and the diverse group of people who are addressed on a particular occasion. Here we do find a distinction between town and country:

> It makes a great difference whether there are few present or many, educated or uneducated [*docti an indocti*] or a mixture of both; townspeople or country people [*urbani an rustici*] or both at once, and whether the assembly is a mixture of all kinds of people.[48]

These various *rudes,* Augustine says, should be addressed in *sermo humilis,* the "low" style of speaking. But the use of *sermo humilis* would not necessarily bridge the gap between educated preacher and inexperienced hearers, for it is not the same as the language of fishermen or working people. *Sermo humilis* is Cicero's term for the language of educated professionals who are keeping it simple, and as any academic knows, it is very easy for an educated speaker to suppose that he or she is speaking simply, only to discover that the vocabulary, sentence structure, and content of this "simple" speech is difficult for most people to follow.

The sermons collected in the Patrologia are those that someone thought worth recording: they were preached by skilled speakers. Averil Cameron called Christian preaching "the hidden iceberg of Christian discourse,"[49] and we have the tip of the iceberg. We have Basil's sermons, but not the sermons of the fifty *chorepiscopi* who were the key to his management of Cappadocia; we know that he said untrained speakers might be dangerous. We cannot reconstruct the sermons of villa chaplains or the instruction given by communities of monks. But the efforts of Caesarius of Arles to regulate preaching in his diocese are a warning that uneducated speakers are not always easy to follow, and may be just wrong.[50]

Educated speakers could be difficult to follow for other reasons, but the sermons we have often show the preacher making a real effort to be understood. Thanks to the shorthand writers, we can hear Augustine, or John Chrysostom, responding to the circumstances and to audience reaction, restating points that have evidently not been grasped, reminding their hearers of what they already know and encouraging them through difficult material.[51] Even Ambrose, preaching in a center of government, made this effort. His style was less brilliant and more formal than that of Augustine or of John Chrysostom, and he probably revised the text of a sermon before it was released, but he was fully aware that his audience did not consist entirely of Milanese intellectuals. When he was preparing a mixed-ability group for baptism, his style was so different that editors could hardly believe the work was authentic Ambrose: another indication that the sermons we have do not exhaust the kind of teaching on offer.[52]

We can also see preachers painfully aware of themselves as performers offering a well-known form of entertainment. Sometimes they exploit this, using a sermon as a rival attraction to the theater or to a pagan festival. Augustine's preaching record stood at just over two hours before the rediscovery of the Mainz sermons: one of these, preached to keep the faithful from celebrating the Kalends, must have taken two and a quarter hours.[53] Entertainment value could be a danger. Augustine, like John Chrysostom, recognized the risk that his preaching would be received only as performance, not as an attempt to modify belief and conduct, and that he himself would revert to the role of the speaker who affirms and is affirmed by his audience. If sermons were rhetoric in that sense, they had failed. But, as Augustine also said, rhetoric can be used to teach truth instead of falsehood; and inherited rhetorical tradition, precisely because it had excluded an uncultured audience, could give value to an audience with a new culture. Listening to educated speakers was itself a prestigious activity. That prestige could be transferred to a congregation of people who knew they lacked traditional culture, but who had more knowledge of Christian tradition than the new *rustici*, the uncomprehending pagans. It might not even matter if the congregation did not understand all the sermon. In late-antique exchanges of letters, it is often the fact of communication that matters as much as the content. Similarly, the fact of preaching demonstrated concern for the audience.

This article has considered the case for saying that Christianity made little difference to urban awareness of *rustici*, who were absent from both the preacher's audience and his text. If that is right, we are dealing with inherited contempt for rustics transposed to pagan opponents, and with rusticity appropriated by the urban male orator to reproach an urban audience or to advertise his own modesty; sermons can tell us about vocabulary used for the country and perceptions of the country, but not about life in the countryside. But both texts and archaeology provide some evidence for preachers trying to reach out beyond the urban elite. Augustine may have failed to find Punic-speaking clergy, but at least he tried; who ever worried about the shortage of Punic-speaking philosophers? "Let my opponent say where the precepts of these gods were read out and regularly heard by the people who worshipped them: we point to churches built for that purpose wherever the Christian religion spreads." If that claim is justified, there really was a late-antique cultural revolution.

NOTES

My warm thanks to Tom Burns, John Eadie, and the participants in *Shifting Frontiers III*. I should like to acknowledge a special debt to Peter Garnsey's seminars on Augustine and to Aideen Hartney's doctoral work on John Chrysostom.

1. Augustine, *City of God* 2.6 (*CCSL* 47: 39): *dicatur in quibus locis haec docentium deorum solebant pracepta recitari et a cultoribus eorum populis frequenter audiri, sicut nos ostendimus ad hoc ecclesias institutas, quaquaversum religio Christiana diffunditur.* All translations are my own.
2. Mystery cults: *City of God* 2.6, 2.26. Philosophers: 2.7.
3. Some recent examples: Averil Cameron, *Christianity and the Rhetoric of Empire* (Berkeley, 1991); Judith Evans Grubbs, *Law and Family in Late Antiquity* (Oxford,

1995); Richard Lim, *Public Disputation, Power, and Social Order in Late Antiquity,* (Berkeley, 1995).

4. On perceptions of the country, see further S. Said, "Rural society in the Greek novel, or The Country seen from the Town," in *Oxford Readings in the Greek Novel,* edited by S. Swain (Oxford 1999), 83–107.
5. Rural synagogues also could have offered practice in listening to exegesis, but very few have been identified and there is a continuing debate on whether non-Jews were encouraged to attend: recent survey in M. Goodman, ed., *Jews in a Graeco-Roman World* (Oxford 1998). I am indebted here to Dr. David Noy.
6. On the complications of "country," see *The Church in Town and Countryside,* ed. D. Baker, Studies in Church History 16, (Oxford, 1979), especially Wolf Liebeschuetz, "Problems Arising from the Conversion of Syria," 17–24; Clare Stancliffe, "From Town to Country: The Christianisation of the Touraine 370–600," 43–59; Ian Wood, "Early Merovingian Devotion in Town and Country," 61–76. For an overview, see P. D. A. Garnsey and C. R. Whittaker, "Rural life in the later Roman empire," in *Cambridge Ancient History* XIII, rev. ed., ed. A. M. Cameron and P. D. A. Garnsey (Cambridge, 1998), 277–311.
7. *De haeresibus* 87 (*CCSL* 46: 339). *est quaedam haeresis rusticana in campo nostro, id est Hipponiensi, vel potius fuit; paulatim enim diminuta in una exigua villa remanserat, in qua quidem paucissimi, sed omnes hoc fuerunt. [. . .] Abeloim vocabantur, Punica declinatione nominis.*
8. *Enarrationes in psalmos* 134.22 (*CCSL* 40: 1954): *quanti fundi, quanta loca deserta modo veniunt! [. . .] veniunt subito de silva, de deserto, de remotissimis et arduis montibus ad ecclesiam.*
9. *Life of Melania* (Latin version) 21; E. A. Clark, *The Life of Melania the Younger* (Edwin Mellen, 1984), 215.
10. Fergus Millar, *The Roman Near East* (Harvard, 1993), 232–34, and recently in "Il ruolo delle lingue semitiche nel vicino oriente tardo-romano (V-VI secolo)," in *Mediterraneo Antico* 1, no. 1 (1998): 71–94. I am most grateful to Professor Millar for an offprint.
11. *Epistulae ad Romanos inchoata expositio* 13 (*CSEL* 84: 161): *in quorundam rusticanorum collocutione, cum alter alteri dixisset: salus, quaesivit ab eo, qui et Latine nosset et Punice, quid esset salus; responsum est: tria.*
12. *Epistulae ad Romanos inchoata expositio* 13 (*CSEL* 84: 162). *interrogati rustici nostri quid sint, punice respondentes: chanani, corrupta scilicet in talibus solet una littera, quid aliud respondent quam: chananaei?*
13. *Ep.* 209.2 (*CSEL* 57.2: 348), cf. *Ep.* 20* 3.3 (*CSEL* 88: 96). I am indebted to David Riggs for the reference.
14. Robert Markus, "Country Bishops in Byzantine Africa," *SCH* 16 (above, note 6), 1–15, especially 4–5 on the numbers of country bishops in the fourth and fifth centuries. Donatists in the countryside, S. Lancel, *Actes de la conférence de Carthage en 411* (1972-) 1.181; see also I.141n.1.
15. *Ep.* 84.2 (*CSEL* 34.2: 393): *sed cum Latina lingua, cuius inopia in nostris regionibus evangelica dispensatio multum laborat, illic autem eiusdem linguae usus omnino sit -*

itane censes nos saluti plebis domini oportere consulere, ut hanc facultatem illuc mittamus et hinc auferamus, ubi eam magno cordis aestu requirimus? The Maurist editors suggested *sed cum calleat Latinam linguam;* Arnoldus (1680) conjectured *Punicae linguae.*

16. O. Perler and J.-L.Maier, *Les Voyages de Saint Augustin* (Paris, 1969); Boseth, 407–8. The rediscovered sermons are now published in *Augustin d'Hippone, Vingt-six sermons au peuple d'Afrique retrouvés à Mayence*, édités et commentés par Francois Dolbeau (Paris, 1996), and translated, with an introduction and a concordance of numbers, by Edmund Hill OP in *Works of St Augustine* III.11 (A new translation for the twenty-first century ed. Joseph E. Rotelle (New York, 1997).
17. *quid te delectat in rebus humanis? circumspice ordinem rerum, pulchritudinem cultorum agrorum, exstirpatarum silvarum, insitorum fructuosorum, quaeque in agris videmus et amamus, ordinem ipsum rei publicae, moles aedificiorum, varietates artium, copiam linguarum, profunditatem memoriae, eloquentiae ubertatem:* Mainz sermon 61.9 (= Dolbeau 25 = *ser.* 360B), first published as F. Dolbeau, "Nouveaux sermons de saint Augustin pour la conversion des paiens et des donatistes," *Revue des Etudes Augustiniennes* 37, no. 1 (1991): 58–77; Augustine's preaching tour, 53–56.
18. *Sermo* 254.2 (*PL* 38: 1182): *stercus non loco suo positum immunditia est.*
19. Augustine, *Enarrationes in psalmos* 80.1 (*CCSL* 39: 1119–20): *Titulum habet psalmus iste: In finem pro torcularibus, quinta sabbati, psalmus ipsi Asaph.* [. . .] *cum de torcularibus locuturi sumus, nemo vestrum aliquid exspectet nos dicturos esse de lacu, de prelo, de fiscinis, quia nec ipse psalmus hoc habet, et ideo magis indicat mysterium. nam et si aliquid tale psalmui textus contineret, non deesset qui putaret ad litteram esse accipienda torcularia, nec aliquid illic amplius requirendum, nec mystice aliquid positum, et sacrate significatum; sed diceret: Simpliciter psalmus de torcularibus loquitur, et tu mihi nescio quid aliud suspicaris.*
20. *Sermo* 13.4 (*PL* 38: 108).
21. A. H. M. Jones, *The Later Roman Empire*, 2 vols. (Oxford, 1964), 1:vi-vii.
22. "The Preacher's Audience (AD 350–400)," *Journal of Theological Studies* 40 (1989): 503–11. See also *Christianity and Paganism in the Fourth to Eighth Centuries* (Yale, 1997), 10–11nn. 26–27.
23. Ibid., 504.
24. *Homily 5 on Titus* (*PG* 62:693–94).
25. *Homily 7 on Colossians* (*PG* 62:350). I am indebted to Aideen Hartney for pointing out this passage.
26. Beggars at the door, *Homily 5 on Genesis* 3 (*PG* 54:602–3); the poor at the altar, *Homily 11 on 1 Thessalonians* 4 (*PG* 62:466).
27. This impression is confirmed by A. Olivar, *La Predicación cristiana antiqua* (Barcelona, 1991), 763–65, with special reference to John Chrysostom. It cannot be checked in machine-searchable texts such as CETEDOC, but valuable information is available from the database-in-progress of homilies (currently those delivered at Constantinople) compiled by Pauline Allen and Wendy Mayer, to whom I am much indebted for advice. For an overview of this project, see their article "Computer and Homily:

Accessing the Everyday Life of Early Christians," *Vigiliae Christianae* 47 (1993): 26–80.

28. A. Mandouze, *Saint Augustin: l'aventure de la raison et de la grâce* (Paris, 1968), 591–663; Wendy Mayer, "John Chrysostom and His Audience," *Studia Patristica* 31 (1995): 70–75.
29. Augustine, *Tractatus in evangelium Johannis 7.2* (*CCSL* 36:68): *quantum pertinet ad numerum fratrum, difficile est ut quisquam illa celebritate raptus fuerit e viris; quantum autem ad sororum numerum, contristat nos, et hoc magis dolendum est, quia non ipsae potius ad ecclesiam currunt, quas debuit si non timor, certe verecundia de publico revocare.*
30. See John Rettig's note in his translation, *St Augustine: Tractates on the Gospel of John* 1–10 (*Fathers of the Church*, CUA, 1988), 158.
31. Mainz sermon 42.11 (= Dolbeau 13 = *sermo* 159A).
32. Modes of address: Olivar 1991 (note 26 above), 879–89. On the use of gendered language, see also G. Clark, "Adam's Engendering," in *Gender and Christian Religion*, ed. R. N. Swanson, Studies in Church History, 34 (Boydell and Brewer, 1998), 13–22.
33. *Homily 59.2 on Matthew* (*PG* 58: 651).
34. *quid facit agricola? interrogo vos qui agricolae estis, quid facit agricola? puto quia agrum colit: sermo* 87.2 (*PL* 38:531). I differ here from M. Pellegrino (*Sermons of Saint Augustine*, note 15 above, 1:87), who thinks that the farmers had come in for a special reason.
35. John Chrysostom, *Homily to the people of Antioch* (*On the Statues*) 19.1 (*PG* 49:188).
36. Cf. Fr. Eligius Dekkers, "Les limites sociales et linguistiques de la pastorale liturgique de saint Jean Chrysostome," *Augustinianum* 20 (1980): 119–29.
37. *Eight Baptismal Catecheses* 8.2.4, ed. A.Wenger, *Sources Chrétiennes* 50 (1957): 248–49.
38. On John's use of the angelic life, see Amanda Berry Wylie, *John Chrysostom amd his homilies on the Acts of the Apostles: reclaiming ancestral models for the Christian people* (diss. Princeton 1992). On the precise status (clerical or ascetic) of the "men from the country," see F. van de Paverd, *St John Chrysostom, The Homilies on the Statues: an introduction* (Rome, 1991), 255–89. I owe the reference to Dr. Wendy Mayer.
39. J. N. D. Kelly, *Golden Mouth* (London, 1995), 166–68 surveys the arguments for a date 400–1.
40. R. Nürnberg, *"Non decet neque necessarium est ut mulieres doceant," Jahrbuch für Antike und Christentum* 31 (1988): 51–73.
41. G. Clark, "The Old Adam: Patristics and the (Un)making of Masculinity," in *Thinking Men: Masculinity and Its Self-representation in the Classical Tradition*, ed. L. Foxhall (London, 1998), 170–82.
42. See further G. Clark, *Porphyry: On Abstinence from Killing Animals*, fc. (London-Ithaca, 1999).
43. *Hexaemeron* 3.1 (*PG* 29:53, *SC* 26 bis:191). On Basil's audience, see also Richard Lim, "The Politics of Interpretation in Basil's *Hexaemeron*," *Vigiliae Christianae* 44 (1990): 351–70.
44. Arsenius 6, *PG* 65:89a; cf. Arsenius 5, ib. 88d-89a, in which secular education is also contrasted with *agroikoi*. See further D. Burton-Christie, *The Word in the Desert* (Oxford, 1993), esp. 57–61.

45. I am indebted here to a comment by Philip Rousseau on an earlier paper. "Speak a Word to Me": see further Burton-Christie (note 44 above), 77–79, 109–10.
46. *Tractatus* 2.11.1 (*CCSL* 22: 183) on Isaiah 5.
47. *de cat.rud* is discussed by Brian Stock, *Augustine the Reader* (Harvard, 1996), 181–90. In the sixth century, Martin of Braga used *de cat.rud.* as the basis for his treatise *de castigatione rusticorum.*
48. *De catechizandis rudibus* 15 (*CCSL* 46: 147): *multumque interest... utrum pauci adsint an multi; docti an indocti an ex utroque genere mixti; urbani an rustici an hi et illi simul; an populus ex omni hominum genere temperatus sit.* Augustine later extends this to include differences of age and sex.
49. *Christianity and the Rhetoric of Empire* (Berkeley, 1991), 79.
50. Chorepiscopi: Philip Rousseau, *Basil of Caesarea* (Berkeley, 1994), 42; Rousseau also has reservations about the MacMullen thesis, note 68. Caesarius and preaching: W. Klingshirn, *Caesarius of Arles* (Cambridge, 1994), 9–15, 146–51.
51. Edmund Hill's translations of Augustine's sermons, in the *Augustine for the 21st Century* series, are especially good at catching this approachable quality.
52. On the authenticity of *de sacramentis,* see B. Botte's introduction to his edition of *Ambroise de Milan: Des Sacrements, Des Mystères, Explication du Symbole* (Sources Chrétiennes 23 bis, 1961). On Ambrose's preaching, see G. Nauroy, "L'écriture dans la pastorale d'Ambroise de Milan," in *Le monde latin antique et la Bible,* ed. J. Fontaine and E. Pietri (Paris, 1985), 371–408. Philip Rousseau, "The Preacher's Audience: A More Optimistic View," in *Ancient History in a Modern University II,* ed. T. Hillard et al. (Grand Rapids, 1998), 391–400, uses Ambrose as a counter to MacMullen's argument from John Chrysostom: I am indebted to Professor Rousseau for an offprint.
53. Mainz, 62; the record was previously held by *en. in ps.* 93 (*CCSL* 39: 1300–30). For theatricality in John Chrysostom, see Blake Leyerle, *Displays of Holiness* (Berkeley, fc): I am most grateful to Prof. Leyerle for allowing me to read the ms before publication.

The Continuity of Paganism between the Cities and Countryside of Late Roman Africa

DAVID RIGGS

THE IMPETUS FOR THIS ARTICLE IS MY FRUSTRATION WITH THE CONVENTIONAL representation of pagan religion, which continues to inform so many accounts of Christianization in the Roman world. Namely, that "paganism was a mosaic of established religions linked to the political order" which "could be suitably practiced only within the framework of the State, municipal or imperial."[1] It logically follows from this view, of course, that once the emperors had severed pagan religion from its political context, it was no longer a force to be reckoned with, and as a consequence scholars either ignore or marginalize any "unofficial" expressions of pagan worship that might have survived beyond the fourth century.[2] This is especially true with regard to the cultic practices of the provincial countryside. For such practices, when mentioned at all, are routinely characterized as the stubborn superstitions of an under-Romanized and ignorant peasantry, who by their nature were bound to continue in remote places regardless of whether Greco-Roman paganism or Christianity dominated society, and who were, therefore, a minor concern to the church.[3]

The evidence for pagan religion in the central North African provinces of Proconsularis, Byzacena, and Numidia, however, reveals the shortcomings of this view.[4] For one thing, the epigraphic and archaeological records clearly show that the official cults were merely one of several important contexts within which North Africans worshipped their gods. Indeed, what is most striking about the traces of Romano-African religious life that survive is not the exceeding importance of public religion, but rather the prevailing belief among individuals that their gods were willing and able to meet all their needs.[5] As a consequence of this belief, we find a plurality of cultic activities that were as manifold as the daily preoccupations of individuals. For just as concern for the well-being of one's city prompted participation in its official cults, so one's concerns about other matters such as health, profit, love, weather, employment, travel, social status, personal safety, and the harvest also inspired diverse acts of piety in various contexts. And unless we are prepared to minimize the importance of such concerns to the men and women of Roman Africa, then we must recognize that it was through all of these various contexts that the gods dominated the daily lives of individuals.

Ultimately, then, instead of treating Romano-African paganism as a religious system intimately linked to the political order, it appears more faithful to the evidence to conceptualize it in terms of a decentralized and complex system of patronage between individuals and their patron gods, which permeated all levels of society and, therefore, offered worshippers access to divine providence on a number of different levels in their public and private lives. Accordingly, this patronage relationship could take on important collective meaning and shape in the political life of a city without it losing its transcendent nature and significance. In other words, the political sphere was embedded in the religious system, and not vice versa.

It is also important to emphasize (as others have recently) the extent to which pagan religion in Roman North Africa was a uniquely "Romano-African" construct; that is, one created by provincials who actively integrated native and Roman elements in accordance with their dual sense of identity as both "Africans" and "Romans."[6] In this regard, pagan religion in Roman Africa cannot be easily cast in terms of distinctly "Roman" or "indigenous" traditions. I would, in addition, stress that "Romano-African" religion was not a phenomenon created simply among the sophisticated urban élites.[7] For although there may have been a number of native Africans whose religious outlook differed very little from their Punic or Libyan ancestors, there were many individuals among the non-élite classes who were willing to actively integrate new and old religious traditions into their personal piety.

If we consider the place of rural worship in this religious milieu (which will be our focus from this point), the first thing to keep in mind is the extraordinary degree to which life in the cities and the countryside of central North Africa was interconnected in the Imperial period. Statements like the following by the notable church historian W. H. C. Frend do not fairly represent the urban-rural relationship in our chosen area of study. He writes:

> Romans, Greeks and Jews might contest for supremacy of the cities, but beyond the city walls was barbarism, represented by a succession of conquering and conquered races, retaining their own customs, crafts and languages . . . between town and countryside, citizen and barbarian, there was little love lost.[8]

In our present case, such an impression is belied by certain interrelated developments in North Africa during the Roman empire, which transformed settlement patterns and greatly encouraged the integration of urban and rural milieu.

Perhaps the most important of these developments was the phenomenal expansion of agricultural production. Already one of the major granaries of the empire in the first century, the African provinces soon became equally famous for their prosperous olive cultivation, and from about the early third century the region emerged as the "epicentre of Mediterranean trade."[9] The intensification of agrarian exploitation and the thriving agricultural industry it generated had many profound effects on culture and society. On the one hand, the profits from this economy permitted an extraordinary expansion of urban construction unparalleled in other Western provinces. By the third century, central North Africa had thus become marked by a rather dense network of Romano-African towns (of various size and status), which continued to grow during the fourth century, and remained prosperous on the eve of the Vandal invasion.[10]

Key for our present discussion is that this flowering of urbanization brought an increasing number of peasants within comfortable walking distance of Romanized civic centers. This, in turn, generated a more significant ebb and flow between town and countryside as rural populations took advantage of urban markets, frequented various amusements, and participated in religious festivals.[11] In addition, it is important to note that, unlike the large metropoleis Carthage and Cirta, most of the prosperous Romano-African cities were essentially the "civilized nuclei" of agricultural districts.[12] The built-up residential sectors of these cities were often small and might be limited to households of the local élite whose farms funded the public buildings, temples, monuments, and various amenities. The majority of the city's population were farmers who lived and worked in the fields of the adjacent municipal territory, and looked to the nearby civic center for their commercial, religious, social, and legal interests. Or, some scholars have suggested that, considering the exceptionally small territoria characteristic of African towns, perhaps some individuals commuted each day between urban dwellings and their fields.[13] In any case, the point remains that most people breathed in a steady dose of both town and country air.

Equally important is how the prospering agricultural economy, within the context of the spread of Romanization, tended to bring the urban world into the countryside. At the center of much of this phenomenon were the ubiquitous rural estates, which provided the framework for so much of Africa's agrarian production. These estates, whether owned by the state or private landholders, represented the most important focal points for everyday life outside the cities. In many cases the estate might be an important place of retreat for its owner or lessor, and so the central villa could grow to include many of the monumental features of Romano-African civic life, which he or she cherished. We also know from certain North African martyr accounts that it was not uncommon for Roman administrators to conduct official proceedings on rural estates.[14]

What is perhaps even more significant, however, is that the prosperity of the agricultural economy also enabled many among the rural population in central North Africa to make their own contributions to the spread of Romano-African urbanization. We find numerous cases where, instead of clinging exclusively to Libyan or Punic traditions, farmers (who in many instances included Roman citizens) were quite keen to augment their rural settlements with the features of Roman civic life. Whether on private or imperial estates, in municipal territoria, or on the fringes of any of these, various kinds of agrarian communities applied their disposable income toward the development of quasi-civic centers complete with colonnades, arches, and most especially, temples.[15] Some of these even evolved, eventually, into full-fledged towns. The Kasserine survey, for instance, has brought to light a community on the periphery of the municipal territory of Cillium in Byzacena, which possessed a forum, a temple, baths, fountains, and a street grid, alongside substantial agricultural facilities (including twenty-two olive presses and extensive field and water control systems around the settlement).[16]

Such a site embodies well the intimate symbiosis between urban and rural life, which came to characterize so much of the central African landscape in the Roman period. The simultaneous expansions of urbanization and agricultural production, and the substantial population increase it seems to have fostered, nourished a thick diffusion of Romano-African society and culture, which greatly diminished the social and intellectual distance between town and countryside. In such a context, we would expect to find a significant degree of religious continuity between the cities and the rural districts, especially if we accept the representation of Romano-African paganism that I proposed earlier: i.e., a decentralized system of divine patronage which was rooted in the daily preoccupations of individuals, and accordingly inspired a plurality of important contexts of worship alongside the civic public cults. Not surprisingly, there is plenty of evidence to substantiate our expectation. In the interest of brevity, I shall limit my account of such evidence to a few examples that show that the goddess Caelestis was an important divine patron in both the cities and the countryside of Roman Africa.

Caelestis was a thoroughly "Romano-African" deity. As the great patron goddess of Punic Carthage, she was known as Tanit to her African worshippers, whereas the Romans (who associated her with Jupiter's consort) referred to her as Juno "Caelestis." By the Roman imperial period she was usually identified by the Latin epithet alone, and her status as the chief tutelary deity of Roman Carthage was reinforced in the second century with the dedication of a magnificent new temple complex in the African capital by (in all likelihood) the emperor Marcus Aurelius.[17] She was similarly honored with temples and official cults in many other cities throughout North Africa,[18] while both the epigraphic and archaeological records testify to her veneration in several private contexts among the various urban classes.[19]

Tertullian, however, also described Caelestis as the "promiser of rain" (pluviarum pollicitatrix), and indeed like so many other prominent deities in the Romano-African pantheon her role as a patron of agricultural production was no less prominent than her role as a protector of cities.[20] Her cult thus held great appeal in the central North African countryside. The ephemeral nature of many of these cultic rites, such as the offering of the first fruits of the harvest to the goddess on turf altars, prevents us from ever being able to document the full extent of Caelestis' influence over the rural population.[21] Nevertheless, thanks to the increased affluence and civic ambitions among African tenant-farmers and estate owners, the rural cult of the goddess also inspired monumental forms in the Roman period that do survive in the historical record. We possess an inscription from an imperial estate in Africa Proconsularis, for instance, which records the restoration of a temple to Caelestis Augusta by a local group of coloni. These tenant farmers had not only rebuilt the collapsing temple with their own funds (sua pecunia), but had also adorned the sacred structure with new columns (*ILTun.* 1568). On what appears to be another imperial estate, we again find the commemoration of repair works on a local temple of Caelestis, this time owing to the piety of an imperial slave (or freedman).[22] The remains of a Roman-style temple with colonnades and an assortment of votive steles in the mountainous countryside between present-day Kairouan and Kasserine (at Henchir-es-Srira) has likewise been associated with the worship of Caelestis. The decorative style of the steles found at the site and the names of their dedicants testify, just as the temple architecture does, to the impact of "Romanization" on these rural worshippers. Here, again, it appears as though the cult center served an estate community.[23] We find evidence for another rural temple to Caelestis in an inscription from Henchir-bel-Azeiz (this time from a privately-owned estate), though in this case it is not clear whether it was erected by a group of tenant farmers or by the estate's owner (*AE* 1980, 917).

The evidence from the province of Numidia is much the same. On the estate of a Roman senator between Milevus and Cuicul, the bailiff (a freedman of the senator) constructed a temple of Caelestis for the benefit of the local farming community (*CIL* 8. 8241). An even greater act of euergetism was performed by a landowner from Cirta, however, who built a quasi-civic center for the tenant farmers on his estate complete with "all buildings and columns and colonnades and arches," and erected a temple to Caelestis Augusta to preside over the new settlement (*ILAlg.* II.2. 6225). He also mentions that he has instituted a periodic market-fair to be held on the premises (nundinae) which suggests that the new temple, which had been fitted with benches (sedibus), was meant to accommodate more than just the devotees of the goddess on his estate. Another inscription from an estate situated in the Cirtan region (fundus Seneci [osus]) records the dedication of an unknown monument to Caelestis. The dedicant, a Roman citizen of unknown station, offered his gift "pro salute Imperatoris" (*CIL* 8.6351; *AE* 1991, 1687).

While I have limited myself here to some of the more conspicuous examples of the Caelestis cult in the countryside, the goddess also inspired great devotion in numerous rural sanctuaries of a more modest nature,[24] and scores of votive stelès and altars (with Latin dedications) attest to the personal piety of the worshippers who frequented these sites.[25] To all of this, I would add only that religious euergetism in the countryside was not limited to estate owners, bailiffs, and tenant farmers. We also have examples of municipal senates building temples several kilometers away from their cities, no doubt for the benefit of citizens who lived in the rural districts.[26]

The cult of Caelestis, of course, was not unique. The importance of Saturn (successor of African Ba'al) to religious life in the countryside, for instance, has been demonstrated many times over.[27] However, examples such as the rural shrine (a paganicum) built by "cultores Iovis Optimi Maximi" in the region surrounding Thala, the temple of Pluto dedicated to the tetrarchs on a fundus in Byzacena, the female priesthood of Ceres on the

Saltus Massipianus, or the altar erected to Jupiter (Deo Iovi) by "universi pagani" on a private estate (fundo Tigibelle), show that rural worship was not limited to the cults of Saturn and Caelestis.[28] In fact, archaeological and epigraphic evidence reveals that the cults of Jupiter, Mars, Ceres, Mercury, Magna Mater, Neptune, Pluto, Silvanus, Tellus, Hercules, Minerva, and Liber Pater all extended into the African countryside.[29] Although it is not possible here to illustrate the roles that each of these deities played in rural North Africa, the breadth of this list reinforces the impression given above by the cult of Caelestis: which is, that to characterize Romano-African paganism as primarily an urban phenomenon is to underestimate the potent diversity of this ubiquitous religious system.

• • •

In the early fifth century, Augustine (rather optimistically) assured a Roman official that the anti-Donatist legislation had reaped great rewards, citing the large crowds that had been saved by these laws "on the farms, through the countryside, in the villages, in the citadels, the towns, and the cities" (*Ep.* 85). This is an excellent illustration of how integral the rural milieu was to an African's outlook on everyday life. Romano-African society in the central North African provinces was one that embraced both the cities and the prosperous and densely-populated countryside, and as the case of Caelestis has shown, religion was no less a part of this continuity. This is not to say, of course, that no distinctions can be made between urban and rural expressions of worship. The influence of some gods, like Apollo and Aesculapius for instance, does not seem to have spread beyond certain cities in Roman Africa.[30] But what is important to focus on in the present case is: (1) most of the pagan gods who were honored in civic contexts also received worship to varying degrees among the rural population, while deities like Caelestis and Saturn seem to have been equally influential in both town and country; (2) agrarian prosperity was a powerful impetus for the spread of quasi-urban cult centers into the countryside; and (3) a number of individuals must have worshipped the gods in both urban and rural contexts at various times in their lives.

What then is the significance of all of this as we assess the challenge Romano-African paganism posed to the church's efforts to spread its influence? The simple answer, of course, is that the old religious system was a more formidable rival to the church than is commonly assumed. I have used the analogy of a system of patronage at certain points in this paper to emphasize that the essence of pagan religion was not public ritual, but rather a relationship of dependence between individuals and their divine patrons. Ultimately, this patronage relationship generated many diverse expressions of worship, because it was so closely linked to the various everyday needs and concerns that preoccupied such individuals. Since most of the prominent Romano-African gods maintained a clientele that included many whose lives and interests were often deeply rooted in the countryside, it follows that if the African church wished to supplant the influence of the pagan system of divine patronage in society, it had to confront it equally in both the towns and the rural districts. This is especially true if we consider that, as important as its city-based bishops were, the North African church itself was as much a rural as an urban phenomenon.[31]

In order to lend a more concrete form to the conclusions reached thus far, and to elucidate further the significance of rural contexts of pagan worship for our understanding of the Christianization of central North Africa, I wish to use this final section of the paper to highlight two revealing patristic texts from the early fifth century. First, portions of two canons from a church council held at Carthage in 401:

> 58: There remain still other requirements to be sought from the most pious emperors: that they should command the remaining idols throughout all Africa to be utterly destroyed, for in a number of coastal areas and in various *rural estates* the wickedness of such error flourishes. . . .
>
> 60: This too is to be requested, that, inasmuch as religious banquets (convivia) occur in many places contrary to the decrees, brought together by pagan error, so that now Christians are under pressure from pagans to join in such celebrations (and hence, under Christian emperors, another persecution seems to be carried on in secret), the emperors should order that they be prohibited and banned from both cities and *rural estates*. . . .

We not only find here good testimony to the vitality of rural pagan worship at the beginning of the fifth century, but also an explicit reference to the continuity of paganism between the cities and the countryside of Roman Africa. In addition, the date of these canons is significant. As far as we can tell from the evidence, a formal campaign against pagan religion was not introduced into North Africa until 399, when Honorius sent legislation and imperial agents to Carthage (no doubt at the request of local church leaders). That their first (of many) attempts to persuade the emperor to continue to press the issue included these references to rural paganism shows that the church's agenda for persecution had a dual focus on town and countryside from the outset.

The second text is a sermon Augustine preached in Carthage at some point during the first decade of the fifth century (*Sermo* 62). His message has two themes of interest for us here. On the one hand, he chastises members of the congregation for attending sacrificial banquets at pagan temples. It is clear from the context that these temples, which continued to function in defiance of the recent anti-pagan laws, were those located on rural estates in the Carthaginian countryside. Moreover, Augustine frankly admits that "many pagans have these abominations on their estates" (62.17), "staring us in the face" (62.18). Once again, then, we see the continued vigor of rural paganism in the early fifth century, and its significance within North African society.

On the other hand, Augustine also uses this sermon to respond to the indignation among local landowners over the recent destruction of idols on an estate that the church had come to possess. That Augustine would need to justify such an action is revealing in itself. In doing so, however, he also gives us clear insight into why rural paganism continued to thrive despite the anti-pagan laws and the objections of the church. For he reminds the landowners that the church did not encroach upon pagan cult sites on estates unless it had been given the authority to do so by the estate's owner, and he cites the prevalence of temples and idols in the countryside as proof of this policy. We might also add that it was not just the *pagan* landlords who prevented the suppression of religious freedom on their estates. In a letter to a Christian landowner who had persuaded the tenants on his estate to convert to Catholicism, Augustine commented upon how rare such actions were among the landed aristocracy in the church, and claimed that such inertia emboldened the church's enemies (*Ep.* 58). In this particular case, the enemies he has in mind are probably the Donatists. However, there is little doubt that many Christian landowners were also resistant to cracking down on pagan worship on their estates, whether to avoid antagonizing or losing the tenant farmers upon whom their profits depended or, in an age when Christian polytheism was common, they themselves may have been hesitant to reject those deities who had so faithfully safeguarded their agricultural investments for generations.

There is one final point worth mentioning with regard to Augustine's sermon. Supposedly the Christians who had attended the sacrificial banquets defended themselves by arguing that it was not a god who was honored at such rites, but only the "genius of Carthage" (62.10). We know, however, that unlike many other parts of the empire where genii might represent a rather vague concept of the supernatural, in Africa the genius of a city was consistently associated with a particular deity, and most often the city's chief tutelary deity.[33] Thus, for example, in the city of Sufes (in Byzacena) where sixty Christians were killed around 400 C.E. for desecrating a cult statue of Hercules, we know from epigraphic evidence that local residents considered Hercules to be the "genius" of their city. As Augustine pointed out to the Christian offenders in Carthage, the important thing was not what the genius actually was, but what the pagans believed it to be. And since Caelestis was *the* patron deity of Carthage, and was identified as the "genius civitatis" of other African cities, as well as being called the "genius terrae Africae," it is reasonable to surmise that she was the one being worshipped as the genius of Carthage at these sacrificial banquets in the countryside.[34] If this is the case, then we should view these rural cult sites as one of the important ways in which Caelestis was able to sustain her influence over the city of Carthage long after her official temple had been closed by the authorities in 399—an influence which, according to Salvian, remained powerful even into the 440s (*De Gub. Dei* 8.2).

The continued vitality of Romano-African paganism in the early fifth century was not, of course, sustained only by rural cult sites such as these.

On the one hand, public cults no doubt continued in many African cities unaffected by the anti-pagan legislation thanks to "the evil sloth of the judges, the connivance of the office staffs, and the contempt of the municipal senates" (as an edict posted at Carthage in 408 put it).[35] On the other hand, even in a city like Hippo Regius where Augustine's notable influence probably helped ensure that the official prohibition of paganism was largely enforced, the patronage relationship between the pagans and their gods continued to animate daily life through less conspicuous (though not less significant) contexts such as domestic shrines and private collegia. Thus, in spite of the wishes of the emperor and the bishops, the influence of the Romano-African gods remained a vital force in the fifth century in various areas of life. Yet as we have seen in the course of this paper, we can not hope to detect the true extent of this vitality, or hope to understand the dynamics and effects of Christianization in late Roman Africa, unless we first recognize the essential continuity of Romano-African paganism between the cities and the countryside, and then explore the significance of this latter context for the encounter between pagans and Christians in the *Christiana tempora*.

NOTES

I am grateful to Simon Price and Greg Woolf for reading various drafts of this article.

1. Pierre Chuvin, *A Chronicle of the Last Pagans,* (Cambridge, Mass., 1990), 6; 83. Cf. Paschoud, "L'intolérance chrétienne vue et jugée par les païens," *Cristianesimo nella Storia* 11 (1990): 546; "les païens ne pouvant concevoir les rites traditionnels que dans un cadre officiel, célébrés par le monarque et les dignitaires civils aux frais de l'Etat"; and Claude Lepelley, *Les Cités de l'Afrique Romaine au Bas-empire* (Paris, 1979), 1:333, 1:361–62. Garth Fowden has recently criticized this conventional interpretation in the *Cambridge Ancient History, XIII (a.d. 337–425),* ed. Averil Cameron and Peter Garnsey (Cambridge, 1998), 538.
2. Yet, Glen Bowersock, *Hellenism in Late Antiquity* (Ann Arbor, 1990), and Frank Trombley, *Hellenic Religion and Christianisation c. 370–529,* 2 vols. (Leiden, 1993), have now demonstrated that several pagan cults continued to thrive well into the sixth century in the Greek East without the supporting hand of the state.
3. Most recently, Ramsay MacMullen, *Christianity and Paganism in the Fourth to Eighth*

Centuries (New Haven, 1997), 64–72, describes rural paganism as "superstition," "a substratum of rites which address life's hopes and fears *without* appeal to any one being in particular"; meaning actions like the veneration of nature's elements or dependence on various good-luck charms. He also assumes, therefore, that rural paganism was a minor concern to Christian bishops "whose preoccupations were always city-bent."

4. See Lepelley, *Les Cités*, 37–57, on the fundamental differences in wealth and Romanization between these North African provinces and the Mauretanias to the west, and see David Mattingly, *Tripolitania* (London, 1995), 167, 210ff., for the degree to which Tripolitania differs from the rest of North Africa with respect to its religious history. The province of Numidia was created under Septimius Severus, while Byzacena remained part of Africa Proconsularis until the reign of Diocletian.
5. The thousands of surviving votive dedications, for example, testify both to the faith that people of all social classes had in the providence of the gods, and to the vigor of pagan worship outside the public sphere.
6. See e.g., J. B. Rives, *Religion and Authority in Roman Carthage from Augustine to Constantine* (Oxford, 1995), 100–72; Marcel Le Glay, "Les syncrétismes dans l'Afrique ancienne" in *Les syncrétismes dans les religions de l'antiquité*, ed. F. Dunand, P. Lévêque (Leyde, 1975), 123–51 and Le Glay, "Un centre de syncrétisme en Afrique: Thamugadi de Numidie," *L'Africa Romana* 8 (1991): 67–78. In addition, the evidence cited by Marcel Benabou, (*La résistance africaine à la romanisation* [Paris, 1976], 261–368) is helpful despite the author's misguided attempts to interpret it solely in terms of African "resistance" to Romanization. More generally on Romano-African society as a "new world," see D. Mattingly and B. Hitchner, "Roman Africa: An Archaeological Review," *JRS* 85 (1995): 204ff. For similar conclusions regarding "Gallo-Roman" religion, see Greg Woolf, *Becoming Roman: The Origins of Provincial Civilisation in Gaul* (Cambridge, 1998), 206–37.
7. Rives is concerned primarily with the "agenda of the local elite," while Le Glay (1975: 124) assumes that Romano-African syncreticizm was a "phénomène de classe" since (in his opinion) peasants were little inclined to reflect philosophically about their religious beliefs.
8. Frend, "Town and Countryside in Early Christianity" in *The Church in Town and Countryside*, ed. D. Baker (Oxford, 1979), 36–37.
9. Garnsey and Whittaker in *CAH* 13 (1998): 315. Grain: G. Rickman, *The Corn Supply of Ancient Rome* (Oxford, 1980), 108–12; 231–35; Olive: D. Mattingly *JRA* 1 (1988): 33–56. Cf. Mattingly and Hitchner, *JRS* 85 (1995): 190.
10. See P.-A. Février, "Urbanisation et urbanisme de l'Afrique romaine," *ANRW* II.10, no. 2 (1982): 321–76, on urban density. Lepelley discusses (and greatly advances) the recent shift in perspective on the extent and durability of Romanization in late Roman Africa in *Les Cités* (1979) and "The Survival and fall of the classical city in Late Roman Africa," in *The City in Late Antiquity*, edited by J. W. Rich (London, 1992), 51–71. Mattingly and Hitchner, *JRS* 85 (1995), provide a good general survey of recent scholarship pertaining to this subject (despite their emphasis on archaeological investigation).

11. MacMullen (*Roman Social Relations* [New Haven, 1974], 55), for instance, notes the presence in several Roman cities of a selection of amphitheater seats reserved for the people of a particular rural village (citing CIL 8.3293 from Lambaesis). For markets see MacMullen, "Market-days in the Roman Empire," *Phoenix* 24 (1970): 337ff. and B. D. Shaw, "Rural Markets in North Africa and the Political Economy of the Roman Empire," reprinted in *Rulers, Nomads and Christians in Roman North Africa* (1995), 42ff.
12. R. Duncan-Jones, "City Population in Roman Africa," *JRS* 53 (1963): 85f. Cf. A. N. Sherwin-White, "Geographical factors in Roman Algeria," *JRS* 34 (1944): 10.
13. B. H. Warmington, *The North African Provinces from Diocletian to the Vandal Conquest* (Cambridge, 1954), 55, and Lepelley, *Les Cités* (1979), 47–48. The latter has estimated that in many parts of central North Africa the average municipal territory was only around 140 km^2, which would mean of course that journeys between a town and its rural districts would not normally have been particularly burdensome.
14. *Acta Cypr.* §2; *Passio SS. Maximae, Donatilla et Secunda* §1.
15. See D.P. Kehoe, *The Economics of Agriculture on the Roman Imperial Estates in North Africa* (1988), 188–228.
16. Hitchner, "The Organisation of Rural Settlement in the Cillium-Thelepte Region (Kasserine, Central Tunisia)," *L'Africa Romana* 6 (1989): 391, which provides a more extensive list of finds than I recount here.
17. For the history of the cult of Caelestis see Halsberghe, "Le culte de Dea Caelestis," *ANRW*, ii, 17, no. 4 (1984): 2203–23, and Rives, *Religion and Authority in Roman Carthage*, passim. See Rives (66) regarding her temple at Carthage.
18. For example, the African cities of Cirta (*ILAlg.* II.804; 807), Mustis (*AE* [1968], 595), Thugga (C. Poinssot, *Les Ruines de Dougga* [Tunis, 1958], 41–44), Thuburbo Maius (A. Lezine, *Thuburbo Maius* [Tunis, 1968], 123–24), Lambaesis (AE [1957], 123; *CIL* 8.2592), Thysdrus (M. Le Glay, *Saturne Africain Histoire* [Paris, 1966], 216n. 6), Thala (*CIL* 8.23280; *ILAfr.* 195), Theveste (*ILAlg.* I.2997; 3066), Colonia Iulia Carpi(tanorum) (*CIL* 8.993), Thignica (Le Glay, *Saturne Africain Monuments*, I [Paris, 1961], 125n. 5), Vallis (*ILTun.* 1281), and Simmithus (AE [1993], 1885) have all left evidence of temples or public worship of Caelestis.
19. From the evidence for personal devotion to the goddess among civic populations we might mention examples of her devotees performing religious rites "ex viso," "iussu deae" or "ex praecepto deae" (e.g., *CIL* 8.8433; 26474 [with Poinssot, *op. cit.*, 72]; *ILAfr.* 352; 431; 1052; *ILAlg.* I.3000; II.468), the numerous ex-voto lamps and statuettes dedicated to her (e.g., at Thibaris: Le Glay, *SAM*, I, 101; at Thysdrus: *Mus. Alaoui, Suppl. 1*, 185, 769–773; at Carthage: ibid., 108, 160; and at Thuburbo Maius: ibid., 63, 1385), and the many small votive monuments erected in her honor: such as altars and steles (e.g., *ILAfr.* 226; 227; *CIL* 8.4286; 20743; *AE* [1955], 59; 124; [1957], 58; [1987], 1076; Le Glay, *SAM*, II, 140, nos. 22 and 23; *ILAlg.* II.472; 6864).
20. Tert., *Apolo.* 23.6. Cf. *CIL* 8.4635(=16810) from Naraggara.
21. Food and harvest offerings to the gods are depicted on several stèle reliefs, of which Le Glay, *SAM*, I, pl. X, 4, is a particularly well-preserved example. Cf. Augustine, *Epist.* 46 and Apuleius, *Apolo.* 56. See also *C.Th.* 16.10.12.2 and Maximus of Turin, *Serm.*

107.2 for references to turf altars.

22. *AE* (1957), 92b; Also evidence for worship of Cybele and Saturn at this site, which was located near the border of Proconsularis and Numidia (M. Le Glay, *Bulletin archéologique du Comité des travaux historiques et scientifiques* [1954], 194 and *SAM*, II, 11).
23. The double-cellae temple was jointly dedicated to Caelestis and Saturn. See L. Hautecoeur, "Les ruines de l'Henchir es-Srira, près Hadjeb-el-Aïoun (Tunisie)," *MEFR* 29 (1909): 365–400. Cf. M. Le Glay, *SAM*, I, 307f.; *SAH*, 89.
24. With regard to such cult centers, it is important not to mistake a lack of wealth or resources for a lack of religious sophistication or openness to the influence of Roman ideas.
25. The small rural sanctuary devoted to Caelestis and Saturn at Bir-Derbal is a good example of these less ornate cult sites. It is worth noting that the remains of a lavish residence were discovered in the vicinity of this cult site, which (as Le Glay points out) makes it tempting to relate the sanctuary, and two additional ones found in the immediate area, to an estate community: *SAM*, I, 287–89.
26. The decuriones in Thugga, for example, built a temple to Saturn some eight kilometers south of the city: *SAM* I, 216, no.6.
27. In the case of Saturn, although his role in the countryside has been well covered, his prominence in the public cults of the cities has been largely neglected, as Rives has pointed out (*op. cit.*, 142ff.). For a detailed discussion of Saturn worship in the cities, and of the significance of Roman citizens and Romano-African élites among his devotees, see the author's forthcoming Oxford D. Phil. thesis ("The Religious World of Late Roman Africa: A Reassessment of the Dynamics, Effects and Limits of Christianisation"), chapter I.2.
28. *CIL* 8.23326; 11732; *ILTun.* 267; *AE* (1993), 1755(=*CIL* 8.25966).
29. A fuller treatment of rural paganism in Roman Africa, which takes into account the evidence upon which this list of deities is based, may be found in the author's forthcoming D. Phil. Thesis, chapter I.7.
30. Yet, the African writer Arnobius does refer to a vintage festival in honor of Aesculapius (*Adv. Nat.* VII.32), and *CIL* 8.27356 may signal a rural temple of Aesculapius.
31. This fact is quite evident in the glimpses that Augustine's works give us into the everyday life of the church: see, for instance, *Ep.* 35; 44; 65; 105; 115; 139; 209; 222; 247; 10*; 15*; 20*; and *Civ. dei* XXII.8.
32. CCL 149: 196f (June 401); English translation borrowed (with slight revision) from E. Lane and R. MacMullen, *Paganism and Christianity, 100–425 c.e.: A Sourcebook*_ (Minneapolis, 1992), 287–88.
33. Jules Toutain (*Les cultes païens dans l'empire romaine*, t.1 [Paris, 1907], 450–51) cites examples from Sufes and Sua (Hercules), Bulla Regia (Apollo), and Thysdrus (Mercury); to which we might add Lambaesis and Naraggara (Hercules): *AE* (1973), 632; *ILAlg.* I.1183, Uzappa (Liber Pater): *CIL* 8.11924, Sitifis and Cuicul (Mars): *CIL* 8.8438; *BAC* (1912), 188, Mustis and Thugga (Pluto): *AE* (1968), 595; *CIL* 8.26496, and Thuburbo Maius (Caelestis): Ben Abdallah, *Les Inscriptions*, 328, 336, 343.

34. Caelestis was the "genius" of Thuburbo Maius (see preceding note). For "Genius terrae Africae" see Toutain, t.1, 451, and Rives, *Religion and Authority,* 69. It should be mentioned, however, that an inscription does survive from Dacia which may distinguish between the "genius" of Carthage and Caelestis (ILS 3923), though it is far from certain.
35. *C.Th.* 16.10.19 (= *Sirm. Const.* 12).

From Pagan to Christian in Cities of Roman Anatolia during the Fourth and Fifth Centuries

KENNETH W. HARL

THE SHIFTING RELIGIOUS LANDSCAPES IN ROMAN ANATOLIA DURING THE FOURTH and fifth centuries are but part of a wider story of the Christianization of Asia Minor. I must request the indulgence of archaeologists, as I, a historian and numismatist, shall offer observations on how public buildings, street plans, and shrines were transformed between the first and sixth centuries A.D. A review of the current archaeological record raises significant questions as to changing relationship between cities and their countrysides (the chora), and so the issue as to when and how Christianity might have been received in villages and townships of Anatolia.

Excavations as yet have not revealed the full extent of the shrines and temples in any single city in Asia Minor, including Aphrodisias where Professors Ratté and Smith have plotted a virtually complete map of the city (save for the southeastern quadrant).[1] Even with a glance at any map of Turkey today, one can observe that the two dozen excavated sites (and surveys) are concentrated on the Aegean shore, along with its hinterlands of Lydia, Phrygia, and Caria, and on the southern Mediterranean littoral. Only recently have Professor Fredrik Hiebert and his team from the University of Pennsylvania commenced a survey of the Euxine shore, and Roger Mathews of the British Institute is heading a survey of ancient Paphlagonia. Classical sites in northeastern and eastern Anatolia remain, and probably will remain, largely unknown to us because the principal cities are astride the North Anatolian fault line so that the cities have been prey to repeated earthquakes and rebuilding. Therefore, the densely populated modern Turkish cities of Amasya (Amasia), Tokat (Dazimon), Sivas (Sebasteia), Kasyeri (Caesarea), Divriğli (Tephrice), Erinzcan (Erzica), and Erzurum (Theodosiopolis), boast as their earliest visible monuments enchanting Seljuk, Danishmend, and Mongol medresses and mosques, for these cities are astride the invasion route followed by the Seljuk Turks, victorious over the Byzantines after the Battle or Manzikert in 1071, and by the Mongol army that crushed Seljuk power at Köse Dağin 1243.[2] In short, the present archaeological record of Late Antique Asia Minor parallels the record of the literary sources, inscriptions, and coins that illuminate life in cities of the Mediterranean shores and the hinterlands of the western riverine valleys.

Despite these qualifications, the current archaeological record yields a number of crucial points about religious change in cities and their hinterlands. In contrast to many works published on pagan cults, two main features of religious change can be seen in the cities of Roman Asia Minor. First, public worship in architecture and rites were dignified in Hellenic guises. Second, the civic cults were expanded in their political content by being linked to the veneration of the Roman emperor.[3] This conclusion, based on the physical remains of cities, is at odds with the received opinion since Franz Cumont that has stressed the rise of mystery cults, syncretist confusion of cults (and so the loss of faith in the traditional gods in favor of newcomers), and a flight to irrational, secretive, and private worship over public worship.[4] Such changes have been invoked as creating a religious atmosphere conducive to conversion of pagans to Christianity from the late third through the fifth centuries.

Instead, as pointed out by a number of historians, cities of the Roman world recovered political stability and prosperity during the first century of the Principate under the Julio-Claudian emperors.[5] Then, over the next 165 years, from the Flavian through Severan ages, local elites spent their money on decorating their cities in such splendor that the ruins still awe tourists today. The architectural history of shrines at Anatolian cities thus reveals how public cults were housed in ever more splendid Greek style temples during the Principate. From the reign of Hadrian (117-38) on, many pre-Greek shrines of local or regional importance, such as Labranda in Caria or Aezanis in Phrygia, were transformed into great centers of empire-wide importance. Aezanis was a prime case of how imperial patronage and membership in the Panhellenion changed the local Anatolian divinity into Zeus Aezanitis.[6] The temple and city prospered from the mid-second through the late fifth century, drawing their wealth from pilgrimage and commerce attached to this Hellenized cult. The upper classes of Aezanis, as they prospered, commissioned unique funerary monuments from the second century on, a variation of the so-called North Phrygian tomb doors, finely carved false entrances to family inhumation graves.[7] With the new Hadrianic temple (built in a monumental, almost baroque, Ionic order) came quays, bridges, a market (where the Price Edict was later erected), newly uncovered colonnaded streets, two bath complexes, and the unusual complex of theater and stadium. Aezanis became more than a showcase of fancy building, for she was also a market and religious center drawing residents of villages and satellite towns to celebrate the common cults at high holidays.

The embellishment of buildings and ennobling of festivals at Aezanis were repeated at scores of other shrines.[8] At the common Carian sanctuary of Labranda, the buildings erected by the Hectamonid dynasts of the fourth century B.C. presented the pilgrim with a pleasing mix of Ionic and Anatolian features.[9] This sanctuary, which was administered by the city of Mylasa in the valley below, retained its architectural coherence despite expansion and improvements throughout the early imperial age. Pilgrims who ascended the magnificent pine clad mountain sacred to Carian Zeus, patron of the honey bees, were filled with awe for the antique venerable buildings of Labranda in a fashion similar to Medieval pilgrims who viewed the Romanesque church of Vézelay in an era of high Gothic cathedrals at Paris.

Most dramatic of all was Hierapolis, still a mecca for countless tourists seeking the thermal waters among the bleached limestone cliffs dubbed Pamukkale or "Cotton Fortress" by the first Turkomens arriving in the eleventh century. Four decades of excavations have dramatically increased our knowledge of this sanctuary in southwestern Phrygia on a limestone plateau overlooking the lush Lycus Valley.[10] The thermal springs and cavern exuding noxious gases (celebrated as the Plutonium) were long held as sacred to an Anatolian divinity who was assimilated to his Hellenic counterpart as Apollo Lairbenos.[11] The Attalid kings of Pergamum elevated the mountain shrine to a Greek style city Hierapolis (perhaps in opposition to rival Laodicea ad Lycum, a Seleucid foundation on the plain that dominated the road systems).[12] From the Flavian through Severan ages, Herapolis enjoyed imperial patronage. After most of the Hellenistic city was leveled by an earthquake in 60 A.D., the proconsul of Asia, Sex. Julius Frontinus (c. 85-86), rebuilt the city's two monument gates and the axial street running north from the necropolis to the south end. In the Hadrianic age, a new public center was constructed in the northeastern quarter of the city (recently uncovered by the Italian team), and this center, complete with civic basilica, provided markets and public space for the growing city. The sanctuary of Apollo Lairbenus, toward the center of the city, was also improved. The Plutonium was redecorated and linked to the main temple, and a colossal nymphaeum was added just to the northwest of the temenos wall and along the northern side of the axial street. To the southeast and above the shrine rose a Roman-style theater, opulently decorated in the Antonine and Severan baroque style and conveniently located for housing citizens and pilgrims on high holidays. But the sacred spring and main temple still elude proper study inasmuch as they are the centerpiece of the swimming pool of the Pamukkale Motel, which caters to large tour groups at West European prices. Bronze coins, minted by Hierapolis in 221, reveal that the festival to Apollo Lairbenus was elevated to Actian and Pythian status by the heliocentric emperor Elagabalus (218-22).[13]

The record from Hierapolis also points to the extensive rebuilding that followed each earthquake that struck Anatolia during the Principate. Earthquakes, such as the disastrous one reported by Tacitus that toppled twelve cities of Asia in A.D. 17, shattered and ruined many Hellenistic and pre-Greek cities that were then rebuilt along Roman lines.[14] Surviving city plans not only at Hierapolis, but also major cities such as Sardes or Nicaea show major remodeling along grid systems. Rebuilding occasioned the refurbishing and expansion of cults, and their association with the imperial cult. With the grander shrines came imperial festivals and city titles that marked the city as favored by emperors, and advertised of city games as "panhellenic" and sacred or imperial games such as Actian games. By 235, the worship of the gods of Anatolia had attained its most articulated form, for dedications to city gods, endowments for festivals, and building inscriptions record the boom in construction of shrines and public buildings from the Flavian through early Severan ages. The process can also be documented by depiction of well-known cult statues, such as Artemis Ephesia or Zeus Labrandus, which are depicted as decked out in ever more elaborate costumes (ὁ κόσμος) on civic coins minted between the Augustan and Severan ages.[15]

Since many cities of Asia Minor escaped the worst of the political and military crisis of 235-84, there is little or no evidence that the so-called crisis of the third century generated a rush of disillusioned pagans to Christianity. In contrast to the gloomy images that fill textbooks stand epigraphic dedications to the gods and, above all, civic bronze coins. At cities throughout Asia Minor, the pagan ruling classes down to the reign of Gallienus (253-68) linked the fortunes of their cities with those of the Roman emperor and the gods. On the north paraodos of the theater at Aphrodisias, which served as the archival wall of the city, petitions to successive emperors down to the reigns of Valerian (253-60) and Gallienus, along with polite imperial responses, were duly carved.[16] City notables ever expanded the scale of festivals which played a vital role in linking the religious, social, and economic life of cities with their hinterlands. The process is best glimpsed in the remarkable dedications by the Stratonicean notables who expanded the festivals of the goddess Hecate at the Carian shrine of Lagina and of Zeus Panamaros.[17] As Peter Brown once noted, "The third century, as we know it, does not appear to have happened at Straonikeia."[18] Even more telling is the recently published Hadrianic endowment in which the local benefactor Demosthenes (with the approval of the governor Flavius Aper) specifies the expenditure of the interest on the principal to ensure that Oenoanda, a remote Lycian city in the mountains, had a proper Greek style city festival each summer.[19] Upon this pagan ruling class in the cities Diocletian

(284-305) and later Julian (360-63) had every reason to base their revival of the cults. Therefore, traditional families at such cities as Aezanis, Mylasa, Hierapolis, Stratonicea, and Aphrodisias continued to repair and remodel their shrines, and many cities of Roman Anatolia still presented a pagan image in their architecture and public worship perhaps as late as the mid–fifth century, particularly cities of lesser rank that were not centers of imperial administration or homes to early Christian communities.[20]

This public worship was accompanied by the proliferation of stately funerary monuments so that main gates of each Anatolian city were approached through suburbs of necropoleis by the mid-second century.[21] In part, families stressed the wealth and prestige by erecting such memorials, but funerary monuments were also linked with ancestor worship, and the veneration of traditional mores, by an upper class so vital in maintaining the public worship of the old gods. Most often, as at Hierapolis, the necropolis were located immediately before the main city gates so that visitors passed instantly from the ancestral to the living city. Such cities of the dead must have been integrated with the living city by repeated family celebrations and memorial services. An equally elaborate necropolis survives just outside and below the western district of the Lycian mountain city of Pinara.[22] The streets of the necropolis run along a deep ridge (between city and the face of a cliff) and were lined with traditional house tombs as well as imposing rock tombs cut into the mountain façade opposite the western edge. At the Lycian cities of Tlos, Arycanda, and Myra monumental tombs were either erected or incorporated within the limits of the Roman city proper (although possibly not in the original settlement). In Rough Cilicia, temple tombs to deceased ancestors are easily mistaken as shrines to the gods. Pilgrims left the humid Cilician shore from the port of Seleucia on the Calycadnus (Göksuyu) to visit the great Corinthian temple of Zeus Olbios, an Anatolian cult center nestled in the Taurus foothills among the Mediterranean scrub and pine trees and rechristened in the Roman age as the city of Diocaesarea.[23] These pilgrims trod a route flanked by magnificent necropoleis of temple tombs of satellite townships. These temple tombs, such as those at Imbrigon (Demircili), were arranged along terraced streets with stunning vistas toward the sea so that the pilgrim was treated to a preview of the even more imposing architecture of the sanctuary of Zeus Olbios with its colossal Corinthian temple.

Christians destroyed funerary monuments of their pagan ancestors with the same zeal with which they attacked the shrines of the old gods. Pagan funerary monuments were frequently dumped as fill in foundations of cites remodeled as Christian centers in the fifth and sixth century.[24] This was the case at Amorium, which is currently being excavated by Christopher Lightfoot.[25] In the reign of Zeno (473-91) or Anastasius (491-518), the citadel of Amorium (the *hüyük* of the modern Turkish village of Hisar) was constructed from the debris of the Roman city, and on the northwest slopes it is still possible to glimpse inside the citadel to view pagan funerary monuments of the second and third centuries stacked upon each other. Anatolian Christians long feared the tombs and sarcophagi of their pagan ancestors as the haunts of demons. Hence, they treated the monuments as *spolia*, incised crosses on them to ward off demons, or buried them. At the end of the sixth century, Saint Theodore of Skyeon exorcized from many Christian villagers of Galatia demons who had swarmed out of their resting places, pagan tombs, which had been inadvertently disturbed.[26]

The picture painted is one of a rich pagan heritage that drew together residents of city and countryside in Asia Minor, and this picture raises questions as to the process of Christianizing cities and countryside in the Dominate. Shrines and public buildings (whether pagan or Christian) provided the sacred places where citizens and guests celebrated the divine, and held markets and games that wove residents of cities, villages, and rural demes or townships into a community. The image of the ancient city as a parasite on the countryside, ultimately a Marxist construct, is not very illuminating, and recent studies on ties of patronage between countryside and city convey a much more subtle network of political and social relationships comparable to those of an Italian Renaissance city and its *cantado*. Furthermore, the number of Christians in Asia Minor before 325 is an issue that can be addressed only in part here. Christian funerary monuments from select cities of Phrygia are consistent with the existence of discrete communities of apostolic and heretical churches in central Asia Minor prior to 325.[27] These Greek-speaking Christians, many of whom retained ties with synagogues or practiced the beliefs of their Jewish cousins, were members of a distinct minority that had adapted themselves to the social mores of their cities or towns. Whatever number we wish to accept, in 325 the cities of Asia Minor were pagan in their public architecture and rituals. We have no idea of the size and type of churches anywhere in the Roman world prior to 325 save for the so-called house church excavated at Dura-Europos on the Euphrates frontier.[28]

Once Constantine reunited the Roman Empire in 324, the pagan appearance of Roman cities in Asia Minor began to change, but Constantine and his heirs faced a daunting task. Powerful bishops of an imperial church had the means to construct magnificent basilican churches in downtowns and so attract converts, but it took the bishops between 75 and 200 years to rewrite the architectural and social landscape of Anatolian cities.[29] For even a modest city of 20,000 residents required dozens of major churches, along with chapels, martyria, and lesser shrines. Throughout the fourth and fifth centuries, bishops employed a subtle combination of their access to imperial largess, their own wealth and social rank, and their personal holiness, to build for themselves powerful positions of dominance within their native cities, and they transmitted their position to their successors.[30] A charismatic bishop, and his family, could exert a powerful and immediate impact upon reshaping the architecture and religious beliefs of his city. This process is best documented for the city of Caesarea Mazaca in Cappadocia (today eastern Turkey) by the voluminous writing of members of this city's great episcopal family of Caesarea, notably the brilliant brothers Saint Basil of Caesarea (c. 330–79) and Saint Gregory of Nyssa (c. 330–95). Members of this family, who were long respected for their piety and the antiquity of their faith by fellow Christians, after 325 assumed leadership not only of a church enriched by the patronage of the imperial court at Constantinople and swollen with recent converts, but of the entire city of Caesarea Mazaca as well. For the father and namesake of Saint Gregory Nazianzus, a prominent pagan magistrate and civic patron, converted when he beheld a vision "at the very time it happened that a number of bishops were hurrying to the Council of Nicaea" in 325.[31] This processional display of religious and imperial power so filled Gregory with awe that he converted to the new faith, and by 328 he was a bishop of his native city. The elder Gregory was rapidly ordained a deacon and then a bishop, and given his social position and wealth he carried many of his fellow citizens over to the new faith, offering his city its first church in thanks for his conversion in 329—fewer than four years after his conversion. The success of Christianity in the Dominate hinged on the rank, wealth and prestige of its leading members (as at Caesarea) rather than its overall numbers. For most pagans, this was the measure of the power of a cult, the success of its followers, rather than mere numbers. It was this reasoning that explains why so many pagans would have considered the new faith once the emperor Constantine embraced it.

The current archaeological record for the period between Constantine (306-37) and Justinian (527-65) suggests three phases (rather than strict periods) in the Christianization of sacred places within and around cities of Asia Minor. In the initial phase, dating between the mid-fourth and late fifth century (depending on local circumstances), Roman imperial authorities assisted in the construction of the first significant basilican churches (often positioned to interrupt the pagan public areas or to draw crowds away from well known pagan shrines). Emperors and bishops often moved cautiously, if deliberately, in constructing the first churches, because, until the imperial church was in a position to attract crowds, and so win converts, Christianity remained a minority faith in many cities.

This first phase can be documented earliest at major cities where a basilica was given to the Christian community by such emperors as Constantine (306-37), Constantius II (337-61) or Theodosius I (379-95). The basilica quite often was a remodeled imperial or public building of the second or third century. Until recently such seemed to have been the case of the celebrated Church of Mary Theotokos at Ephesus, often dated to the reign of Constantius II (337-61). This church, in the harbor district and just off the axial Arcadiane, was constructed into the south stoa of the Temple to Hadrian Olympius, which was built in 130-32 and enclosed by a temenos wall with stoa before 200. The present church was constructed in the western half of the southern stoa, and the eastern arm was remodeled as the residence of the bishop (*episkopeion*). Each end of the southern stoa ended in an apsidal exedra, possibly the location of statues of Caracalla and Geta who were hailed the "New Sons" (υέοι ῾Ηλιοι) on city coins bearing the title of a third neocorate.[32] This church of Mary Theotokos has been usually dated to the mid–fourth century, and its prime location interrupted the previous layout of religious and public space, drawing visitors arriving at the harbor to the new imperially sponsored basilican church.

Doubts have been recently raised over the dating of this present church, because ceramics and coins point to a date around 500 A.D. for the construction of the outer walls (which enclosed the colonnade of the stoa and so turned the columns into the interior partition between nave and aisles). But the dating of the outer walls may not be conclusive, and the stray coins from the floor of the bishop's palace at the eastern end of the former south stoa date from the mid–fourth to mid–sixth century so that the church at the west end of the complex could well be one where the Third Ecumenical Council convened in 431.[33] By 400, the rest of the Olympieion was dismantled, and turned into a quarry, and residents melted many marble blocks into lime—an action readily associated with the visit of the Patriarch John Chrysostom in 401-40. During his visit, John might have also ordered that the Artemisium be demolished so that the removal of two major temples of Ephesus from view might have been taken in tandem with the construction of expansion of churches.[34] Whenever the date of the construction of the first Church of Mary Theotokos, visitors arriving at the harbor of Ephesus would have seen from afar two splendid churches to the patron saints of the city—the church of Saint John just to the north of the late antique city and atop the waterless hill Ayasoluk (the settlement of the Middle and Late Bronze and then the Middle Byzantine Age), and the church of Mary Theotokos in the harbor quarter. Between these monumental basilican churches lay the swamp with the melancholy ruins of the Artemisium. Since Christians had quite early associated Ephesus with the translation of Mary to Heaven and the final resting places of St. Luke and St. John, it was imperative that Constantine, his sons, and their successors rewrite the religious geography of Ephesus and her hinterland just as they initiated Christian building programs at imperial capitals such as Treveri, Milan, Rome, and Constantinople.[35]

Sardes, the ancient Lydian capital, boasted an ancient Jewish community, which received from the city a spacious basilica next to the Severan bath and gymnasium that was opulently remodeled into a synagogue around 300 A.D. This synagogue, along with complaints by the city's Apologist Melito concerning Judaizing practices, suggests that Christians at Sardes were long the poor step children to the synagogue.[36] Given the importance of the Jewish community at Sardes, the emperor Constantius II (337–61) perhaps gave his blessing to a Christian basilican church that overlooked the wealthy residences along the banks of the Pactolus River. This so-called church EM is securely dated to 348–52 by coins found beneath the floor's pavement.[37] Such an adaptation of the basilica, an imperial building, to the place of worship of the New Faith resulted in a steady, but dramatic, transformation of the orientation and look of sacred places within the cities of Anatolia.

If we return to Hierapolis, in the Lycus valley and home of the shrine to Apollo Lairbenus, this city too had early Christian associations, for here St. Philip the Evangelist was martyred for his faith in 80, and from this city his four virgin daughters uttered orthodox prophecies that inspired the later sectarian Montanist seers Priscilla and Maximilla.[38] When Hierapolis was again damaged by earthquake in the later fourth century, the city was rebuilt. The northern baths were converted, in part, into a church and the colonnaded north-south axis road of the pagan city lost some of its primacy. Two basilician churches were constructed just off this axial road, perhaps in the fifth century, and so greeted visitors well before they ever reached the ruined shrine of Apollo. Likewise, the spacious Hadrianic public center of the pagan city was largely abandoned. Instead, the road leading from eastern gate gained precedence, because just outside the eastern gate loomed the martyrium of St. Philip constructed in the late fifth century along an octagonal plan and located over a spring that must have been long venerated.[39]

Therefore, the first Christian churches were often positioned to attract crowds, and to break the symmetry or patterns of movement within cities as at Ephesus. At Hierapolis Christians turned the second century baths into a church; the baths were those that stood before the north gate that led to the axial Flavian street, perhaps in the early fifth century, and so a church henceforth greeted visitors before they ever reached the shrine of Apollo. But if major cities with early Christian associations and with imperial patronage were so remodeled in the fourth and early fifth centuries, many lesser cities yield little trace of early Christian basilicas. In cities such as Aezanis, Aphrodisias, or Mylasa, pagan decurions weathered the crisis of the third century and the conversion of Constantine, and so preserved their shrines to the ancestral gods, and the pagan appearance of their cities.

Constructing basilicae was just a start. During the second phase, prelates and ever more Christian decurions expanded and articulated the places of Christian worship within their cities, and Christianized the haunts of pagans outside the city walls such as springs and mountain tops. Particularly renowned pagan shrines were often completely destroyed and left as memorials of the victory of the New Faith; such was the fate of Ephesus' Artemisium and quite possibly the shrine of Apollo at Hierapolis (although the latter might have been cast down by earthquake). But more temples were converted into churches during the fifth century. At present, Aphrodisias has yielded one of the best examples in the Mediterranean world of how a temple was converted into a church.[40] The pagans of Aphrodisias most likely blundered into backing the usurper Illus (484-88) against the emperor Zeno.[41] Zeno seized on this action as the justification to apply imperial bans on pagan worship against this rebel city and the stubborn pagan elite. Aphrodite's temple disappeared within a basilica, because the colonnades of a pagan temple were remodeled to serve as the inner partition between nave and aisles of the church. The Temple was reoriented west, and the city plan of Aphrodisias, save for the southeastern quarter, has revealed how roads were reoriented to the west side of the former temple. A bishop's palace was built next to the bouleuterion (or city council hall), and streets were remodeled accordingly, notably the boulevard leading from the public places of the north and south stoa and the baths of Hadrian (and so past the bishop's palace) to the hippodrome (which was incorporated as part of the late Roman wall as well as a center of chariot races). The Sebasteion, a monumental hallway dedicated to the imperial cult, was converted into public use, for coin finds from late fifth to early seventh century suggest that the lower level was turned into shops, and several relief panels of the upper level depicting figures of cult statues were chiseled out, although personifications and mythological incidents were left intact out of a sense of good taste.[42] Similar measures were taken to convert into churches two other celebrated temples of Zeus discussed earlier, those at Aezanis and Diocaesearea; the Temple of Cybele and Augustus at Ancyra (Ankara) should be added to this group. Such architectural rewrites of cities were repeated at scores of cities, but what is remarkable is that so many remodelings were conducted two or three generations after the laws of Theodosius I had outlawed pagan worship in 391-92.

A variation on this process comes from the Cilician city of Canytelis, which was rebuilt as Neapolis during the reign of Theodosius II (408-450).[43] The Hellenistic and Roman city was oriented around a great chasm, held to be sacred to Zeus Olbios, and in the fifth century three basilican churches were constructed (largely from spoilia taken from pagan buildings) to ring the natural phenomenon, and so re-sanctify the chasm as a Christian site. The case of Neapolis was also part of a wider story to Christianize and thus, re-sanctify springs, holy mountains, and extraordinary natural features long venerated since the Hittite era. This process can be documented only from the fifth century on, and some details are captured in the lives of saints, notably St. Theodore of Sykeon, or the missionary activity of Bishop John of Ephesus. Christian aetiological legends were invented about pagan locales, such as the springs located near the martyrium of St. Philip the Evangelist outside the east gate Hierapolis or the "Sleeper's Cave" on the eastern slopes of Mount Pion outside of Ephesus. In the phantasmagoric landscape Phrygian Highlands just north of Afyon, rock cut churches in such valleys as Ayazin date from the late fifth century at earliest. Many pagan shrines such as early rock carved Phrygian monuments to Cybele today known as Arslankaya and Büyük Kaplikaya near Doğer are still inaccessible to the modern traveler, and they apparently escaped notice of bishops and holy men long after the cities of the Justinianic age boasted cathedral churches.[44] A comparable architectural rewrite of the sacred landscape of the Anatolian peninsula occurred in the twelfth through fourteenth centuries when the *türbeler* and *tekkeler* (funerary memorials to pious Muslims) played the role of medresses and mosques in Seljuk cities.

The final phase of Christianizing cities climaxed in the reign of Justinian (527-65) as many cities constructed magnificent domed cathedral churches modeled after great domed churches of Constantinople such as Saint Polyeuctus, Hagia Eirene, or Hagia Sophia.[45] As yet few of these churches have received study inasmuch as attention is paid to the Classical monuments at most sites. In 535/36, with Justinian's blessings and money, Bishop Hypatius commenced construction on the St. John's, crowning the arid hillock Ayasuluk with a three-storied cathedral church with six domes.[46] With so awesome a cathedral church, the next bishop John of Amida (542-71), a moderate Severan Monophysite, conducted vigorous missionary campaigns, reputedly converting 80,000 souls in the diocesis of Asiana; razing numerous temples and groves; and building 96 churches and 12 monasteries.[47] At Hierapolis, this third phase is represented by what must have been similarly magnificent cathedral the southwest district just off the axial north-south Flavian road, and just south of the sanctuary of Apollo. On the southern shores of Anatolia 2 such cathedral churches await proper study. The first is at Xanthus, a Lycian city known for her Classical and Hellenistic monuments. A cathedral church, possibly of late fifth or early sixth century date, was built over a residential district of Hellenistic origin and off a major colonnaded street.[48] On the Pamphylian shore, none of the pagan shrines of Perge has yet been located, and the foundations of 6 churches await proper study; but in the lower city, what was probably a cathedral church of late fifth or early sixth-century date, is just off the axial road from the Hellenistic monumental gate to the nymphaeum at the base of the acropolis.[49] By the death of Justinian, most cities in Asia Minor had a definitively Christian topography, and their skylines were dominated by domed churches.

This picture presented of redesigning cities with churches raises questions as to the role played by ascetics and monks in converting peasants of Anatolia. The archetypical militant holy man and missionary is the Syriac hermit Barsuma, who was favored by the empress Eudocia, wife the emperor Theodosius II (408-50). Barsuma and his equally formidable followers armed with cudgels descended on pagan villagers who were terrified by his mere appearance into embracing Christ. Barsuma had his Anatolian analogues in St. Hypatius operating in Bithynia in the fifth century or the Galatian Saint Theodore of Sykeon in the sixth century.[50] Each was credited with converting villagers by miracles, exorcisms, and destruction of idols much in the fashion of the prophets of the Old Testament. But there is limited literary and archaeological documentation for the role of ascetics and monastic communities in converting the villages and towns of Anatolia from the late fourth through sixth centuries.

St. Basil of Caesarea penned his disciplinary manual *Aesthica,* in part, to put the monks of Cappadocia under strict episcopal authority—an understandable precaution given conditions in Asia Minor. In contrast to the arid deserts of Egypt and Syria that were home to so many ascetics, in Asia Minor, Sozomen, the ecclesiastical historian of the Theodosian age, noted that ascetics lived in villages and towns rather than in solitude due to the severe winters on the Anatolian plateau.[51] But climate was only part of the story, for the churches of Asia Minor prior to Constantine's conversion (whatever their strict confessional lines) were largely Jewish in origin, and they shared in the ascetic and prophetic traditions of Pharisee Judaism of the Diaspora. Among Christian communities of Western Asia Minor, rigorist sectarians such as Montanists in the second and third centuries or Novatians in the fourth century valued abstinence and continence, whereas Encratites practiced the strictest of sexual continence since the second century. The imperial church of Constantine, based on those churches of Apostolic origins and headed by monarchical bishops with the canon of the New Testament, faced many competing and well established "heretical" churches in the search for ascetic purity. Many Anatolian Christians with puritanical leanings could well have gravitated to the so-called heretical confessions, and if it is often quite difficult to determine the confessional loyalties (if this were even a meaningful issue) of the first ascetics and monks mentioned in literary sources from the 340s on.

It has been long argued that the phantasmagoric landscapes of Cappadocia and Lycaonia invited ascetics and monks to make their homes there, often by carving out cave dwelling from the soft tuf. In the Middle Byzantine Age, between the mid–ninth and late eleventh century, monastic communities and churches have been claimed at such sites as Madenşehir, cradled in an awesome volcanic crater Kara Dağringed by four peaks and dominating the high Lycaonian plateau. These chapels and churches were constructed perhaps from the seventh or eighth centuries atop a city of refugė established by those departing the classical city of Barata at the base of Kara Dağand approximately 30 km northwest of Larbanda (modern Karaman) in ancient Lycaonia. The site is still to be studied adequately, and many of the churches noted by William Ramsay and Gertrude Bell have all but disappeared.[52] Likewise, it is argued that monastic communities abounded in the deep riverine valleys cut out of high plains, such as the lush Peristrema valley (Ihlara) near modern Aksaray, the Seljuk caravan center, or in the erosion basins of the "fairy chimney" rock formations of eastern Cappadocia around Göreme, Uçhisar, Ortaköy, Çavusin, and Zelve. In the opinion of Stephen Mitchell, "It seems inconceivable that many of these [monasteries] did not trace their origin back to the age of Basil and Gregory Nazianzus, who were active precisely in this region, but the claim is very difficult to prove."[53] But a picture of Byzantine Cappadocia studded with monastic churches cut from volcanic rock is perhaps largely an illusion. Robert Ousterhout has completed a survey of one such monastic community, Çanli Kilise, southeast of Aksaray, and his survey conclusively proves that this settlement was hardly monastic.[54] In Ousterhout's opinion, the main churches here and in the Peristremea, whether cut from rock or freestanding, are architecturally inspired from the capital and were most likely prestige churches of lay donors or private chapels.

In short, the evidence from the Middle Byzantine Age points to what can be inferred from the letters of the Cappadocian fathers, namely monastic communities were but part of a wider effort directed by prelates to Christianize cities and countryside. Instead, greater weight should be given to bishops backed with imperial money rather than the dramatic miracles of an inspired Stylite ascetic. Sometimes, cities, towns, and villages were converted suddenly as in 325 Orcistus, when a *vicus* of the presumably still pagan city of Nacoleia just north of Amorium, obtained her independence when the Christian decurions swore sanguinely that no pagans dwelled among the true believers.[55] Saint Basil, Bishop of Caesarea, reports in his letters similar grants of civic status to "petty communities" (αἱ μικροπλεῖται) in an effort to spread the faith from these new episcopal seats.[56] Such sees needed churches and associated buildings, and so one such country church may be Kizil Kilese "Red Church" presently in a field of grain and poppies at eastern base of the mountain occupied by Güzelyurt (Gelveri). Another was perhaps the complex at Alahan, atop the slopes of the Taurus range, which was abandoned at the end of the sixth century.[57] In his letters, Saint Basil reveals how he labored to organize parish, episcopal, and monastic hierarchies for Cappadocia, and such organization required the remodeling of sacred space in cities into a Christian theater complete with churches and festivals that drew pagans from city and countryside to the celebration of the New Faith, and so gained converts. The most telling case of episcopal initiative is commemorated on the memorial inscription of M. Julius Eugenius (c. 315-45), who served as bishop of Laodicea Combusta, in Lycaonia, for some twenty-five years. Julius Eugenius transformed the architecture of the sacred space in his native city Laodicea Combusta (modern Ladik, just west of Konya in west central Anatolia) with a zeal for building that would have earned him condemnation for *lithomania* by his fellow Christian moralists. Yet, Julius Eugenius employed his passion for building in his labors to convert pagans and heretics, and by his patronage transformed the traditional decurional virtues of civic patriotism (φιλοπατρίς) and search for social recognition (φιλοοτιμία) into service to God. In his own words, Julius Eugenius reports:

> Marcus Julius Eugenius, son of Cyrillus Celer of Kouessos, a member of the Laodicean council, served as an officer on the staff of the governor of Pisidia and married Flavia Julia Flaviana, daughter of Gaius Julius Nestorianus, a man of Roman senatorial rank; and I served with distinction. When a command had meanwhile gone forth in the time of [the emperor] Maximinus [II Daia, 309-13] that Christians should offer sacrifice and not quit the service, I endured many tortures under Diogenes governor of Pisidia and I contrived to quit the service, and I maintained the faith of the Christians; and when I spent a short time in the city of the Laodiceans, I was made bishop of the city by the will of Almighty God. I have administered the episcopate for twenty-five full years with great distinction, and I rebuilt from its foundations the entire church and all its adornment around it, consisting of stoas, tetrastoas, paintings, mosaics, a fountain and outer gateway, which I furnished with all construction and masonry, and, in a word, with everything. Being about to

> leave the life of this world, I made for myself a protection and sarcophagus on which I caused the above to be inscribed, for the distinction of the church and my family.[58]

This essay closes with suggestions rather than conclusions. In reevaluating the Christianizing of Anatolian cities and their hinterlands, it is important to consider the scale of change, the numbers and types of churches needed, the sources for funding churches, the impact of building programs, and the use of churches in the recasting of public and religious festivals. Such considerations require a new look at archaeology of the Middle Byzantine period to elucidate the scale of the task confronting emperors and bishops in the late Roman era. For even at modest Middle Byzantine settlements such as Çanli Kilise and Madenşehir between thirty and sixty churches and chapels have been detected. As for city and countryside in the Dominate, they were, as in the Principate, cemented together by patronage, religious rites and markets into a coherent community. Christianizing the city was inevitably pursued in tandem with Christianizing the hinterland. Constantine and his heirs faced a daunting task in their rewrite of the sacred geography of Asia Minor, let alone the entire Roman world, but to this end Constantine dedicated his New Rome, Constantinople, in 330 as a model for prelates and decurions, such as those of Orcistus, to follow in recreating their cities for the worship of the New Faith.

NOTES

1. My thanks to the directors of excavations and surveys who have generously shared their impressions about their sites as well as to the staff of the American Research Institute in Turkey, Ankara, and the British Institute of Archaeology, Ankara.
2. See survey of Byzantine monuments of Pontus by J. Crow and A. A. M. Bryer, "Survey in Trabzon and Gümüşhane Vilayets, Turkey, 1992–1994," *DOP* 51 (1997): 283–89; cf. A. A. M. Bryer and D. Winfield, *The Byzantine Monuments and Historical Topography of the Pontos* (Washington, D.C., 1985).
3. See S. F. R. Price, *Rituals and Power: The Roman Imperial Cult in Asia Minor* (Cambridge, 1986).
4. See the fundamental studies by F. Cumont, *Les mystères de Mithra*, 2d ed. (Paris, 1902)

and *Les religions orientales dans le paganisme romain,* 4th ed. (Paris, 1941). See reservations by R. MacMullen, *Paganism in the Roman Empire* (New Haven, 1981), 112–30.

5. See T. R. S. Broughton, "Roman Asia Minor," in *Economic Survey of Ancient Rome,* edited by F. Frank (Baltimore, 1938), 4:591–902, for masterful collection of the evidence.
6. See A. J. Spawforth and S. Walker, "The World of the Panhellenion," *JRS* 75 (1985): 81 and 89. For development of the shrine, see R. Naumann, *Der Zeustempel zu Aizanoi* (Berlin, 1979), 32–68.
7. See M. Waelkens, *Die kleinasiatische Türnsteine* (Mainz, 1986), 10–11 and 47–48, and pl. 107, types E and F; cf. *MAMA* 9:xlviii-xlix.
8. See Naumann, *Zeustempel,* 67–69, for comparable Hadrianic temples. The stately peripteros Corinthian temple at Euromus, a minor Carian city just west of Mylasa (Milas), points to similar patronage by Hadrian of another shrine of Zeus.
9. See Hellström and T. Thiène, *Labranda: Swedish Excavations and Researches Vol. I, Part 3: The Temple of Zeus* (Lund/Stockholm, 1982), 45–53, and note critique by S. Hornblower, *Mausolus* (Oxford, 1982), 278–312. For the cult, see A. Laumonier, *Les cultes indigènes en Carie* (Paris, 1958), 101–10.
10. For survey of the city's monuments and excavations, see P. Verzone, *L'urbanistica di Hierapolis di Frigia* (Rome, 1972).
11. Strabo 13. 4. 14.
12. For preliminary survey of Laodicea, see J. des Gagniers et al., *Laodicée du Lycos: La Nymphée* (Quebec/Paris, 1968).
13. See K. W. Harl, *Civic Coins and Civic Politics in the Roman East a.d. 180–275* (Berkeley, 1987), 68–69, and the catalogue of coins by A. Johnston, "Hierapolis Revisited," *NC* 144 (1984): 52–80.
14. Tac., *Ann.* 2. 47. 1–5; the twelve cities were Sardes, Magnesia sub Sipylum, Temnus, Philadelphia, Aegeae, Apollonis, Mostene (Hyrcanis), Hierocaesarea, Myrina, Cyme, and Tmolus. Comparable rebuilding at Hierapolis followed an earthquake of c. 60 a.d.; see W. Ruge, "Hierapolis," *RE* VIII (Stuttgart, 1912), col. 1404. Between 120 and 129, the earthquake that leveled the Bithynian cities of Nicaea and Nicomedia occasioned rebuilding by Hadrian. See *CIG* 3745 (Nicaea), and 1720 and 3771 (Nicomedia), and cf. Euseb., *HE* 8. 1. 10, with discussion by O. Stein, "Nikaia," *RE* XVIII (Stuttgart, 1937), col. 230–31, and W. Ruge, "Nikomedia," *RE* XVIII (Stuttgart, 1937), col. 474.
15. See R. Fleischer, *Artemis von Ephesos und verwandte Kultstatuen aus Anatolien und Syrien* (Leiden, 1973).
16. See J. Reynolds, *Aphrodisias and Rome: Documents from the Excavations of the Theatre at Aphrodisias Conducted by Professor Kenan T. Erim, Together with some Related Texts* (London, 1982, *JRS* Monograph 1).
17. See corpus of inscriptions of Lagina in M. C. Ŝahin, *Die Inschriften von Stratonikeia* 2 vols. (Bonn, 1981–90). The inscriptions of Panamara are yet to be published, although Professor Ŝahin has recorded a number of important ones.
18. P. Brown, *The Making of Late Antiquity* (Cambridge, Mass., 1977), 51.
19. See S. Mitchell, "Festivals, Games, and Civic Life in Roman Asia Minor," *JRS* 80 (1990): 183–93.

20. See G. W. Bowersock, *Hellenism in Late Antiquity* (Ann Arbor, 1993), 1–3; the majority of cities in Asia Minor probably fell into this category.
21. See collection of the evidence for temple tombs by S. H. Cormack, "*Non Inter Nota Sepulcra:* Roman Temple Tombs of South West Asia Minor," 2 vols. (Ph.D. Diss., Yale, 1992). For rock carved tombs and tumuli, see J. Fedak, *Monumental Tombs of the Hellenistic Age* (Toronto, 1990), 46–56 and 74–101.
22. See W. Wurtster and W. Wörrle, "Die Stadt Pinara," *AA* (1978): 74–101.
23. See C. Williams, "The Corinthian Temple of Zeus Olbios at Uzuncaburç," *AJA* 78 (1974): 404–15; the temple was erected in the second quarter of the third century b.c.
24. See J. Alchermos, "*Spolia* in Roman Cities of the Late Empire: Legislative Rationales and Architectural Reuse," *DOP* 48 (1994): 167–78.
25. See C. S. Lightfoot and E. A. Ivison, "Amorium 1995: The Eighth Preliminary Report," *Anatolian Studies* 46 (1996): 91–110, and "The Amorium Project: The 1995 Excavation Season," *DOP* 51 (1997): 291–300.
26. Vita Theod. Sky., 116–17, and see discussion by S. Mitchell, *Anatolia: Land, Men, and Gods in Asia Minor Volume II: The Rise of the Church* (Oxford, 1993), 139–44.
27. Analysis of inscriptions based on forthcoming study. For corpus of inscriptions from the Upper Tembris valley from Altintaş, see E. Gibson, *The "Christians for Christians" Inscriptions from Phrygia* (Missoula, 1978). For translations of important published pre-Nicene Christian inscriptions, see G. J. Johnson, *Early-Christian Epitaphs from Anatolia* (Atlanta, 1995).
28. For "house church" of Dura, see C. H. Kraeling, *The Excavations of Dura-Europos, Final Report Volume VIII Part II: The Christian Buildings* (New Haven, 1967). See also Lact., *Mort Pers.*, 12–13 and Euseb., *HE* 8. 2, but the type of church at Nicomedia razed by the Diocletian's soldiers in 303 is unknown. The unnamed Christian town in Phrygia torched by Tetrarchic soldiers is probably a fiction; see Euseb., *HE* 8. 11. 1 and Lact., *Div. Inst.* 5. 11. See Mitchell, *Anatolia* II, p. 57, n. 34, and R. L. Fox, *Pagans and Christians* (New York, 1986), 771n. 4, for suggestions to identify the town as either Eumenia or Orcistus. See Procopius, *Anecdota* 11. 23, for a similar story told of a Montanist town during a persecution initiated by Justinian.
29. See F. W. Deichmann, "Frühchristliche Kirche in antiken Heiligtümern," *Jahrbuch des deutschen archäologischen Instituts* 54 (1939): 105–36.
30. See P. Brown, *Power and Persuasion in Late Antiquity: Towards a Christian Empire* (Madison, 1988).
31. Greg. Naz., *Or.* 18. 111–12 = Migne, PG 37. 997b-1000b.
32. See *SNGvAulock* 1904; *SNGCop* 436, and *BMCIonia*, p. 89, no. 292.
33. See S. Karwiese, "The Church of Mary and the Temple of Hadrian Olympios," in *Ephesos, Metropolis of Asia*, ed. H. Koester (Cambridge, Mass., 1995), 315–17. In Karwiese's view, the location of the principal church of Mary Theotokos was moved from an as yet undetected location to the present location during the reign of Anastasius (491–518). A possible split within the hierarchy might have resulted in the building of two new churches, the current church of Mary Theotokos and the St. John's, which replaced the unlocated, earlier basilican church of Mary Theotokos. This

undocumented, and so unprovable, suggestion is unlikely given that the bishop's palace was constructed as part of the main complex of the current church of Mary Theotokos. See reservations expressed by V. Limberis, "The Council of Ephesos: The Demise of the See of Ephesos and the Rise of the Cult of the Theotokos," in *Ephesos,* 322n. 5.

34. Palladius, *Dialogus* 13, and see discussion by C. Foss, *Ephesus after Antiquity: A Late Antique, Byzantine, and Turkish City* (Cambridge, 1970), 30–32 and 86n. 83.
35. See R. Krautheimer, *Three Christian Capitals: Topography and Politics* (Berkeley, 1983).
36. See A. Seager and A. T. Kraabel, "The Synagogue of the Jewish Community," in *Sardis from Prehistoric to Roman Times: Results of the Archaeological Exploration of Sardis 1958–1975,* ed. G. M. A. Hanfmann and W. E. Mierse (Cambridge, Mass., 1983), 168–71. For a comparable Jewish community at Aphrodisias, see J. M. Reynolds and R. Tannenbaum, *Jews and God-Fearers at Aphrodisias,* Cambridge Philological Society, Supplementary Vol. 12 (Cambridge, 1978). For Judaizing Christians, see S. E. Johnson, "Christianity at Sardes," in *Early Christian Origins: Studies in Honor of Harold R. Willoughby,* ed. A. Wikgren (Chicago, 1968), 84–90.
37. See G. M. A. Hanfmann and H. Buchwald, "Christianity: Churches and Cemeteries," in *Sardis,* 196–204.
38. *Acts* 21: 8–9, for daughters of the evangelist Philip, and cf. Euseb. *HE* 3. 31. 3. For the location of Montanist churches, see A. Strobel, *Das heilige Land der Montanisten* (Berlin, 1960).
39. See P. Verzone, "Il martyrium ottagono a Hierapolis di Frigia," *Palladio, Rivista di Storia dell'Architettura* 10 (1960): 1–20.
40. See R. Cormack, "Temple as Cathedral," in *Aphrodisias Papers: Recent Work on Architecture and Sculpture,* edited by C. Roueché and K. T. Erim, *JRA* Supp. Series 1 (Ann Arbor, 1990,), 75–88.
41. See F. R. Trombley, *Hellenic Religion and Christianization c. 370–529* (Leiden, 1994), 2:52–73.
42. See R. R. R. Smith, "The Imperial Reliefs from the Sebasteion at Aphrodisias," *JRS* 77 (1987): 88–138, and "The *Ethne* from the Sebasteion at Aphrodisias," *JRS* 78 (1988): 50–77.
43. For a preliminary survey of the churches, see S. Eyice, *Kanlidivan Bazikikalar2* (Ankara, 1977). There is a fourth church of Middle Byzantine date built on piers.
44. See C. H. E. Haspels, *The Highlands of Phrygia* (Princeton, 1971), 13–15, 64–65, and 87–89.
45. For the first domed cathedral in Constantinople as a model, see M. Harrison, A *Temple for Byzantium: The Discovery and Excavation of Anicia Juliana's Palace-Church in Istanbul* (Austin, 1989).
46. See Foss, *Ephesus after Antiquity,* 87–95.
47. John of Ephesus, *HE* 3. 2. 44 and 3. 36 (edition Brooks, 80 and 125–26), and cf. Michael the Syrian, *Chronicon* 9. 26 and 33 (edition Chabot II, 207–8 and 270–71). See discussion by K . W. Harl, "Sacrifice and Pagan Belief in Fifth and Sixth-Century Byzantium," *Past and Present* 128 (1992): 19–20.

48. See C. Foss, "The Lycian Coast in the Byzantine Age," *DOP* 48 (1994): 10–12, and consult the detailed excavation report by H. Canbilen, J-P. Sodini, and P. Lebouteiller, *Anatolia Antiqua* 4 (1996): 201–29.
49. See A. Pekman, *Perge Tarihi History of Perge* (Ankara, 1973), for survey of the excavations and cf. W. E. Kleinbauer, "The Double-Shell Tetraconch Building at Perge in Pamphylia and the Origin of the Architectural Genus," *DOP* 41 (1987): 277–94. I am in debt to Professor Haluk Abbasoğlu, current director of excavation, for offering his opinion about the churches during and after his presentation "The Founding of Perge and its Development in the Hellenistic through Roman Period," at the annual meeting of the Archaeological Institute of America, Washington D.C., 29 December 1998.
50. See Callincus, *Vita Hypatii,* 20, 28, and 42, and *Vita Theod. Syk.* 118, for exorcizing demons that had emerged from sarcophagi. For Christian fears of pagan funerary monuments as inhabited by demons, see H. Saradi-Mendelovici, "Christian Attitudes toward Pagan Monuments in Late Antiquity and Their Legacy in Later Byzantine Centuries," *DOP* 44 (1990): 58–60.
51. Soz., *HE* 6. 34. 7–9, but see qualifications by Mitchell, *Anatolia,* 2:111. For the ascetics of Syria and Egypt, see P. Brown, "The Rise and Function of Holy Men in Late Antiquity," *JRS* 52 (1962): 80–101.
52. W. M. Ramsay and G. Bell, *The Thousand and One Churches* (London, 1909).
53. See Mitchell, *Anatolia,* 2:116.
54. See R. Ousterhout, "Survey of the Byzantine Settlement at Çanli Kilise in Cappadocia: Results of the 1995 and 1996 Seasons," *DOP* 51 (1997): 301–06. More detailed surveys by the same author are "The 1995 Survey at Akhisar-Çanli Kilise," *Araştirma Sonuçlari Toplantisi* 14 (1996): 435–52 and "The 1996 Survey at Akhisar-Çanli Kilise," *Araştirma Sonuçlari Toplantisi* 15 (1998): 45–57.
55. *MAMA* VII. 305, and see W. H. Buckler, "A Charitable Foundation of A.D. 257," *JHS* 57 (1937): 1–10.
56. See Mitchell, *Anatolia,* 2:71–72, and cf. P. Rousseau, *Basil of Caesarea* (Berkeley, 1994), 133–89.
57. For Kizil Kilise, see N. and M. Thierry, *Nouvelles églises rupestres de Cappadoce. Région du Hasan Daği* (Paris, 1963), 25–26 and pl. 6–7. There is no conclusive evidence to identify the complex at Alahan as monastic; see M. Gough, ed., *Alahan: An Early Christian Monastery in Southern Turkey Based on the Work of Michael Gough* (Toronto, 1985), 3–20. See also the survey by M. Harrison, "Churches and Chapels in Central Lycia," *Anatolian Studies* 13 (1963): 117–51.
58. Translation adapted from W. Calder, "Studies in Christian Epigraphy," *JRS* 10 (1920): 45.

"... Nec sedere in villam." Villa-Churches, Rural Piety, and the Priscillianist Controversy

KIM BOWES

WHAT WAS THE RELATIONSHIP BETWEEN PRISCILLIANISM AND VILLAS? DID PRISCILLIANISTS meet and worship in villas? Archaeologists and historians have both made this suggestion more than once, although never in a rigorous manner,[1] and perhaps now is the time for a real appraisal of the evidence.

First, it must be stated that archaeologically, this may be an unanswerable, and indeed, moot question. For how can archaeology uncover heresy? Do certain ceramic profiles or stratigraphic sections reek of heterodoxy? In fact, of Priscillian or Priscillianists, archaeology can tell us nothing. However, recent inquiry has turned to the motivations of Priscillian's accusers, that is, to the socio-ecclesiastical construction of "Priscillianism," and it may be in this area that archaeology can contribute something to the dialogue. For if modern scholarship is right and Priscillianism was a heresy largely constructed from rumor and accusation, it may be that it was thus very much about environment.[2] Archaeology can help us to reconstruct the structural, ecclesiastical, and geographical environment in which both Priscillian and his accusers lived. By understanding this environment, perhaps we can better understand why certain accusations were leveled at Priscillian and why these alleged activities were deemed such a threat.

Two of the more prominent fears associated with Priscillianism were Christian practices in the countryside and unsupervised worship in the home.[3] It is at the juncture of these two environments, the rural and the domestic, where the archaeology of Early Christian Hispania is unexpectedly rich. A surprising number of Early Christian churches in Hispania are constructed in or near rural Roman villas[4] (fig. 1). By examining for the first time the archaeology, architecture, and geography of the villa-church phenomenon, we will find that it constitutes a major part of the Iberian Christian environment and indeed, seems significantly more common in Hispania than elsewhere in the Empire.[5] However, any direct relationship between Priscillianism and these sites is attenuated by the chronological uncertainty surrounding the majority of these villa-churches, and by the nature of the church councils allegedly convened against these churches and Priscillianism. Rather, this examination will illuminate the general character that the villa-church imparted to Iberian Christianity, a character which from the late fourth century onward may have contributed to the specific distrust of rural and domestic worship and thus to the definition of certain activities as "Priscillianist."

There are two basic structural types of villa-churches, the intra-villa church, constructed inside the *villa urbana* or *rustica* by modifying an extant space, and the extra-villa church, a free standing building located 100-500 m from the villa proper. The former category is perhaps the most complex and will be considered first, beginning with Monte de Cegonha, deep in the Baixo Alentejo of Portugal[6] (fig. 2). At some point, perhaps in the fourth century, the Flavian-period villa on the site, whose overall form is unknown, was completely rebuilt along the so-called corridor or façade villa plan with two wings.[7] The south wing was composed of a 10 × 8 m central court, bordered by an apsed hall. The north wing of the villa was separated from the south by a drainage canal, restricting the interaction between the two wings. This north wing was largely occupied by a three-aisled basilica with a tri-partite sanctuary and northern entrance.[8] The earliest floor of this basilica is no longer extant and is assumed to have been wooden, set on a rubble base.[9] This rubble base was later pierced by the addition of graves, which were in turn covered by a later floor.

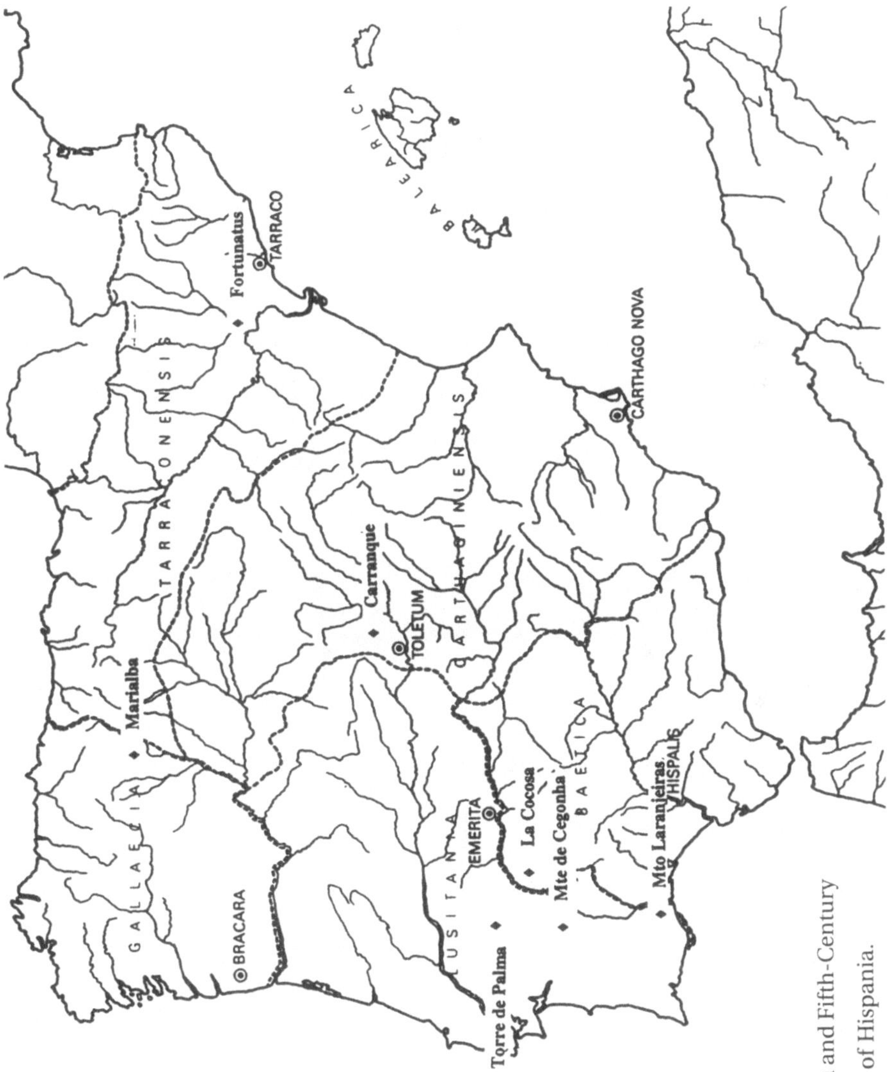

Figure 1. Fourth and Fifth-Century Villa-Churches of Hispania.

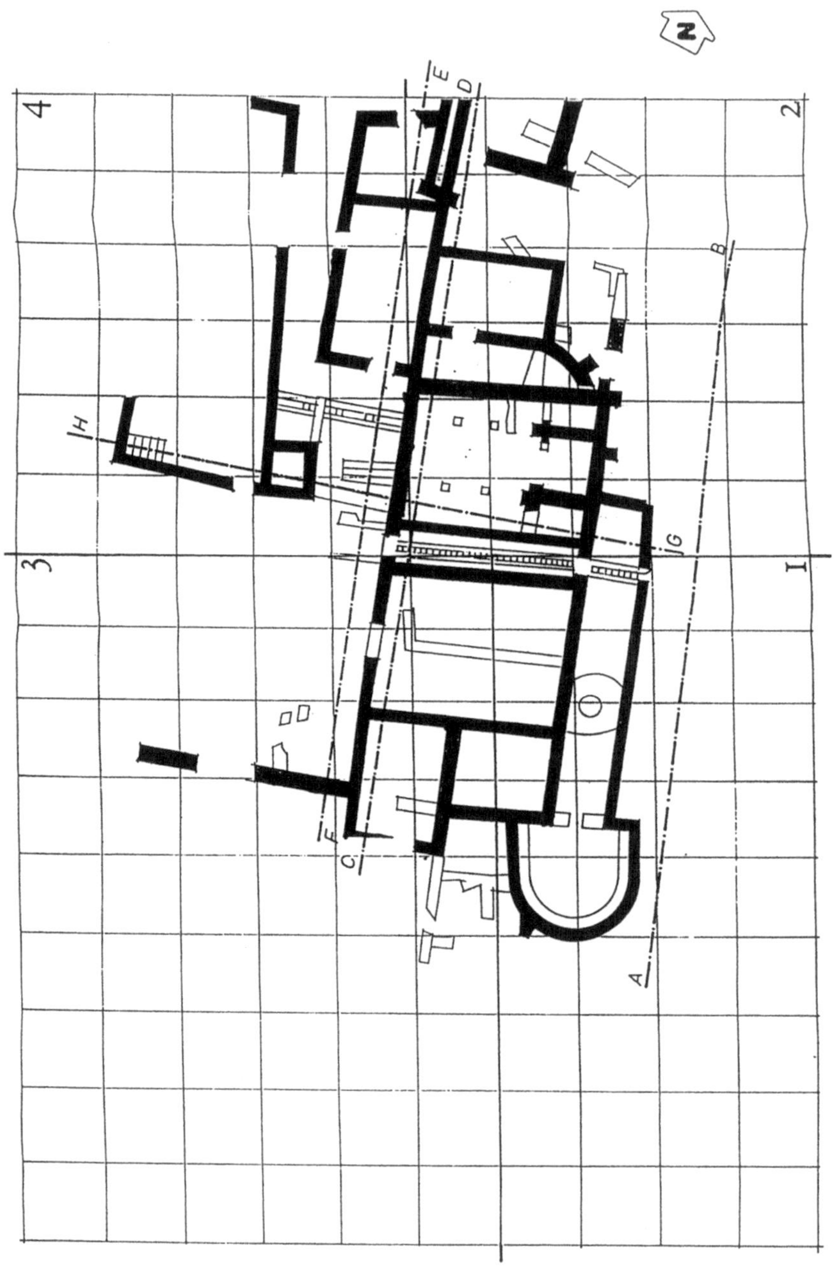

Figure 2. Monte da Cegonha (Vidigueira), Portugal. Villa and church, plan. Courtesy of Rafael Alfenim and Conceição Lopes, unpublished.

The villa and church of Montinho das Laranjeiras are located to the south of Cegonha, on the banks of the Guadiana in southern Portugal. Largely destroyed by roadwork and flooding, very little remains of the villa or the church. However, nineteenth-century excavations generally outlined a large complex, seemingly a villa,[10] and excavations in the last four years have detailed a large, well-constructed corridor of fourth-century date to the south of the church[11] (fig. 3). The church itself is composed of an uneven cross plan, with a sanctuary, baptismal font, and a burial chamber.[12] The nineteenth-century excavations revealed mosaics of fish and a vase near the baptistery[13] and geometric mosaics were recently discovered in the burial chamber. While the current excavations have not determined the relationship between the church and the surrounding villa, some of the church walls may have been integrated into the villa fabric.[14] The current excavator of Montinho das Laranjeiras, Justino Maciel, has dated the church to the sixth century, based on the cross-plan and supposed connections with Galla Placidia and Ravennate churches.[15] However, the mosaics found in the nineteenth-century excavations as well as those in the burial chamber find their

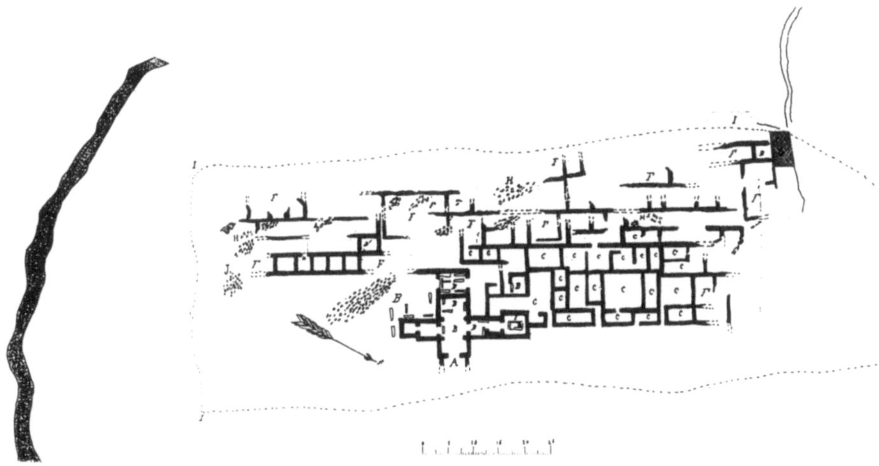

Figure 3. Montinho das Laranjeiras (Alcoutim), Portugal. Villa and church, plan from nineteenth-century excavations of Estacio da Veiga. (from M.L.E.V.A. Santos, *Arqueologia Romana do Algarve*, II, p. 378).

closest parallels with fourth- and fifth-century examples,[16] and the latest sigillata similarly date to the early to mid–fifth century.[17] A coin of Licinius found inside one of the graves further supports this date.[18] Thus, it is possible that Montinho das Laranjeiras is another fourth/fifth-century church associated with a villa-type community.

In the northeast of Tarraconensis, near modern-day Fraga, yet another church is constructed within the heart of a villa.[19] The so-called Villa Fortunatus was a typical peristyle villa with an additional western atrium and eastern bath suite (fig. 4). Late in the fourth century or early in the fifth, the center room off the peristyle was rebuilt and a new mosaic installed, inscribed with the owner's name, Fortunatus, and a chrismon. Excavations in the late 1980s by Francesc Tuset suggest that at this time, a large hall in the western wing was converted into a Christian church.[20] This area received a tripartite sanctuary and a crypt, and two doors were opened in the lateral walls.[21] During this first phase of the church, the cubicula to the north

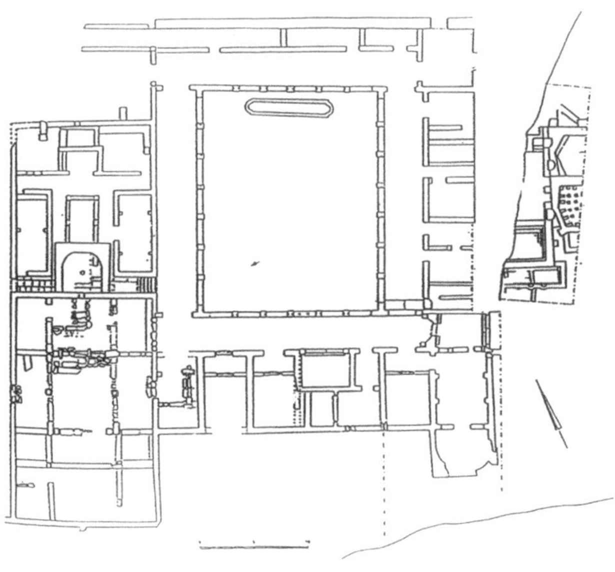

Figure 4. Villa Fortunatus (Fraga), Spain. Villa and church, plan. From Tuset, appearing in Guardia Pons, *Los Mosaicos de la Antigüedad Tardía en Hispania*, fig. 7.

seemed to have continued in use, their mosaic floors conserving depictions of pagan love scenes. Tuset's re-excavations have tentatively placed both the Fortunatus mosaic and the first Christian phase in the late fourth or very early fifth century.[22]

Turning to the extra-villa churches, the church of Torre de Palma, in the Alto Alentejo, is associated with one of the largest excavated villas in the Iberian Peninsula[23] (fig. 5). The villa's fourth-century fabric consisted of a peristyle with accompanying tri-apsed hall, large granary and olive press, and a detached bath complex. Later, a large house fronted by a courtyard was constructed to the northeast of the villa, (not on plan) and the detached bath complex was heavily modified. The church itself was constructed approximately 50 m from the later house in the pagan, villa necropolis. The surviving basilica is of the double-apsed variety, with a second set of opposed apses to the west. Recent excavations by the University of Louisville revealed a deposit of ten Constantinian-aged bronze coins in the mortar of the floor in front of the altar. The latest of these coins dates from 354–57, leading the excavators to propose a late fourth/early fifth-century date for the church. However, the long circulation of fourth century coins dictate that this date can only be a *terminus post quem* for what could potentially be a much younger building.[24]

If we move to the east into the Spanish Extremadura, the villa of La Cocosa may offer another Christian villa site, this time specifically associated with funerary cult. The villa was excavated in late 1940s and only partially published.[25] A large peristyle emerged from those excavations, with accompanying baths, servants quarters, and agricultural structures (fig. 6); 250 m to the southwest of the villa urbana, an 11 × 7 m quadrilobed structure was constructed, oriented east-west, and containing a single east-west oriented sarcophagus beneath the apse floor (fig. 7). The structure seems to have been vaulted and either the vault or walls covered with mosaics. A later baptistery was attached to the south wall and a complex of unknown function added to the north. The quadrilobed building seems to be a small Christian church, specifically associated with the cult of the dead. With no stratigraphy or ceramic studies, the modern scholar has been left with only the building plan as a chronological indicator. The probability of vaulting,

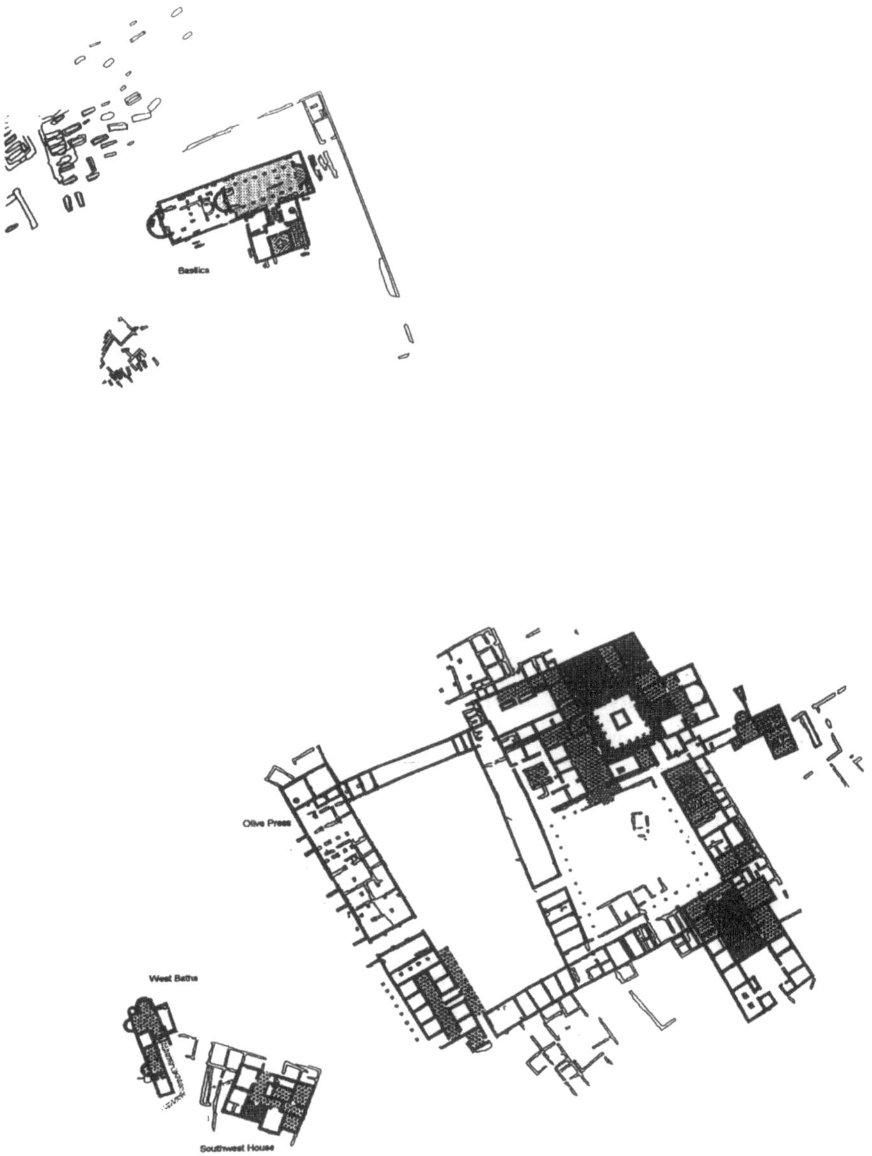

Figure 5. Torre de Palma (Monforte), Portugal. Villa and church, plan. From Maloney and Hale, in *JRA*, 1996, fig. 16.

Figure 6. La Cocosa (Badajoz), Spain. Villa and church, plan. Not to scale. Plan by Bowes after Palol, *Arqueología Cristiana,* figs. 47 and 49, and Schlunk and Hauschild, *Die Denkmäler der frühchristlichen und westgotischen Zeit,* fig. 6.

use of multiple apses, and glass mosaics have led most scholars to place the building in the fourth–fifth centuries.[26]

Finally, current excavations directed by Dimas Fernández-Galiano in the villa of Maternus, Carranque in the province of Toledo, are revealing what may be one of the most luxurious villa-churches.[27] About 400 m from the main villa, an enigmatic basilican structure has come to light, linked by a series of porticoes to a possible mausoleum. Only brief publications have appeared on this structure, but the most recent claims that it is a late fourth-century church, probably funereal in nature.[28] The structure was certainly used as a church at some point in its history, as marble carvings depicting a chi-rho have been found in the abandonment layers. However, it is not clear

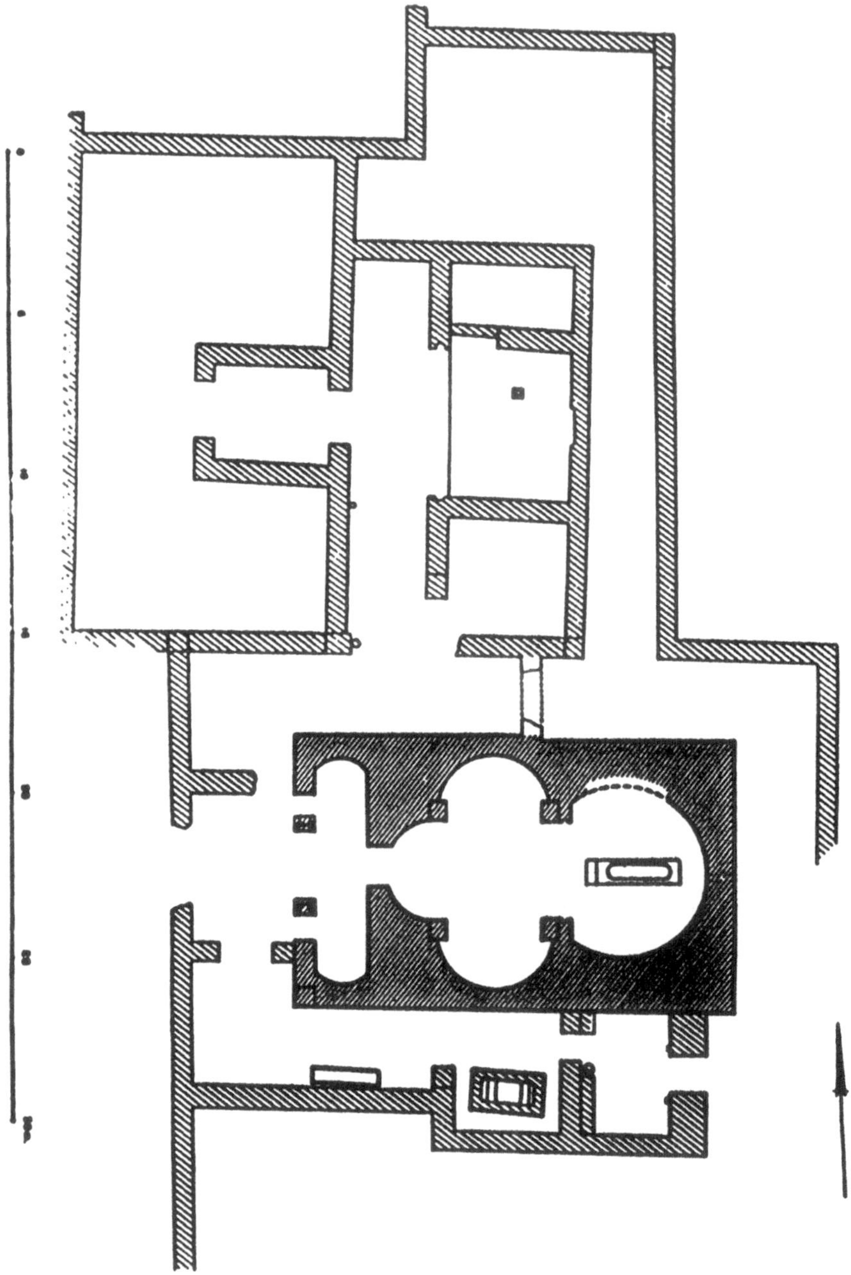

Figure 7. "Capella" de La Cocosa. Church, plan from Schlunk and Hauschild, *Die Denkmäler der frühchristlichen und westgotischen Zeit*, fig. 6.

if the building was designed as a church from the beginning. The presence of marble from imperial quarries and a mosaic inscription in the villa itself have led the excavators to attribute both villa and the possible church to Maternus Cynegius, consul of the year 388 and one of the many Hispanic members of the Theodosian court.[29]

There are other Early Christian villa-churches that I have omitted here, such as Marialba,[30] whose villa remains unexcavated, or those that definitively date to the sixth or seventh centuries, but I think that the preceding list does show the frequency with which Iberian churches were constructed within or near a Roman villa. However, the mere adjacency of villa and church is of rather limited significance. Churches constructed near or in abandoned villae, and churches constructed in functioning villae are fundamentally different phenomena, and I would suggest that it is only the latter category that interests us here.[31] Thus, we must rigorously examine the datable evidence for both villa and church and determine if the lives of the two coincide.

In each of the cases I have mentioned, there is a certain amount of archaeological evidence for the continuation of the life of the villa during the earliest church phase. The south wing of Monte de Cegonha was clearly conceived with the north, basilican wing and the ceramic profiles, while not yet published, show no marked differences between the two wings.[32] At Torre de Palma, recent excavations have revealed that the large house near the church, and the bath complex some 200 m to the southwest, may be contemporary with the church. It is not known if the peristyle villa continued in occupation, but the many patches in the mosaic floors suggest the possibility of continued habitation.[33] At Montinho das Laranjeiras, the fourth/fifth-century date suggested by the mosaics is matched by similarly aged ceramics and fourth-century coins found in both villa and church excavations.[34] La Cocosa may be the most problematic case, as we have only the early excavator's claim that he found evidence of occupation well into the Visigothic period.[35] However, the construction of a later, enigmatic biapsed hall in the villa itself suggests continued, later domestic use.[36]

Thus, while no site provides conclusive archaeological evidence of continuity, in each case there are certain indications that the occupation of the villa coincided with the earliest phase of the church. It must be noted, however, that the absolute dates of this phase are somewhat uncertain, a fact that must be kept in mind when we consider any potential relationship with Priscillianism.[37]

But even if these churches were constructed in working villas, what population did they serve? This is often difficult to establish, although frequently scholars posit the family oratory as a likely function.[38] However, if we examine only the intra-villa churches, the most likely candidates for domestic oratories, the churches' size and entrance/egress patterns both suggest that these basilicas are more than private chapels. For instance, the church at Monte de Cegonha occupies about 13 percent of the villa as excavated. The church was only accessible from outside the domestic core, suggesting permeability to extra-household members.[39] A similar situation exists at Villa Fortunatus, where the original church also occupies about 13 percent of the *villa urbana*, and where the first Christian phase saw the addition of both east and west doors, leading to both domestic center and extra-villa environments, respectively.[40] Thus, it seems likely that these churches serviced both the family of the *dominus* and very likely a portion of the neighboring population.

Some have also suggested the *extra*-villa basilicas were constructed as parochial churches.[41] The construction of parochial churches assumes a firmly established, widespread Christianity, and requires the existence of some kind of parochial structure. However, the church councils of the fourth and early fifth century are silent on matters of parish organization. The only canons scholars have cited as evidence for such organization are precisely those condemning villa-churches.[42] It seems then, that the parish system in Hispania, as with so many other provinces, was in its infancy until the mid–late fifth century.[43] Furthermore, as Pablo Díaz has shown, the later, sixth-century church councils, testaments, and hagiographies provide ample evidence of the continued independence of villa-churches from the episcopal and even parochial hierarchy.[44] It is thus far more likely that these churches fell principally under the authority of the *dominus* himself.

The case of Torre de Palma suggests a better model for the origins and functions of the extra-villa churches. Beneath the basilica floor was found the remains of a two-roomed, rectangular structure. Since earlier excavations found an altar to Mars as agricultural deity near the site, these foundations may represent an earlier pagan villa-temple that was later replaced by the Christian church.[45] The pagan villa-temple, although it has never been comprehensively studied, was a common component of both Iberian and Gallic villa life.[46] Usually constructed at some 100-300 m from the villa proper and sometimes serving funeral as well as cultic functions, these temples were usually dedicated to agrarian or water deities and seemed to have served both *dominus* and *coloni*.[47] Both in its geography, funeral function, and semi-public use, the villa-temple thus parallels the later villa-church. This suggests a certain degree of continuity in the villa's religious experience, an experience that always seems to have featured both the *dominus* as impresario, and extra-household members.

If the Christianity of Hispania was particularly marked by the villa-church, can this phenomenon be linked in any way to the allegations of Priscillianism? Certain canons in the so-called anti-Priscillianist councils of Zaragoza and Toledo reveal a fear of the villa-church based on characteristics that we have found in the archaeological evidence. Canons 2 and 4 of the Council of Zaragoza prohibit the faithful from convening in other's villas, (*ad alieneas villas agendorum conveniant,*) or remaining in villas (*sedere in villam*) during Lent and Christmas.[48] The first canon characterizes this villa Christianity as collective (*ad alienas villas*) rather than purely familial, a precept continued from canon 1 which further prohibits women from attending prayer meetings with *alieni*, or non-family members.[49] The additional descriptive *villas agendorum*, or "villas of the powerful," vividly describes communities led by a *dominus*. Contrary to other scholars' interpretation that the faithful retreated to villas during holidays, the use of the phrase *sedere in villam* also indicates that these communities were permanent.[50] The suspicion with which this type of villa community was regarded is abundantly clear. Villa worship was associated with non-orthodox or pagan practice (*suspicionibus*), particularly the practice of walking barefooted, (*nudis pedibus incedere*) which Virginia Burrus, Henry Chadwick and others have suggested probably pertains to pagan crop rituals.[51]

The council of Toledo in 400 makes more explicit reference to churches *per say* in villas, and seems to have come to terms with their existence, but instead of banning them outright, insists on episcopal involvement in their liturgy. Canon 5 requires any cleric who is in a castle or town or villa (*aut casteli aut vicus ut villae*) to attend church every day, while Canon 9 states that if the ritual of the *lucenarium* is celebrated in a villa, a bishop, presbyter, or deacon must be present.[52]

Taken together, the canons of the councils of Zaragoza and Toledo attest to the presence of extra-episcopal villa-churches that were viewed as a threat to episcopal control. Their rural setting suggested non-orthodox practices specifically associated with agricultural rituals. The link with the domestic sphere placed them outside the public, regulating eye and they seem to have co-opted traditional episcopal activities, such as the Lenten and Christmas services.

The question then arises, how closely were these councils and their canons tied to Priscillianist allegations? Traditional historiography has labeled both the councils of Zaragoza and Toledo as "anti-Priscillianist" councils, and assumed, particularly in the case of Zaragoza, that their canons were reflective of perceived Priscillianist activities or beliefs.[53] However, recent scholarship has noted quite rightly that none of the above cited canons mentions Priscillianism specifically, that, not all of the canons in either council were written to combat Priscillianism, and that some instead may have reflected general, community concerns.[54]

Thus, while the above canonical descriptions bear a striking resemblance to the archaeological remains of villa-churches, namely quasi-independent, rural churches with permanent communities made up of both *dominus* and locals, I do *not* believe that we can view this conjunction as evidence for Priscillianist activities in villas. Not only is the chronological evidence for these churches too imprecise, as we have seen, but the councils' reaction to villa-churches is only loosely tied to the heresy itself. Thus, I think that any attempt to connect these sites with the Priscillianists must be rejected.

If there is a relationship between the allegations and rumors of Priscillianism and the villa-churches of Hispania, it is complex one. One point of connection may be the ecclesiastical geography of Late Antique Hispania in which both the rumors of heresy were perpetuated and the villa-church grew and flourished. Most villa-churches are located in areas where rumors of early Priscillianism were propagated, namely Lusitania, where the allegations originated, and north-east Tarraconensis, where suspicions of Priscillianism were described by Consentius in the early fifth century.[55] Southern Lusitania, however, is clearly the locus of the phenomenon.[56] The Christian communities of southern Lusitania were principally governed by the bishops in Emerita Augusta (Merida) and Ossonoba (Faro). However, the episcopal structure of this area was particularly sparse. In fact, in the fourth and fifth centuries, there is definitive evidence of only three bishops for the whole of southern Lusitania, leaving the bishops in Emerita, Ossonoba, and Olisipo to monitor between them an area of over 52,000 km^2.[57] The sixth century saw only slight improvement in this episcopal lacuna, with the addition of documented bishoprics in Ebora (Evora) and Pax Iulia (Beja). If indeed our villa-churches date to the late fourth–fifth centuries, the inclusion of anti-villa church legislation during this period may have been due to the increasing presence of such churches in these territories , the increasing episcopal awareness of them, and the converse inability to control them.

Indeed, if we further examine the populations and geography of Lusitania, both the formation of villa-churches and the episcopates' fear of them is hardly surprising. Occupying around 120,000 km^2, the province boasted only three *conventi* and 50 identified *oppida.* [58] Compared with Baetica, for instance, the truly rural character of Lusitania is obvious. That rural landscape, however, is emerging as a much richer and more complex environment than the huge latifundia imagined by earlier historiography.[59] The latest field surveys around Beja, Caceres, and Merida indicate a surprisingly densely settled landscape with smaller sites every 1.5 to 3.2 km, punctuated by larger, villa-type sites.[60] The Beja survey suggests that not only did the villas see their apogee in the Late Empire, but that many of the smaller sites also continued, although the duration of that occupation is not always clear.[61]

Furthermore, as several scholars have noted, the villa communities of Hispania and the aristocracy that ran them seemed to have been powerful, particularly independent entities, enmeshed in a web of local politics and concerns.[62] Not only Orosius' description of private, estate-stocked armies points in this direction,[63] but even Consentius' narrative of the so-called Priscillianist enclaves in Tarragona betray a local landowner/clergy, controlling the definitions of orthodoxy in their spheres of influences, and closing ranks around those who would question their authority. This is a world in which city and country were simultaneously linked by social and economic ties, yet psychologically, the country could stand apart, an enclosed world delimited by the *dominus*, tied to his prosperity and subject to his laws and his faith.

Thus, if the phenomenon of villa-churches in Hispania can inform our understanding of Priscillianism, it is not in a simple, cause-effect way, but as a reflection of the Christian environment generally current in Hispania in the fourth and fifth centuries. The accusations of Priscillianism were born in the growing pains of a new faith and the struggle to implement that faith in an environment where the power of the local Christian *domini* was more immediate than that of a still distant but growing episcopate. The villa churches similarly suggest a semi-independent, rural Christianity, tied to the *dominus* and the *fundus*, and founded in areas with few urban entities and even fewer bishoprics. As the *villae urbanae* disappeared, as their churches were gradually converted into parish churches, and the ecclesiastical and landowning aristocracy merged into one,[64] the distrust with which these churches were regarded diminished, although it never disappeared completely. In the fourth and fifth centuries, however, these quasi-independent communities, probably specifically dedicated to rural concerns and patronized by a powerful, local elite, were inherently suspicious, perhaps suspicious enough to fuel the rumors and accusations which would long be termed Priscillianism.

REFERENCES

Alarcão, J., J.-G. Gorges, V. Mantas, M. Salinas de Frías, P. Sillières, and A. Tranoy. 1990. Propositions pour un nouveau tracé des limites anciennes de la Lusitanie romaine. In *Les villes de Lusitanie romaine*, 319–29. Paris.

Alarcão, J, R. Étienne, and F. Mayet. 1990. *Les Villas Romaines de São Cucufate*. Paris.

Alfenim, Rafael, and Conceição Lopes. 1986, 1988, 1991. Interim reports on excavation of

Monte da Cegonha. Archive, Instituto Português do Patrimonio Arquitectónico. Evora.

Alfenim, Rafael, and Conceição Lopes. 1992. A basílica paleocristã/Visigótica do Monte da Cegonha (Vidigueira). *IV Reunión d'Arqueologia Cristiana Hispánica*, 1994, 389–99. Lisbon.

———. La villa romaine de Monte da Cegonha. *Dossier d'Archéologie* 198:64–67.

Almeida, Fernando. 1972–74. Torre de Palma (Portugal). A basílica páleocristã e visigótica. *Archivo Español de Arqueologia* 45–47 (125–30):103–12.

Alonso, Justo Fernandez. 1955. *La Cura Pastoral en la España Romanovisigoda*. Rome.

Arce, Javier. 1986. Las metamorfosis de Carranque (Toledo). *Madrider Mitteilungen* 27:365–74.

———. 1997. *El Último Siglo de la España Romana (284–409)*. 2 ed. Madrid.

Bigador, R. 1933. *La Iglesia Propia en España*, Analecta Gregoriana. 5. Rome.

Blazquez, J. M. 1980. Los mosaicos romanos de Torre de Palma (Monforte, Portugal). *Archivo Español de Arqueologia* 53:125–50.

Breyfogle, Todd. 1995. Magic, Women and Heresy in the Late Empire: The Case of the Priscillianists. In *Ancient Magic and Ritual Power.* Edited by M. Meyer and P. Mirecki, 335–54. Leiden.

Burrus, Virginia. 1995. *The Making of a Heretic: Gender, Authority and the Priscillianist Controversy.* Berkeley.

Carro Otero, José. 1970. Estudio anatomicoantropológico de los restos humanos del templo de Marialba. *Legio VII Gemina*, 525–48. Leon.

Chadwick, Henry. 1978. *Priscillian of Avila.* Oxford.

———. 1983. New Letters of St. Augustine. *Journal of Theological Studies* 34 (2):425–452.

Coutinho, Helder. 1992. Sigillata Clara do Montinho das Larenjeiras (Escavações de 1990). *IV Reunió d'Arqueologia Cristiana Hispànica*, 1995, 507–514. Lisbon.

———.1997. *Terrra Sigillata Clara do Montinho das Laranjeiras. 1990 e 1991*. Alcoutim.

David, Pierre. 1947. Les paroisses rurales dans l'occident latin du IVe au VIe siècle. In *Études historiques sur la Galice et le Portugal*, 7–18. Paris.

Díaz, Pablo. 1986. Iglesia propia y gran propiedad en la autobiografia de Valerio del Bierzo. *I Congreso International Astorga Romana*, 297–303. Astorga.

———.1992–93. Propiedad y explotación de la tierra en la Lusitania tardoantigua. *Historia Antigua* 10–11:297–309. (*Actas de la Mesa Redona Internacional. El Medio Rural en Lustitania Romana. Formas de Habitat y Occupacion del Suelo*).

Díaz y Díaz, Manuel. 1980. A proposito del concilio de Zaragoza de 380 y su canon VI. *I Concilio Caesaraugustano. MDC Aniversario*, 225–35. Zaragoza.

Encarnação, José de. 1977. Epigrafia do Nordeste Alentejano. *Conimbriga* 16:59–82.

Escribano Paño, Maria Victoria. 1988. *Iglesia y Estado en el Certamen Priscilianista. Causa Ecclesiae y Iudicium Publicum, Monografias de Historia Antigua.* Zaragoza.

Escribano Paño, María Victoria. 1992. Cristianización y liderazgo en la Lusitania tardía. *IV Reunió d'Arqueologia Cristiana Hispànica*, 1992, 267–75. Lisbon.

Fernández Castro, Maria. 1981. Villa romana y basilica cristiana en Hispania. In *La Religion Romana en Hispania.* 381–89. Madrid.

Fernández Corrales, José Maria. 1988. *El Asentamiento Romano en Extremadura y su*

Analisis Espacial. Cáceres.

Fernández-Galiano, Dimas. 1991. La villa de Materno, Carranque (Toledo). *Revista de Arqueología* 12 (127):26–36.

———. 1994. The villa of Maternus at Carranque. *Fifth International Colloquium on Ancient Mosaics,*199–227. Bath.

———. 1998. La villa romana de Carranque. *La Lonja* (Sept-Nov):437–40.

———. 1999. La villa romana de Carranque. in *Hispania. El Legado de Roma,* 287–89. Merida.

Fernández-Galiano, Dimas, Belen Patón Lorca, and Cesar Maria Batalla Carchenilla. 1990. Mosaicos de la villa de Carranque: un programa iconográfico. *VI Coloquio Internacional sobre Mosaico Antiguo,* 1994, 317–26. Palencia-Merida.

Ferriero, Alberto. 1993. Sexual depravity, doctrinal error and character assassination in the fourth century: Jerome against the Priscillianists. *Studia Patristica* 28:29–38.

Fontaine, Jacques. 1981. Panorama espiritual del occidente peninsular en los siglos IV y V: Por una nueva problematica del Priscillianismo. *Primera Reuniono Gallega de Estudios Clasicos,* 185–201. Edited by M.C. Díaz y Díaz. Santiago de Compostela.

Fouet, Georges. 1984. Le sanctuaire gallo-romain de Valentine (Haute-Garonne). *Gallia* 42 (1):153–73.

García Iglesias, Luis. 1980. Sobre el canon IV del primer concilio de Zaragoza. *I Concilio Caesaraugustano. MDC Aniversario,* 189–200. Zaragoza.

Garcia-Moreno, Luis. 1991. Élites e iglesia hispanas en la transición del imperio romano al reino visigodo. In *La Conversión de Roma. Cristianismo y Paganismo,* 223–57. Edited by J. M. Candou, et al. Madrid.

Gorges, Jean-Gérard. 1986–7. Villas romaines en Lusitanie. *Bulletin des études portugaises et brésiliennes* 46–47:149–70.

———.1990. Villes et villas de Lusitanie. In *Les villes de Lusitanie romaine,* 91–113. Paris.

Guardia Pons, Milagros. 1992. *Los Mosaicos de la Antigüedad Tardía en Hispania.* Barcelona.

Hauschild, Theodor. 1969. Untersuchungen in der Märtyrerkirche von Marialbe (Prov. Leon) und im Mausoleum von las Vegas de Pueblenueva (Prov. Toledo). *Actas del VIII Congreso International de Arqueologia Cristiana,* 327–32. Barcelona.

———.1970. Die Märtyrer-Kirche von Marialba bei León. *Legio VII Gemina,* 513–21. León.

———.1978. Técnicas y maneras de construir en la arquitectura paleocristana hispánica. *II Reunió d'Arqueologia Paleocristiana Hispanica,* 1982, 71–86. Barcelona.

Heleno, Manuel. 1962. A 'villa' lusitano-romana de Torre de Palma (Monforte). *O Arqueólogo Português. New Series* 4:313–38.

Heinemeir, Jan, et al, 1997. AMS C-14 dating of lime mortar. *Nuclear Instruments and Methods in Physics Research. Section B,* 123:487–95.

Huffstot, John S. 1998. Votive (?) use of coins in fourth-century Lusitania: the builders' deposit in the Torre de Palma basilica. *Revista Portuguesa de Arqueologia* 1 (1):221–26.

Huffstott, Luz, and John Huffstott. 1992. Prisciliano, um caso arqueológico. *IV Reunió d'Arqueologia Cristiana Hispánica,* 1995, 443–47. Lisbon.

Lopes, Conceição. 1989. Sigillata de Montans no Monte da Cegonha (Vidigueira).

Conimbriga 28:223–28.

———. 1995. L'occupation du sol dans le territoire de Pax Iulia. *Itinéraires lusitaniens,* 1997, 157–78. Bordeaux.

———. 1996. O território de Pax Iulia: limites e caracterização. *Arquivo de Beja, Series III* 2–3:63–74.

Lopes, Conceição, and Rafael Alfenim. 1992. A villa romana do Monte da Cegonha. *Arqueologia en el Entorno del Bajo Guadiana,* 1994, 485–502. Huelva.

Maciel, Justino. 1992. A 'villa' romana fluvial do Montinho das Laranjeiras, junto no Guadiana (Algarve). *Arqueologia en el Entorno del Bajo Guadiana,* 1994, 469–484. Huelva.

———. 1994–96. Interim reports on excavation of Montinho das Laranjeiras. Archive, Instituto Português da Arqueologia. Lisbon.

———. 1996. *Antiguidade Tardia e Paleocristianismo en Portugal.* Lisbon.

Maloney, Stephanie. 1992. The Early Christian basilican complex of Torre de Palma (Monforte, Alto Alentejo, Portugal). *IV Reunión d'Arqueologia Cristiana Hispánica,* 1995, 449–458. Lisbon.

Maloney, Stephanie, and John Hale. 1996. The villa of Torre de Palma (Alto Alentejo). *Journal of Roman Archaeology* 9:275–94.

Mantas, Vasco. 1986. Implantação rural romana en torno da villa de S. Cucufate. *Arquivo de Beja, Series II* 3:199–214.

Menendez Pidal, Ramón, ed. 1940. *Historia de España. España Visigoda.* Vol. 3. Madrid.

Navarro Sáez, Rosario. 1999. Vil.la Fortunatus. In *Del Romà al Romànic. Historia, Art i Cultura de la Tarraconense Mediterrània entre els Segles IV i X,* 147–50. Barcelona.

Palol, Pedro de. 1967. *Arqueologia Cristiana de la España Romana. Siglos IV-VI.* Madrid/Valladolid.

———. 1967. La Arqueología paleocristiana en España: estado de la cuestión. *Actas de la I.Reunión Nacional de Arqueología Paleocristiana,* 17–25. Vitoria.

———. 1986. La arqueología cristiana en la hispania romana y visigoda. Descubrimientos recientes y nuevos puntos de vista. *Actes du XI congres international d'archeologie chretienne:* Vol. 2. 1989, 1975–2057. Lyon.

———. 1999. Basilica de la Vil.la Fortunatus. in *Del Romà al Romànic. Historia, Art i Cultura de la Tarraconense Mediterrània entre els Segles IV i X,* 193–94. Barcelona.

Patón Lorca, Belén. 1992. La villa romana de Carranque. Arquitectura y mosaicos. *Revista de Arqueología* 13(129):30–38.

Percival, John. 1976. *The Roman Villa: A Historical Introduction.* London.

———. 1997. Villas and Monasteries in Late Roman Gaul. *Journal of Ecclesiastical History* 48 (1):1–21.

Puertas, Rafael. 1972. Trabajos de planimetria y excavacion en la 'Villa Fortunatus,' Fraga (Huesca). *Noticiario Arqueológica Hispanico, Arqueología* 1:69–81.

Rodriguez Días, Alonso. 1986. *Arqueología de Tierra de Barros.* Badajoz.

Sánchez, Ángela Alonso. 1983. Las estancias absidiadas en las villae romanas de Extremadura. *Norba* 4:199–206.

Santos, Maria L.E.V.A. dos. 1972. *Arqueologia Romana do Algarve.* Vol. 2. Lisbon.

Schlunk, Helmut, and Theodor Hauschild. 1978. *Die Denkmäler der frühchristlichen und westgotischen Zeit.* Mainz am Rhein.

Serra Ráfols, José. 1943. La Villa Fortunatus, de Fraga. *Ampurias, Revista de Arqueología, Prehistoria y Etnología* 5:11–35.

———. 1945. Informe a la Excma. Diputacion Provincial de Badajoz sobre los restos romanos de la dehesa de La Cocosa: Acuerdos de la sesion ordinaria de la comision gobierno de la Diputacion provincial de Badajoz. November 17. Caja 1336.3.

———. 1949. La capilla funeraria de la dehesa de "La Cocosa." *Revista de Estudios Extremeños* 5:105–16.

———. 1952. *La 'villa' romana de la Dehesa de 'La Cocosa.'* Badajoz.

Sotomayor, Manuel, Teodoro Gonzalez Garcia, and Pablo Lopez de Osaba. 1979. *Historia de la Iglesia en España. La iglesia en la España romana y visigoda.* Edited by R. Garcia Villoslada. Madrid.

Torres, M. 1928. El origen del sistema de iglesias propias en España. *Arquivo de la Historia del Derecho Español,* 5.

Ulbert, Thilo. 1978. *Frühchristiliche Basiliken mit Doppelapsiden auf der iberischen Halbinsel.* Berlin.

Van Dam, Raymond. 1985. *Leadership and Community in Late Antique Gaul.* Berkeley.

———. 1986. "Sheep in Wolves' Clothing": The Letters of Consentius to Augustine. *Journal of Ecclesiastical History* 37 (4): 515–35.

Viñayo, Antonio. 1970. Las tombas del ábside del templo paleocristiano de Marialba y el martirologio Leonés. *Legio VII Gemina,* 550–68. Leon.

Vives, J. 1963. *Concilios Visigóticos e Hispano-Romanos.* Barcelona.

Vollman, B. 1974. Priscillianus. in *Realenzyklopädie der classischen Altertumswissenschaft.* suppl. XIV, 485–559. Edited by Pauly Wissowa. Munich.

NOTES

Most of the sites discussed in this essay are not fully published and thus I am greatly indebted to the excavators for sharing with me unpublished information. I am particularly grateful to Drs. Rafael Alfenim, Dimas Fernández-Galiano, Theodor Hauschild, Luz and John Huffstot, Conceição Lopes, Justino Maciel, Stephanie Maloney and Francesc Tuset. Thanks also to Javier Arce and Lois Drewer for healthy debate.

1. For instance, J. Fontaine, "Panorama espiritual del occidente peninsular en los siglos IV y V: Por una nueva problematica del Priscillianismo," *Primera Reuniono Gallega de Estudios Clasicos,* edited by M.C. Díaz y Díaz (Santiago de Compostela, 1981), 185–201; M. V. Escribano Paño, *Iglesia y Estado en el Certamen Priscilianista. Causa Ecclesiae y Iudicium Publicum* (Zaragoza, 1988), 192. For the designation of a specific villa as a Priscillianist meeting place, see L. Huffstott and J. Huffstott, "Prisciliano, um caso

arqueológico," *IV Reunió d'Arqueologia Cristiana Hispánica* (Lisbon, 1992), 443–47.

2. Much recent scholarship is moving in this direction. See V. Burrus, *The Making of a Heretic: Gender, Authority and the Priscillianist Controversy* (Berkeley, 1995), *passim;* R. Van Dam, "'Sheep in Wolves' Clothing': The Letters of Consentius to Augustine," *Journal of Ecclesiastical History* 37 (1986): 515–35; A. Ferriero, "Sexual Depravity, Doctrinal Error and Character Assassination in the Fourth Century: Jerome Against the Priscillianists," *Studia Patristica* 28 (1993): 29–38.
3. Burrus (1995), *passim.*
4. This coincidence was already noted by Palol in 1967. See P. d. Palol, "La arqueología paleocristiana en España: estado de la cuestión," *Actas de la I. Reunión Nacional de Arqueología Paleocristiana* (Vitoria, 1967), 18.
5. I have found evidence of approximately eleven villa-churches on the Iberian Peninsula, versus four examples in Gaul, and two in Italy. These figures are based on sites where villa and church show at least some evidence of contemporaneous occupation.
6. R. Alfenim and C. Lopes, "A basílica paleocristã/Visigótica do Monte da Cegonha (Vidigueira)," *IV Reunión d'Arqueologia Cristiana Hispánica* (Lisbon, 1992), 389–99; R. Alfenim and C. Lopes, "La villa romaine de Monte da Cegonha," *Dossier d'Archéologie* 198 (1994): 64–67; C. Lopes, "Sigillata de Montans no Monte da Cegonha (Vidigueira)," *Conimbriga* 28 (1989): 223–28; C. Lopes and R. Alfenim, "A villa romana do Monte da Cegonha," *Arqueología en el Entorno del Bajo Guadiana* (Huelva, 1992), 485–502.
7. See R. Alfenim and C. Lopes (1992). The dating of this phase is made difficult by mixed stratigraphy and the small amount of fourth- and fifth-century ceramics. (Personal communication and 1986 and 1988 Interim Reports, Archive, Instituto Português do Patrimonio Arquitectónico, Evora.)
8. A north entrance is assumed, since no evidence for entrances on other sides is possible. The extant south wall is preserved well above floor level with no evidence of a door, and the ground level on the west side is too low to accommodate a door without a step. Since no step was found, the largely destroyed north wall remains as the only possibility. See C. Lopes and R. Alfenim (1992), 491.
9. Interim Report, Archive, Instituto Português do Patrimonio Arquitectónico, Evora and personal communication by the excavators.
10. M. L. E. V. A. Santos, *Arqueologia Romana do Algarve,* vol. 2 (Lisbon, 1972), 373–77.
11. Interim Reports, Archive, Instituto Português da Arqueologia (Lisbon, 1996).
12. J. Maciel, "A 'villa' romana fluvial do Montinho das Laranjeiras, junto no Guadiana (Algarve)," *Arqueologia en el Entorno del Bajo Guadiana* (Huelva, 1992), 469–84; J. Maciel, *Antiguidade Tardia e Paleocristianismo en Portugal* (Lisbon, 1996), 93–100.
13. A careful reading of the nineteenth-century excavation notes indicate that the font was cut into the mosaic floor, and not itself paved with mosaics, as some authors have assumed. See M. L. E. V. A. Santos (1972), 374.
14. The excavator has found no evidence of the continuation of the walls of the church into the villa. However, numerous modern fence walls extend from the church walls to the villa (e.g. the SW wall) and these may be placed on earlier walls. These areas

have not been fully excavated.

15. J. Maciel (1996), 98–100.
16. No mosaics from the mainland of the Iberian Peninsula have been found to date later than the early to mid–fifth century. Only the Balearic Islands have produced sixth-century mosaics, and both a different style and great geographic distance separates them from those at Laranjeiras. See H. Schlunk and T. Hauschild, *Die Denkmäler der frühchristlichen und westgotischen Zeit* (Mainz am Rhein, 1978), 185; T. Hauschild, "Técnicas y maneras de construir en la arquitectura paleocristana hispánica," *II Reunió d'Arqueologia Paleocristiana Hispanica* (Barcelona, 1978), 83.
17. H. Coutinho, "Sigillata Clara do Montinho das Larenjeiras (Escavações de 1990)," *IV Reunió d'Arqueologia Cristiana Hispànica* (Lisbon, 1992), 507–14; H. Coutinho, *Terrra Sigillata Clara do Montinho das Laranjeiras. 1990 e 1991* (Alcoutim, 1997), 22–26.
18. See J. Maciel (1992), 36.
19. The original excavations of the site were carried out in the early part of the century under private patronage and never published. From 1945 to 1949, José Serra Ráfols surveyed and published the site. See J. Serra Ráfols, "La Villa Fortunatus, de Fraga," *Ampurias, Revista de Arqueología, Prehistoria y Etnología* 5 (1943): 11–35. Re-excavations were carried out by Rafael Puertas and Francesc Tuset, although the latter were not fully published. See R. Puertas, "Trabajos de planimetria y excavacion en la 'Villa Fortunatus,' Fraga (Huesca)," *Noticiario Arqueológica Hispanico, Arqueología* 1 (1972): 69–81; M. Guardia Pons, *Los Mosaicos de la Antigüedad Tardía en Hispania* (Barcelona, 1992), 83–100; P. d. Palol, "La arqueología cristiana en la hispania romana y visigoda. Descubrimientos recientes y nuevos puntos de vista," *Actes du XI congres international d'archeologie chretienne*, vol. 2 (Lyon, 1986), 2001–3; R.Navarro Sáez, "Vil.la Fortunatus," in *Del Romà al Romànic. Historia, Art i Cultura de la Tarraconense Mediterrània entre els Segles IV i X* (Barcelona, 1999), 147–50 and P. de Palol, "Basilica de la Vil.la Fortunatus," *Del Romà al Romànic. Historia, Art i Cultura de la Tarraconense Mediterrània entre els Segles IV i X* (Barcelona, 1999), 193–94.
20. See M. Guardia Pons (1992), 83–87.
21. Puertas suggested the church may have been part of an earlier, pre-church phase, but Tuset's excavations seem to have definitively attributed the stairs and lower chamber to the first, church phase. See R. Puertas (1986), 75; P. d. Palol (1986), 2001.
22. See M. Guardia Pons (1992), 87 and 97–98. There is no stratified ceramic material to date this construction.
23. See F. Almeida, "Torre de Palma (Portugal). A basílica páleocristã e visigótica," *Archivo Español de Arqueologia* 45–47 (1972–74): 103–112; M. Heleno, "A 'villa' lusitano-romana de Torre de Palma (Monforte)," *O Arqueólogo Português. New Series* 4 (1962): 313–38; T. Ulbert, *Frühchristiliche Basiliken mit Doppelapsiden auf der iberischen Halbinsel* (Berlin, 1978), 96–109; J. M. Blazquez, "Los mosaicos romanos de Torre de Palma (Monforte, Portugal)," *Archivo Español de Arqueologia* 53 (1980): 125–50; S. Maloney, "The Early Christian basilican complex of Torre de Palma (Monforte, Alto Alentejo, Portugal)," *IV Reunión d'Arqueologia Cristiana Hispánica* (Lisbon, 1992), 449–58; S. Maloney and J. Hale, "The Villa of Torre de Palma (Alto Alentejo)," *Journal*

of Roman Archaeology 9 (1996): 275–94; J. S. Huffstot, "Votive (?) Use of Coins in Fourth-Century Lusitania: The Builders' Deposit in the Torre de Palma Basilica," *Revista Portuguesa de Arqueologia* 1 (1998): 221–26.

24. For the coin evidence, see S. Maloney (1992).
25. J. Serra Ráfols, "Informe a la Excma. Diputacion Provincial de Badajoz sobre los restos romanos de la dehesa de La Cocosa," Archivo de Badajoz, Acuerdos de la sesion ordinaria de la comision gobierno de la Diputacion provincial de Badajoz, November 17, 1945. Caja 1336.3; J. Serra Ráfols, "La capilla funeraria de la dehesa de 'La Cocosa,'" *Revista de Estudios Extremeños* 5 (1949): 105–16; J. Serra Ráfols, *La 'villa' romana de la Dehesa de 'La Cocosa'* (Badajoz, 1952).
26. The most recent opinions favor a mid-fourth to mid-fifth-century date. See T. Hauschild (1978), 82; H. Schlunk and T. Hauschild (1978), 11–12; P. d. Palol, *Arqueologia Cristiana de la España Romana. Siglos IV-VI* (Madrid, 1967), 143. The excavator himself favored a sixth-century date based on perceived Byzantine influence. See J. Serra Ráfols (1952), 119–30 and 164–65.
27. D. Fernández-Galiano, "The villa of Maternus at Carranque," *Fifth International Colloquium on Ancient Mosaics* (Bath, 1994), 119–227; D. Fernández-Galiano, "La villa de Materno, Carranque (Toledo)," *Revista de Arqueología* 12 (1991): 26–36; D. Fernández-Galiano, "La villa romana de Carranque," *La Lonja* (Sept.-Nov., 1998): 437–40; D. Fernández-Galiano, B. Patón Lorca, and C. M. Batalla Carchenilla, "Mosaicos de la villa de Carranque: un programa iconográfico," *VI Coloquio Internacional sobre Mosaico Antiguo* (Palencia-Merida, 1990), 317–26; B. Patón Lorca, "La villa romana de Carranque. Arquitectura y mosaicos," *Revista de Arqueología* 13 (1992): 30–38.
28. D. Fernandéz-Galiano, 1998; *idem*, "La villa romana de Carranque," in *Hispania. El Legado de Roma* (Merida, 1999), 487–89, and cat. nos. 262–64, 266.
29. This attribution has been disputed, particularly by J. Arce, "Las metamorfosis de Carranque (Toledo)," *Madrider Mitteilungen* 27 (1986): 365–74, although the recent discovery of Theodosian mason marks makes the possibility of Maternus Cynegius as patron more likely.
30. T. Hauschild, "Die Märtyrer-Kirche von Marialba bei León," *Legio VII Gemina* (León, 1970), 313–21; *idem*, "Untersuchungen in der Märtyrerkirche von Marialba (Prov. Leon) und im Mausoleum von las Vegas de Pueblanueva (Prov. Toledo)," *Actas del VIII Congreso International de Arqueologia Cristiana* (Barcelona, 1969), 327–32; J. Carro Otero, "Estudio Anatomicoantropológico de los restos humanos del templo de Marialba," *Legio VII Gemina* (Leon, 1970), 525–48; A. Viñayo," Las tombas del ábside del templo paleocristiano de Marialba y el martirologio Leonés," *Legio VII Gemina* (Leon, 1970), 550–68.
31. See J. Percival, *The Roman Villa: A Historical Introduction* (London, 1976), 198; idem, "Villas and Monasteries in Late Roman Gaul," *Journal of Ecclesiastical History* 48 (1997): 1–21.
32. See R. Alfenim and C. Lopes (1992), 391, and personal communication.
33. Thanks to Stephanie Maloney and Äsa Ringbom for providing information on the

recent excavations.

34. See notes 17 and 18 above.
35. J. Serra Ráfols (1952), 166.
36. The fact that this building was placed inside the villa urbana has suggested to some that it post-dated the villa. See J. Serra Ráfols (1952), 67. However, the orientation and more importantly the door of this enigmatic structure aligns with the door leading to rooms off the peristyle, indicating the structure was planned to relate with extant, functioning villa buildings. Furthermore, the most recent, and to my mind, most sensible hypothesis of the apsed structure's function as audience hall, further indicates the continuation of domestic functions. T. Ulbert (1978), 109; A. Sánchez, "Las estancias absidiadas en las villae romanas de Extremadura," *Norba* 4 (1983): 205.
37. I am working with a Finnish team who have pioneered a new, more precise method for the dating of mortar, to provide more secure dating for each of the sites mentioned. For the method, see J. Heinemeir et al., "AMS C-14 Dating of Lime Mortar," *Nuclear Instruments and Methods in Physics Research. Section B* 123 (1997): 487–95.
38. For oratories, see R. Alfenim and C. Lopes (1992): 298.
39. See note 8 above.
40. P. d. Palol (1989), 2001.
41. See M. Fernandez Castro, "Villa romana y basilica cristiana en Hispania," in *La Religion Romana en Hispania* (Madrid, 1981), 386. Also, J. Maciel (1996), 112ff.
42. For this assumption, see J. F. Alonso, *La Cura Pastoral en la España Romanovisigoda* (Rome, 1955), 202. Alonso then goes on to say that these same canons indicate the presence of "iglesias propias" which fall outside the episcopal system. See also R. Menendez Pidal, *Historia de España. España Visigoda* (Madrid, 1940), 303.
43. The early sixth-century council of Tarragona gives the first real evidence for parochial organization. See J. Vives, *Concilios Visigóticos e Hispano-Romanos* (Barcelona, 1963), 36, c. 7 and 8, among many. For the undeveloped state of the Iberian church in the fourth and early fifth centuries, see J. Arce, *El Último Siglo de la España Romana (284–409)*, 2nd. ed. (Madrid, 1997), 148; P. David, "Les paroisses rurales dans l'occident latin du IVe au VIe siècle," in *Études historiques sur la Galice et le Portugal* (Paris, 1947), 13.
44. P. Díaz, "Iglesia propia y gran propiedad en la autobiografia de Valerio del Bierzo," *I Congreso International Astorga Romana* (1986), 297–303. In this respect, the villa-church seems to be the forerunner of the so-called "iglesia propia," or private foundation church. This phenomenon was particularly common in Spain during the Early Middle Ages, but its origins have been associated with the fourth century, anti-villa church canons. Like the villa-church, the "iglesias propias" maintained a disturbing amount of independence from the episcopate and were chiefly run by their founders. See R. Bigador, *La Iglesia Propia en España*, Analecta Gregoriana, 5 (Rome, 1933); M. Torres, "El origen del sistema de iglesias propias en España," *Arquivo de la Historia del Derecho Español*, vol. 5 (1928). The assimilation of the archaeological evidence into the history of the "iglesia propia" is an important, future task.
45. For the altar, see J. d'Encarnação, "Epigrafia do Nordeste Alentejano," *Conimbriga* 16

(1977): 59–82.

46. Examples include, in Hispania, Milreu, San Cucufate, Olhão and perhaps the unpublished Los Castillejos. In Gaul, Valentine, Newel and Montmaurin. In Britian, Lullingstone, Rapsely and Chedworth.
47. See G. Fouet, "Le sanctuaire gallo-romain de Valentine (Haute-Garonne)," *Gallia* 42 (1984): 153–73.
48. J. Vives (1963), 16–17, c. 2 and 4. A Theodosian code edict from 407 (*C. Th.* 16.5.49) specifically bans Priscillianists from meeting in villas.
49. For *alieni,* see V. Burrus (1995), 33–43.
50. For the supposition of villa retreats, see M. V. Escribano Paño (1988), 193; H. Chadwick, *Priscillian of Avila* (Oxford, 1978), 8–9.
51. V. Burrus (1995), 66–67; H. Chadwick (1978), 17–19; T. Breyfogle, "Magic, Women and Heresy in the Late Empire: The Case of the Priscillianists," in *Ancient Magic and Ritual Power,* ed. M. Meyer and P. Mirecki (Leiden, 1995), 141.
52. J. Vives (1963), 21, c.5 and 9. The former canon also betrays the lacuna of a true diocesan structure guiding their activities. Rather than terming the clerics' area of responsibility as *parochiae,* the canon uses an enumeration of traditional site categories, *castellum, vicus,* or *villa.*
53. For example, Chadwick, 12–29 (Zaragoza) and 170–74 (Toledo), and on Zaragoza, see B. Vollman, "Priscillianus," in *Realenzyklopädie der classischen Altertumswissenschaft,* suppl. 14, ed. Pauly Wissowa (Munich, 1974), 498–502 and 546–51.
54. See L. García Iglesias, "Sobre el canon IV del primer concilio de Zaragoza," *I Concilio Caesaraugustano. MDC Aniversario* (Zaragoza, 1980), 189–200; M. Díaz y Díaz, "A proposito del concilio de Zaragoza de 380 y su canon VI," *I Concilio Caesaraugustano. MDC Aniversario* (Zaragoza, 1980), 225–35.
55. For Lusitanian Priscillianism, see V. Burrus (1995), 27; M. V. Escribano Paño, "Cristianizaci6n y liderazgo en la Lusitania tardía," *IV Reunió d'Arqueologia Cristiana Hispànica* (Lisbon, 1992), 267–75. For Tarraconensis, see Augustine, Ep. 11*, and H. Chadwick, "New Letters of St. Augustine," *Journal of Theological Studies* 34 (1983): 434–36. For the excellent suggestion that the letters do not point to the existence of Priscillianism *per say* in Tarragona, see R. Van Dam (1986), 515–35.
56. Burrus has even claimed that Priscillianism only existed in Lusitania and Baetica and that the heresy did not extend to either Aquitaine or Galicia. See V. Burrus (1995), chap. 4.
57. This includes the bishoprics of Merida, Ossonoba and Olisipo (Lisbon).There is some disagreement as to whether the "Elbora" mentioned in the Council of Elvira was Ebora, modern day Evora. The great majority of scholars have placed this 'Elbora' near Caesarobriga. However, some still hold out hope for an Alentejan "Elbora." See J. Maciel (1996), 37n. 173; M. Sotomayor, T. Gonzalez Garcia, and P. Lopez de Osaba, *Historia de la Iglesia en España. La iglesia en la España romana y visigoda* (Madrid, 1979), 91.
58. For the most recent assessment of the boundaries, urbanization, and size of Lusitania, see J. Alarcão, J.-G. Gorges, V. Mantas, M. S. Frías, P. Sillières, and A. Tranoy,

"Propositions pour un nouveau tracé des limites anciennes de la Lusitanie romaine," in *Les villes de Lusitanie romaine, Collection de la Maison des Pays Ibériques* (Paris, 1990), 319–29. See also J.-G. Gorges, "Villes et villas de Lusitanie," in *Les villes de Lusitanie romaine, Collection de la Maison des Payes Ibériques* 42 (Paris, 1990), 95.

59. See particularly C. Lopes, "L'occupation du sol dans le territoire de Pax Iulia," *Itinéraires lusitaniens* (Bordeaux, 1995), 167ff.

60. For Beja, see J. Alarcão, R. Étienne, and F. Mayet, *Les Villas Romaines de São Cucufate* (Paris, 1990), 150–87; C. Lopes, "O território de Pax Iulia: limites e caracterização," *Arquivo de Beja, Series III* 2–3 (1996): 63–74; C. Lopes (1995); V. Mantas, "Implantação rural romana en torno da villa de S. Cucufate," *Arquivo de Beja, Series II* 3 (1986): 199–214; A. Rodriguez Días, *Arqueología de Tierra de Barros*, Badajoz, 1986; J. M. Fernández Corrales, *El Asentamiento Romano en Extremadura y su Analisis Espacial*, Caceres (1988).

61. See J.-G. Gorges, "Villas romaines en Lusitanie," *Bulletin des études portugaises et brésiliennes* 46–47 (1986–87): 156ff; J. Alarcão, R. Étienne, and F. Mayet (1990), 181–82. The Tierra de Barros and Cáceres area surveys were not able to give dates of settlements.

62. See R. Van Dam (1985), 27–42; L. Garcia-Moreno, "Élites e iglesia hispanas en la transición del imperio romano al reino visigodo," in *La Conversión de Roma. Cristianismo y Paganismo*, ed. J. M. Candou et al. (Madrid, 1991), 231–39; P. Díaz, "Propiedad y explotación de la tierra en la Lusitania tardoantigua," *Historia Antigua* 10–11 (1992–93). (*Actas de la Mesa Redona Internacional. El Medio Rural en Lusitania Romana. Formas de Habitat y Ocupación del Suelo*, 297–309).

63. For estate armies, see J. Arce (1997), 76–80.

64. On this process, see particularly Garcia-Moreno (1991), 232 and *passim*.

Christianizing the Syrian Countryside: An Archaeological and Architectural Approach

FRANK L. KIDNER

RECENTLY FRANK TROMBLEY HAS ARGUED THAT "THE CHRISTIANIZATION OF THE Syrian countryside is of archetypal significance for understanding that process elsewhere," in part because of "abundantly detailed narrative sources and numerous dated inscriptions which permit analysis down to the village level."[1] In this article I wish to both endorse and expand upon Trombley's point by arguing that the process so richly documented in textual and epigraphic sources needs to be supplemented by a careful examination of the extensive standing remains of the region since the built environment of the Syrian countryside is an equally rich and revealing but surprisingly neglected source for understanding how the area became Christian. A study of Christianization from this perspective takes us across several past and present "frontiers." As far as the past is concerned, it allows us to assess the shifting boundaries between urban and rural Christian cultures as manifested in the distinct configurations of their built environments and the exchanges between them. In the present, from the perspective of historians of Late Antiquity, it involves crossing disciplinary frontiers by using the insights of archaeologists, architects, and communications theorists to address a problem normally taken up by historians using the classical types of historical sources to which Trombley points. In the end, I will argue that the north Syrian standing remains reveal a complex interrelationship between domestic and church architecture, and between urban and rural architectural traditions, which point to many visual, formal, and spatial similarities. At the same time, we can see visual, formal, and spatial rupture between dwellings and churches, and between urban and rural architectural traditions. We shall see that the simultaneity of both rupture and union at the level of architecture helps to explain the Christianization of the region. What I do in this paper is frankly exploratory since historians (I am one) have not usually tried to expand their own text oriented studies of the Christianizing process with insights drawn from other disciplines concentrating on analyses of past built environments.

My examination will center on the villages of the Belus Massif, a limestone plateau some 35 miles to the east of Antioch, which stretches 70 miles from near Cyrrhus in the north to Apamea in the south, is about 40 miles across at its widest point, and occasionally reaches a height between 24,000 and 3,000 feet. It rises abruptly from the Orontes and Afrin valleys in the west and then descends more gently to the plains in the east near Aleppo (Beroea) and Qinnesrin (Chalcis sub Belo) (figure 1). In Late Antiquity it was divided administratively between Apamea in the south and Antioch in the west. For the most part, I shall concentrate on the territory under the jurisdiction of Antioch, the Antiochene, which covered all of the Belus Massif except for the central and southern parts of today's Jebel Zawiye. It is in this territory that the first rural Christian monuments in the region are found. I begin with a sketch of the region before the arrival of Christianity and then move to the moment when Christian structures first appeared there, concentrating on two of them: the single aisle church and the three-aisle colonnaded basilica. My main concern will be to relate them to previous, locally established models for domestic architecture. Next, I argue that conceptual and explanatory frameworks drawn from the disciplines I have already mentioned allow us to see how Christian manipulation of the local built environment related to the overall process of Christianization. I shall then look briefly at church architecture in the centuries after Christianity's first appearance in the region to see what changed or remained the same. Finally,

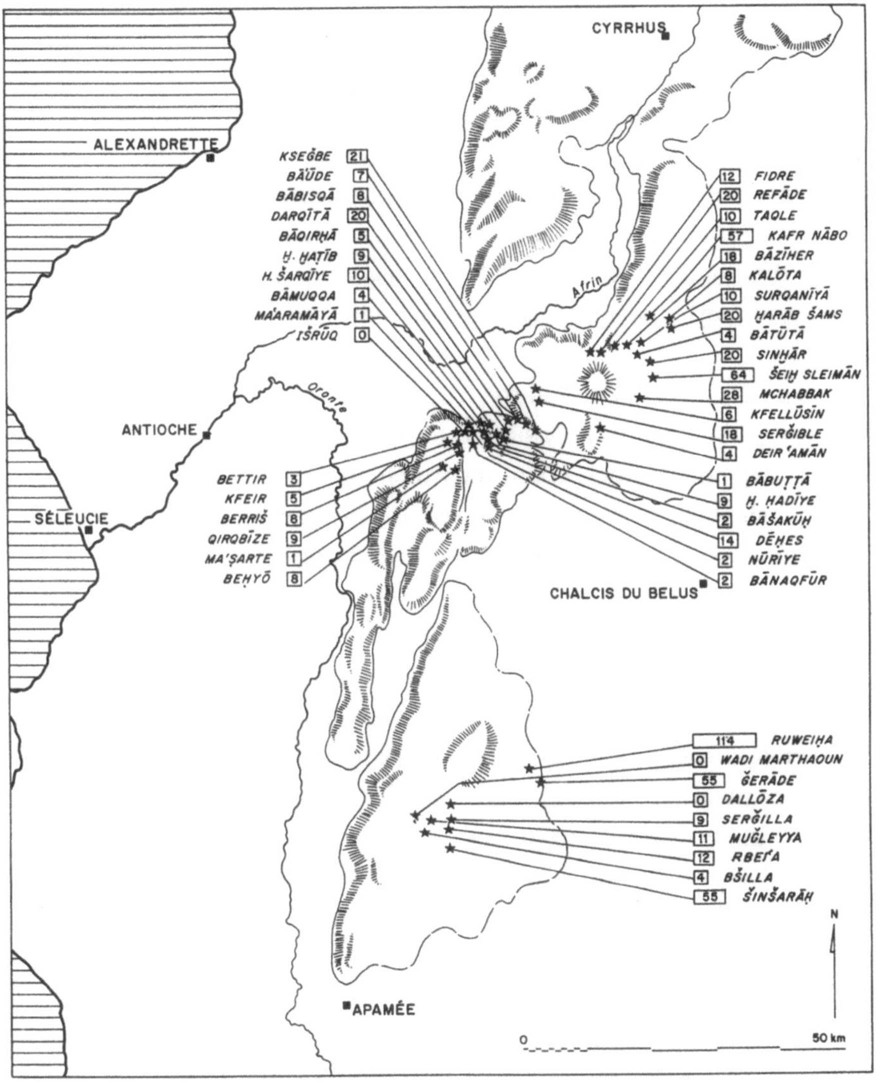

Figure 1. The villages of Belus Massif.

I shall draw some general conclusions from the totality of the architectural evidence.

The Belus Massif has always been marginal agricultural land, but in the late Roman and early Byzantine periods it supported some seven hundred villages, which housed an astonishingly dense population of remarkable prosperity. The region's wealth resulted from two factors: its location in the middle of an exceptionally urbanized part of the eastern Empire, and the two centuries' long peace that followed Galerius' war against the Persians in the late third and early fourth centuries. Proximity to great urban markets and prolonged peace stimulated a massive settlement of the area beginning in the late third century. The greatest period of growth and expansion started during the reign of Constantine I, and lasted for over two centuries until about 550, with the most vigorous activity occurring during the fifth century.[2]

When farmers moved into the Belus uplands from older settlements in the surrounding plains, they started to sell their agricultural surplus in the form of olive oil, livestock, grain, and fruit in the surrounding buoyant urban markets. The Belus was thus urbanized as a result of its close ties to a thriving regional economy based on great cities, but it was not urban in and of itself, despite the characterizations of some earlier scholars who referred to the local settlements as the "dead cities." The settlements there were distinctively rural complexes set apart from the urban environment. The plateau was relatively inaccessible from the outside; the villages in it were connected to each other and to the plains below only by a series of tracks leading to main paved roads. But it was down these tracks that increasing amounts of agricultural surplus moved toward market. The sale proceeds then funded the extensive building activity in the villages.

The systematic analysis of the Massif's standing remains began in the middle of the last century and has continued to the end of this one. It has resulted in a series of outstanding older studies by archaeologists, architects, and art historians, the most important of which were published by Count Melchior de Vogüé, Howard Crosby Butler and the other members of the two Princeton expeditions to Syria, Jean Lassus, and Georges Tchalenko.[3] More recent work by Georges Tate and Christine Strube has moved in two directions. Tate has published the first volume of an *Annales*-inspired demographic and economic study of the region based on a computer generated analysis of domestic architecture.[4] Strube has done important work on architectural decoration, which continues the art historical analyses begun by her distinguished predecessors.[5] In this essay I shall draw on all these studies to show how data presented in them can expand our understanding of the Christianizing process in the region.

Any analysis of the earliest building activity in the Belus Massif must now begin with the recent work of Georges Tate of the Institut Français d'Archéologie du Proche-Orient (IFAPO). Tate has revised our understanding of the area's village architecture in fundamental ways. In particular, he has called into question earlier views that the domestic architecture of the region reflected economically specialized rural communities made up of tenant farmers, small independent owner-occupiers, and trades or craftsmen, which were headed by a local aristocracy of rich landlords living in sumptuous "villas." An extensive analysis of domestic architecture shows that the villages were overwhelmingly peopled by independent peasant farmers who either owned or rented their lands and who lived in work-a-day peasant houses, which they also most likely owned. Although there is evidence of large estates, with one exception they seem not to have consisted of consolidated holdings dominating whole villages or regions.[6] Tate thinks this indicates that there was not much difference between the economic and social conditions of peasants working strips of domain land and those in the free κώμαι. Finally, there is no real evidence that the phenomenon of patronage, mentioned by Libanios as a growing fact of rural life, played any significant role in the Belus villages, nor is there any evidence that a landed aristocracy was resident there. The "villas" identified in earlier studies are, in fact, simply larger versions of the farm house. The Massif was therefore the home almost exclusively of small or medium owner-occupiers and tenants of considerable means.[7]

From the beginning the farm house dominated the local landscape, making up something like 95 percent of the built environment. Before the construction of churches, the only public buildings in the region were temples, baths, and "androns." To date eighteen temples have been identified either inside or outside villages. Later, churches and chapels would number well over one hundred. Baths occur in only seven sites, all large or medium sized. There are five, and possibly eight, structures that are usually called androns. Of the five certain ones, three date to before 300 C.E. The other two were most likely built in the mid–fifth century C.E. They are almost certainly public buildings, although their actual function is unclear; they may have been community centers, or perhaps, banquet halls. Most of them have their principal room on the second story like dwellings, but unlike dwellings they are not shut off from the rest of the community by an enclosure wall.[8] In every village where one or more of these structures were built, dwellings overwhelmingly outnumbered them.

The form and "look" of local farms were set when occupation of the Belus first began in the Roman period and remained absolutely fixed for the next five hundred years.[9] Construction techniques and decorative schemes changed over the centuries, and some houses were clearly costlier than others, but their basic design remained unaltered. The farm was a distinctly local, rural dwelling type. No urban parallels have been found in the scant information we have on the domestic architecture of Antioch, its suburb Daphne, and Apamea. The only possible urban evidence for making a connection between the built environments of city and country is found on the border of the Yaqto mosaic from Antioch, which shows the city and Daphne as they appeared in 450. One section consists of a public square with a structure almost identical to the well preserved andron at Serjilla in the southern part of the Belus. But, as we just saw, the few androns we know of, while bearing some resemblance to farm houses, were public not domestic structures. This is the closest we can come to any documented connection between urban and rural "civil" architecture.[10]

Farms were actually ensembles of buildings enclosed within a wall, which shut them off from the outside world (fig. 2). Access was through one or more gates in the boundary wall. Boundary walls and all buildings within them were made of the local limestone, which was cut into blocks and laid down without the use of mortar or clamps. The main building in the ensemble was the domicile. Its rear wall served as part of the overall boundary wall. It was rectangular, had two stories, and was often aligned on an east-west axis with its front facing south. The front consisted of a projecting ground level portico surmounted by a gallery. The portico was usually pillared while the gallery might be pillared or columned. In either case the second story uprights supported an architrave at roof level. The spaces between the uprights on the second floor gallery were usually filled with large stone slabs

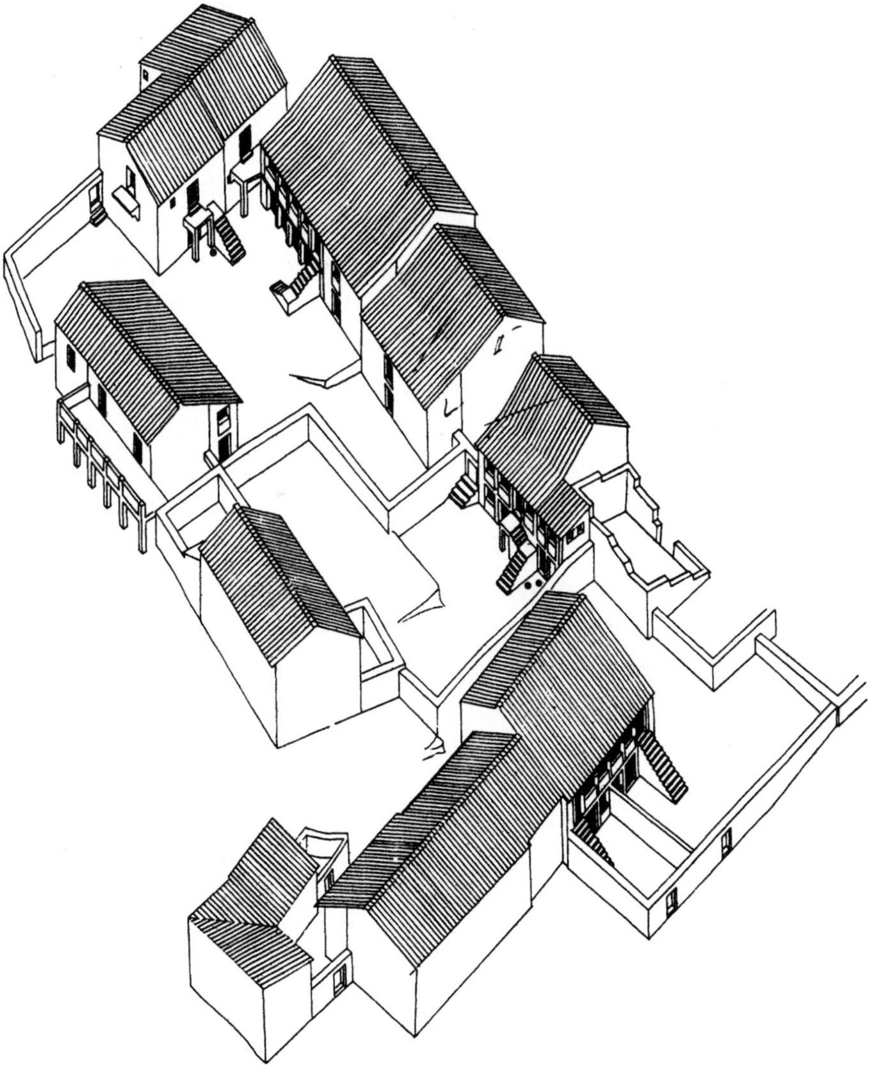

Figure 2. Isometric drawing from Tate.

creating a balcony. The roof was pitched, resting on a wooden frame, and was tiled. The building's ground floor housed the farm's livestock and was also used as a storage area. Its flooring was sometimes stamped earth, but it could be paved with stone or with a simple mortar. Living quarters were on the second floor. Access to them was usually gained by stone stairs cut into the facade of the building or projecting outward from it. These stairs led to the gallery. Second story rooms were mostly of the same modest size and were accessible only from a single door opening onto the gallery; it is rare to find a door leading from the interior of one room to another. There are traces of shelves, niches, and cupboards in many of these second story rooms, but there is no indication of specialized use for any of them, and none can be identified as a kitchen, a sleeping as opposed to a living room, or the like. Most of them were floored with wood, although some had stone floors resting on corbels and wide-spanned arches rising from the ground floor.

Dwellings seem at first to have consisted of one or two rooms on each floor. Later, many were expanded with the addition of one or more two-story units. Subsequent renovations could lead in some cases to very large buildings of ten rooms or more on each floor, but expansion never involved a change in basic plan and did not bring specialization of rooms with it. It almost certainly resulted from the demographic expansion in the Massif during the fourth and fifth centuries as households grew in size. We do not know exactly how people living in these units were related; a reasonable guess is that they constituted real or fictive family groups of some kind or another. The sameness of the dwelling rooms, however, points to a certain egalitarianism. Nobody seems to have had larger, more elaborate, or specialized living quarters.

The main building within the wall was almost always fronted by a courtyard which could be paved with large stones. Around the courtyard were ancillary buildings, which probably served as storage rooms or animal shelters. Some may have served as kitchens. In or near the bounded area one also often finds oil or grape presses.

The wall surrounding these ensembles cut them off from the rest of the village. Thus villages consisted of island-like farm units. They dotted the village landscape in no apparent order since no grid plan or other overall organizing device shaped the village as a whole. There are no streets between the houses, simply unpaved passageways. The only recognizable overall pattern in the villages is a tendency toward closure to the outside world. The village periphery is usually made up of the solid rear walls of farm units, which present their largely blank façades to anyone approaching them. No village in the Belus was fortified, almost certainly because of the long period of peace during the era of greatest expansion, but the village as a whole offered the same guarded stance to the outside as the farm units themselves.[11]

It was into this well established and remarkably monochromatic built environment that Christianity made its way in the early fourth century, just as the region began its remarkable demographic and economic expansion. The first sign of Christians in the Belus Massif occurs in an inscription dated to 326-27. The first recognizable Christian grave dates to 369. The first recognizable church structures date from the same century when two different types of churches started to be built in the region: the single-aisle church and the colonnaded three-aisle basilica. In one way or another both clearly resembled local styles of domestic architecture.

The resemblance between local dwellings and the region's earliest ecclesiastical structures fits well with a number of well-known works on early Christian architecture, all of which employ what we can call a "developmental model" for organizing and analyzing the extant textual, epigraphic, and material evidence. This model conceives of the history of Christian architecture as a series of stages emerging gradually over time, each of which is characterized by distinctive kinds of church structures. Normally a distinction is made between pre- and post-Constantinian churches since the emperor's conversion and his subsequent patronage of the Christians led to widespread use of a new Christian building, the basilica. For English speakers Richard Krautheimer's study of Paleo-Christian and Byzantine architecture is the standard account using this model.[12] The most recent is that of Michael White.[13]

The developmental model is concerned mainly with long term trends in Christian architecture and less with locating churches in the complete architectural context in which they existed. In part, this is the result of gaps in our evidence—contexts often are not there to be studied. But it also results from the basic logic underlying this type of analysis which puts a premium on issues of chronology and sequence. White's recent study serves as an instructive example of how a sophisticated version of the model works.

White argues for a three-staged development of pre-Constantinian church architecture. In each stage developments reflect changes in the social conditions of the communities making them. The first stage, the house church, attested to in the Pauline corpus, consisted of architecturally unmodified houses as the typical Christian meeting place. The size of communities and their liturgical practices required nothing more than access to a member's house when it was time to assemble. The second stage, that of the "house of the church (*domus ecclesiae*)," which is found across the empire from Lullingstone in Britain to Dura Europos on the Euphrates, involved the modification of already existing houses into places used exclusively for church purposes. This points to larger communities, changes in liturgical practice, and to some kind of group ownership of buildings resulting from donation, patronage, or purchase. The final stage, that of the "hall of the church (*aula ecclesiae*)," involved the construction of places for Christian assembly that were even larger than those found in the *domus ecclesiae*. These "halls" resulted from yet more changes in the social circumstances and liturgical practices of the community.

The basic strength of White's work is to link church construction to the changing social conditions of specific Christian communities and to the larger urban environment where many other groups engaged in similar acquisition and subsequent remodeling of houses as community meeting places. His social contextualization is done, however, within the overarching developmental model, which posits an orderly evolution from one stage to the next. Thus the last stage, the hall of the church, "evolved through a continued, natural course of adaptation" from the earlier house of the church.[14] Sometimes hall churches were the product of still further remodeling of older meeting places. In these cases "natural adaptation" is evident and to some degree predetermined. Sometimes, however, they were entirely new buildings that from the first were intended only for Christian worship. Here adaptation resulted from a conscious decision to maintain continuity with older, domestically rooted structures. White's example of the first kind of development is the villa under the basilica Euphrasiana at Porec (Parentium) in Croatia. His example of the second is the church at Qirqbize in the Jebel il-A'la region of the Belus Massif.

The first detailed analysis of the Qirqbize structure was carried out by Georges Tchalenko, who argued that it was the oldest church in the region, dating to the early fourth century.[15] The building is strikingly similar to the large dwelling found immediately to the east and also to the general plan for dwellings in this part of Syria. It is a rectangular structure with a pitched roof that originally was covered by tiles supported on a wooden frame. Its two entries are on the long south side, which is preceded by a portico. The south side faces a courtyard and the whole complex is bounded by a wall. Tchalenko pointed out, quite correctly, that all of these features mimic the adjacent house, making it nearly indistinguishable. Tchalenko also argued that in its original form the interior consisted simply of a single room with a raised platform at the east end. As it now stands, a "triumphal" arch is there, as well as a bema, a horseshoe-shaped construction in the center of the building, which is found in a number of churches in the region. In Tchalenko's analysis, these were both later additions to the structure whose simple original form gives us the architectural minimum necessary for the Christian cult. Tchalenko also argued that it is the earliest example in north Syria of the house church, finding precedents for the large room not only in dwellings but also in the andron, which can be viewed as a community house of some sort. The one at Berrish-North stands only a few miles away and antedates the church. White adopts Tchalenko's analysis, and calls the church an *aula ecclesiae*. But whatever the Qirqbize structure is called, according to this interpretation it is a late but clear example of the last pre-Constantinian stage of church architecture, which evolved in an orderly way from the private house to which it continued to have strong formal ties. A real break with earlier architectural traditions, it is argued, came only with the introduction of the basilica during the reign of Constantine I.[16]

The Qirqbize church is one of several single-aisle churches in the central region of the Belus which was at first the privileged area for this kind of building. Later, it would be used throughout the Massif, sometimes in monastic complexes where it was particularly favored, and sometimes as the community church in small villages. It is also found in chapels.[17] But it was never the dominant type of church. That distinction goes to the colonnaded three-aisle basilica of which over one hundred examples are known. More importantly, the Qirqbize church probably was *not* the earliest type in the region. Christine Strube has made a convincing case that it should be dated to the end of the fourth century and not to the beginning as Tchalenko and White have argued.[18] She also has shown that the triumphal arch is probably not a later addition to the church, but was placed in the east end at the time of its construction. Therefore, we do not have a pristine example of a "hall church" in the Belus before Christians there started to use the basilical form. We have instead a late fourth century "hall" that from the beginning incorporated a standard basilical feature, the east end arch. All of this means that the sequence presented by Krautheimer, Tchalenko, and White in fact does not work in the Belus Massif. On the contrary, it seems clear that the first churches were basilicas, and that the "hall church" appeared after or at best simultaneously with them and was influenced by them. This sets the developmental model on its head.

It is to the basilicas than I now turn since they illustrate even more strikingly than the single-aisle church how already established forms of domestic architecture did and did not influence these new Christian structures, and how this in turn can help us to understand the Christianization process in the region. As I turn to them I shall also shift from an analytic framework centered on the long term development of Christian buildings to one that considers them as part of a local repertory of structures making up the overall built environment of the village. The developmental model we have explored so far is of use to the historian looking back on the period of Christian origins because in very general terms it explains how Christian architecture came to be what it was over roughly three centuries. But its perspective is "presentist," since it focuses on a problem that is clear to us in retrospect but could not have been clear to people in the Late Antique world, few if any of whom would have known of various types of churches built over several centuries in widely different provinces of the Empire. The perspective I propose to adopt recognizes this and thus concentrates on church architecture from the locals' point of view by treating it as an ensemble with which everyone in the community would be familiar. Shifting this way from a chronologically based developmental perspective to a holistic one makes it easier to see how the first churches in the Belus villages would have been assessed and understood by the people who used them.

It is likely that the first churches in the Belus were built in Jebel Sim'an, the northernmost part of the Massif. They stand in the villages of Burj Heidar, Batuta, Sinhar, and Fafertin. All are datable to the second half of the fourth century, and the one at Fafertin is securely dated to 372.[19] All are colonnaded three-aisle basilicas. We do not know why they were built in these villages or who financed their construction, but a safe guess is that urban clergy took the lead on both accounts. An inscription found at Fafertin may mention a bishop Antiochos and definitely mentions a certain Maris who is identified as a periodeutes, that is a circuit riding priest in the region acting under a bishop.[20]

From the local point of view, the colonnaded three-aisle basilica was an architectural alien which must have been imported from Antioch, the metropolitan see of the Belus, or from other nearby urban centers.[21] Except for a rectangular shape and pitched roof, it bore no real resemblance either inside or out to the established built environment of the Massif. The curious thing, however, is to see how quickly the exterior of the basilica, like that of the single-aisle church, was systematically modified to resemble as closely as possible the dominant architectural form in the region, the farm house complex. It is as if the church, the "house" of the new religious community, reshaped itself in a thorough-going way to accommodate prior local traditions. Yet, at the same time, church interiors remained radically unlike the interiors of any other building in the community.

Let us begin with outsides.[22] The first cluster of churches in the Jebel Sim'an share a number of striking and idiosyncratic features. In overall size they mimic the farm since the width and length of the church are roughly the same as nearby dwellings while the heights of the central and side aisles correspond to those of their rooms and south portico/balconies respectively. Their north and west ends are closed; access to the interior is only from the long south side through two doors. One thus entered the church from the "wrong" place since the point of entry accords poorly with the emphatic interior east-west axis. If, however, one has farm house plans in mind, the entry is exactly right. This clearly was the perspective of local designers; they even regularly made the south aisle wider than its northern counterpart to accommodate it. To carry the fit between house and church further, churches usually have south courtyards, often with ancillary buildings (later, baptisteries) inside them. Finally, the ensemble is bounded by a wall with an entry gate.

The main problem for this mimetic strategy, of course, was the east-end apse of the church. There almost certainly had never been anything like it in the earlier built environment, even in temple architecture.[23] At Fafertin, where the east end may have been built by urban workers, the apse was semi-exposed, emerging like an architectural sore thumb from between two flanking rooms.[24] In the other three cases, at Burj Heidar, Batuta, and Sinhar, where the architects and workmen were clearly local, the problem was solved by camouflage: the apse was placed behind a rectilinear chevet so that the rectangular shape of the building could be maintained as far as possible. Tchalenko explains the enclosure of the apse as an architectural necessity. Since its half dome was built of stone blocks placed without the use of mortar or clamps, a counter force was necessary to stabilize the construction, which in part took the form of the straight east wall.[25] My point is somewhat different. Leaving aside the specific technical problems posed by construction techniques, the end result was a hidden apse and a church exterior looking as much like a farm complex as possible. That the look of the church mattered is shown by a late fifth or early sixth century church at Gubelle where mortar was used to build the apse which at first projected out from the east end of the building and was fully visible. Later, two rooms were built to the north and south of it and a rectilinear chevet was put in place as the optic values of old models asserted themselves and, finally, carried the day (fig. 3).[26]

Church interiors were another story. Upon entering the church one faced directly the parallel arcaded colonnades and their clerestory, a form as alien to previous traditions as the apse. Despite the local builders' obvious unfamiliarity with it and the equally obvious deficiencies in its execution, it was

GÜBELLE

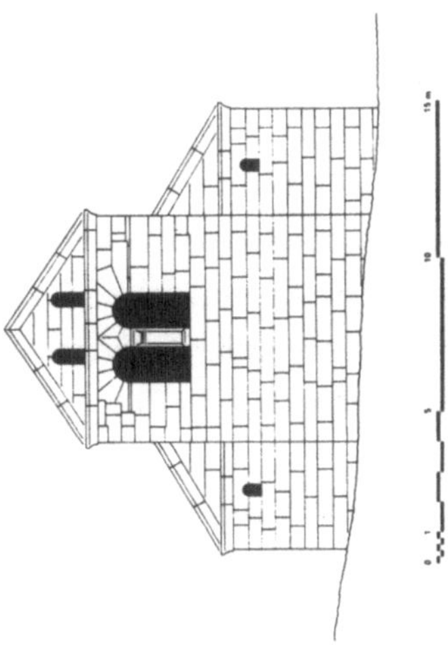

184. L'église: façade Ouest.

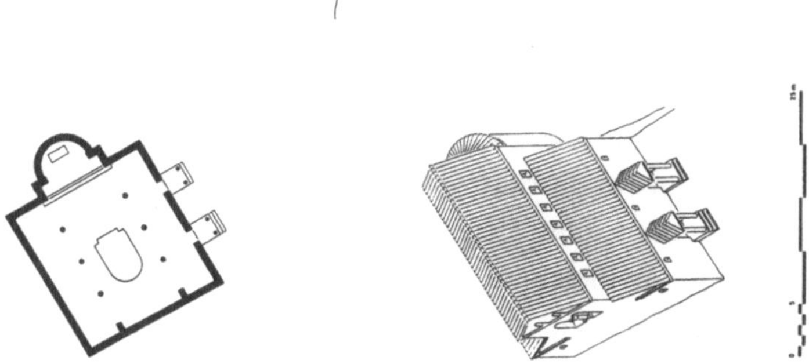

185. L'église: plan et perspective de l'état initial.

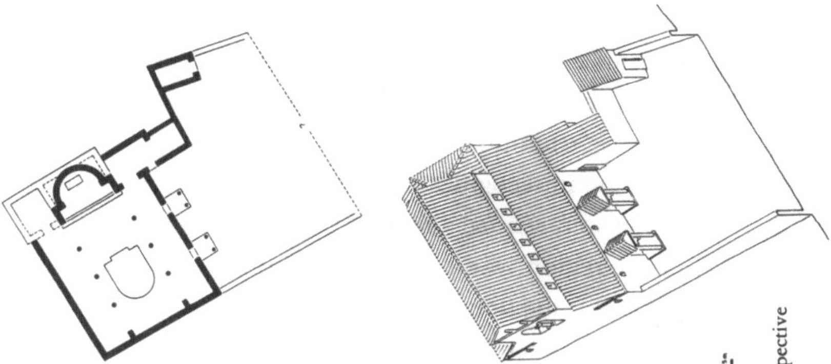

186. L'église: plan et perspective de l'état final.

Figure 3. Plan of the Church.

produced in all the earliest basilicas of the type: the colonnaded architrave, an element frequently used in house balconies, was never employed in church interiors in this part of the Belus Massif. Passing through the colonnade, clerics took up positions in the east end of the church while all the laity probably assembled in the western area.[27] Facing east, worshippers would see the imposing "triumphal" arch and beyond it the interior of the apse. The apse would be unrecognizable within the lexicon of local architectural forms, but the arch echoed a feature found on the ground floors of some dwellings in the region where wide-spanned arches resting on low piers were used to support the flooring of the second story living quarters.[28] Although the pilasters flanking and supporting the arch were higher than those used in houses, the overall form would be far more familiar than that of the apse beyond. But it was a form found at ground level, the place of store rooms or animals, not of humans, who lived in the upper story of their houses and usually assembled on the second floor of the andron. Moreover, the church floor, a ground floor, on which the worshipper stood, could be paved with stones or with a simple mortar—techniques that were also used for the animal part of the dwelling. Only one formal feature inside the church spoke of continuity with the pervading built environment—the pitched and tiled roof resting on a wooden frame. Everything else was radically new or strangely out of place.

Now, what are we to make of all of this? In the existing literature on the Belus Massif, many of the inter-relationships between dwellings and churches have already been noted, but little has been done to integrate them into an overall analysis of the ways in which changes in the built environment related to the Christianization of the region. To date, most studies have dealt with issues of architectural form as the setting for liturgical practice, with developments in decorative systems, or with demographic and economic change in the region. Here, I want to argue that another way to make sense out of the architectural evidence is to develop new conceptual and explanatory frameworks, which concentrate on the general issue of architecture as a type of nonverbal communication, and the more specific ones of architectural space and form, as these have been examined by archaeologists, architects, and communication theorists.[29]

We can begin with the commonplace observation that built structures shape those living in and near them. More specifically, the ensemble or repertory of buildings in any given community, which we can call the built environment, reflects, maintains, creates, or subverts social order by delineating and categorizing space. In fact, as a specific form or component of material culture, the built environment can be thought of as the "objectification of social being."[30] As such it creates, reiterates, or calls into question such basic categories, spaces, or oppositions as inside/outside, public/private, male/female, culture/nature, and the like. Because it deals with social being, the messages contained in the built environment are primarily public ones aimed at the community as a whole and concerned with collective understandings. However, along with collective understandings, individual and idiosyncratic ones occur as well. Because both kinds of responses to messages are possible, we have to say that the built environment can suggest or order certain kinds of message reception, but cannot compel acceptance of them—it can only persuade with greater or lesser force. I would argue that the persuasive quality of its messages was particularly strong in a place like the Belus Massif, where the repertory or "palette" of built structures was remarkably stable and limited over a very long period.

Because the built environment offers architecturally transmitted information about social experience, we can say that it constitutes a distinctive form of language, if we define "language" very broadly as anything (ritual gesture, work practices, customs, institutional arrangements, and so on) that shapes experience of the world in understandable and plausible ways.[31] This shaping involves sorting out the component parts of the world using such things as association, contrast, and context to create satisfactory and usable patterns and categories for social life. The built environment does all of this by reinforcing, or subverting, already established social mappings, or by creating new ones. But this architectural "language" is both nonverbal and material; it therefore operates in its own distinctive ways.

One noteworthy feature of architectural language is that it lacks the linearity and precision of verbal communication. Its messages, therefore, are received often as overall impressions or clusters of cues letting people know what kind of setting they are in, who is expected in the setting, and what kind of behavior is permitted there. It can do this with proxemic, that is spatially framed, cues resulting from the delineation of overall space. Operating in this manner it addresses issues of access, inclusion, or exclusion as regards the elements in the built environment. Architectural language can also send its cues in a categorical way by making distinctions between different types of structures. Spatial and categorical cues usually work together to communicate information about the kinds of people and behaviors expected or permitted in the component parts of the built environment. For example, students at a university (a) know whether the room they have entered is a lecture hall or a seminar room, (b) know whom to expect in the space, and (c) know about appropriate and inappropriate behaviors therein. They know this because the clusters of cues they receive are appropriated on the basis of prior cultural understandings.

Messages can come from two levels of the built environment, the semi-fixed and the fixed. In our example, the semi-fixed level would include such things as tables, chairs, blackboards, cabinets, and the like. The room itself is the fixed element.[32] Cues sent from these two levels are usually taken for granted, until something challenges them and calls them into question.[31] The relative importance of semi-fixed and fixed cues depends on cultural settings. In the Belus villages, where the repertory of the built environment was so limited and its elements so standardized and invariant, fixed elements were particularly prominent in message communication.

We have already seen that the built environment cannot compel a particular reception of its messages, it can only try to persuade with greater or lesser force. Its persuasiveness, however, is considerable because it can construct messages simultaneously in two different but interlocking ways—vision and touch. This results in message redundancy, and redundancy increases force. Architecture also increases its communicative power by presenting social order in a uniquely three dimensional or "environmental" way, that is in concrete and enveloping fashion, creating what we might call a "buildingscape" which finds its nearest analogue in the local landscape. The analogy to landscape calls attention to another feature of the built environment, its qualities of fixity and permanence. The materiality of architecture gives it solidity and endurance which allows its messages to be repeated continuously over an extended period of time and thus to cast them as invariable cues for local understandings of society.[34]

The distinctive characteristics of architectural language result in its sharing many qualities with ritual. The concreteness, persistence, and invariability of architectural messages work to convey a sense of ultimate reliability. In this way the messages are akin to the sacred propositions embodied in ritual and are thus one of the most powerful factors in shaping peoples' sense of themselves and the world around them.[35] I would suggest that this was particularly the case in the Belus Massif where literacy was sporadic. In the absence of well established practices of writing and reading, ritual and architecture, working in tandem, were central to the establishment of basic codes of meaning.[35] Application of these insights to the built environment of the Belus plateau helps us to understand what was at stake when the new architectural structures of Christianity were introduced.

As we have seen, before the arrival of Christianity the built environment of the Belus consisted almost entirely of dwelling complexes organized into villages. The overall nature of the dwelling and the shape of villages as a whole point to significant concerns with issues of social categorization manifested in careful delineation of boundaries between dwellings and controlled access from the outside to domestic spaces. Within the dwelling, issues of boundaries and access setting off different categories of space continued to be paramount and were encoded in a fixed, invariable repertory of architectural forms. Surrounded and enclosed by their farm walls, people lived in carefully marked spaces while animals, tools, and stores were placed in equally delimited and marked off ones of their own. Overall, this points to separation and categorization as paramount organizing principles of community life. These principles were realized by means of a proper use of architectural forms gathered into distinctive ensembles. The forms and their ensembles did not simply give voice to the principles or execute them in stone, they also created and maintained them.

This, however, is only half of the picture. In fact, villages were also utterly homogeneous and unseparated. Dwellings and the spaces in them were all fundamentally alike. From the beginning of settlement they repeated themselves endlessly as villages grew, using the same repertories and following the same overall organizational blueprint. This points to an architecturally created understanding of community as "united because identical" in all its component parts. The invariability of architectural forms and blueprints, in conjunction with the careful boundaries drawn by them between different kinds of architectural spaces, indicate that the creation of new spaces involving any novelty in form, or any repositioning of forms in new ensembles, would constitute a sharp challenge to usual ways of conceptualizing the built environment of the village.

The appearance of the basilica in the Belus region precipitated a crisis between old and new ways of mapping the human community. The older world had been powerfully shaped by an architectural environment that was well-established, well-articulated, and remarkably unchanging. It conveyed deeply reliable information about who villagers were, and how they related to each other and the world around them. The basilica, as architecture, made claims to present information of the same order. But its information was novel and alien, since it defined itself by means of an architectural language that was either strangely misused or entirely foreign from the villagers' point of view.

The crisis was resolved almost immediately by means of a complex and finally ambiguous negotiation between architectural languages and their messages. Churches roughly of the same dimension as nearby houses were, like them, set off from the outside world by a boundary wall. The wall was a clear sign that the church was not a completely new and alien phenomenon in the village. By such means the church began to present itself as a dwelling and told the village that the people of the church were somehow organized in ways like the people of the house. It sent messages of both accommodation to and assimilation of the pre-existing village environment, which had the strength of being couched in deeply familiar architectural language. This is all the more remarkable when one considers that the traditional sacred structure in the region, the temple, which was usually raised on a podium and was prostyle in antis, bore scant resemblance to village dwellings.[37] As villagers passed through the church's wall gate, entered the courtyard, and then made their way to the south entrances of the main rectangular structure, they continued to find themselves in a setting of forms and architectural elements aimed at assimilation and accommodation. Even the church proper was a house—or nearly so. While wall, courtyard, and point of entry spoke of dwellings, the line of clerestory windows and the ground floor doors spoke of something else.

That something else became strikingly clear once the building was entered. Here, as we have seen, newness was almost completely triumphant and nothing could be taken for granted. Traditionally, scholars interested in the message of newness have concentrated on the ritual enacted within the church. Concern with architectural form has been shaped within this general perspective, and has been largely confined either to analyses of the building's "symbolic" content—the so-called triumphal arch as a symbol of Christ's cosmic rule, the east oriented apse as a symbol of his resurrection, and so on—or to an analysis of how a building's form and its later modifications were related to developing liturgical practice. But these perspectives, while legitimate, are not sufficient. The church structure in and of itself, as an enveloping and enduring built environment, worked to convey messages about the meaning of the new religion and the people who adhered to it. This meaning was neither confined to nor even primarily concerned with the "symbolic" content of the new architectural order. Rather, it offered a new map of the human community as it created a new type of architectural space in which human beings could and should assemble. It reorganized and restructured the community by making this space out of unknown and repositioned architectural forms, which defined it both as radical novelty, as in the central use of the colonnaded arcade, and as a startling reassembling and repositioning of the old, as in the use of ground floor arches modified into "triumphal" ones. Thus the new architectural ensemble of church interiors was not simply the background for the primary message of liturgical performance. It was, in fact, the equal partner of liturgy, conveying the same order of information in the same basic ways. It interlocked with ritual action thus creating a final and still more powerful redundancy. When taken together, the interior and exterior of the church building spoke of the Christian community in terms of newness and sameness, continuity and rupture, accommodation, assimilation, and supersession with unique power and in ways that no text or inscription can reveal.

Up to now I have focused on the earliest Christian structures in the Belus region, the basilicas of Jebel Sim'an, because they show us in remarkably clear fashion how Christianity first inserted itself into the built environment of rural, northwestern Syria. At this point I want to turn to a brief discussion of what came afterward, architecturally speaking. Christian architecture was introduced in the villages starting in the fourth century, but it continued to spread and to take root for several more centuries before the Arab conquest. This process, like the moment of introduction, is well documented in the standing remains of the region. An examination of the structures can show us what changed and what remained the same in the architectural language of the new religion.

One of the most noticeable features of the on-going Christian built environment is the continuing dominance of the basilical church. Throughout the fifth and sixth centuries, when churches were being built in ever greater numbers, the colonnaded three-aisle basilica clearly remained the form of choice. This is all the more interesting when we compare the development of church architecture in the nearby cities; there a variety of church forms proliferated: cross shaped churches, and central plan ones, as well as basilicas.[38] With the exception of the great cross shaped structure at Qalat Sim'an, dedicated to St. Simeon Stylites the Elder, and the sixth century octagonal church at Mujleyya in the southern area of Gebel Zawiye, none of these forms were adopted in the Belus.[39] In the villages, the only alternative form deployed, as we have seen, was the single-aisle church.

Although the full repertory of urban Christian architecture never caught on in the hinterland, certain features of the basilica, which were not originally present there and had their origins in the urban world, were introduced. The most frequent was the west end door. It made its first appearance at a very large church built in Brad, the administrative center of the Antiochene, in 402, under the supervision of the architect Julianos. The church's west end doors resolved the problem of entrance in relation to axis and was widely copied throughout the region. But its appearance did not eliminate the earlier south doors. The Julianos church had four of them, as opposed to three west ones, and they faced a courtyard.[40] Later churches continued to be built without west end doors, or with both west and south ones. South doors, however, almost always continued to be the principal points of entry.[41]

The Julianos church was clearly inspired by urban models, and in fact urban workmen were almost certainly used to build at least parts of it. But local initiative seems to have been paramount. A number of commemorative inscriptions found at the site name well-off members of the village who paid for various parts of the structure. None of them are identifiable as urban civil or ecclesiastical officials.[42] This pattern is borne out by the few other inscriptions we have dealing with donors and finances. They mention village leaders of various kinds (γέροντες, δεκάπροτες), local notables (a "Lord" Flavianos at Kharab Shams), or local ecclesiastics (a [church?] accountant at Rayan). Our most complete information comes from an inscription of 507 found at the church in Khirbet Hasan in the central area of the region. The church's construction costs were set at 580 nomismata and 430 bushels (μόδιοι) of beans, wheat, and lentils. No donors are listed so it is probable that the costs were raised by the community as a whole.[43] At the very beginning of Christianization church construction probably was initiated by people like the *periodeutes* mentioned at Fafertin. Later on, the overall impression is that locals took the lead and most likely determined the type of building to be constructed. Their tastes were largely conservative. Only one structure in the Belus broke significantly with the patterns laid down by the first Belus basilicas. This was St. Simeon's great shrine church at Qalat Sim'an. Cross shaped, it was formed by four three-aisle basilicas projecting out from a central octagon surrounding the saint's column, the base of which is still visible today. The east basilica constituted the church proper. Its east end consisted of three apses which were completely visible from the outside. It was almost certainly built with imperial and ecclesiastical financing with the Emperor Zeno and the Patriarch of Antioch as the most likely donors. It is the most striking example we have of an urban intrusion into the region's built environment. For our purposes, therefore, the question centers on the degree of influence the shrine had on village architecture. The answer is, "some."

Qalat Sim'an's chief influence was decorative. Window and door moldings, column capitals, and the like were imitated and expanded upon throughout the region in the years after its construction. These borrowings and developments became a hallmark of sixth-century churches. One other feature also was picked up, the exposed apse at the east end of the church. It had been very infrequent in the years before St. Simeon's was built, appearing only in 4 or 5 churches.[44] In the sixth century a few more adopted it, sometimes modeling it very closely on Qalat Sima'an. But the projecting apse was never a common feature in the region. Jean-Pierre Sodini's survey of 102 churches show that it appeared only in 10, and these were clustered mainly in Gebel Zawiye to the south.[45] Rectilinear chevets continued to be the rule; like those of the first basilicas, they served to maintain the rectangular shape of the church exterior.

Another innovation of the fifth century also deserves mention, the appearance of a church modeled in part on earlier temples. The first example is the basilica at Qalb Lozeh.[46] The church was built shortly before Qalat Sim'an and probably had some influence on it. It stands just a few hundred yards from Qirqbize. The church proper follows the standard plan of the three-aisle basilica with east orientation. Two of its distinctive features are its very rich exterior decoration and its projecting apse. Of greater interest, however, is the placement of the church. Here there are no courtyards or ancillary buildings. Rather the church sits in the center of an open space bounded on all four sides by a wall whose west side is pierced by a "propylaeon." The resemblance to local temple architecture is unmistakable; the open space reproduces the old temenos and the wall its peribolos. We find the same arrangement later in the sixth century to the south at Ruweiha in the Church of Bizzos. Here the only differences are the presence of two tombs in the "temenos" and a "propylaeon" on the south rather than the west side.[47] In many ways these churches represent significant departures from earlier local models of the basilica, but they never cut all their ties with tradition. Both have prominent south doors, and the southern section of the "temenos" at the Bizzos church constitutes the largest open space inside the enclosure wall. The single "propylaeon" on the south side also reinforces the clear south orientation of the ensemble. Thus, the farm complex continued to function in these churches as a shadowy but recognizable template.

Qalb Lozeh and the Church of Bizzos were not really village churches;

most probably they were regional shrines housing important relics. This may help to explain the self-conscious adoption of temple features. But puzzles still remain. The association of church and temple was somewhat looser in the Belus than in other parts of the Empire. For example, we have no instances of temples being turned into churches, although some, like the Julianos church at Brad, were built on temple sites and incorporated spolia from them.[48] Why churches should be built that imitate temple settings but not their forms is something of a mystery. Nevertheless, the overall implication is clear: at a relatively late stage in the Christianization of the Belus a decision was made to extend the architectural strategy of assimilation and appropriation in directions that went far beyond the first churches' borrowing of features from the farm house. In the churches at Qalb Lozeh and Ruwieha the old gods, now demoted to *daimones*, were met symbolically on their home turf and defeated. But this maneuver came late and was never pursued with complete thoroughness. The great temple site atop Mount Koryphaios to the south of St. Simeon's, which was dedicated to Zeus Madbachos and a local god, Selamanes, was never conquered architecturally. The Christians contented themselves with a ring of churches and monasteries on the mountain's lower slopes as a kind of *cordon sanitaire*.[49]

Finally, one further feature of these churches deserves comment, their use of broad spanned arches resting on piers as a substitute for the colonnaded arcade. Qalb Lozeh offers the earliest example of this feature, which was imitated in some local churches like Ruweiha. It was also used in urban settings from nearby Cyrrhus in the north to far away Ravenna in the west.[50] We thus have an interesting example of an architectural form invented in the countryside moving to an urban setting; architectural exchange between town and country, as it developed in the built environment of the Christians, could run both ways.

Of equal interest from my point of view is the fact that the broad spanned arch introduced yet another feature of local domestic architecture into the church. We have already seen that these arches were sometimes used on the ground floors of dwellings as supports for the second story floor. They were the nearest analogue in the local architectural repertory to the triumphal arch of the basilica. Now, at a quite late date, they were introduced in something very near their pristine form into the church interior. Some historians of architecture have argued that they were used to open the sight lines from the side aisles to the main one. I am struck by the way they continue to appropriate and relocate local architectural elements in the interests of an overall scheme of architectural communication based on simultaneous strategies of assimilation and rupture, either through innovation or displacement. The complexity of the scheme is revealed both by its initial features and the variations played on them over a long period of time.

Throughout this article I have argued that Christianity made its way into the north Syrian villages by means of an architectural strategy, involving both accommodation to prior models from the built environment and breaks with them. The overall, if implicit, message conveyed by the strategy was that Christianity was something old and something new, something familiar and something foreign. The idea that the Christianization of the Roman Empire involved a simultaneous fusion with and distancing from older cultural traditions has, of course, been argued before. To give one recent example, Averil Cameron has explored how Christian discourse, using a language of separation from the discourses of the surrounding Greco-Roman world, nevertheless engaged in powerful strategies of accommodation with them.[51] One can think in this context of Theodoret of Cyrrhus' complicated account of the monkish "philosophers" who carried out some of the earliest Christian missions in the Belus region.[52] Peter Brown has also recently emphasized the "facilitating" role between Christianity and paganism of someone like Simeon Stylites, that seemingly ultra-Christian figure, who fifty-odd years after the first colonnaded basilicas were built in Jebel Sim'an stood atop his pillar only a few miles away.[53] Like Brown and Cameron, I am struck by the extraordinary variety of strategies employed by the Christians as they moved into the northern Syrian countryside. Like them, I see a basic pattern of accommodation and separation as the old built environment of the Belus Massif was accepted and changed. But if an examination of the architectural dimensions of the Christianizing process in this one part of the Late Roman Empire does not offer us a wholly new general model for understanding it, the approach taken in this paper does make us aware of the huge complexity of the process in ways that go well beyond what we can learn from textual and epigraphic evidence. Architectural change represented one of the very deepest, most powerful, and distinctive aspects of Christianization which transformed churches, villages, and the people living in them as it worked itself out.

NOTES

My thanks go to Gil Stein (Northwestern) and Kathleen James (U.C. Berkeley) for very fruitful bibliographic suggestions, and to my colleagues William Bonds, Richard Hoffman, and Barbara Loomis whose comments on earlier drafts of this paper were helpful in many ways. Thanks also to Mr. Waleed Omar in Damascus for his indispensable help during two trips to the Belus region, and to Giovanni Ruffini, my research assistant, for many hours of spade work in several Bay Area libraries. Whatever is wrong or wrongheaded here, of course, belongs only to me. Finally, I wish to thank San Francisco State University for a 1996 Summer Stipend in support of my research.

1. Frank R. Trombley, *Hellenic Religion and Christianization, c. 370–529,* 2 vols. (Leiden: 1993–94), 2:204.
2. Tate, *Les Campagnes de la Syrie du Nord du IIe au VIIe siècle* (Paris, 1992), 167–88.
3. Melchior de Vogüé, *Syrie centrale, architecture civile et réligieuse du Ier au VIIe siècle,* 2 vols. (Paris, 1865–77); *Publications of an American Archaeological Expedition to Syria,* 4 vols. (New York, 1903–30); *Publications of the Princeton University Archaeological Expeditions to Syria,* 4 vols. (Leiden, 1907–49); Howard Crosby Butler, *Early Churches in Syria* (Princeton, 1929); Jean Lassus, *Sanctuaires chrétiens de Syrie* (Paris, 1947); Georges Tchalenko, *Villages antiques de la Syrie du nord,* 3 vols. (Paris, 1953–58); Georges Tchalenko, *Eglises de village de la Syrie du nord,* 2 vols. (Paris, 1979–80); Georges Tchalenko, *Eglises syriennes à béma* (Paris, 1990). For the tangled publication history of the last two titles see the review by Christine Strube in *Jahrbuch für Antike und Christentum* 35 (1992): 222–28.
4. See note 2 above. Convenient recent summaries and appreciations of the work of Tate and his predecessors can be found in two articles by Clive Foss, "Syria in Transition, a.d. 550–750: An Archaeological Approach," *Dumbarton Oaks Papers* 51 (1989): 189–289, and "The Near Eastern Countryside in Late Antiquity: A Review Article," in *The Roman and Byzantine Near East: Some Recent Archaeological Research,* ed. J. H. Humphrey (Ann Arbor, 1995), 213–34. Tate has also published preliminary summaries of his work in "Archéologie sérielle et histoire rurale: le cas du massif calcaire dans la Syrie du nord," *Castrum 2. Structures de l'habitat et occupation du sol dans les pays méditerranéens: les méthodes de l'apport de l'archéologie extensive,* ed. Ghislaine Noyé (Rome and Madrid, 1988), 107–14, and "La Syrie à l'époque byzantine: Essai de synthèse," in *Archéologie et histoire de la Syrie.* II: *La Syrie de l'époque achéménide à*

l'avènement de l'Islam, ed. Jean-Marie Dentzer and Winfried Orthmann (Saarbrücken, 1989), 97–116. A more recent analysis of one village can be found in Georges Tate and Alice Naccache, "Le village antique de Deir Sunbul," *Mélanges de l'Université de Saint-Joseph* (1991–92): 370–490. In addition, see Christine Strube, *Die "Toten Städte": Stadt und Land in Nordsyrien während der Spätantike* (Mainz, 1996), which incorporates Tate's work.

5. Christine Strube, *Baudekoration im Nordsyrischen Kalksteinmassiv.* I: *Kapitell-, Tür- und Gesimsformen der Kirchen des 4. und 5. Jahrhunderts N. Chr.* (Mainz, 1993).
6. The one known exception is the village of Baziher. A cadastral inscription dating from the Tetrarchy states that it was the domain of a certain Zaero. Its physical appearance, however, is indistinguishable from neighboring sites. Tate, *Campagnes,* 265–66.
7. Ibid., 269–70, and passim; Tate, "La Syrie à l'époque byzantine . . . ," 105–6.
8. Tate, *Campagnes,* 65, 69–78; Strube, *Toten,* 11–14, 19–20.
9. For what follows, see Tate, *Campagnes,* 13–18, 29–84, 224–26, 238–39.
10. Jean Lassus, "Sur les maisons d'Antioche," in *Apamée de Syrie: Actes du Colloque tenu à Bruxelles les 29, 30 et 31 mai 1980,* ed. Jeanine Balty (Brussels, 1984), 361–72, pl. LXXIII-LXXV. (Fouilles d'Apamée de Syrie. Miscellanea, Fascicule 13.); Foss, "Syria in Transition," 217–26.
11. Tate, *Campagnes,* 213–26.
12. Richard Krautheimer, *Early Christian and Byzantine Architecture,* 4th ed. rev. (with Slobodan Curcic) (New Haven, 1986), 23–37.
13. L. Michael White, *The Social Origins of Christian Architecture,* 2 vols. (Valley Forge, 1997), esp. I:102–39, II:1–32.
14. Ibid., I:128.
15. Tchalenko, *Villages,* I, 17–18, 319–42, and *Eglises syriennes,* 151–56, *Eglises de village . . . Album,* 87–93, *Eglises de village . . . Planches,* 232–43.
16. Against this standard view, White argues interestingly for some continuity between the hall church and the basilica, pointing to the similarities between the earlier large assembly spaces and those of the basilica, but even he stresses the considerable discontinuity between the basilica and what came before (White, I:127–39; II:6–9).
17. Jean-Pierre Sodini, "Les Eglises de Syrie du Nord," in Dentzer and Orthmann, 347–72; Strube, *Toten,* 19–23, 34.
18. Christine Strube, "Hauskirche und einschiffige Kirche in Syrien: Beobachtungen zu den Kirchen von Marmaya, Nurie und Banaqfur," in Otto Feld and Urs Peschlow, eds., *Studien zur spätantiken und byzantinischen Kunst: Friedrich Wilhelm Deichmann gewidmet,* 3 vols. (Bonn, 1986), I:109–23, pls. 29–37, and *Baudekoration,* 68–76. Georges Tate also assigns a late date to the church (*Campagnes,* 120).
19. This is so if one accepts Strube's late dating of the Qirqbize church and a late date for the West church at Baqirha in the Jebel Barisha region of the Massif. Although Tchalenko and Strube disagree on the dating of the church at Qirqbize, they both accept an early fifth-century date (416 c.e.) for the church at Baqirha (Tchalenko, *Eglises syriennes,* 131–34; Strube, *Baudekoration,* I:77–79). Some years ago, however, a member of Tchalenko's team published the inscription used by Tchalenko and Strube

to date the Baqirha church, but read the date as 405 in the Caesarian Era of Antioch which translates to 357 in the Common Era (J. Jarry, "Nouvelles Inscriptions de Syrie du Nord," *Zeitschrift für Papyrologie und Epigraphik* 47 [1982]: 75). This much earlier date has recently been accepted by Pauline Donceel-Voûte, *Les Pavements des églises byzantines de Syrie et du Liban.* I: *Décor, archéologie, et liturgie* (Louvain-La-Neuve,1988), 31–33. This is not the place to resolve the discrepancy, although a recent preliminary examination of the inscription *in situ* leads me to accept Jarry's date. If it proves to be correct then it is still further evidence that the first Christian structures in the Belus Massif were colonnaded basilicas.

20. William Kelly Prentice, *Greek and Latin Inscriptions: Northern Syria* (Leiden, 1922), 202. This volume appears in *Publications of the Princeton University Archaeological Expeditions to Syria in 1904–5 and 1909* as Division III, Section B, Part 6.
21. Unfortunately we know first hand about only one fourth century church in Antioch, the shrine (martyrion) of St. Babylas, a local bishop, which was built around 379 in a suburb of the ancient city and excavated earlier in this century. It is cross-shaped and most probably modeled on Constantine I's Church of the Apostles (the Apostoleion) in Constantinople. Constantine himself started a church in Antioch in 327, Hagia Harmonia, which was completed in 341 by his son Constantius II. Nothing of it remains today, but contemporaries describe an octagonal structure of considerable grandeur and opulence. Finally, a basilical church has been excavated at Ma'chouqa, a site 3 kilometers northeast of Antioch. It is datable to the fifth or sixth century (Krautheimer, 75–78; Donceel-Voûte, 174–77). In Apamea three churches have been fully or partially excavated in the southern section of the city. None date to the fourth century and none are basilical in plan. The remains of a large basilica have been identified near the north gate but it has yet to be excavated and dated (See Foss, "Syria in Transition," 211–17). Finally, a wide arched basilica stands in Cyrrhus, but it can hardly be dated to before the late fifth or early sixth century (Peter Grossman, *S. Michele in Africisco zu Ravenna* {Mainz:1973], 58–63). Thus, on the basis of current archaeological evidence a fourth century north Syrian urban origin for the Belus basilicas must be conjectural. But the conjecture is reasonable.
22. For what follows see Lassus, 23; Tchalenko, *Eglises syriennes*, 25–45, and *Eglises de village . . . Planches*, 17–52, *Villages*, I, 201, 201n. 2; Strube, *Baudekoration*, I:28–34, and *Toten*, 32–33.
23. To some degree this is also a matter of conjecture. Unfortunately, of the eighteen temple sites identified in the region almost all are very ruinous or have disappeared. The two best preserved sites, the temple at Burj Baqirha and the temple-tomb at Deir Mismis, however, do not use apses or conches.
24. Strube, *Baudekoration*, 33–34, and *Toten*, 33.
25. Tchalenko, *Eglises syriennes*, 42.
26. Ibid., 73–76.
27. I am setting aside the question of who stood exactly where in these churches along with the problem of the bema, a horseshoe shaped construction in the center of the main aisle. These matters pertain to the history of liturgical practice but not to an

examination of the optics of architectural form.

28. The ground floor wide-spanned arch is most commonly found in Jebel Zawiye, the southernmost part of the Massif, but is attested throughout the region.

29. For what follows I draw in one way or another on the following: Michelle Hegmon, "Social Integration and Architecture," in *The Architecture of Social Integration in Prehistoric Pueblos*, ed. William D. Lipe and Michelle Hegmon (Cortez, 1989), 5–14; Ian Hodder, "Material Culture Texts and Social Change: A Theoretical Discussion and some Archaeological Examples," *Proceedings of the Prehistoric Society* 54 (1988): 67–75, "Post-Modernism, Post-Structuralism and Post-Processual Archaeology," in *The Meanings of Things: Material Culture and Symbolic Expression*, ed. Hodder (London, 1989), 64–78, and *Reading the Past: Current approaches to interpretation in archaeology*, 2d ed. (Cambridge, 1991), esp. chap. 7, "Contextual Archaeology"; Amos Rapoport, *The Meaning of the Built Environment: A Nonverbal Communication Approach*, 2d ed. (Tucson, 1990), and "The Levels of Meaning in the Built Environment," in *Cross-Cultural Perspectives in Nonverbal Communication*, ed. Fernando Poyatos (Lewiston, 1988), 317–36; Roy A. Rappaport, "The Obvious Aspects of Ritual," in his *Ecology, Meaning, and Religion* (Richmond, 1979), 172–221; Polly Wiessner, "Is There a Unity to Style?" in *The Uses of Style in Archaeology*, ed. Margaret W. Conkey and Christine A. Hastorf (Cambridge, 1990); Victor A. Buchli, "Interpreting Material Culture: The Trouble with Text," Felipe Criado, "The Visibility of the Archaeological Record and the Interpretation of Social Reality," and Michael Parker Pearson, "Tombs and Territories: Material Culture and Multiple Interpretation," all in *Interpreting Archaeology: Finding Meaning in the Past*, ed. Ian Hodder et al. (London, 1995), 181–209.

The classic example along the lines of the approach I attempt here is Pierre Bourdieu, "La maison kabyle ou le monde renversé," in *Echanges et communications: Mélanges offerts à Claude Lévi-Strauss à l'occasion de son 60ème anniversaire*, 2 vols., ed. Jean Pouillon and Pierre Maranda (The Hague, 1970), II, 739–758. For an abbreviated English translation of the same see P. Bourdieu, "The Berber House" in *Rules and Meaning*, ed. Mary Douglas (Harmondsworth, 1973), 98–110. For other historians' attempts to apply some of the conceptual and theoretical positions discussed in the literature cited here see Andrew Wallace-Hadrill, "The Social Structure of the Roman House," *Papers of the British School at Rome* 56 (1988): 43–97, reprinted in his *Houses and Society in Pompeii and Herculaneum* (Princeton, 1994), and Ray Laurence, *Roman Pompeii: Space and Society* (London, 1994).

30. The phrase is Felipe Criado's (Criado, 196).

31. This definition and the examples are William Sewell's. See his *Work and Revolution in France: The Language of Labor from the Old Regime to 1848* (Cambridge, 1980), 12. We can add "architectural arrangements" to the list of examples.

32. Rapoport, *Meaning*, chaps. 2–4.

33. The messages of material culture are sometimes described as "subconscious" (see, for example, Hodder, "Post-Modernism" 73). I think Victor Buchli offers a better formulation of the issue when he states that the messages ". . . are taken for granted until a rule is misapplied" (Buchli, 187).

34. For a discussion of the ways buildings cue interpretations and thereby set parameters for appropriating their messages see Hodder "Material Culture Texts," 67–69.
35. Hegmon, 8, citing Roy A. Rappaport, "The Sacred in Human Evolution," *Annual Review of Anthropology* 2 (1971): 23–44; see also Rappaport, "The Obvious Aspects of Ritual," *passim.*
36. On the importance of architecture and ritual in pre-literate societies see Hodder, 74.
37. Strube has documented decorative borrowings between temples and early dwellings in the region. A similar interchange occurred when churches were built. See *Toten Städte,* 27–28, and *Baudekoration,* passim. These borrowings, however, were of a different order from those which the basilica took over from the house.
38. See note 21 above.
39. Another possible exception is the sixth-century polygonal structure at Deir Seta, although its function is unclear.
40. Tchalenko, *Eglises syriennes,* 19–24, and *Eglises de village . . . Planches,* 4–16; Strube, *Baudekoration,* 40–47. The Julianos church also had two north doors which like the south ones faced a courtyard. From then on north doors also are copied in a number of churches although north courtyards are rare.
41. Tchalenko, *Eglises syriennes,* 75.
42. Ibid., 21–22.
43. Sodini, 348; Strube, *Toten,* 77.
44. The others are Fafertin (372), the East Church at Babisqa (390–407), the church at Kaukanaya in the Gebel Zawiye (fifth century), and the church of St. Phocas at Basufan (491–92). The last may have been influenced by St. Simeon's.
45. Sodini, 358.
46. Tchalenko, *Eglises syriennes,* 163–66, and *Eglises de villages . . . Planches,* 256–62; Strube, *Baudekoration,* 94–115.
47. Tchalenko, *Eglises syriennes,* 183, 189–92, *Eglises de village . . . Planches,* 282–95.
48. Temple conversion anywhere in Syria is rare. Two known examples are the tychaion at Mesmiye in the Hauran, and the cella of the temple of Bel at Palmyra (Lassus, 247–48). In Jebel Sim'an, the fifth-century church at Qalat Kalota incorporates part of the walls of two temples in its own north and west walls, as well as temple spolia (*Publications of the Princeton University Archaeological Expedition . . .*, Division II, Section B, Part 6, Plate XXVI.)
49. The Muslims, however, have built a local shrine just to the north of its peribolos.
50. See the reference to Peter Grossman in note 21 above. Jean Lassus was one of the first to recognize the similarity to "civil architecture" (Lassus, 76).
51. Averil Cameron, *Christianity and the Rhetoric of Empire: The Development of Christian Discourse* (Berkeley, 1991).
52. See Theodoret of Cyrrhus, *A History of the Monks in Syria,* trans. R.M. Price (Kalamazoo, 1985).
53. Peter Brown, "The Christian Holy Man in Late Antiquity," in his *Authority and the Sacred: Aspects of the Christianization of the Roman World* (Cambridge, 1995), 57–78.